A HISTORY OF THE INDIAN
NOVEL IN ENGLISH

A History of the Indian Novel in English traces the development of the Indian novel from its beginnings in the late nineteenth century to the present day. Starting with an extensive introduction that charts important theoretical contributions to the field, this *History* includes twenty-five chapters that shed light on the legacy of Indian writing in English. Organized thematically, these chapters examine how English was "made Indian" by writers who used the language to address specifically Indian concerns. These included the question of what it means to be modern as well as how the novel could be used for anticolonial activism. By the 1980s, the Indian novel in English was a global phenomenon, and India is now the third-largest publisher of English-language books. Written by a host of leading scholars, this *History* invites readers to question conventional accounts of India's literary history.

ULKA ANJARIA is Associate Professor of English at Brandeis University. She is the author of *Realism in the Twentieth-Century Indian Novel: Colonial Difference and Literary Form* and has published in such journals as *South Asian Popular Culture*, *NOVEL: A Forum on Fiction*, and *Economic and Political Weekly*. She was the recipient of an ACLS/Charles A. Ryskamp fellowship in 2014 for her current book project on realism in contemporary Indian literature, film, and television.

A HISTORY OF THE INDIAN NOVEL IN ENGLISH

EDITED BY

ULKA ANJARIA

Brandeis University

CAMBRIDGE
UNIVERSITY PRESS

CAMBRIDGE
UNIVERSITY PRESS

32 Avenue of the Americas, New York, NY 10013-2473, USA

Cambridge University Press is part of the University of Cambridge.

It furthers the University's mission by disseminating knowledge in the pursuit of
education, learning, and research at the highest international levels of excellence.

www.cambridge.org
Information on this title: www.cambridge.org/9781107079960

First published 2015

Printed in Great Britain by Clays Ltd, St Ives plc

A catalog record for this publication is available from the British Library.

Library of Congress Cataloging in Publication Data
A history of the Indian novel in English / edited by Ulka Anjaria, Brandeis University.
        pages   cm
        ISBN 978-1-107-07996-0 (hardback)
  1. Indic fiction (English) – History and criticism.   I. Anjaria, Ulka, 1979– editor.
        PR9492.2.H57   2015
        823.009′954–dc23   2015004873

ISBN 978-1-107-07996-0 Hardback

Cambridge University Press has no responsibility for the persistence or accuracy of URLs
for external or third-party Internet Web sites referred to in this publication and does not
guarantee that any content on such Web sites is, or will remain, accurate or appropriate.

Contents

v

Figures

Notes on Contributors

ULKA ANJARIA is Associate Professor of English at Brandeis University, with research interests in South Asian literature and film, the global novel, and literary realism. She is the author of *Realism in the Twentieth-Century Indian Novel: Colonial Difference and Literary Form* (Cambridge University Press, 2012) and has published in journals such as *South Asian Popular Culture, NOVEL: A Forum on Fiction*, and *Economic and Political Weekly*. She was the recipient of an ACLS/ Charles A. Ryskamp fellowship in 2014 for her current book project on realism in contemporary Indian literature, film, and television.

BARNITA BAGCHI teaches and researches comparative literature at Utrecht University, the Netherlands. She studied at Jadavpur, Oxford, and Cambridge universities and has previously taught at the Institute of Development Studies, Kolkata. She has research interests in eighteenth-century British literature, South Asian (especially Bengali) narrative, and the transnational history of culture and education. Her publications include a critical edition and part-translation of Rokeya Hossain's *Sultana's Dream and Padmarag* (Penguin, 2005), the edited volume *The Politics of the (Im)possible: Utopia and Dystopia Reconsidered* (Sage, 2012), and the coedited volume *Connecting Histories of Education: Transnational and Cross-Cultural Exchanges in (Post)-Colonial Education* (Berghahn, 2014).

EITAN BAR-YOSEF is Associate Professor in the Department of Foreign Literatures and Linguistics, Ben-Gurion University of the Negev, Israel. His books and articles include *The Holy Land in English Culture, 1799–1917: Palestine and the Question of Orientalism* (Oxford University Press, 2005); *Vila ba-jungel: africa ba-trabut ha-israelit* [A Villa in the Jungle: Africa in Israeli Culture] (Van-Leer Institute and Hakibbutz Hemeuchad Press, 2013); and "Zionism, Apartheid, Blackface: *Cry the Beloved Country* on the Israeli Stage" in *Representations* (2013). He is currently the editor of the journal *Teoria U-vikoret* [Theory and Criticism], published by the Van-Leer Institute, Jerusalem.

AYELET BEN-YISHAI is on the faculty at the Department of English Language and Literature at the University of Haifa. She holds a Ph.D. in comparative literature from the University of California, Berkeley, and degrees in comparative literature and law from Hebrew University, Jerusalem. She is the author of *Common Precedents: The Presentness of the Past in Victorian Law and Fiction* (Oxford University Press, 2013) and has published in a range of journals, including *Nineteenth-Century Literature*, *Modern Fiction Studies*, and *The Journal of Law, Culture and the Humanities*.

SHAMEEM BLACK is a Fellow in the Department of Gender, Media and Cultural Studies at the Australian National University. Her interests include Anglophone literatures of South Asia and its diaspora, contemporary fiction and globalization, humanitarian crisis and transitional justice, and cosmopolitan ethics and sympathy. Her work has recently appeared in the *Journal of Human Rights*, *Social Text*, and *Public Culture*, among others. She is the author of *Fiction Across Borders: Imagining the Lives of Others in Late Twentieth-Century Novels* (Columbia University Press, 2010). Her current research concerns the imaginative life of yoga in a globalizing world.

MRINALINI CHAKRAVORTY is Associate Professor of English at the University of Virginia. She holds degrees from the University of Colorado, Boulder, and the University of California, Irvine. Her research interests include postcolonial literature and film; race, gender and sexuality; and cultural studies. She is the author of *In Stereotype: South Asia in the Global Literary Imaginary* (Columbia University Press, 2014). She has also published in *PMLA*, *differences*, *ARIEL*, and *Modern Fiction Studies*.

SUPRIYA CHAUDHURI is Professor Emerita in the Department of English at Jadavpur University, Kolkata. She was educated at Presidency College, Calcutta, and the University of Oxford and has held visiting appointments at the Universities of Cambridge and Paris. She has written on Renaissance studies, cultural history, cinema, sport, and modernism and has translated for the series *Oxford Tagore Translations*. Her recent publications include *Petrarch: The Self and the World* (coedited with Sukanta Chaudhuri, Jadavpur University Press, 2012) and *Sport,*

Literature, Society: Cultural Historical Studies (coedited with Alexis Tadié and J. A. Mangan, Routledge, 2014).

COREY K. CREEKMUR is Associate Professor of Cinematic Arts and English at the University of Iowa. He received his Ph.D. from the University of Illinois and has research interests in American film, popular Hindi cinema, queer theory, psychoanalysis, and comics. He is coeditor of *The International Film Musical* (with Linda Mokdad, Edinburgh University Press, 2012) and *Cinema, Law, and the State in Asia* (with Mark Sidel, Palgrave Macmillan, 2007), and he has published essays in many other collections. He is also the general editor of the Comics Culture series for Rutgers University Press.

KAVITA DAIYA is Associate Professor of English and Director of the M.A. program in English at George Washington University, with expertise in modern British and postcolonial literatures, gender and sexuality studies, Asian American literature and cinema, global modernisms, and ethnic studies. She received her Ph.D. from the University of Chicago and is the author of *Violent Belongings: Partition, Gender and National Culture in Postcolonial India* (Temple University Press, [2008] 2011; Yoda Press, 2013). She directs a Digital Humanities initiative on histories of migration and violence (www.1947Partition.org) and serves as associate editor of *South Asian Review*, the journal of the South Asian Literary Association.

VINAY DHARWADKER is Professor in the Department of Comparative Literature and Folklore Studies, University of Wisconsin-Madison. He translates from Hindi, Marathi, Urdu, Punjabi, and Sanksrit. His scholarship focuses on South Asian literature (all periods and genres), theory, modernism, cosmopolitanism, and globalization. He is the author of *Kabir: The Weaver's Songs* (Penguin Classics, 2003); the South Asia editor of *The North Anthology of World Literature*, 3rd ed. (2012); and the cotranslator, with Aparna Dharwadker, of Mohan Rakesh, *One Day in the Season of Rain* (Penguin Modern Classics, 2015).

SÉBASTIEN DOUBINSKY teaches French and English literature in the Department of Aesthetics and Communication at Aarhus University, Denmark. He is coeditor of *Reading Literature Today: Two Complementary Essays and a Conversation* (with Tabish Khair, Sage, 2011) and author of articles such as "What One Tells the Poet about Irony: A Reflection on Irony and Literary Objects in Rimbaud's Poem 'What One Tells the Poet about Flowers,'" published in *Ironistik: Ironi i et multidisciplinaert perspektiv* (ed. Merete Birkelund, 2013). He also writes fiction and poetry in French and English.

TORAL JATIN GAJARAWALA is Associate Professor of English and Comparative Literature at New York University. Her research interests include theories of the novel and narrative, postcolonial studies, subaltern studies, and the relationship between aesthetics and politics. She has published in such journals as *PMLA*, *Modern Language Quarterly*, and the *Journal of Narrative Theory* and is the author of *Untouchable Fictions: Literary Realism and the Crisis of Caste* (Fordham University Press, 2012).

SANGITA GOPAL is Associate Professor of English at the University of Oregon. She is the author of *Conjugations: Marriage and Form in New Bollywood Cinema* (University of Chicago Press, 2011) and coeditor of *Intermedia in South Asia: The Fourth Screen* (with Rajinder Dudrah, Anustup Basu, and Amit Rai, Routledge, 2012) and *Global Bollywood: Travels of Hindi Film Music* (with Sujata Moorti, University of Minnesota Press, 2008). She has published articles in *Comparative Literature*, *Feminist Studies*, *Camera Obscura*, and the *Journal of Commonwealth and Postcolonial Studies*, among others. She is currently working on a book on women's cinema in India.

PRIYA JOSHI is Associate Professor of English at Temple University. She received her Ph.D. from Columbia University and is the author of *In Another Country: Colonialism, Culture and the English Novel in India* (Columbia University Press, 2002), winner of the MLA First Book Prize, the Sonya Rudikoff Prize for best first book in Victorian studies, and a *Choice* Outstanding Academic Title award, as well as *Bollywood's India: A Public Fantasy* (Columbia University Press, 2015), which continues her scholarship on South Asian modernities and popular culture. Joshi's research has been supported by the National Endowment for the Humanities and the American Institute of Indian Studies.

ANANYA JAHANARA KABIR is Professor of English Literature at King's College, London. She is the author of *Territory of Desire: Representing the Valley of Kashmir* (University of Minnesota Press, 2009), which was shortlisted for the 2010 European Society for Studies in English Prize, as well as *Partition's Post-Amnesias: 1947, 1971 and Modern South Asia* (Women Unlimited, 2013). She has also coedited several volumes, including *Postcolonial Approaches to the European Middle Ages: Translating Cultures* (with Deanne Williams, Cambridge

University Press, 2005) and *Diaspora and Multi-Locality: Writing British Asian Cities* (with Sean McLoughlin, William Gould, and Emma Tomalin, Routledge, 2013).

SUVIR KAUL is the A. M. Rosenthal Professor of English at the University of Pennsylvania. He is the author of *Eighteenth-Century British Literature and Postcolonial Studies* (Edinburgh University Press, 2009); *Poems of Nation, Anthems of Empire* (University of Virginia Press, 2000); and *Thomas Gray and Literary Authority* (Stanford University Press, 1992). He has also edited *The Partitions of Memory: The Afterlife of the Division of India* (Permanent Black, 2001) and coedited *Postcolonial Studies and Beyond* (with Ania Loomba, Antoinette Burton, Matti Bunzl, and Jed Esty, Duke University Press, 2005). *Of Gardens and Graves: Reflections on Kashmir* is forthcoming from Three Essays Press, New Delhi.

TABISH KHAIR is Associate Professor in the Department of Aesthetics and Communication at Aarhus University, Denmark, and is also a poet and novelist. He is the author of many books, including *The Gothic, Postcolonialism and Otherness: Ghosts from Elsewhere* (Palgrave Macmillan, 2009); *Babu Fictions: Alienation in Indian English Novels* (Oxford University Press, 2001); and, more recently, *The Thing About Thugs* (HarperCollins, 2010) – which was selected as Oprah's "Book of the Week" – and *How to Fight Islamist Terror from the Missionary Position* (Interlink and Corsair, 2014).

SAIKAT MAJUMDAR, Assistant Professor of English at Stanford University, is the author of *Prose of the World: Modernism and the Banality of Empire* (Columbia University Press, 2013), a finalist for the Modernist Studies Association's 2014 Book Award, and a novel, *Silverfish* (HarperCollins, 2007). His current book project, *The Amateur*, is about the literary public intellectual from the global British Empire as an amateur and autodidactic figure; an essay from this book appeared in the March 2015 issue of *PMLA*. His second novel, *The Firebird*, was published by Hachette.

VIJAY MISHRA is Professor of English Literature and Australian Research Council Professorial Fellow at Murdoch University, Australia. He is also a Fellow of the Australian Humanities Academy.

SATYA P. MOHANTY is Professor of English at Cornell University, where he has taught since 1983. He is the author of *Literary Theory and the Claims of History: Postmodernism, Objectivity, Multicultural Politics* (Cornell University Press, 1997), in which he first outlined a "postpositivist realist" theory of literature, identity, and culture. He is the editor of *Colonialism, Modernity, Literature: A View from India* (Palgrave Macmillan, 2011) and coeditor of *The Future of Diversity: Academic Leaders on American Higher Education* (Palgrave Macmillan, 2010). His new book, *Thinking Across Cultures*, is forthcoming from Duke University Press.

UPAMANYU PABLO MUKHERJEE is a professor in the Program of English and Comparative Literary Studies at the University of Warwick. He studies Victorian and contemporary imperial and anti-imperial cultures, postcolonial theory, crime fiction, world literature, and environmental literatures. He is the author of *Natural Disasters and Victorian Empire: Famines, Fevers and the Literary Cultures of South Asia* (Palgrave Macmillan, 2013); *Postcolonial Environments: Nature, Culture and the Contemporary Indian Novel in English* (Palgrave Macmillan, 2010); and *Crime and Empire: Representing India in the Nineteenth Century* (Oxford University Press, 2003).

RUKMINI BHAYA NAIR is Professor of Linguistics and English at the Indian Institute of Technology, Delhi. She received her Ph.D. from the University of Cambridge and another honorary doctorate from the University of Antwerp for her contributions to linguistic theory. Author of several scholarly books, including *Narrative Gravity: Conversation, Cognition, Culture* (Routledge, 2003) and *Poetry in a Time of Terror: Essays in the Postcolonial Preternatural* (Oxford University Press, 2009), Nair has taught at universities ranging from Singapore to Stanford. An award-winning poet who has published three volumes with Penguin India, Nair's first novel, *Mad Girl's Love Song* (HarperCollins, 2013), was long-listed for the 2014 DSC Prize.

RASHMI SADANA is Assistant Professor of Anthropology at George Mason University. She received her Ph.D. from the University of California, Berkeley, and is the author of *English Heart, Hindi Heartland: The Political Life of Literature in India* (University of California Press, 2012), an ethnography of Delhi's literary sphere. She is coeditor (with Vasudha Dalmia) of *The Cambridge Companion to Modern Indian Culture* (Cambridge University Press, 2012) and writes a regular column for the Indian newspaper *DNA*. Her current project considers new forms of sociality, urban space, and design as seen through the prism of Delhi's metro system.

RUMINA SETHI, Professor in the Department of English and Cultural Studies, Panjab University, Chandigarh, India, wrote her doctoral thesis at Trinity College, Cambridge. She has held academic fellowships at the University of Oxford and the Rockefeller Foundation at Bellagio, Italy. She is the author of *Myths of the Nation* (Oxford University Press, Clarendon, 1999) and *The Politics of Postcolonialism* (Pluto, 2011). She has published extensively in *South Asian Review*, the *Journal of Gender Studies*, *Modern Asian Studies*, *Textual Practice*, *New Formations*, the *Journal of Contemporary Thought*, *World Literature Written in English*, and *Postcolonial Text* and is presently editor of the journal *Dialog*.

SNEHAL SHINGAVI is Assistant Professor of English at the University of Texas, Austin. He received his Ph.D. from the University of California, Berkeley, and is the author of *The Mahatma Misunderstood: The Politics and Forms of Literary Nationalism in India* (Anthem, 2013). He has also translated several works from Hindi and Urdu to English, including *Angaaray*, the 1932 collection of Urdu short stories by Sajjad Zaheer, Ahmed Ali, and others (Penguin, 2014); *Sevasadan* by Premchand (Oxford University Press, 2005); and the forthcoming *Shekhar: A Life* by Agyeya (Penguin, 2016).

ELI PARK SORENSEN is Assistant Professor in the College of Liberal Studies at Seoul National University, South Korea. He specializes in comparative literature, postcolonial thought, literary theory, and cultural studies. He is the author of *Postcolonial Studies and the Literary: Theory, Interpretation and the Novel* (Palgrave Macmillan, 2010) and has published in journals such as *NOVEL: A Forum on Fiction*, the *Journal of Narrative Theory*, *Paragraph*, *Modern Drama*, *Research in African Literatures*, *Partial Answers*, and *Forum for Modern Language Studies*.

ALEX TICKELL lectures in English and is director of the Postcolonial Literatures Research Group at the Open University, UK. His research interests include South Asian literary history and contemporary Indian fiction. He is the author of *Terrorism, Insurgency and Indian-English Literature, 1830–1947* (Routledge, 2012) and a Routledge guide, *Arundhati Roy's* The God of Small Things (Routledge, 2007). Tickell is editor of *The Oxford History of the Novel in English* (Vol. 10, forthcoming with Oxford University Press), on the novel in South and South-East Asia since 1945. He is also currently editing a volume titled *South-Asian Fiction in English: Contemporary Transformations* (forthcoming, Palgrave).

E. DAWSON VARUGHESE is an independent researcher, most recently a Visiting Research Fellow at the Institute of English Studies, London. She is the author of *Beyond the Postcolonial: World Englishes Literature* (Palgrave Macmillan, 2012) and *Reading New India: Post-Millennial Indian Fiction in English* (Bloomsbury, 2013). Her forthcoming books are titled *Genre Fiction of New India: Post-Millennial Receptions of "Weird" Narratives* (Routledge, 2016) and a coauthored volume, *Indian Writing in English and Issues of Visual Representation: Judging More than a Book by Its Cover* (Palgrave Macmillan, 2015).

Acknowledgments

A work like this is entirely a cooperative endeavor, and so first and foremost I would like to thank the twenty-seven contributors who made this possible. These scholars took time out of their busy schedules to write these chapters and to read and respond to my many emails. They put up with my sometimes dramatic cuts and responded to edits and other suggestions with the open-mindedness and good spirit that represent the best of scholarly collaboration.

I want to thank Michaela Henry for her excellent work editing and proofreading the manuscript. Her involvement in the project was made possible by the English Department at Brandeis University, along with a Manuscript Completion Grant from the Dean's Office at Brandeis, for which I am extremely grateful.

I also want to thank Brandeis University, and in particular the English Department, for their continual support of me and my work, with special thanks to John Plotz, Paul Morrison, and Lisa Pannella. Michele Elam was, once again, generous with her mentorship and advice. Thanks to the Vadehra Art Gallery for their permission to use the cover image and to Mr. Satheesh for his help with the high-resolution file.

Thank you to Ray Ryan at Cambridge University Press for inviting me to undertake this project and to Caitlin Gallagher for her help with the production process.

And, of course, thanks to my family, who sustain my every day: Rehaan, Naseem, and Jonathan.

Introduction: *Literary Pasts, Presents, and Futures*

Ulka Anjaria

Literary histories can seem self-evident, tracing a linear development from "the beginning" straight through to the present day. It is thus that one might imagine a history of the Indian novel in English, which by most accounts – indeed, comparatively within the larger span of Indian literature – is a brief one. This history would begin with the nineteenth-century indigenous elite's first dabblings in the writing of English, influenced by colonial education and the allure of modernity and driven by reformist impulses. It might then take us to the movement known as "progressive writing" in the early twentieth century, when the novel was put to the service of a range of nationalist visions, and then to the early postcolonial decades, a period when English novels and their *bhasha* (vernacular-language[1]) counterparts went in a number of directions. It would then linger a bit at 1981, when, it is said, the Indian English novel finally found form with the publication of Salman Rushdie's *Midnight's Children*. Such a history would trace Rushdie's impact on the genre during the 1980s and 1990s and contrast the more commercial forms of contemporary Indian English writing since 2000 to the literary heavy-weights of the preceding generation.

The current volume seeks to complicate, enrich, and at times challenge this conventional account. The straightforward historical trajectory, based in three formative periods that cover around a century, mark the Indian English novel at three definitive moments: its emergence, its "realist" phase, and its "modernist" one. Each period can be understood as a response to – even critique of – the former; at the same time, because of the global status and marketability of the third phase, its significance might be taken to have vastly surpassed those of the other two. However, this narrative has significant limitations. First, *A History of the Indian Novel in English* suggests that what happens to the novel *between* and *within* these supposedly distinct eras is as important as the eras themselves. Second, it argues that a solely historical approach has the potential to reduce authors to their

I

explicit political positions or to the ethos of their age, thus precluding attention to literary form – to questions of genre, narrative, and literary aesthetics – and to the multiple ways in which literature *means*. A straightforward historical narrative also potentially occludes the question of the contemporary novel, which, the following chapters variously suggest, is not necessarily a continuation of or development on the Rushdie generation; modernism is not always surpassed by postmodernism; literary histories might not always unfold linearly. And, lastly and perhaps most importantly, this book demonstrates that the story of the Anglophone novel cannot be isolated and told as if it were a self-contained history. Rather, the English novel developed in relation to the rich history of the Indian novel – and indeed Indian literature more generally – in other languages. This runs counter to some conventional critical wisdom, which uses the current global importance of English to make a case for the inherent distinction of the English novel in India.

These are distinct arguments but, I believe, not unrelated. They all serve to call into question the historical narrative, along with our conventional tools for generating literary histories in the first place. They draw attention to how traditions not only *develop* but intersect and interact and gain richness and meaning from contemporaneous trends and transhistorical forms, rather than only as revisions of their own pasts. They compel us to focus on genre, form, and aesthetics rather than reduce literary works to expressions of their age. And by focusing on the contemporary *qua* contemporary – rather than as a continuation of an already-existing narrative – they allow us to challenge the teleology of literary history, to refuse to be contained by the logic of progressive time.

But linear histories are compelling things. This is especially true in the Indian context, in which the various literary traditions require specialist knowledge (or, at the very least, reading ability), lending the practice of literary history a certain practicality that comparative studies lack. The particular paradigms of postcolonial theory have also done much to determine what Indian literature – and the Indian novel in particular – *is* as an object. The post-1980s Indian novel's own investment in the hold of the (colonial, national) past on India's present has affected our readings of the entire genre to such a degree that the field of Indian novel studies is almost entirely dependent on a critique of historicity. While this approach has been useful in theorizing the relationship between literature and history in a broad sense, it has also resulted in some significant blind spots and erasures in terms of the texts it foregrounds and the themes it makes legible.[2] This historical framework has also meant that form and aesthetics have been undervalued, and the field has at times neared a straightforward historical determinism or literary sociology.

The following introduction thus proceeds in five sections. The first sketches out a chronology of the Indian novel in English based on the progression of the subgenre from the nineteenth century to the twenty-first century and presents the volume's chapters in relation to this chronology. The second, third, and fourth sections suggest ways of enriching this history through attention to the interactions between the Indian English novel and the bhashas; a renewed focus on literary form; and a consideration of the particular ontology of the contemporary. These sections attempt to foreground some themes that appear throughout the chapters – to draw them together and to suggest alternative groupings than those based solely on historical progress. Lastly, the final section collects some notes on terminology and explains the structure of the book.

A History of the Indian Novel in English

The first three chapters of this volume trace some of the first instances of the Indian novel in English, from Bankimchandra Chattopadhyay's *Rajmohan's Wife* (1864), discussed by Supriya Chaudhuri in Chapter 1; Lal Behari Day's *Bengal Peasant Life* (1878), analyzed by Satya P. Mohanty in Chapter 2; and Krupabai Satthianadhan's *Saguna: A Story of Native Christian Life* (1887–88) and Rokeya Sakhawat Hossain's "Sultana's Dream" (1905), which are only two of the range of women's texts Barnita Bagchi reads in Chapter 3. All of these works – as discussed further in this introduction – were highly experimental and emerged in dialogue with their vernacular contemporaries. Hossain's text – more a novella than a novel – takes us into the twentieth century, but the notable shift in the thematics of the Indian novel, to which both Snehal Shingavi and Rumina Sethi alert us in Chapters 4 and 5, respectively, takes place with nationalism and the rise of the "progressive" and "Gandhian" novels about fifteen years later as subgenres of the nationalist novel more generally. Anglophone authors Ahmed Ali, Mulk Raj Anand, and Raja Rao were central to these movements, and it was in this realist turn, which consolidated some of the disparate trends of the nineteenth century, that, many say, the Indian English novel was truly born. This is also when the gaze of Anglophone writers (as of nationalist leaders: Mohandas K. Gandhi, Jawaharlal Nehru, and Mohammad Ali Jinnah all studied law in England) turned westward, with both Ahmed Ali and Mulk Raj Anand gaining patronage from E. M. Forster and spending several years in London

(D. Anderson, 81–2; M. Anand, *Conversations*); Raja Rao wrote his "Gandhian" novel *Kanthapura* in France (R. Rao, "Entering" 537).

Yet these writers were also contemporaneous with the flourishing of high modernism in the west, and as Vinay Dharwadker suggests in Chapter 6, the experimental realism of Anand and other progressive writers might also be seen as a version of modernism defined by a particular kind of cultural critique founded in anti-colonial nationalism. Indeed, we can follow this line of thinking beyond independence as well, as the Indian English novel goes in a number of experimental directions. The event of Partition, for instance, as Ananya Jahanara Kabir argues in Chapter 7, marks the novel in profound ways both in terms of new themes but also formally, resulting in new aesthetic modes that last until the end of the twentieth century. The legacy of Partition remains immanent in the domestic novels that Suvir Kaul discusses in Chapter 8, in which Muslim writers struggle to reconcile the harsh realities of postcolonial Muslim life with the urgent need for religious reform, especially around women's rights. Anita Desai and Shashi Deshpande also wrote their early works during this period, focusing on gender and women's subordination within the household. But overall, these individual authors never cohered into a movement or notable trend. While they were and continue to be well-known, in Indian literary studies they remain largely in the shadow of contemporary bhasha novelists, such as Phaniswarnath Renu, author of *Maila Anchal* (Hindi, 1954), Srilal Shukla, of *Raag Darbari* (Hindi, 1968), U. R. Anantha Murthy, author of *Samskara* (Kannada, 1965), Sunil Gangopadhyay, Mahasweta Devi, and others. In Chapter 9, Rashmi Sadana discusses the politics and aesthetics of translation, which, she argues, was an essential mediating lens through which these bhasha writers gained national exposure.

If Partition marks the incipient moment of postcolonial disillusion – the beginning of the end of nationalist idealism – then Indira Gandhi's declaration of Emergency in 1975 represents its death knell. It was Salman Rushdie's *Midnight's Children* (1981) that gave form to this sense of disillusion, changing the course of the Indian English novel from that point forward. *Midnight's Children* was marked by a profound critique of the dominant nationalist narrative, emphasizing the constructedness and precarity not only of India's nationalist history but of history itself. All of Rushdie's novels are characterized by a resistance to metanarratives, a playful textuality, and a critique of the realist fallacy. Thus started a new phase in the Indian novel, which has alternatively been called "modernist" (Walkowitz), "postmodernist" (Afzal-Khan; Bhabha, "How Newness");

Hutcheon 92; M. Mukherjee, "Anxiety" 2609), and properly "postcolonial" (Bahri; McLeod; During 46; Tiffin). As Arundhati Roy quoted in her epigraph to *The God of Small Things* in 1997, summarizing the literary ethos of the 1980s and 1990s: "Never again will a single story be told as though it's the only one."[3]

Chapters 10, 11, and 12 consider the Emergency from refreshingly original perspectives; rather than focusing solely on Salman Rushdie's representation of the event in *Midnight's Children* – as the brilliantly termed "sperectomy: the draining-out of hope" (503) – Ayelet Ben-Yishai and Eitan Bar-Yosef consider Emergency through the fictional and nonfictional writings of Nayantara Sahgal; and Eli Park Sorensen situates Rohinton Mistry's Emergency writings within Mistry's larger interest in form and totality. Vijay Mishra takes a unique perspective on Rushdie's works themselves through a formal reading of their aural quality, which resists the allure of national allegory that underlies so much Rushdie criticism. It is a similar resistance to allegory that animates the next three chapters as well: in Chapter 13 Saikat Majumdar illuminates an interest in privacy and an aesthetic of the ordinary in the writings of Shashi Deshpande and Sunetra Gupta; Kavita Daiya reorients critical attention from the big "P" of Politics to small acts of intimacy in Chapter 14; and in Chapter 15, Alex Tickell explicitly engages the gap between nationalist historiography and the lived histories of India's present in his analysis of the meta-historical novels of Amitav Ghosh, Githa Hariharan, and M. G. Vassanji.

The remaining chapters bring these various questions to the present, approaching the contentious question of contemporaneity in the new Indian novel from a range of perspectives. In Chapters 16 and 17, respectively, Rukmini Bhaya Nair is interested in linguistic experiment and Mrinalini Chakravorty in aesthetic innovation. In Chapter 18, Upamanyu Pablo Mukherjee sees the contemporary novel as struggling to represent the increasing violence neoliberalism wages on the poor; and Shameem Black suggests, in Chapter 19, that the novel might be engaged in imagining a "post-humanitarian" ethical space that exposes the complicity between the discourse of human rights and the very violence it was built to condemn. The next five chapters consider different forms of novel-writing that have emerged over the last decade: Priya Joshi on pulp fiction (Chapter 20), E. Dawson Varughese on "chick lit" (Chapter 21), Tabish Khair and Sébastien Doubinsky on fantasy fiction (Chapter 22), Corey K. Creekmur on the graphic novel (Chapter 23), and Sangita Gopal on "filmi lit" – or novels written with a film adaptation and screenplay already in mind (Chapter 24). The final chapter by Toral Gajarawala considers the question of caste in relation to the contemporary, offering a hypothesis on the new forms that political critique will take once the older aesthetics of literary radicalism give way to the more ambivalent politics of ressentiment.

These twenty-five chapters tell a convincing story of the development of the Indian novel in English from the late nineteenth century until the present. But they do a good deal more. The discussion that follows offers some language to begin to flesh out the theoretical questions that the timeline of literary history might unintentionally preclude.

Bhasha Modernities and the Question of English

Across the board, the Indian novel had its more spectacular start in the bhashas – Malayalam, Odia, Marathi, Bengali – than in English. English was of course a colonial language, brought to India by colonial education and instituted by means of a deliberate policy, as articulated most famously by Thomas Babington Macaulay in 1835, "to form a class who may be interpreters between [the British] and the millions whom we govern; a class of persons, Indian in blood and colour, but English in taste, in opinions, in morals, and in intellect" (237). With literacy rates in any language at 3.5 percent in 1881 (P. Joshi, *In Another* 42 and 268–9, n. 13), and even lower in English, one can see how tracing the rise of the English novel might simply offer a highly selective genealogy of India's native elite.

Yet in fact, although Governor-General Lord Bentnick did largely adopt Macaulay's policy as outlined in his Minute on Indian Education, the actual process of "forming" this class was not as seamless as he might have imagined it. For one, the question of whether or not to structure education in English or the vernacular languages was not one that all colonial officials agreed on. Although English was seen as a means to wrench native elites out of what were seen as their inherent cultural limitations, some officials saw vernacular education as better equipped to transmit the moral learning that was part of the civilizing mission. Indeed, India's modern written bhashas emerged in the very crucible of colonial modernity, and thus any false opposition between India's "authentic" or untouched bhashas and the colonial language of English is in fact inaccurate. In this way, *both* English and the vernaculars were the site of the consolidation of colonial power – and the site of potential resistance as well. An 1887 Minute from the governor-general warned that "the general extension in India of secular education has, in some measure, resulted in the growth of tendencies unfavourable to discipline and favourable to irreverence in the rising generation"; the Christian Vernacular Education Society for India used this as evidence that English education was potentially dangerous to British interests.[4] However, the bhashas were the site of significant projects of reform and dissent as well. In fact, what we see across nineteenth-century bhasha writings is a profound sense of literary experiment, evident in the writings of Bengali author Bankimchandra Chattopadhyay, whom Sudipta Kaviraj reads as reflective of the "unhappy consciousness" characteristic of colonial modernity (*Unhappy*), and in the epistemic experiments of Fakir Mohan Senapati in his Odia novel *Chha Mana Atha Guntha*, to name only two. Bilingual writers characterize these ambivalences more literally in their movements between languages, as seen with bilingual poets Michael Madhusadan Dutt (R. Chaudhuri, *Gentlemen* 86–126) and Henry Derozio (R. Chaudhuri, "Politics"; and "Cutlets") and in the embattled writings of Toru Dutt, Krupabai Satthianadan, and Rabindranath Tagore. As the range of these early authors shows, neither writing in English nor in the vernaculars expressed straightforward political or ideological alliance with colonialism but rather evinced a complex interrogation of the contradictions of colonial modernity itself (A. Chaudhuri, "Modernity" xix).

Thus early English fiction did not emerge in a distinct sphere of its own but rather in relation to and in dialogue with innovations in the bhashas that were taking place at the same time (M. Mukherjee, *Perishable* 9). Often, individual authors wrote in both English and one of the bhashas. Thus, less than a decade after publishing his one and only novel in English, Bankimchandra Chattopadhyay founded a Bengali magazine, *Bangadarshan*, in which he hoped to invigorate the Bengali language in public life, where English had largely found sway.[5] Likewise, Rokeya Sakhawat Hossain wrote both in Bengali and English – and Toru Dutt in French as well. These examples show how the modernity that emerged in India was always already polyglossic. Thus we not only dispel associations of foreignness attached to the nineteenth-century Anglophone novel in India but also see how an analysis of the English novel cannot be separated from accounts of colonial modernity across languages.

Interchange among the various linguistic traditions continued beyond the nineteenth century. While early twentieth-century Anglophone writers Mulk Raj Anand, Ahmed Ali, and Raja Rao are often lumped together as nationalist/socialist writers who wrote in English, this grouping provides only a partial understanding of the richness of literary cultures in this period. Anand and Ali were both affiliated with the All-India Progressive Writers' Association (AIPWA), which brought together authors writing in a range of languages, including Sajjad Zaheer in Urdu and Premchand in Hindi.[6] As Snehal Shingavi discusses in Chapter 4, Ahmed Ali wrote in both Urdu and English and was involved equally in literary debates with his fellow Urdu writers as he was with other English writers.[7] Raja Rao, too, wrote in Kannada and French along with English (Amur; Jamkhandi 133). Seeing these authors as essentially linked just because they wrote in English overlooks the richness of engagement of both figures in their respective languages. In the postcolonial decades as well, the "existentialist" (P. Gupta 53) Hindi writer Nirmal Verma spent most of his life abroad, often set his works in Europe, and has admitted significant influence from western literature (P. Gupta 53) rather than from the Hindi novel. Kiran Nagarkar's first novel, *Saat Sakkam Trechalis* (*Seven Sixes are Forty-Three*, 1974) was written in Marathi, and only later did he switch to English (Lukmani xii). Partition literature, as discussed in Chapter 7 by Ananya Jahanara Kabir, also crossed linguistic boundaries; a novelist such as Qurratulain Hyder crafted her own English translation of her Urdu *Aag ka darya*, demonstrating engagement in both languages' literary and public spheres. And, as Rashmi Sadana's chapter shows, some of the most significant works of this period were written in the bhashas and disseminated in translation.

These myriad, interlingual histories tend to get obscured in contemporary literary criticism, which often privileges English as a distinct and more cosmopolitan language than any of the bhashas. This is in part because of the slippage between English and cosmopolitanism advanced by many English-language novels themselves: for instance, in the "altered vision" (5) with which Aadam Aziz returns to Kashmir in the first pages of *Midnight's Children*, a perspective that makes him "[resolve] never again to kiss earth for any god or man" (4). From this moment onward in the Indian novel, travel (and English) is cast as broadening and perspective-changing, constructing, in turn, staying home (and, consequently, writing in the bhashas) as myopic and provincial. Rushdie stated this view more directly in his Foreword to *Mirrorwork*, an anthology of writing from India from 1947–1997 that he edited, in which he included only one piece – out of thirty-two – in translation; the others were all originally written in English:

> The prose writing – both fiction and non-fiction – created in this period by Indian writers *working in English*, is proving to be a stronger and more important body of work than most of what has been produced in

the 16 "official languages" of India, the so-called "vernacular languages," during the same time; and, indeed, this new, and still burgeoning, "Indo-Anglian" literature represents perhaps the most valuable contribution India has yet made to the world of books. (Rushdie, Introduction viii, emphasis in original)

While celebrating English over the bhashas, Rushdie simultaneously asserts its marginality, as by putting the phrase "official languages" in quotes, he suggests at least to the book's non-Indian readership that English is only recognized "unofficially" by the Indian state and thus that writing in English carries an inherently non-nationalist or cosmopolitan imaginary.[8] From this perspective, English is not only global but inherently progressive; this is not the progressivism of social realism but a righteous refusal of the narrowness of nationalist belonging.

The backlash to comments like Rushdie's from academics in India "defending" the vernaculars led to a further entrenchment of the national-cosmopolitan agon. Path-breaking literary critic Meenakshi Mukherjee – who worked at Jawaharlal Nehru University (JNU) in Delhi and then at the University of Hyderabad until her death in 2009 – coolly suggested that "in the English texts of India there may be a greater pull towards a homogenisation of reality, an essentialising of India, a certain flattening out of the complicated and conflicting contours, the ambiguous and shifting relations that exist between individuals and groups in a plural community" ("Anxiety" 2608). Yet those are precisely the authors that are more widely read, "interviewed ... [and] invited for readings" (M. Mukherjee, "Local" 51).[9] In response, several English authors took increasingly entrenched positions in defense of English. Vikram Chandra, for instance, argued that Indian critics such as Mukherjee, whom he dubbed "commissars" and "self-proclaimed guardians of purity and Indianness," have constructed a "cult of authenticity" around a nationalist fantasy of Indianness ("Cult").[10] Through this type of polarizing debate, the stakes of the question rose dramatically, crescendoing into rigid – and ultimately useless – binaries: authentic versus traitorous; *desi* versus *pardesi*. Backed by the very material realities of market inequality and access to international celebrity-status, the English writers who "won" the debates framed their position in such a way that increasingly, any call for attention to vernacular writing was cast as backward, provincial, and an expression of a knee-jerk nationalism.

This valuation of Indian English writers over bhasha writing was only strengthened by an increasing interest in the west – the place where, until very recently, literary fortunes were made – in a certain type of writing coming from India, often marked by an easily digestible blend of exotic difference and legibility (in short, different but not *too* different): "otherness [that] is validated only if it fits into certain pre-established paradigms of expectation: a magic realist ambience, mystical spice women, small town eccentrics, the saga of women's suffering, folk tale elements blended into contemporary narrative, so on and so forth" (M. Mukherjee, "Local" 52). This contradictory desire was encapsulated in a June 1997 issue of *The New Yorker* that featured eleven of "India's leading novelists" (Buford 6) – all writing in English – who, the article's author reported, represented, "in a hopeful, even exhilarating way: the shape of a future Indian literature" (8). In the photograph of the eleven writers, they are all dressed in shades of black, suggesting a kind of staged hipness; yet despite this well-meaning attempt to convey the modernity and futurity of the Indian novel, the cover of the issue still relied on tired, Orientalist imagery for representing India, showing the surprise on the intrepid, white explorers' faces when they find a statue of Ganesh not staring ahead with his usual composure but reading – and reading fiction, to boot (see Figure 1). English – in particular the "Indian English" celebrated so enthusiastically by the article – provides precisely that mix of difference and legibility that makes Indian writing marketable to an audience unfamiliar with India. This is not the "small-town tedium, frustrated youth, couples incapable of communicating with each other, the impossible gulfs between aspiration and reality" of the Hindi novel *Raag Darbari* – the "India that the West does not like to think about for too long" – but "the florid, sensuous, inclusive, multicultural world of the post-Rushdie, postcolonial novel," through which "the West can settle down to contemplate, not India, but its latest reinterpretation of itself" (Orsini, "India" 88).[11] One might say that Chinua Achebe's determination that the African writer "should aim at fashioning an English which is at once universal and able to carry his peculiar experience" (63) was commodified and neatly assimilated in this period into a particularly American multiculturalism that values the exotic only when it appears in faintly familiar garb.

And yet, although the ripple-effect of these debates continues to affect not only what gets published but what authors write in the first place, it appears that the relationship of English to the vernaculars in contemporary writing has begun to shift in the last decade or so. For one, today's authors seem to be more attentive to the political – if not expressly historical – relationship between English and the vernaculars, now that the euphoria surrounding cosmopolitanism's children has somewhat died

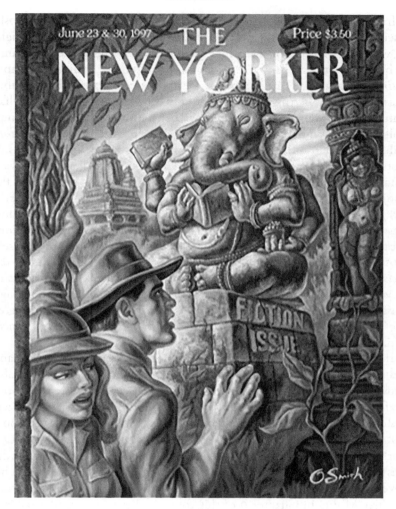

Figure 1. The June 23 and 30, 1997, *New Yorker* cover featuring Indian fiction.
© The New Yorker.

down. Thus, for instance, although Booker-winning author Aravind Adiga writes his novels in English, he has published articles celebrating regional writing[12] and has professed that when he is in Bangalore, he only reads the Kannada-language press.[13] His second and least globally known work, the interconnected short stories *Between the Assassinations* (2009), is recognized in India as having a particular regional quality that distinguishes it from his other novels. Likewise, Chetan Bhagat, who as Priya Joshi discusses in Chapter 20 writes deliberately in opposition to the "highbrow" literary culture of the earlier Indian novel, writes a weekly column in both the English daily *The Times of India* and the Hindi newspaper *Dainik Bhaskar*. All Bhagat's books are translated into Hindi and other bhashas; and the settings of some of the recent ones in Tier-II cities like Ahmedabad, Varanasi, and Chennai (rather than the more cosmopolitan Kolkata and Mumbai) speak to his desire to reach a wider audience *within* India rather than outside of it. This is something we see in the works of bestselling contemporary author Anuja Chauhan as well, who brings a notable Punjabi inflection to her light, "rom-com" novels resonant of the Punjabi idiom of many popular Hindi romance films (A. Roy, "What's" 155). Although at times they appear similar, I suggest that these examples constitute a phenomenon different from Rushdie's "chutnification" because the intended audience is not the cosmopolitan elite but precisely those Indian readers who might potentially read in English *and* one of the bhashas (Subramanian). Thus, today's texts no longer ask their readers to be versed in the hybrid history of Moorish Spain or the Jallianwala Bagh massacre but in Facebook, Premier League cricket, and Bollywood gossip. They carve out a new space where English and the bhashas can meet again.[14]

In Bhagat and Chauhan, we also see a closer tie between literature and India's most significant mass cultural product: Hindi popular film, also known as Bollywood. Although connections between literature and popular film have existed in the past, with notable Hindi and Urdu writers such as Saadat Hasan Manto, Ismat Chughtai, Krishan Chandar (R. Bose 62), K. A. Abbas (Khair, "Indian" 73, n. 14), Javed Akhtar, and Gulzar working in both domains, in English, the divide has been historically greater. Likewise, although Rushdie includes many filmic references in his novels (described in detail by Stadtler), his true interest – as pointed out by Vijay Mishra in Chapter 11 of this volume – lies in auteur filmmaking, and he uses Bollywood as a cultural source mostly generative of parody. In Chapter 24, Sangita Gopal shows how the connections between popular film and literature have only heightened in recent years, with novels like Bhagat's seemingly written for film, and their adaptations becoming huge box office successes. Again, what looks like a crass commercialization might simultaneously be seen as another instance of a renewed relationship between English and the vernaculars.

Moreover, today's English fiction actively rejects the westward orientation that was clear – if not necessary (for publishing purposes) – among the earlier generation. Bestselling novelists such as Anuja Chauhan, Chetan Bhagat, Ashok Banker, Amish Tripathi, and others do not market their books to the west; many of them have not even been published outside of India – something unthinkable for an earlier generation. Likewise, notably absent in these books are glossaries or other attempts at translating food or other cultural items to a western reader. The assumption, then, that writing in English means a western orientation or foreign intended audience is no longer valid; in consequence, the terms of the earlier debate – the sense of English as a "foreign" language on one hand and a cosmopolitan one on the other – have largely dissolved.

This shift corresponds with a larger change in urban Indians' self-perception vis-à-vis their own national history as well as the west that has largely grown out of the liberalization of the Indian economy in the early 1990s.[15] This has also resulted in a de-fetishization of the diaspora, as the lifestyle for the wealthy in India's big cities is no longer radically different from how emigrants might live abroad. The changes in urban India's consumer economy, in addition to new multinational companies hiring both Indians and foreigners, means that there is more back-and-forth movement between India and its diaspora. The wide availability of imported products and a new "global" urban aesthetics (such as malls, multiplex cinemas, coffee shops, and so on) have further reduced this gap. The image at the beginning of *The Satanic Verses* of diaspora as a moment of utter freedom – a space where "anything becomes possible" (*Satanic* 5) – repeated in various ways in more recent novels, such as Jhumpa Lahiri's *The Lowland* (2013) – has now been reevaluated. It is not that the allure of diaspora no longer exists, but its experience is no longer represented as a sea change. In Aravind Adiga's *The White Tiger* (2008), Ashok, Balram's boss, has lived in the United States; therefore, unlike the rest of his family, he wears different clothes, knows the correct pronunciation of "pizza," and is slightly more liberal than his brothers in his treatment of his driver. But the novel simultaneously suggests that (westernized) liberal condescension is just as bad as (homegrown) feudal hegemony; thus, it is Ashok who becomes Balram's eventual victim. Aesthetically as well, in a graphic novel such as Sarnath Banerjee's *Corridor* (2004), which Corey K. Creekmur discusses in Chapter 23, New Delhi's streetscapes elicit the same feeling of alienation that might arise in any modern city and thus "challenge the negative images of the postcolonial metropolis as a 'third world' megalopolis with problems ranging from the ill-health of its urban poor, and increasing numbers of inhabitants to slumification" (Standten 512). It is thus not that contemporary novels efface the cultural differences between "east" and "west," but they de-fetishize them; they render them banal.

Today's authors also not only move but *move back*: Chetan Bhagat and Aravind Adiga both lived for many years abroad but now live in India. This kind of movement complicates the one-way trajectory that was true for most of the *New Yorker*-featured writers. But at the same time, contemporary writing cannot be reduced to these sociological trends. I suggest that these new itineraries are accompanied by new literary concerns and, perhaps more importantly, new literary forms, which have emerged in relation to these changes. In turn, these forms require new methodologies that might entail breaks from more classically postcolonial theoretical concerns.

Reading the Postcolonial

The publication of *Midnight's Children* a short two years after Edward Said's *Orientalism* (1979) also had a determining influence on the field of Indian novel criticism. Just when the Indian novel in English was being feted as a radical reimagining of the postcolonial condition, *Orientalism* and its interlocutors were contributing to a rethinking of the role of literature and the academic disciplines more broadly in the formation and consolidation of empire. At the same time as Rushdie was offering his critique of nationalist history through a rupture of realist aesthetics, the field of postcolonial theory was beginning to develop, increasingly influenced by French poststructuralism. Thus, at the incipient moment when the Indian novel in English became an object of study, texts were determined to be always effects of power, and literary qualities such as form or aesthetics to bear political and historical weight. At first, this meant reexaminations of English novels through a postcolonial lens, with the intent of exposing how great works of Western literature contributed to the consolidation of the colonial episteme, as in Gayatri Chakravorty Spivak's ground-breaking reading of *Jane Eyre* ("Three"), Edward Said's reading of *Mansfield Park* (*Culture*), the many studies of Joseph Conrad's *Heart of Darkness* and others. These analyses supplemented similar findings in other fields: Thomas Metcalf's study of colonial architecture in India (*Imperial*), Mary Louise Pratt's discussion of travel writing ("Scratches"), and Timothy Mitchell's analysis of photography and the world's fairs (*Colonising*) all confirmed the epistemic violence inherent in representation. But literary critics soon transposed this methodology to Indian novels, exposing their relationship if not to colonialism, then to the nation, as a site of knowledge-formation no less insidious than its predecessor. This approach was immensely useful in seeing how the idea of the nation renders significant exclusions of even those minorities it claims to represent: of religious, gendered, casteized others. Textual analyses such as Gauri Viswanathan's reading of Mulk Raj Anand's *Untouchable* (Viswanathan 220) and Aamir Mufti's of Manto in "A Greater Short-Story Writer Than God" are brilliant examples of how this national-discourse analysis, as an elaboration on colonial discourse analysis, was put to excellent use.

This methodology became the paradigm for postcolonial readings of Indian literature, with the nation-state increasingly targeted as the site of the consolidation of normalizing discourse; yet its repetition – as it was deployed in relation to more texts and additional marginalized populations – quickly turned into a kind of interpretation-machine that verged on monotony. Likewise, novels that contested or criticized the nation – following the trail blazed by *Midnight's Children* – were more often read, circulated, and commented on as if that itself was the basis for aesthetic and scholarly legitimacy. The postcolonial "canon" was formed in this heady mix of modernist aesthetics and a cosmopolitanist critique of nationalist hegemony. The linguistic decision to write in English thus gained a thematic counterpart, and a critique of the nation became central to what the Indian novel was seen to "do."

This situation was only exacerbated by the centrality of the diasporic subject in criticism on the Indian novel. For not only did the most well-known authors of the 1980s and 1990s live abroad, but the shapers of the critical field often did as well. This is not to say that literary critics can only write from their own subject-positions, or that a diasporic critic can only be critical of national belonging, but that is, largely, what happened: the incessant questioning of the nation *in a theoretical sense* inadvertently ended up taking as its paradigmatic agent a diasporic writer and critic – a fact that in turn influenced the texts that were studied and the methodologies used to study them. Critics' locations shaped the development of the field, resulting in a skewing of its scholarly priorities. As Meenakshi Mukherjee explained:

> After the initial euphoria subsided, doubts have begun to creep in about the adequacy of this global [postcolonial] discourse with its emphasis on dislocation, diaspora, race and multiculturalism of an immigrant variety to enable us to engage with the issues that are locally relevant to us in India.... What is sometimes forgotten is that metaphors like centre and margin are language specific as well as location specific. A Hindi or Bangla writer in India today may be quite surprised to know that he or she is

supposed to inhabit the periphery. Read by tens of thousands of people at home, figuring centrally in literary and sometimes political controversies over issues that are important in the country, they are naturally seen as being situated at the hub of a complex and populous culture. ("Local" 49)

In this passage, Mukherjee suggests that the discourse of postcolonial theory did not apply to the "Hindi or Bangla writer" because, in a sense, it was conceived not to explain such a writer but the "displaced" cosmopolitan of the Indian English literary and critical imagination. For this reason, the celebration of the "margins" devolved into a sustained critique of the Indian nation itself from the perspective of its outside. Being "handcuffed to history" became a peculiarly Indian condition and "shame" a Pakistani cultural trait; translation and interpretation (as in "the interpreter of maladies") were inherently valued over what was cast as their nativist or patriotic alternatives. Meanwhile, bhasha writers, although of course equally critical of current conditions, were largely excluded from this new canon, as they framed their critiques in a very different idiom, often targeting, for instance, the Indian *state*, as in Mahasweta Devi's critiques of developmentalism in her Bengali short stories or Srilal Shukla's scathing satire of the postcolonial bureaucracy in *Raag Darbari* (1968). Upamanyu Chatterjee made a similar critique of India's civil service in his English-language novel *English, August* (1988), but that novel, lacking in the particular vocabulary of diaspora and the problem of nationhood, failed to capture either an international readership or significant critical attention in postcolonial literary studies.

This thematic focus on the nation has overdetermined the development of the field we now know as Indian novel criticism to such an extent that, I would argue, it is often difficult to write outside of it. In addition to the privileging of English over the bhashas, it has also privileged certain kinds of methodologies and critical approaches, hinging on keywords such as displacement (M. Mukherjee, "Theme" 226), nation, diaspora, hybridity, alterity, and subaltern. Recent panels of the South Asian Literary Association (SALA), for instance – an allied organization of the Modern Language Association (MLA) – shows an overwhelming interest in such key words and phrases, featuring topics such as "The Nation and Its Discontents," which was the theme of the 2014 annual conference or, in 2015, panels such as: "Unfinished South Asian Pasts," "Canada and U.S. West Coast as Sites of Memory," "Borders, Boundaries and Margins," and "South Asians in Africa."[16] Although wide-ranging in terms of topic, these themes all center around the question of national boundaries, figured through diasporic identities, and the continuing hold of the past on the present – rather than the myriad other approaches that might potentially be mobilized on behalf of the study of South Asian literature.

One of the primary problems with this approach is that literature as a discursive formation can do little else than either consolidate or contest the nationalist project. In both cases, literature is a discursive accompaniment to a larger political or cultural endeavor. This calls for a particular kind of critical practice that paradoxically both inflates and diminishes the status of the text: the former because it invests texts with cultural and political significance far beyond "merely" literature but the latter because once the text *is* cultural and political, it is simultaneously no longer *literature*, with all the contradictions, ambivalences, and obscurities that constitute that field. Literature thus loses its complexity, its ability to mediate, to refract, to imagine, to create.

These somewhat overdetermined approaches have led to a loss in actual *reading* of the Indian novel. This is not unique to postcolonial criticism but is an overall trend in literary studies more broadly following the demise of New Criticism and the rise of "theory," but it is one that, to my mind, this subfield has suffered quite acutely. As Jane Gallop writes, in the rush to celebrate the end of the New Criticism, literary critics have given up on the methodology that distinguishes them from other disciplines: close reading, which she describes broadly as an "enhanced, intensified reading" (183) that makes visible certain features not immediately evident in a text. Gallop's words sound a striking note in an institutional atmosphere more plagued than ever with doubts about the "value" of the humanities for undergraduates and doctoral students. If all we do, she argues, is a "weaker sort" of what historians do better, what will be the continuing role of our field? This is true in South Asian studies in particular, which is such a rich, interdisciplinary area in part because our historians and our anthropologists do such a fantastic job of reading literary texts. Historian Ayesha Jalal has written convincingly on both Iqbal (*Self*) and, more recently, Saadat Hasan Manto (*Pity*), for example; political scientist Sudipta Kaviraj authored a fascinating book on Bankimchandra (*Unhappy*); many anthropologists have written on popular film. All this scholarship is notable for the lucid way it relates literature to other aspects of cultural life, using literary texts to enhance topics of their authors' specific disciplinary expertise. Yet what, then, remains the task of the literary critic?

This is not a call for a return to close reading per se, or to somehow suggest that the solution to the crisis in the humanities lies in a particular critical methodology. Rather, I seek to draw attention to the numerous ways we might attend to those attributes that distinguish the literary text from other kinds of writing or discourse for the purpose of a reinvigoration of our field. Ellen Rooney makes a similar argument in her defense of literary form, arguing that without attending to the role of form in the production of meaning, literary critics are left to find meaning in what texts explicitly say:

> The effects of the attenuation of the category of form include the reduction of every text to its ideological or historical context, or to an exemplar of a prior theory (content) – form reduced to an epiphenomenon; the rapid exhaustion of the entire roster of political and theoretical problematics "applied" in this manner, with the attendant miasma theoretical incoherence; the trivialization of the concept of textuality ... and the generalization of reading-as-paraphrase, which robs cultural *and* literary studies of the power to make any essential contribution to critical work already moving confidently ahead in history, sociology, anthropology, and communications. (26)

Rooney's "formalism" is similar to Gallup's "close reading"; while both concepts seem to have lost much of their legitimacy in literary studies for what is perceived as their irreconcilability with politics and history, they both stand for modes of *reading* that attend to the way content is mediated in literary texts in unique and discernible ways. *Reading* is in this sense an alternative to paraphrase: it requires the recognition of textuality in the production of meaning, of the importance of genre and medium, and of the materiality of the written word. These do not lead to the disabling of the political or historical significance of a text but rather assert that the fields of politics and history are in fact open rather than determined in advance. As Rooney writes, "the work of formalism is to resist the application of 'theoretical themes' as master codes that reduce every text (whatever its provenance) to an illustration of theory itself" (31). She calls on critics to explore instead "how 'the actions of texts elude and resist the critical arguments imposed upon them'" (38). This is not, therefore, a return to something like New Criticism, an erasure of historical context, a resurrection of the politics-aesthetics divide, or a manifesto for the aesthetic autonomy of the literary text. Rather, in its best form, it is a means of elaborating *better* political, historically sensitive readings of works through attention to the medium-specificity of the literary text itself. Reading stands as a metonymy for the future of our field.

Admittedly, a return to reading is not a particularly saleable concept in today's academic culture, and it goes quite radically against the grain of postcolonial literary criticism as it has been practiced over the past several decades. Moreover, I do not mean to deny the incredible value of cultural studies, book histories, genre studies, and thematic analyses of Indian novels, whose importance will only be renewed as the category of the "Indian novel" is put under pressure and as new themes and imaginaries are folded into the genre. In fact, it is this last proposition that impels this critique: as the novel becomes democratized, as it interacts with forms such as popular film and comics, as the world of criticism expands with blogs and Twitter hosting book reviews that are more accessible to more people, it seems all the more important to take heed of the specificities of literary writing and reading, with the hope that attention to the complexities, nuances, and ambivalences of literature can inform this new democratized book culture rather than represent an outdated practice happily left behind.

Few of the chapters in this book engage this question explicitly, but by and large there is an impressive investment in *reading* as a powerful analytic and interpretive practice – although, again, from a range of critical perspectives. Toral Gajarawala, for instance, is attentive to the circulation of ressentiment in typical dialogue spoken by unnamed speakers in Uday Prakash's *The Girl With the Golden Parasol*; Gajarawala reads not only the dialogue for what it conveys but the ellipses and unspoken text for what they betray about the "general social malaise" of the campus culture the novel describes. Alex Tickell leads us through the contentious terrain of Indian historiographical fiction through a sensitive close reading of A. K. Ramanujan's poem, "Some Indian Uses of History on a Rainy Day," which he gleans not for evidence but as the source of theory itself, in the juxtaposition of its various incongruous images. Shameem Black uses an extended reading of *The God of Small Things* to show how the novel asserts "smallness" as an alternative to globally-circulating humanitarian discourses. Eli Park Sorensen finds several metatextual moments in Rohinton Mistry's novels in which characters comment on the author's own artistry and reads those moments as essential mediations between form and content. And Vijay Mishra's chapter on Rushdie argues against a purely ideological analysis, suggesting that we attend to the formal elaborations of his works as well. Thus, rather than reading *The Satanic Verses*' "Mera joota hai japani" as a nationalist counterpoint to James Thompson's "Rule Britannia!" Mishra suggests that the tonal qualities of both texts, as they are shouted and sung, reflect Rushdie's engagement with "a corporeal disconnectedness where the body utters sounds without immediately connecting them to their thematic referents." Thus, for Mishra, Rushdie's cosmopolitanism is visible not only in his themes but in the formal structure of his novels as well.

These approaches offer a challenge to our sedimented methodologies for studying the Indian novel, especially as the forms of the novel grow and proliferate in the twenty-first century. New forms of the Indian novel – the popular, the filmi, the fantastical, the graphic – will put further pressure on the practice of literary reading, potentially marking the full demise of these older methodologies that postcolonial theory set into motion. That is up to readers and scholars to decide. Are we content to relinquish the uniqueness of the literary critical approach as the boundaries between literature and popular culture diminish even further? Are contemporary literary texts more easily assimilated to a larger sphere of cultural production? Or, alternatively, is there something we can continue to contribute by practicing – and teaching – reading as a methodology that brings contemporary texts in dialogue not only with their predecessors in India but with the historical concerns of the novel in its longer history, and with contemporary literature around the world? Is there something genre, form, text, and language continue to offer us, not only as scholars but as part of an ever-expanding reading public more generally?

Contemporaneity and History

> Here, at the twilight of the twentieth century and the dawn of the twenty-first, even names like Gandhi, Tolstoy, Premchand, and Tagore have begun to disappear from people's memories. The best-selling book in stores today? *The Road Ahead*, by Bill Gates.
>
> – Uday Prakash, *Peeli chatri wali ladki* [*The Girl with the Golden Parasol*] (pp. 11–12)

Just as the term "history" implies a neatly packaged narrative with few loose ends – a chronology that is as much a structuring principle as an accurate account of change over time – contemporaneity implies the opposite: an uncontrollable mess of synchronous elements that are ever-unfolding and, by their very nature, impossible to contain and classify. Contemporaneity signals something irreducible to narrative time; it highlights the productive dialectic that underlies this whole book, between diachrony and synchrony, containment and excess. The contemporary also stands outside conventional periodization in literary studies – one can be a "medievalist" or a "Victorianist" but hardly a *contemporaneist* – and thus refuses our conventional academic signs of expertise. It is only now that dissertations and books are being written that try to theorize the contemporary itself as a phenomenon, but the status of that enterprise within existing institutional structures is yet to be determined.

It is unsurprising, when seen from this perspective, that almost half the chapters in this volume somehow take up the question of the contemporary novel; this is, literally and critically, the future of the field. Indeed, by diffusing its own organizational principle in this way – by allowing history to morph into contemporaneity – this volume hopes to raise important methodological questions that bring together long-standing debates in the field – as discussed earlier – with the new pressures of studying contemporary literature: When is a genre or type of text new, and how do we grasp its newness? How do we begin to construct categories and language to define new texts? How do we understand trends when those trends are still being shaped and formed? What is the status of time-honored categories like realism and modernism in the face of the contemporary? How do we conceive of the relationship between literature and global capitalism, the global war on terror, and neoliberalism?

Certain trends do seem apparent. We might say, for instance, from a survey of the contemporary chapters, that Aravind Adiga's *The White Tiger* seems to be playing a similar role in the periodization of the contemporary Indian novel in English as *Midnight's Children* did for the earlier generation, as it features as a key text in a number of different chapters. We could also identify an "anti-literary" trend – to use Priya Joshi's phrase in Chapter 20 – in which the modernist sensibilities of postcolonial literature seem to have given way to its commercialization. Relatedly, we can see some elements of the Bharatiya Janata Party's (BJP) "India Shining" rhetoric – central to its 2004 national election campaign – in many new works: an overcoming of the postcolonial melancholy that was sometimes evident in the earlier generation, yes, but also a celebration of India's putative global status, an abandonment of social and political aims, a loss of faith in the state and in Nehruvian secularism, a concomitant celebration of capitalism, as well as an increasing use of Hindu nationalist tropes and themes. However, the chapters on these texts simultaneously suggest that it would be a mistake to lament the loss of sensibilities whose alternatives are as-yet unknown. Thus, the other side of the contemporary is a set of unresolved questions about literary futurity in India.

In this sense, contemporaneity is another kind of rejoinder to the diaspora-driven methodologies within postcolonial studies discussed earlier. Part of what contemporaneity offers as a methodology is attention to the "nowness" of literary and cultural production, but where does that nowness reside? Significantly, the answer to that question, as contemporary novels demonstrate almost across the board, is that the "now" resides no longer in Europe or the United States but in India itself. The present and future of the Indian novel is in India, both because the Indian English readership is growing dramatically and India is on its way to becoming the largest global publisher of English-language fiction[17] and because, inasmuch as writers and scholars have criticized the recent electoral victory of the BJP for its communal agenda, this victory very much emblematizes a new sensibility for urban India: one of "aspirations," as Vijay Prashad has characterized it ("India's Left"), and of futurity. At long last, India is no longer a place one must leave in order to live the good life; the aspiration is no longer the United States or Canada but a posh apartment in Mumbai or Bangalore. India itself is the site of literary futurity. This is why a novel like Jhumpa Lahiri's *The Lowland* (2013) – despite its very favorable reviews – seems decidedly out of date, almost as if the setting in the 1970s reflected not merely the author's interest in the Naxalite movement in Calcutta but her desire to tell a markedly 1970s story: of violence, displacement, and, finally, tentative reconciliation to a new land. *The Lowland* is thus uniquely melancholic, not only, I argue, for the loss of home but for the loss of the diasporic novel itself as the primary form of postcoloniality. For Lahiri's (and her characters') is not the dominant migrant story anymore. Today's stories are those of Aravind Adiga and Chetan Bhagat, authors who lived abroad and returned to India; of Manu Joseph and Arundhati Roy, authors who never left; and of new liberal arts institutions being opened in India, while in the United States the very idea of the liberal arts is under threat. This is not to say there are not continued problems and hardships in India, or a continuing allure of the west, but rather that the future now has potentially multiple paths. This is also not to overstate the difference location makes in producing critical knowledge – nor to re-fetishize the "local" or the "authentic." Rather, it is to offer new theoretical frameworks for understanding the relationship of the present to the past outside of the unilinear narrative of diaspora that has long shaped critical questions in the field.

Contemporaneity also serves as a rejoinder to postcoloniality's fixation with – almost, I would venture, its fetishization of – the past. Consider powerful images like Salman Rushdie's Saleem Sinai being "handcuffed to history" (*Midnight's* 3) or Arundhati Roy's "History House" – a place where "human history, masquerading as God's purpose, reveal[s] herself to an under-age audience" (A. Roy, *God* 309). Even the novels of Amitav Ghosh, which use history so compellingly to question the hold of the nation on the writing of historical truths, are still deeply invested in unearthing alternative *pasts* as a means of restitution against what are implied to be the provincialisms of the present. As Alex Tickell reminds us in his chapter, the past is consistently the site of tension in India's present. Yet this relationship of postcolonial writing to the past, while productive for all these reasons, also precludes other kinds of engagements with the present and the future; from the perspective of the past, the present is haunted by a specter that is silently shaping its form. This has made it difficult to consider the contemporary *qua* contemporary, and it has largely disabled the aesthetic means of imagining a livable future in literature.

I see the contemporary as the site of an important contradiction, then, between postcolonial literary criticism and the future of Indian literature. Yet it also raises a new series of questions – for instance, regarding the status of "literature," which in its modernist (and postcolonial) incarnation has always retained a respectable distance from the contemporary, unlike its lowbrow counterpart, popular culture. Thus, new novels include what some have criticized as neoliberal themes: the valorization of the "self-made man" in Aravind Adiga's *The White Tiger*, the celebration of capitalist workspaces and middle-class leisure in "chick lit" and other mass market fictions, and the revival of a Hindu cultural superiority in some fantasy. The kind of explicitly political writing we saw in the early twentieth century – progressive literature – is hard to find today. Is a rejection of the past merely an uncritical embrace of the "shining India" of right-wing rhetoric? Is it part of a new culture of unthinking presentism, an unceasing embrace of the new, as suggested by Rahul's sardonic comment, in Uday Prakash's novel *The Girl with the Golden Parasol* and quoted in the epigraph to this section? Are we in the throes of a literary neoliberalism? These are questions central to any study of the literary contemporary. They apply to new literary histories as well as new literatures.

Terminology and Structure of the Book

What I hope is unique about the individual chapters and the way they fit together (and, at times, productively misfit) is their engagement across literary traditions, their refusal of English's distinction, and, in some cases, their specific attention to form and genre. Those impulses drove the design of the table of contents, the choice of contributors, and the productive discussions I had with individual authors around the process of revising and editing each chapter. At the same time, readers will note a diversity of approaches to the questions I have raised here. The volume's twenty-five authors come from eight different countries, spread over four continents. This is truly an international field. I have taken this range of institutional backgrounds as an asset rather than an unwieldiness that might need to be contained. It speaks to the heterogeneity not only of the field but of the subject itself.

At the same time, and while I strove for broad coverage of themes, writers, and social locations, this is not a truly comprehensive history of the Indian novel in English. There are several notable absences in terms of topics: English writings from Kashmir and the Northeast, postcolonial science fiction, literature and the environment, the satirical novel, the cricket novel, the Indian Bildungsroman, the queer novel, the "theory" novel, crime fiction, noir fiction, and "terrorist" novels – to name only a few. As this list demonstrates, the potential topics for this kind of study are endless – and I was, in the interest of word count, limited to twenty-five chapters. The volume's significance, then, is less to be found in the number of topics covered than in the range and diversity of approaches to the particular ones addressed here.

Likewise, as will be clear from a brief glance at the table of contents, the volume is not rigidly divided by author, with only a few exceptions: that is, it is not structured with a chapter on Toru Dutt, one on R. K. Narayan, one on Aravind Adiga, and so on.[18] Rather, it is organized thematically. This is a deliberate attempt to decenter individual auteurs and situate them instead within larger historical, political, and aesthetic trends. The result of this decision, however, is that there are several authors and texts that appear in more than one chapter. When this happens, readers should register it as significant, as, especially in the last section, it marks one way of gauging the potential importance of contemporary authors for whom there is not yet a canon. For teachers as well, it will be useful to locate these overlaps, as they show the range of approaches to a single text: Mulk Raj Anand's writings are discussed – to give just one example – in chapters on the progressive novel, the Gandhian novel, the modernist novel, the experimental novel, and caste. The validity of all these approaches to Anand might have been occluded if there had been one chapter grouping all his novels under a single rubric.

In addition to individual topics, the conception of the volume – like all others – also carries some significant exclusions. The partiality of the term "English" was discussed earlier; "novel" too limits the possible texts that we might have included, especially in a context such as India where the novel was a relatively late literary development.[19] But "Indian" also marks certain limits – the most significant of those being the literatures of Pakistan and Bangladesh. Indeed, the national boundedness of this history is complicated by the fact that the India that exists today is not the same India that existed before 1947. Thus, Ahmed Ali, for instance, is considered in this volume an Indian writer even though he moved to Pakistan in 1948; Bapsi Sidhwa, discussed by Kavita Daiya in Chapter 14, was born in Karachi and has lived in both postcolonial India and Pakistan, as has Salman Rushdie. Bankimchandra Chattopadhyay spent several years in Khulna, in East Bengal (later to become part of Bangladesh): that is, as Supriya Chaudhuri documents in Chapter 1, where he started writing his only English novel. "India" as a category that crosses from the nineteenth century to the twenty-first century is thus more genealogical than precisely historical. This is more than a technicality, as restricting the scope to only India results in a loss of analytic depth as well: postcolonial Pakistani and Bangladeshi literatures are connected in many ways to Indian literature, and to any reader or scholar of South Asia (clearly the more accurate term in this regard), it seems artificial – even, to channel Urdu writer Saadat Hasan Manto, absurd[20] – to discount those rich connections for the sake of two arbitrary national borders. This cross-fertilization of subcontinental histories is evident in the novels of Salman Rushdie and Amitav Ghosh, for instance, and, as Alex Tickell shows in his chapter, it is also the subject of increasing anxiety among Hindu nationalists in India, who would rather read India as synonymous with Hindu. (As recent attacks on Buddhist sites in Pakistan have shown, the policing of transnational identities takes place on the other side of the border as well.) Yet, I would argue that despite what seems like increased religious nationalism in both countries, the connections among today's South Asian writers are stronger than ever. This is in part because of the recent explosion of literary festivals in both countries, which allows for greater contact and conversation between Indian and Pakistani writers especially.[21] But it can also be traced to some of the new geopolitical anxieties that concern contemporary novels, such as the global war on terror, climate change, and new forms of transnationalism and finance capitalism, anxieties that are not easily contained by national borders. In Chapter 17, Mrinalini Chakravorty gestures toward such a connection in her reference to contemporary Pakistani author Mohsin Hamid's *How To Get Filthy Rich in Rising Asia* (2013) as an example of a work that has much in common, stylistically and aesthetically, with contemporary Indian novels. Certainly other Pakistani and Bangladeshi authors, such as Kamila Shamsie, Mohammad Hanif, Tahmima Anam, and Zia Haider Rahman, share many features with the various authors discussed here.[22] The exclusion of their writings from this

volume, therefore, should be taken not as a statement on the definitive-
ness of national boundaries but as the consequence of an insufficient,
provisional grouping that demands further inquiry and even radical
questioning.

And a few notes on terminology. It is inevitable in a book with
twenty-five chapters all written by different scholars with different national
and institutional backgrounds that there will be differences in terminology from one chapter to the next. I have resisted the urge to standardize
the use of key terms across the chapters, except in cases when not doing so
might cause some confusion. I have, for instance, tried to retain a specific
meaning for the term "postcolonial" – as opposed to "post-colonial" –
where I have been able. I have managed to standardize its usage to the
extent that the non-hyphenated term refers more often to the theoretical
body of work and critical lens that view colonialism as an epistemic shift
with reverberations that extend beyond the historical end of colonial rule.
The term "postcolonial" also refers to a body of literature that registers the
deep impression of history – in particular the histories of colonialism and
nationalism – on the present. In Fernando Coronil's words: "The *post-*
of postcolonialism became at once a temporal and an epistemic marker,
a critical lens through which to view the complicity between knowledge
and power in multiple domains, past and present" (636). By contrast,
"post-colonial" usually serves as a historical designation and applies to the
period following independence in 1947.

Another important terminological clarification involves the term the
"Indian novel in English" that is the key part of the book's title. As readers
will notice, different authors use different variants of the term: the Indian
English novel; Indian writing in English (a term used often in India, des-
ignated by the acronym IWE); Indo-Anglian fiction; the Anglophone
novel or the Indian Anglophone novel. These are all widely circulating
terms with a variety of connotations and associated meanings, and scholars in the field of Indian novel studies tend to have individual preferences.
It would give a false sense of the unity of this group for me to ask authors
to change their usage according to one standard.

I have also designed the Works Cited section somewhat uniquely, to
be a useful resource to readers of this volume, by dividing it into primary and secondary sources, both of which are for reference but are also
meant to be browsed. The Primary Sources section lists the wide range
of novels discussed and referenced in these chapters, and at quick glance
should give a sense of the scope of the texts covered. In the spirit of our
collective commitment to reading Indian novels in English alongside

their contemporaries in the vernaculars, I have included all Indian bhasha texts that are referenced by the chapter authors in the Primary Sources list as well. In addition, this list includes three additional categories of texts: nonfictional writings by important fiction authors that are used in the chapters as primary texts; Indian films mentioned in the chapters; and relevant South Asian (but non-Indian) texts, such as Pakistani novels, referenced by the chapter authors. Thus, the Primary Sources list does not only include Indian novels in English but represents the rich milieu of primary texts out of which the Indian novel in English emerged and within which – as the chapters suggest – it still lives.

The list of Secondary Sources might also be browsed, in addition to being used for reference, as it shows the very rich range of theoretical engagements with the Indian novel deployed by our twenty-five contributors. Even a quick glance over the extensive list of secondary sources will demonstrate the widest possible engagements with the Indian novel in English: from novel theory to more general social theory to postcolonial criticism to the rich body of new monographs in the field – published by our authors and by other contemporary scholars – that has emerged in the last several decades. It is thus not only a reference list but a useful archive-in-progress of scholarship in the field.

It is in this final sense that this volume seeks to be a survey, not as containing a full or methodical account of every Indian novel in English, but through its theoretical engagement, its vastness and range, its mix of canonical and experimental approaches, and its explorations of the diachronic and synchronic, as conveying a sense of the utter expansiveness of the field of Indian novel studies and, in what I hope I can say on behalf of all the chapter authors, as a commitment to its future. As much as this book shows how much excellent work has been done, it also reminds us how much work there still remains to do: how many new works to be read, approaches to be outlined, connections to be made, and subtleties to be gleaned. This is a "history" of the Indian novel in English that is as much an anticipation for its continuing future study.

Notes

1 *Bhasha* means "language" in Hindi, but can be used to represent the Indian vernaculars more specifically. Most critics prefer the term *bhasha* to "vernacular," which has associations with the ordinary as opposed to the literary – along with a more recent history of being a degraded mode within colonial discourse.

2 To give a concrete example of one such erasure: Toral Gajarawala has shown how the centrality of Partition in postcolonial literary criticism has led to

the occlusion of Dalit subjectivity, for whom Partition was not a central or seminal event (*Untouchable* 178–82).

3 Roy cites John Berger as the source of this quotation. It is possible to generalize that the successful bhasha novels discussed earlier identified the ethos of postcolonial disillusionment much earlier than their English-language counterparts but, unlike *Midnight's Children*, simply never reached a global audience. As Meenakshi Mukherjee argues, in mid-twentieth-century works such as *Maila Anchal* and *Raag Darbari*, "The serious discourse of nationalism of an earlier period gets transformed into comedy. The charged and emotive words of the freedom fighters emptily echo in the mouths of the scheming politicians" ("Narrating" 143). But even as early as the early postcolonial years, Mukherjee notices, English-language texts tended to efface detail and accuracy for the sake of appealing to a broader audience, thus overshadowing their bhasha contemporaries: "[R. K. Narayan's fictional town of] Malgudi is Hindu upper-caste pan-India, resistant to change, eternal and immutable – very different, say from Maryaganj in Phanishwar Renu's *Maila Anchal* … or Purnea in Satinath Bhaduri's *Jagori* (Bengali: 1946), both in north Bihar, variegated in terms of caste and sub-caste, language and dialect, and in the throes of constant turmoil" ("Anxiety" 2608).

4 Christian Vernacular Education Society for India: Thirtieth Annual Report, for the year ending March 31, 1888. London: Christian Vernacular Education Society, 1888. British Library, IOR/L/PJ/6/240 – File 1796.

5 See "Bangadarshaner Patra-Suchana," Bankim's Foreword to *Bangadarshan*, also discussed by Supriya Chaudhuri in Chapter 1 of this volume.

6 There was an international aspect to the AIPWA as well, as detailed by Coppola ("All-India" 17–31).

7 The debates among Urdu writers involved the nature of progressivism and are discussed by Ahmed Ali in an interview he gave to Carlo Coppola (Coppola, "Ahmed Ali in Conversation") as well as in Ali, Afterword. Snehal Shingavi also discusses these debates in his book, *The Mahatma Misunderstood*, in which he details the importance of seeing Ali's English novel, *Twilight in Delhi*, as engaged in literary debates within the *Urdu* public sphere, which allows for an entirely different reading of the novel than as the communal, backward-looking, "Muslim" novel that most Anglophone critics find it to be (Shingavi 124–5 and 133).

8 In fact, English has a higher position than the "16" other languages, being, along with Hindi, one of India's two national languages. The point is not to demonize Rushdie, however, which has been done by many, but rather to underline that leaving aside his particularly strong language in this Introduction, his views on the superiority of Indian English writing over bhasha writing is not unique. Bharati Mukherjee, another Indian English diasporic writer, said that by living in the diaspora, "I have joined imaginative forces with an anonymous driven underclass of semi-assimilated Indians with sentimental attachment to a distant homeland, but no real desire for permanent return.... Instead of seeing my Indianness as a fragile identity to

be preserved against obliteration … I see it now as a set of fluid identities to be celebrated" (quoted in M. Mukherjee, "Anxiety" 2610). In her introduction to the reference book *South Asian Novelists in India: An A-to-Z Guide*, Sanga similarly writes: "Also unmistakable is the enduring quality of writing in English" (Introduction xiii); other, similarly subtle valorizations of English writing appear widely.

9 Mukherjee criticized specific English-language authors such as Chitra Banerjee Divakaruni and Suhaila Abdulali for their use of "the kind of exotic rhetoric to evoke the native country that would have embarrassed a home-based Indian writer" ("Local" 55) and Vikram Chandra for his use of Sanskrit-derived titles for his chapters in *Love and Longing in Bombay* (1997).

10 See N. Majumdar; and Rajan and Sharma (159–65) for useful summaries of these debates.

11 Rajan and Sharma similarly recount how some U.S. readers of *The God of Small Things* found its use of Indian English alienating, as it "distracted them from getting the meaning." In its audiobook version, however, the novel was more accessible; when "read in a well-modulated but slightly accented voice, many … nodes of cultural differences were delicately mediated" (153).

12 For instance http://www.outlookindia.com/article/A-Storyteller-In-Search -Of-An-Ending/284084, accessed July 16, 2014.

13 http://www.thedailybeast.com/articles/2012/02/19/why-i-ve-learned -many-languages-by-aravind-adiga.html, accessed September 10, 2014.

14 India has had, of course, a strong tradition of pulp fictions, but, as Tabish Khair points out, almost none in English ("Indian" 59).

15 William Mazzarella describes the "euphoria" that undergirded India's economic liberalization as "ar[ising] out of a sense of *temporal overcoming*, a rejection of the historical stalemate that the developmentalist/modernizing paradigm had bequeathed" (89).

16 http://www.southasianliteraryassociation.org/news/calls-for-papers/, accessed July 17, 2014.

17 Many articles cite India as currently the third-largest publisher of English-language books (for instance, http://www.thenational.ae/news/ world/south-asia/publishers-get-a-measure-of-indias-booming-english-boo k-market, accessed October 20, 2014; and http://www.theguardian.com/ books/2009/apr/22/books-india-china, accessed October 20, 2014); however, author and publisher Urvashi Butalia points out that there is no accurate measure of the size of India's publishing industry (http://forbesindia .com/blog/life/the-changing-face-of-indian-publishing/, accessed October 20, 2014).

18 Piciucco (ed.) is, for example, structured this way; likewise, the majority of chapters in Arvind Krishna Mehrotra's *A History of Indian Literature in English* include names of authors in their titles.

19 The range of possibilities for a volume such as this without the two restrictive categories "novel" or "English" is demonstrated, for instance, in critical studies such as *A History of Indian Literature in English*, edited by Aravind

Krishna Mehrotra, or *A History of Indian English Literature*, edited by M. K. Naik, both of which cover nonfictional prose, poetry, and drama in addition to novels. Even more expansive is Sisir Kumar Das's multi-volume opus, *A History of Indian Literature*, which covers all literary genres in all of India's official languages and more. In his book, Snehal Shingavi discusses how critics' fixation with the English novel produces certain narratives about Indian literature at the exclusion of others (*Mahatma* 3). However, I prefer to see the limitations on this volume both as restrictive and also potentially productive of new critical methodologies and new insights into the novel genre that would not be visible if it included criticism on Indian writing more generally.

20 Manto wrote a searing satire of the absurdity of Partition in his Urdu story "Toba Tek Singh" (1953), which is set in a mental asylum that is to be partitioned on August 15, 1947 – a historical fact that the "lunatics" are simply unable to fathom.

21 The Jaipur Literature Festival, founded in 2006, is the largest in the subcontinent, but the Lahore Literary Festival, first held in 2013, is particularly groundbreaking for bringing writers from both sides of the border to Pakistan (http://www.nytimes.com/2013/03/07/world/asia/pakistan-under-cultural-siege-is-buoyed-by-book-festivals.html?pagewanted=all&_r=0, accessed September 27, 2014).

22 There has been far too little written on Bangladeshi writing in English, but a recent article in *Caravan* magazine outlines some of the critical approaches to the recently emerging field (http://caravanmagazine.in/books/east-east?page=0,0, accessed August 7, 2014).

CHAPTER I

Beginnings: Rajmohan's Wife and the Novel in India

Supriya Chaudhuri

Rajmohan's Wife, published in 1864 by Bankimchandra Chattopadhyay (1838–94), is generally regarded as the first Indian novel in English, significant not only because its author was the greatest Bengali novelist of the nineteenth century but also because it speaks to an emergent genre in the literature of colonial modernity. Unlike earlier short fiction in English, such as the futuristic novellas *A Journal of 48 Hours of the Year 1945* (1835) by Kylas Chunder Dutt and *The Republic of Orissa: A Page from the Annals of the Twentieth Century* (1845) by Shoshee Chunder Dutt, *Rajmohan's Wife* has affinities with the domestic and social novel in the vernacular, inaugurated by Peary Chand Mitra's *Alaler Gharer Dulal* (*The Spoilt Son of a Rich Family* [1855–57, Bengali]), and anticipates some of the major developments of the novel as a genre.[1]

Rajmohan's Wife stands at other intersections too: between "original" composition and translation, between realism and romance, between linguistic choices in periodical publication, and between modernity and tradition. Though it may strike us today as a novel without a posterity, it serves as witness to these relations at a critical moment of genre formation and of the construction of the colonial subject, and it offers lessons to later novelists, including Bankim himself. Sadly, the neglect of this work by his critics and biographers is a mark of the discomfort that overcomes literary historians when classifying the relatively minor English-language productions of major Indian writers such as Bankim, Michael Madhusudan Dutt, and Rabindranath Tagore.

The Colonial Public Sphere and the Politics of Print

The extent to which writing in the modern Indian languages was being transformed by contact with the West was a source of deep cultural anxieties as well as new modes of literary self-representation in the nineteenth century. New vernacular literatures attempted to acclimatize

Enlightenment ideas within native literary idioms, while Western genres had to accommodate the desires, aspirations, and experiences of the native bourgeoisie. Bankim's own writings, decisively shaped by progressive Western thinkers such as Jeremy Bentham, John Stuart Mill, and Auguste Comte, reflect the critical tensions that developed after the Revolt of 1857 between Western liberal thought, repressive government, religious and social reform, and traditionalist reaction and introspection. In literary terms, Bankim's novels show the influence of Shakespeare, Scott, and the Romantic poets as well as the Sanskrit *kavya* tradition. Strongly critical of the hypocrisy of the colonial middle class, he nevertheless felt what Sudipta Kaviraj calls "the peculiar melancholy of living in an alien and intractable history" (Kaviraj, *Unhappy* 161), so that the choice of modernity seems also to be the choice of subjection as its condition. Kaviraj regards this inability to turn away from either side of a divided history as a sign of the Hegelian "unhappy consciousness," expressed in profound estrangement from the system within which Bankim functioned as an educated collaborator (*Unhappy* 168). Bankim's most characteristic mode, therefore, is irony, a rhetorical doubling most evident in the essays he published in *Bangadarshan*, the Bengali journal he founded in 1872.

A member of the colonial bourgeoisie by birth and training, Bankimchandra was an early beneficiary of colonial higher education, when in 1858 he became one of the first two graduates of the newly founded University of Calcutta, and entered the civil service. But he was already widely read in his grandfather's Sanskrit library and was writing poems and essays in Bengali. He began *Rajmohan's Wife* in 1863, near the end of his tenure as deputy magistrate in Khulna, East Bengal. The novel was serialized in 1864 in an English-language weekly, the *Indian Field*, edited by Kishori Chand Mitra (Peary Chand's brother), who had been dismissed from the colonial civil service for his support of the legislative reforms proposed in Sir Barnes Peacock's Bill of 1857, extending the right of jurisdiction over Europeans to native magistrates. C. E. Buckland reports that "while at Khulna, Bankim Chandra began a serial story named 'Rajmohan's wife' in the *Indian Field* newspaper, then edited by Kisori Chand Mitra. This was his first public literary effort" (Buckland 1078).

However, by 1856, Bankim had already won acclaim for his Bengali poetry and prose, published in Ishvarchandra Gupta's journals *Sambad Prabhakar* and *Sambad Sadhuranjan*. In 1863–4, he was also working on what was to be his first published novel in Bengali, *Durgeshnandini* (*The Chieftain's Daughter*, 1865). Early copies of the *Indian Field* have not survived, but as late as March 1872, Bankim was writing to Dr. Sambhu

Chandra Mookerjee, editor of the English-language *Mookerjee's Magazine*:

> For the English Magazine, I can undertake to supply you with novels, tales, sketches and squibs. I can also take up political questions, as you wish. Malicious fortune has made me a sort of jack of all trades and I can turn up any kind of work, from transcendental metaphysics to verse-making. The Novel is to me the most difficult work of all, as it requires a good deal of time and undivided attention to elaborate the conception and to subordinate the incidents and characters to the central idea.[2]

In fact, Bankim contributed a couple of essays, but no novels in English to *Mookerjee's Magazine*. His Bengali novels *Durgeshnandini, Kapalkundala* (1866), and *Mrinalini* (1869) had already been published to general acclaim, and although he continued to correspond in English, he urged Sambhu Chandra that "we ought *to disanglicise* ourselves, so to speak, to a certain extent, and to speak to the masses in their own language. I therefore project a Bengali Magazine."[3] That Bengali magazine was the epoch-making *Bangadarshan*, arriving to "ravish the heart of Bengal," as Rabindranath Tagore described it some forty years later (*Jivansmrti* 333). In his foreword to the journal ("Bangadarshaner Patra-Suchana" 245), Bankim argued that "until well-educated, enlightened Bengalis start expressing their own opinions in the Bengali language, there is no hope of progress for the Bengali race."[4] In colonial India, English was the compulsory medium of public discourse, and for those who had received a "modern" – that is, English – education, language was constitutive of social identity:

> No work of any kind is done in the medium of Bengali amongst the modern set. Scholarly discussion is carried on in English. Public affairs, meetings, lectures, addresses, proceedings, are all in English.... If you do not speak in English, the English do not understand you; if the English do not understand you, they grant you no self-respect or dignity; if you have no self-respect or dignity with the English, you have none anywhere. ("Bangadarshaner Patra-Suchana" 245)

Yet, as Bankim knew, "there is not much possibility of social improvement as a result of advice that is not heard or understood by most people of our land" ("Bangadarshaner Patra-Suchana" 245). It was as necessary to address fellow Indians in their mother tongue as it was to speak to Englishmen in English. Bankim's own practice points to a two-way process of linguistic transfer, a traffic in ideas and moral sentiments. If John Stuart Mill is the subject of an essay in *Bangadarshan*, Hindu philosophy could be the theme of a contribution to *Mookerjee's Magazine*, and translation or adaptation remained the only means of sharing the creative resources of either language.

The politics of print, thus, demanded that the linguistic domains of English and Bengali be crossed and re-crossed by writers anxious to speak both to the rulers and the ruled. Bankim made no public renunciation of English to turn to the riches of his native tongue, as Michael Madhusudan Dutt claimed to have done in a celebrated sonnet (M. Dutt 159 [Sonnet 3]). Nevertheless, he cited Madhusudan as an example when he counseled his younger contemporary, the economic historian and colonial administrator Romesh Chunder Dutt, to use Bengali rather than English for his creative work (cited in A. Bhattacharya 167–8). In a brief skit, "Bangala Sahityer Adar [The Prestige of Bengali Literature]," he contrasted the English-educated but crass Babu with his Bengali-reading wife, who possesses a finer literary taste ("Bangala" 41–3). Eventually, Bankim not only adopted Bengali as his preferred language of creative expression, he also sought to make it a supple and powerful instrument of social commentary. Seen in the context of Lord Lytton's Vernacular Press Act of 1878, which sought to curb the freedom of the native press, Bankim's decision had larger political implications. The fact that *Rajmohan's Wife* remains his only English novel is part of a complex linguistic history made up of many strands and is not simply a mark of literary failure.

Translation and Cultural Transactions

Rajmohan's Wife is a text that carries the task of translation as its burden. On the one hand, it attempts to adapt the rhetorical devices of Sanskrit poetry to events and characters in a contemporary social setting, and on the other, it is driven by the classic concerns of the high bourgeois novel of nineteenth-century Europe: property, sex, and marriage. It is thus closely affiliated with the emergent Indian novel in the modern vernaculars, and if it had achieved a wider readership, it might have set the Indian novel in English on a parallel line of development.

The novel's transmission history is also a history of translation. In the preface to his 1935 edition, Brajendra Nath Banerji reported his discovery of all but the first three issues of the *Indian Field* for 1864 (containing Bankim's novel) bound in with issues of the *Hindoo Patriot* for that year. Since the first three chapters were missing, Brajendra Nath substituted for them "a version as close to Bankim's own as could be desired," drawing on Bankim's own Bengali translation of the first seven chapters of *Rajmohan's Wife,* incorporated by his nephew Sachishchandra Chattopadhyay into the novel *Vari-Vahini.* Retranslated into English, probably by Brajendra Nath, the three first chapters supplied "the missing beginning of Bankim's English novel" (Banerji xiii).[5] In 1935, this composite text was published in the well-known Calcutta journal the *Modern Review,* appearing in book form from their office the same year.

The semi-translated character of *Rajmohan's Wife* is a reminder that in this early period of writing, and for a public divided by language, translation was a constant, necessary recourse. Two of Bankim's novels, *Kapalkundala* (1866) and *Bishabriksha* (1873), had been translated into English by 1885, but Bankim declared himself dissatisfied with the published versions and attempted his own rendering of *Bishabriksha.*[6] In 1891, near the end of his life, he showed Sureshchandra Samajpati an English version of *Debi Chaudhurani* (1884). The few chapters that survive of this reportedly complete and corrected manuscript are more like purposive adaptations than translations, as Julius Lipner has recently emphasized (Lipner 30–3).[7] Moreover, the unsigned article on "Bengali Literature" that appeared in the *Calcutta Review* of 1871 (No. 104), attributed to Bankim by his editors, contains a long summary and partial translation of *Kapalkundala* (B. Chattopadhyay, "Bengali Literature" 120–3 and 291).

Translation, then, was as constitutive of the literary culture of nineteenth-century India as it is of a "global" postmodernity. Often it seems expressive of a larger anxiety regarding the possibility of adequate representation of the colonial subject. H. A. D. Phillips, in the introduction to his translation of Bankim's *Kapalkundala,* urged Bengali fiction writers to provide an exhaustive list of native cultural practices and domestic objects (Phillips xxviii–xxix). Transactions between languages function as transactions between cultures, constantly importing material from one realm into another. *Rajmohan's Wife* is remarkable in its attempt to render as closely and vividly as possible the nature of women's talk and the colloquial everyday – a point worth noting, considering that Bankim has been criticized for the archaic diction of some of his melodramatic scenes, liberally employing personal pronouns such as "thee," "thou," and "thy." Yet given the difficulty of finding a linguistic equivalent in English for the vernacular "life-world," the general readability of *Rajmohan's Wife* is something of an achievement.

The Novel and Colonial Society

Bankim's novel is set in rural East Bengal, in a small village called Radhaganj on the banks of the Madhumati, one of the principal rivers of the Khulna division (Hunter 233). Most of the characters belong to the upper bourgeoisie, in particular a single Hindu Kayastha extended family "of menial origin," but now possessed of great wealth by the cunning defalcations (from his former master's widow) of its founder, Bangshibadan Ghose. Bangshibadan's sons, Ramkanta, Ramkanai, and Ramgopal, "purchased zemindaris, built fine houses, and assumed the state and style that belonged to their wealth" (*Rajmohan's Wife* 16).[8] Bankim's ironic treatment of this family's rise from humble origins to wealth and status suggests that he may have had a longer social narrative in mind when he began writing the novel. In fact, Bangshibadan's heirs are typical in their uneasy bridging of the traditional–modern, rural–urban, and East–West divides. The eldest son, Ramkanta, a conservative bigot, "had viewed with eyes of jealousy the encroachments that were being made in the ancient manners and usages by the influence of Western civilization and had steadily forborne to send his son to an English school, which he condemned as a thing not only useless but positively mischievous" (16–17). This son is Mathur Ghose, the novel's villain, who had early on learned "the science of chicane, fraud and torture" (17). By contrast, a wasteful and profligate modernity is exhibited in the second son, Ramkanai, who indulges his taste for fine living in the colonial metropolis of Calcutta, surrounded by parasites who draw him into mercantile speculation and bring "his mismanaged and neglected estates to the hammer" (17). Ramkanai's son, Madhav, has obtained "as good an education as he could receive in Calcutta" (17), as well as a beautiful, city-bred bride, Hemangini, the younger sister of Matangini, the novel's fiery heroine. Madhav inherits the property of his childless uncle Ramgopal (the third brother, about whose habits we have no information) and is persuaded by his wife to take her sister's husband Rajmohan into his employment in their ancestral village, Radhaganj.

This web of relations is representative of the native bourgeoisie in the post–Permanent Settlement era, and the opposed figures of Ramkanta and Ramkanai, and their sons Mathur and Madhav, offer alternatives of ideology and *habitus*. Ramkanta's obscurantism and Mathur's villainy are paired, while the profligate, city-loving Ramkanai, representing the class of spendthrift zamindars and dissolute *babus* who became the butt of nineteenth-century Bengali satire, has sired the handsome, educated, and refined Madhav. Satire was a powerful instrument in the making of the early Bengali novel, from the satirical sketch or *naksha* instanced in Bhabanicharan Bandyopadhyay's *Naba Babu Bilas* (*A Pleasant Tale of the New Babu*, 1825) and Kaliprasanna Sinha's *Hutom Pyanchar Naksha* (*Sketches by Hutom the Owl*, 1862), to Peary Chand Mitra's moral fable, *Alaler Gharer Dulal.* While much of this satire targets the dissolute, self-indulgent residents of the city of Calcutta, Bankim's own satirical essays in Bengali, as well as "The Confession of a Young Bengal," which he contributed to *Mookerjee's Magazine* in English, criticize both urban fashion and rural obscurantism.[9] But *Rajmohan's Wife* uses a melodramatic plot based on simple black-and-white contrasts. Mathur, prosperous but repellent, hires a gang of dacoits to steal his uncle's will, the key to Madhav's inheritance, and holds both Madhav and Matangini captive in his warehouse. Madhav, "mild and easily yielding by nature" (50), and given to weeping as he broods over his misfortunes (96), is honorable and tender in his relations with Matangini, rallies his household against the dacoits, and exhibits uncommon resolution when he is kidnapped. The lone British official, "a shrewd and restlessly active Irishman" (124), is, unlike parallel figures in Bankim's Bengali novels, the agent of colonial justice; his impending arrival leads the wicked Mathur to kill himself. The scales are thus weighted in favor of English education and the rigor of colonial law. Yet this ideological slant, however influenced by choice of language and audience, is tempered by the novel's pervasive irony and Bankim's imaginative investment in the character of his heroine Matangini.

In her edition of the novel, Meenakshi Mukherjee suggests that Bankim completed *Rajmohan's Wife* in a hurry, having lost interest in a limited English-speaking audience and outgrown this act of bad faith (M. Mukherjee, "Afterword" 131). Less persuasively, Makarand Paranjape claims the text as a national allegory in Fredric Jameson's sense:

> All third-world texts are necessarily, I want to argue, allegorical, and in a very specific way: they are to be read as what I will call *national allegories*, even when, or perhaps I should say, particularly when their forms develop out of predominantly western machineries of representation, such as the novel. (Jameson, "Third-World" 69)

Building on Jameson's sweeping generalization, Paranjape casts Matangini as the new Indian nation, born out of the opposition between evil obscurantism (Mathur) and Anglicized refinement (Madhav). Whatever the merits of Jameson's characterization of "third-world texts" (critiqued, for example, by Aijaz Ahmad in a celebrated essay [Ahmad, "Jameson's"]), it is difficult to be convinced by the "culturalist-allegorical" reading of the novel that Paranjape presents. The fact that some characters have a representative function – historically or generically – does not mean that the novel as a whole is allegorical, even in Jameson's somewhat loose sense. Rather, the initial morality-tale structure is left behind as the novel penetrates the domestic interiors of the Hindu middle class on the one hand, and the dark, dacoit-infested hinterland of rural East Bengal on the other. In doing so, it combines realism with romance, everyday life with gothic horror, bourgeois respectability with crime and passion: an uneven blend but one that actually works to resist, rather than confirm, Jameson's categorization. *Rajmohan's Wife*, "Bankim's initial and tentative attempt to write fiction on a Victorian narrative model to which colonial education had exposed a new generation of urban Indians" – as Mukherjee describes it ("Afterword" 129) – is remarkable in its refusal to dissolve history into myth, event into symbol, individual fate into national destiny.

Persons, Objects, and *Habitus*

The novel focuses on the social and domestic *habitus* of persons, answering a need that Bankim correctly saw as central to the realism of the nineteenth-century novel. The techniques of realist description are grounded in the careful detailing of inanimate things: settings, objects, dress, and domestic interiors. It is these that give substance to the imagined lives of human individuals, threatening at times to overwhelm their actions or feelings, or to become their sole index and witness. *Rajmohan's Wife* allows passion and melodrama full room, but Bankim is attentive to his representational project, describing the appearance of individual characters in specific material surroundings and producing a marvelous realist centerpiece, the description of the four sections, or *mahals*, of Mathur Ghose's house in the thirteenth chapter. This lays the ground for Nagendra's three-sectioned (*tin-mahalla*) house in Bankim's later novel *Bishabriksha* (1873), both evidencing a newly aspirational bourgeois ethic.[10] But unlike Nagendra's tastefully appointed residence, Mathur's rural mansion combines an outward lack of care and cleanliness with the primitive accumulation of money and goods in its storehouse:

> The house of Mathur Ghose was a genuine example of mofussil magnificence united with mofussil want of cleanliness.
>
> From the far-off paddy fields you could descry through intervening foliage, its high palisades and blackened walls. On a nearer view might be seen

pieces of plaster of venerable antiquity prepared to bid farewell to their old and weather-beaten tenement.... Not unfrequently a young shoot of a bur or a less noble vegetable had struck its roots in the crevices between the layers of brick, realizing, rather on an humble scale, the Persian monarch's dream of a hanging garden. (*Rajmohan's Wife* 74)

By contrast, the hero Madhav is seen in a richly furnished setting, filled with signs of a refined bourgeois sensibility that can afford to look away from the evidence of its operations:

Madhav Ghose was alone. He sat reclining on a mahogany couch covered with satin. A single but well-fed light illumined the chamber. Some two or three English books were scattered over the couch, and one of these Madhav held in his hand but he hardly read it. He sat with his abstracted gaze fixed on the dark but star-besprinkled heavens which were visible through the open windows. (95)

Such details enlist the material world into the service of a notation of manners and sensibility, just as later accounts of the inner, women's quarters of both residences "furnish" that material context with human substance.

This semiotic practice, deriving from the mid-Victorian realist novel, is combined in Bankim's novel with descriptions modeled on classical Indian rhetoric, as in the account of Matangini's beauty (a passage retranslated from Bengali, perhaps embellished by the author). These luxuriant images are reminiscent of those in Sanskrit *kavya* or in medieval Vaishnava love-poetry:

Some sorrow or deep anxiety had dimmed the lustre of her fair complexion. Yet her bloom was as full of charm as that of the land-lotus half-scorched and half-radiant under the noonday sun. Her long locks were tied up in a careless knot on her shoulder; but some loose tresses had thrown away that bondage and were straying over her forehead and cheeks. Her faultlessly drawn arched eyebrows were quivering with bashfulness under a full and wide forehead. The eyes were often only half seen under their drooping lids. But when they were raised for a glance, lightning seemed to play in a summer cloud. (3)

There is nothing quite so metaphorically "wrought" elsewhere in the novel: Matangini, a "perfect flower of beauty," bred in the civilized environs of Calcutta rather than in rustic East Bengal, is a heroine who recalls the love-quests of Krishna's consort Radha and her *gopis*, at the same time as she gestures toward a future that is, for women, still to be born. Both possibilities are implicit in Bankim's description of Matangini's journey to Madhav's house at dead of night, when she conceals herself from detection by immersing herself in a pool: "apprehensive lest the fair complexion of her lily face betray her, she unloosed the knot of her hair and spread the dark luxuriant tresses on all sides of her head, so that not even the closest scrutiny could now distinguish from above the dark hair floating over the darkened pool" (42). The account of Matangini's midnight excursion is clearly influenced by the *abhisarika* figure of Sanskrit love poetry. Yet she also exhibits a modern resolution and daring, taking extreme risks to warn her sister and frankly confessing her love to Madhav.

As a character, Matangini is the focus of a special project of Bankim's imagination, the liminal woman standing at a remove from orthodox society: threatening, attractive, and ultimately unassimilable. Yet even this idealized and romantic figure is embedded in a carefully detailed social and physical context. Matangini is confined in an unhappy marriage to a brutal husband who beats and threatens to kill her, and her situation is brought out through her initial conversation with Kanak, with whom she is contrasted by an elaborate semiotics of costume. So too Mathur, dark, portly, and unattractive, wears fine clothes of Dacca muslin, a gold chain, an amulet, and studs, as well as rings on each finger; Madhav, handsome but passive, is unostentatiously well-dressed, wearing only a single ring. Both men wear "English shoes." These details, like the account of the garden itself, enter into an elaborate register of material indices signaling social place, individual temperament, and the contrast of country and city. A contemporary parallel to the "directedness" of such object-description may be found in the *naksha* or satirical sketch targeting the *babu* culture of Calcutta and the visual art of the Kalighat *patuas*.[11] Nevertheless, Bankim's adaptation of this technique to domestic fiction in English aligns it with Victorian realism as well as with an older rhetoric of image and desire: "There was a fire in that voluptuous eye, – there was a glow on that moonbeam brow ... as she stood leaning with her well-rounded arm on the damask-covered back of the sofa" (55). Both have a place within the new representational project of constructing the life-worlds of the colonial gentry.

Space, Plot, and the Colonial Uncanny

Set "on the banks of the Madhumati" (3), *Rajmohan's Wife* articulates a localized east-west binary, contrasting rural East Bengal with the western metropolis of Calcutta. Lacking the grand geographical sweep of Bankim's historical novels, its spatial trajectory extends from humble domestic settings to the dacoits' lair on the riverbank, a place of "peculiar and almost frightful solitude" (89). Yet space and plot, we realize, are etymologically related: the carefully described ground plan of Mathur's house alerts us to a narrative *thinking through space.*

Inside and outside have complementary functions: Matangini is first glimpsed in the humble domestic interior of a "mat-walled" (30) hut flanked by kitchen gardens, and Madhav and Mathur chat on the terrace of a substantial brick-built house, while their womenfolk occupy themselves indoors. This apparent security is contrasted with the wilderness outside, through which Matangini journeys to Madhav's house at dead of night, and where the dacoits have their hideout in the impenetrable underwood on the riverbank. Within the frame of bourgeois domesticity, we pass from the outer apartments of Mathur Ghose's house to the women's quarters where his elder wife Tara plaits her daughter's hair, and his younger wife Champak applies lac-dye to her feet. Despite the uneasy tensions between these two claimants for Mathur's attention, it is in these regions governed by women that Matangini finds succor when she escapes from her murderous husband. Tara, who shelters Matangini and rescues Madhav from his dungeon, a "gloomy and low-roofed room, whose sombre and massive walls looked more grim in the dim light" (104), emerges as a type of feminine valor.

The bourgeois respectability of Mathur Ghose's house is contiguous – spatially as well as morally – with the storehouse where he keeps his goods and imprisons not just Madhav but the object of his lust, Matangini. So too, in the rural heart of Bengal, is village domesticity contiguous with outlaw gangs – dacoits who lurk on the forested outskirts and carry out raids on prosperous households. That Matangini is saved from death by the dacoit's sudden entry into her room suggests that the "inside-outside" binary is only nominal. Darkness inhabits both interior and exterior, the wilderness and the human heart. Yet Bankim achieves much rhetorical purchase by his splendid descriptions of Matangini's midnight sojourn: "The knotted trunks of huge trees showed like so many unearthly forms watching her progress in malignant silence. . . . All the wild tales she had heard of fierce visages and ghostly grins that had appalled to death the belated traveller, rushed to her imagination" (40).

Matangini's superstitious fears are linked to the rich store of country legends about ghosts and dacoits mined by Bankim's contemporary, the humorist Trailokyanath Mukhopadhyay (*Bhut*). Yet the villainous *sardar* and his principal aide Bhiku are vividly sketched as they discuss terms with Rajmohan, smoke *ganja* in their hideout, and sardonically dismiss the folly of the householder. In fact the *sardar*, who eventually escapes punishment, is a more representative specimen of his tribe than the idealized dacoits of *Debi Chaudhurani*. A shrewd and practical criminal, he becomes a fit tool of bourgeois cunning when Mathur employs him to steal that classic Victorian plot device, a will (used again in Bankim's novel *Krishnakanter Will* [1878]).

Rajmohan's Wife thus opposes the structures of bourgeois domesticity and colonial law to the dark regions "without the law," where robbers and specters reign. This latter might be described as the colonial uncanny. For superstitious village folk, the uncanny resides in a world of ghosts and predators prowling the unlit, untilled spaces beyond household and plough land. But while ghosts might be outside the magistrate's purview, dacoits – legendary robbers living by their own savage codes in forest settlements – were certainly subject to the full rigor of colonial law, as William Henry Sleeman's tireless prosecutions in northern India showed. Tales of dacoits and thugs become part of a colonial repertoire of sensational narrative (Sleeman; Taylor). Bankim himself had to deal with the repeated depredations of dacoits in Khulna, and *Rajmohan's Wife* employs the *frisson* of the supernatural as well as the real terror of the dark regions outside the law to produce for its readers an early version of the "uncanny" of colonial India, a parallel to Victorian gothic.

The Lives of Women and the Future of the Novel

The twentieth chapter of *Rajmohan's Wife*, in which Matangini rejects Mathur, is editorially titled "Some Women are the Equals of Some Men." The novel has already given centrality and visibility to the lives of women: Matangini's energy, resolution, and courage are a match for the villainy of Rajmohan and Mathur. Although she frankly declares her love to Madhav in a melodramatic midnight encounter, the novel's conventional morality will not allow their love to be consummated. At the close, there is little Matangini can do but die. Yet she has been the center of the novel's world, both as agent and as victim. Moreover, she is part of a larger company of women, finding assistance and succor among her fellows when she escapes from Rajmohan's murderous attack. Even as Bankim penetrates the inner quarters of the Ghose family, he examines women's lives with unerring precision. Earlier, the relatively minor character Kanak is described as married, according to Kulin custom, to an absent husband with many wives.

The interest Bankim shows in his protagonist Matangini is deeply rooted in the project of constituting the female subject in colonial India (T. Sarkar; Chakrabarty, *Provincializing*). This was more a *male* social and discursive imperative than a task for women themselves. Education, social reform, the age of consent, and companionate marriage were issues of public debate and of legislative endeavor. In literature, these are visible themes through which a certain notion of selfhood, male as well as female, might be constructed. The history of nationalist self-consciousness in India is doubly worked out through the histories of women: *women* as agents and subjects and *woman* as idea and representation. Bankim's novels are remarkable in their representation of relatively free and self-determining women protagonists, even if he was unable to fit them into social space. For him, the feminine was itself a liminal category, an undetermined social and historical site. "Women are the prime movers of the verbs" (Kaviraj, *Unhappy* 18) in his fiction, yet his heroines stand at the boundary of a social world incapable of accommodating them. The importance of the free woman in Bankim's fictional imaginary, signaled by the radical content of his 1875 essay, "Samya [Equality]," is at odds with his deeply conservative social views, as with his acquiescence in the patriarchal social order and in colonial rule.[12] The woman protagonist in *Rajmohan's Wife* signals a dangerous excess that domesticity cannot absorb: she is central but excluded, placed at the heart of the narrative but tragically unfulfilled.

In choosing this figure, and placing her in a complex domestic and social setting, *Rajmohan's Wife* is a novel that speaks to an emergent genre in the Indian vernaculars. Not only is it closely tied by features of plot and character to Bankim's own later fiction, it anticipates some concerns – especially the central importance of women – of the early novel in Bengali, Marathi, and Malayalam. It is not a "false start because the author chose to write in English" (M. Mukherjee, "Afterword" 131) but an indication of the road that the novel would actually take. A local variant of the realist or sensational Victorian novel about property, sex, and marriage might have helped domicile the English *language* itself in India; but Bankim abandoned the project after this single attempt, and *Rajmohan's Wife* does not appear to have attracted many readers. There are few contemporary references to it, and it had no real successors. When the Indian novel in English took off in the early twentieth century through the work of Mulk Raj Anand and Raja Rao, it had already been co-opted into a quite different social and nationalist project, better suited to produce Jameson's model of a "national allegory."

Notes

1 For accounts of the development of the Indian novel, see M. Mukherjee, "Epic," and S. Chaudhuri, "Bengali." Contenders for the title of the first Indian novel include *The Revelations of an Orderly* ([1846] 1849) by Panchkouree Khan (evidently a pseudonym), *Phulmani o Karunar Bibaran* (1852, Bengali) by Hannah Catherine Mullens, and *Yamuna Paryatan* (1857, Marathi) by Baba Padmanji.
2 Letter to Sambhu Chandra Mookerjee, March 27, 1872 (*Bankim Rachanabali*, vol. 3, 171).
3 Letter to Sambhu Chandra Mookerjee, March 14, 1872 (*Bankim Rachanabali*, vol. 3, 170). Emphasis in original.
4 All translations from Bengali are my own unless otherwise indicated.
5 Banerji's preface is printed in Meenakshi Mukherjee's edition (Penguin/Ravi Dayal) of *Rajmohan's Wife*. All in-text citations of the novel are from this edition by page number. For Bankim's Bengali translation of the first seven chapters of *Rajmohan's Wife* (converted to nine in Bengali), see *Bankim Rachanabali*, vol. 2, 923–41.
6 Bankim reportedly translated *Bishabriksha* under the title *The Bane of Life*. See S. Chattopadhyay, 87.
7 For the surviving chapters of *Debi Chaudhurani* in Bankim's translation, see *Bankim Rachanabali*, vol. 3, 273–88.
8 A "zemindari" (or zamindari) was the title to land-rents, and the zamindar a landholder. Under the Permanent Settlement of Bengal, also called the Cornwallis Code (1793), zamindars secured permanent tenure of the lands for which they had earlier been merely revenue-collecting intermediaries under the Mughal emperor. This created a new zamindari class, which saw land as a commodity.
9 See *Bankim Rachanabali*, vol. 3, 137–41 and 292.
10 See S. Chaudhuri, "Phantasmagorias" 183.
11 See K. Sinha, *Satik Hutom*; and K. Sinha, *Sketches*. For the art of the Kalighat *patuas*, see J. Jain, *Kalighat*.
12 Bankim's essay "Samya [Equality]," published in *Bangadarshan* in 1875, was inspired by John Stuart Mill's *The Subjection of Women* (1869) (*Bankim Rachanabali*, vol. 2, 328–51).

CHAPTER 2

The Epistemic Work of Literary Realism: Two Novels from Colonial India

Satya P. Mohanty

Early in the 1870s, in response to a competition for a prize to be awarded for the best novel on the "Rural Population and Working Classes of Bengal," Lal Behari Day (1824–92) wrote his novel *Govinda Samanta*, or *Bengal Peasant Life* (1878). Day, who had converted to Christianity in his youth and spent much of his life as a pastor and missionary in small towns in Bengal, chose to write in English. The novel won the prize and was widely reviewed, and it is indeed remarkable for its naturalistic portrayal of the life of peasants. Its ethnographic efforts won the admiration of Charles Darwin, who wrote about how much "pleasure and instruction" he derived from reading it (quoted in Saha viii).

Approaching Day's novel in the twenty-first century, when our knowledge of Indian history and society has gained considerable depth, it would be instructive to ask what it in fact says about the life of Bengali (or Indian) peasants in colonial India. How does it present "Bengal Peasant Life"? Is, for instance, its ethnographic effort, its attempt to portray peasant life with sympathetic knowledge, linked to the author's ideological investments and anxieties? Is its effort to write realistically – avoiding conventional exaggerations – successful? What, we may ask, is the novel primarily about?

My questions point to hermeneutical issues that literary scholars have been discussing for a few decades now. In this chapter, I propose to read Day's novel as a particular, and indeed ideological, way of referring to colonial Indian society. My suggestion is that it would be more instructive to read Day comparatively, in the Indian multilingual literary and cultural context, than it would to place him in the history of the Indian novel in English. To explore part of this suggestion, I read Day's text together with a novel written some twenty-five years later in an Indian language, Oriya (now officially spelled Odia). The Odia novel, *Chha Mana Atha Guntha* (*Six Acres and a Third*, 1897–99), by Fakir Mohan Senapati (1843–1918), is clearly not written with English readers in mind, and its representation of rural Indian society is mediated – self-consciously, even obsessively – by a narrator who questions the colonialist assumptions of those of his Odia readers who were "English-educated." Juxtaposing these two novels suggests a way to address the question of how to read Day's work from our vantage point in history. At bottom is another, more basic, literary-critical question: In politically charged times such as the colonial period in India, how do realistic novels *refer* to the reality around them?

Reference: A Theoretical Detour

Reference, in literature, history, or science, is not direct or unmediated, as many thinkers have pointed out. Summarizing work from a variety of philosophers, let me present three basic theses that suggest how a partial theory of literary (specifically, novelistic) reference can be developed. This will allow me to place Day's and Senapati's literary endeavors in the wider context of the literary representation of colonial rule.

1. Words, concepts, and even theories refer to aspects of the world, but in necessarily mediated ways. *There is no unmediated reference.* As Charles Sanders Peirce argued, the referential relation is never "dyadic" – between (what he calls) a First and a Second, a Sign and its Object – but always inevitably mediated and transformed by a Third, an Interpretant. Peirce was elaborating a theory of signs, but he saw such a theory as part of an epistemological project.[1] Later thinkers as varied in their backgrounds as Heidegger and Quine made the same point: the empiricist vision of knowledge based on pure observation is wrong, because even scientific observation in the laboratory is profoundly mediated by our background assumptions and tacit theoretical commitments.

2. *Many significant instances of reference, especially in scientific discourse or literary texts, do not involve simple empirical givens, static and unique objects in the world, but rather complex objects of inquiry.* Considering the culturally mediated process of signification, Peirce pointed out that what he called the Object of the Sign was itself more than the observable datum of the empiricist. Objects, for Peirce, are always and already interpreted by both the Sign and the Interpretant; they are thus dynamic rather than static, engaged by and defined within the process of signification. The postpositivist philosopher of science Richard Boyd similarly argues for a dialectical view of the object, or referent, of scientific-theoretical terms. In detecting key features of the natural world, Boyd and others argue,

scientific inquiry relies on theoretical terms that point or refer (often inadequately) to objects as mediated and theory-laden as "electron," "DNA," "gold," and "reptile." These objects themselves undergo change and refinement as our epistemic practices evolve, and – Boyd suggests, much like Peirce – we should thus not construe such objects in empiricist terms as mere givens.[2]

3. If the objects of reference are complex objects of human inquiry, part of an evolving epistemological engagement, it will follow that in many instances it is misleading to see reference as influential literary theorists such as Paul de Man sometimes tend to do, as an all-or-nothing affair. Either we have an instance of referential success, de Man and others assume, or else reference fails. Instead, the more mediated and dialectical notion of reference I am retrieving from Peirce and postpositivist thinkers like Boyd suggests that *reference should be seen as existing in degrees.* Boyd provides a theoretical account of this phenomenon that can be useful for literary scholars. Reference, says Boyd, provides degrees of "epistemic access" to central aspects and properties of the world. Differences in referential practice do not point merely to differences in social or intellectual convention, because in some crucial instances they are based on better and more accurate knowledge. Referential vagueness, imprecision, indeterminacy, and even failure can sometimes give way to increasing degrees of success, precisely because of the growth of knowledge, of our socially coordinated knowledge-seeking practices:

> Scientific terms must be understood as providing the sort of epistemic access appropriate to the level of epistemic success typical of scientific discoveries. Historical evidence suggests that the theories which are accepted by the scientific community are rarely entirely correct in every respect, even when they reflect the discovery of fundamentally important truths. What is typical of successful scientific investigations is successive improvements in partial but significant knowledge: scientific progress typically arises from the replacement of revealing (though only approximately accurate) theories with more revealing (and more nearly accurate) theories. Similarly, it is true that the history of science reveals a number of plausible but fundamentally mistaken "false starts" which are only corrected over time (for example, Darwin's belief in inheritance of acquired characteristics, or the theory of vital forces). Thus the sort of success which is characteristic of epistemic access in the case of a theoretical term in science involves the capacity of the scientific community, typically and over time, to acquire increasingly accurate knowledge about the referent of that term. (Boyd 506–7)

Does literary reference really also work in this way, to facilitate what Boyd calls epistemic access? When we are analyzing literary texts, can we talk meaningfully about "successive improvements" in knowledge and the socially coordinated practices of a community of knowers? My view is that what we call "literary reference" is a very heterogeneous phenomenon, defined in a number of different generic modes and contexts, and so it would be foolish to try to find its essential and unitary definition. Literary reference is, rather, best seen as a cluster concept, a grouping of roughly similar phenomena that we observe and study in a number of very different literary contexts. The nineteenth-century realist novel, for instance, obviously refers to its social world differently than does a devotional lyric circulated privately among members of a royal court. Both the intended audiences and the stylistic features shape the layered ways in which texts refer, and our goal as theorists of literary reference is less to seek its singular essence and more to work modestly and inductively to identify and analyze these constitutive layers.

At least in some crucial instances in literary history, I would like to argue, Boyd's view of the progressive refinement of reference seems to hold. Writers sometimes seem to comment on previous writers and attempt to provide fuller, less partial, and thus more accurate reference of social reality. But this process of critique and revision, which is often evident in the history of literary realism, for instance, is where we also see how complexly mediated reference is: how the referent is itself theory-laden. The improvement of reference we see in these contexts leads to greater accuracy or objectivity, but it is not because the object simply unveils itself in its innocence. Rather, even in the realist novel, literary reference reveals the role of social ideology or theoretical bias in *every* representation of the object, of the world. But some ideologies and biases produce better and more accurate knowledge, less distortion and mystification. It is through the analysis of ideological distortion and error that complex realist novels reveal the possibility of accurate and objective knowledge – a knowledge that is often as much about the mediating ideologies as it is about the object of representation.

Novelistic Discourse and Epistemic Access

Juxtaposing Day and Senapati provides a good way to explore this claim, examining how realist novels refer and whether there is epistemic, not just artistic, progress in the way literature represents the world. It is often recognized by literary historians of India that Fakir Mohan Senapati's Odia

novel *Six Acres and a Third* is perhaps the first truly sophisticated example of realism in the history of the Indian novel.³ Sisir Kumar Das, in
his monumental *History of Indian Literature, 1800–1910*, calls Senapati's
novel the "culmination of the tradition of realism" in modern Indian literature. "All these plays and novels contain elements of realism in varying
degrees," Das says about earlier realist texts, "but none can match Fakir
Mohan's novel in respect of its minute details of social life and economic
undercurrents regulating human relationships and the variety of characters representing traditional occupational groups" (296). Das is right
about Senapati's achievements, of course, but if we look more closely at
how Senapati is actively revising and rewriting Lal Behari Day, we will
see something far more important about Senapati's project and about the
development of literary realism in the context of colonial Indian society.⁴
One of Senapati's primary achievements as a realist writer is evident in
the way he analyzes the *ideological underpinnings* of the literary representation of (colonial) Indian society. He succeeds as a realist because he
focuses less on the "what" of representation and reference and more on
the "how," on the mediating perceptions, values, and judgments that constitute the "object" of literary representation. He is thus a realist not only
in the literary-critical meaning of the term but also in the philosophical
sense: he goes beneath the surface of description to analyze social *causes*.
His narrative discourse identifies the distorting ideologies that accompany
social representations and, in this way, attempts a more self-reflective and
accurate account. His realism is thus less descriptive and more analytical, and we will see this clearly in the way his novel implicitly comments
on Day's.

Like *Bengal Peasant Life*, Senapati's novel, written in Odia, is also about
life in an eastern Indian village. It is historically and socially very specific,
however, as it refuses to accept Orientalist images of the timeless Indian
village and presents in their place a complex account of social exploitation under colonial rule. But colonial rulers – that is, the British – rarely
appear directly in the novel. Instead, what we get is an unsentimental
analysis of the unequal relations between Indian (or Odia) peasants and
landlords, as well as between the educated intelligentsia and the ordinary Indian (Odia). *Bengal Peasant Life* is one of the earliest examples
of literary realism in India, and it is often cited as exerting an influence
on Senapati's realist mode, but what has not been analyzed adequately
is exactly how and why Senapati rewrites ideological elements of Day's
descriptive-realist text. Day's novel, as has been pointed out by some critics (Mohapatra and Nayak 29–40), is written in what might be called a

submissive tone, presenting colorful sociological details about Bengali village life to its colonial readership. Like many realists before him, in India and elsewhere, Day wishes to write in a plain and unvarnished style, rejecting "anything marvellous or wonderful" in favor of the authentic reality of Indian (Bengali) village life. "My great Indian predecessors," as Day begins his book,

> the latchet of whose shoes I do not pretend to be worthy to unloose – Valmiki, Vyas, and the compilers of the Puranas, have treated of kings with ten heads and twenty arms; of a monkey carrying the sun in his armpit; of demons churning the universal ocean with a mountain for a churn-staff. (Day 5–6)

Instead, says Day, he will provide a "plain and unvarnished tale of a plain peasant, living in this plain country of Bengal … told in a plain manner" (7). This assertion of realism will sound familiar to readers of realist novels from just about every literary tradition. What Senapati – who begins writing twenty-five or so years later – seizes on, however, is that while Day's style may be "plain and unvarnished," his representation of the Indian village is anything but "plain" – that is, unmediated or ideologically innocent.

Writing in Odia rather than English, in a lively colloquial style as opposed to the tame prose of his predecessor, Senapati is at pains to redefine realism as much more than a plain unadorned representation written in simple language. This is evident in a scene in *Six Acres and a Third* where ordinary village women are bathing at the village pond – a scene that is clearly a deliberate rewriting of a similar chapter in Day's novel. In both texts, we listen in on the conversation among the women and learn details of their domestic lives. Here is an excerpt from Day's novel, with its unabashed anthropological tone:

> A woman who is rubbing her feet sees another woman preparing to go, and says to her,
>
> "Sister, why are you going away so soon? You have not to cook; why are you then going so soon?"
>
> "Sister, I shall have to cook to-day. The elder *bou* is not well to-day: she was taken ill last night."
>
> "But you have not to cook much. You have no feast in your house?"
>
> "No; no feast, certainly. But my sister has come from Devagrama with her son. And the fisherman has given us a large *rohita*, which must be cooked."
>
> "Oh! You have guests in your house. And what are you going to cook?"

"I am going to cook *dal* of *mashkalai*, one *tarkari*, *badi* fried, fish fried, fish with peppercorns, fish with tamarind, and another dish, of which my sister's son is very fond, namely, *amda* with poppy-seed."

"The everlasting *badi* and poppy-seed. You banias are very fond of these two things. We Brahmans do not like either of them."

"The reason why you Brahmans do not like *badis* is that you do not know how to make them well. If you once taste our *badi* you will not forget it for seven months. You would wish to eat it every day. As for poppy-seed, what excellent curry it makes.... Though you are a Brahman, once taste my *badi*. *Badi* will not destroy your caste."

So saying, the banker woman went away with the *kalasi* on her waist. (Day 121)

Much of Day's novel is written in this embarrassingly turgid style, where the main goal seems to be to convert the village women into specimens of this or that caste, this or that sub-region of Bengal, so that his reader may be entertained by these cultural details. The ethnographic desire to represent village women accurately is compromised by the ideological assumption that reality will reveal itself automatically if the veil is lifted and the women are put on display. Senapati, however, begins with an entirely different premise. For one thing, his rendition of this conversation is indirect, presented not as direct dialogue but rather in the narrator's inimitable voice. The humor is that of the village storyteller reveling in his oral performance:

The gathering at the ghat became very large when the women came to bathe before cooking their daytime meals. If there had been a daily newspaper in Gobindapur, its editor would have had no difficulty gathering stories for his paper; all he would have had to do was sit at the ghat, paper and pencil in hand. He would have found out, for instance, what had been cooked the previous night, at whose house, and what was going to be cooked there today; who went to sleep at what time; how many mosquitoes bit whom; who ran out of salt; who had borrowed oil from whom; how Rama's mother's young daughter-in-law was a shrew, and how she talked back to her mother-in-law, although she married only the other day; when Kamali would go back to her in-laws; how Saraswati was a nice girl and how her cooking was good, her manners excellent....

Padi started a brief lecture as she sat in the water cleaning her teeth. The sum and substance of it was that no one in the village was a better cook than she. She went on tirelessly, pouring out much relevant and irrelevant information. A few pretty women went on rubbing their faces with their sari-ends, in order to look even prettier. Lakshmi's nose, adorned with a nose-jewel, had already become red from too much rubbing. Sitting at

the water's edge, scrubbing her heavy brass armlets with half a basketful
of sand, Bimali was engaged in a long tirade against some unnamed person, using words not to be found in any dictionary. The gist of it was that
somebody's cow had eaten her pumpkin-creepers last night. Bimali proceeded to offer some stinking stuff as food to three generations of the cow
owner's ancestors, going on and on about the fertile soil in her back garden: the wretched cow had not merely devoured the shiny pumpkins that
grew there but had destroyed the possibility of it producing many more
such delicious pumpkins. With the help of several cogent arguments and
examples, she also demonstrated that this cow must be given as a gift to a
Brahmin, otherwise a terrible calamity would befall the owner. If a violent
quarrel between Markandia's mother and Jasoda had not suddenly erupted
and put an end to all the talk, we could have gathered many more such
items of news. (Senapati 105–6)

At first, the differences between the two depictions of this scene appear to
be mainly those of *tone*, but what soon emerges is that Senapati is trying
to reframe the women's discourse through the humorous *and critical* voice
of his narrator. Day's narrator presents his account of the Indian village
to the English-educated Indian reader as well as the colonial readership
in England, and his approach to his subject is that of a benign tourist
or ethnographer. You would never suspect from Day's account that he is
writing about mid-nineteenth-century Indian society, a period when anti-
colonial and nationalist ideas were spreading across the country. Day is
aware of the 1857 rebellion, and even anxious about it, for the missionary
Day writes the same year to the District Magistrate to apply for a license
to keep a gun (Macpherson 73–4). But this anxiety – shared by almost
everyone associated with the colonial rulers in India and reported by the
English press – is actively repressed in his letters and his novel. Pretending
to be plain and unvarnished, Day's descriptive realism hides the fact that
its own plainness or neutrality might be ideologically motivated, for the
narrative information it provides is clearly partial and resolutely apolitical. Even though racial tensions are high in post-1857 colonial India, and
the Indian countryside must have seemed dangerous and hostile, Day's
(English?) reader is invited in to hitherto invisible and private spaces,
almost as a friend from another land. In the chapter "Malati's Marriage,"
for instance, the narrator takes the reader deeper and deeper into native
spaces: "But while the hymeneal party are making preparations to take
Kanchanpur by storm, the reader must accompany me for a few min-
utes to the house of the bride, and see for himself" (Day 63). Both native
informant and tour guide, Day's narrator frames and presents his narrative
as innocent of ideological motive.

Senapati's text, by contrast, foregrounds the ideological dimension of literary representation in colonial India. Senapati is writing, after all, in Odia for educated Odia readers, some of whom will not only know English but will also have been coopted by colonial values and ideology. So his narrator (one of the genuine achievements of the nineteenth-century Indian novel) is a sly, clever, and critical commentator, mediating between the Odia villagers he is talking about and the English-educated Odia middle class who will read his account. His tone is satirical and subversive; he is less the teller of a simple story about Odia peasant life and more a self-conscious, trickster-like critic of colonial relations and attitudes. So his analysis is not limited to the obvious disparities between British and Indian; it is just as interested in the cultural reproduction of these relations among different classes of Indians:

> There was only one pond in Gobindapur, and everyone in the village used it. It was fairly large, covering ten to twelve batis, with banks ten to twelve arm-lengths high, and was known as Asura pond. In the middle once stood sixteen stone pillars, on which lamps were lighted. We are unable to recount the true story of who had it dug, or when. It is said that demons, the Asuras, dug it themselves. That could well be true. Could humans like us dig such an immense pond? Here is a brief history of Asura pond, as told to us by Ekadusia, the ninety-five-year-old weaver.
>
> The demon Banasura ordered that the pond be dug, but did not pick up shovels and baskets to dig it himself. On his orders, a host of demons came one night and did the work. But when day broke, it had not yet been completed: there was a gap of twelve to fourteen arm-lengths in the south bank, which had not been filled in. By now, it was morning, and the villagers were already up and about. Where could the demons go? They dug a tunnel connecting the pond to the banks of the river Ganga, escaped through it, bathed in the holy river, and then disappeared. During the Baruni Festival on the Ganga, the holy waters of the river used to gush through the tunnel into the pond. But, as the villagers became sinful, the river no longer did this. English-educated babus, do not be too critical of our local historian, Ekadusia Chandra. If you are, half of what Marshman and Tod have written will not survive the light of scrutiny. (Senapati 101–2)

Notice the revision of one of the central norms of realist literary discourse. The legends and religious mythology Day wanted to banish from his text are brought back in – rehabilitating, in the process, the illiterate village historian Ekadusia Chandra and humorously questioning the legitimacy of Marshman and Tod, influential colonial authorities on Indian culture. But the most obvious object of satire, the object that frames the discourse, is the English-educated Indian babu, who imitates colonial values mindlessly and accepts uncritically the condescending attitudes toward indigenous Odia or Indian culture. The irreverent tone of this passage is present throughout the novel, and if we are to analyze the main way that Senapati revises Day's representation of village life in India, we would have to focus primarily on the mediating role of the narrator in framing the object of literary representation.

Day's representation of the Bengali village women effectively dehistoricizes their lives; his narrator's gaze swerves up from the Indian village to a timeless world where social life is drained of political specificity. Numerous references and quotations, from Virgil to more recent English poets, situate his tale in the European pastoral tradition. References to Greece and Egypt, to various classical and contemporary European models, dominate Day's novel. The village landlord's daughter, for instance, is supposed to remind us of ancient Egypt:

> Her head was uncovered; her body covered in every part with ornaments.... The silver anklets of her feet made a tinkling noise.... All eyes were directed towards her. She had no kalasi at her waist, was attended by two maid-servants, and looked as proud as, to compare small things with great, Pharaoh's daughter might have looked when she went to make her ablution in the Nile. (Day 123–4)

These references rewrite contemporary social reality through a select set of literary allusions; they draw on primarily European cultural images to posit a false universality, masking conquest and providing the ideological frame of historical innocence through which readers are asked to view the Indian peasant. Colonial rule is rarely mentioned, and if it is, it is made to seem utterly natural, never a political issue. The peasants grumble about the landlord Jaya Chand and the British indigo planter, for instance, but "Kompani Bahadur" (the East India Company and, by extension, the British colonial system) is always praised as the bearer of the highest standards of fairness and justice, even when its middlemen are not honest: "The fact is," says Govinda at a political meeting, "though the *Kompani Bahadur* is just and merciful, it has made laws on the supposition that the jamidars [landlords] have common honesty and humanity. The *Kompani Bahadur* never dreamt that jamidars would be so wicked" (Day 185).

Senapati's garrulous narrator, however, cannot seem to keep colonial rule and its exploitative nature out of his mind, try as hard as he might. Here he is, talking about the pond, before the women appear:

> There is another equally irrefutable proof to support this contention [that there are fish in the pond]. Look over there! Four kaduakhumpi

birds are hopping about like gotipuas, like traditional dancing boys. The birds are happy and excited because they are able to spear and eat the little fish that live in the mud. Some might remark that these birds are so cruel, so wicked, that they get pleasure from spearing and eating creatures smaller than themselves! What can we say? You may describe the kaduakhumpi birds as cruel, wicked, satanic, or whatever else you like; the birds will never file a defamation suit against you. But don't you know that among your fellow human beings, the bravery, honor, respectability, indeed, the attractiveness of an individual all depend upon the number of necks he can wring?

Some sixteen to twenty cranes, white and brown, churn the mud like lowly farmhands, from morning till night. This is the third proof that there are fish in the pond. A pair of kingfishers suddenly arrive out of nowhere, dive into the water a couple of times, stuff themselves with food, and swiftly fly away. Sitting on the bank, a lone kingfisher suns itself, wings spread like the gown of a memsahib. O stupid Hindu cranes, look at these English kingfishers, who arrive out of nowhere with empty pockets, fill themselves with all manner of fish from the pond, and then fly away. You nest in the banyan tree near the pond, but after churning the mud and water all day long, all you get are a few miserable small fish. You are living in critical times now; more and more kingfishers will swoop down on the pond and carry off the best fish. You have no hope, no future, unless you go abroad and learn how to swim in the ocean.

The kite is smart and clever; it perches quietly on a branch, like a Brahmin guru, and from there swoops down into the pond to snatch a big fish. That lasts it for the whole day. Brahmin gurus perch on their verandahs, descending on their disciples once a year, like the kite. (Senapati 103–4)

The loquacious narrator cannot seem to confine himself to the story he is telling. As we see in almost every chapter in the novel, his rambling voice often modulates into high-pitched anger. That anger is directed against those who use power to exploit the vulnerable and the laboring poor; and colonial rule is placed on a continuum that includes the rapacious Brahmin priest and the long-beaked kaduakhumpi bird.

Conclusion

Reading Lal Behari Day and Fakir Mohan Senapati together in this way leads us to ask whether their narrative discourses, which so closely resemble each other in many ways (especially in these two chapters), share a common referent. And, if so, is this referent "village life in India"? Clearly, this would be a very partial and inadequate explanation. For Senapati's novel historicizes and politicizes Day's discourse, and it does this by drawing attention to the crucial role of the narrative's mediating values and attitudes. Senapati's narrative discourse takes us beneath the surface of descriptive realism to reveal the ideological elisions and historical silences in Day's text. Using Boyd's terms, we might say that Senapati's discourse, in resituating Day's account of village life, improves it; it provides a critical and reflective, and hence more objective, definition of the referent of both texts: village life in *colonial* Indian society.[5] When we approach both novels this way, we notice the referential continuities, and a more complex and general referent emerges in the background: *colonial relations, both literary and ideological.* The object of representation, very narrowly defined, may be Indian village women bathing at the pond, but any reader who focuses on that alone will miss the substance of what is going on in these novels.

To talk more adequately about these "realist" texts, what we need is an account of not just the objects of the social world but also the mediating layers, the referential lenses, through which those objects come into view. These lenses are what Peirce calls the Interpretant. They are not extraneous to the object of signification – you will recall from my earlier account – but rather essential to it. Reference, on this view, is not about simple empirical givens (the minute details of social life, for instance), which the realist writer tries to represent (describe) accurately. Rather, the writer brings the object of signification into our view, into discourse, by working on the referential mediations themselves. The Interpretant (here, the narrator in his mediating role) is not a person but an interpretive perspective, and this perspective is not just conventional; it has an epistemic dimension. That is because it facilitates better or worse accounts, greater or lesser degrees of access to reality, which in turn is not simply waiting out there for us to hold up a mirror to it. It is this focus on the epistemic dimension of reference that marks the sharpest contrast between the realist theory I am outlining and defending and the skeptical poststructuralist view of realism and reference as reductive and necessarily simplistic.

At crucial moments in literary and cultural history, such as this formative moment in the history of the realist novel in India, we can point to *advances* in the referential function of literature, and, as such, suggest new ways of doing comparative (Indian) literary study. Common referents can help provide a comparative framework that takes us beyond the limits of local literary and linguistic traditions and raises the stakes of literary analysis. Working with a realist theory of literary reference will enable us to see common textual referents as productive sites of theoretical encounter, ideological contestation and revision. However, once we enlarge the analysis in these ways, we can appreciate the dynamic relationships in which literary production is always embedded. What I called "advances" in the referential function of literature, for instance, cannot be seen as purely literary advances; they cannot be understood in only linguistic or formal terms. Senapati's critique of Day's account of Indian peasants is a critique of social ideology, of the ideology that inheres in our representational habits. Given the analytical values and critical attitudes he presents, Senapati's loquacious and wily narrator embodies an epistemic achievement, not just a literary one. It would not be inaccurate to say that this narrator is Senapati's (and the early Indian novel's) contribution to an anticolonial and demystificatory social thought. Our evaluation of Senapati's achievement is in turn not a purely literary-critical one, for it depends crucially on our growing historical knowledge of colonial Indian society and culture and the crucial role of peasant resistance, the kind of knowledge that is in part fundamentally interdisciplinary.

My realist-pragmatist account of the mediated nature of literary reference is, then, an attempt to reassert the epistemic dimension of literature. Our appreciation of this dimension of literary texts will be limited if we see reference as a static and reductive process. This view of reference and my comparative analysis of Day and Senapati both suggest the need to avoid literary-historical readings of Lal Behari Day that would situate him only in relation to other texts written in English. A more adequate reading would put Day in agonistic dialogue with Indian-language writers such as Fakir Mohan Senapati – those who were "talking back," often from cultural and linguistic spaces that colonial rule had marginalized.

Notes

1 I am summarizing and drawing on my extended discussion of Peirce in Mohanty, *Literary*, chapter 2. All quotations and page references are provided in that chapter.

2 See especially Boyd, "Metaphor." For more sources on the competing realist and poststructuralist views on reference, see Mohanty, *Literary*, chapter 1 (on Paul de Man) and chapter 2 (on Bakhtin, Peirce, and Putnam).

3 The most recent translation of Senapati's novel *Chha Mana Atha Guntha* (*Six Acres and a Third*, with an Introduction by Satya P. Mohanty) was published by the University of California Press in 2005 (reprinted by Penguin India in 2006); the translators are Rabi Shankar Mishra, Satya P. Mohanty, Jatindra Nayak, and Paul St. Pierre.

4 Some of the passages that follow are adapted from my introduction to *Six Acres and a Third* and from Mohanty, "Dynamics." For more on Senapati, see the essays in Mohanty (ed.), *Colonialism*.

5 Senapati's account is more "objective" than Day's, but that is not to say that it is completely "neutral," shorn of all evaluative or ideological content. For a brief discussion of the postpositivist view of objectivity as itself theory-laden and evaluative, see my "Can Our Values."

CHAPTER 3

"Because Novels Are True, and Histories Are False": Indian Women Writing Fiction in English, 1860–1918

Barnita Bagchi

While visiting England in the early 1870s, the prodigiously talented teen-age writer Toru Dutt met "Lord L." – or Lord Lawrence, former viceroy of India. He asked her what book she and her sister Aru were reading. The book in question was a novel, *John Halifax, Gentleman* (1856), by Dinah Maria Mulock. Lord L. replied, "Ah! you should not read novels too much, you should read histories." While Aru did not reply, Toru answered, "We like to read novels." On being asked why, she responded, smiling, "Because novels are true, and histories are false" (H. Das 23). Here, Toru Dutt was articulating and helping to constitute a kind of cultural modernity in which the truth of the novel, a particular form of fiction, was crucial. This truth was particularly seized upon by women, who were making strides toward fuller participation in the public sphere, including in the construction of knowledge. Fiction written by women in English and other languages in India, whether in the form of full-fledged novels or as shorter fiction, contributed to a renewal of language, identity, and history.

Already by 1875, quite a few pieces of English-language fiction had been written and published by Indians. Notable among these is Shoshee Chunder Dutt's "The Republic of Orissa" (1845). Shoshee Chunder Dutt (1824–85) was a cousin of Toru's, and he, like Toru's father, had converted to Christianity. (Toru's father Govin Chunder, along with his brothers and nephew, published a collection of poetry titled *The Dutt Family Album* in 1870.) Meanwhile, Bankimchandra Chattopadhyay's novel in English, *Rajmohan's Wife*, had come out in 1864. Dutt was one of several Indian women novelists writing in the period 1860 to 1918, along with Krupabai Satthianadhan, Rokeya Sakhawat Hossain, and Swarnakumari Devi Ghosal. These writers, from a range of backgrounds – Hindu, Christian, Brahmo, and Muslim – also published in a range of genres, encompassing, for example, the Gothic novel (Toru Dutt), novels of sensibility (Toru Dutt), speculative and utopian fiction (Rokeya Hossain), the Bildungsroman (Dutt, Satthianadhan, Hossain, Ghosal), love stories (Ghosal, Hossain), and novels about religious conversion (Satthianadhan). The spectrum is thus wide, but the gendered voices of female agency are heard in all the fictions in question. Throughout their works, the authors express their visions not just of India but of the world, making wide claim to agency and articulation. Their fiction is also richly and subversively multilingual, spanning Indian *bhashas*,[1] English, and other European languages, including French.

The history of Indian fiction in English by women needs to be seen, then, as part of the connected cultural histories of world literature. In that context, Toru's remark on novels and history echoes the comments made by Jane Austen's highly ordinary yet subversive heroine Catherine Morland in *Northanger Abbey* (1817), on why she dislikes reading history: "The men all so good for nothing, and hardly any women at all – it is very tiresome: and yet I often think it odd that it should be so dull, for a great deal of it must be invention" (88). The narrator of *Northanger Abbey* says, equally, that novels express the highest powers of the human mind in the best chosen language:

> "Oh! it is only a novel!" replies the young lady; while she lays down her book with affected indifference, or momentary shame... or, in short, only some work in which the greatest powers of the mind are displayed, in which the most thorough knowledge of human nature, the happiest delineation of its varieties, the liveliest effusions of wit and humour are conveyed to the world in the best chosen language. (22)

The observations of Catherine and the narrator of *Northanger Abbey* resemble the pithy daring of Toru's remark. Unfortunately, at this time such potentially subversive remarks as Toru's were constantly troped in a discourse of Orientalism; accordingly, Toru's correspondent and friend Clarisse Bader reduced her preference for fiction and legend to her status as an Oriental woman: "Toru Dutt, in replying with such a paradox, proved a true daughter of this poetical Hindu race who prefer Legend to History" (H. Das 24). However, far more relevant, in my view, was Toru's ability to see, like Austen, that the novel as a form provided a space for the production of a particular kind of truth, one accessible to marginal or subaltern groups such as women because of its still relatively non-canonical status. The distinguished sociologist and gender historian Meera Kosambi has termed Marathi upper-caste reformist women writers such as Ramabai and Kashibai Kanitkar, whom we encounter later in this chapter, "gendered subalterns" (*Women* 5). I argue that this term applies to all the women writers examined in this chapter. They are women who, to varying degrees, contest patriarchy, colonial racism, and the orthodoxies of brahminical Hinduism, many of them from their positions as religious minorities.

At the heart of the novels are vivid and gendered imaginings of selves and subjects. Reform is crucial to these enterprising undertakings – reform of the self and of society, including of patriarchy and racism. The fiction of Toru Dutt, Krupabai Satthianadhan, Rokeya Sakhawat Hossain, and Swarnakumari Devi Ghosal, set in the interstices of the private and public spheres, participates in the larger, multivalent reform of gender relations and other matters in late nineteenth-century Indian society. The focus of reform in these fictions often concerns women's education, livelihoods, and claims to spaces in the public sphere. However, reform in these novels also takes the shape of concerns over affect, finding love, or seeking conjugal, romantic, or sexual fulfilment in ways that stretch and question patriarchy. The much-derided cultural figure of the woman novel-reader (so present, implicitly, in Lord L.'s remark to Toru and her sister, for example), steeped in socially unsanctioned enjoyment, is turned around in many of these fictions to present instead a self-cultivating, virtuous, developing female subject who seeks reform of many aspects of Indian society, even while seeking to engage in a very personal/individual process of self-reform and self-education.

Toru Dutt: Romance and Cosmopolitanism

Toru Dutt (1856–77) herself did not publish her fiction in her own short lifetime, although she did publish and gain a reputation for her poetry. Toru was a cosmopolitan, transnational writer whose fame spanned India, Great Britain, France, and the United States. Born to a gifted literary family, Toru's prodigious talents were encouraged by her father, although she only saw one of her works published during her lifetime: *A Sheaf Gleaned in French Fields* (1876), a volume of French poetry translated by her and her elder sister Aru. Renowned British critic and poet Edmund Gosse reviewed the book favorably in 1877.[2] After her death, Toru's collection of Sanskrit translations, *Ancient Ballads and Legends of Hindustan*, was published in 1882 with an introductory memoir by Edmund Gosse.

Toru's cosmopolitan interest in literature and her transnational friendships with other intellectual women were fostered by a four-year stay in Europe. After the tragic death of her brother Abju, the family traveled to Europe, where they stayed from 1869 to 1873. They lived in France, and Toru's interest and proficiency in French grew, leading to her 1876 publication. From 1871 to 1873, Toru and Aru attended the Higher Lectures for Women at Cambridge University. While living in Cambridge, Toru became very good friends with Mary Anne Martin, the daughter of John Martin of Sidney Sussex College. Toru and Mary Anne corresponded with each other after Toru's return to India until her death. After her return to India, Toru learned Sanskrit and became busy with translations and adaptations from ancient Sanskrit literature. She also wrote memorable English-language poetry evoking the Dutt family's environs, including the beautiful gardens of the family retreat at Baugmaree. Toru also became friends through correspondence with Clarisse Bader, the French writer mentioned earlier, whom she had come to admire after reading Bader's book *La Femme dans L'Inde Antique*. Toru's French was so accomplished that she completed a full novel in that language. This work, *Le Journal de Mademoiselle D'Arvers*, was published in Paris in 1879, with a prefatory piece by Clarisse Bader on the life and oeuvre of Toru Dutt, whom the front matter of the book describes as a *"jeune et célèbre Hindoue de Calcutta, morte en 1877."*

Toru's cosmopolitan linguistic multiplicity manifested itself in her choosing to write in both English and French, as well as in her translating poetry from French and Sanskrit into English. Her father, Govin, published her unfinished English novel *Bianca, or, the Young Spanish Maiden* in *Bengal Magazine* after her death.[3] Prophetically, melancholy, death, and tragedy brood over this novel from its beginning to its incomplete end. The tale is about a half-Spanish, half-British young woman, Bianca. Her sister Inez has just died, and she and her Spanish father are continuing to live in exile in England. The novel is written in a highly affective register, with a jealous, over-possessive father who resents his surviving daughter being courted by the British aristocrat Lord Moore. In the delicate, sensitive, intelligent Bianca, who is steeped in French poetry and is very much an outsider in England, we see valuable traces of Toru creating a blossoming young female self. Bianca quotes to her father this beautiful description of dawn in a poem by the French poet and novelist Claude Adhémar André Theuriet (1833–1907):

> Je m'endors, et là-bas le frissonnant matin
> Baigne les pampres verts d'une rougeur furtive,
> Et toujours cette odeur amoureuse m'arrive
> Avec le dernier chant d'un rossignol lointain
> Et les premiers cris de la grive.
>
> (T. Dutt, *Collected* 118)[4]

In addition to voicing the poem within her novel through the character Bianca, in her personal life Toru quoted this poem in a letter to Mary Jane Martin (H. Das 135)[5] and praised and quoted these lines in the original French in *A Sheaf Gleaned in French Fields* (305). Such repeated quotations make it clear that Toru fashioned Bianca as a young woman who shared many of her own aesthetic preferences. Moreover, Bianca's transnational positionality also echoes Toru's cosmopolitan identity. When Bianca nearly dies after an illness, her father consents to her engagement to Lord Moore. Lord Moore's mother, however, calls Bianca a "wild girl" and "as proud as if she were the Queen of Spain" (T. Dutt, *Collected* 114).[6] Toru's awareness of English snobbery and xenophobia is obvious in such passages.

The themes of melancholy, tragedy, madness, and death also dominate Toru's French novel, *Le Journal de Mademoiselle d'Arvers*, even while it weaves a story of romantic love. N. Kamala has argued that Toru could only have written such a story of romantic, sexual, and affective awakening in a language such as French (Kamala 109). Placing her stories in European contexts also allowed Toru to more easily utilize plots of sensibility and the Gothic that she gleaned from reading European novels. Again, like Bianca, the heroine of Toru's French novel also bears strong resemblances to Toru herself, in physical description, sensitivity, and intelligence. Toru Dutt's oeuvre, as we saw, bridges the worlds of Indian and European sensibilities, as well as languages, notably English, French, Sanskrit, and her mother tongue, Bengali. Her novels, which are heroine-centered, constitute a distinctive and unique part of the larger line of nineteenth-century Indian women writers' fictions delineating female growth and development. Writing as she did in both prose and poetry, Toru Dutt's experiments in creativity are cosmopolitan, multilingual, and bold.

Krupabai Satthianadhan and Ramabai: Conversion and Reform

Krupabai Satthianadhan (1862–94) was a younger contemporary of Toru Dutt; she too died tragically young, at the age of thirty-two. Like Toru, she was Christian. When considering Satthianadhan's remarkable fiction, it is illuminating to juxtapose her oeuvre with that of another even more celebrated Indian Christian woman writer, Pandita Ramabai, also known as Ramabai Saraswati and Ramabai Medhavi Dongre (1858–1922). A high-caste Indian Hindu widow who converted to Christianity in 1886,

Pandita Ramabai played a multifaceted role as a writer, essayist, campaigner for women's education, and founder of multiple developmental organizations (including a school and homes for widows, prostitutes, and the destitute). There are some striking similarities between Ramabai's and Krupabai's lives: both intended to study medicine; both had to give up their plans due to health reasons. Ramabai had a hearing impairment, and Krupabai, who won a scholarship to study medicine in England, was not allowed to go because of her failing health; she later enrolled at Madras Christian College for the same purpose but had to give up her studies as a result of a health breakdown. Satthianadhan, like Ramabai, was an actor in the educational and welfarist sphere: the former, after marrying Reverend Samuel Satthianadhan, started a school for Muslim girls in Ootacamund, with help from the Church Missionary Society, and she taught girls in other schools as well. Both published their writings at roughly the same time.

In 1883, supported by the Anglican order, Ramabai set sail for England, where she was to remain until a visit to the United States in 1886. In England, she converted to Anglican Christianity, although she later adopted a non-denominational form of Christianity as her faith. Ramabai makes a scathing critique of brahminical patriarchal Hinduism in her book *High-Caste Hindu Woman* (1887), which offers a novelized portrait of the sufferings of the upper-caste Hindu widow in ways that parallel, but also contrast with, Krupabai Satthianadhan's 1894 novel *Kamala*. In 1889, Ramabai published a Marathi travelogue, *United Stateschi Lokasthiti ani Pravasavritta*, loosely translatable as *The Peoples of the United States*, which was published in Bombay. This text offers a wonderfully detailed and acute portrait of U.S. society in the late nineteenth century. On her return to Maharashtra, Ramabai established institutions in Mumbai, Pune, and Kedgaon, such as Sharada Sadan (a school and home for child widows), followed by Mukti Sadan and Kripa Sadan (which served lower-caste women, rescued sex workers, and offered training and refuge to blind and other disabled women).

Satthianadhan's first novel *Saguna: A Story of Native Christian Life* was serialized in the Madras Christian College Magazine in 1887–88, and her second novel, *Kamala: A Story of Hindu Life*, was published in 1894 in Madras. While *Saguna* tells the semi-autobiographical story of a young Indian woman who converts to Christianity, *Kamala* is the story of an upper-caste Hindu child wife and, later, widow. Although Kamala refuses the chance to escape the sufferings of her life by remarrying, the novel is not primarily judgmental. Instead, it offers a sympathetic anatomy of

Kamala's life. Her ultimate satisfaction comes from her many acts of philanthropy and charity.

A posthumous collection of Satthianadhan's miscellaneous writings and reviews of her books that I discovered shows how sophisticated the literary reviewing sphere was in relation to Indian women's writing in English by the closing decade of the nineteenth century and how attentive writers and publishers in India were to culling and publicizing such reception of literature (Satthianadhan, *Miscellaneous* 118–29). Take this excerpted review:

> India has given its native poetess in the late Toru Dutt, and in Krupabai Satthianadhan, who last autumn laid down the pen for ever at the early age of thirty-two, we have the first native lady who had ever attempted fiction in the sense understood of the modern novel. Her last work "Kamala" has been issued posthumously, and has just reached this country, where it deserves attention as showing in a manner that the most sympathetic European could never convey, the everyday life and thought of the average purdah woman of the East.[7]

The term "New Woman" is used with ease when discussing Satthianadhan's heroines:

> *Saguna*, her first book, may be described as a study of the "New Woman" as she is in Indian surroundings. It is to some extent biographical.... The story which relies on characterisation rather than plot is told in the first person.... We get many glimpses of inner native life and thought almost unknown to European readers. Many of her descriptions of scenery, household routine, and pleasures, and jealously believed legends are fascinating reading, and she possesses a vein of incisive satire.[8]

Thus, although literary scholars are currently excavating these early Indian women writers' texts, part of that excavation should entail recognizing that such texts and their writers had attained a high reputation even in their own times.

Toru Dutt and Krupabai Satthianadhan were both members of literary families, although in the case of Satthianadhan it was the family that she married into that was active in the literary sphere (de Souza). For instance, Padmini Sengupta, Krupabai's step-daughter, wrote several biographies of distinguished Indian women, such as Toru Dutt,[9] while Padmini's mother Kamala, Krupabai's husband's second wife, edited the *Indian Ladies' Magazine*, in which Rokeya Sakhawat Hossain published her now-classic feminist utopian narrative "Sultana's Dream" (1905). Kamala edited this distinguished magazine first with her husband, from 1901 until 1906, when Samuel died. Undaunted, she continued to publish the magazine until 1913 and revived it after it was discontinued in 1918, in 1919, and again from 1927 to 1934. Sarojini Naidu was one of the other contributors to *The Indian Ladies' Magazine*, a remarkable periodical that is now beginning to receive the scholarly attention it deserves.[10]

Rokeya Sakhawat Hossain: Feminist Utopias

Rokeya Sakhawat Hossain (1880–1932) was an educator, creative writer, essayist, and feminist. In 1911, she founded a school for girls in Kolkata, which still exists today. Her feminist utopian narrative "Sultana's Dream" (1905), written in English, is a masterpiece, as is her Bengali novel *Padmarag* (1924): the latter envisages a utopian community of reformist women. By 1901, Hossain had emerged as a full-fledged writer in Bengali and had been published in a wide range of periodicals, such as *Mahila, Nabanoor, Bangiya Musalman Sahitya Patrika, Saogat*, and *Mohammadi*. A biting, humorous, witty writer, Hossain, like Satthianadhan and Ramabai, used her writing in tandem with and as a form of action in the educational and welfarist public spheres. Besides "Sultana's Dream" and *Padmarag*, she wrote many other short satirical parables and fables. Elsewhere I have analyzed two such notable pieces, "The Fruit of Knowledge" and "The Fruit of Freedom," which demonstrate the richness of her novelistic imagination (Bagchi, "Hannah Arendt").

"A terrible revenge!" said Hossain's husband when he read his wife's narrative, "Sultana's Dream." *The Indian Ladies' Magazine* published the story, written in English by a woman who had no formal education in that language – her brother had helped her learn the language at home. "Sultana's Dream" remains widely read and loved, retaining its status as one of the most successful pieces of Indian writing in English. In the story, the driving force behind the utopian feminist country of Ladyland and its success is women's education. In particular, Hossain emphasizes women's scientific cultivation and condemns male militarism. In her inverted world, the men, mostly brawn, remain confined to the *mardana* and perform the quotidian chores, while the women, mostly brain, govern the country wisely and well, headed by a queen who is aided by the Lady-Principals of the two women's universities.

As a fable, "Sultana's Dream" has a succinct plotline. In Ladyland, the women are busy cultivating their minds, thanks to a queen who decrees universal female education and bans child marriage. In the two universities created exclusively for women, innovative schemes are drawn up, one of which allows water to be drawn directly from clouds, while another permits solar heat to be collected and stored. When the country is threatened with defeat in war by a rival nation, the Lady-Principals of the universities step into the breach, making the withdrawal of men into the *mardana* a precondition for agreeing to rescue the country. The enemy is attacked with missiles fashioned from the concentrated heat developed by the women's universities and is defeated. Since the men are now safely in the *mardana*, the women continue to govern the country, now called Ladyland, creating a utopia where science, technology, and virtue work together harmoniously.

By contrast, *Padmarag* (1924, but believed to have been written before 1916 [B. Ray 444]) is generically hybrid. It is a short novel with much melodrama and romance. It is also a polemical, passionate work on feminism, social welfare, and education. Thus, contrasting with the melodrama is a realistic and gritty strand, particularly in its depiction of a female-administered school and institution, Tarini Bhavan, founded and led by a Brahmo widow, Dina-tarini Sen. Hossain, richly endowed with her own experience of running a pioneering school for Muslim girls, includes wryly humorous descriptions of the trials faced by the administrators of a girls' school. She also gives us vignettes of working women and reformist women writing, teaching, typing, and taking care of other duties, trying to create a utopia in a humdrum world.

Moreover, Hossain in this novel offers a series of portraits of abusive familial, marital, and sexual practices that lead women to madness, the brink of death or suicide, as happens in the case of the eponymous heroine of the work, Zainab, who is also known as "Padmarag" and "Siddika." These critiques are conveyed through a series of pathos-inducing narratives, of women who are "biye fail" – a pun on "biye," or marriage, and "BA," the academic degree. While Siddika/Zainab/Padmarag has undergone much suffering before she comes to Tarini Bhavan, she comes to realize that other teachers also have suffering and pathos in their pasts, despite maintaining remarkably cheerful outer demeanors. Listening to their stories bonds Siddika with these other women.

By the end of the novella, Siddika, inspired by the other inhabitants of Tarini Bhavan, has initiated a process of self-development and the fervent quest for a useful vocation that will help others. Most of her friends hope that she and her benevolent, kind-hearted fiancé, Latif Almas, from whom she has been estranged due to both chance and machination, will reunite and live happily ever after. But Siddika is adamant in her resolve to reject married domesticity. Hossain thus gives her heroine a novel ending: Siddika decides to go back to Chuadanga, bring up her brother's eight-year-old son, and supervise the estate there. She declares that she will spare no effort to awaken Muslim women. Thus, although she leaves Tarini Bhavan, she does so for a far more difficult existence.

Bridging fantastic and realistic utopian modes, with a flair for satire and humor, Hossain's literary oeuvre is fascinating for its stylistic and generic innovations. Equally, her literary works offer striking insights into how an educational leader and pioneering activist for girls' and women's education could also keep her literary creativity alive.

Swarnakumari Devi Ghosal: An Unfinished Song

If a Brahmo woman leads Hossain's fictional community Tarini Bhavan, the Brahmo writer Swarnakumari Devi Ghosal (1855–1932) had crafted an impressive place for herself in the literary sphere in Bengal by the late nineteenth century. She was an elder sister of the writer Rabindranath Tagore, and some of her works, translated from the original Bengali, were also published in English. Ghosal edited the Bengali literary monthly *Bharati* from 1884, on and off, for nearly thirty years. Although she wrote twenty-five works in Bengali, her finest work is the novel *Kahake* (1898), which she herself translated into English, and which was published in London as *The Unfinished Song* (1913). This is a novel of manners and a whimsical, subtle love story about Moni, a sensitive, intelligent young woman seeking to find true love in the heart of the artificial, Anglicized Bengali drawing rooms of early twentieth-century Calcutta. At first, Moni falls in love with Romanath, but, on discovering that he had made promises of love to a young Englishwoman whom he then spurned, she cannot accept his advances. Since this causes the gossip mills to grind furiously, Moni's father decides to take her back to their country home and arrange her marriage. Meanwhile, Moni falls in love with a young doctor. It is symptomatic of the doctor's character that he considers George Eliot, a woman writer, to be as great as William Shakespeare, and that he views Eliot's women characters, such as Maggie Tulliver and Dorothea Brooke, who are searching for love and meaning in their lives, with great sympathy.

Here, as in other novels by early Indian women, such as Kashibai Kanitkar's Marathi novel *Ranga Rao* (1886–1903), we see how Indian and British societies, literatures, and ideals are discussed and debated in women's fiction. Kashibai Kanitkar (1861–1948) has her eponymous hero in *Ranga Rao* hold forth on the Darcy-Elizabeth Bennet union in Austen's *Pride and Prejudice* as an ideal, romantic marriage of choice (Kosambi, ed. 141–2), but, in real life, he learns to reconcile love and negotiated marriage. Meanwhile, Kanitkar, who was corresponding with her husband's friend and her literary mentor Hari Narayan Apte, found that he, excited to discover the first "lady novelist" in Marathi, suggested two possible role models for her writing: George Eliot and Jane Austen. He rejected George Eliot for being too learned and instead suggested that Kanitkar model herself on the supposedly less learned and more modestly domestic Jane Austen (Kosambi, ed. 11).

Like Ramabai, Satthianadhan, and Hossain, Ghosal was active in social reform. She founded the Sakhi Samiti, an organization to help widows and destitute women. In 1889 and 1890, she, along with Pandita Ramabai and other leading women actors in the Indian public sphere, took part in the annual sessions of the Indian National Congress, then still very much a nascent political body. In the preface to her translated novel *The Fatal Garland* (1915), published in London, Ghosal offers valuable and intriguing remarks on her writing and its reception (Ghosal, *Fatal* 11–15). She writes:

> It is now thirty-eight years since the publication of my first novel *Dipnirvan*, and thirty since I took over the editorship of the *Bharati*. At that time the well-known monthly magazine, the *Bangadarshan*, under the guidance of that brilliant writer and novelist, the late Bankim Chandra Chatterjee, had passed away, after inaugurating a new era in Bengali literature; and the *Bharati*, which had been edited for seven years by my eldest brother, Dwijendra Nath Tagore, one of the eminent literary men of Bengal, was also about to retire from the field when I took over the editorship. It is difficult now to imagine the courage then required for a young and inexperienced woman to undertake such an arduous task, and how many difficulties I had to overcome. The literary talent of our Bengali women was at that time almost latent; and if, by any chance, any one among them showed any ability, the public was astonished. (11)

This is a clear-sighted analysis of herself as a woman writer breaking new ground in the male-dominated literary sphere of Bengal. Later in the preface, she also writes:

> The *Adelaide Review* (South Australia) remarked in a review of my book, "An Unfinished Song," that it was curious to find in a book showing such evident traces of English influence on Indian Society, no mention of the English people who reside in India. That newspaper does not know, perhaps, that while Indian and English people live side by side in India, they have really very little social intercourse. In rare cases they make strong and lasting friendships, but the governed and the governing races form, for the

most part, only formal and official relationships. And if this is true today, how much more so was it the case twenty years ago, when that book was written in my own tongue? (*Fatal* 13)

It is notable that while transmitting her story in a transnational, cosmopolitan public sphere by writing it in English, Ghosal is simultaneously protesting against the racism that was integral to colonialism. She further writes:

> There is an Italian saying to the effect that a translator is a traitor; and it is true that to translate the word is only too often to traduce the thought. This is the case with translations made from one European language into another, and infinitely more so when works in Indian literature are translated into English. European nations have more or less the same traditions and ideas, and also a common religion. Their modes of life and thought are very much alike. A literal translation from one European language into another conveys often not only the denotation, but also the connotation of words. But it is very different when an Indian language is translated into English; then the connotation of words is sometimes different, and associations of ideas are sometimes actually opposed. Hence the necessity for encyclopaedic footnotes, and even these fail to convey the actual meaning of a word, and to conjure up the thoughts and sentiments that give to it vitality and importance. (*Fatal* 14)

The complexity and insight of this preface shows that Indian women writers could by 1915 confidently reflect on their own literary journeys and achievements, as well as on the problems that beset them, including what gets transmitted and what gets lost or added in the "carryings over" or "trans-latio" of Indian literature into English. We also see how the question of race was multiplied by patriarchy. Indeed, Rabindranath Tagore was not sympathetic to his sister's international literary ambitions; in February 1914, soon after *An Unfinished Song* was published, he wrote to his friend William Rothenstein: "She is one of those unfortunate beings who has more ambition than abilities.... Her weakness has been taken advantage of by some unscrupulous agents in London and she has had her stories translated and published."[11]

Against both these views, Ghosal believed that women writers could be as great as or greater than the most celebrated male writers. E. M. Lang, introducing *An Unfinished Song*, stated that Ghosal was one of the many early Indian writers who were creating innovative discussions about the comparative reading of literature in ways that were transnational and cosmopolitan, while being impassioned about women's rights to agency and power, literary and otherwise (Ghosal, *Unfinished* 7). It is in this spirit that we can read the following quote from *An Unfinished Song*, from a section in which the relative merits of George Eliot and William Shakespeare are being debated:

> "What is the discussion about? George Eliot? Oh, she is a great woman, we must admit that, I am sorry to say."
>
> "That is a very reluctant admission. Do you not as a man glory in such a genius in woman? She had a truly grand intellect combined with the sympathetic heart and subtle instinct of a true woman. Think of the masterly way in which she shows that every act of man, small or great, springs from a deeper motive, a finer sense of the inner nature. Has any writer of the stronger sex been able to equal her in that?"
>
> "I disagree with you," said my brother-in-law. "Do you mean to say she is as great as Shakespeare, for instance?"
>
> "Of course," was the doctor's warm reply. (Ghosal, *Unfinished* 126–7)

As one of India's leading early women writers claims for a leading British woman writer the highest possible place in the literary canon, Ghosal's creation Moni, along with Saguna, Kamala, Marguerite, and Siddika, deserve their own distinctive and unique niches in our contemporary, emergent canon of Indian writing in English – which, as we saw, also straddles literature in other European languages and in Indian bhashas. Fiction by Indian women continues to be, from the early women writers we encountered in this chapter to contemporary writers such as Arundhati Roy, Sunetra Gupta, Shashi Deshpande, and so many others, an arena of heuristic knowledge and an experimental laboratory in which women try on and experiment with many different kinds of selfhood and course along a variety of paths and journeys of development.

Notes

1 Given that the word "vernacular" originates from the Latin *verna*, meaning "home-born slave" or "native," I prefer the term *bhasha* to describe the range of Indian-language literatures. *Bhasha* means "language" in Sanskrit and a number of other Indian languages.
2 Gosse's review appeared in *The Examiner*, August 26, 1876.
3 *Bengal Magazine* vi, January–April 1878.
4 "I fall asleep, and there the quivering morning/ Bathes the green vines in a shy blush,/ And this loving smell still reaches me/ With the last song of a distant nightingale/ And the first cries of the thrush."
5 Letter to Miss Martin, March 13, 1876, in H. Das 135.
6 Lord Moore's mother never ends up consenting to the marriage, but Lord Moore stands by his intention to marry Bianca. However, at the close of this

unfinished novel, Lord Moore leaves to fight in the Crimean War before the marriage can take place; he places a ring on Bianca's "marriage finger" before he leaves (T. Dutt, *Bianca* 114).

7 Review in *The London* (Sketch), April 17, 1895. Quoted in Satthianadhan, *Miscellaneous* 129.

8 Miss Billington in *The Daily Graphic*. Quoted in Satthianadhan, *Miscellaneous* 123.

9 See Sengupta, *Sarojini*; Sengupta, *Toru*; Sengupta, *Portrait*; and Sengupta, *Pandita*.

10 See, for example, Emily J. Monteiro, "Communal Formations: Development of Gendered Identities in Early Twentieth-Century Women's Periodicals." Ph.D. Dissertation, Texas A&M University, 2013.

11 Rabindranath Tagore, Letter to William Rothenstein, February 1914. Quoted in Tharu and Lalitha, eds., 238.

CHAPTER 4

When the Pen Was a Sword: The Radical Career of the Progressive Novel in India

Snehal Shingavi

Is the Anglophone Indian Novel also a Progressive Novel?

In April of 1936, while India was still under British rule, the All-India Progressive Writers' Association (AIPWA) held its inaugural conference in Lucknow (P. Gopal, *Literary* 17).[1] The goal of the meeting, in part, was to bring together writers on a common platform to defend artistic freedoms against the twin challenges of colonial censorship and religious orthodoxy. But the goals of the AIPWA (also called the "Akhil Bharatiya Pragativadi Lekhak Sangh" in Hindi and the "Taraqqi Pasandi Masneef Tehreek" in Urdu) went beyond free speech issues to embrace a wide range of social and political concerns (Coppola, "Premchand's" 21). The Manifesto of the Progressive Writers' Association read, in part:

1) It is the duty of Indian writers to give expression to the changes in Indian life and to assist the spirit of progress in the country by introducing scientific rationalism in literature. They should undertake to develop an attitude of literary criticism which will discourage the general reactionary and revivalist tendencies on questions like family, religion, sex, war and society, and to combat literary trends reflecting communalism, racial antagonism, sexual libertinism, and exploitation of man by man.

2) It is the object of our association to rescue literature from the conservative classes – to bring the arts into the closest touch with the people....

3) We believe that the new literature of India must deal with the basic problems of our existence today – the problems of hunger and poverty, social backwardness and political subjection.

4) All that arouses in us the critical spirit, which examines customs and institutions in the light of reason, which helps us to act, to organize ourselves, to transform, we accept as progressive. (Malik 651)

In so doing, Indian writers were not only responding to the heady spirit of the agitations for India's independence, but they were also charting a course for the direction of India's future, embracing a wide range of concerns: social redistribution, gender equality, scientific rationality, and political reform (T. Ahmed 11–37). The organization, while initially dominated by Urdu writers, was vast: "almost no contemporaneous Indian writer in any language, including English, would remain unaffected by its reach" (P. Gopal, *Literary* 2). The Progressive Writers' Movement grew over the next decades to become the most important and largest literary movement in South Asia's history.

At the same time, the relationship between the AIPWA and Anglophone novelists was not always a straightforward one. While English may have been the language that most of the early members of the AIPWA spoke with one another, there were very few novelists in the AIPWA who wrote primarily in English. There was a small group of Anglophone writers who never ventured into leftist political territory: Govinddas Vishnoodas Desani, Nirad Chaudhuri, R. K. Narayan. K. S. Venkataramani seems never to have linked up with the AIPWA, despite the fact that his early novels dealt with peasant exploitation in south India; nor did Krishnaswamy Nagarajan, whose *Athavar House* (1937) depicted the effects of capitalism and colonialism. Mulk Raj Anand and Ahmed Ali were both there at the beginning, helping to craft the AIPWA manifesto, and Ali was a part of the infamous *Angaaray* (1932) collective and the editor of the AIPWA's short-lived journal *Indian Writing*, but Anand never joined the AIPWA and Ali was soon edged out by erstwhile comrades (Shingavi 21). Raja Rao, also a radical, published independently of the organs of AIPWA (except for a short story in the short-lived journal *Indian Writing*) and also seems never to have joined.[2] Bhabhani Bhattacharya's early novelistic output bears traces of the political sentiments of the AIPWA, but he never became a member either (Dwivedi 7–8). Even at this early stage, the movement's emphasis (as the AIPWA manifesto put it) on "bring[ing] arts into the closest touch with the people and [making] them the vital organs which will register the actualities of life," and focusing on a population largely illiterate in the vernacular languages and nearly entirely incapable of reading in English, seemed to foreclose the idea of a large membership of Anglophone writers (M. Anand, "Progressive" 21).

This formal separation of Anglophone novelists from the AIPWA has led many to conclude that in these early years, Indian writing in English was dominated by its affiliation to Gandhi (as opposed to the AIPWA's interest in Marx):

The national freedom movement under Mahatma Gandhi called up
a sensitive response in the novelists of the period. From the twenties
onwards, therefore, the Indian English fiction shows a marked impress of
Gandhi's philosophy and personality. The novels of the late thirties and for-
ties reflect the influence of political parties on Indian ethos and the role of
the Indian National Congress under the dynamic leadership of Mahatma
Gandhi. (Yaseen 12)

Other critics, too, have noticed how Gandhi was able to inspire a vast
coalition of writers with disparate political agendas, creating a much larger
coterie of "Gandhian" writers than progressive ones (P. Gopal, *Indian* 46).
One critic went as far as to call Gandhi indispensable in the production
of Indian literature in English: "The works of K. S. Venkataramani, Mulk
Raj Anand and Raja Rao would not perhaps have been possible had the
miracle that was Gandhi not occurred during this period" (Naik, *History*
162). In fact, Khwaja Ahmad Abbas, through his involvement with the
associated Indian People's Theater Association (IPTA), seems to be the
only Anglophone writer with sustained, formal ties to the progressive
movement.

Other critics have attempted to short-circuit these writers' connections
to the AIPWA by calling this period "Nehru's decades" (L. Gandhi 171).
If Gandhi represented the uplift of "women, workers, untouchables, and
peasants" through his constructive programs, "Nehru's Marxism – and his
critique of the nexus between world capitalism and imperialism – gestured towards the viability of a more expansive and politically motivated
internationalism" (L. Gandhi 171). As a result, some critics have found it
easier to explain the political sympathies of the period through nationalist figures rather than the internationalist genealogies of Marxism, realism, and modernism or the vernacular genealogies of politics at the more
local level. In place of either the "Gandhian" or the "Nehruvian" sobri-
quets, the term "progressive" still best captures the Anglophone writing
of this period of late literary nationalism, in part because it so closely
mirrors all of the complexities and contradictions of the Progressive
Writers' Movement as well. First of all, in the early years of the AIPWA,
the Progressives themselves were divided over the question of their allegiances to Gandhi and Nehru, with some seeing the split between the
movement and the nationalist leadership clearly, others attempting to syn-
thesize the two figures, and others opting for a different set of politics
altogether. Secondly, the Gandhi/Nehru dyad too closely mirrors other
dyads – rural/urban, traditional/modern, national/cosmopolitan, pacifist/
Marxist – and none of these are resolved in the Anglophone novel of the

period, which shuttles back and forth between a variety of geographies, political agendas, and aspirations. Finally, and most importantly, the figures of Gandhi and Nehru, while definitely important, overshadow a range of influences, political and aesthetic, that the labile term "progressive" preserves. Tendentiously, it is worth proposing that despite the final takeover of the AIPWA by the Communist Parties of India and Pakistan, the progressive movement of late colonial India was as important as it was precisely because it did not resolve these tensions in a straightforward way (Toor 11–14). Several writers continued to call themselves "progressive" even after leaving the AIPWA.

The Retrospective Politics of Exclusion

One of the reasons it is important to situate Anglophone writing within the orbit of the AIPWA – even though it was not entirely determined by its gravitational pull – is because Anglophone writers have been used as evidence in the partisan debates about the AIPWA to demonstrate that the progressive movement deteriorated into a Communist Party-controlled, Zhdanovite socialist realism, as its intolerance toward "adab baara-e-adab [art for art's sake]" drove serious artists from its ranks (Mufti, "Towards" 252). There is much evidence to support this particular reading of Anglophone Indian fiction. Anand's book, *Apology for Humanism*, attempts to chart out a political course separate from Progressivism, and it has given succor to critics who want to distinguish him from the formal left: "Even in the early days of his career, in the 1930s, for example, when Anand was closely connected with the Progressive Writers' Association (PWA) and personally accepted the idealistic goals of Marxism, he never viewed the writer as one whose purpose was chiefly propagandistic or political" (Fisher 81). Ahmed Ali, who had an explicit falling-out with the leadership of AIPWA, especially Sajjad Zaheer, was explicit that the reason he was quitting the movement was because the AIPWA was too tightly controlled by the agenda of the Communist Party of India: "The fanfare that accompanied the first All-India Progressive Writers' Association meeting in 1936 was largely political and stamped with a certain ideology.... When an open attempt was made in 1938–39 to give the movement a direct communist turn, the creative section moved away from it. Even Premchand would have done so had he been alive, for he was never a communist anyway, though he was progressive in the sense most of us understood the word" (A. Ali, "Progressive Writers" 43–5). The failure to attract a substantial membership of Anglophone writers has led some to conclude that progressive writing was largely confined to the regional or vernacular languages.

That such a view is partisan and related to post-independence debates about literature and politics should be underlined. In fact, the need to separate the Marxists or socialists from the nationalists or the Gandhians was – and continues to be – so powerful that it has led to a mistaken consensus in the Indian academy that the Indian novel in English had a uniquely Gandhian pedigree (Iyengar 271–95). There are at least four reasons why this consensus developed: first, as the Communist Party of India moved into the opposition against the Indian National Congress after independence, earlier political coalitions were beginning to dissolve into partisan rancor; second, in the debates about English in the post-independence period, academics found it easier to make the case for continuing to teach English by showing that novelists were moved by nationalist rather than internationalist concerns (Shingavi 13–28). Moreover, unlike the Hindi or the Urdu novel, the Anglophone Indian novel could find publishers for itself without going through watchful, local patrons who channeled and controlled access to journals and publishing houses. The Anglophone novel found its support through the Fabian politics of E. M. Forster, Graham Greene, and Leonard Woolf, which set it on a parallel but slightly different track than its vernacular cousins. It would, then, be more precise to say that the Anglophone novel of the 1930s and 1940s had a range of influences irreducible to either the long shadow of nationalist politics or the putative orthodoxies of socialist realism, while containing elements of both and others as well: indigenous aesthetic traditions, early experiments in Anglophone writing, local political ideologies, religious forms and figures, and so forth. Unlike the later AIPWA, which became an antagonist with the Halqa-e-Arbab-e-Zauq (the movement for Urdu modernism) and with the Prayogvaadis (the movement for Hindi experimentalism), its Anglophone "fellow travelers" were much more eclectic. So, even before he broke from the AIPWA, Ahmed Ali was able to make claims that would have been indistinguishable from the propagandists of socialist realism of the later AIPWA:

> The artist lives in society, and as its product he cannot escape tendencies which work in that society in that particular period. Feudalism has produced an aristocratic art, democracy a more popular one; capitalism now has produced an exclusive art expressing all despair and contradictions inherent in it; and side by side the proletariat has created and is creating an art of its own, which is more human and free from obscurity and contradictions. (A. Ali, "Progressive View" 67)

Still, the impact of AIPWA on the thought and craft of the Anglophone novelists of the period (as well as their centrality to the development of the AIPWA) is unmistakable, as is their political critique of both British imperialism and comprador religious forces. Ahmed Ali and Mulk Raj Anand, considered two of the "founding fathers" of Anglophone writing in India, were both involved in the earliest stages of organizing the AIPWA. Anand helped pen the first draft of the Manifesto, while Ahmed Ali helped organize meetings in Lucknow. Anand's novels *Untouchable* (1935) and *Coolie* (1936) both draw attention to the plight of young laborers and their exploitation by Hindu orthodoxy and colonial capitalism – although sometimes when writing about them, Anand could be cagy about their politics (M. Anand, "Making"). Ahmed Ali's novel *Twilight in Delhi* (1940) documents the slow devastation suffered by Delhi's cultural establishment as British colonialism reorganized the city for its own imperial purposes. The poet Sarojini Naidu, who was also Gandhi's lieutenant during the Salt Satyagraha (1930), addressed several of the meetings of the AIPWA. And whether Bhattacharya, Rao, Venkataramani, or others ever joined the AIPWA, it would not be difficult to demonstrate that their work, too, dealt with the same issues that the manifesto laid out: "the basic problems of our existence today – the problems of hunger and poverty, social backwardness and political subjugation, so that it may help us to understand these problems and through such understandings help us act" (Coppola, "All-India" 11).[3]

Third, the work of the Anglophone writers in particular was essential to cementing the international relationships the AIPWA cultivated with anti-imperialist and anti-fascist writers' movements, especially in France and England. Finally, and perhaps provocatively, at least one critic has noticed that all the Anglophone writers from this period (Venkataramani, Nagarajan, Narayan, Anand, Rao, Desani, Chaudhuri, and Bhattacharya) came from more modest beginnings than did the vernacular writers who preceded them or the Anglophone writers who followed: "All these writers, belonging to the early twentieth century, learnt their English initially from non-native speakers of English. They did not have the benefit of public school education in their formative years nor were they Oxbridge products. Generally, they all hailed from non-genteel backgrounds. None of them were teachers of English in colleges or universities in India or abroad" (Prabha 33). This class difference, in part, accounts for why so many critics are willing to dismiss these writers for the quality of their craft (which also doubles as a critique of the politics of their narratives) (Prabha 21). Both organizationally and dispositionally, the Anglophone novelists of the 1930s and 1940s belong to the story of the development of progressive writing and the broader movement of artists against British imperialism.

The Origins of Progressive Writing: Local, National, Colonial, International

The AIPWA and the trend toward progressive writing in general were direct results of four historical developments, all of which influenced sections of the Progressive Writers' Movement differently. First and foremost, the growth of a movement for Indian independence from British rule had gained considerable strength by the 1930s and had deep roots in the classes of Indians that produced artists and writers. Not only did the anticolonial movements draw this generation of writers toward a more explicitly political aesthetics, it also redirected its art toward issues of poverty, sexism, illiteracy, caste-based chauvinism, economic exploitation, and the like. Writers from India in almost every language began producing art that attempted to make sense of Indian subjection at the hands of British colonialism. Second, educational opportunities for study in Europe brought Indian writers, in English and in the vernaculars, together with writers from various parts of the world. For Anglophone writers, the most important connections were with England (where writers encountered the Fabian politics of Bloomsbury as well as the Marxism of the Communist Party of Great Britain), France (where they made connections with the anti-fascist international conferences), and Russia (which put Indians in touch with the works of Soviet artists). Anglophone Indian writers were not merely aping developments that were taking place in European letters but were active participants in political and aesthetic debates that were co-constitutive of one another (Gajarawala 71). Third, developments in vernacular literary traditions were already moving in the direction of more experimentation with form and style. A full accounting of these would be nearly impossible, but it could already be seen in the novelistic innovations in *Navodaya* (in Kannada), the psychological realism of Jainendra Kumar, the socially committed realism of Premchand (in Hindi), the politically subversive poetry of Josh Mahilabadi (in Urdu), the social critique of A. Madhaviah (in Tamil), and the innovative realism of the three Bandopadhyays: Tarashankar, Manik, and Bibhutibhushan (in Bangla), just to give a few examples. Anglophone writing emerged out of a class of writers who may have felt less comfortable writing in vernacular languages but who were nonetheless surrounded by developments in the vernacular literatures. The suggestion that progressive writing's grouping together of modernism and realism was merely imitative of European traditions does a disservice to the rich history of innovation in most Indian languages.

Fourth, and perhaps most famously, what launched the AIPWA was the national controversy created by the publication of the infamous Urdu short story collection *Angaaray* (1932) and its proscription by the British authorities five months later (Zaheer, Ali, et.al.). The stories themselves exhibit a range of stylistic and formal choices (modernist stream-of-consciousness, high realism, a one-act play), but they are united around challenging the problems of Muslim orthodoxy (troped as sexism) and colonial rule (troped as poverty). The book created an immediate controversy for its frank discussion of sexuality and the oppression of women within the home, but it was also condemned by the Muslim ulama for three stories (all by Sajjad Zaheer) in particular: in "Neend Nahin Ati [Can't Sleep]," God flirts with prostitutes in heaven; in "Jannat ki Basharat [A Vision of Heaven]," a pious maulvi has an erotic fantasy about houris in heaven; and in "Phir Yeh Hangama [This Trouble Too...]," Gabriel reports that others (presumably the Prophet Muhammad) have mistaken him for Satan (an allusion to the so-called Satanic Verses of the *Qur'an*). Commentators have remarked that it was in fact the involvement of Rashid Jahan, the sole woman in the group, that seems to have drawn the ire of the conservatives most strongly, since the association of women with a kind of radical feminism was perhaps too much for the ulama to tolerate (M. Mukherjee, "Mapping an Elusive" 84). Fatwas were issued against the collective, and at large public meetings of the ulama, the collection was roundly denounced:

> The Central Standing Committee ... at this meeting strongly condemns the heart-rending and filthy pamphlet called Aangarey [sic] compiled by Sajjad Zahir, Ahmed Ali, Rashid Jehan, Mahmudul Zafar which has wounded the feelings of the entire Muslim community by ridiculing God and his Prophet and which is extremely objectionable from the standpoints of both religion and morality. The committee further strongly urges upon the attention of the U.P. [United Provinces] Government that the book be at once proscribed. (G. Kumar 120–1)

Within five months, all but a few extant copies of the book were seized.

The authors of the stories had hoped, as they argued in their "In Defence of *Angāre*. Shall We Submit to Gagging?" printed soon after the controversy around the book was unleashed, that they could reveal the problems extant in Muslim communities and begin a long overdue conversation about them with an eye toward substantive reforms. In response to their critics, they argued:

> The authors of this book do not wish to make any apology for it. They leave it to float or sink of itself. They are not afraid of the consequences of having launched it. They only wish to defend "the right of launching it and all other vessels like it." ... They stand for the right of free criticism and free expression in all matters of the highest importance to the human race in general and the Indian people in particular. They have chosen the particular field of Islam, not because they bear any "special" malice, but because, being born into that particular society, they felt themselves better qualified to speak for that alone. They were more sure of their ground there. (Quoted in Mahmud 451)

It was the combination of the government crackdown on artistic freedoms and the angry spirit of the anticolonial movement that seemed to make the call for a Progressive Writers' Association more urgent, but it also placed the literary output that would follow on a certain track that would be hard to redirect: literature was now to be associated with speaking truth to power, with freedom of expression, and with exposing the intimate problems of everyday life.

Anglophone Novelists and the Contested Terrain of the Progressive Novel

In these early years (roughly 1935–40), the definition of what it meant to be "progressive" was still in flux, and even though most took it as a "kind of euphemism for socialist realism," there were still many in the group who were committed to a politics of social justice but less convinced of the need to defer formal innovation (P. Joshi, *In Another* 208). However, as the movement developed, and it became more important for the Communist Party of India to exert influence in the AIPWA and use it as its cultural arm, the AIPWA began to alienate writers who saw its doctrinaire approach to literary form unacceptable (K. Ali 7). At the same time, writers who remained within the orbit of the AIPWA objected both to the accusation that theirs was not an innovative realist art and that their emphasis on social problems reduced their art to mere propaganda (Coppola, "Ahmed Ali" 114). In fact, part of the reason that the scholarship on the Progressive Writers' Association is so partisan has to do with the fact that the movement would undergo a number of splits, all of which produced different accounts of the history of the association and its aesthetic contributions (K. Ali 7). And, as Meenakshi Mukherjee reports, the debates that started in the 1930s in the ranks of the AIPWA continued to inflect literary debates well after independence as well:

> But opposition between those who used literature to highlight injustice and oppression, and the writers who focused on the predicament of the individual in a fragmented society, persisted for many decades to come. In fact the rift might have even grown wider over the years. Harish Trivedi has pointed out how in 1943 when *Tar Saptak* was published, Agyeya [Sacchidanand Hiranand Vatsyayan] and [Gajanan] Muktibodh could co-exist in the same volume; but in subsequent decades their admirers are in such sharply opposed camps that the importance of one can be claimed only by denying literary merit to the other. (M. Mukherjee, "Mapping an Elusive" 82)

Anglophone writers, too, became partisans in these post-independence literary debates.

Depending on who is asked, Mulk Raj Anand and Ahmed Ali are counted variously as supporters and as detractors of the AIPWA. This is, in part, because of the changing nature of the category "progressive." Mulk Raj Anand's essay, "On the Progressive Writers' Movement," and Ahmed Ali's "Progressive View of Art" are both included in Sudhi Pradhan's collection *Marxist Cultural Movement in India* but without any indication that the writers later objected to the politics they advocated in the included pieces. In his essay, Anand argues for an explicitly Leninist kind of literary criticism and advocates simultaneously for historical materialism and literary freedom (though it contains the germ of the terms that separated him from the later AIPWA):

> Lenin's occasional essays and notes on literature are examples of this method and the viewpoint behind them differs from the approach of the mere sociologist and of the dilettante critic, because, whereas the latter seems to conceive Marxist criticism as the answer to the question to what class a writer belongs, the former judges the artistic quality of a writer's work by relating it to the history of the time in which the writer lived, the conditions under which he worked, the social problems that were pressing for solution during his life, the relationships of the classes of the time, and withal the depths of understanding of the writer and the intensity of his realisation of the social reality of the time. (M. Anand, "Progressive" 9)

Ali, too, begins his essay by talking about the beginnings of "proletarian" art in India, but then lays out the debate over what counted as "progressive":

> At the very out-set I must point out that "progressive" should not be taken to be synonymous with revolutionary. It does, however, mean trying for the betterment of our social life. It implies the banishment of mysticism

(which I have already considered above in more detail) and all that which stands in our way of attaining freedom. It also means the acceptance of realism as a primary factor in the arts and literature....

The word progressive, then, implies the consciousness of what we are, what we were, what we should or can be. It is dynamic in essence and stands for action. In order to appreciate it we must be conscious of our condition today: We are in the mire – we were not in the mire – how can we get out of the mire? (A. Ali, "Progressive View" 78–9)

Both of these essays contain terms that either Sajjad Zaheer's wing of the AIPWA or those who left the AIPWA could find to support their positions. Anand's defense of Lenin's historical materialist reading practice is coupled with his belief that good writing and class allegiances may not work in the same direction. Ali's sense that "progressive" and "revolutionary" art were separate entities did not prevent him from endorsing social realism as the form that literature would need to take in the modern period. At least one critic has suggested that despite his later criticisms of the AIPWA as being too closely dominated by the Communist Party, Ali's early definitions of the term "progressive" were even more restrictive than the communists': "it was his [Ali's] contribution that struck a sectarian, dismissive note" (T. Ahmed 45). At a minimum, though, all critics are forced to acknowledge that Anand, Ali, and many of the Anglophone writers of the period would have been considered progressives by these standards (Prabha 20–36).

The Varied Careers of Anglophone Progressive Novelists

Of the Anglophone writers of the 1930s and 1940s, the most important is clearly Mulk Raj Anand, not only because of the sheer volume of his output but because of his tireless campaigning for Indian writers in English (H. Williams 36). Two of his novels from this period – *Untouchable* (1935) and *Coolie* (1936) – take up protagonists from lower castes and classes and attempt to show the bustling world of colonial modernity from their perspectives. *Untouchable* follows a day in the life of Bakha, a young Dalit boy in a small cantonment town in northern India (most likely based on Bulandshahar). Along the way, Bakha encounters both the chauvinisms of Hindu orthodoxy – being cheated by a merchant, given spoiled leftovers by a caste Hindu housewife, accused of despoiling a temple by his mere presence, and then almost beaten for accidentally touching a Brahmin – as well as the failures of colonial modernity – the failure of the British to establish useful sanitation, the futility of conversion to Christianity, and the pointless desire for British commodities. In a thrilling final section, Bakha encounters both Mahatma Gandhi and a poet, Iqbal Nath Sharshar (a combination of the poet Muhammad Iqbal and the novelist Ratan Nath Sharshar) who convince Bakha that a solution awaits the problem of untouchability in the twin projects of nationalist independence and socialist modernity. In describing his own process in composing *Untouchable*, Anand's connections to the spirit of progressivism are unmistakable:

> I felt that, apart from the exuberance of my own egoism in the *Confession*, I had been trying to be truthful in Gandhi's way. But I had not so far faced our weaknesses. Our inability to revolt. Even the courage to call a spade a spade, as the English do. Unless I could become a revolutionary, I would not be able to free myself from the corrosions behind the façade of the Hindu in me and have a vision of the free life.... I must take out the portion about the sweeper-boy Bakha from the confessional and write about him as a new kind of hero of India, a failure against the twiceborn, but one who makes the effort to come up from the labyrinths. I must create a hero, beyond the weak-kneed me. My nerves tingled at the inspiration which had just come. (M. Anand, *Bubble* 337)

Anand's *Coolie* takes up similar problems in the life of a young laborer, Munoo, who is forced to go from job to job (domestic servant, industrial laborer, rickshaw puller) and discovers along the way the inability of various well-intentioned forces to overcome the strictures of capitalist exploitation of labor.

If Anand is sometimes accused of producing boiler-plate socialist realism, the charge is never leveled at his contemporary Raja Rao, whose novel *Kanthapura* (1938) describes the period of nationalist agitation in a small village in Uttar Kanara immediately following Gandhi's Salt Satyagraha (1930). *Kanthapura* was perhaps a one-of-a-kind experiment in Anglophone writing in India, as Rao attempted to marry the novelistic form to the *sthala-purana*, an oral epic tradition narrating the history of a pilgrimage site. Not only did its breathless polysendetons explode the realist sentence of tight adjectival phrases, but it also allowed for a different pattern of political explanation to enter into the novel. The novel's narrator is a grandmother named Achakka who early on describes how politics entered into the claustrophobic world of women's homes:

> Our Rangamma is no village kid. It is not for nothing she got papers from the city.... But there was one thing she spoke of again and again – and, to tell you the truth, it was after the day the sandal merchant of the North came to sell us his wares and had slept on her veranda and had told her

of the great country across the mountains, the country beyond Kabul and Bukhara and Lahore, the country of the hammer and sickle and electricity – it was then onwards that she began to speak of this country, far, far away; a great country, ten times as big as say Mysore, and there in that country there were women who worked like men, night and day; men and women who worked night and day, and when they felt tired, they went and spent their holiday in a palace – no money for the railway, no money for the palace – and when the women were going to have a child, they had two months' and three months' holiday, and when the children were still young they were given milk by the Government, ... and when they grew older still they went to the Universities free, too, and when they were still more grown-up, they got a job and they got a home to live in and they took a wife to live with and they had many children and they lived on happily ever after. And she told us so many marvellous things about that country. (30–2)

In the place of the usual set-piece of the union militant who excoriates the evils of capitalism, Rao's novel offers the almost fairy-tale version of socialist utopia in the Soviet Union, complete with its emphasis on the centrality of women's rights in the workplace. Unlike the socialist realism of the period, in which political speeches at the end of the novel serve as a kind of pseudo-epiphany, Rao's novel puts its political themes at the beginning and then watches them unfold. And contrary to the claims of some critics who have called the novel "distinctly non-Marxist" and "Gandhian" (Trivedi, "Gandhian" 114), it is clear that the novel holds out the possibility of far more radical solutions than those on offer from Indian nationalism.

Of the authors of this period, perhaps the most controversial to include in the category of "progressive writers" is Ahmed Ali. Because of his early break from the AIPWA (sometime around 1939), Ali's post-*Angaaray* output is largely seen to be either anti-Marxist or apolitical (Sarma 33). At the same time, Ali fiercely defended his own sense of progressive politics and the narrowing of literary horizons to class-based determinations of political ideologies (A. Ali, *Prison* 162–3). His most famous novel, *Twilight in Delhi* (1940), attempts to show just how paralyzed Muslim north India had become by its failure to develop an anticolonial politics that spoke to its own needs, rather than those of the predominantly Hindu Indian National Congress. The novel follows the life of Mir Nihal, a Syed in Delhi, who finds his emotional and urban life slowly vitiated by the invasion of Delhi first by the British (who move the capital there from Calcutta in 1911) and then by India, as Punjabi migrants enter the city seeking better opportunities. As one critic has noted, Mir Nihal's "little world is essentially and intensely Muslim in a way that the countrywide

nationalist movement could not be" (Trivedi, "Ahmed Ali" 64–5), despite
the fact that his hatred for the British outstrips the nationalists'. What
Ali's novel marvelously tracks are the twin failures of Indian nationalism
to speak effectively to Muslim concerns and of Muslim politicians to generate an anticolonial politics that could have produced solidarity with the
larger struggle. In the wake of these twin failures, we watch a bedridden
Mir Nihal slowly die as the cultural and emotional legacy of Delhi draws
its last breaths:

> He lay on his bed in a state of coma, too feelingless to sit up or think. The
> sun went down and hid his face. The rooks cawed and flew away. The spar-
> rows found their nests. And night came striding fast, bringing silence in its
> train, and covered up the empires of the world in its blanket of darkness
> and gloom. (*Twilight* 200)

The conventional images of Urdu poetry, especially from *ghazals* and *sheh-
rashobs*, find their way into Ali's novel as a part of what one critic has
called "indigenizing the novel," also demonstrating just how central the
cultural devastation of Delhi was to Britain's imperial project (P. Joshi, *In
Another* 226).

Unlike the progressive novel in Hindi and Urdu, in which the lines
of affiliation are drawn much more clearly, the Anglophone novel has a
different relationship to the political period, even as the influence of a
suite of political ideas – nationalism, Marxism, feminism, egalitarianism,
literary realism, and so forth – remains unmistakable. Despite the fact
that the AIPWA may have defined progressivism in rather specific ways,
Anglophone writers attempted to carve out a space for their own works
as they traveled along parallel political and literary lines as other writers.
But perhaps even more importantly, Anglophone writers were an indispensable part of the career of the progressive novel, shaping both its international reputation and its theoretical underpinnings as they participated
in both national and international debates about the role of committed
writing in the interwar period. Putting the early Anglophone novel in
relationship to developments in the vernacular literary traditions allows
us to see the various contributions that all made toward the project of a
progressive future for the subcontinent.

Notes

1 Sometimes the scholarly literature uses "PWA" (Progressive Writers'
  Association) in place of "AIPWA." However, since the Pakistani Progressive
  Writers' Association also called itself PWA, I have tried to use "AIPWA" in all
  instances to avoid confusion.

2 Zaheer makes mention of a journal called *New Indian Literature* in his memoirs about this period, which seems to have been set up in 1939, just a year before *Indian Writing* (Zaheer 136). Both claim to be related to the AIPWA, but it is most likely that *Indian Writing* came after Ahmed Ali's split with the AIPWA and that the journal bears the impress of the politics of the period rather than any formal connection to the AIPWA (T. Ahmed 36).

3 Note that Malik's rendering of the manifesto differs from Coppola's. Coppola takes his version from the one published in *The Left Review*, while Malik takes his from the one published in India.

CHAPTER 5

The Road Less Traveled: Modernity and Gandhianism in the Indian English Novel

Rumina Sethi

Modernity did not germinate organically in Indian soil; it was British colonialism that brought modernity to India. Colonialism grafted varieties of new economic, cultural, political, and intellectual structures on what was largely a feudal setup. These new "Western" formations were progressive, to say the least, and continuously created fault lines between the modern and the ancient.[1] The nation, as an artifact of modernity, is also believed to have emerged from colonialism, from the "sense of unity" resulting from being a single colony of the British, who for the first time consolidated the multifarious communities of India (Panikkar, "History"). The ensuing nation was both what Partha Chatterjee calls "derivative" (*Nationalist*) – being modern and secular – and the antithesis of that very modernity, which was based on an indigenous, hence nativist, perception of the nation. The latter representation is ordinarily called cultural nationalism. Some historians have assigned to Indian nationalist history the status of a "palimpsest," characterized by a certain borderlessness, wherein the traces of the new order only partially overwrite the systems of the past (Saberwal 434).

In the 1930s and 1940s, cultural nationalists threw up a ubiquitous model of village societies – the unchanging Indian village republic – that was seized upon by the fiction writers of the period and celebrated in their many works. These were the last two crucial decades of colonial rule in India, when an identifiable nationalist ideology, with Gandhi at its helm, was being shaped to free India from colonial rule and step forward into modernity. During these years, fiction writers employed images of the Indian village community to promote national self-consciousness in literature, which worked well within the parameters of Gandhi's theory of *swaraj* or home rule. Paradoxically, the idea of India as a land of villages was incompatible with a rising modernity that accompanied the birth of the nation. This chapter takes up three Anglophone authors of that era – Raja Rao, R. K. Narayan, and Mulk Raj Anand – to discuss the dynamic ways in which the appropriation of a Gandhian national identity, based on the village model, was contrary to the cosmopolitanism that was a necessary accompaniment of colonial modernity in India.

In many ways, the orientalist and nationalist views together effected the idea of India as a land of villages in their endeavor to define the "real India." While European societies had made the transition from the country to the city, in India, the village continued to exist as a living entity. From the orientalist view, the Indian village was a charming entity, preserved and protected from capitalist modernity. While Europe had traveled the path of aggressive capitalism, particularly in the nineteenth century, establishing colonies overseas, the Indian village appeared as a calm oasis, untouched by civilizational ravages. Much was written about the Indian village community in the accounts of Henry Sumner Maine and Baden-Powell, who created a contrast between modern Europe and ancient India. Almost timeless in conception, the village was to become representatively "Indian" in accounts celebrating Indian nationalism. It symbolized indigenous cultural standards as well as the power of antiquity that could stand up to the modern. The representation of the idealized Indian village as a prehistoric inner world would define the notion of "Indianness" in the writings of many Indian nationalists, from Rammohan Roy to Vivekananda, and from Madanmohan Malaviya to Rabindranath Tagore. Gandhi, of course, became the embodiment of a civil society based on village communities that was premised on spiritualism as opposed to materialism.

Writers such as K. S. Venkataramani, Raja Rao, K. Nagarajan, and R. K. Narayan built remarkable narratives of "real" Indian villages, encoding traditional principles that were purportedly part of Indian village communities. Narayan's Malgudi was almost picture-perfect: the sacred river Sarayu provides the spiritual backdrop to the simplicity of village life in which play out the stories of India's two major epics, the Ramayana and the Mahabharata. So it is with Raja Rao's *Kanthapura* (1938), in which the village is quintessentially "Indian." It seeks sustenance from the *sthala-puranas*, or legendary stories of the land, as much as from the river Himavathy – both presided over by the village goddess, Kenchamma. The idealized village provides the very lexicon of living in K. Nagarajan's *Chronicles of Kedaram* (1961) through the employment of myths of the past in which the river Nilaveni and the Temple Kedareswarar are prominent landmarks.

The Gandhian initiative of associating national life, based on village communities, with the virtues of *swadeshi*, or indigeneity, deeply influenced many pre- and even post-colonial novelists. In *Hind Swaraj*

(1909), which contains Gandhi's vision of India, he idealizes free India as non-industrialized, based largely on his perception of a traditional Indian culture that would tolerate no economic oppression or human degradation of any kind. Condemning modern civilization, Gandhi envisaged the post-independence social order to be built on a more utopian than historical foundation, with a vision of a revitalizing and vigorous ancient Indian village community as a dominant constituent of his social philosophy of state, society, and nation (M. Gandhi 96, 189). " 'We are inheritors of a rural civilization,' " he said. " 'If the village perishes, India will perish too' " (quoted in Fox 59).

The Indian novel of the early decades of the twentieth century sought mainly to express this ideological formation of Gandhian thought. Archaic and prescriptive as this endeavor was, it had to be explored in a new novel form, a genre that came as a benefaction of the British. In other words, Indian national identity, which seemed resurrected from the past, was to inhabit a certain modernity that came with the novel. This complexity came to mark the central contradiction between the tenets of cultural nationalist ideology – which were pre-modern – and the novel form – which was inherently modern, and very British.

Modernity and Antiquity in Raja Rao's *Kanthapura*

Raja Rao wrote *Kanthapura*, his first novel, between 1929 and 1933 in "a thirteenth century castle in the French Alps belonging to the Dauphins of France [where he] slept and worked on the novel in the room of the Queen" (Naik, *Raja Rao* 60). As in A. K. Ramanujan's rendition of Annayya's self-discovery amidst the stacks of a Chicago library wherein he unmasks India, the itinerant Indian novelist writing in the first few decades of the twentieth century was to envision that very "Indianness" by traveling outside his country. For Rao, a journey outward ended up increasing his love for his motherland in the manner of Nehru, who was compelled to go to England to "discover India" (Ramanujan, "Annayya's" 44). For Rao, as for Nehru, India turned out to be more of a construction, an entity into which he could put what he imagined it to be.

Since Rao's literary career overlapped with the stimulus of the Indian freedom struggle, *Kanthapura* became, so to speak, the historical companion to the rise of the nation (Brennan, "National" 49), recounting the story of an idealist, Moorthy, who, following Gandhi, scorns all British-made luxuries and clothes as well as college education for a simple living engaged in constructive work for the Congress Party. Following Benedict Anderson,

Timothy Brennan maintains that the novel is a "mass ceremony" in which one may "read alone with the conviction that millions of others were doing the same, at the same time" ("National" 52). *Kanthapura*, not fortuitously, became Rao's epic enterprise, the instrument of national formation embodying a reverence for the antique and the traditional. He wrote in the novel's foreword:

> There is no village in India, however mean, that has not a rich *sthala-purana*, or legendary history, of its own. Some god or godlike hero has passed by the village – Rama might have rested under this pipal-tree, Sita might have dried her clothes ... on this yellow stone, or the Mahatma himself, on one of his many pilgrimages through the country, might have slept in this hut, the low one, by the village gate. (R. Rao, *Kanthapura* v)

The link with myth and folktale, once incipient in German nationalism, was to become generic and universal by appealing to the people through the novel. The novel would go on to become the vehicle of a great national awakening, although it was brought to India via the British. Yet the novel, especially when it was written in English, could find a readership only among the educated elite. This may well be a statement about the exclusive nature of Indian nationalism itself, which was predicated on awakening the masses to national consciousness yet itself was co-opted, to a large extent, by Western thoughts and ideas.

Kanthapura shows Rao to be extremely adept at reworking English into an Indian medium of expression: his emphasis on bilingualism in the foreword ("we are all instinctively bilingual" [v]) was to become the novelist's credo, raising misgivings about writing/reading in English for an entire generation of Indian novelists succeeding him. In an essay Rao wrote five decades after the publication of his first novel, he recalls the linguistic experiment he had conducted with both a "Macaulayan English" and his native Kannada: "A South Indian Brahmin, nineteen, spoon-fed on English, with just enough Sanskrit to know I knew so little, with an indiscreet education in Kannada, my mother tongue, the French literary scene overpowered me. If I wanted to write, the problem was, what should be the appropriate language of expression, and what my structural models" ("Entering" 537–8). Even though Rao was attempting to write as "authentically" as possible about India, the modernist impulse shaping his art could hardly cut him off from the influence of European writing. He developed, eventually, "the ordinary style of ... story-telling" (*Kanthapura* vi) that was to become, he claims, his natural mode of expression – rather than what was, in fact, a translation from Kannada thought into English prose. This very Indian idiom, comprised of oaths, greetings, abuses, jokes, blessings, mannerisms, and so on, was translated into English, yet allowed to retain a cultural specificity necessary in forging a national spirit that could be called "Indian." Such was the linguistic pluralism of India that Indian novelists had to, oddly, employ the English language to create a sense of unity.

It is thus that the language of the colonizer and the discourse of nationalism have existed side-by-side with representations of the traditional village community, creating the "double discourse of the national and the modern" (G. Kapur 288). The coexistence of the national/modern effects a pastoral "makeover," in many ways, resulting in Kanthapura, Kedaram, or Malgudi. The antiquated images of these village communities are inward-looking and rather regressive, contrary to modernity. However, in so far as modernism, as an aesthetic movement in the West, is characterized by exhibiting the very opposite of modernity – through, for instance, its critique of the myth of progress and the persuasion of the non-material East – the literary representation of the Indian village community performs a mimesis well within the modes of Western thought. Here, the turn toward "Indianness" suggests a journey toward primitivism or a return to innocence in the same way as the author-anthropologist in Western literature imagines Africa to be the West's dark Other.

Amit Chaudhuri has argued that modernism in India did not arrive via the West; it may have been influenced by the West, but it possessed an "authentic Easternness" ("Modernity" xviii). Taking examples from Rabindranath Tagore's writings, Chaudhuri alleges that there always existed "a new space" (xviii) that could accommodate an amalgam of "Western liberal humanism, education and folklore, Hinduism and Protestant-style reform, Bengali, English, Sanskrit and other languages . . . in ways that often blurred the distinctions between what was 'native' and what 'foreign'" (xviii). From this view, India's entry into history was not initiated by the British; India had its own incipient forms of modernity that the British never cared to discover. In some of the Bengali writings Chaudhuri uncovers, he illustrates how the colonizer as oppressor is almost peripheral to the Bengali vision. On the contrary, Anglophone writing in India, he contends, has not been able to rid itself of its "postcolonial" identity and its Eurocentric leanings, which it has derived from colonialism (xx). Had English not arrived, loaded with civilizational values that appear to have ushered in modernity, the development of those "endlessly multifarious, confusing number of tongues" present in India would indeed have shown the complex synthesis of a Western and a non-Western civilization: a "cross-fertilization," in which the dominator-dominated paradigm would not have been so considerably foregrounded (xx–xxi).

That there was a homegrown modernism confounds the argument that nationalism itself was a "derivative discourse" (P. Chatterjee, *Nationalist*) – a prototypically modern movement – as much as one about keeping tradition alive. Despite one's quibbles with Chatterjee's assumption, cultural nationalism – as against its more material, and Marxist, manifestations – has exhibited a tendency to improvise, if not completely imitate, the European history of nationalism, at least among the small percentage of the intelligentsia who entered the Western education system from where they could have imbibed the idea of nationalism. The new novel in English, roughly coterminous with the rise of nationalist sentiment in India, also ended up straddling the double discourse of modernity and tradition. This is probably the reason why the 1930s novel has become a "chronological fix between nationhood and modernity" (G. Kapur 298): it was both the novel about the nation and the result of the experiment of introducing a new genre of writing derived from the British.

This argument does not support the Western standpoint of writing history that, overwhelmingly, "consign[s] … other … nations to an imaginary waiting room of history" (Chakrabarty, *Provincializing* 8). What I am saying is that the nationalist turn toward the outmoded village model was a rather stark and atavistic reaction to colonialism within the discourse of modernity. While Chaudhuri's views may be read alongside those of Chakrabarty, who warns against yielding to Western categories of modernity when writing postcolonial history, neither links the birth and ancestry of the novel in India to colonialism. The "vernacular" novel Chaudhuri valorizes over the one written in English was undoubtedly derivative if it emerged out of the colonial encounter, when the first British novel may have been shipped to India and read by the Bengali intelligentsia. Tagore himself rather candidly confessed: "Ours was not the aesthetic enjoyment of literary art, but the jubilant welcome of a turbulent wave from a situation of stagnation" (quoted in Mehrotra, Introduction 11). Chandu Menon's Malayalam novel, *Indulekha* (1889), had also begun as a translation of Disraeli's *Henrietta Temple* but was later rewritten as an independent work of fiction. It was through colonialism that many Indian writers were first exposed to modernism through the realist novel, the sonnet, and blank verse – initiating what came to be known as the Bengal Renaissance.

Chaudhuri's story of modernism in India is an account of the "self-division" of the creative writer, the "tension between rejection and recuperation" of his indigenous tradition. Indisputable though this is, his dismissal of the "narrative of post-coloniality" as simply a confrontation between "English and indigenous forms of knowledge" (*Clearing* 54–5) is not altogether admissible. If the postcolonial narrative of nationalism is sometimes confrontational, it is with the understanding that there is nothing indigenous about the novel form when employed by Indian novelists, even in Bengal, where the earliest Indian novels came to be written in the mid-nineteenth century. It is in the context of the Anglophone novel that postcolonial studies raises questions about the central paradox of representing national identity in the language of the West. Indeed, attention has been drawn to the inconsistency within cultural nationalism itself, which seeks to bring to the fore the hoary past of a people, yet is an extremely modern ideological movement that Europe had experienced in the nineteenth century and that was to become part of the nationalist ideology burgeoning all over its colonial empires. It was incumbent upon this new nation to usher in modes of capitalism, administrative bureaucracy, systems of government, and a variety of other infrastructure already identified as Western.

Raja Rao, as representative of this nationalistic genre of Indian English literature, consciously and self-reflexively attempts to create the Indian style of storytelling, which can only be "interminable," "endless," and "colourful" (*Kanthapura* v–vi) by virtue of being "Indian." "Indianness," that mammoth abstraction, was an accompaniment to a nascent nationalism. Although in postcolonial India – especially in departments of English where postmodernism has attained academic currency – the construction of "Indianness" has drawn much flak, it must be understood that the focus on indigeneity became virtually a commonplace for the writer of the Indian novel in English because Indian nationalism coincided with the rise and subsequent growth of that very genre. Despite taking Western modernity onboard, the essential themes of the 1930s novel had to be coeval with the civilizational consciousness of being homogeneously "Indian." Thus it is that Rao's hero, Moorthy, scarcely notices Ratna, who is in love with him, so deeply is he consumed with the "primordial radiance" he acquires after a day of fasting (*Kanthapura* 68). Love stories written after India's independence, such as the one between Bharati and Sriram in R. K. Narayan's *Waiting for the Mahatma* (1955), were also turned into novels of national awakening, where even the title reflects the overarching significance of national themes over those of love. Although the argument here closely approximates Jameson's controversial hypothesis that "the story of the private individual destiny is always an allegory of the embattled situation of the public third-world culture and society" ("Third-World" 69), the oppressor-oppressed relationship remained nonetheless primary to the novel about nationalism.

Narayan's Invention of Tradition

There is another variety of Indianness witnessed in Rao's contemporary R. K. Narayan. Once mocked by Naipaul for remarking that "India will go on," Narayan's fictional world indeed appears to be "abstracted" from his country (Naipaul, *India* 27). His fiction perpetuates the feeling of everlasting calm without any fear of political contingency. The world that Narayan built in the 1930s consists of "the small and pacific South Indian town, little men, little schemes, the comedy of restricted lives and high philosophical speculation, real power surrendered long ago to the British rulers, who were far away and only dimly perceived" (Naipaul, *India* 28). Naipaul defines Narayan's complacency as a kind of "certitude" supported by a "Hindu equilibrium" (28). From a modernist standpoint, this involves the shedding of one's sense of history. Then, and only then, can a contemplative idler like Srinivas, the hero of *Mr. Sampath* (1949), not be overwhelmed by his circumstances. The roll of novels that Narayan produced after his first – *Swami and Friends* (1935), which managed to survive in the publishing industry of the West – embody a picture of timeless rustic charm in which history plays no part. That Malgudi, the setting for most of his novels, is more imagined than real, does not help. Detached from history, Narayan's novels are suited to perpetuating an ontological belief in a placid India.[2]

Is this "authorial reticence" or "strategic ingenuousness" (A. Chaudhuri, *Clearing* 243)? Narayan may be accused of masquerading as both. Our impression of the silent, unassuming writer, whom nobody would publish until the intervention of Graham Greene, jostles with our consciousness of his artistic craft that could create an array of simple fictional characters, leading critics to comment on the extreme insignificance of his universe. In Narayan's works, there are no wars, no magnificent love stories, not even a carefully crafted ideology. He almost appears to have stumbled into novel-writing unwittingly. In many ways, Narayan approximates the image of the unspeaking common man – so commemoratively created by his cartoonist brother, R. K. Laxman – by scarcely obtruding his space, so deep is he an observer of, so to speak, the marketplace.

Could this apparent apathy be a sign of engineered innocence? A device to create ironic detachment from the eternity of India? The weightlessness of Narayan's writing, which Naipaul deplores, may well be his technique to displace the sheer strain of big, nationalistic themes. The marketplace, which is his inspiration, appears with such regularity that the hustle and bustle of life is more likely an attempt to frustrate the obsession his contemporaries display with the freedom of their country. For Narayan, the life that his characters live is more in keeping with routine than the grandiose gestures of some of his peers.

Narayan began his profession at a time when India needed to claim a host of larger-than-life heroes and heroines. It was part of the national-ist enterprise – which included writing – to speak of an otherworldliness that could forsake the dross and materiality of a bourgeois existence that had become identified with the British. The exploration of the spiritual potential of India by the predecessors of the 1930s generation of writ-ers had propped up a brahminical tradition that alone could represent Indian metaphysics. Rabindranath Tagore, Madanmohan Malaviya, and Bankimchandra Chattopadhyay had already stressed the values imbibed from the family, the village, and the caste system that assumed a brah-minical tradition to be at its core. Hindu traditionalists like Vivekananda, Aurobindo Ghose, and Annie Besant attempted to excite national pride through the Ramakrishna Mission school of Vedantism, a culturally asser-tive neo-Hinduism, and the Theosophical Society. The ideological forma-tion of an "eternal" tradition stood as a safeguard against the actual history of those times, which was in turmoil. It is not surprising that Raja Rao's heroes, even in his post-independence novels, are idealized, antithetical figures who oppose Western civilization.

Narayan, in so many ways, shifts that ponderous burden by creating a humble village, Malgudi. Unfortunately, critics have clubbed Malgudi with, say, Kanthapura, as a representative portrayal of "a microcosmic image of the macrocosmic world" (Ramamurti 63), thus sacrificing a deeper understanding of the nature of this village community. Malgudi, undoubtedly, is an Indian village, but it is not a celebration of the imme-morial in a world of flux, although the latter assumption may not be altogether irrelevant, as Narayan is unable to completely overcome the homogeneity of an essentialized India. Narayan's writing does approach timelessness in so far as history and change are viewed as temporary, even illusionary, and needing to revert to solidity and custom.[3] In *The Man-Eater of Malgudi* (1961), for example, Narayan safeguards tradition in the form of an elephant, which Vasu, a taxidermist, proposes to destroy in order to shock India into the twentieth century. As Vasu fatally knocks himself senseless, Narayan celebrates the victory of tradition that cannot accommodate Nehru's five-year plans for India's growth.

However, at another level, the profits Vasu would acquire from the sale of the elephant's tusks, hair, and legs implicitly recall the mercantile motives of the East India Company. Malgudi, this typical Indian village, also exhibits an urban character: it possesses a post office and a bank, a missionary school, shops, official colonial-style bungalows, and even a club. These exclusive symbols of colonial rule, which turn Malgudi tantalizingly into a "creature of colonialism" (Khilnani 110), are regular fixtures in Narayan's novels, hinting at an easy camaraderie with at least the more agreeable aspects of British rule. Quite non-Gandhian in conception, there is also the discomfiture of the eponymous English teacher, Krishna, who cannot correlate the peace and tranquility derived from the poetry of the Romantics, unequalled in the world, with the turmoil of the Indian struggle for freedom, premised on ousting those very British concepts (Narayan, *English Teacher* 178). One may claim, then, that Narayan's vision is narrower than Rao's, although his world is more accessible. Unlike Moorthy, Narayan's heroes are small-time crooks, tourist guides, or teachers of English in rural mission schools. To this effect, their ordinariness is reflected in the titles of his novels: *The Bachelor of Arts* (1937), *The Painter of Signs* (1976), *The Vendor of Sweets* (1967), and *The Financial Expert* (1952). Rao's Moorthy is a quite different "mahatma," for instance, from Raju in *The Guide* (1958) or Jagan in *The Vendor of Sweets*; while Moorthy follows the principles of renunciation, Raju and Jagan are counterfeit gurus, the former a drifter who falls in love with a married woman, and the latter someone who cannot set off on pilgrimage without his checkbook.

At times, even the employment of myth becomes ambivalent when it is rehearsed outside time and place: in *The Painter of Signs*, Daisy agrees to wed Raman on the condition that he will never stand in her way, in the manner of King Santanu, who unprotestingly allowed his celestial wife to murder even their own children. That Narayan's ironic tonalities are at work is indicated by the urgent concerns of the 1970s when Prime Minister Indira Gandhi had become obsessed with forced sterilization programs to stem the rapid growth of India's population. One wonders whether Narayan is pleading for the virtue of traditional wisdom or the absurdity of its application in the context of the state of emergency imposed by Mrs. Gandhi. *Waiting for the Mahatma*, again, is difficult to interpret unambiguously. In one sense, Gandhi's spinning wheel is a devotional symbol: "Spin and read Bhagavad Gita, and utter *Ram Nam* continuously, and then you will know what to do in life" (Narayan, *Waiting* 96). Even the act of going to prison is not political; it is a mysterious, religious instruction that Bharati obeys without argument. In another sense, however, Gandhi's *satyagraha*, or struggle for truth, is viewed as an "extra adventure" from which Sriram, the hero, who is entrusted with the task of painting "Quit India" everywhere, wants to retreat into a life of "quiet charm ... verging on stagnation" (223–4). Sriram's inconstant nature borders on sheer absurdity as he cuts off the tail of the letter "Q" from the nation's most evocative slogan in an endeavor to prevent the national consumption of paint. It is in *The Guide*, perhaps, that we get a real glimpse of Narayan's ironic, but nuanced, insight when he creates a tourist guide who veritably invents tradition, a history-that-does-not-exist, to attract tourists. What could be a more telling comment on the construction of nationalist histories during an inchoate phase of ideological formation?

In many inscrutable ways, then, Narayan may even be called "international" rather than "national" because he exists, almost interstitially, outside the binaries of East, West; high, low; native, foreign; fantasy, reality; and elite, democratic. Narayan's writing, in tune with the "palimpsest" view of history, turns out to be unselfconsciously "realistic," neither succumbing to Western modernity nor falling back on constructions of a pristine Indian tradition. Few would realize that many of Narayan's protagonists, such as Swami and Chandran, are Brahmins who find themselves displaced from a tradition of veneration in a rapidly changing new nation-state (P. Mishra 199).

Anand's Revolutionary Socialism

The third notable writer of this generation is Mulk Raj Anand, a realist. In his own account, "The Sources of Protest in My Novels," Anand recalls spending time at Gandhi's Sabarmati Ashram in 1927, following Gandhi's advice to go to the people before writing any further: "All experience, then, became the reservoir from which I wrote my fictions, hoping to transform the raw material of life freely into communicable forms" (123). The material of his fiction thus turned out to be the life of the "folk," those from the "lower depths," "whom [he] knew intimately" (M. Anand, "Sources" 123). *Untouchable* (1935), the story of the misfortunes of Bakha, a young, low-caste sweeper, was Anand's first "protest" novel. Significantly, Anand's progressive thinking emerged before he had read Marx. To this extent, Anand is not concerned with representing an "Indian" village even though his characters are primarily peasants. And even though *Untouchable* was inspired by a story about an outcaste named Uka that Gandhi had written for *Young India* and was revised after Gandhi advised Anand to "cut down more than a hundred pages" from what appeared to be the account of "a Bloomsbury intellectual" (M. Anand, "On the Genesis" 135), he could not treat Gandhi's teachings as either metaphysics or visionary politics. Gandhianism, as such, was never ideologically assimilated by Anand.

While it is arguable whether *Untouchable* is a "Marxist, humanist, or Gandhian document" (Verma 144), it is clear that Anand's message lies less in an appeal through spiritual or religious reform than in a radical indictment of the prevailing differences that exist in society leading to the miserable conditions of the downtrodden. Outlining social realism, he declares that the revolutionary novelist's technique is altogether different from "political tracts about the poor" in which the rich are depicted to be "decadent villains":

> The very contrary is true.... It is a method to ensure the deepest, broadest and most sensitive imaginative awareness of men at a given time and place by the writer, so that it bears the reader forward by its inherent logic: it aims at the fullest and richest representation of historical man as he develops in the society of his time, through all the gamut of inner and outer conflict, a full-blown character with all his strengths and weaknesses. (Anand, quoted in Cowasjee 78)

What emerges with considerable accuracy is a picture of low Indian life. Correspondingly, the depiction of the little people of India is more rounded and uncertain than glorified. While Anand has often been accused of mixing propaganda with art, his characters are not larger than life or vehicles of the author's political consciousness. Anand's characters might be oversimplified symbols of the class struggle, but they are significant in breaking stereotypes. *The Village* (1939), for instance, breaks away from the standard characterization of Indian villages as untouched and unaffected symbols of "true" India. A definite infiltration of modernity is evinced in the novel in the sound of the railway whistle that frightens Nihal Singh – the protagonist Lalu's father – in spite of its familiarity, or in Lalu's dreams of modern brick houses in which he has seen European workmen live. On a personal level, Lalu violates orthodoxy even more vehemently by cutting off his long hair against the religious injunction of the Sikhs, for which his face is blackened and he is paraded around the village on a donkey's back. His alienation from his environment grows, and he discovers his disenchantment with his village as well as with his friends, who seem to fade away as he leaves home to become a recruit in the Indian army.

The experience of the First World War is one of utter loneliness and confusion for Lalu; the "grey[ness]" and "vast[ness]" of the bleak French sea and sky (M. Anand, *Across* 97–8), symbols of change and disillusionment, suggest the loss of innocence of rural existence. The second part of the trilogy, *Across the Black Waters* (1940), invokes comparisons between traditional and superstitious village life and the unique freedom that allows the soldiers to experience for the first time the pleasures of eating beef, free sex, and a ritual-free living. In neither text are there any Hindu concepts to explain either Lalu's isolation at home and abroad, or the inhuman laws followed by the governments of France, England, and Germany. Lastly, Lalu's return to the village is mapped out in *The Sword and the Sickle* (1942), which represents a new identity outside tradition, a journey from the purgatory of the war to revolutionary socialism. Although Lalu returns to find more poverty, greater exploitation, and corruption, he also senses a need for social resistance against them. In this changed world, he takes a plunge and becomes a passionate revolutionary. This marks the beginning of a struggle characterized by sheer lack of direction for the peasantry who blindly follow the maverick Marxist, Count Rampal, and the academic but ineffective Verma Sahib.

Yet colonialism, as treated by Anand, is not only critiqued as the onset of political and economic oppression, it is also seen as the harbinger of a certain "intellectual cosmopolitanism" (Majeed xii–xiii) of texts and ideas that provided writers with a breadth of material across traditions.[4] In *The Sword and the Sickle*, he argues both as an artist and as a Marxist, surrendering finally to a socialist dream:

> You can't just pick up a stave, shout a slogan and march forward to Revolution! ... You can't open hostilities against the most organized and deeply entrenched Imperialism ... without any systematic or carefully considered plan for organizing, instructing and steeling the workers for a prolonged and stubborn struggle! Comrade Lenin called such primitivism in Russia a "disease"; in our country it is an epidemic. (*Sword* 339)

While Anand is conscious of the evils of colonialism, he also considers it to demarcate a long period of aesthetic and intellectual inventiveness based on reforming and modernizing orthodoxy and tradition. The new scientific concepts of that time created an alienation from, and a disinclination to pursue, the convictions of the past. In modernity, thus, Anand seeks to find alternatives to the miseries of the lower castes, although his ideas about modernity are not implicated in the colonial project or derived from European sources; they are, instead, part of "a global phenomenon of cultural production, dissemination, and exchange occurring synchronously and unevenly around the world" (A. Sharma 15). Anand's secularism is not an aesthetic mimesis but a selective appropriation of available polyglot discourses and their political application to his own personal experience.

Thus, the war of the peasantry is hardly against the British. On the contrary, it is the cruel and oppressive system of feudalism that Anand holds accountable. Colonial suppression is something the peasants understand only as part of a narrower reality of being the underdog. Except for *Private Life of an Indian Prince* (1953), in which the hero is a prince browbeaten by both the English regency and the Indian nationalists, most of Anand's novels depict people who are affected only indirectly by the British and whose more immediate concerns are the local overlords and their corrupt policies. In effect, he reveals those realities that tend to be disregarded in romantic representations of India, which he believes are clothed in stereotypical ideologies. Gandhi's own romanticism is brought out in *Untouchable*. His speech on religious tolerance and cow protection is almost unintelligible to the village Dalits who want to hear about the opening of temples, schools, and waterworks to lower castes. A similar situation arises in *The Sword and the Sickle* when Lalu tries to draw Gandhi's attention to the peasants' hardships. But Gandhi can only extol the virtues of nonviolence, spinning, soul-force, repression of sexual urges, and the therapeutic values of suffering, none of which are related to Lalu's dilemmas. Anand's Gandhi is an "inveterate, non-stop talker," deriving evident pleasure in hearing his own voice (*Sword* 195).

Despite Anand's reservations about Gandhi, there is little doubt about his passion for political freedom. What he questions is Gandhi's reliance on a pre-industrialized, fundamental Hindu tradition – almost a kind of "second colonization" (Nandy xi), which effaces one's sense of history. Anand, who was associated with the Bloomsbury group during his years in London (1925–45), wrote: "I wanted to liberate the unconscious via the Shakti-Shakta Tantric thought and dig down to the depths" (M. Anand, "Reason" 612). Even though London was at the heart of colonial culture, it was nonetheless an international milieu in which orthodoxy was contested and oppression interrogated. It was the metropolis that opened a world Anand could identify with, where human equality, liberty, and egalitarianism existed in contrast to the stranglehold of caste, tradition, and superstition he saw in his own country. In some ways, then, Anand's personal politics espouse an anti-colonial modernity and embrace the city rather than the village.

Although a good deal of the literary corpus of these 1930s novelists was to come after that decade, it was a time when a complex mix of ideas was first generated in the new genre of novel writing in the English language. In this intellectual ferment, cultural self-expression, infused largely with incipient national feeling, struggled for power with the antithetical cosmopolitan energies coming from the metropolis. In so many ways, the embrace of the novel was symptomatic of the seductive influence of Europe, yet the retreat into one's own cultural artifacts, for instance in the form of representations of a characteristic Indian village, could be, at best, only strategic devices to resist Eurocentrism.

Notes

1 Several British and Indian historians, such as Kopf (*British Orientalism*), Heimsath, R. Majumdar (ed.), and S. Sarkar, have demonstrated that the emergence of Indian nationalism was marked by the cultural antagonism between tradition and modernity.
2 See Narasimhaiah; Cronin; and M. Mukherjee (*Twice Born*). More contemporary critics endorse the view that Narayan's novels depict a world that exists "independently of the colonial power," despite being written during the phase of "intense nationalist activity" (Boehmer 176).
3 Meenakshi Mukherjee has figured that "Order – Dislocation of order – Re-integration of order" is the governing strain of most Narayan novels (*Twice Born* 205).
4 I use the term "intellectual cosmopolitanism" to mean the comprehensive range of new material that colonialism provided, enabling writers to move across literary traditions. See Majeed.

CHAPTER 6

The Modernist Novel in India: Paradigms and Practices

Vinay Dharwadker

Locating Indian Modernism

The historical origins of Indian modernism in literature and the arts lie in the extraordinary transformation of society and culture that begins in the early nineteenth century, while the East India Company is still in the process of establishing its military dominance and political hegemony on the subcontinent. In the perspective of literary history, this social transformation is driven, to a significant extent, by a dialectic of discourses across cultures that has been at work since the European Renaissance. As the action of opposing forces within a society, this generalized dialectic has four simultaneous, dynamic components: 1) Europe's long-standing critique of Indian society and culture, stemming from Europe's self-definition of its autonomous modernity; 2) India's counter-critique of Europe, which starts early in the nineteenth century; 3) Europe's self-critique, in response to the encounter in the colony; and 4) Indian self-critique, developed "*outside* the purview of the state and the European missionaries" and based on a Kantian "*public* use of . . . reason" under a republican ideal, which accepts many points in the European critique and seeks responsively to transform Indian ways of life (P. Chatterjee, *Nation* 7; Kant 55; emphases in originals). Once this quadrangular dialectic is active in the colony by the 1810s, it triggers a succession of organized and concerted movements of social reform, which deeply influence political, legal, economic, religious, aesthetic, and cultural phenomena in modern India, down to the present (Dharwadker, "Historical" 238–43). The process of reform launched in the early nineteenth century constitutes a social modernism that has clearly enunciated goals: among them, to change women's life-conditions inside and outside the home; to provide for the literacy and education of girls and for the habilitation and remarriage of widows; to end child marriage, polygamy, and polyandry, *purdah*, the immolation of *satis*, "blind" superstition, ritual pollution and untouchability, and discrimination based on caste; to produce new translations and interpretations of Hindu scripture, theology, and philosophy; to reconcile differences among religions, increase their mutual understanding and respect, and defuse communal violence; to reform ancient Indian law; to comprehensively historicize the subcontinent's past; and to revitalize its crafts and arts (see Kopf, *Brahmo*).

Indian literary and aesthetic modernism acquires concrete historical forms in the final decades of the nineteenth century. Given that writers, artists, and thinkers in the Indian languages refer almost always to *adhunikta* (modernity, as a condition or phenomenon) rather than to *adhuniktavad* (modernism, as an ideology or a movement), the most inclusive conception of modernism applicable to the subcontinent is the one that Frederico de Onis offers for *modernismo* in the Spanish world: there is no "difference between 'Modernism' and 'modernity,'" because those who named these phenomena understood that "*Modernism is essentially ... the search for modernity*" (Calinescu 77–8). In the Indian case, the "search for modernity" in literature and art grows out of and returns repeatedly to society's corresponding search, which is given shape, substance, and direction by the general and specific tasks of social reform. The subcontinent's literary and aesthetic modernism therefore is a synecdoche for its social modernism; from the 1880s onward, it evolves in four main phases that define the historical trajectory of the modernist novel.

Against this backdrop, Indian literary modernism, at a minimum, is deeply inflected by three factors that are absent from Europe's definition of its own modernity. First, as just indicated, all forms and phases of Indian modernism in literature and art are causally embedded in a specific *social modernism*, which diverges from European social modernism. Second, the varieties of Indian modernism cannot be extricated from their beginnings under *colonialism*, an encounter between Europe and India in the colony that has no parallels in Europe and that simultaneously induces four Indian "responses": complicity with empire, anticolonial nationalism (based on the imagined community of the nation yet-to-be), village-centered anti-modernism, and city-centered modernist cosmopolitanism (Dharwadker, "Historical" 238–53). Third, the great bulk of what constitutes Indian *tradition* occupies a past outside the historical domain of European colonization, so that Indian modernism's anti-traditionalism does not necessarily reproduce the anti-traditionalism of Europe's modernism. Tradition is important in this respect because its rejection – whether in Europe or in India – defines not only the primary axis of modernity, modernism, and modernization but also modernity's openness to the future and modernism's commitment to experimentation.

Phases of Modernism

A historical and theoretical framework of this sort makes it possible to identify not only distinct phases of modernism in Indian literature and art but also seminal moments in the history of modern fiction on a subcontinental scale, as well as paradigmatic instances of the modernist novel. Of the four phases, the earliest stretches approximately from 1882 to 1916 and may be labeled the phase of "realism and reform." During these decades, most of the creative energy in Indian literature is focused on prose fiction and establishes the genres of novel, novella, and short story in the print medium. The inaugural moment is provided by Bankimchandra Chattopadhyay's *Anandamath* (1882) and the closing moments by Rabindranath Tagore's *Home and the World* (1914–15) and *Quartet* (1916) in Bengali. Besides Chattopadhyay and Tagore, major figures across genres include Muhammad Iqbal (Urdu) and Premchand (Urdu and Hindi). The most prominent concerns of the period are pinpointed in Chattopadhyay's anticolonial nationalism, Tagore's universal spiritual humanism, and Premchand's idealist realism; the privileged literary locations are village, countryside, and country estate (on Tagore, see Dharwadker, "Constructions" 478–80; on Premchand, see Trivedi, "Progress," especially 975–80 and 1008–11). The significant modernist innovations include a thoroughgoing critique of tradition; radical breaks from select portions of the past; the aestheticization of colonial conflicts in the face of censorship; the first full constructions of past and future nation as an imagined community; and an extensive intellectual and artistic interrogation of science and technology, rationality, religious faith, secularism, and modern political systems. In fiction, these decades witness the invention of the Indian short story; a consolidation of the novel as an Indian genre; a valorization of women's writing and autonomy; and experiments with narrators, focalization, and narrative continuity. This phase is vital for the formation of Indian realism: the representation of everyday life in contemporary home, family, village, town, and city; of male and female characters with interior lives; of women's interiority and heroism in domestic space and outside; and of novelistic action that provides the foundation for future developments in social, psychological, historical, and "mythic" realism (Dharwadker, "Internationalization" 65–71).

The second phase of Indian modernism, from about 1922 to 1945, may be identified as "nationalism and experimentation." It covers the later careers of Tagore, Premchand, and Iqbal and the early or middle careers of such modernists as Jibanananda Das and Buddhadev Bose (Bengali); Mulk Raj Anand, R. K. Narayan, and Raja Rao (English), Agyeya and Muktibodh (Hindi), and B. S. Mardhekar (Marathi). Politically, this phase opens in 1920, with the first national *satyagraha* under Gandhi, and closes in 1947 with Partition and independence; aesthetically, its transformative early moment is the first Bauhaus art exhibition outside Europe, held in Calcutta in 1922 (Mitter 15). This period is characterized by extensive exposure of Indian modernists to Europe and their European counterparts (especially through travel) and by the emergence of well-defined movements, such as the Bengali avant-garde in Calcutta around *Kallol* magazine; *prayogavad* (experimentalism) in Hindi around Agyeya's *Tar-saptak* (1943) anthology; and *pragativad* (progressivism), the all-important subcontinent-wide phenomenon, launched momentously by the Progressive Writers' Association in 1936. Writing in these decades highlights the industrial landscape; the Indian metropolis (Bombay, Calcutta); city-country relations; village-to-city migration and city-to-village "return"; and the deserted village, the "village without walls," the village as nation, and the nation as village (for examples, see Jussawalla [ed.]; and Dharwadker and Ramanujan [eds.]). There is a resurgence of poetry as a social force (100 years after the Bengal Renaissance); prose and verse share the literary center-stage; and critical and theoretical work on literature, poetics, the arts, and history surrounds fiction and poetry. This is the first self-styled modernism, and its accomplishments include: an extensive breaking of inherited forms and aesthetic ideals; widespread experimentation with language, technique, structure, genre, and mode of representation; and the first comprehensive literary critique of industrialization and capitalism. In fiction, this quarter century witnesses the invention of subaltern-centered realism, experiments in stream-of-consciousness narrative, the use of interior monologue, attempts at automatic writing and split-consciousness writing, and the development of Indian socialist realism. Gandhi, Marx, and Freud become the common reference points and lead to a concerted exploration of the individualism-freedom-nation nexus, focusing on private interiority, the unconscious, and the future nation.

The third phase of modernism, "freedom and nation-building," runs roughly from 1950 to 1975; politically, it starts with independence and ends with Indira Gandhi's emergency regime. Among the important modernists in these early postcolonial decades are Mahasweta Devi and Badal Sircar (Bengali), Mohan Rakesh, Mannu Bhandari, and Rajendra Yadav (Hindi), Saadat Hasan Manto, Qurratulain Hyder, and Ismat Chughtai (Urdu), Amrita Pritam (Punjabi), U. R. Anantha Murthy and Girish Karnad (Kannada), Kamala Markandaya, Anita Desai, and Nissim Ezekiel (English), A. K. Ramanujan (English and Kannada), and Arun Kolatkar (English and Marathi). The major new references are Nehru, Sartre, and Camus; the chief political alignments are with socialism, Nehruvian secularism, and nation-building; the principal literary movements are *nai kavita, nai kahani,* and *naya upanyasa* (new poetry, new short story, and new novel) and their equivalents in various languages, and the main counter-movements concern women's writing, Dalit prose and poetry, anti-aestheticism, anti-poetry, and protest literature (for examples, see Jussawalla [ed.]; and Dharwadker and Ramanujan [eds.]). Drama is empowered and shares the stage equally with fiction and poetry, even as literary locations shift to "middle" India, to the new linguistic states (created from 1956 onward), and to the margins of the new nation (city slums, tribal areas, borderlands). Significant modernist innovations include: a remapping of Indian traditions in relation to nation-building, a critique of the new nation-state and its disappointments, and experiments in multi-generational narratives, high aestheticism, existentialist realism, ethnographic realism, and documentary realism.

The fourth phase of modernism, from about 1980 to the present, is characterized by "diaspora and cosmopolitanism"; in this perspective, for reasons of legal structure, state-society relations, economy, technology, social practices, and infrastructure, India as such does not shift to "postmodernism." The inaugural text of this phase is Salman Rushdie's *Midnight's Children* (1981); its notable innovators include Vikram Seth, Rohinton Mistry, Amitav Ghosh, Arundhati Roy, and Jhumpa Lahiri (English), as well as older figures such as Raghuvir Sahay, Usha Priyamvada, and Nirmal Verma (Hindi), and Mahasweta Devi and Sunil Gangopadhyay (Bengali). The literary focus now shifts to magic realism and to migration, subaltern history, and globalization; novel and prose are revitalized, despite the dominance of media culture, the eclipse of poetry, and the partial eclipse of drama. These late postcolonial decades experience a radical displacement of realistic representation, a questioning of rationality and causality, a rebellion against legal, political, and cultural authority, a fresh rewriting of history and inherited pasts, and critiques of religious fundamentalism, cultural nationalism, and failed nation-states. Modernists of the diaspora map out itinerant and transnational cultures,

Table 1 *The Paradigms of Modernist Fiction*

Phase	Paradigm	Representative text or writer
I	Anticolonial nationalism	Bankimchandra Chattopadhyay, *Anandamath* (Bengali, 1882)
	Cosmopolitan modernity	Rabindranath Tagore, *Ghare-baire* (Bengali, 1914–15)
II	Social realism; idealist realism	Premchand (Hindi)
	Subaltern fiction	Mulk Raj Anand, *Untouchable* (English, 1935)
	Gandhian nationalism	Raja Rao, *Kanthapura* (English, 1938)
III	Village	Vyankatesh Madgulkar, *Bangarwadi* (Marathi, 1954)
	Stream-of-consciousness narrative	Qurratulain Hyder, *Aag ka dariya* (Urdu, 1959)
	Partition	Yashpal, *Jutha sach* (Hindi, 1958–60)
	Existentialist realism	U. R. Anantha Murthy, *Samskara* (Kannada, 1964)
	City; psychological realism	Anita Desai (English)
	Ethnographic realism	Mahasweta Devi (Bengali)
	Feminist cosmopolitanism	Amrita Pritam (Punjabi)
IV	National allegory	Salman Rushdie, *Midnight's Children* (English, 1981)
	Postcolonial cosmopolitanism	Amitav Ghosh (English)
	Diaspora	Jhumpa Lahiri (English)
	Dalit narrative	Om Prakash Valmiki (Hindi)

dislocation and fragmentation, and home and hybridity; they revise the genres of novel and short story, the relation of self and history, and the distinction between fiction and nonfiction in ways that align them with "geomodernism" (see Rushdie and West [eds.] for examples; Dharwadker, "Historical" 253–9; Doyle and Winkiel [eds.]).

These four phases shape the paradigms of modernist fiction and the novel in India and, with modifications, across South Asia. Some of the generic, thematic, and modal paradigms created since the 1880s, together with suggestive examples, are listed in Table 1. A panoramic survey of this kind can provide only a general orientation to the varieties of the Indian novel in the past century and a quarter; to chart their evolution, it would be necessary to explore several paradigms and more than one phase. The tabulation above, for example, does not immediately indicate how multifariously the concerns of Indian social modernism are integrated with the narrative paradigms of the modernist novel. Given the constraints of space, it is best to examine one representative paradigm in sufficient detail to reveal the important features of the larger historical process. The most useful example is modernist realism, which dominates the Indian novel for much of the twentieth century. In the rest of this chapter, I therefore concentrate on this phenomenon, on Mulk Raj Anand's modernist realism in *Untouchable* (1935) during the second phase, and on the convergence of his practice with Premchand's theoretical reflections on realism a decade earlier. Since my discussion juxtaposes new material and new theoretical arguments, it offers a fresh perspective on the history of the modernist novel.

Theorizing Modernist Realism

Realism in literature, especially in modernist fiction, may be conceptualized as a textual effect, a verbal style, an authorial stance, a form, a genre, or a mode of representation – the six most common bases for such an exercise. When we equate realism with verisimilitude, we essentially claim that a given work is realistic because it induces the *effect* of resemblance to reality in our readerly imaginations. That is, a text is verisimilar when its words stimulate us into experiencing a scene, a setting, and action, or a set of characters in virtuality the way we experience their real-life counterparts in actuality, through sense-perception, sensation, feeling, emotion, and thought. In contrast, when we locate a novel's realism in its *style*, we put aside the effect of verisimilitude and identify the verbal elements – lexicon, syntax, figuration, textual organization, technique, devices – that are, presumably, the sources of a moving virtual experience. Both verisimilitude and realistic style require consideration of the author and his or her intention and practice, but attention to the author's *stance* as the determining element in a work's realism introduces a more complicated quadrangulation of factors. To define such a stance, we need to assess not only the relation of the *author* to the style of the *text*, and the style's relation to verisimilitude in the imagination of the *reader*, but also the author's attitude toward the interior and exterior *reality* being represented.

Textual affect, verbal style, and authorial disposition toward reality and its representation furnish three productive approaches to the analysis of realism, but by themselves they do not reveal or explain the foundations of realism, particularly in the modernist novel. As a consequence, we also need to conceptualize realism as a *form*, which necessarily has separable outer and inner aspects. If a novel employs realism as its form, then its outer form usually is that of (written) prose discourse of significant magnitude, and style emerges as the outer form's crafted surface. In exceptions such as Alexander Pushkin's *Eugene Onegin* (1833) and Vikram Seth's *The Golden Gate* (1986), of course, the outer form is verse, and it is structured in chapters composed of individual units on the prosodic frame of a rhymed, tetrametric sonnet. A novel's outer form itself is modulated by its inner form – the "soul or shaping principle," metaphorically the in-built motor that drives its action as well as aesthetics, its shape as well as substance (Frye 52). V. S. Naipaul's *A House for Mr. Biswas* (1957) has realism as its inner form at the deepest level, whereas Salman Rushdie's *The Satanic Verses* (1988) does not, and the two novels therefore have rather different outer forms, which move us equally profoundly but in rather different modernist ways.

When realism is not merely a stylistic feature but serves as the engine that drives a novel's entire contraption, it plants its author's orientation toward reality and representation, textual generation and textual effect, at the core of the enterprise. The most important components of this machine then prove to be the novelist's *conception of reality* per se and his or her *method of representation* – the process of depicting that reality and the sources, materials, means, and ends of the depiction. For Balzac, for instance – decades before the onset of Euro-American modernism – realism as the inner form of the ninety-one novels, novellas, and tales that make up his monumental *La Comédie Humaine*, and especially of a representative novel such as *Lost Illusions* (1837), dictates not only the choice of subject matter, setting, characters, style, and organization but also the emplotment, characterization, and thematization, as well as the scope and density of verisimilar representation.

Realism, however, can also constitute a novel's genre, and since form and genre are not interchangeable, realism as genre pushes a work beyond its inner and outer forms (which are aesthetic) to the functions imposed on it by the marketplace (which are not merely aesthetic). That is, when realism defines a novel's form, it is driven by literary codes, but when it defines the work's genre, it is also driven by market elements. In Vikram Seth's *A Suitable Boy* (1993), modernist realism serves as a principle of genre rather than form; the novel's limited aesthetic impact but disproportionate commercial success highlight its contrast with *The Golden Gate* (1986), in which realism serves as the inner form and hence works at a much higher aesthetic temperature. Once we have distinguished realism as a genre, it is easy to see that the three most frequently identified varieties of realistic representation – social realism, psychological realism, and historical realism – are not merely authorial dispositions, styles, or targets of verisimilitude, or even outer or inner forms: they are *subgenres* of realistic fiction, demarcated by disparate combinations of theme, focalization, repertoire of devices, and object of representation.

Finally, when a novelist treats realism as a *mode of representation*, he or she lifts it out of the domains of form and genre and situates it in relation to its deliberative and epistemological functions. A novel that is modally realistic usually layers its mimesis (its "showing," its faithful depiction of reality) as well as its diegesis (its "telling," its description and narration) with meta-discourse about the nature of representation, the relation of text to represented reality, and even the general features of realism (its goals, limits, and failures). In *Adam Bede* (1859), George Eliot famously raises the thematic genre of "the provincial English novel" to the level of modal representation, when she uses Chapter 17 to offer an extended meta-discursive account of realism. As a mode of representation that is antithetical to other modes, such as allegory, realism has to secure several platforms for itself: the reality that undergirds it; the relation of reality to time and history; and the causality that structures the real. As a consequence, when Rushdie, for example, rejects realism as his mode of representation in *The Satanic Verses*, he is compelled to insert meta-discursive passages explaining his alternative conceptions of reality, representation, causality, temporality, and historicity. Most important, modal realism meta-discursively underscores the facticity of its own discourse, and hence its claims to represent the "truth" about "things as they are." Before modernism, Balzac and Zola explicitly adhere to empiricism as the epistemological foundation of their respective versions of fact-based and science-driven realism; Zola goes further by adopting Darwinian natural selection as the ontological basis of his naturalism, which enables him to define the *experimental* novel practically in the laboratory sense of the term. Similarly, when Virginia Woolf invents her stream-of-consciousness method, she anchors it in William James' empirical and theoretical psychology – which separately influences the phenomenology of Husserl, whose analysis of "the natural attitude" in *Ideas* (1913) then provides a perfect epistemology for Woolf's mode of representation in modernist times.

Anand's Modernist Realism

Published in England with a preface by E. M. Forster, some seventy years after Bankimchandra Chattopadhyay's *Rajmohan's Wife* (1864), Mulk Raj Anand's *Untouchable* (1935) historically re-inaugurates the Indian English novel in the twentieth century. But despite the absence of immediate precedents, Anand and his novel arrive "fully formed" – stylistically, conceptually, politically, and aesthetically – with respect to his realistic stance. For its protagonist, Bakha, the overall action represented in the novel corresponds to about fifteen hours on one day (from early morning to nightfall) in real time. It is narrated in the third person by an anonymous, omniscient narrator, and the narrative is laid out in a relatively plain verbal style; both the lexicon and the syntax define a middle diction in prose, maintaining a "naturalness" in the written form without lapsing into either formality or colloquialism. A high proportion of the narrative is diegetic, combining functional description with functional narration. The descriptive passages are almost always literal and unembellished, presenting settings, objects, characters, and events with very little figuration; the novel's opening sentences, for instance, define the book's overall paradigm:

> The outcastes' colony was a group of mud-walled houses that clustered together in two rows, under the shadow both of the town and the cantonment, but outside their boundaries and separate from them. There lived the scavengers, the leather-workers, the washermen, the barbers, the water-carriers, the grass-cutters and other outcastes from Hindu society. A brook ran near the lane, once with crystal-clear water, now soiled by the dirt and filth of the public latrines situated about it, the odour of the hides and skins of dead carcasses left to dry on its banks, the dung of donkeys, sheep, horses, cows and buffaloes heaped up to be made into fuel cakes, and the biting, choking, pungent fumes that oozed from its sides. (1)

When a rare figure does surface in the prose, it is compact and unintrusive: "The cup of Bakha's life was filled to overflowing with the happiness of the lucid, shining afternoon, as the bowl of the sky was filled with a clear and warm sunshine" (101). Likewise, the narration itself is brisk and referential, focused on what is happening – on getting the story told:

> When the chimney had consumed the last basket of straw and refuse Bakha closed its mouth and retreated. He felt thirsty. The edges of his lips were dry. He put back the shovel, the basket, the broom and the brushes in their place. Then he moved towards the door of his hut, sniffing the air full of smoke from the chimney, brushing his clothes and smoothing them

out. His thirst became overpowering as he entered the room. Looking dazedly at the utensils lying about in a corner, he felt he wanted tea. But as he surveyed the room he heard his father still snoring under his patched quilt. (13)

However, as these typical lines indicate, Anand constantly blends narration and description, so that the verbal medium creates the illusion of transparency. At the level of style, his extraordinary accomplishment as a realist is that he uses diegesis to fuse his characters' interiority and exteriority. He conveys what is outside them, and what they feel and think in response to it, through a single continuum of third-person description and narration, without resorting either to interior monologue or to a dramatic mode of representation. When he does incorporate mimesis, it remains secondary to the diegesis, and comes in the form of dialogue, imitative of conversation in real life. His fusion of Bakha's interior and exterior worlds, and especially of unequal proportions of diegesis and mimesis, indexes a complex authorial stance, in which – to put it in Hegelian terms – the unification of subject and object paves the ground for a true apprehension of reality.

Anand's style and stance furnish his novel's outer form. The narration on the surface is almost wholly linear, following the existential chronology of events through the daylight hours and maintaining Bakha's consciousness mostly in the narrative present, without flashbacks or significant intrusions of memory. If the clock of the reality represented in the novel ticks through approximately fifteen hours, the clock of the narration itself moves through roughly half that time (thus contravening Laurence Sterne's demonstration in *Tristram Shandy* [1759–67] that a true narration can never catch up with what it seeks to narrate). Anand nevertheless produces the impression of both fullness and continuity: *Untouchable* runs from beginning to end without chapter divisions, but it contains fifteen breaks in the narrative (indicated by double-spacing on the page), and yet nothing significant in the day's events, as Bakha experiences them, is lost. With each discontinuity, the narration leaps forward in time, consistently blending internal and external worlds to keep up the impression of verisimilitude and unvarnished reality in the reader's mind.

The novel's anonymous, omniscient narrator – who is practically impossible to distinguish from its implied author – functions as the conduit between its inner and outer forms. He has unimpeded access to each character's interior life, as also to the exterior world within the fiction, as each individual character experiences it and as it stands outside the characters' collective experience in virtuality. Anand, however, stops short of going all the way that modernism seems to demand, by projecting a narrator who, though omniscient, is mostly non-reflexive, so that there is no "mirror in the text," no *mise en abyme*, no "problematization" of reality or of its representation. However, as I indicate in this chapter, this omission is deliberate and fundamental to the novel's *raison d'être*. The narrator's limited self-consciousness is aimed only at his implied readers and serves the novel's anticipated audience in the international marketplace. The absence of self-reflexivity in the narrator – which stands in tension with modernist experimentalism – is consistent with the fact that he is a reliable narrator who needs to remain un-intrusive, un-ambivalent, and un-ironic throughout the novel. Given his characteristics and his relation to the imagined characters and their world, the realism that he mobilizes is a fusion of social realism and psychological realism – varieties that are distinguished, in any case, by differences of focus and emphasis rather than by substantive differences of kind.

Untouchable maximizes the force of verisimilitude by presenting us with an implied author who is an insider, by birth and life-experience, to the society and the culture he represents in the text. Of course, Anand, the flesh-and-blood writer behind the implied author, is not a scavenger in real life, but he *is* a subaltern member – from a degraded caste of Hindu coppersmiths – of the society that so-called untouchables also inhabit. The novel's overall image of its author is that of someone who knows the object of representation intimately in real life, which is the ultimate validation of its realism. At the same time, this is someone who is also a virtual insider to the English language and its literary culture, not by birth or station but by education and cultivation. He appears inside the text implicitly as a participant-observer, a reliable reporter, a knowledgeable translator whom we would now call a hybrid, though not in the sense of someone stuck "in-between" but someone who serves actively as a "go-between." Anand's implied author addresses three distinct implied readers simultaneously. Two of them are Indian readers educated in English and accustomed to the novel in this language: the reader who belongs to the Punjab, or is familiar with it, and the reader who is Indian but is unfamiliar with everyday life in the subcontinent's northern region. The third implied reader is someone who is not Indian, or does not know India well, who therefore needs additional translation and commentary in the text in order to understand its references and nuances. The limited amount of meta-discourse interspersed throughout the narrative is addressed to the second and third of these implied readers. Keeping his meta-discourse to a minimum, Anand makes sure that the flow of the narrative remains uninterrupted, thus reinforcing the resemblance to reality.

Underneath this thick web of devices, the specific inner form of *Untouchable* is synecdoche: a part represents a whole, one day for Bakha stands for his entire life. More generally, the novel has the principle of metonymic representation as its inner form, so that Bakha and his life are represented by all the things with which they are associated – place, occupation, diurnal routine, social codes and circumstances, historical moment, colonial rule, religion, modernization, and so on. Synecdoche and metonymy – rather than metaphor or allegory – drive the narrator and narrative, unfolding part after part in sequence to fill out the whole. In Anand's case, this syntagmatic unfolding is teleological; the novel's *telos* or goal, the element that drives the protagonist and his life, is Bakha's desire "to produce, out of the society [he *has*] to live in, a vision of the society [he *wants*] to live in" (Frye 349, emphasis added). This *telos* of social transformation makes *Untouchable* a "reformist" novel to its core. But given Anand's theoretical reticence about his mode of representation, the connection between realism and reform – between aesthetic practice and societal change – does not become visible until we juxtapose him with a more self-reflexive practitioner of realism, such as Premchand.

Premchand's Theory of Realism

Although Anand and Premchand are unequal in their accomplishments, they share a number of attributes. Besides being innovators of Indian modernist fiction (in English and in Hindi and Urdu, respectively), both have origins in subaltern caste communities (coppersmith and *kayastha*), are deeply affected by nineteenth-century reformist movements as well as Gandhian politics, become anti-colonial public intellectuals, and exhibit strong socialist sympathies. In January 1925, Premchand published a first version of an essay entitled "Upanyasa [The Novel]" in Hindi, which offers a compact but conceptually complete theoretical account of realism and the realistic novel in the context of Indian modernism. Anand probably did not read the essay before he wrote his novel in 1933, but Premchand's discussion impinges, directly and indirectly, on many aspects of *Untouchable*.

Premchand begins "Upanyasa" by defining the novel as a "picture or depiction of human conduct and character"; its "original essence or fundamental principle" is "to shed light on human nature and to open up its secrets and mysteries" (291). His conception of character and of what is human emphasizes variability rather than fixity:

> Just as the faces of no two human beings match, so their actions and personalities, too, do not match.... [But even] as the characters of all human beings contain so much that is the same, they also contain some differences. The novel's principal duty is to depict this identity and diversity of character, this absence of unqualified difference, this sameness-in-difference and difference-in-sameness. (291)

The question that follows is whether "the novelist who has studied human characters and their conduct" should or should not "place them before the reader" exactly as they are (292):

> This question has led to the division of novelists into two classes: the idealists and the realists. The realist places characters before the reader in their stark, actual form. He is not concerned with whether goodness of character has bad outcomes, or badness of character produces good results. His characters complete their playful dance of life according to their deficiencies and assets; and because the world is such that the fruit of goodness is not always good, and the fruit of badness is not necessarily bad – in fact, the results are contrary – so [in realist fiction] good men endure blows, suffer torments, experience hardships, and tolerate insults, putting up with consequences that are the inverse of their goodness; whereas bad men find comfort and pleasure, become famous, and are celebrated, and their evil yields fruits that are the opposite. (292)

"The laws of Nature," Premchand continues, "are very strange." As a result, "the realist is trapped by the chains of experience, and because reprehensible characters predominate in the world ... so realism is a portrayal of our weaknesses, our hostilities, and our cruelties stripped naked." It is then possible for realism to become "destructive," in part because it may show "only evil all around us." However, even though "realism is extremely useful in turning our attention to society's flawed institutions and practices" (292),

> human nature also has the special feature that a re-vivification of the deceit, baseness, and cunning around it cannot make it happy at heart. It wishes to soar into a world where, for a short while, it is liberated from these low-grade emotions, where it can forget that it is strapped with anxieties, where it can witness noble and emotionally sympathetic creatures who are fully alive, where there is no predominance of crookedness and guile, enmity and indifference. It carries the thought in its heart that if, in tales and anecdotes too, we have to endure the company of the same people with whom we have to deal night and day, then why read such books at all? (292–3)

In Premchand's perspective, idealism – in the moral and ethical sense – "makes up for this shortcoming in realism":

> Idealism acquaints us with characters whose hearts have a sacrosanct purity, who are devoid of selfishness and lust, who are saintly by nature. Even though such characters are not adept in the ways of the world, even though their straightforwardness lets them down in their practical dealings, folks who are sick and tired of deviousness take a special pleasure in witnessing them in their sincerity and lack of worldly knowledge. If realism opens our eyes, then idealism lifts and transports us to a place that engages our hearts and minds deeply. (293)

This line of reasoning leads him to a generalization that stands at the center of his theoretical position:

> That is why I think novels that fuse realism and idealism belong to the highest category. You can call this fusion *idealistic realism*. Realism should be employed to bring ideals to life, and this is the distinctive property of the good novel. The novelist's greatest bequest is the creation of characters who enrapture the reader with their good thoughts and good actions. (293)

Yet such a fusion of realism and idealism is all the more difficult in the mid-1920s, when "conditions are changing at such a frantic pace, so many new ideas are being conceived, that perhaps no writer can manage to keep literature's ideal in mind." One of the consequences of such a rapid transformation is that "knowledgeable writers, not only in India but even in Europe, preach one ideology or another in their works" (295). The promotion of a partisan ideology conflicts directly with aestheticism, but Premchand nevertheless holds that:

> a skillful artist composes even an ideologically motivated work so beautifully that he can keep playing out the conflict of fundamental human tendencies. "Art for art's sake" is best practiced at a time when a nation is prosperous and happy. But today, when we see ourselves trapped in so many kinds of political and social bondage, at every turn our gaze encounters terrible scenes of suffering and poverty. When we hear the rending wail of utter deprivation, how is it possible for the heart of any thinking being not to be struck by horror? (295–6)

In these passages, translated here for the first time, Premchand speaks eloquently for a particular vision of modernist realism and its significance in the second phase of Indian modernism. As the translator of Eliot's *Silas Marner* and twenty-three of Tolstoy's stories into Hindi, he addresses his European precursors retrospectively, at the same time that – as the premier fiction writer in Indian modernism's second phase, with a full bilingual oeuvre in Hindi and Urdu – he also addresses younger novelists, such as Anand, prospectively. By juxtaposing my narrative analysis and my translation, and by turning to the original works, readers will be able to ascertain for themselves how precisely Anand's English text – unawares – traces every step in the moral, social, political, and aesthetic logic of Premchand's Hindi essay, written a decade earlier. As Victor Shklovsky might have said, *Untouchable* is the most typical novel of idealistic realism in modernist literature.

CHAPTER 7

"Handcuffed to History": Partition and the Indian Novel in English

Ananya Jahanara Kabir

Oh spell it out, spell it out: at the precise instant of India's arrival at independence, I tumbled forth into the world. There were gasps. And, outside the window, fireworks and crowds. A few seconds later, my father broke his big toe; but his accident was a mere trifle when set beside what had befallen me in that benighted moment, because thanks to the occult tyrannies of those blandly saluting clocks I had been mysteriously handcuffed to history, my destinies indissolubly chained to those of my country.

– Salman Rushdie, *Midnight's Children* (p. 3)

With these now-famous words begins one of the most iconic Indian novels written in English, a work that is widely recognized as having changed the course of not just the novel from India but postcolonial writing from South Asia at large. Is it mere coincidence that *Midnight's Children*, which in 1981 announced to an unsuspecting world a new idiom of fiction altogether – brash, jocular, daring, and deeply clever – should center thus on "the precise instant of India's arrival at independence"? The response I would offer, and which forms the basic premise of this chapter, is: no. This novel, unfettered as it seems by the need to genuflect to established models of correctness and decorum presented to the Indian novelist by the weight of colonial history, is actually as "handcuffed" to that history as its protagonist. Specifically, it is handcuffed to that pivotal moment when the colonial era ended and the postcolonial moment began – a moment that, for India and Pakistan (and, in a more complicated way, for Bangladesh), brought together the triumph of independence with its dark side, the trauma of Partition. In these opening sentences, Rushdie already signals this duality through the juxtaposition of celebratory and auspicious signifiers (fireworks, crowds, the birth of a child) with hints of inauspiciousness, inexplicability, and coercion (accidents, however bathetic, "occult tyrannies," handcuffs, and chains). This is a duality that unfolds in its full tragicomic magnificence in the course of the novel.

119

In this chapter I argue that Rushdie's *Midnight's Children* is neither the first nor the only Indian novel in English to be thus handcuffed to the history of Partition – though it is certainly the first novel to announce this condition so meta-fictively. The historical processes that culminated with the simultaneity of Partition and independence in 1947 are, in a way, the same as those that gave birth to the Indian novel in English: India's crystallization as part of the British Empire, the decision to make British India the laboratory for Western-style liberal education, including the use of English as the medium of instruction; the creation of a colonized intelligentsia that, by the early twentieth century, was articulating its aspirations in anti-colonial terms; and the use of the same mechanisms of liberalism and empire to experiment with different forms of decolonized subjectivity (A. Kabir, "Postcolonial"). Even as Partition instantiated a swerve in the utopian conception of the decolonized subject, it left its indelible mark on the form and preoccupations of the Indian English novel. It is my contention that, at different historical phases, starting with the anticolonial movement that led to the emergence of the nation in 1947, the novel has borne the impress of Partition as an event, a memory, and even a premonition. In other words, the Indian novel in English is handcuffed to the history of Partition in two ways. It is shaped by the politics that resulted in Partition and that created a specific post-Partition subject, exemplified by the Indian Muslim as minority figure; and it is shaped by the ways in which Partition has been remembered, forgotten and re-remembered by successive generations of writers: a process that I have elsewhere detailed as "Partition's post-amnesia" (A. Kabir, *Partition's*).[1]

The relationship between Partition and the Indian novel that I will trace is thus deeper than the novel as a form of Partition narrative. The recording, or attempted recollection, of epochal traumatic events is ideally suited to the temporal scope and heteroglossia of the novel form, and the novel has lent itself well to this service by representing the causes and impact of 1947 on social formations in different parts of India and its diaspora. Despite persistent claims of silence around the event, a large number of Partition narratives now exist, in English as well as various other South Asian languages, and this number will no doubt continue to expand. I am not so concerned here with an analysis of this primarily narrative and memorializing function of novels about Partition. Rather, my claim is for a radically formative relationship between the Indian novel in English and Partition. "What good are Partitions?" asks a recent research project on this subject.[2] This question may seem aberrant to Indians accustomed to mourning the lost possibilities of a conjoint existence with what became

Pakistan (and subsequently, Bangladesh). Yet it is a useful one that forces us to confront the innovative and fundamentally transformative force of the Partition of British India. On the most basic level, the Indian novel in English could be defined as such because an "India" emerged; inasmuch as this India was irretrievably formed through the historical choices that led to Partition and the collective trauma that resulted, it was an India that its novels inevitably mimicked, even if setting out to critique it (P. Gopal, *Indian*). Those novels whose authors wrote in English carried on their shoulders the additional burden of that language, which developed into the expressive medium through which to declare the novel form's association with a defiantly secular world (George).

Such assertions did not come without contradictions; the amnesias and post-amnesias unleashed by Partition found in these novels their reflection, their form, and their subject matter. Thus, although Partition *narratives* are not my focus in this chapter, I will organize its argument through iconic novels that have engaged centrally with Partition – the processes leading up to it and the impact radiating away from it. In these novels, an overt preoccupation with Partition (including as an event that is approaching) is actually a guide to their authors' sustained engagement with the challenge of flexing form to reflect this unprecedented content, as well as to register the fundamental impact on subjectivity as the interface between public and private memorial-affective domains. We are thereby able to isolate discrete stages in the evolution of the deeper relationship I have proposed between the event and the literary form. From this perspective, the Indian novel in English itself represents what one recent scholar of Karachi's divided families has termed "Partition effects," or "the ways in which Partition is rhetorically invoked and socially remembered" (Zamindar 238); indeed, the Partition effect in this case is the novel itself, emerging as a multivalent record of Partition's reformulation of social memory. This argument is no simplistic return to Fredric Jameson's much-debated claim that all third world writing aspires to the condition of national allegory (Jameson, "Third-World"); rather, I demonstrate that this genre uses the possibility and potential of allegory to stage a complex confrontation with the historical processes of subject formation that are grouped around the shorthand term "Partition" and the date August 15, 1947.

I thereby engage with the following major themes: myths of pre-Partition existence and their imagined survival; the nation as a new (but impossible) object of love; and the persistence of memory, including forms of "postmemory." The novelists I engage with represent three distinct post-Partition generations and include Qurratulain Hyder, Ahmed Ali, Humayun Kabir, Salman Rushdie, Rohinton Mistry, Amitav Ghosh, Anita Desai, Kiran Desai, and Siddhartha Deb. The texture of their narratives, the relationship of diegetic temporality to the recollection of past events, and the degree of meta-critical self-consciousness differ according to the generation to which the writer in question belongs; indeed, these cohorts form in concert with the historical events that enable a generational identity to crystallize. The chapter will attempt to map out these differences. At the same time, all these novelists share an interest in exploiting and indeed revivifying the formal and epistemological capacities of the novel to evoke alternative worlds: other possibilities to the turns taken by history. They use the novel not merely to "mourn," as now-accepted theories of trauma would routinely assert; they use it to dream, to long, and to wonder "what if?"[3] To admit affection and affiliations to conditions of existence that were lost to the decolonized world, they tap into vernacular reservoirs of affect; through the use of English, nevertheless, they situate themselves within a certain lineage of South Asian modernity as the psyche's compensation for loss. My assessment of Partition's impact on the Indian English novel thus also participates in a wider reconsideration of Partition as "traumatic" for South Asia: how we might move beyond European-derived models for articulating and analyzing trauma – even while acknowledging their formative impact – to incorporate into our hermeneutic toolkits the concomitant operation of a range of vernacular affective resources (A. Kabir, "Affect"; Sangari; Ewing).

Harbingers of a Melancholic Modernity

What kind of a novel emerges through the compromised memory of the elusive fragrance of flowers? The answer would be *Aag ka darya* (1959), Qurratulain Hyder's tour de force in Urdu, which she herself "transcreated" into English in 1998 as *River of Fire*. From an aristocratic north Indian Muslim family, Hyder moved to Pakistan shortly after 1947 but moved back to India following the publication of *Aag ka darya*, presumably on the strength of what she has elsewhere called "a conviction born of that love that some even call treason. This treason or treachery is nothing but a longing for the fragrance of jasmine blossoms" (quoted in Hussein xxiv). The longing that she goes so far as to call "treachery" is personified in Hyder's novel as Champa, an "utterly enchanting" woman (76): earthy, barefoot, golden-skinned, bearing the vernacular name for magnolia, a flower that occurs in horticultural and poetic contiguity to the jasmine (*bela*). She represents the wet earth, organic and fragrant with monsoon rains. In her first appearance in this novel, which begins in the forest of Shravasti in the fourth century BCE and ends in 1958 (the year of its actual completion), Champa, standing under a kadam tree, inspires the young ascetic manqué Gautam Nilambar to create the bas-relief Sudarshan Yakshini: "tree sprite, good to behold" (Hyder 37–41). His hands are mutilated soon thereafter by Chandragupta Maurya's invading imperial army. Gautam, who opens the novel with this immersion in the sensorium of the jungle, ages into a feckless rake. These alienations triggered by political violence foreshadow the novel's later tragedies, culminating in Partition's rupturing of kinships and friendships. The characters' reappearance down the epochs until the present, in dialectical concert with history, lends a mythical, cyclical quality to this final devastation, even as Gautam's closing return to the forest, through which Buddhist nuns still pass, suggests a panacea for modern times.

Aag ka darya exemplifies the early postcolonial novel in India as the novel of premonition. The novelist becomes the exegete of the complex patterns of history that characters swirl in and out of, endowed with a seeming awareness of their allegorical, extra-fictional burden. In other novels dealing with the impact of Partition, the narrative focus is not so temporally and allegorically ambitious, being restricted to the fortunes of an extended family across a few generations – as in Attia Hosain's *Sunlight on a Broken Column* (1961) – or the changing relationships within a single village – as in Khushwant Singh's *Train to Pakistan* (1956). Yet all these novels are marked by an acute sense of historical prescience. Narratologically, this sense is consolidated through the authors' adherence to social realism, but with a twist. Passages of thick description bestow value on the homes, lifestyles, and mores of an age that is coded as pre-modern, either because "feudal" or "rural" (or both), and which the end of the narrative will redefine as "the time before Partition." Denouement and closure invariably coincide with the revelation of Partition as an event that defies narrative capture. Instead, the moment around 1947 is coded as an aporia, which emerges as a watershed between epochs. Dramatic narratological changes, such as fragmentation, compression, or simply the onrush of conclusion, all work to endow the pre-Partition period with alterity. This is a world that has just slipped out of reach and left us blinking in the harsh daylight of a postcolonial modernity. Whether it is a ray of sunlight that illuminates the architectural remnants of the feudal past, or a rushing train that, having taught entire villages to synchronize life to Weberian modernity, now transports slaughtered bodies across new national borders: carefully chosen tropes striate these novels written in the wake of Partition with an ambivalence toward the modern.

Let us recall that the novel is the modern, rational genre par excellence. In British India, the novel in English became both the site and the product of modernity as something to be aspired to.[4] The bookish, intellectual protagonists – the Lailas (as in Hosain's *Sunlight on a Broken Column*) and the Iqbals (as in Singh's *Train to Pakistan*) – who populate post-Partition novels are continuations and remnants of that aspirational modernity. Yet Partition also created a mindset that rationalized multiple alienations through recourse to "modernity." We return to Hyder's branding as "treason" her longing for the fragrance of jasmine. A certain poetics of place, coded through jasmine, had to be banished as "treacherous" to this mindset: treacherous because of its ability to trigger attachments to sites of identity-formation beyond the nation (village, birthplace, ancestral home, region). The colonial process of forming the modern subject had meant the superseding of these sites by the sacrosanct idea of the nation. However, Partition rendered many of these actual sites "across the border" and thus geopolitically out of reach. The reality of the estranged homeland became a cipher for a melancholic modernity even as narrative teleology branded those homelands as atavistic. The banished recurred: tantalizing, fleeting, seasonal, and local. The memories of the sensorium, diffused through the scent of the monsoon-drenched earth, the flower names through localized pronunciations labeled as "dialect," the folksongs that paid homage to the onomatopoeia of songbirds, were intangibles that kept intruding against the structure of compensation that the nation-state offered and that the novel form echoed. Narrative focalization through protagonists whose filiations conjoin them to the worlds that are now lost but whose affiliations are internationalist, usually thanks to a Socialist worldview, encourages us readers to pitch our fortunes with theirs, and with the post-Partition, decolonized nation. The polyphony of the novel, manifested here in the split between filiation and affiliation (Said, *World* 6 et passim), allowed the simultaneous evocation of both compensation and longing.

Indian novels written in the first decades after decolonization are – not surprisingly – marked by the major event of this period: the emergence of the independent nation in the midst of epistemic and physical violence. Embedded within their often overtly optimistic social realist narratives are lyrical strands that sound out a consistent minor key of melancholia, which a vernacular hermeneutics would resolve as the manifestation of *viraha*: a Sufi/Bhakti trope for separation from one's lover, who can stand in for guru, saint, or even god (or God). Kumkum

Sangari has demonstrated how post-Partition Hindi films drew on *viraha* to structure the unspeakable longing for lost worlds that the new nation made impossible to love anymore; the *viraha* mode typically shaped the song sequences that are structurally indispensable to Indian film. Something similar happened to the novel. Elsewhere, I have explored the ubiquitous affect of *viraha* within post-Partition nation-building and its concomitant cultural production in both decolonized India and Pakistan (A. Kabir, *Partition's*, esp. 104–19). Here, I simply reiterate that while the form, language, and epistemological framework of the Indian English novel made it the vehicle of a forward-looking postcolonial modernity, the multiple affect-worlds inhabited by authors, their exposure to vernacular sacral hermeneutics, and their personal estrangements as a consequence of living through (anti)colonial modernity, injected the novel with an anti-rational streak. This recourse to *viraha* as a vernacular equivalent of melancholia also marks novels predating 1947. Unable to be "about" Partition (because they were written before the event took place), these novels, such as Humayun Kabir's *Men and Rivers* (1945) and Ahmed Ali's *Twilight in Delhi* (1940), presage the event by narrating the precarious existence of modernity's various non-Anglophone others (peasants, feudal noblemen) at the mercy of natural and historical forces.[5] Together with the tendency toward premonition, *viraha* allows the Indian novel to step into the postcolonial era bearing this dual valence of being ostensibly rational and deeply mythical. This duality is the very quality of its modernity.

The Big Fat Indian (Partition) Novel

The transcreation of *Aag ka darya* into its English version, *River of Fire*, in 1998 suggests that the preoccupations of novelists who wrote contemporaneously to Partition remained in their minds with the passing of decades. This may not be too unexpected, given this generation's firsthand experience of the process of decolonization. What is arguably more worthy of attention is the persistence of Partition as a theme in the work of a new generation of novelists, who emerged dramatically in the interim to change Indian literature and its perception both at home and abroad. These now-iconic novels, which include not only Salman Rushdie's *Midnight's Children*, mentioned at the start of this chapter, but also Vikram Seth's *A Suitable Boy* (1993), Rohinton Mistry's *Such a Long Journey* (1991), and Amitav Ghosh's *The Shadow Lines* (1988), heralded a new phase of global visibility for Indian English fiction. They also handsomely contributed to the development of postcolonial theory in academia.[6] Moreover, this was also a period when the first forays into writing critically about Partition were made, largely through feminist engagements with the silence around women's experiences during 1947 (Butalia; Bhasin and Menon). Within this landscape of discursive transformation, therefore, what seems to remain constant is a thematic interest in Partition. Nevertheless, as the feminist work of retrieval of Partition memories also demonstrates, this is actually a time of finding new ways to articulate and reassess those foundational traumas. Hence my emphasis – as evident in my comments on *Midnight's Children* in the introduction – on this thematic mobilization as but a clue to the deeper phenomenological relationship between the event, its ongoing, semi-private memorialization, and the novel form as it evolves in postcolonial India. A generation on from Partition and independence, those who write novels find themselves needing to work out the form and style that best carries those traumatic burdens that they have inherited from their parents and the postcolonial nation's first cohort of intellectuals.

Within the opening wedding scene in *A Suitable Boy*, we read of an abrupt mood-change suffered by Mrs. Tandon, the grandmother of the protagonist Bhaskar: "the pleasant chatter of the garden in Brahmpur was amplified into the cries of the blood-mad mobs on the streets of Lahore, the lights into fire" (23). The trigger for Mrs. Tandon's momentary transportation from wedding festivities to Partition violence is the casual mention of Pakistan by one of the guests, the aristocratic Nawab Sahib: "She had been willing to tolerate talking to the Nawab Sahib though he was a Muslim, but when he mentioned comings and goings from Pakistan, it was too much for her imagination. She felt ill" (23). We encounter here the psychosomatics of a trauma that is folded into the interior of the psyche but which cannot bear the weight of arbitrary recall. The narrator notes that neither her son Kedarnath nor his wife Veena seem (to her) similarly affected, as they rebuild their lives in the new India; and her grandson Bhaskar, who "had of course only been six at the time" (23), can hardly be expected to do so either. Yet is it the author, the same age as Bhaskar, who articulates her trauma to the world: "daily, sometimes hourly, in her imagination she returned to what she still thought of as her city and her home. It had been beautiful before it had become so suddenly hideous; it had appeared completely secure so shortly before it was lost for ever" (23). Seth assumes the responsibility of recording this loss, turning to the conceit of the omniscient narrator to excavate Mrs. Tandon's interiority. Classic realism remains the vehicle of choice to transmit experiences that are already moving into postmemory. At the same time, the impressive bulk of the novel insists, somewhat defiantly, on the solidity of the present.

Seth, as the grandson of Hindu migrants to India in the wake of Partition violence, writes a tome of more than 1,000 pages that chronicles the nation in reassuringly realist style; Rushdie, the grandson of Muslims who stayed in India despite Partition violence, writes his own version of the nation's formative years in a magic realist romp that leaves us unsure about the novel's status as tragedy or comedy and that begins and ends with the narrator's fragmenting, hole-ridden body (A. Kabir, "Subjectivities"). I interpret these marked stylistic divergences as reflecting a range of creative responses to the (post)memory of Partition, in which the differences calibrate the precise subjectivities of the novelists concerned. To pinpoint the correspondence between style and subjectivity would then be the task of literary criticism. These divergences also register on a level that we may call each novel's philosophical orientation: while Seth turns to the world of Urdu poetry in *A Suitable Boy*, Rushdie's creative inspiration comes from the popular worlds of Bombay cinema, advertising jingles, and the crowds on the street. These alternative reservoirs of cultural expression enter the novel as compensations for those worlds lost by an earlier generation through Partition; they are the new trajectories taken by *viraha*. For another writer of this generation, Amitav Ghosh – whose family, too, was impacted by Partition – it is the philosophy of history itself that is called upon to comment on and reassess the meaning of the nation's birth in the midst of violence and mass migrations. *The Shadow Lines*, Ghosh's earliest sustained engagement with the theme, narrates Partition within a wider context that includes World War II, colonialism, and the connectedness of traumatic events before and after 1947 – including the plunder of a sacred relic from the Hazratbal shrine in Srinagar and the emergence of Bangladesh in 1971 after a prolonged civil war between the eastern and western wings of Pakistan.

The necessity of bringing the birth of Bangladesh into dialogue with the memory of Partition is an obvious way in which the relationship between Partition and the novel changes after 1971. The presentation of these two epochal events as *linked* participates in an overall desire of this second post-Partition generation to be encyclopedic.[7] If novels of the previous generation were long, as seen in *River of Fire*, it was because of their vast diegetic temporal span; in contrast, what we may term "the big fat Indian novels" of the 1980s onward achieve narrative extent through complexly intertwined stories and a fascination with detail. This obsessive recourse to the "meanwhile" – which Mieke Bal uses to consolidate Benedict

Anderson's argument for print capitalism's capacity to produce imagined communities – projects polyphony and multiplicity as core characteristics of the Indian nation (M. Bal; B. Anderson). Yet it also signals a certain anxiety – reflected, too, in the love of linguistic play displayed by these authors. This anxiety may be traced to the novel form's ability to offer a malleable record of the novelists' private knowledge of "Partition effects" on families, as well as the ways in which they have been shaped by those family stories. In opening up these inner worlds to the public gaze, the Indian English novel during the 1980s and 1990s creates space for a range of minority subjectivities whose stories interrupt the master narrative of the nation's triumphalist trajectory toward independence. A range of odd and unconventional families emerges as writers such as Seth, Rushdie, Mistry, and Ghosh experiment, often through humor, wit, and self-deprecation, with the line between the possible and the real that constitutes the fictional pact between reader and author. Simultaneous to this flaunting of seemingly vulnerable selves, they claim legitimacy within the public sphere through the power inherent in the use of the English language, and an alliance with the doctrine of Nehruvian secularism, which was the leading philosophy in the first fifty years of the nation's existence (Khilnani; A. Sen).

Geo-Desire and the (Continued) Search for the Sacred

As Neelam Srivastava has convincingly demonstrated, the fiercely loyal alliance with secularist doctrine is historically linked to the development of a postcolonial Anglophone literary sphere. What I want to emphasize is that this alliance is born out of the need to compensate for the alienations of late colonial modernity that are, in turn, resolved by the memorializing mind as logically culminating in Partition. As these processes of remembering and forgetting move into subsequent generations, we note an increase in the imaginative reliance on certain secularist myths – the ancient modernity of India, the democratic nature of the crowd, the spiritual wellsprings of folk culture, the panacea of Sufism – that serve as the affective antinomies of modernist self-fashioning.[8] These myths are sustained by the same psychosocial need that wants to carve out space for a sacred center within the teleological progression of narratives otherwise concerned with encoding the post-Partition Indian subject as secular, modern, and free from a dependence on spiritual succor. These sacred centers are discernible in all the later works by the authors who made such an impact during the 1980s and 1990s with their big Partition novels. The clearest examples would be the detailed description of the Parsi temple in Mistry's *Such A Long Journey* – literally a refuge in the midst of the narrative's comings and goings through the geography of Bombay – and the mysterious episode of Ayesha and the pilgrims who drown (or not) in the Arabian Sea as they hope to find it parting for their pilgrimage to Mecca in *The Satanic Verses* (1988). For others, such as Seth and Ghosh, the search for the sacred invests narratives with the expansiveness of extra-territorial history. In Seth's *Two Lives* (2005), for instance, this investment takes the form of excavating interpersonal connections unanticipated by nationalist frameworks; for Ghosh, it is through an increasing interest in the phenomenology of interconnected oceans, as evinced in his recent Ibis Trilogy.[9]

The second generation of novelists writing after Partition has thus moved to the exploration of what Michael Rothberg has termed "multidirectional memories" – memories of concurrent traumas and displacements that emerge through a planetary rather than nationalist vision (A. Kabir, *Partition's* 24–35). Through characterization and plot, these traumas, which typically involve the contemporaneous events of the Second World War (leading to the Holocaust) and the decolonization of British India (leading to Partition), are revealed as interconnected. Their memorialization is proposed, as it is in the works examined by Rothberg, not as competitive but as complementary. Among the latest generation of post-Partition novelists in South Asia, it is only Kamila Shamsie of Pakistan whose work has progressed in this vein, as most evidently marked by her magisterial *Burnt Shadows* (2009), which moves from bombed-out Hiroshima to Delhi during Partition, and from postcolonial Pakistan to post-9/11 New York and Afghanistan. Shamsie's Indian counterparts, however, have preferred a regional rather than a planetary frame to explore the legacy of Partition. They engage the same search for the sacred as their predecessors, but they focus on the home and the hometown in order to emphasize an inability to feel at home. Narratives unfold to reveal anterior family histories of movement outward from ancestral lands typically through a combination of Partition-induced migration and the demands of bureaucracy on freshly decolonized subjects. Grandfathers and fathers are invoked as those who set into motion processes of displacement and compensatory Anglicization. Misfit protagonists record alternative processes of belonging unfolding through the lives of others – contemporaries who are presented through easier relationships to the space they inhabit. In an age of fiercely competitive vernacular politics of recognition, these protagonists' – and their creators' – fluency in English emerges as the burden and voice of a secularism that nevertheless cannot be abandoned. Narrative scope shrinks, as memorialization turns inward to ponder the webs of longing that still interpellate the post-Partition subject.

Significantly, the more memorable of these novels work out what Kiran Desai calls the "inheritance of loss" – Desai's novel of the same title (2006), and Siddhartha Deb's *The Point of Return* (2002) – by situating their narratives on India's northeastern flank. Compensating in part for a Punjab-centrism that was an earlier predilection of Partition memorialization, this shift of geographical focus is the consequence of an interest not only in the formation of Bangladesh as a complication of Partition's psychosocial effects but also on the even more elusive story of the subcontinent's northeastern corner. Colonial and postcolonial gerrymandering left this region a tangle of borders, in some cases drawing the epistemologically estranged "there" into confusing proximity with the "here": "They stepped out to look at Bangladesh," reports *The Point of Return* (49), speaking of a break in a car journey taken by the narrator's father and his colleague. "Looking at Bangladesh" forces the pre-Partition "then" into dialogue with the "now," even as the intervening events of 1971 cast before and after, here and there, into cartographic and memorial confusion. Attempted journeys back lead to dead ends; Deb's narrator "wanted to photograph the bridge and the shrine, the lime trees that appear in thick bunches on the hillside, the plains of Bangladesh that seem faraway and mysterious from the road" (41), but narrative circumstances intervene to prevent him from doing so. Novels such as Deb's consciously thwart readerly expectations of narrative progress, emplotment, and resolution by interrupting narrative with reflective and lyrical segments. A story emerges, but it is one of the painful, never entirely successful processes of articulating one's post-Partition subjectivity by embracing what anterior generations had deliberately shut out as part of the "quest to find a place in the modern world" (Deb 28). These are records of the failure of narrative to retrieve a pre-Partition utopia, whole and untainted.

This return to a past moment, not in order to reclaim lost worlds but to remember what had to be forgotten at a certain foundational post-Partition moment, is what I have explicated as "post-amnesia." The logic of intergenerational dialogue places the baton of post-amnesia in the hands of the generation writing after the postcolonial big hitters: Rushdie, Ghosh, Seth; it is exemplified by Kiran Desai's novel, read as a response to her mother Anita Desai's contemplative and lyrical recall of Partition, *Clear Light of Day* (1980). There, ruminations on memory, violence, and Anglophone modernity had been articulated along a recognizable axis of faded high cultural glamor (Old Delhi and Urdu poetry); the daughter's novel shifts to the lesser-feted north Bengal, and the impact of Partition on the marginalized cultures and aspirations of the mountainous zone bordering the ancient hegemony of the Indo-Gangetic plains. This shift recalibrates the persistence of *viraha*, which now becomes a new way of talking about nature's triumph over cartography: "A great amount of warring, betraying, bartering had occurred; between Nepal, England, Tibet, India, Sikkim, Bhutan; Darjeeling stolen from here, Kalimpong plucked from there – despite, ah, despite the mist charging down like a dragon, dissolving, undoing, making ridiculous the drawing of borders" (K. Desai 9). The meeting of mountain and mist parallels the confluence of rivers, estuaries, and seas explored extensively by Ghosh and reveals how post-amnesia can manifest itself, too, in new developments within the work of more established novelists. This is a geo-desire born out of post-amnesia, which stakes a claim to difference through its refusal to self-sublimate into a pastoral romanticism. If the subject of post-amnesia is guided by the potential of geo-desire, it is through lyrical and shard-like interventions into the novel's narrative flow; narrative flow is not so infused by it that the subject can be apotheosized. There is a promise of transcendence, but it is always deferred and shown as somewhere else, within the reach of someone else.

Conclusion

"Restorying Partition can never be easy." Thus declares the Curator's Note prefacing one of the most recent experiments in the realm of Indian English fiction: *This Side That Side: Restorying Partition, An Anthology of Graphic Narratives* (V. Ghosh 12). A collaborative effort that pairs writers and illustrators from South Asia and its diaspora, anthologized by an Indian resident in New Delhi, and published by an independent press, this black-and-white assemblage of diverse voices and illustrative styles seems to be the latest embodiment of the evolving relationship between Partition and the Indian English novel. The collection is not only a Maus-like distillation into image-text but a polyphony of many voices and – their visual counterpart – many pens. It is not a single narrative but a veritable collage of fragments produced across borders; yet this centrifugal blasting out of history is restrained by two reassuring covers, a centralizing editorial presence, the reassuring solidity of a printing press, and the lasting materiality of a book that approximates the size and shape of a novel. *This Side That Side* is thus a development that testifies to the radical potential of Partition to elicit solutions for the shifting ground of collective memory as new generations of Indian writers move ever further away from the limiting event through which the nation was born. It also confirms the limits of that radicalism – unable, as it seems, to abandon all forms of epistemological security. The English language and the genre of the novel – even one that leaves its vestigial shape behind as it tries to flee the building: these are, ultimately, the most lasting ways in which Partition has left those who want to tell the tale still handcuffed to its history. From this perspective, it may not be too bold to view the literary history of the Indian novel in English as a record of the imagination working with and against those handcuffs.

Notes

1 On the Muslim as minority figure, see Mufti, *Enlightenment*. I have developed this argument's implications for post-Partition subject-formation in A. Kabir, "Secret."

2 I refer to Radhika Mohanram's research project, "Partitions: What are they good for?" At http://www.partitions-net.com (accessed August 29, 2014).

3 For new work away from these assertions, see Buelens, Durrant, and Eaglestone (eds.).

4 On the novel, rationalism, and modernity, see Ermarth. On the novel and modernity in British India, see P. Joshi, *In Another*; A. Kabir, "Postcolonial"; and Chakravorty.

5 See also A. Kabir, *Partition's* 192–6.

6 E.g., the influential citation of Rushdie's *The Satanic Verses* in Bhabha, "How Newness."

7 I have offered a detailed analysis of 1947 and 1971 as linked events in A. Kabir, *Partition's*.

8 For a fuller working out of these antinomies, see A. Kabir, *Partition's* 83–127.

9 So far, the Ibis Trilogy includes *Sea of Poppies* (2008) and *River of Smoke* (2011). See also Ghosh's earlier *The Hungry Tide* (2004).

CHAPTER 8

Women, Reform, and Nationalism in Three Novels of Muslim Life

Suvir Kaul

> It is a well known fact that man is superior to woman in every respect. He is a representative of God on earth and being born with His light in him deserves the respect and obedience that he demands. He is not expected to show his gratitude or even a kind word of appreciation to a woman: it is his birthright to get everything from her. "Might is right" is the policy of this world.
>
> – Iqbalunnisa Hussain, *Purdah and Polygamy* (p. 49)

In the late nineteenth century and after, Indian anti-colonialists and nationalists argued that social and familial norms were in need of reform and that they, rather than the British, should be the men to undertake such efforts. The British had been wary of legislating Hindu and Muslim family laws, but once they moved against the Hindu practice of sati in 1839, "reform" was firmly on their agenda and became a cornerstone of their putative civilizing mission. Hindus and Muslims, both because they were wary of further colonial intervention in domestic matters and because reformers within each religion were active against corrupt and discriminatory practices, reexamined women's lives and gender relations as they imagined the future. The remarriage of widows and the marriage of underage children became topics for furious discussion – as did, particularly for Muslims, the practice of polygyny. Muslim men were not the only ones to take multiple wives in India, but, as Asiya Alam reminds us, "polygyny came to be inextricably linked to the social identity of Muslims" (635–6). Colonial administrators had written critically about Muslim polygyny, and such criticism, Alam shows, intensified ongoing discussions among Muslims about theological and historical justifications for, as well as the abuses of, polygyny. The primary question was at what pace – if at all – to accommodate changes in Muslim social practices, particularly since such changes were seen as associated with British (and increasingly Hindu) forms of sociality.

Debating Purdah and Polygamy

For the most part, reformers as well as traditionalist defenders of purdah and polygamy debated each other in pamphlets, prose tracts, and fiction written in Urdu. However, writing in English appealed to another influential and international readership, and it is this readership that Iqbalunnisa Hussain addressed in her novel, *Purdah and Polygamy* (1944). The novel is an astonishing indictment of the conditions of life for women in a property-owning Hyderabadi family. This tone is set in its opening paragraph, which describes Dilkusha, their "imposing" home, as a building whose "high blind walls made a stranger take it for an unguarded jail, and literally so it was for its women folk" (*Purdah* 1). All the women who live in this building maintain purdah, which they and their men understand to be crucial to the maintenance of their gentility and their religious purity. However, as the story develops, it becomes clear that they do so with different degrees of conviction; in general, the novel makes clear that both purdah and polygyny are coercive and deny women's individuality.

Hussain's convictions are also available in her book of essays *Changing India: A Muslim Woman Speaks*, which makes clear her concern about the future of Muslim lives in India.[1] In "There is no Polygamy in Islam," she argues that the Koran provided no justification for men marrying more than once (*Changing* 29), and, in "Purdah and Progress," she turns to contemporary socio-historical developments to explain her views (*Changing* 45). Hussain notes the historical "advantages" that have followed from purdah: Muslim women have learned to be "obedient and loyal wives, devoted mothers and helpful and considerate sisters" (46), but she argues that purdah combined with "illiteracy and ignorance has cramped their personalities" (47). She insists that removal of the purdah system is crucial to the regeneration of the once "great Muslim nation" (48) and advocates judicious, ameliorist action: women should be moved out of purdah "gradually and indirectly by providing [them] chances of useful education and opportunities for vocational education" (49).

In contrast to the cautious (though challenging) positions developed in these essays, *Purdah and Polygamy* is much less forgiving of traditional verities, and is an unyielding saga of oppressed women. In the first two chapters, we are told, in matter-of-fact tones, about the landlord Umar's life and death, his property, and his wife Zuhra, his son Kabeer, and Jamila, his twelve-year old daughter, who, once her father falls ill with cancer, is married off to a cousin. The most emotively powerful section of the novel describes the humiliating rituals that Zuhra has to undergo upon

Umar's death. She is told that her fate is the cause of her husband's death, her sister-in-law smashes the bangles on her wrist that betoken marriage, her bright clothes are taken away and replaced with a widow's whites, her face is covered so that no married woman might look upon it and know ill luck herself, and she is not allowed to touch her husband for fear of polluting his body. All this happens alongside conspicuous expenditure, as elaborate funeral feasts are held for hundreds of invited mourners. This juxtaposition of female abjection and public posturing becomes one of the signature themes of the novel: women must be taught their place within the household even as family status is confirmed in wasteful ceremonials.

The novel's primary concern is the lives of women, in particular the way men treat them and the way they treat each other. At every turn, the novel shows women at the receiving end of male power and duplicity: when Zuhra finances a lavish wedding for Kabeer by selling property, she does so at a loss, as "the capitalists and exploiters of the town," once they heard that a woman was selling property, "stuck together and offered a rock-bottom price" (*Purdah* 33). Within the household, every ritual occasion is marked by displays designed to humiliate vulnerable women. When Nazni, Kabeer's wife, comes to his home after marriage, Zuhra does all she can to demean her and thus demonstrate her power. The only comfort Kabeer can offer his new wife is to point out that his mother is old and has not long to live: "Soon you will be mistress of the house. She has reached that position after passing through similar days. You must strive to achieve it." Nazni's response is equally self-deprecating: "One must not expect a bed of roses in this life" (63). This is one of the many maxims articulated by women as they try to come to terms with their difficult lives; for them, suffering is to be expected, even embraced, as the proper moral condition of femininity.

Hussain deftly weaves larger conflicts about the coming of "modern" ways into the power plays that characterize life within the family. Zuhra objects to Kabeer accompanying Nazni to a cinema hall because "a woman going to the pictures can neither be virtuous nor an obedient wife" (63). When Nazni's father has her heart ailment examined by a male specialist, Zuhra's response is uncompromising: "A man can't own a woman as his wife after she has been touched by a man." She approves of "men in former days who used to cut off that part of the body which was touched by a stranger." Kabeer says that he too felt "repulsion" when the doctor examined Nazni; "I felt that I could not be proud of her any more," he concludes (65). Kabeer's "repulsion" leads to his taking a second wife and Zuhra offers a simple justification: Kabeer must marry again to lessen

Nazni's domestic burdens because "an extra healthy woman at home is no more than an extra servant" (68).

Kabeer sees his new wife Munira's face only after they are married, and finds her "repulsive" (71) but takes her to his bed anyway. Kabeer mollifies Nazni by describing his new wife as "that wretched negress" and "not suitable even to wash your bathroom" (90–1), his phrases bringing together the color- and caste-consciousness that define bigotry in India. (Later, he refines his description: "Negresses don't have long teeth, so ape is better" [101].) Nazni's thoughts at this point are a reminder of the quasi-scriptural basis of women's oppression: she believes she must be reconciled to him because "The woman who makes her husband sorry goes to the Seventh Hell where the fire burns eternally. She is burnt alive and is recreated and burnt again" (91). Her grandmother's injunctions further underline her duty: a man can do anything he likes, she says, and "Your only duty is to obey him" (123).

Passages like this, and the miserable lack of choice for women, emphasize the claustrophobic world of the household. However, there are occasional glimpses of different viewpoints, as when Nazni's brother insists that she should not return to her betraying husband: "She is no more his wife. A man remarries to prove the disloyalty, incapacity, ill-temper and barrenness of the first wife.... No respectable woman would humiliate herself by calling him her husband" (113). His father is pleased to take these ideals as a sign of his son's education but then insists that such independence is "not practical for a woman, specially a Muslim girl. She is weak both bodily and mentally and should be kept under restrictions." His son, however, blames the male monopoly on "freedom" (114). Such conversations, set-pieces in which ideas of change are debated, are very important to the reformist motivation of this novel, although they are far more occasional than those that range over the tussles, slights, and duties that comprise women's lives.

Kabeer's disappointment in his second wife leads him to consider another, this time "a girl of his choice" (126). Maghbool, his third wife, is educated and a poet, skilled at accounts, needlework, and painting, but she is twenty years old and beyond the socially acceptable age of marriage. She is shocked when her father accepts a proposal from a twice-married man only because he is propertied but understands that refusing this marriage will mean going "against the established dogmas" (142). Her mother offers no sympathy either. At moments like these, *Purdah and Polygamy* makes clear that a girl's education is no guarantee against her being treated, on both social and theological grounds, as a liability in her natal home. These are convictions shared across generations and internalized by vulnerable young women including Maghbool. Nazni is furious at Kabeer's third marriage, but she realizes, as do all the women, that she must "yield and adjust herself to the circumstances" (180). Once Maghbool discovers Dilkusha's miseries, she accuses her father of having transferred her from "a semi-prison to a real one" (191). He is amused by her anger and responds with commonplaces about ideal female behavior. Inevitably, Kabeer is challenged by Maghbool's intelligence and begins to dislike her. He is particularly peeved that Maghbool writes and publishes poetry (using income arranged by her father).

At the end of *Purdah and Polygamy*, Kabeer dies after witnessing the injuries to his son Akram, who is beaten up because of his friendship with an Anglo-Indian employee, Rose. At Kabeer's deathbed, his family discovers that he has taken a fourth wife, Noorjehan, the young granddaughter of a tenant who owes him rent. Maghbool leaves the house in protest, and Zuhra dies not long after. The closing sentences of the novel tell us that, finally, "Nazni achieved the coveted position" of senior woman in the house, and "Munira and Noorjehan being helpless lived under Nazni's regime" (310). This dispiriting conclusion suggests little alleviation of the ugliness that has marked the lives of the women of Dilkusha.

Purdah and Polygamy is deeply political in its insistence on identifying two socio-religious practices – purdah and polygyny – that deny women individuality and rights, but the novel is unwilling, or unable, to delineate improved futures. Maghbool leaves, and presumably continues to write and publish, but Hussain offers no vignettes of emancipated lives. In her own life, Hussain had traversed the vast distance between purdah, early marriage, and partial education to the wider worlds of international education, travel, and nationalist social and political advocacy, but that trajectory finds no parallel in her novel. Jessica Berman has argued, sensitively, that the novel shows that "women need not leave the zenana to raise concerns of national import and that their emerging modernity develops by way of their participation in traditional sites and rhetorical practices" (143). However, the problem is that *Purdah and Polygamy* suggests none of the highly visible contemporary currents of "emerging modernity" (Gandhian and progressive politics, Westernized education, movements for social reform) then changing the Hyderabadi and Indian public and domestic spheres and thereby reads as a *cri de coeur* about the forms of women's oppression rather than a novel that locates possibilities of change in an India mobilizing against colonialism, or indeed in parallel energies and relations within the household. It may well be that Hussain's observational realism was so scrupulous that she could not, in 1944, see progressive change in the public sphere altering the traditionalism of a *rentier* family, whose properties, the diminishing remnants of a feudal inheritance, insulated them from contact with modernizing political or professional energies in Hyderabad or in India.[2]

Women Outside the Home

In contrast, the characters who populate two novels by Zeenuth Futehally and Attia Hosain are aware of and shaped by socio-political change. Their lives are marked by historically representative debates and antagonisms, and their hesitations and triumphs follow from such engagement. These are Muslim women and men who shape the future of their families, communities, and nations (the idea of Pakistan becomes a reality), and they are energetic, vital, and forward-looking. These novels understand that the future of any community is intertwined with the drive toward nationhood, and even when they tell love stories of family relations, they derive their narrative energy from the power of anti-colonial political movements as they swirl around and into domestic spaces. Zeenuth Futehally's *Zohra* (1951) is a remarkable portrait of a girl growing into adulthood, marriage, and the discovery of a life outside the home. It charts her love for and differences with her husband, and then her great and unconsummated desire for her husband's brother. The novel is notable for sections that show both her response to the attentions of men other than her husband and her struggles to maintain her commitment to her marriage. These experiences are treated with great sensitivity and seriousness, and, in doing so, the narrative normalizes female desire (no small achievement in a novel then or now).[3]

Zohra belongs to an aristocratic Hyderabadi family (her mother traces her ancestry to the Mughal emperors) who fled Delhi after the British took power in 1857 and moved to Hyderabad, which retained "some vestige of Muslim rule and culture" (Futehally 12).[4] The narrative points out that Hyderabadi culture has become "a fusion of Hindu and Muslim, the philosophic and the poetic," to which is "now added a more vital stream from the West – the scientific" (11). Futehally deftly makes the education of women one fulcrum of the difficulties and promise of "modernization" that her novel explores. Zohra's father encourages her education, much to her mother's chagrin, for she believes that "learned girls never settle down happily to married life" (13). He enables his daughter to learn English, for it is the "gateway to modern thought" (14). Zohra grows up in purdah, but her education makes her a suitable bride for a man who will not keep his wife secluded. She resists proposals for an early marriage, and, in a sign of the times, her desire for independence is articulated in terms of her desire to work with Mahatma Gandhi, or perhaps to "find shelter" with Rabindranath Tagore in Shantiniketan, "the center of the revival of national culture" (38). She hopes that such an adventure might lead her to a man to "really fall in love with" (39) but realizes that she cannot possibly cause her parents emotional distress by breaking away. This sense of familial obligation is a crucial determinant of Zohra's life, as is the twinning of desire with the political energies of nationalism.

Zohra is married to Bashir, who has been educated in England and is an academic committed to science education. He is taken by her beauty and shyness, which leads him to think: "whatever else might be said against the purdah system – and there was much – it certainly enhanced feminine appeal to a remarkable degree" (71). Zohra moves to his home, where she meets Bashir's traditionalist mother and his very fashionable sister Safia, whose activities match those of her husband, a Westernized bureaucrat. Bashir makes clear that he too wishes his wife to accompany him outside the house; for him, this is part of the "revolution of thought, revolution of methods, revolution of systems" that he believes scientific advance has brought to Europe. When Zohra asks him if revolution is not what Gandhi is bringing to India, he says that he has lost faith in Gandhi's methods, as they are too slow moving (83). Not long after they are married, Bashir takes her off to Mussoorie on a delayed honeymoon.

Mussoorie marks Zohra's entry into the world but also the discovery of her differences with Bashir. She is more observant than he is (he does not pray) and more spiritual in her responses: where he sees mountains valuable for their minerals, she sees natural beauty. For Bashir, a modernizing India cannot afford mysticism and spirituality, which are versions of superstition; for Zohra, Gandhi's "soul force" brings the spiritual and the political together (93). A novelist less canny than Futehally might have allowed this debate to be couched in terms that enact the conventional gender divide between "scientific" man and "spiritual" woman. Here, by contrast, both lay claim to different contemporary conceptions of a national future and of the methods appropriate to its achievement. Remarkably for novels at this time, when husband and wife quarrel, they are equally articulate, and they argue about ideas! It becomes increasingly clear how many of Zohra's ideas are connected to the work of nationalist poets and thinkers. As she continues to engage the world around her, her responses are honed both by her understanding of women's subordination as well as by her intellectual commitment to nationalist ideals.

Mussoorie and its social freedoms precipitate in Zohra another kind of awakening, that of sexual desire outside of marriage. She warms to a young man named Siraj, whom she sees as "so irresponsibly charming and ... such a change from her serious husband, that she could not help being attracted" (99). What begins in flirtation turns more serious when Siraj asks her to elope with him. Zohra confesses that all of this is "new and bewildering" but refuses (107). Even as Bashir senses something, he maintains a distance, as he feels that jealousy is not "worthy" (112). He does bring Siraj up later, and Zohra admits her attraction but says that it now "belongs to the past" (112). Bashir's controlled, even impersonal, response bothers Zohra, even as she is grateful for his affection. Once again, quite remarkably for its moment, the novel makes clear that she is not contrite, and in fact emphasizes the maturity of experience and "self-confidence" (112) Zohra gains from Siraj's attention.

Zohra's growing independence of mind, as well as her fierce affective bond with her first child, cause her to rail against patriarchal divorce laws, which grant a father automatic custody: she tells an uncomprehending Bashir that if men had wanted to put "a woman into bondage, there could have been no heavier chains to bind her down. For the sake of her child, a woman would hold onto her husband, even if she disliked him a thousand times" (140–1). For Futehally, women's personal experiences can lead to political insights, and the novel offers a powerful refutation of the traditional insistence on the divide between the home and the world. Zohra's maturity is a product of both her domestic and her public engagements; indeed, her radical insights are generated from her meditations upon the place of women within the family. She is also attuned to changes in her world – following Gandhi's call, Zohra buys khadi saris, which she thinks "look so pure ... as if they have a soul" (146).

Her soulfulness is what finally distances her from Bashir, as does the arrival of his younger brother Hamid from his studies in England. Whereas Bashir has a technocratic understanding of India's myriad social problems and their solution, which is European science, Hamid, aware of the role of scientific advance in enabling war, believes that a Gandhian "revolution" addresses both social and spiritual concerns. As Bashir develops his professional career, Hamid – to his mother's dismay – opens a bookshop that stocks "leftist literature" that will, as Bashir puts it dismissively, "undermine our youth with your impractical ideas, and help to create chaos and disorder." Hamid argues that he accepts none "of the prevalent *isms*" but believes in freedom of thought and action. "Regimentation of spirit is intolerable," he insists, and he believes that Gandhian principles will help "evolve a way of our own" that includes a sense of the beauty of life itself (169). Zohra, not surprisingly, is attracted by Hamid's questing spirit.

The second half of *Zohra* develops into a tale of complex desires, particularly as Zohra comes to admire Hamid's world, his progressive friends, and his desire to identify with his surroundings. They share conversations about art, history, and contemporary politics, and she finds herself both "thrilled and alarmed" by her feelings for him (215). She says nothing to him, until one day he tells her he loves her. Her own joyful response courses like sunlight through her body: "To Zohra it was as if all her life she had waited to hear those three simple words from Hamid's lips. They were like the 'open sesame' to the meaning of life for her" (244). "I feel I have loved you all my life," she tells Hamid, and they enter a phase of liminal happiness, "like care-free children, happy in their newly-acquired joy" (247). Both Hamid and Zohra are caught between desire and obligation. She struggles to understand their love as "the expression of one's deeper self," "the ecstasy of the heart," but he recognizes the impossibility of spending time together without becoming physically intimate (248).

Futehally's narrative allows Hamid and Zohra space in which to discuss their feelings and to do so as part of their continuing conversations about the social conventions that govern love and marriage. They do not act on their desire, but their tense and loving conversations allow them to explore personal relations, ethics, and Sufi conceptions of love and belonging. Ironically, Bashir, who once again senses his wife's attraction for another man, this time his brother, responds by attacking Hamid's ideals and politics. In an extraordinary vignette, Bashir insists on debating the difference between Muslim and Hindu society in India and on arguing the grounds of Islamic superiority against Hamid's insistence that both history and Gandhian politics indicate a commonality of cultures and peoples. They furiously debate India's future and that of a Muslim-ruled "independent" state like Hyderabad. Hamid is clear that in a democracy, "Hyderabadi Muslims have no right to rule the Hindu majority," but for Bashir, democracy means that Muslims, "the race of conquerors," must now imagine a future in which they will not "be under the Hindus." Their differences have never been clearer, and Bashir denounces Hamid as having no right to call himself a Muslim. Zohra, stung by his offensive tone, briefly takes Hamid's side, and the conversation ends in a pall of resentment (251–7).

Since the situation has become intolerable for all of them, Hamid chooses to leave the family home to join the Gandhian anti-colonial movement. Zohra is devastated and tells him that if she cannot live with the man she loves she would rather live alone (262–3). Hamid pleads with her to stay with Bashir for the sake of her children and family propriety. Her response is near-blasphemous: "I have not seen God," she says, "but I have seen you." Her conclusion is as despairing as it is pointed, and it sums up one of the central insights of the novel: "There must be something wrong with our moral code or with the laws of nature" (265). In an effort to repair his relationship with Zohra, Bashir takes her to Europe, where he encourages her to use cosmetics, learn dancing, and drink alcohol, all of which he believes will allow them to live at ease there. Zohra begins to enjoy the social scene in Paris until a Frenchman who has squired her about forces himself on her. That ugly moment prompts grave self-examination and she decides to give up on her newly-fashionable self and return to Hyderabad and home.

Through Bashir, Hamid, and Zohra, Futehally explores the participation of Muslim elites in civic and political life and the passage of women into the public sphere. Bashir is appointed vice-chancellor of his university; Hamid writes a novel that furthers his reformist agenda; Zohra, moved by the plight of the poor, becomes a social worker. Her debates with Bashir continue to map the dynamism of change in 1930s India. However, in 1935, Zohra, who works with the plague-struck poor, contracts it herself. She sickens into a slow decline. Bashir eventually sends for Hamid, knowing that his presence will bring her cheer. Hamid's company allows Zohra to meditate on the passions that have defined her life and to recognize the strength of her feelings for both men. Before she dies, she makes Hamid promise that he will marry and also make sure that her daughter Shahedah is allowed to choose her husband (and thus a life different from her mother's).

Independence and Partition

Attia Hosain's *Sunlight on a Broken Column* (1961) is, like Futehally's *Zohra*, a novel that determinedly connects the home with the world and traces, in the lives of women, pathways of social change. Hosain writes of the differing fortunes of an extended taluqdari family (the taluqdars were the landowning gentry of Awadh in north-central India) and expands her canvas to include the many servants and retainers whose labor and devotion made their lives extremely comfortable. The patriarch of this family, Syed

Mohammad Hasan (Baba Jan), socializes with other Hindu and Muslim taluqdars, whose wealth and authority support all kinds of feudal excesses, but also with an English lawyer who has interests in Sanskrit, Persian, and Arabic and lives like an Indian aristocrat. Other men in the family are similarly cultured, if not as elite: for instance Mohsin, a landowner himself, does no work, believes women should know their limits, and thinks it his right to ignore his wife, visit dancing girls in the city, and seduce vulnerable servant girls. Baba Jan, influenced by late nineteenth-century ideas of reform, had educated his sons in English universities, and Hamid, his older son, is a bureaucrat in the Indian Civil Service – so thoroughly Anglicized that, as his niece puts it, when "he came home it was like meeting a stranger masquerading as one of the family" (Hosain 86). He is at odds with Baba Jan's world, an inheritor of its male privileges but indifferent to its traditional forms and rituals. He grooms his wife and children out of orthodoxy and into his own image of modernity.

Hosain describes a privileged world, deeply conservative at the same time as it is cosmopolitan, but mobile enough culturally and politically to allow some of the younger women in the family access to advanced education not only in Urdu, Persian, and Arabic but also English. However, the education of women is a source of tension, and the novel opens with a quick contrast between fifteen-year old Laila, the "bookworm" (14), and her cousin Zahra, who, in her mother's words, is ready for marriage, as she "has read the Quran ... knows her religious duties ... [and] can sew and cook, and at the Muslim School she learned a little English, which is what the young men want now" (24).[5] Hosain stages contentious family discussions about the education of girls, appropriate dress codes, and the proprieties of arranged marriage in order to show that change is coming, surely but unevenly, to these lives. It is not only what happens outside the home that matters; within, the way that women conduct themselves – the volume of their voices and laughter, their subservience to men and their opinions, the diligence with which they maintain purdah – is an index of their acceptance of or challenge to normative notions of femininity. Laila's unmarried aunt Abida, herself a well-read scholar of poetry, supervises Laila's education but makes it clear that the "traditions of the family" are never to be forgotten (39).

As she grows into adulthood, Laila's political sympathies turn nationalist as she sees satyagrahis being beaten by the police. From older cousins she learns about divergent political and religious affiliations among Muslims but also about Russian communism. She is sent to a women's college and becomes part of a cohort of students who are caught up in politics. Nita Chatterji speaks for a newly professionalizing class of Hindu women who believe in anti-colonial activism; Nadira, who is staunch in her Muslim faith, fears the coming of what she can only think of as Hindu rule; Joan is an Anglo-Indian who believes in the "rightness and greatness of the British Empire" (Hosain 126). Laila is uncertain about her politics but reacts sharply against social injunctions that vilify a Muslim girl from her college who eloped with a Hindu boy, was abandoned by him and both his and her families, and eventually committed suicide; Laila defies her aunt by insisting that the girl was "*not* wicked" (133) but had acted for love. Moments like this cause Laila to become increasingly intolerant of social hypocrisies and to feel rebellious – but without, she acknowledges, "an outlet" (139).

Hosain's novelistic method personalizes political events and issues and brings them home, with public transitions energizing private conversations and events: each social gathering Laila attends becomes, as she puts it, a mirror of the contentious world and of conflicting values (176). Political actions now take center stage in the novel. Police crack down on a student protest against the visiting viceroy, and Laila's cousin Asad is wounded. Nita Chatterji is also beaten and dies two days later. For Laila, Nita's death is "a martyrdom" (166), but she herself, in adherence to her uncle's wishes, stays away from such activism. The world of the taluqdars is changing too as older forms of authority give way to new business elites. Elections are held, and they precipitate sharper differences between Muslims and Hindus; when the Congress sweeps the elections, the taluqdars fear reforms that will disempower landowners like themselves (262).

Change is coming, but older divisions hold. Laila's cousin Kemal and a Hindu friend Sita were in love while they were both students in London and dealt with English racism against "coloured people" (178), but once home, Sita refuses to marry a Muslim. Laila falls in love with Ameer Hussain, a university lecturer in history, even though her aunt Saira considers him unsuitable, as his mother's family are "ordinary people" with "no breeding" (199). The social circle of these cousins and their friends fragments as new political and personal differences surface between them and between children and parents. Laila, now twenty, inhabits a changed world from the one she knew as a fifteen-year old. She still values older rituals and courtesies but knows that very different notions of personal desire, citizenship, and nationality are ascendant.

Hosain tells the end of her story in retrospect: in 1952, Laila returns on a farewell visit to her childhood home and meditates on the last fifteen years. Urban development has now swallowed the estates surrounding her family home. Independence comes with the "putrescent culmination, the violent orgasm of hate" (283) that was Partition. Once Uncle Hamid dies, his heir Saleem moves to Pakistan, which allows the government to classify their ancestral home as "evacuee property" and take it over. The family is divided as Saleem's brother Kemal and his mother choose to stay. Partition casts a long shadow over Muslims in India, their loyalties and faith open to challenge, even those who are committed to the only home they know. As before, Hosain registers the scale and violence of political events by personalizing them – for, as Laila observes bitterly, Partition has reduced millions of uprooted human lives to numerical figures (272).

As Laila reflects on these enormous changes, we learn that she had, in the face of family opposition, married Ameer in 1937. They had been happy together and lived in the company of poets, writers, and political theorists who, like themselves, did not have much but were full of progressive ideas and energy. After the birth of their daughter, Shahla (who is now fourteen), Ameer joined the wartime army, was taken prisoner, and killed while trying to escape. Laila had been helped through her grief by Asad, who, as a Congress activist, had been jailed, worked with the poor and then with refugee populations, and now was moving up the party hierarchy in Delhi. Still single, he has let Laila know that he has long cared for her. In the poignant yet hopeful closing of the novel, as Laila sits in the home that is now a marker of a lost past, he comes to meet her and hears her say, "I have been waiting for you, Asad. I am ready to leave now" (319). A more egalitarian, democratic future lies ahead.

Each of the three novels discussed here dramatizes for us the contested issues that defined ideas of women's emancipation within the Muslim family and, by extension, in the world at large. *Purdah and Polygamy* interrogates the social norms and theological sanctions that constrict women's lives; *Zohra* and *Sunlight on a Broken Column* ask similar questions but with a confidence in new possibilities opened up by the entry of women into public spaces and by the remaking of these spaces by anticolonial nationalists. These two novels are deeply concerned with appropriate forms of national belonging and of citizenship, and each sees the emancipation of women as a foundational necessity for both political and personal demands for freedom. Both Futehally's and Hosain's idiom and their storytelling methods derive from their immersion into the intricacies of relationships within families, and their novels are energized by the worldly vocabularies in which historical and political change were articulated in the lead-up to national independence. They are wonderful accounts of the ways in which Muslim women and men (but not only Muslim women and men) forged the modernity of mid-twentieth century India; indeed, it is very much the case that each novel is a signal intervention in that political, intellectual, and creative process.

Notes

1 Hussain's life was an instantiation of her belief that education was the key to the emancipation of women, and that men must allow women "to take an active part in the educational, social, and economical activities of their community.... Regeneration of the Muslim nation is possible only when its women are educated, and are made efficient and independent" (*Changing* 23).

2 In its representation of a remarkably insular mode of living, *Purdah and Polygamy* parallels Ahmed Ali's *Twilight in Delhi* (1940): it has only three non-Muslim characters, all Christians, just as Ali's novel mentions precisely one Hindu, a Dr. Mittra. Ali's novel is written in a very different idiom, of course, but it too despairs that the diminishing ashraf culture of Delhi it mourns can offer no political opposition to the British or generate any reformist energy against the myriad corruptions that bedevil the community.

3 For a supple analysis of the novel, see Hai, "Adultery."

4 The novel was reissued in a corrected edition by Rummana Futehally Denby (Delhi: Oxford University Press, 2004), but these "corrections" occasionally dilute the force of the original. For instance, the phrase I quote above is reduced to "some vestige of Muslim culture" (9).

5 Not surprisingly, once Zahra is married to a more Anglicized husband, she learns to play "the part of the perfect modern wife as she had once played the part of the dutiful purdah girl" (140). In this, she fulfills her primary obligation to be as her husband wishes.

CHAPTER 9

Found in Translation: Self, Caste, and Other in Three Modern Texts

Rashmi Sadana

One cannot be for or against modernity; one can only devise strategies for coping with it.

– Partha Chatterjee, *Our Modernity* (p. 19)

Translation in the Indian Context

Speaking at a "Translating India" conference at the Sahitya Akademi (India's National Academy of Letters) in 2001, the celebrated Kannada writer U. R. Anantha Murthy began with this provocation: "Which work is worth translating? It should be a book *not written to be translated*. People have begun to write to be translated – a bad tendency. A work should belong deeply to its own culture, and a writer should have no consciousness of the reader. A writer should be speaking to herself."[1] Anantha Murthy was critiquing the tendency he saw among bhasha (literally meaning "tongue," and the colloquial term used to refer to Indian languages *other* than English) writers who feel they must be translated into English to be recognized. It is the effect this realization has on the writing process that disturbed him, akin to the internal colonialism that has long plagued the Indian elite. If a writer's very interiority becomes compromised by this realization, what then will be the consequences for literary art? What he prescribed at the conference was for writers to use their language in a way that would require people to learn the original language to read the work. It is this type of writing, he argued – "the untranslatable work" – that is a worthwhile task for the translator. A work should be thoroughly immersed in the worldview of the original language; it should strive to be fully of that world as experienced and understood by the author. It should be so steeped in that world that when it *is* translated, English itself should gain the qualities of the source language.

147

It is in this respect that I see all translations of Indian novels into English as a contribution to Indian writing in English and not merely translated texts. Translations originate with a non-English language vision of the world, but the process of translating brings that vision into the English language and in conversation with an Indian English worldview, transmitting the qualities, as it were, of the source language.[2] What is lost in translation is found in English, even if that original worldview gets altered. English is part of a multilingual sphere, allowing Indians not only – as in colonial times – to "look outward," or, as a language of the elite, to "look inward" and create Indian English texts; English also enables a "looking across" to other Indian literary modernities. English takes from these modernities, in Bengali, Kannada, and Hindi, as will be demonstrated here, as well as in other bhashas that get translated into English. And in the process of the translation of thousands of bhasha texts into English, which often enables translations of texts between bhasha languages as well (from Tamil to Bengali via English, for instance), English has become India's literary link language. It is also, through English translation, that an *Indian* literary canon has come into being.

Nevertheless, translation in the Indian context has been vexed, to say the least. Perhaps it could not be otherwise, considering there are twenty-two official languages and little institutional support for the translating enterprise. As a result, the quality of translation tends to be poor, often too literal without being literary, diminishing the original work in the process and, most unfortunately, enabling English-language readers to believe these works and literary cultures may be dismissed. Yet after independence, the Sahitya Akademi was instituted precisely to enable an Indian literature to emerge from the country's rich and diverse linguistic strands. Its mandate was not to publish translations in English but rather to promote Indian languages *other* than English.[3] This slighting of English made sense after 150 years of British rule; however, English was also a unifying language, especially for the highly literate, so in fact English became necessary for the very promotion of Indian literature in languages other than English.[4]

Most, if not all, Indians are multilingual, with Hindi being the most common link language in terms of casual conversation. However, for the highly literate and educated, it is not uncommon to read English as well, since the colonial education system privileged this language from the mid-nineteenth century onward, and the postcolonial state continued this practice. English was and is the language of upward mobility, and that has not changed to this day – although who vies for English has.

Translation is also an index of which books become canonized. The more languages a text is translated into, the further its geographic reach and the more celebrated the work and its author. This question of reach, of who gets to read texts and how far they are from the author's domicile, has been central in the construction of what we think of today as global literature. Indians have, since the mid-nineteenth century, seen English as a "window to the world," and that has been true for the elites, including writers, most of all. The Urdu writer Ahmed Ali went as far as to admit in the preface to his 1940 novel *Twilight in Delhi* that he wrote it in English rather than Urdu precisely so that people beyond the mountains that encircled his home would read it (A. Ali, *Twilight* xvi). In thinking about Indian novels in translation vis-à-vis the Indian novel in English, I would argue that bhasha writing is key to understanding Indian modernity in terms of the social issues being addressed, the mindsets being explored, and the literary "solutions" provided. In this chapter, I consider three English translations – of a Bengali novel, a Kannada novella, and a Hindi autobiography – which all went on to become modern classics, largely due to their life after English translation.[5] There has been a long debate about whether bhasha texts are better able to reveal the complexities and nuances of Indian social realities – for instance, more than their counterparts originally written in English. I won't get into those debates here, but instead hope to show how these three works illuminate the daily life of caste close to the grain of non-English thought-worlds and experiences.[6] By looking at how caste is rendered in bhasha literature in three distinct periods (nationalist, post-colonial, liberalized), this analysis is meant to highlight just what it is – in terms of form, content, style – that is brought into English, but also the significance of translation to the life of the text.

The first text is *Gora* (a colloquial term for "fair" or "whitey") by the grand man of Indian letters, Rabindranath Tagore (1861–1941). The novel was published in Bengali in 1909, and a somewhat stodgy English translation by an unnamed translator was published by London's Macmillan and Co. in 1924. *Gora* was retranslated by literary critic Sujit Mukherjee (1930–2003) and published by the Sahitya Akademi in 1997.[7] The second novel is *Samskara* by U. R. Anantha Murthy (1932–2014), published in Kannada in 1965; the scholar-poet A. K. Ramanujan's (1929–93) English translation of it appeared in 1976. Both Tagore and Anantha Murthy are Brahmin writers, and their two respective novels revolve around questions of brahminical culture and identity, although in very different ways. *Gora* is about the nineteenth-century social reform movement the Brahmo Samaj, and it is a story of incipient Indian nationalism in the face of Western influences. The central character is an Irish orphan who is unaware of his true origins, despite his fair skin – hence, a *gora*. *Samskara* is about a Brahmin caught in the immorality of his own desires and the deep casteism of his village in the early to mid-twentieth century. The novella is steeped in traditional mindsets and the violent disjunctures built into those traditions. The third text is by Omprakash Valmiki (1950–2013): an autobiography entitled *Joothan*, which was published in 1997 and translated from the Hindi by the English professor Arun Prabha Mukherjee (b. 1946).[8] "Joothan" means "leftovers" and refers to the refuse – literally the leftovers on a plate of food – sometimes allotted to India's historically lowest social stratum, the Dalits, by upper castes who believe they are spiritually, morally, and socially cleaner and superior to them. The story is unsentimentally recounted in the first person by a Dalit writer, and its power is in line with the traditions of slave narratives and anti-apartheid literature. It is the ordinary, everyday social exclusion of Dalits that is highlighted in Valmiki's text, along with the narrator's deep sense of resentment and betrayal by caste Hindu society. What stands out in viewing the English translations of these three texts is how each work transforms the question of caste for its time by linking it to the formation of a fluid, modern individual identity, subject to interpretation. Further, there is a movement between the texts, as the qualities and nature of caste change in terms of the kinds of existential struggles we see in the protagonists. In *Gora*, Tagore links upper-caste identity to nationalism, while in *Samskara*, Anantha Murthy unveils the hypocrisies of village social hierarchies on the cusp of modernity. In *Joothan*, Valmiki rejects canonical literary pretension altogether by offering an alternate yet parallel vision of life in Hindi.

Colonial Modernity in Tagore's *Gora*

Although we see the Indian novel in English as India's projection of elite understandings of its own modernity, India's literary modernity – in its most complex forms – takes first expression in its bhasha literatures. How could it be otherwise, considering it was bhasha intellectuals who had to wrangle with modernity's impact on their own languages and literary traditions?[9] Tagore's *Gora*, originally published in 1909, is one such novel. The fact that it was re-translated in the 1990s is also a signal of its importance to contemporary issues, especially concerning the place of disadvantaged groups (including Muslims and Dalits) in the face of rising Hindu nationalism. Gora's question, "Who is an Indian?" is all the more resonant after the lead-up to and destruction of the Babri Masjid in December 1992, the rise of the Bharatiya Janata Party (BJP), and the massacre of Muslims in Gujarat in 2002.[10] Sujit Mukherjee notes that the 1924 English translation of *Gora* was both unrivaled for seventy-three years and deemed by Bengalis a terrible translation. Yet the 1924 translation of the novel was reprinted fifteen times between 1924 and 1976, attesting to its resonance with English-language readers. Mukherjee's own 1997 English translation of *Gora* had three reprints within its first five years of publication (S. Mukherjee 100). Its continuous readership speaks to the fact that the relationship between Hinduism and nationalism still pivots on the caste question.

Gora is set in the upper middle-class bourgeois milieu of colonial Calcutta, in the part of the country that first had to deal with the questions of self and modernity when its religions were under siege and its cultural practices and traditions denigrated by foreigners – while at the same time, its elites were gaining exposure to new ideas and ways of being. *Gora* captures the anxiety and possibility of this era from the perspective of its urban elite.

Nearly 500 pages long and recounted in seventy-five short chapters, *Gora* often reads like a play, a living room drama of ideas.[11] It is the story of the Irish orphan (unbeknownst to him), Gaurmohan or Gora, who is raised by orthodox Brahmins to uphold tradition and stringent caste observances, whereby birth dictates levels of purity and pollution and the rules of commensality to be followed for one's entire life. This ironic setup – an outcaste's devotion to caste – is played out through Gora's relationship to a Brahmo Samajist[12] family and his growing friendship with the daughter of that household, Sucharita. What makes Gora compelling to some is that he is devoted not merely to caste but to nation, and for most of the novel he is convinced that the latter is dependent on the former.

Gora is firstly a novel of manners and is a paean to companionate marriage, as the questions of who one is and what one believes become central to the matter of who should and should not be paired off together. Social manners become avenues of expressing one's beliefs, identity, and essence. In an early scene in the novel – of middle-class tea drinking – the issue of who will take food from whom initiates a core debate about caste and modernity as the orthodox Gora stands his ground in the free-tea-drinking Brahmo household he has come to visit:

> After Sucharita had poured several cups of tea, she looked towards Poresh Babu for guidance. She was not certain about whom to offer tea and

whom not. Baradasundari had no such compunctions and addressed Gora bluntly: "I don't suppose you will have any of these things."

"No," said Gora unceremoniously.

BARADA: Why? Will you lose caste?

GORA: Yes.

BARADA: Then you believe in caste distinction.

GORA: I didn't create caste distinction, so it doesn't depend on my belief. But I do believe in it since I also abide by the belief of my community.

BARADA: Must you follow the community in everything?

GORA: Not to follow the community means breaking it up.

BARADA: What harm can there be in breaking it?

GORA: No more harm than there is in chopping off the branch on which we are all sitting. (Tagore, *Gora* 51)

The crux of Gora's argument is not only about caste but also about how caste and nation are interlinked. By the time Tagore is writing, the Indian nationalist movement has become an anti-colonial one, but Indians are still very much at odds about how to assert their cultural identity – as a regressive Hinduism in spite of modern influences or as a reform- ist culture bringing in "the best of both worlds" to create a new, third way forward? It is this possible opening in Gora himself where Sucharita will come to have respect and love for him, even though, as a Brahmo Samajist, she is against caste discriminations. For Gora, it is his friendship with the liberal-minded Hindu Binoy, and ultimately the influence of his adoptive mother, Anandamoyi, who rejects orthodoxy, that punctures his self-assuredness. He also comes to question the sycophants who follow him and is ultimately faced with the reality of his own identity.

Thus, in the novel, individual identity is continually linked to a strug- gle for national consciousness. This struggle plays out as a debate between orthodox revivalism and liberal reformism. This debate, as Sudipta Kaviraj has argued, is in fact a "conceptual translation problem" at the heart of *Gora*, which does not refer to the novel's linguistic translation but rather concerns the "problem of tolerance between neighbouring communities who share a social world" ("Languages" 101). Throughout, Tagore reveals the self not as a static thing but as a process of discovery. Ultimately, the inner form of the novel is a process of an individual's journeying toward himself. Yet, as Meenakshi Mukherjee observes, "Meaning in this novel lies not in individual utterances, but in their dialogical negotiations" (Introduction xi). In this respect, the novel itself becomes a mediator between modernity and tradition. Ultimately, the novel is a repudiation of caste distinctions, as it attempts to forge an Indian nationalism free from notions of difference. In English translation, the sense of urgency in the novel to create a pan-Indian identity becomes at once more intense and more illusory.

Brahminism as the Anti-Modern in Anantha Murthy's *Samskara*

The questions of community and the inner violence of caste are at the heart of U. R. Anantha Murthy's *Samskara*. As Ramanujan points out in the afterword to his translation, the book was not well received in all quarters, especially among south Indian Brahmins (Afterword 146). Ramanujan himself has been known and heralded as a translator who brought the bhasha traditions of classical India to a wider audience and brought much distinction to them as a result. The fact that *Samskara*'s English translation has been a mainstay of syllabi on Hinduism in the United States in particular certainly has something to do with the fact that Ramanujan was based at the University of Chicago for the bulk of his career. Books not only emerge from institutions (publishers in particular), but they also often travel because of them (in this case, universities). Institutional associations, often linked to known individuals, become not only markers of distinction but also *bearers* of distinction.

Samskara is the story of how the death of one man, a childless Brahmin called Naranappa, puts his fellow Brahmins in a moral quandary about who should perform his last rites. Naranappa had defied his brahmin-ness by all forms of licentious, and, according to the Hindu upper-caste schema, sacrilegious behavior – which included abandoning his Brahmin wife and living with his low-caste mistress, Chandri – all in a Brahmin colony (*agrahara*) in an early to mid-twentieth century village in Karnataka. The setup betrays the deep modernity of the novel, which is a moral questioning of identity and existence. If *Gora* questions, and ultimately rejects, a brahminical (Vedic) past as the sole basis for a modern Indian identity, *Samskara* questions a brahminical present that is in fact opposed to the very creation of a modern Indian identity and yet must acquiesce to it.

Naranappa's doppelganger is Praneshacharya – the Brahmin who must ultimately figure out a material and spiritual response to the problem set before his community by the dead man. What soon becomes clear is that where Naranappa's life left off, Praneshacharya must not merely pick up the pieces of that life but, in a fashion, continue it as his own. As in *Gora*, this short novel recounts the inner struggle of one man and his coming to terms with the nature of his own identity. Praneshacharya sees the challenge for what it is in the novella's opening pages, as he considers the dilemma of Naranappa's life and death in an address to his fellow Brahmins:

> That he's a smear on the good name of the agrahara, it's a deep question – I have no clear answer. For one thing, he may have rejected brahminhood, but brahminhood never left him. No one ever excommunicated him officially. He didn't die an outcaste; so he remains a brahmin in his death. Only another brahmin has any right to touch his body. If we let someone else do it, we'd be sullying our brahminhood. Yet I hesitate, I can't tell you dogmatically: go ahead with the rite. I hesitate because you've all seen the way he lived. What shall we do? What do the Law Books really say, is there any real absolution for such violations? (*Samskara* 9)

Praneshacharya's questioning may be contrasted with Chandri's certitude after seeing Naranappa's dead body:

> Chandri came out without a word. What was she going to do? Only one thought burned clear: it's rotting there, that thing, it's stinking there, its belly swollen. That's not her lover, Naranappa. It's neither brahmin nor shudra. A carcass. A stinking rotting carcass. (70)

Praneshacharya will delve into the questions he poses as he comes to be faced with some of the similar choices as Naranappa, especially regarding his own lust and desire for Chandri. Praneshacharya's struggle is not about whether to uphold traditions but, more specifically, whether to keep following self-discipline; in this way, tradition is something very personal and subject to failure and regret. And it is this questioning that is indicative of a modern sensibility; Brahminism here represents the anti-modern in that it does not recommend such questioning. Near the end of the book, Praneshacharya torments himself as follows:

> But if I don't tell the agrahara brahmins, if Naranappa's body is not properly cremated, I cannot escape fear. If I decide to live with Chandri without telling anyone, the decision is not complete, not fearless. I must come now to a final decision. All things indirect must become direct. Must pierce straight in the eye. But it's agony either way. If I hide things, all through life I'll be agonized by the fear of discovery, by some onlooking eye. If I don't, I'll muddy the lives of others by opening up and exposing the truth to the very eyes my brahminhood has lived and grown by. Have I the authority to include another's life in my decision? The pain of it, the cowardice of it. O God, take from me the burden of decision. (132)

As Ramanujan points out in his afterword, we only see Praneshacharya in a liminal state in the novella – a state of questioning and continually mutating rather than arriving or deciding (143). For Ramanujan, this state is where the allegorical character of Praneshacharya – a Brahmin type – confronts the realism of the text, referring to the complex, layered, changing social reality laid out by Anantha Murthy. Ramanujan, who as a poet and scholar brought both literary and academic skills to bear on his translation, states in his translator's note that "a translator hopes not only to translate a text, but ... to translate a non-native reader into a native one" ("Translator's" viii). In this respect, the translation of the novella is complete, even if its characters' journeys may not be.

The Rise of a Modern Dalit Consciousness in Valmiki's *Joothan*

The story of *Joothan*'s publication is contained in the text itself. It compellingly details Omprakash Valmiki's coming into a Dalit consciousness but also the practicalities involved in moving from the world of scavengers to the world of Hindi letters. Here, self-questioning takes on myriad forms as the narrator moves out from his community. The autobiography details the humiliations faced by the narrator growing up in a Chuhra community – describing poverty but, more profoundly, what it felt like to be at the bottom of the social hierarchy. In the opening pages, the narrator says, "There was muck strewn everywhere. The stench was so overpowering that one would choke within a minute. The pigs wandering in narrow lanes, naked children, dogs, daily fights" (Valmiki 1). But then, more damningly, he observes:

> We would often have to work without pay. Nobody dared to refuse this unpaid work for which we got neither money nor grain. Instead, we got sworn at and abused.... The Chuhras were not seen as human. They were simply things for use. Their utility lasted until the work was done. Use them and then throw them away. (2)

As the narrator moves out of his community and engages with broader Hindu society, his own consciousness about his place in society takes shape. For instance, the serving of tea in *Gora* reappears in a scene recounted in *Joothan* a century later. Here, the narrator of *Joothan* confronts a friend who has a budding interest in him and who assumes he is a Brahmin:

> Gathering my courage, I said, "That day when Professor Kamble came to your place..."
> Before I could finish Savita interrupted with, "That Mahar... SC [Scheduled Caste]?"

The way she said it made me flush with anger, "Yes, the same..." I replied bitterly.

Surprised, Savita asked, "Why are you thinking of this today?"

My voice hardened, "You had given him tea in a different cup?"

"Yes, the SCs and the Muslims who come to our house, we keep their dishes separate," Savita replied evenly.

"Do you think this discrimination is right?" I asked. She felt the sharp edge in my voice now.

"Oh... why, are you mad? How can we feed them in the same dishes?" (Valmiki 97)

Soon the narrator exposes his Dalit identity to his friend:

I said as plainly as I could that I was born in a Chuhra family of U.P.

Savita appeared grave. Her eyes were filled with tears and she said tearfully, "You are lying, right?"

"No, Savi... it is the truth... you ought to know this." I had convinced her.

She started to cry, as though my being an SC was a crime. She sobbed for a long time. Suddenly the distance between us had increased. The hatred of thousands of years had entered our hearts. (98)

The two never meet again after this episode, which is typical of the kind of everyday disappointments and betrayals that the narrator recounts. Nonetheless, much of the book is about the narrator's appreciation of a growing Dalit consciousness through Marathi Dalit writers and the work of B. R. Ambedkar. The narrator relays his growing political consciousness as follows:

Dr. Ambedkar's life-long struggle had shaken me up. I spent many days and nights in great turmoil. The restlessness inside me had increased. My stone-like silence had suddenly begun to melt. I proceeded to read all of Ambedkar's books that I found in the library.

...

A new word, "Dalit," entered my vocabulary, a word that is not a substitute for "Harijan," but an expression of rage of millions of untouchables. A new direction was opening for me. I was also beginning to realize that the education imparted in schools and colleges did not make us secular but turned us into narrow-minded, fundamentalist Hindus. The deeper I was getting into this literature, the more articulate my rage became. I began to debate with my college friends, and put my doubts before my teachers. (72)

Joothan shows up Hindu caste society for all its prejudices, but it also indicts the divisions between lower castes, including Dalits. The autobiography is thus also a kind of intellectual history.

The very writing and publication of Dalit autobiographies is a political act, and the same could be said for their translations into English. Debjani Ganguly, in her analysis of *Joothan*, further argues that Dalit life narratives are not merely testimonials but rather that the literary aspects of the narratives bestow "personhood" on the suffering Dalit. Translating these texts affirms their worth, for one thing, even as it might strip away the very social oppression contained in the original. Reflecting on her translation, Arun Mukherjee writes that the autobiography uses "the sociolect of the Dalit to describe the degradation of their daily activities," which posed "a problem for the translator in rendering the socially marked differences between the levels of Hindi in English where the Dalit words have no equivalent" (Mukherjee, Mukherjee and Godard 3). For Mukherjee, there are two aspects of the translation – the communicative function and the politics of language – and it is the latter that matters most in the case of translating Dalit literature, since having these texts be part of the canon of postcolonial literature reorients the very parameters of that canon, which had been "previously focused on works by high-caste Indian writers" (3).

I asked Arun Mukherjee what led her to translate *Joothan*.[13] Mukherjee is a professor of English at York University in Toronto, and she told me that she had been dissatisfied with postcolonial studies, how its notion of resistance and struggle was focused on elite narratives fueled almost exclusively by the writings of Mohandas K. Gandhi and Jawaharlal Nehru. When people want to know about caste or oppression, she explained, there is a bias against teaching translations in English departments, so they would rather read the perspectives on these issues by writers such as Mulk Raj Anand, Arundhati Roy, or Vikram Seth – all of whom, in different ways, have written sympathetic portrayals of Dalit characters in their novels.[14] Furthermore, Mukherjee pointed out, Dalit literature in translation works against the main theoretical framework of postcolonial studies, which highlights the problems inherent in the colonizer/colonized relationship rather than homegrown power imbalances and injustices such as those found in caste hierarchies. Thus, Mukherjee had been looking for an "oppositional perspective" in literature. She began with "a faded image of B. R. Ambedkar" from having grown up in India and became motivated, in the 1980s, to look up his works in the library in Toronto. She read Ambedkar's tract on "What Gandhi and Congress have done to the Untouchables," a piece that impacted her hugely because it went against the usual narratives about Gandhi and Nehru as Indian nationalist heroes and icons. It offered a more complex view of how the nationalist movement was in fact an upper-caste movement with upper-caste interests.

Mukherjee narrated to me the development of her own consciousness about oppositional voices and literature. She explained how at that same time in Canada, aboriginal writers were up in arms about white representations of aboriginal life – what were largely romanticized portrayals, more patronizing than political. Aboriginal writers responded by saying, effectively, "Leave the representation to us," in what became an issue of the appropriation of voice. Mukherjee saw parallels to the situation of Dalits in India and wrote to her friend Rajendra Yadav (1929–2013), the Hindi writer and editor of the leading Hindi literary magazine *Hans*. She asked Yadav for recommendations of stories by Dalit writers in Hindi. Yadav told her that Hindi had yet to produce Dalit writers as Marathi had. On subsequent visits to Delhi, Mukherjee would meet with Yadav in his office in Daryaganj; and on one such visit in 1998, he handed her a copy of *Joothan* and said, "Isa purhiya [Read this]." She read it and immediately knew she wanted to translate it. She then contacted Omprakash Valmiki and went to spend three days with him in Dehradun, a city north of Delhi, at the foot of the Himalayas, where he lived. Valmiki was steeped in Ambedkarite thought, and Mukherjee was also coming under the influence of Dr. Ambedkar. Mukherjee herself is a Brahmin – like all the translators mentioned in this chapter – but unlike A. K. Ramanujan and Sujit Mukherjee, she was translating a writer who had the opposite caste identity as her. Her own political consciousness not only led her to the text of *Joothan* but informed her very practice of translation. In her introduction to her translation of *Joothan*, she writes of the importance of self-representation in Dalit literature as a counter to being portrayed by others for too long and of the necessity of the authenticity of Dalit voices based on their own experiences. This, she told me, made her take fewer liberties with the text as she translated it, focusing her energies on staying especially close to the author's voice.

Conclusion

The English translations of *Gora*, *Samskara*, and *Joothan* have had a significant impact on Indian literature and its perception abroad. As I have tried to show in this chapter, this impact has to do with each text's interrogation of the social problem of caste as it relates to modern identity. *Gora* links caste to the question of nationality, an important move to be registered in the English-reading, anti-nationalist, yet often caste-supporting intelligentsia, whether pre- or post-independence. *Samskara*, which I would argue is the most adventurous of the three texts – modernist more than modern in the way it eschews both tradition and modernity – enacts a kind of societal transformation in its very telling. Here, caste is existential dilemma, with an uneasy, labored journey out of village social worlds. *Joothan* is a clear-eyed rejection of the histories of those worlds, yet the narrator is entangled in the present-day consequences of them, frustratingly so, in an already fully modernized world. *Joothan* has contributed not only to the formation of the idea of Dalit literature (first, most centrally in Hindi, and with the English translation, in south India and internationally) but also to the burgeoning academic field of Dalit studies, in some ways similar to the centrality of nineteenth-century slave narratives in African-American studies. Nevertheless, the very question of translating India's bhasha works into English should not only or merely be seen as liberatory.

To return to Anantha Murthy, then, it is clear that other linguistic worldviews must also contribute to the world's so-called universals. As he reminds Indians, "The more literate we are, the fewer languages we know. Consider the south Indian bus depot worker who speaks Kannada, Malayalam, Tamil and a bit of English versus the multinational bureaucrat who knows only English."[15] His example is more a condemnation of monolingualism than of English per se. Thus, he emphasizes that translations of bhasha literatures into English are not only for a distant Anglophone literary audience in Manchester or Minnesota, let's say, but for other Indians too. Sometimes they are mostly for them. In the case of *Joothan*, we see that it is the English translation that enables the book to get translated into Tamil and Malayalam. It is in this respect that English has most certainly become India's literary link language. But it has also become something more than that. It has become the purveyor of different Indian modernities. It is this capaciousness of English, its oft remarked-on ability to bring in and take on vocabulary from foreign languages, that we should see more of in the Indian literary landscape: a literary English infused with ideas, sentiments, and views drawn from Hindi, Telugu, Tamil, Bengali, Marathi, Kannada, Gujarati, Malayalam, Oriya, and so on. Would this be a complete modernity? No. But it would be closer to an Indian one.

Notes

1 U. R. Anantha Murthy, speaking at "Translating India: A Seminar on Translation," New Delhi, Sahitya Akademi, January 15–17, 2001.

2 Which is not to say "that our uncertainties will be reduced by access to thought-worlds" other than our own, but rather, following Clifford Geertz, "they will be multiplied" (45).

3 From the 1970s onwards publishers such as Orient Longman, Katha, and Kali for Women have also brought out many English translations of bhasha texts. For Katha in particular, translation has been part of its mandate.

4 For an ethnographic portrait and analysis of the Sahitya Akademi, see chapter 5 of my book (Sadana, *English*).

5 These three translations are just some of numerous examples I could have chosen from the pantheon of Indian novels in translation.

6 For an analysis of the multi-layered politics of authenticity in Indian literature and a discussion of key arguments in the debates over linguistic authenticity, see chapters 7 and 8 of my book (Sadana, *English*).

7 Rita Kothari observes that the difference between the unnamed translator of the first *Gora* in English and the not only named but well-known translator (Sujit Mukherjee) of the second version as well as the excellent introduction (by Meenakshi Mukherjee) accompanying it are evidence in and of themselves of how "English translation activity in India has come a long way" (68). Only after independence in 1947, she argues, was there a real push by the state and institutions such as the Sahitya Akademi to improve the quality of translations and showcase the literature of the linguistic regions.

8 The English translation of *Joothan* was first published by Samya publishers in Kolkata, and another re-edited version of that translation was subsequently published by Columbia University Press. Arun Mukherjee has discussed her dismay over the Columbia version of her translation for the way it over explains Indian English words and phrases to an American audience, thereby changing and "otherizing" the text in ways she did not approve. See Mukherjee, Mukherjee and Godard (13–14).

9 It is important to note that many bhasha writers were influenced by the English language and its literature and sometimes experimented with writing in English.

10 For more on "the puzzle of India's unity" during this period, see chapter 4 ("Who is an Indian?") of Khilnani.

11 In fact, *Gora* was staged as a Hindi play (written by Geetanjali Shree and directed by Anuradha Kapur) in the 1990s, when, as Vasudha Dalmia notes, "The novel's political concerns acquired new significance ... as Hindu-Muslim tensions were brought to an escalation, which was to peak in the destruction of the Babri Masjid" (322). See Dalmia (322–51) for a full discussion of this production of *Gora*.

12 The Brahmo Samaj was the first modern religious movement in India to respond to the colonial circumstance of the presence of the English East

India Company and the activities of evangelical Christian missionaries. The Brahmo Samaj sought to reform the Hindu religion by eliminating idol worship, ignoring caste boundaries, and supporting female education. See Kopf (*Brahmo*).

13 Phone interview with Arun Mukherjee on December 18, 2013.
14 For example, see Mulk Raj Anand's *Untouchable* (1935), Arundhati Roy's *The God of Small Things* (1997), and Vikram Seth's *A Suitable Boy* (1993). For Arun Mukherjee's Ambedkarite critique of *Untouchable*, see A. Mukherjee, "Exclusions."
15 U. R. Anantha Murthy, speaking at "Translating India: A Seminar on Translation," New Delhi, Sahitya Akademi, January 15–17, 2001.

CHAPTER 10

Emergency Fictions

Ayelet Ben-Yishai and Eitan Bar-Yosef

Rohinton Mistry's powerful 1995 novel *A Fine Balance* concludes with the story of the State of Emergency imposed by Prime Minister Indira Gandhi from June 1975 to March 1977. Ishvar and his nephew Om, the novel's protagonists, undergo all the horrors of Gandhi's Emergency – violent displacements, arrests, and forced "family planning" procedures – all in the name of progress and modernity. In the novel's climax, the two men are captured and sent to a sterilization camp. Om, in retribution for defiantly spitting at the local racketeer who had murdered his father, is castrated; Ishvar undergoes a "nussbandi" (vasectomy) operation, but the sterilization procedure – simple and painless according to government spokesmen – goes terribly wrong: gangrene spreads through Ishvar's legs, which are then duly amputated. By the time they return from the camp, Om and Ishvar discover that their friend and benefactor, Ashraf Chacha, has been beaten to death.

Yet the trains run on time throughout, creating an evident tension between the Emergency – by definition a period of crisis, of irregular and unusual events – and the stable, recurring regularity of the trains' strange punctuality. Indeed, the entire chapter narrating these utmost horrors (climactic even within this unrelenting novel) is permeated with an odd sense of regularity, stability, commensurability, and cyclicality. It begins, appropriately enough, with the arrival of the train carrying Om and Ishvar into town. To their surprise, their friend is there to meet them:

> "How did you know we were coming today?"
>
> "I didn't," he smiled. "But I knew it would be this week. And the train rolls in at the same hour every day." (Mistry, *Fine* 505)

We would like to thank Franziska Tsufim and Valeria Khaskin for their assistance with the research for this chapter, which was supported by the Israel Science Foundation (Grant No. 236/12).

This image of Ashraf Chacha at the railway station establishes the iterative mood of the entire chapter, where an event described only once (Chacha waiting at the train station) evokes a regular repetition of the selfsame event (the men soon realize that Chacha waited there, at the same time, every day of the week). Indeed, depicting the city, the people, or the weather, the chapter is replete with images characterized by successive cyclical repetitions.

The effect is curious: against this resigned, iterative background, the Emergency does not create a sharp contrast. In fact, it just seems like more of the same: "Market day was noisier than usual because the Family Planning Centre was promoting its sterilization camp from a booth in the square" (513). It is always noisy on market day, and the Emergency makes it just a little bit more so. More broadly, and yet following a similar logic, the Emergency only slightly exacerbates the already difficult lives of the population, reframing it in the context of sterilization. This is especially true of the lower castes and classes: the novel implies that the poor and disenfranchised have always been at the mercy of the powers that rule them; for them it is immaterial whether the violence that oppresses them originates from the local zamindar, as it has from time immemorial, or from the central government in New Delhi, as it does now.[1] The image of the train – on time only during the Emergency – establishes the anti-climactic, *anti-emergency* tone of this chapter, and even of the novel as a whole.

While it might seem far-fetched to conclude that the Emergency is just another iteration of lower-caste oppression, Mistry's brand of realism brings to the fore what we recognize as the central tension in the representation, fictional and nonfictional, of the Emergency – a tension between a discourse of crisis, excess, and anomaly and one of cohesion and historical continuity. In fact, we argue that this tension exists not only in hindsight, when we set out to consider the period's legacy; rather, it was constitutive of the Emergency itself. Indeed, the very tension is continuous, visible in the literature written just before the "crisis" and immediately after it. In other words, the stakes of this discursive battle are not only in determining the ways in which the Emergency will be remembered but, even more so, in understanding how the Emergency was understood – or what the Emergency actually *was* – as it was taking place.

Anthropologist Emma Tarlo claims that our contemporary understanding of the Emergency has been "mythologized" through two narratives (2). The first was the official narrative propagated at the time of the Emergency by Indira Gandhi, her son Sanjay, and numerous politicians, bureaucrats, and journalists. According to this narrative, "by controlling population growth, increasing production, boosting agriculture, encouraging industry, abolishing socially backward customs, clearing slums and rooting out corruption, India could achieve new levels of greatness. Modernity was the goal and the Emergency was the means to attain it" (29).

The second narrative, created post-Emergency by Indira Gandhi's opponents, focuses on the authoritarian and anti-democratic means of the Emergency, presenting the measures taken in its name as an outcome of Gandhi's personal political crisis rather than a national or social one. This narrative, Tarlo argues, was initially constructed through three "overlapping genres": "the political exposé aimed at making visible what was previously hidden; the prison memoir providing the intimate account of personal experience, and the public judgement aimed at interrogation of the guilty" (33–4). Nevertheless, following Gandhi's surprising return to power in 1980 and her assassination in 1984, the Emergency seems to have been relegated to the status of anomaly in India's democratic history – all but erased from public and academic discourses (although not, significantly, from literary fiction): "As a moment of national shame, a blot on India's democratic record, the Emergency has been built more as a moment for forgetting than as one for remembering" (Tarlo 19).

Tarlo argues that these two narratives, locked into their partisan rhetoric, cannot provide a reliable account of the meaning of the Emergency for non-elite and marginalized members of society. However, whereas Tarlo treats these narratives as transparently representing reality and thus questions their reliability, we propose to examine how these claims for reliability were established to begin with – how these two narratives, existing side by side, constructed their claims for representing reality. Problematizing their overly simple division into two opposing, consecutive narratives that exist on either side of a clear-cut break, we contend that despite their many differences, both narratives were predicated on a similar discursive tension between crisis and continuity, a tension constitutive of the ongoing struggle for India's political future.

Political accounts of the Emergency commonly tell the story of two rivals pitted against each other: Indira Gandhi and Jayaprakash (known as "JP") Narayan. When writing about the literature of this period, however, one is tempted to stage a drama between a different set of rivals: Indira Gandhi and her cousin, novelist and political writer Nayantara Sahgal. Scions of the most venerable political family in India, and coming of age during the struggle for India's independence, one cousin became the first woman prime minister of the largest democracy in the world, while the other became one of her strongest critics. Playing a central role in the story of the Indian Emergency, whether as its key political player or as a dominant literary and journalistic figure, each of these two women makes a claim for the reality and realism of her vision. More precisely, they articulate competing claims for an authentic Indian nationality and politics: both the political dyad (Gandhi/JP) and the literary one (Gandhi/Sahgal) clash over the true propagation of a Nehruvian and Gandhian legacy. Despite their antinomy, these competing legacies both rely on a shared rhetoric of continuity and coherence. Like the real-life cousins, they are inextricably connected and depend on each other to articulate the force of their claims.

In order to tease out this discursive and familial rivalry – its origins, manifestations, and implications – we will focus on Sahgal's novels, written in the 1970s and early 1980s. While Sahgal is not the only novelist to write about the Emergency, her work is worthy of special critical attention both because she was part of the Nehru-Gandhi dynasty and, more importantly, because no other writer has paid such sustained attention to the period and its actors in both fiction and nonfiction. The most intriguing element of Sahgal's Emergency writing lies, we argue, in its frustration of a coherent chronological order: as we shall see, her most compressed and persistent critique of the Emergency can be found in a novel published *before* the Emergency – while her attempts to revisit its meaning will continue almost forty years later, as late as 2012.

Emergency Fiction

The Emergency began in the early hours of June 26, 1975. Speaking on All India Radio, Mrs. Gandhi informed a stunned nation that President Fakhruddin had proclaimed a State of Emergency: "There is nothing to panic about," she said, explaining that this was a necessary response to "the deep and widespread conspiracy which has been brewing ever since I began to introduce certain progressive measures of benefit to the common man and woman of India" (quoted in Guha, *India* 491).

Following this announcement, Mrs. Gandhi acted swiftly and ruthlessly. Across the country, tens of thousands were detained without trial and sent to overcrowded jails, where many were tortured. One of her father's closest friends, the universally-loved, former independence activist JP Narayan, along with other oppositional leaders, were arrested and kept in government rest houses near Delhi. Elections for the parliament and state governments were suspended; the constitution was amended; houses and bazaars were demolished in the name of slum eradication or "beautification." The Emergency ended as abruptly as it began: on January 18, 1977 the Prime Minister astonished the nation yet again when she announced that Parliament was to be dissolved and elections were to be held.

Indira Gandhi's own justification of the Emergency signified a dramatic break from the past ("Modernity was the goal") but at the same time relied on a dynastic logic – her allegiance to her father – to validate and fortify her rule. Indeed, this was only one element in a much broader discursive preoccupation, which read the Emergency in terms and tropes of family. Central was Mrs. Gandhi's own self-fashioning as Mother of India, reluctantly administering the "bitter pills" of harsh Emergency measures to her ailing child (quoted in Guha, *India* 493). Ironically, this image of "mother-knows-best" was propagated just as Gandhi was increasingly relying on the advice and support of her second son, Sanjay, despite his well-known history of failure and corruption. Even more ironically and poignantly linked to family life was Sanjay's major contribution to the events: the implementation of so-called family planning programs across the country, relying on sterilization, primarily through vasectomies, and leading to widespread coercion.

The first English novel to feature the Emergency was famously Salman Rushdie's 1981 *Midnight's Children*.[2] Rushdie's representation of the Emergency, and of Indira Gandhi, is all crisis and hyperbole, the narrative and the India it represents hurtling toward nothing less than complete disintegration and annihilation. Put in the terms we have been developing here, Rushdie perfects the crisis discourse of the Emergency and pays little attention to the continuities. By contrast, Nayantara Sahgal's writing is relentlessly realistic, a hunkering down in its almost pedestrian commitment to the reality of crisis. This realism (like that of Mistry, writing in her wake) has the ability to contain both crisis and continuity and thus to address the event's political complexity. Moreover, we argue, Sahgal bases her credibility on this realism, establishing a plausible continuity with a past and thus offering a conceivable possibility of an alternative future.

Sahgal's novels, her personal and family life, and the central actors and events of Indian history and politics are all inseparable. Her first memoir, *Prison and Chocolate Cake*, published in 1954, when she was 27, provides a fascinating glimpse into the unusual world of a young woman coming of age at the heart of the Indian independence movement: a girl for whom Mahatma Gandhi was a household guest, whose beloved uncle was India's first prime minister and whose mother was its first ambassador to the United Nations. Positioned firmly within the Indian political and literary elite, Sahgal's writings reflect and cultivate this elitism. Searching for a subaltern perspective is fruitless (it is simply not there), and to fault her for this lack is beside the point.[3] Indeed, Sahgal's elite viewpoint is important precisely because it reveals not only the locus from which the Emergency originated – Dhar calls it an "elite game" (T. N. Dhar 153) – but also the place from which it has been written into history. The stakes of the Indian Emergency *and* its representation were always higher for the elite, even though, as usual, it was the non-elites who paid the price.

The early memoir also carries a wistful tone: after all, Sahgal was at boarding school and in the United States when history was being made by her family. She was at Wellesley, for example, when her cousin Indira served time in the prison of the memoir's title. One gets the impression that Sahgal intends at least some of the memoir to reinscribe herself into the family lore and, by extension, in the nation's history. This personal and somewhat childish desire takes on an increasingly political meaning when, twenty-five years after her first memoir, Sahgal writes her cousin's political biography. While ostensibly a critique of Indira Gandhi's authoritarian politics, the 1978 biography takes on a sour-grapes tone, often becoming strident and bitter, as when she devalorizes Indira's prison experiences (*Emergence* 16–7). At other points, the biography is downright disingenuous, especially when Sahgal elides or hides her personal stakes in the family battle over Nehru's political succession: the sidelining of her mother by her cousin.

Interestingly, Sahgal published two similar versions of this biography – the first, *Indira Gandhi's Emergence and Style*, came out in New Delhi in 1978, immediately after the Emergency. The second, *Indira Gandhi: Her Road to Power*, published in New York in 1982, targeted a Western audience: it contained glossaries of "Indian Words" and "Indian Personalities" and included several additional chapters that chronicled Mrs. Gandhi's return to power and the death of her son and heir-apparent, Sanjay, in 1980. These biographies were expanded from a series of talks Sahgal gave in London and in the United States as early as 1974, a year *before* the Emergency was declared. Writing and rewriting her cousin's biography thus became very much a preoccupation of Sahgal's throughout the 1970s, at the same time that she was writing many of the novels discussed here. Significantly, the displacement of the political/family nexus into the realm of fiction in *The Day in Shadow* (1971), *A Situation in New Delhi* (completed in 1974, published in 1977), and *Rich Like Us* (1985) seems to have provided Sahgal with a way out of personal animosity. As we shall see, strong plots, round characters, and precise narrative form, together

with an acute sensitivity to the gender politics of (elite) Indian families
and (elite) civil society, imbue Sahgal's novels with a political complexity
lacking from her nonfiction and from many journalistic accounts of the
Emergency.[4]

Prefiguring Emergency

Sahgal's *The Day in Shadow* was published four years before the Emergency
and ostensibly does not belong to the literature of the event. Yet, through
this fictionalized story of her own failed marriage, Sahgal portrays Indian
society and political culture as losing its ethical and historical moorings,
presciently laying out the themes that would become central to the writing
of the Emergency. The novel's protagonist, Simrit, is positioned between
two men: Som, her ruthless husband, a businessman poised to make a lot
of money from selling arms in the new Indian political economy, and Raj,
a Christian member of parliament, who is portrayed as an ethical anach-
ronism in an increasingly corrupt world. Subjected to a cruel divorce settlement by her husband, Simrit turns to his opposite, Raj.

Raj is not only set against Som but is also part of another political
dyad. His belief in ethical government, Gandhian values, and Nehruvian
politics[5] is contrasted with that of Sumer Singh, the up-and-coming politician who dismisses the past and is poised to sell off the country's assets
(in this case, oil) in the interest of power and greed. The personal and the
political are thus intertwined in character, in plot, and in ideology: the
gender and communal politics that doom Simrit to a cruel divorce settlement are but part of a general retreat from Gandhian values that the novel
laments. Indeed, as Pranav Jani has noted, the novel's centripetal movement "consistently forces Simrit to exteriorize her sorrow, to recognize
that her private oppression is linked to larger structures" (110). Through its
repeated doublings, the novel thus not only brings the political realm to
bear on the private one but exposes the political stakes of the very division
between the two.

Raj's character links the two dyads – political and personal – but also
embodies yet another duality that is central to the ideology espoused by
this novel and by the ones that follow. By virtue of not being Hindu,
Raj occupies the privileged space of outsider-insider: "That's what happens when you belong to a minority. You look at things from the outside.
You don't take them for granted, you keep sounding them out" (*Day* 103).
In a sense, this is what Sahgal's novels do at their best – stage adversarial
ideological struggles to "sound out" or question antinomies that are taken

for granted. It is what enables Raj, unlike Simrit, to be a pragmatist and an idealist at the same time and to present a hope for the future through a Gandhian ideological connection to the past.

The Day in Shadow thus lays the ground for the story Sahgal is to tell of the Emergency in two ways. On the one hand, by tracing a wide retreat from Gandhian values in the elite public and private spheres and the subsequent rise of a new, corrupt, self-serving elite that would later lead to the authoritarianism of the Emergency, the novel depicts a break – a crisis – in Indian politics. On the other hand, the novel employs the character of Raj to establish a counter-narrative, the road of continuity not taken, and uses it to contextualize the rapid changes that are taking Indian society away from Sahgal's ideal. The novel does not seem hopeful about Raj's chances of overcoming the forces of power and corruption, but his constant presence as the linchpin of the novel's two narratives underscores his importance. Sahgal thus historicizes the ostensibly inevitable onward rush of "progress" headed for crisis with an alternative discourse of continuity with the past, bringing out "the divergence between the promise the new free India had held and the dismal rot that had actually set in it" (T. N. Dhar 137). Most saliently, the other road, *even when not taken*, is still present in the novels. The result is the continued presence of a political alternative, presented as an option that is always available to those who wish to take it up.

Truth Vindicated

Sahgal's *Rich Like Us* (1985) recounts the events of the Emergency from within its midst. Indeed, this novel reaps what *The Day in Shadow* sows, displaying the political and social disaster brought about by a power-hungry and corrupt elite whose rise she records in the earlier novel. *Rich Like Us* thus validates and vindicates Sahgal's political prescience (of which, as we will show, she was proud, even boastful) while indicting her cousin's transgressions: the horrors of the Emergency in the post-Emergency novel confirm her predictions in the first, pre-Emergency one, written well before the events. Moreover, the confirmation of her predictions provides additional support for Sahgal's implicit claim – made in the novel and in her concurrently published nonfiction – as to the illegitimacy of Indira Gandhi as true ideological successor to her father Nehru and to the (Mahatma) Gandhian legacy. Finally, her prescience also establishes ideological and political continuity in Sahgal's work; in a time of changing allegiances and wavering principles, Sahgal's voice remains constant and, by implication, true.

In the novel's past, Rose, a Cockney shopgirl, meets Ram, a sophisticated Indian merchant who visits Britain in the 1940s; she comes to India to be his second wife. Through her naive honesty, inherent good nature and common sense, she manages to make peace with his first wife, disarm her hostile father-in-law, keep the family together, and secure their finances. In the novel's present, during the Emergency, Ram is incapacitated by a stroke, and Rose is left at the mercy of his son, Dev, a member of the "fast crowd" profiting from the Emergency through his proximity to "the PM's son" and his corrupt car-manufacturing scam (*Rich* 9). "'This Emergency is just what we needed,'" says Dev, "'The troublemakers are in jail.... [This] means things can go full steam ahead without delays and weighing pros and cons forever. Strikes are banned. It's going to be very good for business'" (8).

Explicit when describing and denouncing the corruption and illicit relations between the political leadership, the civil service, and the moneyed elite, the novel barely addresses those aspects of the Emergency that targeted the less-privileged – namely, slum eradication and sterilization. Although the novel's only subaltern, "the beggar," does speak, he is not named and is never really developed as a character. Instead, Sahgal ironically prefers to posit Rose in the role of the non-elite outsider – Rose who is British but lower-class – and it is she who functions as the novel's noble savage, seeing through the webs of lies and deceit spread ever more tightly and widely in the Emergency.

Indeed, dramatizing the interdependence of the foreign and the local – inscribed in the novel's dedication, "To the Indo-British experience and what its sharers have learned from each other" – Rose is yet another of Sahgal's insider-outsiders. Despite being an outsider in terms of class, nation, gender, and education, she manages to preserve the family's modest wealth because she continues the commonsensical commercial legacy of Ram's father, advocating hard work and modest gains rather than grandiose schemes. All this leads to Rose's murder at the novel's end, at the hands of her stepson or his henchmen: speaking her mind, she risks exposing the corrupt commercial scams that are at the foundation of the Emergency and the source of the son's new-found wealth. As T. N. Dhar notes, "the covered-up history of the family [i.e., Rose's murder] metaphorically represents the covered-up history of the nation" (150).

If Rose is an outsider who makes her way in, her younger friend Sonali is the consummate insider: daughter of an elite Kashmiri family and fast-rising star in the Indian Civil Service (ICS), Sonali struggles with the increasingly terrifying gap between her ideals and workday reality.

Demoted, Sonali needs to become an outsider – in this case by leaving the ICS – in order to begin questioning everything she has taken for granted, including the ICS itself: "We could afford to remind ourselves of a past … and we joined ours seamlessly to the present. The civil service was part of the join" (*Rich* 148). Sonali examines this "seamless join," the connection with a past that she takes for granted through a close scrutiny of her personal and national history. Unlike her previous novels, Sahgal interweaves the individual story of the characters with its larger historical context. Indeed, it seems that because the events of *Rich Like Us* take place during the Emergency itself, a time when no alternative narrative was possible, Sahgal turns to the *longue durée* of Indian history to imagine such an alternative. This is done through the elaborate story of Rose's past in India and in England, as well as by Sonali's historical inquiry into her father's legacy, in the form of a trunk of his documents. The novel thus pits two discourses against each other, bearing out Tarlo's claim of opposing partisan narratives. The first comprises the narrative of the Emergency officials and their hangers-on: fraudulent and superficial, it is espoused, for example, by the Minister who speaks – at the dedication ceremony for yet another corrupt manufacturing scheme – "in mellifluous Hindi about the Vedas, the undimmed glory of India's heritage, the high place of selflessness and sacrifice in her tradition and the brightness of the future assured by the emergency" (43). This official discursive claim for a historical legacy, manifestly counterfeit, serves in the novel as a foil for the second discourse, one of true and authentic historical continuity personified by the novel's two protagonists and narrators, Sonali and Rose.

The two women grow closer to each other until Sonali takes over Rose's narrative at the novel's tragic end, adopting the legacy of being able to inhabit a contradiction ("living on a see-saw") that Rose had "handed on in her lifetime" (*Rich* 225). Sonali's examination of her family's privilege and its historical context makes her realize the homologous pain and suffering of those living under other kinds of oppression, in other times and places, such as bride-burning, the torture of people by the police, and the liquidation of small farms by big landlords (T. N. Dhar 152). Sonali's inquiry reveals the gap between the complexity of "real" history and the counterfeit rhetoric, such as that espoused by the minister in the quote from earlier. Musing over the improbability of Rose's "accidental" death, Sonali understands the connection between a local, criminal untruth and a larger, historical one; as she proclaims at the novel's end: "Here in this house the revision of history had begun and there would be no end to the lies" (223).

In *Rich Like Us*, the Emergency is a struggle over history, its meaning in the Indian polity, and its continuity with the past. The novel makes explicit that India's future depends on the legacy India chooses, which must both come from the outside and be incorporated within; as Sonali muses, "Immersed in the past, I was preparing all the while for the future.... Though it was really Rose's legacy again ... [that was] reminding me I was young and alive, with my own century stretched before me, waiting to be lived" (234). At the same time, the novel fails to follow its own prescription. Unlike Rose's and Sonali's ability to contain historical complexity, the novel itself is invested in a Manichean view of history, represented – as we have shown – by the stark and often superficial oppositions of authentic/counterfeit and right/wrong. The result is a novel that, while structurally gesturing toward a complex understanding of history and the tension between continuity and crisis, ultimately offers a reading of history – specifically, of the Emergency – that takes on many of the characteristics of the superficiality it criticizes.

Configuring Emergency

Although *Rich Like Us* is set explicitly during the Emergency, we would like to suggest that the novel that offers the most significant insight into the convoluted stakes of the Emergency is *A Situation in New Delhi* (1977). Despite being written *before* the Emergency (it was completed in early 1975) and published immediately in its wake, the novel uncannily anticipates many of the Emergency's events and tropes, giving truth to Sahgal's claims of her own prescience and political acuity: writing in 1977, Sahgal boasts that "the 'situation' creeping up on us in *A Situation in New Delhi* – a book I had completed writing in January 1975 – was upon us in June, and I myself was hung with it" (Sahgal, *Voice* 20). Most powerfully, the novel's very existence as simultaneously pre- and post-Emergency performs the constancy and continuity with the past that we claim to be at the heart of the Emergency discourse and the temporal maneuvers involved in renegotiating an Indian political legacy.

The novel opens with the death of Shivraj, an idealized and barely fictionalized Nehru, and focuses on his close circle of family and confidants, who contend with the after-effects of this immense loss in their personal and political realms. In keeping with Sahgal's propensity for dual forms and themes, this novel also has two narrative forms. The first, associated with Shivraj's sister Devi, is dominant in the first part of the novel and continues the pedestrian realism of *The Day in Shadow*. This narrative, like much realism, offers the quotidian as an institutional structure that can contain change and preserve continuity in crisis. The leader is gone, but nothing falls apart because of the structure in place, a structure Devi describes as "the bigger, slower human process of a struggle that learns through its own experience" (*Situation* 90). This institutional thinking is presented as Shivraj's explicit legacy: "He wanted mainly to live long enough for free institutions to become part of the soil, become a way of life and thinking that no future could destroy" (93).

In contrast, the novel posits another narrative; however, unlike the two works discussed earlier, the second narrative in *Situation* is not the official, authoritarian one associated with corruption and power. Like the first, this second narrative too opposes the post-Shivraj regime, yet is far more radical and urgent in its quasi-Naxalite politics. Also realistic, its discourse is urgent, highlighting action and escalation, revolution and violence. It is associated with youth, and especially with Rishad, Devi's son. By juxtaposing these two oppositional narratives, Sahgal historicizes "freedom," the central concept of the generation of independence and one that was to become so again under Emergency. For Rishad this freedom – now incorporated in the quotidian – has become empty, if not worse: "Even his mother feels things should go on more or less as before. The star of her generation had been freedom.... But Rishad had been born free, in a world he could not accept" (70). For his mother, freedom has a past, present, and future: "Well, they had talked of freedom so much. Its absence, its coming, what they would do with it when it came. Her growing up, her career, her whole life had been ordered by the freedom to come" (74). But for Rishad, freedom has no revolutionary force, reifying the present rather than opening up a future: "It was pre-history, an event whose antiquity had no relation to the present and with which he had no ties" (74). Freedom, the novel insists, means different things to different people at different times, a truth also recognized by Sonali in the later novel.

Through these narrative temporalities, Sahgal conducts an internal debate on Nehru's legacy and its temporal allegiances – to the past and to the future for sure, but also to the relative speed and rate of progress. As the novel progresses, the sense of urgency gains over the more sober quotidian discourse until, finally, crisis takes over – in the form of a tragic bombing – marking the novel's pessimistic end. Nevertheless, despite its dual narrative form, *A Situation in New Delhi* is not invested in binary oppositions in the same way as *The Day in Shadow* and *Rich Like Us*. Instead, the novel focuses on a more subtle struggle, one about which it provides no clear answers: the struggle over Nehru's legacy. Both in form and content, then, the novel is more interested in offering a reflexive analysis of how things come to be than in staging a Manichean battle. All this makes *A Situation in New Delhi*, to our mind, the most subtle and interesting of Sahgal's novels in its understanding of history, as well as the most intricate formal instance of the discursive struggle that was the Emergency.

Literary critic T. N. Dhar argues that Sahgal's novels reaffirm "that the Indian tradition would provide a safeguard against violent socio-political alternatives" (149). While we would agree, it also seems – somewhat ironically – that Indira Gandhi would also have signed on to such a statement; after all, her claims were that the Emergency was the "bitter pill" declared precisely to safeguard the nation and tradition from those who would break from it violently. Indeed, both Emergency narratives – the official and the oppositional – espoused a future based on a strong connection with the past. They only differed over which one was the rightful representative of this past. Put in the terms of *A Situation in New Delhi*, the real debate is not between those who would follow Shivraj and those who want to break with his ways. Rather, the strife is internal and comprehensive, a difference over what following "Shivraj" means. It is a struggle over the meaning of "Nehru" in post-Nehruvian times.

Finally, the overdetermination of family in this contested legacy, in the novel's plot and characters but also in the convoluted kinship relations between its author and her historical subject matter, becomes especially vexed when juxtaposed with the Emergency's discursive preoccupation with tropes of family and family life (the relationship between the fictional Devi and the real-life Pandit being but one example). This problematizes the way we understand the novel, but it also has an unexpected upside if we read the various texts through one other. Nowhere is this more visible than in the somewhat crude, quasi-sisterly rivalry in the second generation of India's elite that emerges from Sahgal's biographies. Mirrored and problematized in the novel, and then refracted in the "family" discourse of the Emergency, this rivalry offers readers of *A Situation in New Delhi* an uncanny opportunity to contemplate the rhetoric that ties family and politics, in their most literal and figurative meanings – a rhetoric still highly relevant to Indian politics and culture.

Coda

In 2012, at the age of eighty-eight, Sahgal published yet another, third, edition of the biography of her cousin, now titled *Indira Gandhi: Tryst with Power.* Evoking Nehru's famous "Tryst with Destiny" speech at the moment of India's independence, its title restores Mrs. Gandhi to the place Sahgal spent many years trying to wrest away from her: Nehru's legacy and Indian history. Still, the second part of the title, "with Power," suggests that the tryst was not destined, that it had to be gained, and sustained, through the exercise of power. Indeed, in the twelve-page postscript to this edition, titled "Completing the Picture," Sahgal admits the dual and ambivalent nature of Indira Gandhi's personality – and of her regime. She reflects on her cousin in a tone that serves to soften and complicate, if not rewrite altogether, the harshness and unequivocal condemnation of the 367 pages (and forty-odd years) that preceded it: "To the onlooker the heart of the paradox may well have been Indira Gandhi's belief that she was following in her father's footsteps, when in fact her behaviour in power marked a complete break from his," writes Sahgal. "She did not see it in this way.... She saw herself as a guardian of the Congress tradition" (370). Recognizing the dialectic of crisis and continuity which we have described here as a central feature of Indira Gandhi and her rule, Sahgal acknowledges that the true meaning of Gandhi's duality is determined discursively: "In life as in fiction, point of view decides which way the story goes and both stories found their convinced reading public" (372).

Most crucial, to our mind, is the fact that the softened equivocation does not replace her harsh indictment of Mrs. Gandhi (indeed, the original text has not been changed, only supplemented). The existence of both indictment and equivocation, side by side in this latest iteration of the biography, reproduces the intricate relationship between the two opposing narrative modes that we have been tracing. It also adds yet another twist to the ongoing writing and rewriting of this political and cultural legacy. What might initially appear as a fissure between two discourses on opposite sides of an ideological and temporal divide is in fact a common, if complex and open-ended, discursive arena, which invites ongoing reconsideration.

This continuing need for reassessment brings us back to Rohinton Mistry's powerful intervention with which we began: following in Sahgal's wake, Mistry sustains and extends her realist form while adding another layer of content that is so poignantly missing from Sahgal's elite perspective: the lives of the poor and low-caste. Reading these fictions alongside each other establishes the Emergency as an important interpretative site: an exceptionally violent episode, marked as a one-off crisis; but at the same time a continuous renegotiation, iterative and intricate, of the modern Indian polity.

Notes

1 As Emma Tarlo has noted, the experience of home and slum demolitions during the Emergency may have shocked the elite, but it was "all too familiar to the inhabitants of slums and resettlement colonies" (225).
2 Much less famously, Manohar Malgonkar's *The Garland Keepers*, published in 1980, makes use of the post-Emergency exposés of corruption and power as a backdrop for a very entertaining political thriller. Additional novels about the Emergency published in the 1980s and beyond include Balwant Gargi, *The Naked Triangle* (1979), Raj Gill, *The Torch Bearer* (1983), O. V. Vijayan, *The Saga of Dharmapuri* (1988) and *After the Hanging and Other Stories* (1989), Shashi Tharoor, *The Great Indian Novel* (1989), Arun Joshi, *The City and the River* (1990), and Ranjit Lal, *The Crow Chronicles* (1996).
3 See Jani; and Uraizee, who try to do both of these, and T. N. Dhar (147), who defends Sahgal on this point. We agree with Jasbir Jain's claim that "this limitation has become a strength" (115).
4 This is not to say that the family feud is absent from these novels. Many of them contain an idolized Nehru-figure and a responsible, idealized, ethical female civil-servant/politician character modeled on Sahgal's mother.
5 For an in-depth discussion of the novel's nationalist, cosmopolitan, and feminist politics, see scholarship by Jani; Jain (*Nayantara*); and T. N. Dhar.

CHAPTER II

Cosmopolitanism and the Sonic Imaginary in Salman Rushdie

Vijay Mishra

> Gibreel, the tuneless soloist, had been cavorting in moonlight as he sang his impromptu gazal.
>
> – Salman Rushdie, *The Satanic Verses* (p. 3)

Like a ghostly specter, modernity's greatest art form, cinema, haunts and invades Salman Rushdie's critical as well as creative corpus. The haunting presence is not limited just to cinema's visual presence; it is there through its sonic style as well. No better proof of this is available than in Rushdie's own notes and papers. In the Emory University Salman Rushdie archive, ten great films are mentioned on a single typed sheet (written quite possibly at the time Rushdie had finished a first draft of *The Satanic Verses* [1988] – that is, in February–March 1988).[1] The films noted on Rushdie's list were made between 1954 and 1965 – a period marked by a modernist, cosmopolitan, art-house aesthetics that pushed the European avant-garde (with its surrealist foundations) to the limit.[2] One of the striking features of these films, which include Fellini's *8½* (1963) and Godard's *Alphaville* (1965), is the space given to cities. But their representation is not simply visual; there is a symphonic architecture about them, as music both mediates and provides extradiegetic acoustics for the mechanical sounds of the city (cars, trains) and the organic sounds of the human world. Visual literalism works with sonic literalism as cities reconfigure cinema aesthetics. Rushdie's Emory list, with its avant-garde, city bias, resurfaces in *The Satanic Verses* as it receives near replication in Saladin Chamcha's list of his favorite films. Responding to Gibreel Farishta, Saladin Chamcha ("Spoono") offers a list of films that are all "conventional cosmopolitan": "*Potemkin, Kane, Otto e Mezzo, The Seven Samurai, Alphaville, El Angel Exterminador.*" Gibreel is critical of Saladin's choices ("You've been brainwashed.... All this Western art-house crap," he says) because his own "top ten of everything came from 'back home,' and was aggressively lowbrow. *Mother India, Mr India, Shree Charsawbees.*" In a curious reversal of aesthetic judgment, Gibreel tells Saladin that his conventional cosmopolitan choice reflected a head "so full of junk ... you forgot everything worth knowing" (454).

Rushdie's interest in modernity's most powerful and pervasive art form, and in cities too,[3] takes me to the crux of this chapter, which concerns the persistence of cinematic effects – the moving image but also, and more importantly in the reading offered here, the soundtrack – in Rushdie's novels. I want to contextualize Rushdie's writings in Saladin Chamcha's conventional cultural cosmopolitanism by drawing attention to the role of cinema's sonic style (source music, diegetic music, underscore, extradiegetic music, *musique concrète*, and so on) in Rushdie. The city boy and the sonic: both come together in a draft summary of Rushdie's *The Ground Beneath Her Feet* (1999) for publishers deposited in the Rushdie digital archive at Emory:

> I'm a city boy myself. And the music in my novel is as urban, as metropolitan a kind of magic as the mythic Orpheus is pastoral. I have always tried to find in my books a poetry of the city. Ormus Cama sings the city, and so, I hope, will the book in which he appears. Cocteau put Orpheus on a French motorbike. *Orfeu Negro* took him into the Rio carnival. This is Orpheus in Bombay, London, New York. Orpheus is the city of words. Orpheus is Alphaville.

The Ground Beneath Her Feet is clearly a paean to the cosmopolitan city, and capturing sonality, the poetry of the city – Orpheus the lyre-player's city meanderings – is one of its aims. Elsewhere too sonality characterizes the Rushdie aesthetic, a fact that – and given Rushdie's declared interest in cinema – necessitates an exploration beyond Rushdie's fictionality, beyond a reading of his works via homologous correspondences between novelistic representation and cinematic representation, to his interest in "auteur music" – a term used to refer to the sonic as a defining characteristic of an auteur. How auteur music functions as a key supplement to visual representation necessitates finessing my earlier readings, which were restricted to correspondences between cinema and the novel, examining as these did the crossovers between the literary author and the cinematic auteur, where Rushdie's use of narrative design as shooting script was one of the points of entry (V. Mishra, "Rushdie"; and V. Mishra, "Salman").

I shift the argument at this juncture to suggest that the corporeal – the body – makes its way into aural representation, dislodges the mind/body binary, and suggestively moves us toward the idea of the body itself as an epistemological entrepreneur, a "thinking" subject. Just as auteur theory is based on the recognition of a director's style as his/her signature, so a film-maker's work may be recognized through a film's sonic style. Critiquing the limits of auteur theory and especially its emphasis on cinematic for-malism, James Wierzbicki, in his essay "Sonic Style in Cinema," examines the deliberate use of sounds by auteurs. He cites Jack Sullivan's definition of music for Alfred Hitchcock, which "encompassed street noise, dialogue (especially voice-over), sounds of the natural world … sonic effects of all sorts … [and] silence, the sudden, awesome absence of music, capable of delivering the most powerful music frisson of all" (8). Sound adds an extra layer of meaning to both narrative and image – a classic instance of which is Ravi Shankar's use of a single extended note on the sitar and shehnai in Satyajit Ray's *Pather Panchali*. The emotional weight of the moment, its timeless, transcendental quality – what Andrey Tarkovsky called "sculpt-ing in time" (quoted in Fairweather 32) – is transmitted here through sonic effect.

In this respect, the cosmopolitanism that marks Saladin Chamcha's choice of films may be viewed as a sonic cosmopolitanism – a mod-ernist audio-visuality that informs Rushdie's style as the sonic world becomes crucial to the writer's aesthetic vision. It does not follow as a matter of course that sonic cosmopolitanism is the only – or indeed the primary – cosmopolitan register in Rushdie's works; other cosmo-politanisms expressed as cosmopolitan worldliness (Brennan, *Salman*), the hybrid postcolonial (Bhabha, *Location*), the comparative intertex-tual (Cundy), the cosmopolitan intellectual as exile, "history's bas-tard" (Dutheil), the post-religious (Suleri), and the post-humanist (Said, *Culture*) have had greater runs on the board when it comes to Rushdie criticism. Another cosmopolitanism – the visual, the "picto-rial turn" – in the context of this chapter requires a closer look. In Ana Mendes' 2012 edited volume, the visual is discussed at length by all the contributing authors. Given space constraints, I shall limit myself to a discussion of ekphrasis, the technique of visual and descriptive juxtaposition best explored in Rushdie criticism with reference to the Millais painting, *The Boyhood of Raleigh*, in Saleem Sinai's bedroom. In Rushdie, this and other ekphrastic "acts" are not instances of tech-nical virtuosity but sites where, in W. J. T. Mitchell's words, "polit-ical, institutional, and social antagonisms play themselves out in the materiality of representation" (91). This brings into the text a second, visual text with its own affects on the reader – affects not necessarily corresponding to either the character-viewer's or the narrator's description of it. Further, as Stephen Morton argues in his contribution to the volume, the visual provides Rushdie with a "conceptual space" ("Beyond" 32) in which to show the place of painting and film in literary modernity and at the same time challenge the canonical fetish for descriptive prose. It follows that the references to the Moor Boabdil's last sigh upon the surrender of Granada in *The Moor's Last Sigh* (1995) cannot be disentangled from the representation of that event in the Spanish painter Francisco Bayeu's ceiling fresco *Surrender of Granada* (1763) or in Francisco Pradilla's nationalist painting, *Sigh of the Moor* (1892). In Vassilena Parashkevova's exceptional chapter in the Mendes volume, these paintings function as visual palimpsests to the novelistic art of verbal representation. Ekphrasis is not the only technique of visual representation we find in Rushdie – verbal description as cinematic shooting script is another – but it is certainly one with a more powerful ideological function inasmuch as it unsettles and questions what Ramone in the Mendes volume has called "Eurocentric storytelling forms and structures" (99).

The argument in favor of a sonic cosmopolitanism is not meant to replace other cosmopolitanisms and certainly not to subordinate the visual to the sonic in Rushdie. Rather, it is meant to show the manner in which the Rushdie aesthetic draws quite consciously on sounds, and specifically sounds as they function in cinema. A direct lineage of Rushdie's sonic cosmopolitanism may be traced back to those modernist musicians who used non-musical sounds – of railways, machines, and the like – to create musical pieces. Their compositions were referred to as *musique concrète*. The father of the form, Peter Schaeffer, titled his 1948 seminal composition "Cinq études des bruits" ("Five Studies of Noises"), the first of which was "made up of noises associated with the railway" (Kickasola 63). The effect may be read as the aural version of literary defamiliarization because it too broke the normal relay of reception (the anticipation of the familiar) by directing us toward sounds not normally associated with a sonic aesthetic, whether musical or poetic. As we shall later see, for Rushdie, *musique concrète* constitutes a parallel sonic repertoire alongside the familiarly onomatopoeic, a kind of literary version of the filmmaker's "sonic palette" (Kulezic-Wilson 76) in which an acoustic universe of sounds, rhythms, and noises are part of the literary soundscape. Yet, in Rushdie we do not discover a recurring musical leitmotif as such; there is no sound that functions as a controlling metaphor that would constitute an acoustic fingerprint of the author.

Remembering Max Ophüls

My point of entry into Rushdie's sonic collage is the name Max Ophuls (Maximilian Ophuls, the "u" without the umlaut) in Rushdie's *Shalimar the Clown* (2005). Max Ophuls, an ex-American ambassador to India, is dead before the second page of the novel is finished: "The ambassador was slaughtered on her [his daughter India's] doorstep like a halal chicken dinner, bleeding to death from a deep neck wound caused by a single slash of the assassin's blade" (*Shalimar* 4). What follows in the next forty-odd pages of the section entitled "India" is a long tracking shot that recounts Ophuls's life during the two days prior to his brutal killing. Why have I used the language of cinema to explain the manner in which the narrative leading to his death is recounted? The reason, already foreshadowed, lies in Rushdie's investment in the cosmopolitan sonic imaginary and its expression in cinema. As already noted, to Rushdie, cinematic techniques are essentially novelistic, since for him the camera functions as the character or narrator's point of view ("pee oh vee," as we read in *The Satanic Verses* [110]). Conversely, in a homage to cinema, in fiction too the shot (tracking, dolly, crane, shot-reverse, the axial cut, and so on) "alter[s]" and even "condense[s]" "[London] according to the imperatives of film" (*Satanic* 436). So, in the case of the first section of *Shalimar the Clown* (note that the novel does not carry a "Contents" page), the narrative is tracked with an implicit homage to a great director who made films in German, French, and English and after whom the character in the novel is named.

Maximilian Ophüls, originally Maximilian Oppenheimer, of Jewish heritage, was born in Germany in 1902 and died in Germany in 1957 while working on his French film *The Lovers of Montparnasse*. In America, between 1941 and 1950 (having escaped from Nazi-occupied France), he made four films: *The Exile* (1947), *Letters from an Unknown Woman* (1948), *Caught* (1949), and *The Reckless Moment* (1949). I mention these films so as to "locate" the name of Rushdie's character and then move on to a poetics of Rushdie's works, which, for the purposes of this short and theoretically tentative chapter, takes me to the links between his novels and sound, including the cinema soundtrack. Daniel Morgan argues – using Ophüls as his proof text – that "camera movements are in some way deeply, perhaps inextricably, interwoven with concerns with ethics ... [and] tracking shots (after Godard) are matters of morality" (128). Aesthetics and ethics in this argument are closely connected. My point, however, is not that Rushdie's novelistic tracking is like Ophüls's extensive use of tracking shots and thus primarily a matter "of ethics" (Morgan 132) but that sound-scapes in Rushdie invoke an auditory literalism borrowed from cinema. Naming the ambassador "Ophuls" is both an homage to that form and an acknowledgment of the aesthetic as well as ethical links between form and content.

Let's turn to the first five lines of *The Satanic Verses*, which begins with a crane shot of Gibreel Farishta, "the tuneless soloist," singing a "gazal." What might not be obvious to a reader is the relationship between Gibreel's song and its "sonic visualization." To underline this point, let us offer the song in verse:

> To be born again,
> first you have to die.
> Ho ji! Ho ji!
> To land upon the bosomy earth,
> first one needs to fly.
> Tat-taa! Taka-thun!
> How to ever smile again,
> if first you won't cry?
> How to win the darling's love, mister,
> without a sigh?
> Baba, if you want to get born again.
>   (*Satanic* 3)

As a ghazal – that great Indo-Persian lyrical genre with a very precise prosody and restricted subject matter – this is inconsolably mundane, but that is not the aesthetic point. We can, through a little effort, locate enough real Bollywood filmi ghazals that carry the sentiments echoed in the verse: marnā terī galī meṁ, jīnā terī galī meṁ ("to die in your neighborhood, to live in it"), cal uḍjā re paṁcī ab ye deś huā begānā ("fly away O bird, for this land is now alien"), hai sab se madhur vo gīt jinhe ham dard ke sur meṁ gāte haiṁ ("our sweetest songs are those that tell/of saddest thought" [this straight from Shelley]), āh lekin kaun samjhe kaun jāne dil kā hāl ("who understands a sigh, who understands the pain of the heart?"). What we get is the presence of sounds, of notes that recall any number of songs that Gibreel "only mimed to playback singers" (*Satanic* 3) in Bollywood movies. It is the soundtrack of films, here intradiegetic, that becomes a foundational reference. For Farishta is the delusionary actor too who only mimes songs and the voices of others, including those of Angel Gabriel (Gibreel). This song, how-ever, is not disconnected from noise; no foley art is required for the post-production insertion of sonic effects to create a fall to the ground or the voice of the chorus. Gibreel himself breaks the song, first with "ho ji" ("you there, I say" but also the opening strains of the well-known rāga bhairavī in *Baiju Bawra* [1952]: ho jī ho ... tū gaṅgā kī mauj meṁ) and then with "Tat-taa! Taka-thun!" (*Satanic* 3), a common opening tāl on the tabla, the Indian percussion. And this sound ends in the ono-matopoeic sound of someone falling in Hindi, "*Dharrraaammm!*" (4) – the word itself given in italics and with a conscious allusion to *musique concrète* in cinema. Struck by their tonality, the sounds function as an earlier bow-wow theory of language when, before Saussure, the origin of language was in onomatopoeia: dogs barked because "bark" is the sound they made, and so on. The sounds here capture, in some sense, the materiality of the signifier, without the triad of signifier/signified/concept, and thus they engender a "sonic discomfort" (van Elferen 179). There is a vast repertoire of onomatopoeic sounds that reinforce the corporeal, the material, and the body in Rushdie.[4] Here, I wish to highlight only one: "abracadabra." In *Midnight's Children* (1981), this sound is not the cabbalistic formula derived from the name of the supreme god of the Basilidan Gnostics, containing the number 365, but a sound that captures the motion of trains, becoming its sonic equiva-lent. Saleem recalls: "And then we were in a third-class railway carriage heading south south south, and in the quinquesyllabic monotony of the wheels I heard the secret word: abracadabra abracadabra abraca-dabra sang the wheels as they bore us back-to-Bom" (*Midnight's* 519). One can hear the symphony of the motion of the train wheels, which in cinematic tracking would fuse the "real" sounds of the wheels with their orchestral equivalents, morphing the tedious and monotonous sound of train wheels into what may be called musical incantations.

"O, My Shoes Are Japanese"

I began with Farishta's song; let me proceed with the tracking of another song. This song, commented upon by almost everyone, is "O, my shoes are Japanese," which is Farishta's translation of "the old song into English in semi-conscious deference to the uprushing host-nation" (*Satanic* 5). The translation, rewritten as verse, is as follows:

> O, my shoes are Japanese,
> These trousers English, if you please.
> On my head, red Russian hat;
> My heart's Indian for all that. (5)

A postcolonial critical reading would thematize this song along the
cosmopolitan lines (or after the narrator's directive) given in the senten-
tia "deference to the uprushing host-nation": Farishta, the deracinated
Indian, is comfortable with his hybrid self and symbolically presages a
new age of multiple identity formation. What is less often written about
is the invocation of another form of narrative assemblage in which the
soundtrack is divorced from meaning. In the film from which the song is
borrowed – Raj Kapoor's *Shree 420* (1955), a film not mentioned by name
until much later ("while Gibreel yowled an air [aria] from the movie *Shree
420*" [*Satanic* 421]) – the song, merā jūtā hai jāpānī, is sung by the picaro
figure who, en route to Bombay, reads on a road sign: "Bombay 420,"
meaning that the city is 420 miles away. This is an in-house joke – and
again, commented on by many – but the song itself has nothing to do
with either the Indian Penal Code 420 or the traditional account of the
picaro figure on the road, a figure going back to the Spanish picaresque
novels, although in the verses that follow, verses cast in a comic-parodic
mode, the hero's estrangement from the world is evident enough. So in a
sense it is not so much the principle of cultural hybridity, so enthusiastically celebrated in postcolonial criticism, that is addressed here; rather
it is a studied incorporation of the structural principle of "assemblage,"
the disjunction between sound and meaning, as well as, because of playback singing, a *schizophonia* ("the separation of sound from its origin by
means of recording technology" [van Elferen 180][5]) that characterizes the
Bollywood film.

An informed reader singing along with Farishta (songs, in a variation
on Lionel Trilling's statement about books, read us after all [Trilling 23][6])
tracks the song with interest. In *The Satanic Verses*, the God/Satan binary
("Ooparvala ... The Fellow Upstairs" and "Neechayvala, the Guy from
Underneath" [*Satanic* 329]) is rendered through a deflationary Bollywood
rhetoric borrowed from the second and third verses of the "My shoes
are Japanese" song. Here, ūparvālā/ooparvala ("the fellow upstairs") is
the person who alone knows the destination of the picaro figure, as he
declares that he has taken off on an open road. Of course, in this "The
Satanic Comedy," an early title of the novel clearly borrowed from Dante,[7]
Rushdie is on the Neechayvala's side, the word itself not a legitimate
opposite of Ooparvala in the Hindi/Urdu lexicon and hence a Rushdie
neologism. Further – and if we want to stage the song differently, moving
from auditory literalism to instrumental literalism – the rāga in which the
original song is composed is rāga bhairavī, which is the signature rāga of
Raj Kapoor, the film director and actor, in his major corpus, from *Aag*

(1948) to *Mera Naam Joker* (1970). Thus, Farishta's song has an aesthetic valence that transcends the outwardly political and insinuates a postcolonial genesis of secrecy not recuperable through a simple declaration of the song's cultural cosmopolitanism.

The tracking shot in the opening pages of *The Satanic Verses* also involves Saladin Chamcha who, in response to Gibreel Farishta's tuneless song, offers, in a shot-reverse-shot mode, "an old song, too, lyrics by Mr James Thomson, seventeen-hundred to seventeen-forty-eight" (*Satanic* 6). Here, of course, the "old song" invokes a militaristic temper, the colonized celebrating (without, one suspects, any ironic intent) a hymn to imperialism. The old song is by James Thomson (1700–48), Scottish by birth but known best as an English poet and dramatist who wrote *The Seasons* (1726–30). In 1740, he co-wrote (with Daniel Mallet) a masque called *Alfred*, which carried a poem celebrating British naval successes by invoking Britain's great Saxon king, Alfred. The lines sung by Saladin Chamcha, " 'at Heaven's command,' … 'arooooose from out the aaaazure main' … 'And guardian aaaaangels sung the strain'" (6), are from the poem, now commonly known as "Rule Britannia!" The first verse of "Rule Britannia!" reads:

> When Britain first, at Heaven's command,
> Arose from out the azure main;
> This was the charter of the land,
> And guardian angels sang this strain:
> "Rule, Britannia! rule the waves:
> Britons never will be slaves."

The verse soon began to lead an independent life of its own, separate from the masque, and became a jingoistic song of imperial power (and latterly of English soccer hooligans) with changes made to the last two lines to read, "Rule Britannia, Britannia rules the waves/ Britons never, never, never shall be slaves." The verse also has had a wide provenance in music history, with the likes of Handel, Beethoven, Wagner, Johann Strauss, and Arthur Sullivan including it in their musical compositions.

At this point in the novel, Saladin's "wild recital" of heavy, quasi-militaristic notes competes with the Bollywood folk style of "O, my shoes are Japanese." "Horrified" by Saladin's colonial obsequiousness to the Pax Britannica (that wonderful age of peace for a V. S. Naipaul), Gibreel Farishta "sang louder and louder of Japanese shoes, Russian hats, inviolately subcontinental hearts" (*Satanic* 6). There are no intonational or suprasegmental marks accompanying Farishta's Indian song (the original sung by the master playback singer of the sentimental song Mukesh); Saladin's vowels, however, are over extended with long o's and a's. Andrew Teverson's observation is to the point here: "Rushdie exploits the plasticity of his language in order to shape and reshape the way we hear it ... to recreate something of their aural quality" (23). The unruly world of sounds, so central to the discourse of poetry and Shakespeare's dramatic verse, received first sonically and only then visually in the case of the Hindi ghazal (which in fact merā jūtā hai jāpānī is not) and the English poem, brings another hermeneutical principle to our understanding of Rushdie. Whereas an ideological reading, quite correctly, would place the two songs in structural opposition to each other – a monological imperialist dogma against postcolonial cosmopolitan dialogism – a turn to tonality captures what may be called a corporeal disconnectedness in which the body utters sounds without immediately connecting them to their thematic referents – where one displays, with Jumpy Joshi, borrowing from W. B. Yeats' "The Second Coming," "such *passionate intensity*" (*Satanic* 286). ("The best lack all conviction, while the worst/Are full of passionate intensity.") It should not surprise us that the central problematic of the novel – demonic sacralization in Islam, or at least the Prophet's momentary attraction to it – first surfaces as a barely discernible sound: Rekha Merchant (she on the flying Bokhara carpet) cursing "in a language [Gibreel] did not understand," a language of "all harshnesses and sibilance," which carried the unnerving sound/word "*Al-Lat*" (*Satanic* 8). Al-Lat, literally "The Goddess" (cf "Al-Lah" meaning the God), is the great pre-Islamic Arabian mother goddess (whom the Greeks called Lato) representing the Sun. This Arab pagan goddess, a key figure in the censored satanic verses in the *sūra* called "The Star" (Al-Najm'), surfaces as no more than onomatopoeia and for the common reader is therefore no different from other unruly sounds, including the songs of Farishta and Saladin.[8]

A Turn to High Culture

The visualization of the sonic may be traced back to Rushdie's earlier works as well. In *Midnight's Children*, Saleem's sister Jamila Singer (the Brass Monkey) becomes " 'Pakistan's Angel,' 'The Voice of the Nation,' the 'Bulbul-e-Din' or nightingale-of-the faith" (*Midnight's* 359), who sings behind a lengthy veil held by two female attendants. The veil has an aperture through which Jamila sings, a point that takes us back to the perforated sheet through which her grandfather had treated her grandmother's illness in Kashmir. Interesting as this narrative allusion is, what is of value for the tracking of sound in this chapter is the manner in which Jamila Singer, who specializes in patriotic songs during the 1965 India-Pakistan war, plays out the other real singer in Pakistan who earlier left an illustrious actor-singer career in Bombay for the newly-created Indian Muslim nation. The singer was Noor Jehan (1926–2000), the Malika-e-Tarannum (the Queen of Melody) and the Tamgha-e-Imtiaz (the Pride of Performance) of Pakistan who sang the patriotic song "aye watan ke sajīle javān/mere naghme tumhāre liye hai" ("O you stylish soldiers of the land/ My verses are for you"). Like Noor Jehan's rendition of the Faiz Ahmed Faiz song (1962), this patriotic song too would have been familiar to Rushdie. Jamila's singing in the film version of *Midnight's Children* (dir. Deepa Mehta, 2012) is certainly modeled on Noor Jehan. So when she sings in the hall of private audience in the presence of the Pakistani military brass, the regimented approbation, so different from the wah-wahing of a rowdy crowd, captures a controlled, patterned applause. The difference between the earthy, simultaneous approbation captured in the word wah-wahing (to say "wah-wah," a common response of praise from the audience in Urdu) and a controlled approbation is vast, which is why the comparison is made in the novel.

Whereas no chaste Urdu song is actually given in *Midnight's Children* (although we can assume that Jamila Singer sings many on Voice Of Pakistan Radio [*Midnight's* 359]), a real ghazal (a nazm, to be precise) is sung by Rekha Merchant (*Satanic* 345), and it is a ghazal composed by the great Urdu poet Faiz Ahmed Faiz (1911–84), fondly remembered in Rushdie's memoir *Joseph Anton* (2012). The song sung by Rekha Merchant, "Do not ask of me, my love," is one of Faiz's best-known lyrics, and it appeared in his first volume of poems, *Naqsh-e-faryādī* ("A Lover's Complaint," 1941). The poem has twenty lines, of which the first and last are the same. Rushdie translates lines 1 and 17–20, which, in the original, are:

> mujh se pahalī sī mohabbat merī mahbūb na māng…
> ab bhī dilkaś hai terā husn magar kyā kīje
> aur bhī du:kh hai zamāne meṁ mohabbat ke sivā
> rāhte aur bhī hai vasl kī rāhat ke sivā
> mujh se pahalī sī mohabbat merī mahbūb na māng

Rushdie's translation:

> Do not ask of me, my love,
> that love I once had for you…
> How lovely you are still, my love,

but I am helpless too;
for the world has other sorrows than love,
and other pleasures too.
Do not ask of me, my love,
that love I once had for you. (345–5)

On Rushdie's translation, which is a variant of Mahmood Jamal's translation,[9] Professor Harish Trivedi writes, "It's a lame and perfunctory translation, I think; no spark in it, no feeling, and those two rhyming 'too' are
just too bad."[10] Line 19 is reduced, in translation, to "And other pleasures
too," when the full force of the line lies in its reference to the power of
love-in-separation, a not-uncommon motif in Urdu poetry more generally. The poem achieved a wider audience through Noor Jehan's "playback" rendition of it (with some variation) in the Pakistani film *Qaidi*
(1962). It is very likely that Rushdie recalls Noor Jehan's singing as Rekha
Merchant is given this great poem to sing.

But what of the frame of reference of Rekha Merchant's song? Gibreel
sits on a bench in a small London park. The memory of Rekha Merchant,
his former lover who had thrown herself and her children from a Bombay
high-rise – the same Rekha he had seen on the Bokhara carpet as he fell
from the exploding plane, uttering the satanic "Al-Lat" – the same Rekha
returns. He walks through the city streets and Rekha's vision follows him.
She is no tuneless soloist as she sings, accompanied by a harmonium, not
only Faiz Ahmed Faiz but also great Bollywood songs. Saladin Chamcha
had sung from Raj Kapoor's *Shree 420* in translation; Rekha sings a song,
in the vernacular, from the K. Asif epic *Mughal-e-Azam* (1960), the story
of the great Mughal Emperor Akbar's son Salim's (later Jehangir's) passion
for the court dancer-courtesan Anarkali: a much loved and filmed story.
Rushdie gives the reader the opening line of the song – "Pyaar kiya to
darna kya?" – and its translation too: "Why be afraid of love?" (*Satanic*
345). Our mental tracking takes us back to Madhubala's dance, the only
part of the original film filmed in color – where she, as Anarkali, throws
the gauntlet of love at Akbar himself. It is a dramatic challenge, a cour-
tesan defying her king as her song reaches the point where it challenges
the King's power: if God alone knows all, why fear his servant even if a
king? Any Bollywood buff would know the scene and would be aware of
the cinematic tracking at work here. With Gibreel, he (for the spectator
as voyeur is male) too would understand the power of love: she had asked
for "such a little thing, after all" (*Satanic* 345). Rekha sings this "defiant air
[aria]" (345), but we are only given the first line of the song, composed by

another great Urdu poet, Shakeel Badayuni. With the Faiz song, we get a full verse.

The Faiz song has an important thematic function as well, as it leads to the invocation of the name of a poet at the genesis of Islam. The poet's name is Baal. He is "the precocious polemicist" (*Satanic* 100) we encountered earlier in the novel; he is the troublesome satirist that Mahound fears. He asks the foundational question, "What kind of an idea are you?" (345) because Rushdie had defined the poet's role as "to name the unnameable, to point at frauds, to take sides, start arguments, shape the world and stop it from going to sleep" (100). And, continues Rushdie, "if rivers of blood flow from the cuts his verses inflict, then they will nourish him" (100). The unruly poet also voices; he is heard; he works through an auditory literalism, and it is sound that is feared. Like numbers, which for Rushdie are prior to cognition (numbers too, like songs, read us), sounds produce affects that require careful tracking by the reader.

Mother Tongue as Palimpsest

Sonality, then, becomes a key feature of Rushdie's writing. But with the tracking of sounds, there is always, as in Farishta's own tuneless singing, the relic of another language, which in Rushdie is either Bombay Hindi or its higher linguistic register, Urdu, the language of both film lyrics and of Faiz Ahmed Faiz. It is a register that leads Rushdie to play with homonyms such as "khana" in "Pagal Khana" (*Satanic* 352, 356), in which "khānā" is Hindi for food but Urdu for both food and a house or place of business (because the phoneme "kh" in the latter is the Persian and not the Sanskrit/Hindi "kh"). In the Rushdie archive, there are eight typed pages with cancellations and marginalia in autograph that deal with the composition of *The Satanic Verses*. Here, Rushdie looks at the themes of hybridization and translation that govern the novel. Also noted is the principle of death itself, the idea that we prove the world real (against the world as illusion, one suspects) by dying in it. And death – in the kind of existential fashion seen in Tolstoy's *The Death of Ivan Ilyich* – surfaces in these notes as an experience that is not available to us in our real lives, since we cannot live through our own death. In what are clearly notes toward a reconciliation with his own father, Rushdie gives Saladin Chamcha his native tongue back as he says to his dying father, "ham sab aap ke saath hain, abba. hum sab aap ko pyaar karte hai. bahut pyaar." As Rushdie's typed notes expand on the washing of the body and the stitching of the burial shroud, his hands move toward the margin, and in ink we get "when as a boy he saw his father's penis." In the published version (in the censored archive, so to speak) the original Urdu words are given in translation: "Now Salahuddin found better words, his Urdu returning to him after a long absence. *We're all beside you, Abba. We all love you very much*" (*Satanic* 545). Again, for native informants, the reference to "his Urdu returning" takes them to the words given in the notes, as if the text has been subtitled. In a sense, the turn to the sonic as meaning (semantic) and as sound (onomatopoeia) defines the Rushdie corpus.

The great Indian epic, the Mahābhārata, is replete with the word *uvāca*, "said," foregrounding in this linguistic act the utterance, the voice, and the sound and suggesting that descriptions and dialogue are to be heard: discourse tracked by sound. There is nothing new in Rushdie's sonic cosmopolitanism; the point here is that Rushdie insinuates a new genealogy of the Indian novel that privileges, in some ways, the sonic. Rushdie's use of tracking, going back to Maximilian Ophüls, is marked by the use of the soundtrack to bring together the sounds of Bombay as a melting pot, in which "Hinglish" (the Indian variety of English) functions as a social semiotic, alongside the polytheistic chants to the many Indian gods. Rushdie's fiction thus becomes both representation and sound – sonic ekphrasis or sonic fingerprint that captures the "visceral sensuality of form" (Kulezic-Wilson 85) – what Isabella van Elferen attributes to David Lynch's films: "obsessively dismantling signification, schizophonically challenging origin, and trans-diegetically erasing the limits of perception" (186). The image transforms itself into descriptive prose, sound into interference through noise, abracadabra into the motion of a locomotive. For Rushdie, to capture writing as corporeal expression, Saussure had to be transgressed, and a bow-wow theory of language, however dated and wrong, foregrounded. Through the use of a multiplicity of sounds, the *musique concrète* of people and their cinema, including Bollywood, Rushdie endorses an aesthetic regime that takes us back to debates about the ethics of formal experimentation so central to modernity. As Morgan has argued with reference to Ophüls, there may well be an ethics of the sound, of onomatopoeia, or of the utterance, which requires investigating in the context of the Salman Rushdie corpus. In this argument, the sonic in art (music for instance) not only mediates the organic and the mechanical (the human/animal and the sound of machines) but introduces, after Jacques Rancière, a *dissensus*, the placing of different logics on the same stage, "the commensurability of incommensurables" (Rancière 11) that cuts across the hierarchy of representation – image over sound.

This is precisely the challenge posed by Max Ophüls's tracking shots and Rushdie's visualization of the sonic. Of Stanley Kubrick, Kate McQuiston asks, "What makes a Kubrick film sound like a Kubrick film?" (139). Of Rushdie, we can similarly ask, "What makes a Rushdie novel sound like a Rushdie fiction?" This chapter has offered a tentative answer by suggesting links between Rushdie's "sonal auteurism" and a modernist cosmopolitan sonic imaginary that is Rushdie's remarkable contribution to the Indian novel in English.

Notes

1 Salman Rushdie Papers, Box 22, folder 7, "The Satanic Verses, Notes, MS and TS [1 of 2]," Subseries 2.1, Manuscript, Archives, and Rare Book Library [MARBL], Emory University. Hereafter MARBL. The ten films are: *Pather Panchali* (about which Rushdie said in a recent interview: "*Pather Panchali* [*Song of the Little Road*, dir. Satyajit Ray, 1955] is the film that I would choose when asked for the greatest film ever made.... *Citizen Kane* would probably come second" [*Emory Quadrangle*, Fall 2010, p. 13]), *The Seven Samurai* (dir. Akira Kurosawa, 1954), *The Seventh Seal* (dir. Ingmar Bergman, 1957), *Ashes and Diamonds* (dir. Andrej Wajda, 1958), *8½* (dir. Federico Fellini, 1963), *L'Avventura* (dir. Michelangelo Antonioni, 1960), *Alphaville* (dir. Jean-Luc Godard, 1965), *Marienbad* (dir. Alain Resnais, 1961), *Jules et Jim* (dir. François Truffaut, 1962), and *The Exterminating Angel* (dir. Luis Buñuel, 1962). *Citizen Kane* (dir. Orson Welles, 1941) is not mentioned in this list; its inclusion in the *Emory Quadrangle* interview seems like an afterthought and, effectively, expands Rushdie's list to eleven. Parts of this argument have been published in V. Mishra, "Tuneless."
2 Of the films mentioned on the original, single typed sheet, only two films, Kurosawa's *The Seven Samurai* and Ray's *Pather Panchali*, are non-European, with only *The Seven Samurai* and *The Seventh Seal* located in the distant past.
3 MARBL also carries an interview in which, when asked what he would like to come back as, Rushdie replied, "a city."
4 A quick look at *Grimus* (1975), *Midnight's Children* (1981), *Shame* (1983), *The Satanic Verses*, and *The Moor's Last Sigh* releases many sounds: abracadabra (*MC* 519, *TSV* 365), Abyssinia (*Grimus* 28; "I'll be seein' ya"), achha (*MC* 444, *TSV* 34), ai (*Shame* 228), ai-o-ai-ooo (*MC* 117), allakazoo, allakazam (*TSV* 344), arré baap (*MC* 46), arré baba (*MC* 274, 526), baap-ré (*MLS* 169), baap-re-baap (*MC* 142, 280; *TSV* 21), bee tee ems (*TSV* 39), bustees (*TSV* 55), chamcha (*TSV*), chhi-chhi (*MC* 365), cho chweet (*MC* 75), chutter-mutter (*MC* 521), dugdugee (*MC* 75, 198), funtoosh (*MC* 69, *TSV* 355), gai-wallah (*MC* 51), teen batti (*MC* 55), Whisky Sisodia (*TSV* 351), Pagal Khana (TSV 352), and hundreds more.
5 Van Elferen is referring to R. Murray Schafer's work here.
6 Trilling notes, "I invert the natural order not out of lack of modesty but taking the cue of W. H. Auden's remark that a real book reads us."

7 "The Satanic Comedy" is an early title of the novel in MARBL.
8 The sound and image are broken apart; this is how Colin MacCabe would have read it.
9 See Acknowledgments to *The Satanic Verses*.
10 Harish Trivedi, personal correspondence.

CHAPTER 12

Postcolonial Realism in the Novels of Rohinton Mistry

Eli Park Sorensen

In his book *The Postcolonial Unconscious*, Neil Lazarus writes that postcolonial scholars today

> ought ... to redress a long-standing imbalance in postcolonial literary studies by focusing anew on realist writing. The point is that, inasmuch as the dominant aesthetic dispositions in postcolonial literary studies have from the outset reflected those in post-structuralist theory generally, the categorical disparagement of realism in the latter field has tended to receive a dutiful – if wholly unjustified and unjustifiable – echo in the former.... There is no good reason for scholars in postcolonial studies to hang on to this dogma today. (82)

It would hardly be an exaggeration to claim that postcolonial studies – as an academic field based mainly in literary departments – has generally demonstrated a lack of interest in the formal complexities of literary realism.[1] To many postcolonial critics, realism as a literary form fits poorly with the field's dogmas and values – the established theoretical concepts that characterize the orthodox postcolonial text analysis. The theoretical vocabulary – mainly derived from poststructuralist theory, as Lazarus points out – has on the one hand been crucial in terms of the formation of postcolonial studies as an academic field; on the other hand, the at times exaggerated use of concepts such as hybridity, mimicry, catachresis, the in-between, and so on means that many postcolonial literary readings have tended to say more about postcolonial studies as an academic institution and as a theoretical orientation than about the texts themselves.[2] Often, postcolonial critics have focused on anti-realist literary forms – that is, forms seen as corresponding to the institutionalized postcolonial vocabulary – whereas literary forms belonging to the so-called realist tradition have typically been read along a thematic register or labeled inherently Eurocentric, essentialist, and homogenizing.[3] Realism as a literary form constitutes, in other words, a kind of blind spot in postcolonial studies, despite the fact that a considerable amount of postcolonial literature belongs to this tradition.[4]

It is from this perspective that the Indian-born Canadian writer Rohinton Mistry's works offer an interesting counterexample. Born in 1952, Mistry left his native India at the age of twenty-three and moved to Canada, where he embarked on a highly successful career as a writer in the late 1980s. However, India – and in particular the city of Mumbai (Bombay) – figures centrally in all his works. In the eleven stories included in the short story anthology *Tales from Firozsha Baag* (1987), Mistry traces the fates of a group of characters connected to the same Mumbai apartment building, called Firozsha Baag. His first novel, *Such a Long Journey* (1991), tells the story of a bank clerk in Mumbai during the Indo-Pakistani war in 1971. In the novel *Family Matters* (2002), we follow an old man with Parkinson's disease living in Mumbai during the 1990s, while Mistry's perhaps most successful novel to date, *A Fine Balance* (1995), focuses on Indira Gandhi's State of Emergency in 1975.

Mistry's novels draw unmistakably on a realist tradition, which perhaps explains why literary criticism on Mistry's works – in contrast to, say, the magical realist works of Salman Rushdie and others – has often revolved around questions of authenticity, accuracy of historical representation, and even questions about the author's right to fictionalize Indian history as a migrant writer.[5] Realism as a literary form quite simply seems to prompt these questions more readily than other literary styles. In *A Fine Balance*, a scene occurs during which Maneck, one of the main characters, reads a stack of old Indian newspapers from the late 1970s. According to the critic Nilufer Bharucha, Maneck here metafictionally *enacts* the technique used by the author of the book: "the diasporic writer, who, like his creation also dusts off old cobwebs and catches up with the happenings in India during his absence from it" (*Rohinton* 164).[6] Bharucha goes on to question the novel's historical accuracy, specificity, and authenticity – labelling Mistry's style "ethnocentric" while dismissing the author's portrait of the lower-caste characters as "cardboard figures" (167). The underlying premise is that Mistry's realist style inadequately portrays the complexity of the Emergency – that is, it is not realistic *enough*. Other critics have argued that Mistry's style is in fact closer to a *critique* of realism. Thus, Sharmani Patricia Gabriel writes that Mistry's *A Fine Balance* "appears to have been influenced by the narrative concerns of nineteenth-century European social realism.... However, although Mistry accedes to the representational power of the realist novel ... he is also aware of the inadequacies of the traditional realist novel" (87). Both critics – along with many others – seem to be troubled by Mistry's style as realism.[7]

The definition of Mistry's style as "not-quite-realism" is a recurrent motif in much literary criticism on the author's work, and it is this problematic that I want to address and explore further in this chapter through a focus on realism as a literary form. My starting point is a return to Georg Lukács's early treatise *The Theory of the Novel* (first published in 1920), which may offer a different – and what I see as a useful – template for a re-conceptualization of realism as a literary form from a postcolonial perspective. Lukács helps us identify a "realist ideal" in Mistry's three novels, *Such a Long Journey*, *A Fine Balance*, and *Family Matters*. Mistry's novels outline a plethora of incidents and events tied together in a plot structure that seemingly offers a causally determining framework which endows each element with meaning; at the same time, the novels also question causal determinations, preventing any straightforward readings of the texts as simply social critiques of a particular historical epoch. Mistry's novels are specifically concerned with the notion of interpretation – the interpretive dynamics that endow life with meaning in a larger, but also more abstract, framework. The texts explore the inscription of lives in trans-individual trajectories – a process that, at the same time, can never become fully organic, and one that remains haunted by irony, discrepancy. Over time, however – that is, through the myriad repetitive patterns and recurring motifs, combined with gradual progress – one senses a dynamic of connectedness and relatedness, a realist ideal that, as Lukács writes, "cancels out the accidental nature of ... experiences and the isolated nature of the events recounted" (*Theory* 125), even if the dynamic at the same time remains the product of novelistic interpretation.

Compositional Structure

In Mistry's tight compositional structure, actions inevitably seem to be followed by consequences, intended or unintended; as Hilary Mantel – commenting on "the cyclical pattern of disaster in which Mistry has trapped his creations" – writes in a review of *A Fine Balance*: "one feels controlled, as if by a bad god." To Mantel, the characters in Mistry's novels are "caught in a vast, predetermined, prepatterned design which the author embroiders fiercely, glibly" (6).[8] Morey further comments that "there is always the faint but unmistakable trace of an 'author' beyond the text, *imposing* a pattern" (*Rohinton* 169), a trace that endows the fictional trajectory with a sense of compositionality.

The compositionality of the novel form is an aspect that lies at the heart of Georg Lukács's reflections in *The Theory of the Novel*.[9] At one point, Lukács writes that "the composition of the novel is the paradoxical fusion of heterogeneous and discrete components into an organic whole which is then abolished over and over again" (84). The novel form, consisting of independent parts that never quite come together in an organic whole, is always threatened by disintegration; this is why the novel's structure, in contrast to older forms such as the epic, must be rigorously composed. Each part or element in the novel, Lukács argues, "must have a strict compositional and architectural significance" (*Theory* 76). In a historical perspective, the genre of the novel is connected to what Lukács calls the age of "transcendental homelessness," a period of secularization during which god or the absolute no longer provides a guarantee for the order of the world: "the novel is the epic of a world that has been abandoned by God" (88). The main task of the novel, Lukács argues, is to represent a world that has become fundamentally un-representable, a world without a central point around which everything else may be organized. The "lack of limits in the novel," Lukács writes, "has a 'bad' infinity about it: therefore it needs certain imposed limits in order to become form" (81). Like the epic and the drama, the novel composes a form that seeks to organize the heterogeneous elements of the world; yet this form, with its regulating laws and structures, remains inorganic, abstract, and contingent (Lukács, *Theory* 70). The novel is thus a kind of "form-giving," a formal composition of regulating laws and compositional principles, or a "process of becoming" (73) that never quite reaches a stable level.

In the first part of *The Theory of the Novel*, Lukács identifies the novel's overall formal dynamic as irony, a kind of constant self-correction, or a "double vision" that continuously questions all the values and truths that the novel may produce (92). He writes:

> The irony of the novel is the self-correction of the world's fragility: inadequate relations can transform themselves into a fanciful yet well-ordered round of misunderstandings and cross-purposes, within which everything is seen as many-sided, within which things appear as isolated and yet connected, as full of value and yet totally devoid of it, as abstract fragments and as concrete autonomous life, as flowering and as decaying, as the infliction of suffering and as suffering itself. (75)

Through irony, the novel form illustrates that it is fundamentally unable to represent the world truthfully – by which it achieves a kind of objectivity, albeit of a negative character, in the sense that the ironic force reveals the antinomies of modernity, the difference between reality and fiction, or between life and meaning (90).

Mistry's fiction is in many ways a prolonged attempt to articulate and overcome the antinomies of postcolonial modernity, such as the rift between grand ideals and the harsh realities of quotidian life. One scene that recurs in different variations in all of his novels involves a minor character typically indulging in some high-flown rhetoric, while the main character is torn between listening and thinking about the practicalities of life. In *Such a Long Journey*, the main character Gustad Noble at one point listens to the street seller Peerbhoy Paanwalla spinning a patriotic yarn about the history of the nation. A little later, "Gustad looked at his watch and reluctantly tore himself away from the group" (309). One finds a similar situation in *A Fine Balance* when the main character reluctantly seeks advice from the pseudo-lawyer Mr. Valmik: "Dina began to wish Mr. Valmik would stop talking in this high-flown manner. It had been entertaining for a while but was rapidly becoming wearisome.... Bombast and rhetoric infected the nation" (553). In *Family Matters*, the amateur actors Bhaskar and Gautam discuss the art of acting, while the main character Yezad "grew impatient, wishing they would stop sounding their own theatrical trumpets" (331). Hired by Yezad to act like local Shiv Sena thugs, Bhaskar and Gautam's play-acting is supposed to "persuade" Mr. Kapur – a local shop owner – to enter politics. However, even if Mr. Kapur is later duped by Bhaskar and Gautam – with fatal consequences when the real representatives of the nationalist Shiv Sena Party later appear in the shop – he is far from alien to the metaphoric power of theater himself. At one point, Mr. Kapur delivers a pompous speech in which he compares Shakespeare to Bombay, both apparently containing "the universe"; all the while "Yezad studied his watch" (303). The ironic scenes taken together draw the contours of one of the main motifs in Mistry's oeuvre, namely the rift between rhetoric and reality, or storytelling and life. It is a rift that is never quite overcome, one that points toward some deeper, more profound structure, a grand pattern, but also toward the very opposite: the confusing, quotidian experience of everyday life unredeemed by the ineffective ramblings of rhetoric.

Looking Too Closely

This realist ideal, a compositional structure that appears to be *least* composed, is one that in many ways corresponds to the formal dynamic that runs through all of Mistry's novels. On a formal level, the novels are deeply concerned with compositionality, patterns, as well as – thematically – the conflict between the problematic individual and the abstractions of history, and the distance or discrepancy between everyday life and the grand truths. If the novel's task in the age of transcendental homelessness is to represent a world that has become fundamentally un-representable, it does so as we have seen by posing a structure of events that – qua being strung together – are interpreted to be causally related; irony prevents the novel from making absolute statements, while temporality creates a glimpse of the organic whole. At the center of this novelistic dialectic is an exploration of the cause-effect relationship – an exploration that in Mistry's works takes on an almost obsessive character. His novels often seem to delineate complex and convoluted trajectories between causes and effects, yet rarely is there a straight line between them. The novels seem less concerned with the discovery of real causes, or origins, than with demonstrating or investigating the nature of this complex relationship.

Mistry's first two novels, *Such a Long Journey* and *A Fine Balance*, both focus on a turbulent epoch in India's modern history, namely the 1970s. Both novels are occupied with the relationship between the individual and the grand historical trajectory. *Such a Long Journey* tells the story of a Parsi family, the Nobles, who inhabit an apartment complex called the Khodadad Building, and in particular of the family patriarch, the bank clerk Gustad Noble. The novel's historical frame is the 1971 Pakistani Civil War – one that eventually involved India – which always simmers in the background of the family Nobles' daily life (Morey, *Rohinton* 72).

Despite Gustad's attempts to keep the reality of history out of his life – symbolized by the paper he keeps on his windows, long after the government-decreed blackout has ended (339) – history unexpectedly forces itself on the Nobles when their close friend and neighbor, Major Jimmy Bilimoria, a military man carrying out covert operations for the Indian government, asks Gustad to deposit a large sum of money in a bank account, illegally. Reluctant at first, Gustad eventually agrees but later feels betrayed and alarmed when he reads in the newspapers about Bilimoria's arrest.

One of the great themes that *Such a Long Journey* explores is the nature of discrepancy – between Gustad as an individual and the national history of India in the early 1970s; between reality and rhetoric; and ultimately between reality and fiction.[10] The novel establishes what appear to be causal connections, yet these connections are at the same time undermined by a haunting uncertainty that runs through the story on several levels – an ironic force that always threatens to tear apart the overall framework in which the individual events and actions are inserted and strung together. When a pavement artist – a character who paints religious figures on a wall next to the Khodadad Building – discusses the nature of imagination with Gustad, the novel enacts a meta-fictive monologue on the nature of what could be Mistry's own novelistic technique:

> You see, I don't like to weaken anyone's faith. Miracle, magic, mechanical trick, coincidence – does it matter what it is, as long as it helps? Why analyse the strength of the imagination, the power of suggestion, power of auto-suggestion, the potency of psychological pressures? Looking too closely is destructive, makes everything disintegrate. As it is, life is difficult enough. Why to simply make it tougher? After all, who is to say what makes a miracle and what makes a coincidence? (289)

Gustad agrees and adds that the wall, previously "a stinking, filthy disgrace," has now "become a beautiful, fragrant place which makes everyone feel good" (289). However, there is a sense in which Gustad does look too closely at the constructions of history. Throughout the novel, he follows the historical developments at a distance – that is, in the papers and through rumors. Gradually, as the novel progresses, Gustad feels disgusted by the official history, its unreliable and deceitful stories. When he finally visits the dying Bilimoria, he learns a very different story from the one he knows. It turns out that Bilimoria apparently was hired by none other than Indira Gandhi herself to raise funds for a guerrilla operation in Pakistan. However, the operation eventually failed when someone accidentally revealed that a large sum of money had been withdrawn from the government's coffers without the proper authorization. Bilimoria becomes a scapegoat – accused, improbably, of having imitated the prime minister's voice through the telephone – and ends up imprisoned and disgraced.

The knowledge of Bilimoria's personal downfall taints Gustad's feeling of national pride. When he reads about the surrender ceremony, a sense of patriotism initially fills him; soon after, however, he reads a short notice stating that Mr. J. Bilimoria had died of a heart attack in prison, after which the "glow of national pride dropped from him like a wet raincoat" (311). Here, the individual and the historical briefly coincide in the novel – a culminating moment of personal experience intertwined with the newspaper stories corroborating the distant, official narrative. Whether Bilimoria's version of the historical events is true or not is never confirmed, yet it is one that illuminates the gap that separates Gustad's everyday life from history.

Tipping the Balance

The dissonance between the individual and the historical is further explored in *A Fine Balance*, whose plot alternates between large, panoramic descriptions of history – this time the 1975 Emergency – and intimate, personal scenes.[11] The novel traces the intricate connections between the grand historical trajectory and the everyday lives of individuals; yet, once again, these connections remain largely abstract or indirect. From the perspective of the individual, history is generally experienced as a distant, parallel narrative, whose effects randomly and accidentally interrupt people's lives; over time, however, the reader – along with some of the characters – gradually senses a larger and deeper pattern of connectivity, one that potentially dissolves the abstractness of history and people's place in it.

The force of history is constantly at work in the novel, yet a clear and coherent vision is permanently absent. Instead, the historical breaks through and erupts in what seems like a random fashion – a terrorizing, accidental force disrupting, for example, the lives of Om and Ishvar, two tailors who eventually end up as beggars. When their home is destroyed (as a direct consequence of a "Slum Beautification" program), Om and Ishvar watch a work crew erecting two hoardings upon which,

> they pasted the Prime Minister's face ... then debated about the accompanying message. There was a variety to choose from.... The workers were unanimous concerning the first slogan: THE CITY BELONGS TO YOU! KEEP IT BEAUTIFUL! The second was posing some difficulty. The supervisor wanted to use FOOD FOR THE HUNGRY! HOMES FOR THE HOMELESS! His subordinates advised him that something else would be more appropriate; they recommended THE NATION IS ON THE MOVE! (Mistry, *Fine* 299)

The fragility of this symbolic manifestation of political power furthermore becomes evident in a scene during which Om and Ishvar listen to a speech by the prime minister. Accompanying the prime minister is a gigantic cardboard version of herself, which begins to sway violently when a helicopter drops leaflets (about the Twenty-Point Program) and rose petals: "But the Prime Minister's eighty-foot cutout began to sway in the tempest of the helicopter's blades.... The cutout started to topple slowly, face forward. Those in the vicinity of the cardboard-and-plywood giant ran for their lives" (264). The meaning of the political event is here comically severed from the individual yet at the same time ironically reinforced, almost too literally.

There are innumerable, similarly comical – as well as more serious or even tragic – scenes in the novel, in which the individual and the historical are juxtaposed or collide, thus creating unexpected ironic effects and patterns. Other, perhaps deeper, patterns of ironic juxtapositions emerge over time – some clearly intended or causally connected; some of a more accidental nature. It is precisely the grey area between accidental events and possibly motivated ones that Mistry is particularly keen to explore. According to Lukács, the accidental – or what he calls the "demonic" (*Theory* 87) – hints at hidden connections, yet these are connections that can never fully be acknowledged. At one point in *Such a Long Journey*, Dinshawji – Gustad's close friend and colleague at the bank – reflects on the disappearance and changes of names, and the transformation of the things, places, and lives to which the changed names refer. While Gustad and Dinshawji discuss the metaphysics of naming, a man is hit by a car and immediately we are thrown back into the busy streets of Mumbai again (73–4). *A Fine Balance* pursues the accidental with even greater insistence. The novel's plot is constantly punctuated by accidents, especially traffic accidents – for example Rustom, the husband of the main character Dina, is hit by a truck after he has bought some ice cream; Om is hit by a truck, albeit not fatally; when Maneck, another main character in the novel, arrives at his college for the first time, an old man is run down by a bus; and finally the beggar, Shankar, is instantly killed when he is hit by a double-decker bus (*Fine* 45; 189; 232; 491).

It is difficult if not impossible to differentiate between the novel's many incidents – that is, between motivated, causally related events on one hand and random, accidental events with no further significance on the other. Yet what prevents the novel form from disintegrating into heterogeneous, unrelated parts is the novel's deliberate and persistent creation of repetitive patterns, hidden structures, and connections revealed over time. From an individual perspective, one may trace the effects of history back to their original causes – although only in an abstract sense, as the episode in the prologue demonstrates, when a body is found on the tracks: it is an accident that *may* be related to the Emergency but that has concrete consequences involving both tragedy on an individual level and – in a more trivial sense – the delay of the train (*Fine* 3–6).

From a larger perspective, the individual narratives all connect back to the background of India's post-independence history, and more specifically the early 1970s and the Emergency, as Peter Morey observes:

> All characters and relationships are affected by the machinations of the capitalist economy: from the piece-working tailors and their well-intentioned

employer Dina, who is nonetheless implicated as an exploiter of cheap, non-unionized labour ... to the beggars whose place in the warped economy of beggary is determined by the severity of their mutilation.... [It] emphasizes the text's interest in moral culpability and the impossibility of total insulation against the taint of money in a society where anything or anyone can be bought and sold. (*Fictions* 182)

As I have argued elsewhere, the novel at one and the same time creates a sense of relatedness and points toward the underlying conditions upon which this sense of relatedness is premised (Sorensen, *Postcolonial* 126–9). In a Lukácsian perspective, the formal dynamic of *A Fine Balance* involves a chain or a series of events interpreted to be causally connected but which is always questioned and potentially reaffirmed through the novel's many pages. The text's inscription in what Morey calls "the machinations of the capitalist economy" is thus never a stable, straightforward process, and to ignore the latter aspect is also at the same time to ignore what constitutes an important element of what I would characterize as the novel's realist dynamic.

Accommodating the Past

Similar to *Such a Long Journey* and *A Fine Balance*, Mistry's third novel, *Family Matters*, explores the complicated relationship between the individual and history, albeit arguably in a less direct way. The historical frame is the mid-1990s, some twenty years after the turbulent epoch of the 1970s, which Mistry described in the two previous novels. On an individual level, the novel tells the story of Nariman Vakeel, a former professor of English literature, now aging, fragile, and unable to take care of himself due to Parkinson's disease.

Vakeel's life is in many ways representative of the many conflicts and problems haunting the Parsi community in the post-independence era, including a dwindling population – due to falling birth rates, the influence of Western ideas, and secularization – and the possibility of extinction in the near future (Mistry, *Family* 411–7). The events of Vakeel's life have been largely tragic, not only for himself but for several people around him: his wife and the woman he loved (dying together as they fell from a rooftop following a fight), as well as his wife's child, Coomy, who never stops feeling resentment over what he did to her mother – a feeling that only becomes more intense as she herself ages.

The potential of time is a central theme of Mistry's third novel. *Family Matters* is deeply concerned with the themes of aging and retrospection and questions of guilt, forgiveness, and atonement. Only the youngest child, Roxana, seems unscathed by the debris of her father's life. But when Coomy sends Vakeel to live at her place, the relationship – and the small family budget – becomes severely strained. In a larger sense, Vakeel is a representative of the past itself, a country's fading memory, as well as the lessons of the past. The hardship of accommodating the helpless Vakeel eventually becomes a metaphor for a family's – and, in a larger perspective, a community's and a nation's – difficulties in handling the past and for a generation about to repeat the errors and failures of previous generations. For example, when, late in the novel, Yezad's son Murad decides to invite a non-Parsi girlfriend to his birthday party, Yezad strongly objects by insisting on orthodox Parsi rules, thus echoing Vakeel's situation two generations earlier (493–6).

As the novel progresses, Yezad increasingly emerges as the novel's main protagonist. The story zooms in on his at times desperate attempts to keep the family afloat, but his salary working as a shop assistant in a small sports equipment store is barely sufficient. The store is owned by Mr. Kapur, a Hindu who loves Mumbai – or Bombay, as he insists on calling it – more than anything else in the world. Mr. Kapur repeatedly tells the story of his family's escape from Punjab in 1947, how they arrived in the city of Bombay, and how his father became a wealthy man: "My father started over, with zero, and became prosperous," says Mr. Kapur. "Only city in the world where this is possible" (151). Also working in the shop is a severely traumatized Muslim who survived a violent attack by nationalist Hindus in 1992. Although the novel's historical background is more diffuse than in *Such a Long Journey* and *A Fine Balance*, many of the events relate back to one particular event, namely the attack and destruction of the Babri mosque in 1992, which subsequently led to many clashes between Hindus and Muslims and further stimulated a growing nationalist sentiment.[12] As a cosmopolitan idealist who believes Bombay represents (or ought to represent) a peaceful, harmonious haven for all ethnicities, Mr. Kapur initially plans to enter local politics to fight against sectarian violence – a plan that, as described earlier, Yezad supports in his own somewhat roguish way, with tragic consequences.

After witnessing a beautiful scene at a train station where people – regardless of ethnicity or religion – are lifted up on top of the train roof, Mr. Kapur composes an inspired vision of harmonious, peaceful coexistence: "This beautiful city of seven islands … this enigma of cosmopolitanism where races and religions live side by side … this dear, dear city now languishes … like a patient in intensive care … put there by small, selfish men" (160). Some 200 pages later in the novel, Mr. Kapur's beautiful vision suffers a blow when he goes to the train station, attempts to join the people on the rooftop, and is rejected. "They looked at me like I was a stranger," he observes sadly. "Others seemed to find me amusing, turning to one another to laugh" (347). Yezad looks at his boss' expensive hairstyle, his fine clothes and Italian leather shoes, and knows that Mr. Kapur's love for the city is largely built on a romantic illusion – nothing but a story that is painfully different from the realities:

> Sometimes, when Mr. Kapur spoke about 1947 and Partition, Yezad felt that Punjabi migrants of a certain age were like Indian authors writing about that period, whether in realist novels of corpse-filled trains or in the magic-realist midnight muddles, all repeating the same catalogue of horrors about slaughter and burning, rape and mutilation, foetuses torn out of wombs, genitals stuffed in the mouths of the castrated. (151)

The indirect comment on Rushdie's as well as Mistry's own works aside, the passage once again stresses the discrepancy between history and storytelling, facts and fiction, but also acknowledges the importance of retelling events "still incomprehensible" (151), especially to later generations who did not witness them directly.

A novel occupied with writing and memory, as well as with the fragile connections between past and present, *Family Matters* particularly examines the complex relationship between causes and effects. At one point Jehangir, Yezad and Roxana's son, is discovered to have received bribes from schoolmates while supervising their homework; soon after, Yezad delivers a grandiose speech to Roxana: "There's only one way to explain it. The same corruption that pollutes the country is right here, in your own family.... Is it any wonder Jehangla took the bribe?" (283). Roxana retorts that their son only took the money "to help his parents with food, and with his Grandpa's medicines" (283). Yezad, in turn, understands Roxana's answer as an accusation – that he cannot provide enough money to sustain the household. A little later in the novel, Yezad gets himself involved in the earlier-mentioned shady activity leading to the death of his boss when attempting to become manager of the sports equipment store, which will earn him a higher salary so that he can pay for his family's expenses. The strained family budget is of course related to the ill health and helplessness of Vakeel, the person possibly the cause of several people's tragic fates. In all these cases, it would be possible to trace a direct chain of what seem to be connected events. At the same time, it is a chain of events haunted by potential contingency, a dynamic exploring, not of how the events are related in an absolute sense but rather of how they are experienced, or interpreted, as part of a larger puzzle.

Conclusion

Near the end of *Family Matters*, the narrative perspective changes from Yezad to the youngest son, Jehangir. At one point, Jehangir looks at an old jigsaw puzzle of Lake Como, which used to occupy him for hours; now, it reminds him of the puzzle of his grandfather's life, and in a larger sense the puzzle of the past itself: "a strange jigsaw puzzle of indefinite size" (491). This image of a jigsaw puzzle with an indefinite number of small pieces is reminiscent of the motif of the patchwork quilt in *A Fine Balance*, as well as of the writings of the Balzacian figure Mr. Vilas, Yezad's friend, in *Family Matters*. Mr. Vilas composes letters for the poor and illiterate: "He heard about all his clients' lives … writing and reading the ongoing drama of family matters, the endless tragedy and comedy," Vilas reflects, and a little later realizes "that collectively, the letters formed a pattern" (142). Similar to the two previous works, *Family Matters* is a novel that attempts to create a sense of reality, its coherences and structures, while at the same time exploring the discrepancies, the crisscrossing narrative lines that make up most of people's lives.

Thus, in response to criticism that reads the realist text either as an outdated form of representation or simply as a direct critique of historical reality, I have argued that Mistry's novels deliberately seek to explore the connections between individuals and collective history. The texts are in one sense a critique of the postcolonial political structures affecting the lives of Indian citizens in the 1970s. However, the novels also explore the leap such a critique inevitably involves. This is ultimately what I would call the "workings" of Mistry's realism. This dynamic comes close to the one we find in Lukács's theory of the novel, which envisions a realist ideal that strives toward the form that appears *least* composed. Mistry's novels explore the different realities of postcolonial modernity through a compositional structure that is, at the same time, always threatened by disintegration. Throughout, the novels constantly waver between descriptions of immediate experiences and larger narrative trajectories of the nation, a people, a family genealogy. As such, Mistry's novelistic dynamic generates a sense of spontaneity – the dissolution of the abstract and the concrete – which thereby potentially cancels out the purely accidental or meaningless, in an aesthetic attempt to reach out for and uncover the hidden structures of life.

Notes

1 For extended discussions of this issue, see in particular Carter; Moss ("Can Rohinton Mistry's"; "Infinity"; and "Plague"); Sorensen (*Postcolonial*); Gunning; and Anjaria (*Realism*).

2 The institutional narrowness of postcolonial studies has led to a disturbing sameness regarding theoretical inquiries and methodological approaches; as Lazarus points out, one finds "to an extraordinary degree, the same questions asked, the same methods, techniques, and conventions used, the same concepts mobilized, the same conclusions drawn" ("Politics" 424).

3 An example of a classic postcolonial critique of realism is the early essay, "Representation and the Colonial Text," by Homi Bhabha.

4 See Moss, "Plague," for a discussion of this issue.

5 Robert L. Ross recounts a BBC TV panel discussion in 1996 (just before the Booker Prize award ceremony) during which Germaine Greer allegedly said: "I hate [*A Fine Balance*]. I absolutely hate it.... I just don't recognize this dismal, dreary city. It's a Canadian book about India. What could be worse?" (Ross 240). Greer had spent a few months teaching at a college in Mumbai and did not recognize the dismal poverty described in Mistry's *A Fine Balance*. To Greer's relief, Graham Swift won that year's Booker Prize for the novel *Last Orders*. A few years later, Mistry incorporated the incident into his book *Family Matters*. Vilas, a local letter writer, has read a novel portraying the Emergency, which according to "a big professor at some big university in England" who has been in India for a short period but nonetheless has become a self-declared expert, is completely out of touch with the realities. Quoting T. S. Eliot, Vilas concludes that "humans cannot tolerate too much reality" (Mistry, *Family* 210).

6 For a more elaborate discussion of Bharucha's argument, see Herbert (23–4).

7 On this issue, see also Almond; Schneller; and Tokaryk. I have written more extensively about this issue in Sorensen (*Postcolonial* 134–7).

8 Also quoted in Morey (*Rohinton* 162).

9 For a more extensive discussion of Lukács's *The Theory of the Novel*, see Sorensen, "Novelistic."

10 For a thorough discussion of the discrepancy between appearance and reality, and representational crisis, in *Such a Long Journey*, see Morey, *Rohinton* 69–93.

11 For a longer discussion of *A Fine Balance*, see Sorensen, *Postcolonial* (121–37).

12 For more on the rise of the regionalist, Hindu nationalist party Shiv Sena, which came to power along with the Bharatiya Janata Party in 1995, see Morey, *Rohinton* 25–132.

CHAPTER 13

Far from the Nation, Closer to Home: Privacy, Domesticity, and Regionalism in Indian English Fiction

Saikat Majumdar

"I try to locate myself outside issues," writes the novelist and scientist Sunetra Gupta, "but not outside politics."[1] This intriguing claim to locate oneself within a domain of the political that lies outside the narrower purview of "issues" raises several questions. What kind of politics are we talking about here, if it is to be understood as distinct from issues? Is it the identification of the political as personal and vice versa, championed by the thinkers of second wave feminism? Or is it the Foucauldian understanding of politics as diffuse rather than centralized? Is it the radical suspicion of sensational events that defined Fernand Braudel's celebration of history "with slow and perceptible rhythms" (Braudel 20)? Or is it simply a withdrawal from the front pages of the newspaper to its innards, to the harder-to-classify human interest stories?

The twentieth century has made it clear that postcolonial novels written in European languages are among the most deeply burdened with the sharp weight of issues. Such novels face at least a double pressure: the metropolitan expectation to provide historical and anthropological knowledge about cultures they "represent" on one hand and, on the other, the ethico-political anxiety that impels such novelists to foreground the most pressing public issues that dominate the national consciousness from which they emerge. Not infrequently, the Anglophone postcolonial novel feels like newsbytes from war-torn lands; too often it glares with the headlines of newspapers, be it the scale and ambition of post-liberation progress, the high points of anticolonial struggle, or the brutal spectacle of trauma.

If, within the history of India, the real and symbolic moment of the birth of the modern nation is the stroke of midnight 1947, the most resplendent moment of triumph of the issue-driven vision of politics for the English novel is also that of its headline-grabbing reincarnation thirty-four years later: the publication of Salman Rushdie's *Midnight's Children* in 1981. The midnight of 1947 was the proverbial moment of the event that led to the birth of the postcolonial nation – the very genesis of post-coloniality, as it were. It is unsurprising that the celebrated novelization of this moment is shaped and driven by the aesthetics of postmodernism, naturally impelled by the need to subvert a modernity felt as hegemonic, as well as by post-modernism's eruptive attachment to historical discourse in its most fantastic and fabulistic, indeed, magic-realist dimensions.

In his edited anthology *The Picador Book of Modern Indian Literature*, the poet, novelist, and critic Amit Chaudhuri argues that delicacy, nuance, and irony, seen as belonging properly to the domain of the English novel and to Enlightenment reason, are usually suspect in postcolonial fiction, which finds a better ally in postmodernist modes of narration, in magic realism, in poststructuralist self-referentiality and the Jamesonian national allegory, which privileges historical discourse over the literary, culminating in the depiction of Indian history as "a fancy-dress party or the Mardi Gras, full of chatter, music, sex, tomfoolery, free drinks, and rock and roll" (A. Chaudhuri, "Salman" 484). While *Midnight's Children* remains the seminal work of the national allegory, several novels have celebrated versions of it since then, such as Vikram Chandra's *Red Earth and Pouring Rain* (1995), Shashi Tharoor's *The Great Indian Novel* (1989), and Mukul Kesavan's *Looking Through Glass* (1995), before the genre gave way to the post-millennial exuberance of the new economy and its accompanying cultural confidence.

In India, the preferred site of the national allegory is a pan-Indian milieu created in the narrative imagination, and the favorite subjects of its historical discourse are the larger, public processes of nationalism, nation-building, and nation-breaking – the development of the nascent republic and its constitutional ideals, riots, wars, and crises in the cabinet government. Fredric Jameson's declaration of the fusion that takes place between private and public lives in "third world" cultures ("Third-World") makes it possible for such larger national phenomena to be conveniently read as entering into an allegorical relation with the private lives of fictional characters, as Saleem Sinai's Bildungsroman echoes the growth of the nation in *Midnight's Children*. The years following its publication, leading up to the mid-1990s, were perhaps the richest for novels that aspired to the model of national allegory in Anglophone India. The decade following this period, leading up to the present day, however, has seen the publication of significant novels deviating from this dominant public-historiographic norm. These include two Booker-winning novels, Arundhati Roy's *The God of Small Things* (1997) and Kiran Desai's *The Inheritance of Loss* (2006), both of which engage in a far more immediate and sensual apprehension of private, regional sensibilities, existing in greater independence from the nationally constructed public space than the national allegory allows. In 2008, the Booker went to another Indian writer, Aravind Adiga, for *The White Tiger*, a novel that troubles the middle-class national narrative from a very different angle – from the dark underbelly of crime and violence hidden by the post-millennial climate of economic boom that has increasingly come to define the domestic and global image of India in the twenty-first century. These significant novelistic achievements notwithstanding, the shadow of the national allegory still looms large on the wider horizon of Anglophone Indian literature and still dominates critical discussion about it.

This even in a context in which, as South Asian historians like Indrani Chatterjee, Sumit Guha, and Partha Chatterjee have convincingly argued, there exists a disjuncture between the socio-historical reality of South Asia and Western conceptions of the public-private divide (see I. Chatterjee). In his study of anticolonial resistance in nineteenth-century India, Partha Chatterjee distinguishes between the inner and the outer domains, into which national culture was split by the narratives constructed by such resistances.[2] Admittedly, the spiritual domain is not exactly the same as, or wholly coincident with, the private self; and the public self is also more than a sum total of "economy and ... statecraft ... science and technology" (P. Chatterjee, *Nation* 6). Moreover, something like a public narrative of spirituality and religion has also been dominant in India. But even so, the parallels between the two models are partially clear, most notably when Chatterjee identifies the home and the family as crucial sites of the inner domain of national culture. This same emphasis on spheres of culture that coincide with the public and outer domains has also been the privileged subject of the national allegories. To follow Chatterjee's arguments, the inner domain, in spite of its marginalization in the official histories of the nation, was, in fact, a crucial if indirect site of national culture – in this case, of anticolonial resistance. "The home, I suggest," writes Chatterjee, "was not a complementary but rather the original site on which the hegemonic project of nationalism was launched" (*Nation* 147). Chatterjee's claim here is something of an exact reversal of the paradigm of the national allegory. Instead of simply reflecting the embattled public history of the nation, the private self constitutes a crucial site of anticolonial struggle. The agents of this struggle are at pains to maintain the private sphere's distinction from the struggles in the outer, public sphere, as indeed the success of the struggle is contingent on the maintenance of this very distinction.

If the frequent conflation of postcolonial and postmodern narrative modes in the national allegories has led to totalizing, rational/secular myths of Indian reality that valorize a certain version of the national public sphere, I would like to argue that it is the aesthetics conventionally associated with modernism that can provide an adequate means of reading the intricacies of the private sphere – the nuances of the local and the regional. Especially when it comes to the refraction of the liminal nature of postcolonial reality through the fractured worldview of Indian English literature, it is such a modernist literary aesthetic that engages with it most enrichingly, at the same time avoiding the totalizing claims of the national allegory. It is a modernism that has a tantalizing continuity with realist and naturalist aesthetics, which it stretches to their limits without marking a rupture in their fabric, as postmodernism would do later in the century. My analysis of the diaphanous worldview of postcolonial modernism takes place in my reading of the work of two Indian English novelists who to my mind tellingly espouse a tradition of postcolonial modernism that has fallen into critical neglect ever since the celebratory publication of *Midnight's Children* in 1981.

"Politics Without Issues": Shashi Deshpande and Sunetra Gupta

Literary modernism has had a contentious relation to postcolonial cultural production. The hegemony of high modernism is often felt as weighing heavily on postcolonial literature energized by impulses of liberation. This has sometimes overshadowed the fact that modernism itself was a late-colonial cultural phenomenon that carried with it uncertainties and ambiguities about the philosophical and political project of the European Enlightenment. But notwithstanding modernism's fractured and self-doubting interiority, it has remained suspicious of the critical discourse of Anglophone postcolonial studies, which has prospered in a climate of postmodernist skepticism of identity and subjective interiority. Part of my goal in this chapter is to recuperate subjective interiority and regional specificity evocative of high modernism that seem to have become somewhat irrelevant to the postcolonial national allegory. It is also an attempt to re-invoke modernism's lingering – indeed, heightened – affiliation with realist and naturalist narrative modes that evoke real time and space in all their visual, tactile, olfactory, and polysensual dimensions.

My example of vitalized aesthetic regionalism expressed through the interiority of subjective consciousness in this chapter is the fiction of two English-language writers from India, Shashi Deshpande and Sunetra Gupta. A potential relation between the aesthetics of modernism and the ethics of alterity can be drawn in a tradition of women's writing about private consciousness, but what is perhaps more intriguing is the way an essentially modernist foregrounding of subjectivity is held in delicate tension with a constantly vigilant awareness of an ethics of otherness inherent in such discourses, in a liminal state in which one is indeed indistinguishable from the other. Of the two, Deshpande has been writing since the mid-1980s, and Gupta published her first novel in the mid-1990s, but they can be seen together as having projected a distinctly modernist aesthetics in their writing, which has amounted to a quiet and implicit critique of the dominant tradition of South Asian Anglophone fiction rooted in the spectacle of the public sphere. This is also no doubt the reason behind their marginalization in the attention South Asian Anglophone fiction has received since 1981, as their aesthetics is clearly out of joint with the Rushdie-Jameson tradition of disruptive, fanciful postmodernism.

The novels of both Deshpande and Gupta are rich with distinctive modernist features and aspirations that have been lastingly disrupted in twentieth-century fiction by a poststructuralist skepticism of the power of language to evoke a sensual world. What comes immediately alive in their work is a clear sense of place – or more properly, a region, one that is both situated in and disperses the idea of the nation, departing from the larger, unified, pan-Indian topos of the post-Rushdie national narrative. Indeed, the Bombay or Bangalore of Deshpande's fiction is as rooted and sensually evoked as some of the most memorable locales in the vernacular literary traditions of India – Bibhutibhushan Bandopadhyay's Nischindipur, Saadat Hasan Manto's Bombay, Qurratulain Hyder's Lucknow, and the south Indian small towns of Ambai. Here, Sunetra Gupta is poised in an interesting space, delicately suspended between the sensual concreteness of places and their heavy memories, which linger over her work, on one hand, and a strong pull toward emotional and philosophical abstraction on the other. For instance, the physical spaces enclosed by London, New York, Princeton, Calcutta, and the house Mandalay in Gupta's novel *A Sin of Colour* (1999) are at the same time real and ethereal, through a tension between physicality and interiority that evokes the aesthetics of literary modernism.

Sensual worlds are evoked in fiction such as Deshpande's and Gupta's not so much through obvious linguistic inventiveness or hybrid language but simply through a certain use of ordinary English words denoting everyday objects and practices. These ordinary words naturalize the hybridity of the urban, middle-class everyday that constitutes an integral part of postcolonial reality in India. The simplest of English words sit easy on such a life, and at the same time they recall their faintly alien lineage. It is a very different kind of hybridity – if hybridity be indeed the word for it – than the Rushdiesque "chutnification" of English, with its scattering of untranslated words and phrases and odd sentence constructions. "Hybridity," Amit Chaudhuri reminds us in his introduction to *The Picador Book of Modern Indian Literature*, "can frequently enter texts in subtly disruptive, rather than obvious, ways; it need not be worn like national costume" ("Construction" xxvi). Such a belief in the evocative ability of everyday words to encode a deep-rooted cultural history, nowhere better expressed in Indian English fiction than in novels such as those by Deshpande and Gupta, is reminiscent of literary modernism, which is a rebuttal of a Saussurean loss of faith in the power of words to capture a real physical world. It is also a reminder that modernist evocation of place owes more to realism than is sometimes attributed. It is rather the celebration of the ordinary that marks the revolutionary innovation of modernism, echoed in its use of ordinary English words, whose curiously hybrid life in postcolonial India parallels the radical nature of this modernism. This hybridity of ordinary English words, at once strongly felt and deeply subdued, echoes Raja Rao's identification of the subtle balance between alienness and familiarity of language in the context of Indian life in his famous foreword to *Kanthapura* (1938).[3]

Crucial here are the idea and the form of the ordinary. It is modernism's commitment to the dailyness and the banality of the world, the "common objects of daily prose, the bicycle and the omnibus" as identified by Virginia Woolf, that forms the texture of its unique and subtle sensitivity to modes of alterity ("Letter" 214). The radical replacement of worthwhile, grand subjects by epiphanies of ordinary train rides and the purchase of breakfast bread seeks to foreground the ineffable otherness latent in such quotidian acts. The strangeness of chronicling such base matter is followed by an inexplicable wonder at its beauty, leading to a destabilization that is both pleasant and eerie. And this is the juxtaposition that postcolonial fiction with a modernist sensibility achieves with a remarkable degree of success. The shy hybridity of cultural translation, as of the color and texture of traditional Bengali dishes, not only into the English language but into a more impersonal, globally intelligible discourse, is paralleled by the delicate celebration of the ordinary as extraordinary: a maidservant mopping the floor, seen in the frieze of a classical dance; the pattern of mehndi, a colorful dye on the hands of a young Maharashtrian girl; or wet hair sticking to one's legs after a drenched tour through a monsoon shower in Calcutta.

Rooted Dislocations

Indeed, born, brought up, and educated in India, Ethiopia, Zambia, Liberia, the United States, and England, Sunetra Gupta's background is highly cosmopolitan and, one may add, diasporic, as much as any author of Indian English fiction. Her protagonists are cosmopolitan as well, but this has not reduced the importance of the local in her fiction and the tactile evocation of specific times and places. Interracial relationships provide the narrative entropy to much of her fiction, such as the betrayed marriage between the youthful and innocent Bengali girl Moni and the English Anthony in the early *Memories of Rain* (1992) or the later *A Sin of Colour*, which is framed by the marriage of the Bengali Debendranath and the English Jennifer but driven by the passionate adultery between Debendranath's niece, the ambitious scientist Niharika, and the married Daniel Faraday. Intercultural relationships and migrations in Gupta, however, have a way of preserving the original cultures in a curious state of purity, unlike the mongrelization of culture celebrated by postmodernism and beyond. This purity is partly achieved through a romantic attachment to the high cultural aspirations of modernity – whether through the sound of Keatsian poetry that brings Moni and Anthony together for the first time, or Moni's love for French cheeses, their musical names as much as their taste and texture, or the strains of Rabindrasangeet – songs of Rabindranath Tagore – that permeate much of Gupta's fiction. This is a cosmopolitanism rooted in the sensibility of the Bengali middle and upper-middle classes, which trace their roots to colonial modernity through the lingering memory of the Bengal Renaissance and which, through this modernity, claim a conflicted affiliation with the European Enlightenment. As such, the diasporic, somewhat dislocated perspectives of the protagonists – and in certain cases, those of the invisible narrator – remain deeply rooted in space, no matter how far, and how often, their bodies are transported across space and time. Such perspectives create relationships with the places that are at once intense and distanced, on the part of the viewer-participant who is both integral and peripheral to those places. Above and beyond the otherness of English in the context of Indian life noted by Raja Rao, the mindboggling cultural diversity *within*

India creates additional distances that must be bridged. This deepens the dislocation in the perspectives and sensibilities of the brooding female protagonists of Gupta's fractured Bildungsromans.

Such dislocated, fractured sensibilities play a crucial role in all of Gupta's novels, especially in *Memories of Rain*, as mentioned earlier, as well as in her second novel, *The Glassblower's Breath* (1993). *The Glassblower's Breath* belongs to its nameless female protagonist – who is narrated in the second person throughout – and her relationship with three men in London, climactically realized on a single day. The aesthetics of literary modernism celebrate the ordinary with a mode of articulation that is far from ordinary – that which Derek Attridge identifies as a "willed interference with the transparency of discourse" (4) – and this greatly heightens the rich dichotomy between the familiar and the alien. This alienness of discourse is striking in Gupta's fiction, through an Empsonian ambiguity and complexity of prose: richly figurative and full of myth, the heavy shadows of memory, and a brooding interiority of consciousness. One significant way Gupta achieves this is in her unusual movement between the first, second, and third persons to refer to the protagonists from whose consciousness the novels are narrated, a strategy that deepens the appearance of distance between that consciousness and the character it shapes. In *Memories of Rain*, Moni is othered throughout by the use of the third person, most intriguingly within her own consciousness. The narrator-protagonist of *The Glassblower's Breath*, so sensually realized through her own desires and her emotionally charged relationship with the three men who surround her, is strangely alienated by the use of the second person within her own narration. This continues all the way to the resonant last sentence of the novel, which is cradled by the paradox of the first and second persons, both directed at the same subject: "And Sparrow, Sparrow will be easy, my love, Jonathan Sparrow, easily erased, who will miss him, who, upon this wide earth, but you?" (266). Modernist fiction is sometimes considered to move between two poles – the extreme subjectivity of D. H. Lawrence and Virginia Woolf, on one hand, and the clinical detachment of Joyce's artist paring his fingernails on the other. Gupta seems heavily tilted toward the subjective – an inclination that, when combined with the lyrical interiority of her consciousness, partly accounts for the relative lack of humor in her work. A figure such as Malik Solanka of Rushdie's novel *Fury* (2001) – a Cambridge academic-turned-maker of Little Brain dolls, protagonists of his popular television program on the history of philosophy – seems unlikely in her world. Gupta seems neither capable of nor inclined toward that kind of mockingly self-ironic gesture that is so representative of postmodernism.

Deep-Rooted Shadows

Shashi Deshpande's female protagonists are perhaps even more memorable in their finely individualized etching and in the dialectic of subjectivity and otherness created by their fictional locations. Deshpande employs interiority and figurative language in her fiction to apprehend the intricate fabric of the Indian extended family, and especially the place of women in this traditional structure, often portrayed as caught between the polarizing obligations to the past and the present. In two of her finest novels, *Roots and Shadows* (1982) and *That Long Silence* (1988), she positions two unforgettable women, Indu and Jaya, within the matrix of the traditional extended family but situated differently with respect to individual achievement, personal freedom, and power. In both cases, the family looms large as a powerful and paradoxical structure, replete in equal amounts with love, care, pettiness, rivalry, dominating patriarchy, the play of materialism and idealism, and ambition and its curtailment. Both texts are rooted in specific cultural and geographical spaces – Bangalore in the first instance and Bombay in the second. In both novels, the modernist motif of a self-conscious immersion in literature and creativity is ironically juxtaposed with a preoccupation with the more commercial form of journalistic writing. The protagonists of both novels – both writers – perceive journalism as a vulgarized, commercial genre that they have to take recourse to for the sake of money, sacrificing their aesthetic integrity in the process. Indu is a successful journalist (and a less successful fiction writer) who returns to visit her father's family – a family she had alienated by an unconventional marriage to a man of another caste – following the death of her grandmother, the matriarch of the family, to find that the deceased has left very substantial properties entirely to her. She is quickly immersed in the complex socio-psychological entanglements that follow. Jaya, less successful and less empowered than Indu, is a failed writer who churns out the occasional women's column in a popular daily. *That Long Silence* is the story of her effort to reconcile herself with the complex reality she faces as a woman and a wife, under the claustrophobic shadows of her past – specifically, the allegations against her husband, a civil servant, of professional malpractice. Both novels recall modernist narrative innovations as they abandon linear, biographic narration in favor of seemingly endless digressions, fragmented interior monologues, and movements back and forth in time following the course of the protagonists' memories and brooding minds. Both novels are unselfconsciously regional, providing no contextual annotations of relations, notions, customs, or rituals that mean little beyond their immediate cultures, much less outside of India. Nor does either protagonist feel compelled to provide the background information necessary for the reader to grasp a coherent chronology of events in the middle of the lyrical, trancelike stream of consciousness, unapologetic introductions of personal dreams and nightmares, and disjointed threads of family narratives. In fact, although both novels have significant movements and reversals at the level of concrete action, the narration rarely represents such movements; much of these are in fact memories of patterns of the past, and events of the present follow the protagonists' intense, rambling reflections on the past. The narratives also embody a profound celebration of the subjective, in its psychological intensity and the pervasive point of view of the narrator-protagonists – once again recalling modernism – unlike the radically depthless and decentered subjecthood common in postmodernist fiction.

The relevance of the critique and subsequent postmodernist decentering of subjectivity in the Indian context has been questioned by Amit Chaudhuri, who has claimed that humanist notions such as those of the self, realism, and authenticity do not have the same position in indigenous cultural reality as they have had in models of Western reason, be it logocentrism, dating back to the Greeks, or the Cartesian Cogito of the European Enlightenment, even as these models have been called into question in the twentieth century. This unique character of humanism is often ignored or overlooked in postcolonial fiction driven by a postmodern skepticism of humanism, which it imports from metropolitan Western culture. Also worth remembering here is the celebration of subjectivity in minority discourses *within* the metropolitan West, as for instance in fiction by Black American women, as a model of writing in which a modernist foregrounding of subjectivity has been integral to the formation of a minority discourse that challenges the hegemony of Eurocentrism. Such fictions as Deshpande's and Gupta's, in this sense, offer us what Jessica Berman, describing a similar dynamic between ethics and aesthetics, subjectivity and otherness in Virginia Woolf, calls "ethical folds": "the ethics of Woolf's writings rest in the folds between ontology and epistemology, between an intimate ethics of eros and a recognition of the public responsibility to respond to the face of the other."[4] Such folds, Berman indicates, are arrived at through a negotiation between Levinasian conceptions of the Other as infinitely foreign and feminist configurations of the ethical relations with the Other through intimacy in a more personal sphere. This is a hallmark of a modernist tradition that, I would suggest, also informs the female protagonists of both Deshpande and Gupta.

In many ways, both Deshpande's and Gupta's novels reflect the elitism of high modernism – Gupta's perhaps in a more obvious way than Deshpande's. This is evident in her narrative and linguistic aesthetics and perhaps most clear in her consistent rejection of linear temporality in favor of the meandering, frequently reversible timelines etched by memory. The two novels most intensely tied to the sensibilities of single protagonists, *Memories of Rain* and *The Glassblower's Breath*, reveal such personal temporalities most noticeably, but they are in fact persistent features of all her novels, whether or not attached to the consciousness of specific characters. However, the elitist inclinations of high modernism are also evident in her subject matter and her characterization. Many of her characters are academics, scientists, writers, and philosophers, preoccupied in a contemplation of their work with a solemnity and a kind of lost idealism that clearly sets itself as different from the deliberate, playful irreverence of much postmodernist fiction. Such are the characters of the novel *Moonlight into Marzipan* (1995) – two scientists, Promothesh and Esha, husband and wife. The poignancy of their tragic story – especially the way the dead Esha's memory haunts Promothesh's life – recalls the intense and somber world of high modernism. Gupta's world is often one where the old British Empire has directly given way to the feudal aristocrats of Bengal, as with the Roy family in *A Sin of Colour*, who come to own the house Mandalay, built by a British officer. The son of the family, Debendranath Roy, goes to Oxford as a student and thus is an example of the privileged upper-middle class of India, whose members have access to the best of the cultural and intellectual traditions of both the old Empire and their native country. The academic career of Debendranath's niece Niharika bears striking correspondence to Gupta herself, who studied at Princeton and Imperial College, London, before becoming a professor of zoology at Oxford. The author's privileged career at some of the best institutions of the Western world is of course fairly typical of a large cross-section of Indian English writers, who usually hail from the educated, urban middle and upper-middle classes – a fact that often finds reflection in the worlds they create. The relation of Indian English writing to modernism – or for that matter, postmodernism – will have to take into account not only the historical position of its authors with respect to the former empire and global canons but also their place within respective colonial and postcolonial societies.

Home Truths

The insightful and in some ways counterintuitive argument about literary modernism's sensitivity toward forms and beings of alterity – made persuasively by Derek Attridge in his work on J. M. Coetzee – cannot, therefore, be easily applied to postcolonial writing, even though it appears on the periphery of global cultural production. Alterity comes alive most significantly in the transnational afterlife of literary modernism through its spectral embodiment of the ordinary. A commitment to the ordinary not only marks the unique dialectic of the familiar and the alien through which literature works, but, more importantly, in the context of English-language fiction from outside the metropolitan West, it evokes the unique hybridity of postcolonial life that has subtly naturalized over time. While there remains a lasting connection between the celebration of the ordinary, the representation of private consciousness, and traditions of women's writing, one should remain careful about easy identifications of such writing with the private sphere or, at a different level, with the "inner domain" of national culture. Indeed, Partha Chatterjee has pointed out that the binaries of inner/outer, spiritual/material, home/world, and feminine/masculine, operating within an incipient, nationalist discourse in nineteenth-century India, in fact confined that discourse within these essentialisms and merely erected a new patriarchy as a hegemonic construct. By contrast, none of Deshpande's and Gupta's female protagonists remain circumscribed within the domestic confines of home; their artistic and professional endeavors, of varying range and intensity, deconstruct the binary of home/world and suggest that the private and the public refract and interact with each other. Their partial disenfranchisement within a patriarchal society is complicated by their educational and professional achievements and their place within the urban middle and upper-middle class. The most marginal elements of their lives, embodied in the ordinary and trivial moments of the everyday and in the undefined liminal spaces between the public and the private, are therefore less the material for minority history than for "subaltern pasts," as Dipesh Chakrabarty has described them. In *Provincializing Europe*, Chakrabarty speaks of those irrational moments of history that cannot be integrated within the dominant, rational, teleological narratives of historicism – those that "are marginalized not because of any conscious intentions but because they represent moments or points at which the archive that the historian mines develops a degree of intractability with respect to the aims of professional history" (101). Subaltern pasts can equally belong to privileged or marginalized populations, and, as an example of the former, Chakrabarty describes superstitious rituals prevalent among upper-class Brahmins in certain parts of India that have been either left out of histori- cist narratives or rationalized and secularized to be made part of such nar- ratives. The headlines of colonial and postcolonial history, celebrated in psychedelic colors in the novelistic national allegories, have dominated the worldview of fictional and historical narratives alike. The subaltern pasts of quotidian, locally embedded lives, significantly evoked by women writ- ers like Sunetra Gupta and Shashi Deshpande, reveal the fissures within this teleology.

If Sunetra Gupta seeks to situate herself outside of the conspicuous con- tours of issues but within the more capacious amorphousness of politics, Shashi Deshpande thematizes this very question in her lyrical and haunt- ing novel *The Binding Vine* (1993), set in late twentieth-century Bombay. While the narrator of the novel, Urmi, grieves for her dead baby daughter, she meets Shakutai, a poor, working-class Maharashtrian woman whose daughter, Kalpana, has been violently raped and hangs between life and death for months in conditions of neglect in state-run hospitals. The abrupt appearance of Shakutai and Kalpana in Urmi's life threatens to turn Urmi's murky and muted embodiment of politics into a clear and tangible narrative of issues. The most haunting yet elusive strain of pol- itics in Urmi's life so far has been her discovery of the poems of Mira, her dead mother-in-law, who had been repeatedly violated by marital rape throughout her life. But Mira's rapes are an elusive and abstract theme in Urmi's life, falteringly grasped through her poems. Kalpana's brutal rape suddenly throws Mira's long-past story into relief. Finally, toward the end of the novel, Kalpana's rape is fully transformed into a political issue as journalists, pressure groups, and lobbyists turn it into a subject of news headlines and legislative action. Nonetheless, the novel ends in great trag- edy for Shakutai. Thus, we are left with a strange and disempowering cyn- icism about the transformation of the elusiveness of the political into the spectacular tangibility of issues. It feels cynical because Deshpande offers no other alternative through which sexual violence might be redressed, yet the actions rooted in concrete, issue-based politics feel strangely unsatisfy- ing and even destructive in the novel.

Perhaps understandably, the Indian novel in English labors under cer- tain obvious historical burdens – the need to represent the spectacular intensity of the anticolonial movement, the resplendent moment of lib- eration, and the throbbing energy of neoliberal progress. In such a cli- mate, the representation of subjective interiority rooted in the domestic and the regional seems not only irrelevant but morally irresponsible as well. Attention to the textures of ordinary life refracted through an idiosyncratic consciousness seems counterintuitive for the Indian English novelist at a time when his mission – as indeed it seems more of a preoccupation of the male novelist – seems inextricably entwined with the still-unfinished business of decolonization and nation-building in its full public glare. This capacity for moral and political idiosyncrasy recalls European modernism's radical introspection within the frames of the ordinary everyday, at a time when the public sphere, within respective national contexts as well as worldwide, was being ripped apart by the seismic tremors of global war, warring political ideologies, stark polarities of unforeseen economic prosperity and depression, and the gradual disintegration of colonial empires around the globe. Immersion in the interiority of subjective consciousness, ironically, seems as suspect today as it did to an irate Georg Lukács in the 1930s, for whom the subjective methods of modernist narration signaled an indulgence of bourgeois subjectivity ("Realism"). Today, when that impatience seems reinforced by the national and global aesthetics of the spectacle, resolute chroniclers of the private, domestic, and regional such as Deshpande and Gupta remind us that these alternative stories continue to live on, and perhaps thrive better as they are pushed out of the public glare of attention.

Notes

1 http://www.sunetragupta.com/glassblowersbreath.asp.
2 "The material is the domain of the 'outside,' of the economy and of statecraft, of science and technology, a domain where the West had proved its superiority and the East had succumbed.... The spiritual, on the other hand, is an 'inner' domain bearing the 'essential' marks of cultural identity" (P. Chatterjee, *Nation* 6).
3 As Rao writes in his Foreword: "One has to convey in a language that is not one's own the spirit that is one's own. One has to convey the various shades and omissions of a certain thought-movement that looks maltreated in an alien language. I use the word 'alien,' yet English is not really an alien language to us. It is the language of our intellectual make-up" (R. Rao, *Kanthapura* v).
4 Jessica Berman, "Ethical Folds." Paper delivered at the Modernist Studies Association Conference, Madison, WI, October 2002.

CHAPTER 14

Ecologies of Intimacy: Gender, Sexuality, and Environment in Indian Fiction

Kavita Daiya

In our time, when intimacy saturates all aspects of the public sphere,
from politics to culture to law, its regimes and temporalities are certainly as instrumental in pacifying the citizenry and securing social
cohesion as were those of the workplace when work ruled the land.

– Laura Kipnis, "Adultery" (p. 29)[1]

Intimacy is not solely a private matter: it may be protected, manipulated, or besieged by the state, framed by art, embellished by memory, or estranged by critique.

– Svetlana Boym, "On Diasporic Intimacy" (p. 228)

Much scholarship both in India and abroad has explored how Anglophone
South Asian fiction represents women and female agency in colonial and
postcolonial India. Including a consideration of writers from the colonial period such as Bankimchandra Chattopadhyay and Rabindranath
Tagore, as well as postcolonial writers such as Attia Hosain, Anita Desai,
Bapsi Sidhwa, Bharati Mukherjee, and Salman Rushdie, literary and cultural criticism on gender in nineteenth and twentieth-century South Asia
has largely revolved around the relationship between women and nationalism in these works. In particular, the work of feminist and subaltern
studies scholars such as Kumkum Sangari and Sudesh Vaid (*Recasting*),
Sangeeta Ray (*En-Gendering*), Gayatri Chakravorty Spivak (*In Other*),
Dipesh Chakrabarty (*Provincializing*), and Partha Chatterjee (*Nation*),
among others, has been influential in two principal ways: first, it has
mapped the aesthetics and politics of texts in which women are represented either as victims of Indian patriarchal discourses or as symbols of
national and cultural community. How ethnicity, religion, caste, and class
shape these representations of women has been important to elucidat-
ing a complex, historical analysis of women in Indian literature. Second,
this work has collectively foregrounded how the modern representation
of Indian women – of their voice and agency – shores up relations of

neocolonial power between men in national and international contexts. This scholarship has thus called for greater self-reflexivity and care around questions of representation, voice, and subalternity in the Indian nation.

In this chapter, I will not review this important and by now canonical scholarly analysis of cultural representations of women and nationalism in modern India; instead, I will use it as a starting point to signal two directions for future scholarly consideration of gender and sexuality in the Indian novel. First, we might now further intervene methodologically in the modes of analysis that dominate our debates about gender. That is, if we shift focus from an analysis of how women are represented (as agents or victims) to an examination of the textual practices that critically illuminate the relations among gendered norms, sexual identities, and sites of power in postcolonial India, we might offer a new, more expansive account of rhetorics of masculinity and femininity as they invent and shape gendered subjectivity and regimes of sexuality in South Asia. In some measure, this imperative appears in the work of such scholars as Mrinalini Sinha in *Colonial Masculinity* and Jasbir Puar in *Terrorist Assemblages*, who, from very different disciplinary contexts and geographies, illuminate the historical, discursive production and policing of South Asian masculinities. Second, I propose that we include in our gender analyses the consideration of "intimacy," and of how our aesthetic texts negotiate normative patriarchal and subversive intimacies. This can illuminate how sexual ideologies and gendered subjectivities are materially and affectively tangled up with institutions of citizenship and belonging. Intimacy appears variously in the great diversity of South Asian literature and culture: simply put, it refers to conventional, heteronormative coupledom and romance. For instance, in *Violent Belongings*, I tracked how the cultural representation of romantic coupledom is often articulated with the performance of ethnicized national citizenship in independent India. More broadly, intimacy also signals the sense of affective belonging to a community or nation, as well as to "a drive that creates spaces around it through practices" (Berlant, "Intimacy" 4). Toward rethinking the varied ecologies of intimacy that inhabit the post-1947 novel and what I call "the postcolonial public sphere," I will sketch in what follows some thoughts about the relationships among intimacy, environment, and South Asian citizenship in post-Partition literature.

Although these questions might be richly studied in earlier literature, I deliberately focus on post-1947 Anglophone Indian writing here – with some digressions outside the demarcations of "Anglophone" and "Indian." The digressions, in a way, signal the impossibility of telling a story about

India that is contained within specific linguistic and political borders. Important scholarship has shown how much post-1947 fiction in English, by writers such as Shashi Deshpande, Anita Desai, Ruth Prawer Jhabvala, Manju Kapur, Amitav Ghosh, Vikram Chandra, Rohinton Mistry, Chitra Banerjee Divakaruni, and others, unveils the complex forms of abjection and violence that saturate women's lives.[2] Extending this terrain, this chapter pursues the interrelationships among gendered subjectivity, queer desires, disability, subaltern belongings, environment, attachment, and political violence in this archive. As Lauren Berlant has argued,

> Rethinking intimacy calls out not only for redescription but for transformative analyses of the rhetorical and material conditions that enable hegemonic fantasies to thrive in the minds and on the bodies of subjects, while, at the same time, attachments are developing that might redirect the different routes taken by history and biography. ("Intimacy" 6)

My hope is that this can allow us to open up new conversations about the cultural work our literary texts perform and enable when they yoke together stories about gender with those about disability, colonial violence, land, and global migration – when they link stories about intimacy with stories about minoritization in the postcolonial city and state.

Intimacy and Disability in Transition

"No!" I scream, unable to bear the thought of an able-bodied future.

– Bapsi Sidhwa, *Cracking India* (p. 23)

Among other post-Partition novels that enunciate a profound alienation from rhetorics of nationality through the zone of intimacy (for instance, Manju Kapur's *Difficult Daughters* [1999] and Shauna Singh Baldwin's *What the Body Remembers* [2000]) is Pakistani writer Bapsi Sidhwa's semi-autobiographical novel *Cracking India* (1991). *Cracking India* describes the traumatic upheaval of the 1947 Partition of India through the eyes of the young child narrator Lenny Sethi, a Parsi girl living in Lahore. Lenny has polio, and her negotiation of the norms around able-bodiedness is central to her critical perspective on ethnic division, decolonization, sexual violence, and migration that accompanied national freedom in South Asia. When the novel begins, we encounter a fragile interethnic community in which intimacy among Hindus, Muslims, Sikhs, Parsis, Indians, and British is a fact of life in Lahore. Lenny is around five years old and, because of polio in her right leg, walks with a limp. Although she is part of a conventional upper-middle class Parsi family, it is Lenny's attachments to other female figures in her life, from her Godmother to her nanny Shanta, that help her survive "the perplexing unrealities" of her own home – and later of the Partition (Sidhwa 11). Her days are spent in the company of Shanta, whom she calls Ayah; their intimacy offers Lenny access to Ayah's subaltern community of servants and traders in Lahore, allowing us to encounter how Partition's politics played out in ordinary lives, across class.

The novel's largely first-person narrative follows Lenny and Ayah as they watch how ethno-nationalist political rhetoric and violence around the imminent Partition unfolds to change their lives in Lahore's Warris Road, Queen's Garden, and other local haunts. As some friends are killed and others flee across the border to India, the birth of the nation generates the fracturing and loss of domestic and familial intimacies for both Lenny and Ayah/Shanta. Ayah's Muslim lover Masseur is murdered, and, subsequently, her one-time friend and admirer Ice-Candy Man arrives with a murderous mob to abduct and rape her. When he tricks the unsuspecting Lenny into revealing Shanta's hiding place and then abducts her, Lenny and Shanta's deep bond is irrevocably and traumatically destroyed. The novel ends with a montage of scenes of unhomeliness and intimate loss: for instance, the family's erstwhile Hindu neighbor's home is turned into a Recovered Women's Camp where female refugees are housed and aided. When Shanta is abducted, Hamida, one of the women from this refugee camp, is hired to be Lenny's nanny. Once Shanta is rescued from a brothel in Lahore by Godmother, she is also placed in this camp; she chooses to go to her family in Amritsar, and a lovelorn Ice-Candy Man follows her.

I have discussed elsewhere the representation of somatic violence in this novel and how it unveils the complexity of violence that comes to be named ethnic, even when it was often more about other things: caste, class, desire, property, and debt (Daiya, *Violent* 54–86). Here, I am interested in the representation of able-bodiedness and disability in *Cracking India*. On the one hand, as the historian Partha Chatterjee (*Nation*) and critic Sangeeta Ray have shown, Indian nationalist discourse often deploys the middle-class Hindu woman as the embodied representative of national culture. Sangeeta Ray has added that Indian nationalist literature does this through the figure of the upper-*caste* Hindu woman. The idealizing image of the Hindu upper-caste woman as embodiment of cultural tradition in turn allows Indian nationalism to assimilate into the discourses of Western modernity while preserving its autonomy through the assertion of cultural difference. *Cracking India* interrupts this rhetoric. Unlike the centrality of the allegorical in Salman Rushdie's depiction of Saleem Sinai in *Midnight's Children* (1981), and although Lenny's eighth birthday falls on Pakistan's independence day – August 14, 1947 – Lenny's multiple marginality, in terms of able-bodiedness, age, gender, as a Parsi, and so on, disrupts any allegorical reading.[3] Instead, in *Cracking India*, Lenny as a narrator is both colonial subject and national critic, a protagonist at odds both with colonialist and with nationalist discourses.[4] For instance, the former is evident when her family doctor Colonel Bharucha roars to Lenny's mother, who is blaming herself for Lenny's polio: "If anyone's to blame, blame the British! There was no polio in India till they brought it here!" (25). This enunciation historicizes Lenny's difference, implicating colonial power in the intimate production of colonial embodiment. Further, Lenny's first person account of how ethno-nationalist politics violently destroys intimacies and intimate communities becomes, as I will show, a powerful indictment of postcolonial nationalism.

Lenny's disability thus does not function as "narrative prosthesis" here – David T. Mitchell and Sharon L. Snyder's resonant term for how the disabled body is used in much modern English literature to shore up dominant conceptions of normalcy and normative embodiment. Unlike the disabled figures in the nineteenth-century literature that Mitchell and Snyder study, Lenny does not die at the end: she is not evacuated in order to restore social life to able-bodied normalcy. Instead, Lenny, as a postcolonial protagonist, critically unveils patriarchal violence and claims non-normative embodiment as privilege. While she understands, even as a five-year old child, that her mother feels responsible for her polio, Lenny likens having polio to "being born under a lucky star" (20). As she asserts, having polio "has many advantages – it permits me access to my mother's bed in the middle of the night" (20). When her "valuable deformity" (15) is not much altered by Dr. Bharucha's cast, she is delighted: "My leg looks functional but ... gratifyingly abnormal – and far from banal!" (24). Lenny's narrative radically posits that in modern neocolonial experience, "normalcy" itself is aporetic, and an able-bodied future is impossible. Following Partition, Lenny's critique of "compulsory able-bodiedness" (McRuer) connects her in solidarity with others displaced within the conventional gendered construction of able-bodied normalcy and postcolonial citizenship. As she says one evening in the Queen's Garden in Lahore about her new, melancholic nanny Hamida – a Partition refugee who cannot return home to her husband and children because she has been raped: "Like Hamida, I do not fit" (249). In this rejection of patriarchal,

compulsory able-bodiedness, Lenny's critique is, to engage Alison Kafer's
work, "feminist, queer, crip." Lenny's hyper-visible, "disabled," and desiring body becomes a site of affective affiliation with the various subaltern
figures in the novel about to become refugees: the forcibly drugged and
married off servant child Pappoo, the abducted and raped Shanta and
Hamida, and the Sikh childhood friend Ranna, who loses his family in
horrific violence in rural Punjab. Of course, to some extent, Lenny's construction of polio as a "valuable deformity" is informed by both her age
and class privilege. Her family's wealth ensures that she continues to have
access to education (through a private tutor), the pleasures of leisure in
the park (through the nanny who pushes her there daily in a stroller), and
intimacy.[5] Yet, the narrative glance askance at both able-bodiedness and
citizenship, through non-normative intimacies, is generative nonetheless
for its interrogation of hegemonic and gendered violence.

The representation of intimacy in the novel is thus multi-faceted.
Lenny's account of the many women raped and abducted in ethnic violence lies alongside her sensitive apprehension of the violence that saturates
her parents' marital intimacy. Outside her home, Lenny hears the wailing of abducted women and refugees in freshly abandoned homes: "The
mystery of the women in the courtyard deepens. At night we hear them
wailing, their cries verging on the inhuman. Sometimes I can't tell where
the cries are coming from. From the women – or from the house next
door infiltrated by our invisible neighbors" (224). Simultaneously,
inside the domestic space of her home are "the caged voices of our parents fighting in their bedroom. Mother crying, wheedling. Father's terse,
brash, indecipherable sentences. Terrifying thumps" (224). In different
unhomely homes then, grief at violence against women is linked; Lenny
senses that infidelity and domestic violence permeate the apparently successful normative coupledom of her parents when she further hears her
mother trying to stop her father from going "to her," and failing: "Father
goes anyway.... Although Father has never raised his hands to us, one
day I surprise Mother at her bath and see the bruises on her body" (224).
Lenny's intimate invasion of the bathroom deprivatizes her mother's experience of domestic violence, and brings her startling, new knowledge of
her mother's wounded embodiment. Thus, the narrative bears witness to
multiple forms of domestic violence and the failure of bourgeois ideologies of marriage.

This knowledge of marital unhappiness shapes Lenny's critique of
refugee women's violent experiences. One night when a female refugee's
crying wakes her up again, Lenny asserts, "My heart is wrung with pity

and horror. I want to leap out of my bed and soothe the wailing woman and slay her tormentors. I've seen Ayah carried away – and it had less to do with fate than with the will of men" (226). Lenny links the gendered violence experienced by female subjects like her mother, Ayah, and Hamida (representing different ethnic groups) and articulates a secular political critique of gendered violence as generated by patriarchal male agency. When later Hamida cries at Lenny's question if she is a "fallen woman," Lenny is devastated: "I get out of bed and press her face into my chest. I rock her, and Hamida's tears soak right through my flannel nightgown.... I can't bear to hurt her: I'd rather bite my tongue than cause pain to her grief-wounded eye" (227). This act of intimate embrace embodies and performs the secular, disentangling it from nationalism; it signifies an affective secular intimacy between Hamida and Lenny, across class and age, across political status and religion. The mention of Hamida's "grief-wounded eye" here and elsewhere in the text evocatively connects her to Lenny, signaling their shared, non-normative embodiment. Like her bond with her childless Godmother, Lenny's affective intimacy here is queer, as defined by Berlant and Warner: it eschews the dominant forms of intimacy tied to coupling, kinship, property, or the nation and presents instead a more optimism-sustaining, political vision of intimacy on the peripheries of the nation (Berlant and Warner 322).[6] This critical preoccupation with embodied experience, gender, and political intimacies also informs the new Partition accounts from India, Pakistan, and Bangladesh gathered in the graphic anthology *This Side That Side: Restorying Partition* (2013), by its curator Vishwajyoti Ghosh.

Rethinking Sexuality and Revolution

> Without enabling narratives, these various shards of resistance never managed to organize themselves into revolutionary challenges. But that doesn't mean there isn't a collective story to tell about them.
>
> – Laura Kipnis, "Adultery" (p. 28)

Arundhati Roy's award-winning novel *The God of Small Things* (1997) is at once about love and the state and about revolutions large and small in those realms. In its experimental form characterized by postmodernist fragmentation, linguistic play, and temporal shifts, it formally enacts the resistance to the oppressive, institutionalized formations of normalcy and hegemonic intimacy that its various protagonists, from Rahel and Estha to Ammu and Velutha, attempt to enunciate. The novel's plot revolves around the relationship between two twins, Rahel and Estha, who have an uncanny ability to read each other's thoughts and finish each other's sentences. First through the depiction of their Syrian Christian mother Ammu's failed marriage and then through other depictions of coupledom saturated with violence and loss, the novel offers a powerful critique of marriage. For example, for Ammu, who divorced her abusive husband "when his bouts of violence began to include the children" (42), a chance glimpse of her wedding photographs incites the thought that she was "being led to the gallows," her elaborate bridal decoration as absurd as "polishing firewood" (43). The stigma of divorce haunts her frustrated and constrained life in the conservative natal home and joint family to which she returns, in small town Ayemenem, Kerala. Similarly, Mammachi, Ammu's enterprising mother and pickle-business owner, Baby Kochamma, her single aunt, and Chacko, her brother, also experience the failure of ideologies of normative coupledom: Mammachi and her children, we discover, were beaten and abused regularly by her entomologist husband Pappachi; Baby Kochamma is embittered by a failed infatuation with the Irish-Jesuit priest Father Mulligan and takes it out on Ammu and her children; and Chacko's interracial marriage with his English wife Margaret ends in divorce, with his daughter Sophie Mol largely alienated from him, so that when he leaves England, he feels "that something had been torn out of him. Something big" (112). Subsequently, under the guise of shared Marxist camaraderie, he sexually exploits the female workers in his mother's factory in Ayemenem. We also see this failure of heteronormative intimacy across generations and continents, as Rahel eventually divorces her Irish American husband Larry McCaslin in Washington DC, and returns to reunite with her brother Estha many years later.

Against this landscape of toxic heteronormative coupledom saturated with unhappiness and violence, *The God of Small Things* affirms the beauty and pleasures of non-normative intimacies that bypass and rupture social norms and power relations in Ayemenem. In particular, the affective and embodied intimacies between and among Ammu, Estha, Rahel, and the "Untouchable" carpenter Velutha are subversive – and at times utopian (74). Estha, Rahel, and Velutha "had grown to be the best of friends" (75). Although "they were forbidden from visiting his house," they do anyway (75); there, he carves small wooden toys for them, makes them fish curry, and participates gamely in their play. Scorned and abused in their own home by all, Ammu, Estha, and Rahel adore Velutha and forge with him a "world of hooked fingers and sudden smiles" – an exilic intimacy that sustains them (167).[7] As Ammu observes one day when Velutha tosses Rahel up in the air and catches her in his arms, Rahel's delight and laughter are mirrored in his smile: "She was surprised at the extent of her daughter's physical ease with him. Surprised that her child seemed to have a sub-world that excluded *her* entirely. A tactile world of smiles and laughter that she, her mother, had no part in" (167). In the context of the prevailing caste strictures, which forbid contact across the castes, this tactile pleasure and intimacy is both aesthetic and political. It is also adjacent to the desire that flashes up between Ammu and Velutha in this moment, when he sees that "Rahel's mother was a woman," and she sees that his body, known to her from childhood, has "changed ... into a man's body" (167–8). Their desire interrogates centuries of "scars ... [and] wounds from old wars and the walking-backwards days" of caste violence and eventually leads to the transgressive utopian tactility of their lovemaking in the History House (167–8).

Many critics have debated and criticized how Roy represents inter-caste love between Ammu and Velutha; these debates, best exemplified in Brinda Bose's engagement ("In Desire") with Aijaz Ahmad's critique ("Reading") of Roy's novel, have dwelt on whether sexual transgression can count as "true" or "proper" political resistance. Here, the question is whether the erotic can be claimed to be tantamount to a "politics"; for a Marxist critic like Ahmad, it cannot. However, to presume that the erotic is extricable from the realm of "pure politics" is itself a hegemonic fantasy that shores up the violence of discourses that privatize intimacy and, in the process, elides the gendered power relations instantiated by the modern state. I propose that we read these moments of transgressive intimacies as what Kipnis calls "shards of resistance" ("Adultery" 28) to hegemonic and heteronormative formations of acceptable intimacies. They may not cohere into a revolutionary challenge to the state and its dominant politics, but nonetheless, they signal dissent in Roy's story about the violence around minoritization – of gender, of childhood, of class, and of caste – in the "History House" of elite heteronormative privilege in the postcolonial state. To appropriate Kipnis' words, then, while "it's easy to miss the aspirations and wishes coded in small gestures of resistance and insurgency" (29), we must revisit Roy's novel as one that is political precisely because it unveils the small insurgencies in the sensual, intimate worlds fashioned by minor subjects like Ammu, Estha, Rahel, and Velutha; as Deepika Bahri relatedly suggests, it shows us how "libidinal pleasure is suffused with the other sorrows and joys of the world" (229). Brinda Bose has well reminded us that "to read [Roy's] novel politically one may need to accept that there are certain kinds of politics that have more to do with interpersonal relations than with grand revolutions ... that erotics can also be a politics" (68).

In *The God of Small Things*, Roy critiques how "History" and the state violently respond to the subversion of non-normative intimacies. When Ammu's mother and aunt learn of her sexual transgression, they engineer – in the name of caste superiority and family honor – what the narrator names "the Terror" (*God* 74). Complicit in this are modern – and terrifying – institutions of the state, which both privatize inter-caste intimacy as individual indiscipline and destroy it as a public affront. While the communist political leader Comrade Pillai refuses to intervene and help Velutha, claiming that the "Party was not constituted to support workers' indiscipline in their private life" (271), Baby Kochamma tells the police that Velutha has raped Ammu and kidnapped her children. Subsequently, a terrible machinery of destruction is set into motion. While "a posse of Touchable Policemen" (287) systematically tortures and beats to death Velutha – named in the novel as the God of Loss and the God of Small Things – in the History House, Baby Kochamma and Chacko expel Ammu from the family home, separating her from her children. The narrator calls the former "History in live performance" (293); this indicts national history as the unfolding of state and collective violence against the resistant, minor subjects who dare to, as Kandice Chuh conceives, "imagine otherwise." The violent taxonomy of caste that dehumanizes particular people as "untouchable" is criticized in the narrator's repeated reference to the non-Dalit characters such as the policemen as "Touchables" – relentlessly also foregrounding the absurdity of caste.[8] Ultimately, Roy's point is similar to that of Hannah Arendt, who illuminated the banality of evil – its systematicity, its economic efficiency, and, in its political institutionalization, its very modernity. The Ayemenem policemen are merely "Servants of the State" (288) and the Touchable agents of "History" and "Terror." For them, Ammu and Velutha's intimacy threatens centuries of caste power and privilege that have now been captured by the state apparatus. Thus, Velutha's painful and prolonged murder is also, in a sense, very intimate: not content to shoot him or arrest him, the slow, deliberate and brutal destruction of Velutha's taut, muscular body signals the deep, affective response to his sexual transgression. In the process, the novel traces how intimacy and state power are intricately connected.

In this context, *The God of Small Things* finds moments of revolutionary intimacies in the beauty of the natural world. Much of what is joyous and life-sustaining for these four protagonists is tied to the pleasure and happiness they derive from their sensory relationship to the landscape and its non-human inhabitants: the ants, the moths, the spider, the toys whittled from wood, the rain, the river. In Rahel's testimony about how their beloved local river is now dirty and polluted, and how Western tourism ushers in what Ramachandra Guha calls "socioenvironmental degradation," we can locate the novel's eco-critical perspective on development and globalization (Guha, *Environmentalism* 111). Bahri has also noted how Roy's lingering descriptions of the landscape suggest that "within nature and its abundance lies the germinative power of recall.... It is nature that provides the living text" to remember terror, and to invent another world (241–2). This shift to an ecological imagination – and indeed, to other spatial formations that dislocate the national, such as the local, regional, and global – is important for understanding new directions in recent Indian fiction. If in colonial India the nation and nationalism largely framed the novelistic representation of gendered experience by writers like Bankimchandra Chattopadhyay and Rabindranath Tagore, much post-Partition fiction that addresses gender critically has also had an ambivalent relationship to the nation-form. Elsewhere I have discussed the critical energies of works like Amitav Ghosh's *The Circle of Reason* (1986) and *The Shadow Lines* (1988), which depict how violence inhabits the relation between female migrants and their fantasies of citizenship as they circulate transnationally in search of better homes, better lives, and nonviolent belongings (Daiya, "No Home"). Like Ghosh's works, which passionately interrogate the rhetorics of nationalism, Roy's novel is distant from the hegemonic national imagination: in it, subjectivity and the experience of citizenship are instead profoundly shaped by the local and regional (Ayemenem, Kerala) via an imperial global in which intimacies traverse England, India and Washington DC, white and brown, Syrian Christian and Dalit, and so on.

In one sense, then, the nation as imagined community that has dominated the story of anti-colonial nationalism, as well as that of postcolonial citizenship and unbelonging in post-Partition novels such as *Midnight's Children* and Anita Desai's *Clear Light of Day* (1980), seems outdated today. Disillusioned with the idea of the nation as a community, Indian writers instead question the dispossessing operations of the state. This largely post-1990 Indian fiction often illuminates how the state apparatus is manifest in, and violently shapes, intimacy, ecology, and gendered subjectivity in ways that are at once intensely local and profoundly part of a global economy. This, I suggest, is a post-nativist articulation by Roy and others that, as Kwame Anthony Appiah argues, is post-colonial because it is not nationalist. It is "based in an appeal to a certain simple respect for human suffering, a fundamental revolt against the endless misery" (Appiah 66). It marks what Appiah calls a condition of pessimism that challenges legitimating narratives of violence and terror in the name of its suffering victims (67).

Conclusion: Indigenous Ecologies, Queer Intimacy, and the Postcolonial City

Feminist and queer scholars such as Laura Kipnis and Lauren Berlant have recently problematized public formations of intimacy in the United States that link it to state domination, alienation, and minoritization. Kipnis has argued that our hegemonic institutions of intimacy today are grounded in the increasing policing and regulation of individual behavior, enforcing compliant citizenship (Kipnis, *Against*). For this regime, romance becomes "a socially sanctioned zone for wishing and desiring, and a repository for excess. Mobilized as it is by unconscious fantasy, it's potentially a profoundly anti-social form as well – when unharnessed from the project of social reproduction" (Kipnis, "Adultery" 43). Extending this useful formulation in the South Asian context, I suggest, can instigate fresh insight into how romance is inflected by state rhetorics about ethnic and religious identities and intimacy norms. Berlant has eloquently argued that we must reframe intimacy in order to recognize "how public institutions use issues of intimate life to normalize particular forms of knowledge and practice and to create compliant subjects." She notes that "discourses of sexual suffering or trauma have so magnetized crises in a whole set of related fields that stories of the intimate have become inseparable from, for example, stories about citizenship, capitalism, aesthetic forms, political violence, and the writing of history" (8). Good citizenship is increasingly bound up with the discourses that police and produce normative intimacy – in particular, in its configuration as monogamous, heterosexual, reproductive coupledom.

Jhumpa Lahiri's short stories in *The Interpreter of Maladies* (1999) illuminate the complex contours of intimacy in middle-class Indian diasporic experience. In the story "This Blessed House," the newly married middle-class protagonists Twinkle and Sanjeev start to discover fractures in their normative arranged marriage when Christian paraphernalia – for instance, a porcelain statue and a bust of Christ – unexpectedly shows up all over their new suburban home. Twinkle, a second-generation Indian American from California, is delighted to discover the Christian objects as their housewarming party begins; she revels in their incongruity and charm and wants to display them. However, for the upwardly mobile Sanjeev's first-generation sensibility, Twinkle's desire to display the unfamiliar and unwanted objects evokes the anxiety of identity. Thus, he rebukes Twinkle: "We're not Christian" (Lahiri, *Interpreter* 137). For Twinkle, the objects offer an invitation to diasporic intimacy – what Svetlana Boym calls "a diasporic intimacy that is not opposed to uprootedness and defamiliarization but constituted by it" (227). Sanjeev, who in some ways eschews conventional norms around middle-class Indian masculinity, as he cooks and cleans in their household, sees the Christian themed items not simply as kitsch but as objects of religious significance for the other. For him, their unwanted presence in his precariously achieved immigrant domesticity signals his exile and makes it unhomely. Lahiri's representation of their dissonant and at times disappointing intimacy unveils how the promise of their normative model minority married life fails them. Likewise, "Mrs. Sen's" is a story that beautifully captures the contingent fragility of non-normative intimacies, through the unlikely bond of friendship that emerges between Mrs. Sen, an unhappy Indian immigrant housewife who is nostalgic for her home in Calcutta, and Eliot, an eleven year-old white child she babysits because his single mother works full time. Their closeness and mutual empathy, across age and race, is suggestively tied to their shared sense of exile from the conventional normalcy of mainstream America in a New England campus town.

As these examples show, middle-class domesticity as it shapes female subjectivity has been the focus of much Anglophone Indian fiction across genres, from the realist fiction of Shashi Deshpande, Anita Desai, and Manju Kapur to the melodramatic, sexually explicit, and popular novels of Shobha Dé. In this context, the stories in Bengali by notable writer and activist Mahasweta Devi become important to engage alongside Anglophone writing: Devi's fiction illuminates the violent economic exploitation of indigenous tribal communities in the postcolonial state – especially the linked dehumanizing sexual exploitation of indigenous women – with the ecological devastation of the land. It passionately exposes how gender and sexuality are tied to the production of value through the mechanisms of state modernity beyond middle-class urban India. In Devi's stories, indigenous, poor women's sick, exploited, aged, and dying bodies are snared in circuits of labor-extracting debt and become the byproducts of capitalist modernity's march to profit. Especially in such stories as "Douloti" and "The Hunt," "India" is present only as an external force that denudes value and renders citizenship rights inaccessible for indigenous and poor women and men. Resonant with Arundhati Roy's eco-critical perspective discussed earlier and with her later essays on Maoist struggles, Devi's stories articulate an indigenous critical consciousness of what Elizabeth Povinelli has called, in a different context, "ongoing state colonialism" (274–5).

The imbrication of ecology, intimacy, and citizenship is also illuminated in Vikram Chandra's evocative *Love and Longing in Bombay*. Although this is a collection of short, interlinked stories rather than a novel, it resonates for our discussion insofar as it presents a montage of urban, counter-hegemonic intimacies that queer Indian citizenship. As in Roy's novel, the nation is largely absent in these stories, replaced by the city of Bombay (now called Mumbai) as the violent ecological force that shapes queer intimacies. In his story "Kama [Desire]," a young son who belongs to a right-wing Hindu nationalist political party murders his father when he discovers that his parents have been swinging sexually with other couples. As we follow the detective Sartaj on his murder investigation, we discover how neoconservative Hindu nationalist politics destroy middle-class intimacies: contrary to the son's idealizing assumptions about normative and chaste Hindu motherhood, his grieving widowed mother is revealed to be a willing, desiring participant in the non-normative sexual practices that led to her husband's murder. Another story, "Artha [Wealth]" revolves around two software engineers, Sandhya, a divorced single mother, and Iqbal, her gay colleague. Among other things, the story is a queer romance between two Indian men, Iqbal and Rakesh. Crossing religious and class boundaries, Iqbal and Rajesh's romantic intimacy is invisible to their families and exists in the peripheral shadows of the city's public spaces. Their queer desire is haunted by their impossible longing for a private domestic space – their own home – in an overcrowded Bombay where real estate prices rival those in New York and where homosexuality is criminalized. The narrative interweaves this account of loss, longing, and sexual minoritization with the relentless displacement of the urban poor that mirrors Devi's images of the theft of rural land, resources, and bodies.

In line with recent Indian fiction that dwells on the material and ecological dimensions of contemporary Indian experience, Chandra's stories also testify to the great game of urban land grab in India: for instance, Rajesh is a thug who also works for the elite builder Ratnani, "destroying houses and huts and slums. Clearing land" (V. Chandra, *Love* 210). When Rajesh disappears one day, Iqbal's vain search for his lost love unveils a local violent nexus between builders, criminals, and the police and the likelihood that Rajesh was killed by Ratnani. Similarly, the guruji who runs a traditional gymnasium or *akhara* for working-class Bombay also tells Iqbal of rapacious builders trying to usurp his land to build high-rises. This shadowy criminal economy around land abuts the "Shining India" of disruptive technological globalization and India's growing IT industry. Sandhya's new software meets covert resistance from the two accountants, Raunakji and Manishji, who haplessly try to sabotage the accounting program's code created by Sandhya and Iqbal. They do so, we discover later, to protect their livelihoods and very existence: they are acutely aware of their own precariousness in the emergent and globalized ecologies of software that are about to render their skills obsolete. This poignant textual moment – in which imperiled male citizens fight a lost war against the onslaught of a globalized economic landscape and its internet ecologies – also resonates with the depiction of the IT world in later fiction, such as Hari Kunzru's novel *Transmission* (2005). In Chandra's stories, then, alongside many other works, we can track the new energies of recent Indian fiction that maps counter-hegemonic intimacies through stories about gendered embodiment, land, displacement, and citizenship that are intensely local, often violent, and profoundly a part of contemporary Indian modernity.

Notes

1 I would like to thank the Penn Humanities Forum of the University of Pennsylvania and the Andrew W. Mellon Foundation for supporting this research. I owe a special thank you to Jim English, Ulka Anjaria, Jennifer Conway, Monica Kim, Kevin Platt, Robert McRuer, Sreyoshi Sarkar, Victoria Barnett-Woods, and the students and colleagues in the British and Postcolonial Studies Cluster here at George Washington University, for their support, critical insight, and generous engagement with this chapter's argument.
2 For instance, in Sunder Rajan (*Real*); P. Gopal (*Literary*); A. Roy (*Patterns*); Kripal and Atrey; Nubile; and S. Singh (ed.).
3 Much has been written about allegory in Salman Rushdie's *Midnight's Children*, such as by Morton (*Salman*); Agarwalla; Sanga (*Salman*); Heffernan; and Mossman.
4 Rashna B. Singh explores the representation of Parsis in relation to nationalism in her article "Traversing."
5 Thanks to Sreyoshi Sarkar for this astute reminder about how age and class location crucially sustain Lenny's view on able-bodiedness, and for her helpful comments about ecology and economy, which have contributed to my subsequent analysis of Vikram Chandra's work.

6 An earlier version of parts of this argument appears in my analysis of public sphere representations of refugee experiences in Daiya, "Refugees."

7 Thanks to Victoria Barnett-Woods for this salient suggestion about how Velutha allows the twins to forge positive, individualized intimacies outside their home. My analysis of Roy's novel is well-influenced by Vicki's thoughtful feedback here and later in this chapter.

8 Toral Gajarawala has noted the limited representation of Dalit subjectivity and agency in this novel (*Untouchable* 226 n.20).

CHAPTER 15

Some Uses of History: Historiography, Politics, and the Indian Novel

Alex Tickell

A foundational assumption of conventional literary history is that, like any other cultural or physical institution, the novel can be plotted through a more or less linear trajectory of formal change. In other words, within the disciplinary project of literary history it is assumed that "history" will describe a certain temporally structured developmental narrative about how the novel has evolved (in this case in an Indian national context). Yet a history of the novel is not quite the same thing as a study of the novel in – or in relation to – history, nor does it always give us the scope to ask questions about how literature interacts with or intervenes in history. Rather than placing the Indian novel in a literary-historical frame, then, this chapter argues for the equal importance of understanding how Indian fiction reflects on history. How, for instance, does the Indian novel relate to variant (and highly culturally specific) modes of *knowing* history? How has it supported particular historiographies and interpretations of history? And how does the novel position itself textually in relation to contested or overwritten historical narratives?

A. K. Ramanujan's poem "Some Indian Uses of History on a Rainy Day" from the collection *Relations* (1971) promises some answers to these questions and suggests, somewhat whimsically, that Indian "uses of history" might be localized and culturally specific. Structured in three stanzas, the poem presents three particular "uses" of history: in the first of these vignettes of historical consciousness, set in Madras in 1965, bank clerks waiting in the rain to get "the single seat / in the seventh bus" remind themselves of the religious devotees who waited, more patiently, for a ceremonial gift from "Old King Harsha" and, as they eventually give up and begin to walk home, console themselves with the measured reflection that "King Harsha's / monks had nothing but their own two feet." In the second stanza, which moves the poem's setting to Egypt "every July," Ramanujan pictures Indian Fulbright scholars, "faces pressed against the past / as against museum glass" in a Cairo museum, "amazed" at the sight "of mummies swathed in millennia / of Calicut muslin." In a final stanza, dated 1935 and now set in the Germany of the Third Reich, a professor of Sanskrit on a cultural exchange becomes lost in nighttime Berlin and is "reduced / to a literal turbanned child" in his struggle to read the German signs and street names around him, until he "suddenly comes home" when he sees "the swastika / on the neighbour's arm / in that roaring bus from a grey / nowhere to a green" (Ramanujan, *Oxford* 74–5).

Ramanujan's poem cannot offer us anything like a comprehensive schema for thinking about Indian literary-fictional engagements with history, but its distinctive emphasis on utility – on history as something to be *used* creatively – reminds us of the complex historical reflexivity that informs the contemporary Indian novel. Moreover, Ramanujan's poem is a fitting starting point here because the different stages or examples of historical consciousness elaborated in each stanza could also be said to rehearse and foreshadow, unconsciously, some of the predominant modes in which Indian novelists have engaged with history in their writing. Thus, in the following pages, "Some Indian Uses of History on a Rainy Day" will provide the opening for a series of connected readings of exemplary Indian novelistic engagements with history and historiography. As we will see, Ramanujan's own interventions in Indian narrative history will also become relevant in the closing discussion of strategic contemporary Indian fictional responses to medieval history.

In part, the sustained historiographic preoccupations of the Indian novel, which will be charted here, can be explained in terms of a postcolonial critical awareness of history's capacity to be used as a discursive support for colonial rule – a way of narrating the colonized out of an integral active role in Indian history and into a static, marginalized part in British "overseas" history. It is exactly this sense of the exclusions of a European version of India's history that Arundhati Roy points to in *The God of Small Things* (1997) when the protagonists, two Syrian Christian children who associate history with an actual deserted plantation house near their own family home in Kerala, are told by their diffident, Oxford-educated uncle that history is a house they are shut out of: " 'We can't go in,' Chako explained, 'because we've been locked out. And when we look in through the windows, all we see are shadows' " (A. Roy, *God* 52). In Indian[1] novels written in the last three decades, this distinctive suspicion of ethnocentric/Eurocentric history intersects with a postmodern historicism, in which the transcendent truth of historical grand narratives is challenged, giving way to a sense of history as provisional, fragmentary, and genealogical. As critics such as Linda Hutcheon have argued, postmodernism generated new literary responses to history in formal innovations, such as historiographic metafiction, through which history could be manipulated as a parallel, more or less fictional, text (Hutcheon).

This is not the place to review the well-rehearsed and increasingly dated debates over alliances and disconnections between the postcolonial and the postmodern, except to underline the fact that in both a suspicion of historical truth claims has given rise, for markedly different reasons, to forms of fiction that subvert, pastiche, and/or metafictionally intervene in history. In contemporary post-liberalization India, the older temporal frames that structured critical paradigms of the postcolonial and post-modern seem, in any case, to be blurring irrevocably. As Rana Dasgupta notes, in cities like Delhi, there is no longer a sense that India is config-ured differently to a culture of late modernity or has to "catch up" with a more technologically advanced West; instead, urban centers such as Delhi and Mumbai now present a vision of networked hypermodernity that increasingly looks toward possible global futures rather than back toward a belated, time-lagged, or postdated past (R. Dasgupta 45). This is not to suggest that history is no longer relevant, or that inequality no longer exists, but to note that in this new urban-global incarnation, older, established historical narratives will be forced to adapt to the accelerated cadences of India's present.

Claiming History

From the first stanza of "Some Indian Uses of History on a Rainy Day," Ramanujan's poem appears not to offer much initial purchase on the question of how the Indian novel has developed historiographically: the opening stanza simply recounts what might be called a moment of poetic consolation, in which Madras office clerks put up with the petty miseries of commuting and decide not to wait for a bus but to walk home instead. Their shared historical memory of "Old King Harsha" is a reference to the Buddhist monarch Harsha or (Harsa) who reigned over much of north India from 606 to 647 CE and was a Sanskrit poet and patron of the arts. His reign was distinguished by his generosity: he set up charitable institutions in his kingdom and allegedly donated food to Brahmins and Buddhist monks daily, as well as holding assemblies at Allahabad every five years where he distributed treasure. In a poem about history, the ref-erence is playfully reflexive in its gesture to a historical Indian sovereign who promoted poetry; as a way of thinking about the historiographic preoccupations of the novel, Ramanujan's opening stanza reminds us of what might be called an "epic historical consciousness" in early nationalist fictions.

Simply put, this epic imaginary, like the anti-colonial economic historiography it accompanied, mined Indian history for politically enabling or culturally affirming connections with the present. In the process, it adapted a rational historicism and read colonial histories of India closely for evidence of a national agency. The best-known example of this fervent turn to history is the nationalist author and father of the Indian historical novel, Bankimchandra Chattopadhyay, who famously demanded that India "must have a history" (Chattopadhyay, "Bangalar Itihash" 290) and whose seminal Bengali novel *Anandamath* (1882) fictionalized an eighteenth-century *sanyasi* rebellion – chronicled in William Wilson Hunter's *Annals of Rural Bengal* (1868) – as an allegory of nationalist awakening. The fascination with history continued in historical romances like K. K. Sinha's *Sanjogita: or the Princess of Aryavarta* (1903) and in the well-documented influence of such works as James Tod's *Annals and Antiquities of Rajasthan* (1829), which stands behind and informs a number of contemporary Indian historical fictions (M. Mukherjee, *Perishable* 59). As Sudipta Kaviraj notes, in late nineteenth-century Bengal, the new nationalist historicism coincided with a gradual "disenchantment" with the world through scientific and increasingly rationalized intellectual influences. Thus, the contemporary development of self-consciously "historical" Indian fiction involved a substantive re-conceptualizing of the role of literature as a specialized vehicle for imaginative thought (Kaviraj, "Two Histories" 548).

However, the initial, nationally inflected preoccupation with history in the early Indian novel is not straightforward, and the "rational" separation of history and epic/myth is transgressed in some fictions, as myth is co-opted to a national imagining. We see this process clearly in what I have called elsewhere "informative romances" (Tickell, "Terrorism"; and *Terrorism*), such as Sarath Kumar Ghosh's *The Prince of Destiny* (1909), in which the hero, the eponymous Prince Barath, seeks his own destiny both as a real political ruler and also as the transcendent reincarnation of the Hindu god Krishna. (The novel appears to waver in its political investment in myth by retaining reincarnation as a possibility.) A differently presented blurring of history and myth occurs in Raja Rao's nationalist novel *Kanthapura* (1938), which is a virtuoso stylistic evocation of a village community in south India brought into history with the arrival of the nationalist movement, which at the same time narrates the contemporary history of the national struggle (led by Gandhi) as a form of devotional epic. It could be argued that in his novel Rao presents anti-colonial agency as a complex negotiation between history as a paradigm of political sovereignty and history as *itihas*, the generic term for epic narratives such as the Ramayana that combine history and myth.

Ramanujan's temporal juxtaposing of King Harsha's monks and Madras commuters circa 1965 seems to tread the same path as these earlier nationalist novels in its distinctive consolatory return to the past in order to bolster a civilizational confidence. Western-style modernity, the poem suggests, has not brought the Madras bank clerks the kinds of advancements (in public transport at least) that Nehru's post-independence vision of a modern hydro-electrified India promised, but in the face of this potentially demeaning developmental realization, history returns the clerks to a magisterial vision of their cultural past, reminding them of the largesse of earlier Indian kings. However, the implied equivalence of King Harsha's "ten thousand" monks and modern bank clerks also subtly disrupts – "provincializes," in Dipesh Chakrabarty's words (*Provincializing*) – Eurocentric models of national history as a linear continuum. Like the monks, the clerks have "nothing but their own two feet," a statement that connects them (or more accurately returns them) to the traditions of religious pilgrimage so deeply scored into India's cultural landscape but also makes them the inheritors of a form of self-reliance reminiscent of the great politically inflected pilgrimages of the nationalist movement.

Recovering Buried History

The second stanza of "Some Indian Uses of History on a Rainy Day" presents the reader with a different relationship of past to present – prefiguring, I will suggest, a later historiographic mode in the Indian novel. Set in an Egyptian museum and undated, this section of Ramanujan's poem is both literally and figuratively archaeological, in the sudden discovery made by the museum-going Indian Fulbright scholars. Looking at the Egyptian exhibits, they suddenly become aware of the ancient trade routes between Egypt and south India in the "millennia" of bandages, made of muslin imported from the Malabar coastal town of Calicut, which have been used to wrap mummified remains. The scene is thus a startling poetic expression of Walter Benjamin's famous point about the irretrievability of certain histories and the danger that "every image of the past that is not recognized by the present as one of its own concerns threatens to disappear irretrievably" (247).

In relation to what we have been calling the historiographic preoccupations of the Indian novel in English, this moment is highly significant because it finds an equivalence in a post-independence shift beyond the boundaries of a cultural nationalism and toward a renewed attention to that which is effaced or re-narrated in the process of achieving national independence. Rajeswari Sunder Rajan, reviewing the politics of the contemporary Indian novel, relates these changes to the well-documented disillusionment with national politics that some commentators have seen as a key characteristic of the "postcolonial" condition and also cites Salman Rushdie's political critique of the Indira Gandhi regime in *Midnight's Children* (1981) as a crucial moment in the self-positioning of Indian novelists. In the latter work, Rushdie was able to stage himself, authorially, in a newly adversarial relation to the state, and thus, as Sunder Rajan argues, "no longer was the postcolonial writer limited to anticolonial resistance – he was now an adversary of his own government, no less" (Sunder Rajan, "After" 210).

In relation to a novelistic historical consciousness, this new interrogative or adversarial stance was not simply the result of a claimed cultural/political dissidence; it developed equally from a celebratory cosmopolitanism and a migrant aesthetics (also often associated with Rushdie) that had little time for the parochial nativism of national allegiance. A further contributing factor in the disillusionment of Indian authors with the claims of nationalist history was a troubled cross-regional awareness of the personal and social costs of the Indo-Pakistani Partition and the continuing traumas and historical erasures precipitated by the splitting of the subcontinent. The novelistic response to Partition is covered elsewhere in this volume, but we must touch on it briefly here because of its shaping influence on the literary-fictional conception of history.

In Amitav Ghosh's early novel *The Shadow Lines* (1988), the uncanny effects of Partition in Bengal are registered in its traumatic, translated family histories and in Ghosh's attention to the routine effacements and amnesias occasioned by newly exclusive national histories. Another contemporary work that bears comparison with Ghosh's writing in its close metahistorical engagement with the past is Mukul Kesavan's *Looking Through Glass* (1995), which sees its protagonist travel back in time, to 1942, to encounter a version of the past that allows a "counterfactual" questioning of the inevitability of the subcontinent's national destinies. Here again an interest in overwritten or effaced histories also has a particular origin in the traumatic process of national division during the Indo-Pakistani Partition. As Priyamvada Gopal notes of the negotiation of history and memory in works such as Kesavan's, "what ... has to be remembered and reinhabited are the heterodoxies and syncretism of the past, not the Past Perfect, but the past in its dynamic untidiness, porousness, and plenitude" (P. Gopal, *Indian* 88). Recalling some of the more formally ambitious Indian novels written in the 1980s and 1990s, it becomes clear that a highly creative adversarial revision of national history and the new sensitivity to a dynamic or porous past are further nuanced by changes in the disciplinary focus of history in India, and the influence of the subaltern studies historians (a group inspired by the work of the Italian Marxist Antonio Gramsci that sought to recuperate a subaltern agency from history that hitherto had been dominated by colonial and elite national interpretations).

Again, it is Amitav Ghosh's writing, in particular his genre-blurring historical travelogue *In an Antique Land* (1993) – that brilliantly rewrites a research project on textual references to a south Indian slave found in the twelfth-century archival depository of a Cairo synagogue – that exemplifies this paradigm of recovered history. Drawing on material that Ghosh had published as a historical essay in the Subaltern Studies series under the title "The Slave of Ms. H. 6" (and then reproduced in an essay collection, *The Imam and the Indian*), *In an Antique Land* is at once the most methodologically historical of Indian Anglophone literary works and the most subtly literary exposition of the subaltern studies agenda. In fact, critics have been quick to register that it is this generic grafting of the literary and historical, allied with a scrupulous attention to the traveling archival text, that has enabled Ghosh to avoid, here, the strategic essentialism that is often seen as a conceptual flaw of the subaltern studies approach (Dixon 35).

As an extended reflection on the forgotten ebb and flow of cosmopolitan trading communities and migrants across the medieval Levant and Indian Ocean, *In an Antique Land* is notable in its historical tracing of the same trade routes (albeit at a later point) to which Ramanujan alludes in his Cairo museum stanza. In both, the epistemic structure of history is read against the grain, and the taken-for-granted national and religious divisions of the modern world are made strange in a highly political process of social-anthropological defamiliarization. The "fragment," or leitmotif, is also important here (Elias 35), as Ghosh writes out of a sense of the textuality of his archival source, but with none of the overburdening investment in the single anecdote or metaphor-laden trace that makes postcolonial theoretical work produced contemporaneously prone to the same generalizations and interpretative maneuvers as some New

Historicist criticism. The richness of Ghosh's historiographic intervention, then, inheres in his use of seemingly traditional historical approaches to reconfigure conventional ethnocentric assumptions about cultural history and its boundaries.

History under Threat

The final stanza of Ramanujan's poem adds a chillingly ironic note to the historical "uses" that preceded it. The vulnerable and disorientated Sanskrit professor who appears here, stumbling through 1930s Berlin, is reminiscent of W. H. Auden's characterization of his own second-war generation, which has been reduced to a kind of troubled childishness by the imminent conflict: "We are, / Lost in a haunted wood, / Children afraid of the night / Who have never been happy or good" (Auden 99). Searching for familiar signs in the alien world around him, the Indian academic "comes home," in another of Ramanujan's moments of recognition, as he suddenly "assimilat[es]" the Nazi swastika on the arm of a fellow bus-passenger. Again, this part of the poem could easily be read as a figurative evocation of how cultures travel and how even the most un-assimilating nationalisms are cross-fertilized by other histories. However, the portentous signifying political weight of the swastika-armband demands more than this reading: it indicates the much more malignant uses to which history can be put in the service of politics.

Earlier, we noted Rajeswari Sunder Rajan's critical insight that one of the singular shifts in political alignment to mark the Indian novel of the Rushdie era was the self-fashioning of the Indian novelist as dissident – or at least as a commentator critical of the state. For Sunder Rajan, this literary politics is effectively different from the kinds of writing produced in more hardline, non-democratic states, because although "it is not a negligible politics," Indian authorial dissidence "must not be aggrandized as a writing that risks repression by the state" ("After" 212). This is a fine distinction about the political contexts of the novel in India, and it helps elucidate the position of the liberal author-intellectual, but it also risks passing too quickly over those instances in India's recent past in which the Indian novel has tackled, directly, issues of governmental repression and forms of cultural-historical censorship. In the context of the revisionist ethno-nationalist history associated with the Sangh Parivar or "family" of political groups on the Hindu right, particularly, the stakes involved in intervening in history in alternative or creative ways are significantly increased and the dialogic possibilities of the novel take on a somewhat greater urgency.

A work that conveys something of this urgency in its title is Githa Hariharan's *In Times of Siege* (2004). Hariharan's novel spans a precise two-month period, August to October 2000 – a window that is significant because it is framed historically by the BJP-coalition government, the NDA (National Democratic Alliance) of 1998 to 2004. When it was elected, the BJP coalition fostered an already widespread populist Hindu majoritarianism, in contrast to which non-Hindu identities were increasingly presented as threats to the integrity of dominant Hindu culture. This tendency found its most terrifying expression in the anti-Muslim pogrom in Gujarat in 2002, in which the Muslim community was targeted by Hindu gangs with the alleged sanction of the police and the state administration. The latter event provides the ultimately redemptive conclusion to another contemporary novel of India with a complex and nuanced awareness of history, M. G. Vassanji's *The Assassin's Song* (2009). As they both enter into a close dialogue with the new interpretations of history promoted by the BJP-led coalition at the turn of the millennium, Hariharan's and Vassanji's novels demand a parallel reading, as the conclusion to this rough diagrammatic account of Indian literary historiography.

Hariharan's *In Times of Siege* tells the story of an unassuming, Delhi-based history professor, Shiv Murthy, who suddenly finds himself targeted by members of a shadowy Hindu nationalist cultural watchdog group, the Itihas Suraksha Manch or "history protection group," who have taken offense at his coursework and accuse him of distorting Indian history.[2] Shiv works for an "open" university, and his collision with the forces of contemporary Indian politics is intensified by the sequestered nature of academic work in which he has little direct contact with his students and is prey to all the familiar alienations of bureaucratized higher education: "he no longer teaches students" but "coordinates resources for his educational clients" (6). In the course of the narrative, Hariharan's middle-aged protagonist faces the old dilemma of principled resistance versus quietist self-preservation. This moral challenge coincides with the absence of Shiv's wife, who is away visiting their daughter in the United States, and the arrival in his home of the daughter of an old friend, the spirited and politically engaged undergraduate Meena, who has broken her leg and who, in the process of convalescence, uses her contacts to organize popular support for Shiv's cause. As the crisis over Shiv's interpretation of medieval Indian history deepens, his relationship with Meena becomes more involved, although ultimately it never becomes an actual affair – resolving, instead, into a subtler, mutually enabling platonic bond.

In Times of Siege is fascinating as a metahistorical work because it rewrites a well-known episode from the governmental record of the BJP coalition: its controversial revision of the Indian school curriculum. When the BJP came to power as part of the NDA in 1998, it presided over a scheduled educational review and used this as an opportunity to push through plans to "Indianise, nationalise and spiritualise" the national curriculum (Panikkar, "Secular" 72–3). The Hindu right, through its volunteer paramilitary wing, the RSS, already promoted a communalized version of history in its own Saraswati Shishu Mandirs and Vidya Bharati schools (Mukherjee, Mukherjee, and Mahajan 18). The results were not felt in Indian society until 2000, when the coalition released its new Curriculum Framework (Joshee 182). This promised a new emphasis on (communal) civic training, but the planned program of civic instruction never materialized (Joshee 182). Instead, it was in the teaching of history that the new reforms had their greatest impact: all previous school history textbooks were scrapped because they were deemed to have too "Western" an outlook and were replaced with books that conformed to the Sangh Parivar's historical perspective. Secular historians quickly pointed out that the new textbooks were factually inaccurate, misleading, and biased toward a chauvinistic Hindu version of history, and these critics, some of whom were eminent scholars, were subsequently branded "anti-Hindu Euro-Indians" and their work scapegoated as "intellectual terrorism unleashed by the left" (Mukherjee, Mukherjee, and Mahajan 37). The BJP's hold on curricular policy decreased after the electoral defeat of the NDA in 2004, but a powerful lobby group still routinely targets histories it sees as offensive to Hindus.

In Hariharan's novel, the educational-historical plot involves a coursebook "lesson" Shiv has written about the twelfth-century poet-leader Basava or Basavanna, who was one of the greatest exponents of the medieval Virasaiva or Lingayata sect and who sought to reform Hinduism through his rejection of caste and his emphasis on personal spiritual observance. Basava acted as prime minister in the central Indian court of king Bijjala but entered self-exile when his Virasaiva followers were punished by the king for contravening orthodox caste rules about intermarriage.[3] The contested historical interpretation of Basava's life is thus not only a focus for political controversy in the novel; it also mirrors details of the contemporary narrative, setting up thematic reflections about the worth of dissent. The resonances between the twelfth-century Basava and his modern academic chronicler become fully established when Shiv vacillates over whether to continue defending his historical research or capitulate to demands from his head of department that he apologize. This equivoca- tion is immediately answered by the adherent of Basava in him – his more heroic conscience: "Basava's man is ready with his rejoinder: Why pretend you are a professor if you can't stand up to someone telling you what to think? How to think? … Do you imagine an ordinary man cannot be a hero?" (65).

While *In Times of Siege* explores history through the context of aca- demic scholarship and reveals the tensions between a productive, research-led historical uncertainty and the monologic demands of Hindu nationalism, M. G. Vassanji's *The Assassin's Song* (2009) approaches his- tory from a more personal angle. The novel tells the story of Karsan Dargawalla, the heir to the priesthood (*gaadi-varas*) of the shrine of a medieval Sufi saint, or *pir*, Nur Fazal. The shrine has been a place of wor- ship in the eponymous Gujarati town of Pirbaag for hundreds of years, but Karsan grows up unsure of his own commitment to the priesthood and skeptical of the renouncing demands of faith in preference to the fas- cinations of secular intellectual history. His disillusionment grows when he leaves India on a scholarship to study at Harvard and, against his father's wishes, decides to stay and pursue an academic career in North America. Karsan's new life in the United States is marked by tragedy, his marriage failing after his young son is killed in a road accident. Without any remaining ties, and after receiving a letter informing him of his father's death and the destruction of Nur Fazal's shrine during the 2002 Gujarat pogrom, Karsan returns to India. There, he takes up an academic residency at Simla to research the background of the saint his family has been connected with for so long, while at the same time trying to rees- tablish a connection with his brother.

In contrast to the claustrophobic dramatic focus of Hariharan's novel, *The Assassin's Song* ranges widely, moving from rural Gujarat to North America and then back to India, and sweeping chronologically from the time of Nur Fazal to the early post-independence decades and the first years of the twenty-first century. It is tempting to ascribe these fictional differences in setting to their authors' backgrounds (Hariharan is a south Indian living in Delhi, and Vassanji is a Tanzanian-Canadian who grew up in the South Asian community in East Africa but has lived in Canada for most of his adult life). However, apart from the way Vassanji's work touches on some characteristically migrant themes and concerns (about memory, guilt, cultural betrayal, and the vicissitudes of migrant identity), these details are ultimately less important than the beleaguered defense of forms of alternative, syncretic history that occurs in both texts.

At the same time, it is essential to realize that in both *In Times of Siege* and *The Assassin's Song*, even as an exclusive Hindu nationalist interpretation of history is critiqued, the religious or miraculous is not rejected conceptually as an aspect of historical consciousness. In Vassanji's novel, the miraculous is contained in an asynchronous sequence of chapters narrated in the third person dealing with the life and miracles of Nur Fazal. By bracketing these chapters against the novel's "disenchanted" present, Vassanji preserves the miraculous as an aspect of history, rather than taking the clumsier option of employing it as a formal component of an overarching magical realism. Hariharan is also unwilling to lose a sense of the confluence of both mythical and historical aspects of the South Asian past, so that as Shiv conducts his research, he finds that "wading through the numerous contradictory accounts of Basava's life means parting several meeting rivers. Separating history and myth, pulling apart history and legend. Deciding which chunks of history will keep the myth earthbound" (Hariharan 90). In the "secular" contemporary sections of Vassanji's text, the miraculous comes directly into question when Karsan realizes that the lamp on Nur Fazal's shrine, which is alleged to burn constantly without ever needing oil, is actually refueled secretly at night by Karsan's mother. Karsan's disillusionment is devastating and leads him to reject the authority of the shrine and question his father, who responds that the illusion is a necessary part of faith: "People need miracles, Karsan. Without miracles they lose their way.... Our message is more subtle – it's about the meaning of existence – but people have a need of miracles" (150).

In both these novels, the answer to the problem of a politically threatened history is not, then, a retreat into an implacably empirical historicism; it is instead a careful mediation of secular and mythical components of history that recognizes the importance of the latter in Indian cultural responses to the past. In this sense, Vassanji, and, to a lesser extent, Hariharan both tackle a problem outlined by the historian Dipesh Chakrabarty, that to understand history in the context of India one may have to develop an incredulity toward a certain historicism, a "metanarrative of [secular] progress," and allow for an untranslatable sense of enchantment – what Chakrabarty calls the "times of gods," which are implicit in locally embedded versions of history ("Time" 50). Hariharan finds this enchantment in the resonant devotional politics of Basava's poems, or *vachanas*, which have a gnomic, aphoristic quality, even as they represent a revolutionary political vision. In Vassanji's case, a similar gesture is apparent in Karsan's decision to return to Pirbaag and take up his birthright and his mantra-like *bol*, even after he has ascertained the "true" historical origins of Nur Fazal in the Iranian Shi'a assassin sect.

Here we perhaps encounter a strategic redeployment of something we have already registered in the second stage of our rudimentary schema, which summarized so-called postnationalist novels. In these texts, as H. S. Komalesha notes, Indian authors retain a fascination for "premodern narrative techniques" because they can be used to "foreground a postmodern disbelief in nation" (158). Developing on this point I would suggest that, in the novels dealing with a more recent communalist threat to history, the recourse to premodern narratives and aphoristic or miraculous ways of thinking is not so much a critical disbelieving gesture as an affirmative "besieged" statement of the need for an expansive historical consciousness – what Hariharan calls in her novel "the right to know a thing in all the ways possible" (195). In a certain way, as rejoinders to aspects of the Sangh's communal project, both Hariharan's and Vassanji's novels call for history as a support for a civic idea – of medieval Indian city-cultures marked by plurality and tolerance – which can countermand the monolithic, purified Vedic golden-age cities of Hindu nationalist history.

Returning to the concluding stanza of Ramanujan's poem, a further irony and foreshadowing of history present themselves in the fact that in 2011, one of Ramanujan's works – a scholarly essay he had written in 1987 titled "Three Hundred Ramayanas: Five Examples and Three Thoughts on Translation" on the numerous variant versions of the Ramayana – was subject to the same treatment that Hariharan describes for Shiv's research. In 2008, Delhi University students belonging to the BJP's student organization, the Akhil Bharatiya Vidyarthi Parishad (ABVP), campaigned against the essay's inclusion in the syllabus, on the grounds that it offended them. At that time, they were unable to have it removed. Three years later, however, in a highly controversial move, the Academic Council of Delhi University decided to ban the essay. For liberal historians, this was a retrograde act, and the blogger and journalist Nilanjana Roy spoke for many when she commented:

> If you find ideas and stories threatening, if your way of life depends on having just one rigid view of faith, or history, or mythology, then there is no possibility of debate.... The goal is never to encourage dissent and conversation, but to shut it down.... In that world, making a university back down on what it allows students to learn is a major victory, and it

holds out the possibility that one day, it will be only this narrow view of
history that will prevail, that we will learn only one kind of history, one
Ramayana. (N. Roy)

Although it is a potentially reductive critical maneuver to cite the
Ramayana as a narrative precursor of the Indian novel, the fact that
it was the Ramayana's narrative multiplicity that was censored in this
case – and that a meticulous, scholarly version of early Indian literary
history was suppressed in the process – should be highly relevant to
any reading of contemporary fiction. Ramanujan did not live to see
the removal of his essay from the Delhi University syllabus, but his
subtle polyglot sensitivity to the different ways in which culture and
history come into confluence stands as a reproof to the emergence of
a "predatory" identity politics (not, of course, exclusive to India) that
seeks to reduce identity to an ethnic singularity (Appadurai 53). Given
the continuing importance of vote banks and the social uncertainties
unleashed by India's globalizing ascendency, the onward rush of India's
present history is likely to see further literary-historiographic engagements of the kind exemplified by Hariharan's and Vassanji's fictions. In
these texts the question will not only be how Indian writers can use history for different dissident imaginaries but also how they can maintain
the right to imagine history as difference.

Notes

1 The designation of the "Indian" novel is notoriously fraught. Many successful
   contemporary novels are written by authors who, although they have a cultural
   or family connection with the subcontinent, live elsewhere. For the purposes of
   this chapter, "Indian novels" describes works set in India, or with an imaginative investment in Indian cultures, rather than texts written by authors resident
   in India.
2 At the time of writing, the historical research of the American academic
   Wendy Doniger has come under similar attack. In 2010, Doniger's book
   The Hindus: An Alternative History (2009) was the subject of a lawsuit
   brought by a Hindu group, the Shiksha Bachao Andolan (Save Education
   Campaign), against Doniger's publishers, Penguin, for its alleged distortions
   and factual inaccuracies. Penguin has now agreed to destroy all available
   copies of Doniger's book. See http://www.theguardian.com/commentis-
   free/2014/feb/12/wendy-doniger-book-hinduism-penguin-hindus, accessed
   April 3, 2014.
3 For a more detailed account of Basava and the Virasaiva sect, see Michael;
   Schouten; and Zvelebil.

CHAPTER 16

Virtue, Virtuosity, and the Virtual: Experiments in the Contemporary Indian English Novel

Rukmini Bhaya Nair

All fiction, arguably, is thought experiment. Fiction, that is, may be held to perform certain crucial tasks that have conventionally been assigned to the domain of the sciences (see Mach 1897 on the *Gendankenexperimente*). By offering us characters, histories, and geographies that, by definition, do not exist in – or alter in subtle and significant ways – the observable scenarios around us, fictional texts invite us to imaginatively theorize crises or problems in the world so that we "re-cognize" them anew.

A central raison d'être of fiction, in short, is that it is an experiment with the conventions and constructs of truth-telling. Genres such as the novel typically require us to consider counterfactual universes and present us with hypotheses that seek to "explain" the phenomena around us. It is in this sense that fictions have trained us in theory down the ages. For example, when the Indian epic Ramayana tells us that the three distinctive stripes on the back of the Indian palm squirrel (species *Funambulus palmarum*) owe their origin to the grateful Rama stroking the back of this creature in a gesture of gratitude because squirrels helped him build a bridge between India and Sri Lanka, it not only offers us an explanation of these markings but also affords us glimpses into a possible ecological worldview that is culturally grounded. Kipling might be said to make a similar move when he asks how the leopard got his spots. These may be prototype "just so" stories, but in their search for causal explanations, they exemplify attempts at theory-building of a novel sort. The present chapter argues that the sophisticated experiments with storytelling conducted by Indian English novelists in the past three decades (namely, the 1980s to the present) extend further a long and distinguished lineage of "experiments with truth" – to use a phrase that Mahatma Gandhi made famous. They seem, however, to possess a generic advantage over Gandhi's autobiographical methods in that they are out-and-out fictions. Thus, their play with history – self-reflexively and artfully using the colonizers' own tongue to construct alternative accounts of recent colonial and postcolonial history – possesses a sort of "wicked freedom"[1] that was perhaps not available to Gandhi. How that freedom is used to meet certain authorial ends will be a central question addressed in this chapter.

The triangulation I suggest between theoretical framing, historical event, and fictional representation in the contemporary Indian English novel brings us quite naturally, I argue, to a means or method we might call "experimental historiography." If historiography is concerned with the perspectives that other disciplines bring to the writing of history, then it seems plausible that the postcolonial novel constitutes a salient extension of this method. By creating characters, perspectives, and styles of narration that self-consciously experiment with the ways in which historical "truth" is presented, these novels mark a paradigm shift in which one kind of history-making has putatively "ended" (see Fukuyama) and others have begun anew.

Speaking of the "ends" of history and of fiction, most critics agree that the Indian novel in English has altered dramatically in its styles, themes, and ideologies in the years following the publication of Salman Rushdie's "magic realist" *Midnight's Children* in 1981. But why has this period, more than thirty years after India's independence, been so crucial in remaking the colonial/postcolonial narrative? Why has it effected such radical changes of attitude toward the "truth" of previous historical accounts? It is not, after all, that a previous generation of novelists did not interrogate the colonial perspective. They emphatically did: Mulk Raj Anand, for example, made the bold, possibly "subalternist," move of choosing the untouchable Bakha as the subject of his first novel, eponymously titled *Untouchable* (1935); around the same time, R. K. Narayan created a whole geography of small-town India where the British barely figured. Raja Rao and G. V. Desani, both trained philosophers, in their turn fashioned languages (in *Kanthapura*, 1938) and personae (in *All About H. Hatterr*, 1948) that were quite orthogonal to "Raj" histories. Written in English though they were, the idiom and the *weltanschauung* of these last two remarkably estranging novels are, to this day, almost impenetrable if their readers unquestioningly accept the historical presuppositions of, let's say, a John Masters, J. G. Farrell, M. M. Kaye, or Paul Scott.[2] So what, if anything, is so different about the experimental methods associated with the post-Rushdie generation of writers?

To begin with, the newer writers make a far more categorical claim to a cosmopolitan consciousness and deliberately project a quite different frame of historical reference. Witness Rushdie, the "leader" of this brigade, headily announcing the advent of a new kind of Indian:

> We are Indians, but there is redefinition. India has now to admit that there are different ways of being Indian, which do not necessarily have to do with being rooted in India. This is a wonderful and exciting realisation. It is a liberating realisation. This is a kind of newness. (quoted in Nair, *Lying* 227)[3]

It is exactly this framing, however, that is controversial. For the newness of which Rushdie speaks with such palpable excitement cannot but imply a certain moral oversight. In its blithe takeover of the task of defining "Indianness," it suggests that those who write in English and live abroad – novelists, in short, like Rushdie himself – are the ones who have commandeered a new experimental space in which fundamental redefinitions will occur. In this sense, Rushdie presents us with a fait accompli: the lab has been set up, the petri dishes and pipettes are in place, and great literary experiments are already in the making. One world has ended; another, coded in a "postcolonial" language, has begun. Rushdie's global stature, coupled with his aggressive championship of this "new English" as the repository of originality and vim in post-independence writing across *all* of India's languages, has led over the past decades, not surprisingly but perhaps unnecessarily, to bitter culture wars between writers who live in India and those who represent India elsewhere. The issue is further complicated by the perception that even English-language writers who live in India tend to be separated from their regional counterparts culturally as well as economically. They often live in the large metropolises and are themselves far from being "rooted." Indeed, there is more than a faint suspicion in popular culture that these "English-types" would sell out to the West if they got the chance. For regional writers, the kinds of lucrative offers received by some English writers are not even a distant dream. Given this complex lattice of hopes and resentments, the type of "non-rooted" writing that Rushdie praises so highly has been severely criticized in India on at least the following five counts:

i. it is self-consciously exotic and panders to Western tastes and markets
ii. it is inauthentic and lacks rootedness
iii. it is stylistically clumsy and/or far too convoluted
iv. it is limited in terms of scope and theme
v. it is so marked by hype and media publicity – so "happening" that it is currently impossible to assess such writing coolly and with objectivity.

At the same time, Indian English writing has been internationally praised for

i. its conceptualization of "India" as a holistic, robust political entity
ii. its modernity and ability to speak vigorously to contemporary concerns
iii. its stylistic innovations and its fearless use of "Indian English"
iv. its vast canvas and adaptation of old cultural myths to new, diasporic contexts
v. its cosmopolitan flavor, its youthful energy, and its ability to reach out to audiences who are now able to experience "India" in a world language.

Virtue's Double-Bind

Even a passing glance at these cursory lists suggests that diametrically opposed sets of hypotheses concerning ethical positioning as well as stylistic choices obtain. In these performative encounters, a series of battles are endlessly rehearsed over the twin towers of location and language, longing and belonging, and, above all, over literary ownership. Which contingent holds the moral right to speak for India – the "rooted" or the "diasporic"? While it is tempting to dismiss the whole debate as a tired and false problematic, such a "non-aligned" response, based on the liberal premise that writers have no truck with place or time – that they are global citizens, wandering gypsies, transcendent universalists, and so on – could appear not just anodyne but inappropriate in the postcolonial context.

Experimentation with language is not, after all, a choice for a postcolonial writer in English; as a child of mixed parentage, she has perforce to theorize and experiment with her linguistic inheritance. She has to remold the traditional form of the "Western" Bildungsroman so that her story announces a personal as well as a historical coming of age – a twin rebirth of both language and being. In this respect, such fiction is auto-ethnographic: a rites-of-passage bi-modality that out of necessity expresses "Indianness" as hybrid, the product of a long-term history of linguistic and cultural interbreeding (Bhabha, *Location*). Further, India's irrepressible multilingualism and the dominant role that English continues to play in virtually all of India's institutions of education, government, and justice imply that there is no escaping the wicked freedoms of endemic glossolalia in independent India.

Rushdie's celebration of diasporic Indianness consequently presents us with a paradox. Its vision of the Indian English novel offers a utopian portrait: that of a linguistically as well as politically "free" world. The trouble is that most Indians "rooted" in India will never have a chance to experience this world. Nor is this world itself exactly free from "wickedness." Consider the cluster of terms – migrant, immigrant, refugee, asylum-seeker, boat-people, guest-worker, resident alien, tourist, traveler, nomad, gypsy, etc. – often implicated in a whole context of material culture such as passports, airlines, tickets, visas, and so forth. Each marks a site of potential violence because national borders tend to be powerfully guarded and controlled, and each points up a conflict inherent to the notion of that "fourth world" of refugees and migrants, to whose "auto-ethnographic" accounts and "agonistic" circumstances critics like Gregory Castle have drawn our attention (xii–xiii). Contested words such as "immigrant" and "refugee" conceal in their everyday usage racial prejudice, denial of lawful rights and injustices of all sorts. So, two main framing questions – moral ones – raised by postcolonial theorists are: Can there really be a "borderless world," or is this merely an illusion underwritten by the rich and powerful nations of the world? In reality, is it not the case that this marvelous world is crisscrossed with barriers and fences for all poor migrants?

The postcolonial fiction writer responds to these questions by suggesting that while the real world may not be free, it is possible to experimentally "free" the imagination and thus connect with issues of political and intellectual emancipation. For example, Maxine Hong Kingston, explicitly inspired by Rushdie's *The Satanic Verses* (1988), announced in 1989 that "The dream of the great American novel is past. We need to write the Global novel" (Kingston 39). But a quarter-century later, Jhumpa Lahiri, speaking at the Jaipur Literature Festival in 2014, records her suspicion of the word "global," suggesting that it is a marketing label and that the term "universal" is more suitable for the "great book" that communicates emotion and experience across cultures in a way that is "comprehensible, resonant and transcendent."[4] We seem to have turned a full circle here; yet these writers' views intersect, I propose, around the identification of an experimental space demarcated by the postcolonial novelist. Both agree that the "undue power" of the English language is "distressing" and that the figure of the immigrant remains central in postcolonial fiction. Certainly there is no denying that this diasporic figure is to be found journeying through the pages of much contemporary Indian fiction, whether in the magic realist fictions of Rushdie or Sealy or the more realist works of Amitav Ghosh or Arundhati Roy. My suggestion is that postcolonial fiction everywhere and in India in particular has over the last few decades "universalized" this figure of the immigrant and made him/her a key site of experimentation.

In addition, the "thought experiment" that the postcolonial novel conducts is to persistently return its reader to a psychological context of moral ambiguity. This ambiguity does not merely characterize the mental/emotional states of the characters in the novel but seems designed to affect readers' judgments. Readers constantly find themselves in a state of being "in two minds" (metaphorically mimicking the "observer's paradox" in physics), caused by the scenes of cultural clash so frequently depicted in these novels. For example, one of my Chinese-American students at a leading U.S. university told me that part of his strategy for reading Indian fiction in English was "siding" with either the older or the younger generation. What he had noticed about "Asian" fictions, he said, is that they often presented generational as well as gendered encounters that had seeded within them yet another "hidden conflict" between Western and Indian worldviews. These stories, he maintained, *forced* him into a terrain of ambiguity where he had to rethink his views not just of the characters but of the authors – as well as of himself. He pointed out that many of the authors were young, successful, cosmopolitan women whose writing could not quite be separated from their careers, who had attended writing schools and who were not shy about drawing media attention to their positioning in "two worlds." This world of flux, where "East meets West," is also mimicked in the auto-ethnographic cross-talk between writer and reader in a book such as Lahiri's *The Interpreter of Maladies* (1999). The aim in this sort of fiction, then, is to create not so much traditional empathy, but rather a deliberate "alienation effect" in its reader.[5] It challenges the reader to a make a moral choice between the virtues of rootedness and those of wandering. In the Indian context, these "wicked" questions also arise naturally in literature, given the entanglement of history with real world developmental challenges.

Virtuoso Performatives

Trawl through the basic themes of Indian fiction in English over the past decades and it seems, at first glance, to bear witness to Lahiri's claim that it tackles "universal" concerns. Here's a rough and ready list of common themes:

1. **KINSHIP/FAMILY** (sub-themes: childhood, motherhood, autobiography, patriarchy, sibling relationships, forbidden relationships across

caste and class boundaries, illegitimacy, miscegenation, family loyalties and conflicts, age, youth, rites of passage)

2. **COMMUNITY/IDENTITY** (sub-themes: membership in a minority group such as the Parsi or Sikh collective; uniqueness as an individual in terms of customs and habits, dress or codes; "hybridity" and the unfulfilled longing to belong)

3. **HISTORY/POLITICS** (sub-themes: "orientalism" or the paradigm of "East" versus "West"; imperialism, nationalism, political violence, and corruption; democracy; freedom; Partition; bureaucratic power and the roles of powerful leaders)

4. **MYTH/RELIGION** (sub-themes: multiple deities, religious festivals and rituals, intertextual references to mythological tales and epics such as the Ramayana and the Mahabharata, rich in narrative symbolism)

5. **LANGUAGE/CULTURE** (sub-themes: the changing role of English in a postcolonial, global context; oral modes of narration; translation and code-mixing; genre intermixing; multiculturalism, pluralism)

6. **SEXUALITY/GENDER** (sub-themes: incest, homoeroticism, infatuation, transgender identities, repressed sexuality; the discovery of one's "true" self)

7. **MIGRANCY/TRAVEL** (sub-themes: borders and boundary crossings, territoriality, estrangement, discovery and learning, finding or not finding oneself; renaming, binary sight, twinning, magic realist transformations, cultural schizophrenia, etc.)

8. **URBAN LIFE/NATURAL LANDSCAPES** (sub-themes: the contrast between life in big, brash cities, such as Bombay or Delhi, and the natural world that exists at their peripheries, such as the rough sea and natural light; watching the stars through an intervening technology such as a telescope; the part played by technology generally in the construction of modernity and "modern India")

9. **SICKNESS/GROWTH** (sub-themes: illness, decay, old age, and death; medical knowledge, transformation, recovery, tradition, and rationality; growing up, coming of age)

Examine these parameters via the traditional route of textual analysis, however, and the sheer linguistic vitality of recent Indian English fiction offers another perspective on how the Indian subcontinent has been imaginatively reworked in these texts. Two instances:

a) Allan Sealy's *The Trotter-nama* (1988): A recurrent motif in this text is the visual representation of a hand with a pointing finger: ☞. This finger is at once accusatory – suggesting blame for historical wrongs such as the theft of a people's birthright during colonization – and directional – suggesting travel and movement in various directions. Informative and iterative, it fulfills a brilliant indexical function, indicating the here-and-now location of historical events ("☞ HERE SUCH AND SUCH PASSED" [Sealy 358]) as well as the unknown future. Finally, it is a sign that stands in stubborn alterity to the textual narrative, for while the story of the text may tell of a missing right hand with a missing finger, the visual image implies that fictional representation could make up for the "missing" parts of the historical narrative. We should also note a strong intertextual connection here, intended or not, with the first chapter of Book 2 of Rushdie's *Midnight's Children*, entitled "The Fisherman's Pointing Finger," whose much-analyzed image refers to an "English" painting that hung over Saleem's crib as a child, where a "fisherman's finger" points to something unseen beyond the horizon.

b) Arundhati Roy's *The God of Small Things* (1997): Roy has maintained that her writing is quite unembellished. It is written out of experience and opposed to magic realism in that it was written straight and she did not change a single word of her text. This may be so, but subjected to close textual analysis, the level of stylistic experimentation in this text matches that of any more fantastical text. These features include:

1. Reverse or mirror writing sometimes embellished with caps ("NAIDNI YUB, NAIDNI EB" [57]), as well as Stand-up Capitals within sentences ("She said it was entirely possible, for instance, that Estha could grow up to be a Male Chauvinist Pig" [79]);
2. Joint words pressing up against each other, mimicking the linguistic word-worlds of children (chinskin, bestfriend [78–9]);
3. Circling repetitions ("He said that there were only black cat-shaped holes in the Universe. There were ... Squashed Miss Mitten-shaped stains in the Universe. ... Squashed crows that had tried to eat the squashed frog-shaped stains in the Universe. Squashed dogs that ate the squashed crow-shaped stains in the Universe" [79]);
4. Single-word sentences; startling juxtapositions ("Feathers. Mangoes. Spit" [79]);
5. Paragraphs a sentence long or less ("All the way to Cochin" [79]);
6. Profuse italics ("And how he fell to the floor with knives in his back and said, '*Et tu, Brute?—Then fall Caesar*'" [79]).

The list could go on. These examples, with a single exception, are from a randomly opened set of pages in Roy's novel. And it is not only in her choice of graphemics that Roy is stylishly self-reflexive. Inductive inference from the many photographs of her in the media, as well as the interviews she gave at the time in which she identifies herself as an "aerobics instructor," appears to support the surmise that a finely judged self-portrait also appears in her novel: "She was in jeans and a white T-shirt.... Her wild hair was tied back to look straight, though it wasn't. A tiny diamond gleamed in one nostril. She had absurdly beautiful collarbones and a nice athletic run" (19).

It is in this sense, I would argue, that Indian novelists of the post-Rushdie generation have instituted themselves not only as authors but also as *actors* within and chief interpreters of their own texts: auto-ethnographic specialists in defining the contradictions of "Indianness." A further sampling:

> **Vikram Chandra:** "I really don't have any idea of who my typical reader is.... One doesn't have control of the story, once you let it loose in the world."[6] **Upamanyu Chatterjee:** "Some part of my writing is certainly my own autobiographical experience [but] there is a large part that has been inspired by the things that I have been told, read about etc."[7] **Amit Chaudhuri:** "Can it be true that Indian writing, that endlessly rich, complex and problematic entity, is to be represented by a handful of writers who write in English?"[8] **Amitav Ghosh:** I cannot accept the label "Commonwealth Writer"; it is both imperialist and limiting.[9] **Githa Hariharan:** "My voice seems right for a medley. This also means that I will never be a totally 'suitable girl' whose work is easily classified."[10] **Mukul Kesavan:** "Complicated nations [such as India] that learn to deal with diversity are better than simplifying ones that try to draw borders round a People."[11] **Arundhati Roy:** "When people ask me, 'Is Rahel you or is Ammu you?' I say yes, but so is Baby Kochamma and so is Comrade Pillai. They are not very nice people, but I am not a very nice person."[12] **Salman Rushdie:** "Any writer wishes to provoke the imagination."[13] **Vikram Seth:** "As long as the writer is not trying deliberately to be obscure, most readers extend a certain tolerance to other literatures."[14] **Shashi Tharoor:** "I reinvented the epic stories of India as an account of the political history of independent India and in the process tried to illuminate some aspects of the Indian condition."[15]

These glimpses, even in the ludic "post-it" style that I have summarized them, demonstrate the cognitive interfaces between the genres of autobiography, face-to-face interview, history writing, and fiction, as well as between English and the other languages of India, that I earlier dubbed "experimental historiography." As Roy puts it in her novel, "an antiquated philosophy... crumbled. Gradually *Chappu Thamburan* [the Lord of Rubbish, a.k.a. the God of Small Things] acquired a new ensemble" (*God* 320).

Indeed, aided by the visually oriented new technologies that will be addressed in the last part of this chapter, Indian novelists have over the last three decades produced a seductive fictional ensemble that effectively breaches the boundaries between autobiography and autograph. Inasmuch as it crosses generic, sexual, cultural, and other boundaries, variable by variable, this writing is as much postmodern as it is postcolonial. In particular, it transgresses the classical boundaries between creative and critical discourses, whose chief metaphor is miscegenation. Most intriguingly, by narrowing the gap between critic and writer, this incarnation of the novel magically disarms its critics, leaving it almost invulnerable – bulletproof. Genres merge in it; autobiography reaches out flirtatiously for its image in fiction.

Virtual Reality

This chapter has argued that the thought experiments conducted in the Indian English novel involve an alchemical conversion from a received historical archive to literature as "sensuous theory" (Nair, *Lying*).[16] Were we to set out a bare-bones event history of post-1980 India, it would reveal a time of considerable trauma: the military takeover of the Golden Temple, the slaying of thousands of Sikhs in the riots of 1984, the assassinations of Indira and Rajiv Gandhi, the bomb blasts in Bombay, the huge shameless scams in which billions of rupees of public money disappeared, the pulling down of Babri Masjid in 1992, the nuclear blast of 1998, the attack on Parliament in 2001, and the Gujarat carnage in 2002. In one way or another, these event-patterns have been repeated in the decade since 2002 as well, seeming to indicate that the modes of experimental historiography that the Indian English novelists of the 1980s and 1990s pioneered are still serviceable today. Rushdie in fact mourned back then that "the country which came into being in 1947 is being transformed into something else" (quoted in Reder 169). What was this mysterious "something else"? Once again, a motley list of factors could account for this transformation in the specific case of the Indian English novel:

1. As an indirect result of two extremely influential books, namely, Edward Said's *Orientalism* (1979) and Rushdie's own *Midnight's Children* (1981) appearing in the West, there occurred what might be

thought of as an inaugural moment in academia. Postcolonial studies curricula were either established or received a boost the world over
from the 1980s on and are still going strong today. Novels produced in
India today continue to provide fine fodder for these curricula.

2. Economically, India began to "liberalize" its economy in the 1980s and
"globalization" became a slogan, creating market forces that resulted in
international publishing houses (Penguin, HarperCollins, Picador) setting up shop in the country.

3. Book launches and media hype became familiar parts of the social
scene as a consequence, and journals in English devoted to reviewing
arose (*The Book Review*, *Biblio*). Today, India hosts numerous international literary festivals as well.

4. Most crucially, the "Technology Missions" of the 1980s and the burgeoning IT industry in India post 1991 created a new relationship to
reading and writing in English.

Some combination of these factors ensured that the book was reinvented
as an elite object of "sensuous" desire in metropolitan India, reproducing
the attractions of the English language as a locus of aspiration among one
of largest young populations anywhere in the world.

One good measure of the success both of intellectual paradigm shifts
and of technological revolutions is precisely their capacity to foster new
creative genres. Just as the Gutenberg printing press once "democratized"
Europe and provided a crucial condition for the rise of the novel, resulting in far-reaching psychological changes in attitudes toward reading,
the conundrum before us today is: Will computer technologies similarly
generate twenty-first-century textual styles with radical epistemological
consequences?

In the period from the 1980s on, India embraced the digital age. These
palpable technological changes have had a significant influence on writing
styles and entertainment genres in the country and include, for example:

1. the revival of the epistolary form, so well-known in the eighteenth-
and nineteenth-century English novel, in the guise of magically fast
and often stunningly informal email;

2. the rise of myriad chat rooms, tantalizingly poised between writing
and speech and – in India – between the twin tongues of English and
Hindi/Bangla/Tamil, and so on, resulting in a vital spread of multilingual conversational discourses into e-space;

3. video games and interactive narrative writing, in which players influence the shape of a text as it is being made;

4. blogs and e-forms of the interview, book extract, and essay, as tools for intellectual/commercial visibility; and

5. SMS, mobile phones, Facebook, and downloads of books, films, music, and videos, which have all come to stay in urban as well as small-town India.

E-modes such as these demonstrate the flexibility with which contemporary language, and especially "world English," is being redesigned and redesignated to use public spaces in the service of private intimacy, and vice versa. It goes without saying that this e-revolution is by no means confined to India; however, given that 65 percent of India's citizens are below the age of thirty-five, one cannot underestimate the zest with which this young population has taken to multimedia formats, ceaselessly and fearlessly experimenting with them and reaching out internationally through them. I would suggest that this has shifted the burden of fictional experimentation from paper to the electronic screen in contemporary India as elsewhere. As Chetan Bhagat, a runaway bestselling author, frankly states in a 2014 interview, "Today, I'm not competing with other authors but with apps, video-games, with movies and TV."[17]

These developments in the technological imaginary have dramatically affected the experiments now being conducted in the space of the Indian English novel, which seems noticeably to have repositioned itself. Ever since Chetan Bhagat burst on the scene with *Five Point Someone* (2004), plain style is "trending." There is a clear shift of thematic focus from an obsession with the historical past to the social anxieties of the present, from the international diasporic stage to the arena of national politics, and from high literary to middle-brow popular culture, while an earlier sensuous love for theory has morphed into a sensuous desire for real and material satisfactions – or, as Bhagat puts it more bluntly in the title of his 2011 novel, for *Revolution 2020: Love, Corruption, Ambition.* Leading a psychological battle for the soul of the Indian English novel just as Rushdie once did, Bhagat, for example, a passionate advocate of English education, stoutly declares in the interview cited earlier that his aim is to get "every kid in India to read an English book." Displaying a clear understanding of the economics as well as the economies of reading, Bhagat's publishers have priced his books remarkably low (about $2 to $5), while he has, in tandem, repeatedly maintained that his quest is not for critical praise but rather for a wide and direct connect with his mostly young readers.[18] In this respect, authors such as Bhagat remain chief interpreters and purveyors of their own texts, but rather than being evaluated in academic journals, they now appear regularly on television channels, advertising their "products" and speaking directly to their audiences and sometimes making stunningly lucrative alliances with Bollywood cinema. The role models among this generation are also changing and reflect a gender divide: women writers (e.g., Anuja Chauhan, Advaita Kala) generally have high-profile careers, are often signed on by big publishing houses, and write in smoother and more sophisticated prose. By contrast, the men are bankers or engineers and write more roughly. Overall, however, these experiments in "post-millennial fiction" (Dawson Varughese) mark a new era in which the novel is less a literary venture and more a "lifestyle thing," with the inevitable consequence that the "wickedness" of the literary freedoms exercised in the earlier texts has been considerably reduced, so that most contemporary fictions in the near future will likely not be controversial in the manner of Rushdie's *The Satanic Verses*.

As is to be expected of a young nation, a central feature of these new novels is romance,[19] but it is romance fast-forwarded – a fact apparent from the length of most of these books, which are popularly known as "metro reads," indicating a novel that lasts the length of a train ride to work and does not tax the reader overmuch. Graphic novels (Amruta Patil) and fantasy literature loosely based on legend (Amish Tripathi) have also acquired a large readership in English. What all these post-liberalization forms of the novel in India share is their rejection of a "literary ideology" and their pragmatic approach to the English language. A remarkable historiographic turn in this new fiction is that the white man and his spectral presence have all but disappeared in them – perhaps a measure of the ebbing away of postcolonial concerns about language mastery so prominent in the linguistically bedazzling novels of the Rushdie generation. Diaspora is no longer a central theme. At the same time, given that the Indian English novel today must cater to both a domestic and an international audience – to an academic *and* a popular culture – a small space still seems reserved for the experimental literary novel. Such novels in the tradition of Amitav Ghosh's troubling tale of intellectual theft in *The Calcutta Chromosome* (1995) include, for example, Samit Basu's science fictions as well as my attempt, in a recent first novel called *Mad Girl's Love Song* (2013), to describe a residual phenomenon I term "cultural schizophrenia," wherein we inhabit one place and time but tend to believe, especially if we are part of only partially decolonized English literature departments, that another temporal location – eighteenth- or nineteenth-century England, say – is where we "really" live. Such literary fiction still struggles with a sense of dislocation and is concerned with "other worlds" in a way that is orthogonal to the spirit of the post-millennial novels described earlier. In a significant way, the current new fictions seem to have divested themselves of these old hauntings that plague the small-audience literary novel. Instead, these are novels meant to be read *alongside* the daily news, and thus we find in them the subject matters of current nationwide daily concern: poverty, social and gender equity, educational aspiration, corporate employment, caste and regional politics, and corruption.

To end with a hopeful prediction, then: perhaps the most important, potentially major source of innovation and "thought experiments" in the Indian English novel is likely to be the rise of Dalit fiction in English, since many Dalit intellectuals feel that the best way to bypass oppression of many kinds, including the linguistic dominance of the classic literary languages of India (Hindi, Marathi, Tamil, and so on, which are often shot through with words expressing prejudice and bias) is to write in English. It is salutary to recall here E. M. Forster's long-ago preface to Mulk Raj Anand's pioneering *Untouchable*. Anand's book, Forster pronounced approvingly, "could only have been written by" an upper-caste Indian and not an untouchable because the former possessed an insider's understanding of "the pollution-complex" while the latter's "indignation and self-pity" would render him incapable (Forster vii). My contention in this chapter has been that these premises are now "re-cognized" quite differently because the conceptual relationships between what I have called "virtue," "virtuosity," and the "virtual" have undergone so many seachanges since that time. An extensive rerouting of the legendary "passage to India" has occurred. Yet these channels remain largely uncharted. In this sense, the possibilities are vast and exciting – even wicked – and challenges cannot but lie ahead for further experiments in the genre of Indian English fiction.[20]

Notes

1 The phrase "wicked freedom" has been coined here as a derivative of the concept of the "wicked problem" in the social sciences (see Rittel and Webber; and Churchman). A wicked problem is one that resists neat resolution as it is interlinked with numerous concepts and admits of multiple causes. The phenomenon of poverty is often cited as an example of such a problem in that it demands urgent redress and yet is intractable in its complexity. Analogously, "wicked freedoms" too are subject to multiple moral and cognitive constraints that ensure that they can never be fully exercised. Our example of wicked freedom in this chapter is the freedom to experiment with the narrative form and design of the postcolonial novel, which brings authors, readers,

and theorists up against all sorts of difficult moral questions and interpretive dilemmas, some of which we explore here.

2 One of the most important of these presuppositions, for example, is that there is a standard form of the English language that records the story of Englishmen and women brought by historical circumstance to the foreign environs of India. Both *Kanthapura* and *All About H. Hatterr* tamper with this stable picture of language and the cohesive role it plays in depicting and coping with adversity. These novels devise radically non-standard forms of English that "free" their characters to think differently, presenting "Indian" and Anglo-Indian perspectives that almost entirely reconfigure the key concepts of "adversity" and "foreignness"; as a consequence, the power relationships presupposed earlier are unexpectedly destabilized, often to comic or ironic effect.

3 See also Bhabha, "How Newness."

4 See http://jaipurliteraturefestival.org/the-global-novel/ for a video report of these remarks.

5 http://faculty.washington.edu/cbehler/glossary/alienationeffect.html.

6 http://www.authortrek.com/vikram-chandra.html, accessed September 4, 2014.

7 Television interview, http://www.ndtv.com/video/player/the-world-this-week/the-world-this-week-english-upamanyu-aired-june-1993/295166, accessed September 4, 2014.

8 A. Chaudhuri, "Modernity" xvii. See also the reviews of Chaudhuri's *The Picador Book of Modern Indian Literature* in *The Hindu* newspaper of August 19, 2001, by Girish Karnad and Leela Gandhi, in which Gandhi, in particular, highlights this quotation (http://www.thehindu.com/2001/08/19/stories/1319067g.htm, accessed October 13, 2014).

9 This is a composite paraphrase based on the extensive media and critical attention paid to Ghosh's refusal to let his publishers nominate his novel *The Glass Palace* for the Commonwealth Writers' Prize. Compare Maharaj: "Late in 2000 Amitav Ghosh withdrew *The Glass Palace* from being considered for the Commonwealth prize, as he regards the notion of the Commonwealth to be a misnomer and anachronistic."

10 Githa Hariharan talks to Rukmini Bhaya Nair, *The Times of India*, Delhi, 1999; see also www.githahariharan.com/downloads/selected_interviews.doc.

11 Kesavan, "To Be."

12 http://www.kyotojournal.org/the-journal/conversations/arundhati-roy-on-fame-writing-and-india/, accessed September 4, 2014.

13 Quoted in http://www.theguardian.com/uk/1989/feb/19/race.world, accessed October 17, 2014.

14 http://www.theatlantic.com/past/docs/unbound/interviews/ba990623.htm, accessed September 4, 2014.

15 http://globetrotter.berkeley.edu/people/Tharoor/tharoor-cono.html, accessed September 4, 2014.

16 Some of the characteristics of sensuous theory, elaborated in Nair, *Lying*, are: it must be recognized as an embedded critique, occurring *within*

literary texts; hence part of its mystique derives from the fact of textual "cross-dressing" or disguise; it might be called literature-infested theory or, conversely, theory-infested literature. It is, however, surprisingly easy to extricate from its literary context – that is, it comes with detachable-attachable hyphens or hooks that enable it to transfer with relative ease from one context to another. It can often figure very high, much higher than conventional forms of criticism, on a quotability index; consequently, the various *bon mots* of sensuous theory may be found circulating madly around the academic globe quite a short while after their publication. Its discourse is likely to be female-centered but not necessarily feminist; its language is almost always beautifully turned out, formally exquisite haute couture, never commonplace.

17 http://www.ndtv.com/video/player/agenda/watch-half-girl-friend-a -gimmick-by-chetan-bhagat-or-a-game-changer/332945.

18 http://www.ndtv.com/video/player/agenda/watch-half-girl-friend-a -gimmick-by-chetan-bhagat-or-a-game-changer/332945.

19 The romantic idée fixe in these works is clearly revealed in their titles. Some examples: *That Kiss in the Rain: Love is the Weather of Life* (by Novoneel Chakraborty, 2010); *Of Course I Love You..! Till I Find Someone Better* (by Durjoy Dutta and Maanvi Ahuja, 2008); *Now That You're Rich ... Let's Fall in Love!* (by Durjoy Dutta and Maanvi Ahuja, 2011).

20 For further reading on related issues of language and authorship in Indian English writing, see Nair, "Acts"; "Bringing"; "Gandhi's"; "Language"; "Life"; "Linguistic"; *Lying*; *Narrative*; "Nature"; "Pedigree"; "Philological"; *Poetry*; "Road"; "Sappho's"; "Singing"; "Text"; "Thinking"; "Twins"; "Voyeur's"; "Writing"; "Yudhishthira's"; *Translation* (ed.); and (with Bhattacharya) "Salman Rushdie."

CHAPTER 17

Of Dystopias and Deliriums: The Millennial Novel in India

Mrinalini Chakravorty

We live in difficult times, in times of monstrous chimeras and evil dreams and criminal follies.

— Joseph Conrad, *Under Western Eyes*[1]

This is no longer the fatal time of the planets, it is not yet the lyrical time of the seasons; it is the universal but absolutely divided time of brightness and darkness.

— Michel Foucault, *Madness and Civilization* (p. 109)

Ever since Saleem Sinai was obliterated — "sucked into the annihilating whirlpool of the multitudes" in *Midnight's Children* (533) — the emergence of a dystopian aesthetics for the Indian novel became virtually guaranteed. The contemporary Anglophone novel in India is decidedly dystopian. This is not to suggest that other genres of the novel — the satiric, comedic, romantic, and epic — have disappeared.[2] Nor is it to overlook the harrowingly pessimistic representations of modernity in the social realism of numerous anti-colonial novels of an earlier era, prior to Rushdie.[3] It is simply to mark a peculiar trend: dystopia is the prevalent mode through which present-day novels from India grapple with the symptoms and conditions of "millennial capitalism" (Comaroff and Comaroff, "Millennial" 291).

In millenarian modernity, capitalist culture is increasingly seen as "messianic, salvific, [and] magical[ly] manifest ..." (Comaroff and Comaroff, "Millennial" 293). Postcolonial dystopian novels contend with the chimeric, trance-like thrall of capital's latest allures by seizing on a surreal representational force, one we might characterize as "delirious." In other words, postcolonial dystopian fictions make delirium — radical ruptures of the real and the rational reflected by rendering form itself as delirious — the basis of their critique of the social damages of late capital.

These fictions align with the energetic play of magical realism inaugurated in India by Rushdie but refashion it in important ways. Just as "magical realism may transfigure a historical account via phantasmagorical narrative excess" (Mikics 382), so too do the new novels of dystopia from India assimilate the phantasms of life under globalization, but this time to narrate a circumstance of historical calamity without analogue. While Saleem's dissolution heralds the arrival of India's multitudes, a possibly utopian sublimation, the surreal fissures in postcolonial dystopian fictions fix the present in states of horror. Magical realist fiction, Wendy Faris argues, allows us to "imagine alternative visions of agency and history" that temper volatile and disjunctive histories (136). Postcolonial dystopias, however, relentlessly convey the hideous urgencies of the historical "now" without gesturing to more serene alternatives. Simply put, postcolonial dystopias turn on a negative dialectics alone that shuttles between thick scenes of grotesque-yet-mundane material damage and their more stylized or aestheticized translations into delirium.

This chapter draws from two recent novels, *Animal's People* (2007) by Indra Sinha and Jeet Thayil's *Narcopolis* (2012), to advance an argument about the prevalence and necessity of dystopian narratives about the global south in the new millennium. The hypotheses given here on dystopia's present formations are meant to: i) reframe the critical history of dystopian fiction in relation to postcolonial Anglophone literature; ii) provoke us to think about dystopia's aesthetic imprint in delirious forms; and iii) consider how literary texts allow us to contemplate the irrevocable destructions wrought by globalized modernity.

Postcolonial Dystopias and the Refusal of Future

Dystopia is usually understood to be "utopia's twentieth-century doppelgänger," one best exemplified by science and political fiction (Gordin, Tilley, and Prakash 1). Celebrated dystopian novels such as Aldous Huxley's *Brave New World*, George Orwell's *1984*, Yevgeny Zamyatin's *We*, and more recent ones by Ursula LeGuin, Margaret Atwood, Octavia Butler, Don DeLillo, and Kazuo Ishiguro among others, distill the terrors of modern life onto a terribly estranged future time. Contemporary in their concerns, the politics of dystopian narratives emerge as a particular aesthetic response to the vagaries of fairly recent capitalist culture. "Although its roots lie in Menippean satire, realism, and the anti-Utopian novels of the nineteenth century," Tom Moylan writes, "the dystopia emerged as a literary form in its own right in the early 1900s, as capital entered a new phase with the onset of monopolized production and as the modern imperialist state extended its internal and external reach" (xi).

Thus dystopia, as Moylan notes, is anti-utopian for it "expresses a simple refusal of modern life" (xii). The inaugural dystopian imaginary makes two bold assertions: that the future is bleak and that modernity is to blame. This stark refusal of modern life that characterizes first generation dystopias is resurgent in dystopian fictions from the postcolony. This is not because postcolonial dystopias arrive late on the scene and are historically lagging. Rather, postcolonial dystopias are invested in recalibrating the telos of capital as it is reflected in the conventional story told about the evolution of the dystopian imaginary.

The dominant strand of traditional or closed dystopias banks on the external, extra-textual effects that narratives of unmitigated disaster may have in realigning readers' ethical and political commitments but is contrasted with what are known as "critical dystopias." A term coined by Lyman Tower Sargent, critical dystopias share with their older predecessors a temporal impulse oriented to the future. Sargent writes that critical dystopias usually represent "a non-existent society ... normally located in time and space that the author intended a contemporaneous reader to view as ... worse than [contemporary] society" (9). Unlike earlier dystopias, critical or open dystopias are seen to emerge from the historical conjunctures of the late twentieth century that pointedly address the transnational restructuring of capitalist economies in the 1980s and '90s (Moylan xii). The critical dystopian imaginary is said to confront a uniquely millennial capitalist present that "critically voice[s] the fears and anxieties of a range of new and fragmented social and sexual constituencies and identities in post-industrial societies" (Wolmark 91)[4] while also preserving a "radical openness" that "maintain[s] [the] utopian impulse within the work" (Baccolini and Moylan 7–8).

The analytic map of dystopia is thus far as follows: while all dystopias tell teleological stories of degeneration – what we might think of as progressive tales of nonprogress – some foreshadow the world's end in apocalypse, while others encapsulate within their negative form what after Jameson we might call "the Utopian wish" (*Archaeologies* 1 and 72).[5] Postcolonial dystopias unsettle this developmental narrative of how dystopia is usually conceived in several ways. Most importantly, postcolonial dystopias do not render present fears onto a futuristic temporal horizon. Instead of being located in "a non-existent society [that is also] in [a] time or space ... worse than contemporary society," postcolonial dystopias are almost always presentist (Sargent quoted in Baccolini and Moylan 7). They cathect the "prophetic" energies of dystopia, as it is generically understood, onto a historically proximal, even concurrent present.

The temporal stretch of postcolonial dystopias is neither toward an immanent future to be feared or a "vanishing present," as Spivak would have it, but an elastic present that is already here and continues to persist.[6] In this sense, postcolonial dystopias rent the baldly Marxian discourse of a critical dystopian imaginary as originally static or alienating and then propelled by an emancipatory, and fundamentally positivist, impulse toward social change that nevertheless holds fast to humanist ideals of a future-yet-to-come.

Postcolonial dystopias reflect instead an irreducible social chasm wherein disaster or historical damage appear as the defining circumstance of the present. Gordin, Tilley, and Prakash note the immediacy of contemporary dystopias: "Crucially," they write, "dystopia – precisely because it is so much more common – bears the aspect of lived *experience*" (2). Unlike first order dystopias, postcolonial dystopias are not located in the future; instead, by "plac[ing] us directly in a dark and depressing reality," they serve as a warning, conjuring the present as continuous with the future "if we do not recognize and treat its symptoms in the here and now" (2). Here we might think of any number of works, such as Arundhati Roy's *The God of Small Things* (1997), Kamila Shamsie's *Burnt Shadows* (2009), Nadeem Aslam's *The Wasted Vigil* (2008), Michael Ondaatje's *Anil's Ghost* (2000), Amitav Ghosh's *The Calcutta Chromosome* (1995), Salman Rushdie's *The Satanic Verses* (1988), and many others that offer witness to the damages of a dystopian present.

To put it another way, postcolonial dystopias reflect the tremendous "simultaneous, synergistic spiraling of wealth and poverty" that is the very condition of the millennial present (Comaroff and Comaroff, "Millennial" 291). They continually draw attention to the fact that the present is a concert of contradictions, swaying strangely between the slippery enigma of liquid capital compelled by a spectral dialectics of desire and consumption and the violent recognition that indeed "there is no such thing as capitalism sans production" and hence, persistently arduous or torturous forms of work (298). The postcolonial dystopian imaginary is thus fully attuned to the "occult economies" (Comaroff and Comaroff, "Millennial" 310) that proliferate the aura of wealth globally while at the same time highlighting the damaging "*experiential* contradictions at the core of neoliberal capitalism" (298).[7] Unlike critical dystopias' preoccupation with the empty recursive fetishes of postmodern life, postcolonial dystopias reinvigorate the ethos of a more militant dystopia of an earlier era. The postcolonial dystopia is also not impelled from within by a utopian wish.

It remains instead fixated on the immiserated conditions of the present, repeatedly culling vertically imposed histories of inescapable grotesque damage. Ultimately then, postcolonial dystopias are Janus faced, stalling the design of progress within discourses about dystopia that view dystopia as impelled from within by its obverse, utopia.

Atrocities of the Now: Two Fictional Examples

The opening lines of *Animal's People* and *Narcopolis* illustrate these distinctive features of dystopias of the postcolony. *Animal's People* tells the story of the fiery gas explosion in Bhopal on the night of December 4, 1984, caused by a blast of toxic gas at the American-owned Union Carbide pesticide factory. The story is narrated from the perspective of Animal, a boy wounded terribly by that event. The novel opens as if in playback; each chapter is a "tape" that supposedly records Animal's story of mutilation. Bhopal, however, is renamed Khaufpur, or "city of terror," and Union Carbide is simply called Kampani, to emphasize the slide between the historical event and the novel's dystopian, universalizing present. The first words Animal speaks are: "I used to be human once. So I'm told. I don't remember it myself, but people who knew me when I was small say I walked on two feet just like a human being" (1). This declaration immediately invokes the ontological crisis at the heart of the novel. We're called to attend to the immense chasm between the Anglophone readers' presumed humanity aligned with various other characters in the novel and Animal's radical alterity. "My name is Animal," Animal repeatedly tells us. "I'm not a fucking human being, I've no wish to be one" (23).

The dystopian force of this novel derives from a repudiation of humanity itself, suggesting that being human is immaterial if it cannot address the problem of subaltern suffering. As Upamanyu Pablo Mukherjee observes, "Animal's proclamation of his nonhuman identity gives voice to a scandal that lurks behind the tragedy of Bhopal – if there are those who, by the dint of their underprivileged location in the hierarchy of the 'new world order,' cannot access the minimum of the rights and privileges that are said to define humanity, what can they be called?" ("Tomorrow" 221) Animal's repeated insistence that "I no longer want to be human" (1); "I'm not a *fucking* human" (24); and that because of his mutilated condition, his is "a story sung by an ulcer" (12), foregrounds the sentient violence of a world split economically between the consuming and the consumed.

The temporal break that is the novel's epicenter, the toxic historical event of Bhopal, becomes the constitutive condition of a continual dystopia without redress. This is how Animal's nightmare begins:

> My story has to start with that night. I don't remember anything about it, though I was there, nevertheless it's where my story has to start. When something big like that night happens, time divides into before and after, the before time breaks up into dreams, the dreams dissolve to darkness. (14)

Animal's amnesia of a "before time" situates the narrative in the present that follows from the break. Animal's forgetting of the past ensures that the focus of the story remains on the immediacy of "that night," when Bhopal became Khaufpur and uncounted thousands, 60,000 or more, were nominated Animal.[8]

If postcolonial dystopias are besieged by atrocities of the "now," they also underscore just how much the millennial moment is complicated by transnational forms of consumption that inscrutably collapse the cultural and economic. Animal's story is always already compromised by the form of its appearance in the novel. The framing device – Animal's tapes that need to be translated and organized – ascertains that readers are made aware of their complicity in the filters that enable and limit their access to Animal. Animal's tape-recording highlights the prurient fascination that Western readers have with disasters elsewhere, a fascination that is easily commodified. The stasis that postcolonial dystopias stage derives from a highly self-conscious rendering of the genre itself so that dystopia generically becomes a part of the problem it represents; dystopias are dystopian because they appear as a macabre and exoticizing cultural form that is voraciously consumed. This is how Chunaram, a go-between, "wheedl[es] [and] plead[s]" with Animal to share his memories with a reporter:

> "Think of the money. Jarnalis is writing a book about Khaufpur. Last night he had your tape translated.... Jarnalis says it's a big chance for you. He will write what you say in his book. Thousands will read it. Maybe you will become famous. Look at him, see his eyes. He says thousands of other people are looking through his eyes. Think of that." (7)

Animal's retort – "Their curiosity feels like acid on my skin" (7) – suggests an analogy between the historical atrocity and the way in which it enters into a consumptive global imaginary. Indeed, this – the symmetry between the moment of dystopic violence and the reinscription of the violence in its mode of narration or translation – reveals why dystopias of the postcolony cannot reimagine themselves as ultimately utopian.

Animal alludes time and again to what, after Spivak, we may call the "epistemic violence" between history and representation that postcolonial dystopias convey but refuse to reconcile (Spivak, "Subaltern" 283).[9] Here is Animal's address to the "eyes," or the gaze of the reader, who in consuming the text enters into its dystopic aporias:

> Do I speak that rough-tongue way? You don't answer. I keep forgetting you do not hear me. The things I say, by the time they reach you they'll have been changed out of Hindi, made into Inglis et français pourquoi pas pareille quelques autres langues? For you they're just words written on a page. Never can you hear my voice, nor can I ever know what pictures you see. (21)

The dystopic imaginary here is expanded through a double-negative dialectic. Dystopia sublimates into more dystopia because the circumstance of the disaster is shown to endlessly repeat in time. In other words, the moment of explosion stretches to include the past, present, and future. Its catastrophic dimensions remain, however, snarled in a thicket of representational interferences. The historical moment cannot, the novel implies, be unmoored from the conditions of its representation and circulation within an already dysfunctional world order. Animal's "rough tongue" is deliberately caustic, signaling its aversion to entering into circuits of how Bhopal is read in structural difference from locations of privilege in the English-speaking world. The opaqueness of translation includes skepticism about how this story written in "Inglis" for an Anglophone audience can be any kind of vehicle for subaltern expression (Spivak "Subaltern").

The untranslatability of Animal's experience suggests that the most unsettling and intrinsic quality of these new dystopias is that they communicate a violation or breach that cannot be compensated. Indeed, as *Animal's People* attests, any attempt to negotiate the violation reproduces the dystopic imaginary as a surface-reality that merely conjures routine horror without repairing it. Following this logic, metaphors in this novel can only lead to catachresis (dystopia), rather than transformations (utopia). For instance, we witness Animal's animality in very literal, albeit ironic, ways. In the post-apocalypse of the "now," Animal scavenges for food:

> In gone times I've felt such hunger, I'd break off lumps of the dry skin and chew it. Want to see? Okay watch, I am reaching down to my heel, feeling for horny edges, I'm sliding the thumbnail under. There, see this lump of skin, hard as a pebble, how easily it breaks off, mmm, chewy as a nut. Nowadays there's no shortage of food, I eat my feet for pleasure. (13)

The dialectic of dystopia in this scene is a stalled, inwardly spiraling one: mimesis itself is in crisis as the distance between ground and figure collapses. Animal signals the conditions of a dispossessed humanity, but his desires and pleasures are ultimately absurd. He is both the symbol and symptom of a coerced cannibalistic self-consumption; yet, because he speaks to a self-interested humanism that can neither see nor hear him, his pleasure is fathomed as abject. Animal's self-production by way of consuming his own body can never translate into utopian notions of fulfillment or transcendence. He animates, the novel implies, a condition of difference that cannot simply be read as human. Animal, in other words, represents the sign of the "colonial wound" that haunts postcolonial dystopias (Mignolo and Tlostanova).

Although distinct in tone, *Narcopolis* adopts a similar dystopian mode to *Animal's People*. Here too the landscape of Bombay is specifically denoted to depict a geography of devastation that is locatable, immediate, and temporally expansive. Modeled as junkie-writing in the style of Burroughs, Bukowski, Baudelaire, or De Quincey, the novel enacts waves of hallucination, each signaling the intoxication of various addicts.[10] However, Bombay remains the definitive lens through which the extravagance and restlessness of a world lived from fix to fix is known. "Bombay, which obliterated its own history by changing its name and surgically altering its face, is the hero or heroin of this story" is how the novel begins (1). Bombay, then, is narcocity: synonymous with heroin first, and then with all other drugs, opium, cocaine, methamphetamines, and Chemical.

The feverish rush of intoxication is displaced onto the city, as every time Dom, our narrator, leaves the drug den known as Rashid's Khana we are given a dizzying tour of Bombay. Hijde-Ki-Galli, Murugan Chawl, Hutatma Chowk, Pila House, Shuklaji Street, Hill Road, Grant Road, Colaba Causeway, the Victorian ruins, Kala Paani – the city's cartography is both named and given catastrophic shape by the ever bingeing addict. Here is how Dom sees Bombay, imploding and apocalyptic, on his "last" day there:

> On that last day – a day of deluge, water stacked in green and brown layers under a floating membrane of debris, the streets and houses flooded and the neighborhood returned to its original aspect of swamp fed by pestilential rain, a place for mangroves and undersea life, not human habitation; ... the city was revealed as the true image of my canceled self: an object of dereliction, deserving only of pity, closed, in all ways, to the world. (207)

In such portrayals scattered throughout the novel, Bombay epitomizes dystopia by which, after all, is meant "bad place." As one reviewer notes, "The sense of place [in *Narcopolis*] is intoxicatingly horrible, and the author's poetic style makes something indecently lush and nightmarish out of the squalor of recent Bombay" (Saunders). All of the novel's cast – Dom, Dimple, Mr. Lee, Xavier, Rashid – dream opium dreams that continuously render the city as an impenetrable, closed place. Bombay as the location of disaster is a place *in extremis*, "chaotic," "obsolete," and in "decay," to use Dom's words (208).[11] In the novel, specters of annihilation are incessantly conjured in the myriad images of the city in rubble, smoldering, and under the sway of a collective murderous rage. "The world is ending," Dimple says of the communal riots of 1993. "Anything can happen to anyone at anytime" (197).

The hazy filter of addiction that is pervasive in *Narcopolis* only intensifies its representation of singular calamities as the horizon of generalized disaster. Addiction here serves as the exemplary dystopic allegory for all circuits of millennial dependency ensnaring the postcolony. It is notable that Rashid's khana's notoriety comes from a cultivated myth about the origins of its opium pipes in ancient, royal China. This myth contrasts the fact conveyed by Dom that the pipes were incidentally brought to the den because of the intimacy between Mr. Lee, a Chinese exile and opium dealer, and Dimple, the hijra who makes pyalis or opium pipes for Rashid. In invoking this tie with Chinese opium, *Narcopolis* plays on an older imperial history that Hema Chari notes "successfully constructed the discourse of opiate dependency and, in turn, of India as the colonial toxin that the imperial self delineated, and disposed of, as the 'other'" (215). However, addiction also figuratively amplifies the novel's attention to a new entanglement of consumption and production that seemingly reaches into all depths of postcolonial life.

So while this novel is about drug dependency, the metaphor of dependency itself proves elastic. It raises important questions about the conditions of the present as yoked to frenzied forms of consumption. The perpetual dependence of addicts in the novel also fuels important questions about forms of labor that enable the continuous cycles of consumption on which addicts thrive. *Narcopolis* reproduces the deadening, routine effects of addiction-as-habit through endless scenes of drug preparation at the den. Readers are repeatedly thrust back into Rashid's khana to witness the slow, excruciatingly repetitious work of how each "hit" is prepared by Dimple and others who are most abjected by society. Here is a typical example, one of many such in the novel, told from the addict-narrator, Dom's, perspective:

> I watched the woman, watched Dimple, and something calmed me in the unhurried way she made the pipe, the way she dipped the cooking needle into a tiny brass pyali with a flat raised edge.... She was rolling the tip of needle in the opium, then lifting it to the lamp where it sputtered and hardened, repeating the procedure until she had a lump the size and color of a walnut, which she mixed against the bowl until it was done. (5)

The circumstance of consumption or intoxication is relentlessly conjoined to the exact and unyieldingly laborious work done to fulfill the addict's unrestrained, excessive desire to consume. The careful labor of making the drug is shown as endemic to the compulsive anticipation it produces in those who wait to consume it as a pleasurable commodity.

The ethical challenge that metaphors of addiction and dependency ultimately forward derives from the equivalence of freewill and choice with neoliberalism's habits of consumption. What is contested is the idea that expressions of freewill, a cornerstone of liberalism's utopian promise, are by themselves beneficial especially if propelled by unchecked desires. In *Narcopolis*, Soporo, a reformed addict turned enigmatic cure-guru with a cult-like status, poses the question crucially for his followers:

> Is it true that taking heroin is an example of free will at its most powerful? ... All users know how addictive the drug is, and dangerous. OD, infection, crime, we know we're risking our lives and yet we choose to do it.... The interesting thing is that ... we choose it and continue to choose it. Is this an example of free will in action? ... Are addicts free? Are they in fact the freest of men? (245–6)

In this moment, the novel casts liberalism's core values – free will and choice – as fatally dystopian. Soporo's meditation points us to the main problem that *Narcopolis* confronts: namely, that freedom experienced through consuming forms of desire is dangerous. The novel suggests that insofar as millennial liberalism extends itself through spectral forms of desire and dependency masquerading as freedom, it convenes dystopias of the present. Picking up on this aspect of the ethical quandary Thayil's dystopia poses for readers, Tom Alter enjoins us to "Read *Narcopolis*" even if, or even so that we are moved to "wish the world it lives in never existed."

Lest we counter that addiction to drugs is an exceptional social problem that Thayil represents and must not be taken as a synecdoche for generalized forms of consumption within economies of transnational capital, the novel deliberately scatters the metaphor. Addiction becomes a common symptom of an ailment, a dystopic condition felt by all in the postcolony: "Then there are the addicts, the hunger addicts and rage addicts and poverty addicts and power addicts, and the pure addicts who are addicted not to substances but to the oblivion and tenderness that substances engender.... An addict ... is like a saint. What is a saint but someone who has cut himself off, voluntarily, voluntarily, from the world's traffic and currency?" (39) The representational scope of addiction, it turns out, is vast and contradictory. It is a contaminating social condition that inflects all aspects of contemporary life – conjuring specters of want (poverty, hunger), accumulation (power), and disenchantment with the present state of things. Yet, the "oblivion" that true addicts feel in *Narcopolis* is an ethical refusal of "the world's traffic and currency" without salvific or utopian subsequence. *Narcopolis* represents the dystopia of the postcolonial present as one without future reprieve. In so doing, postcolonial dystopias resurrect a version of the negative imaginary of first-generation dystopic works by rejecting the forward-looking utopian impulses of critical dystopias that come in the interim in order to preserve the possibility that present cataclysms may be supplanted by an illuminating, progressive future. Postcolonial dystopias are most concerned with marking contemporary failures to imagine any future alternative that could sufficiently ameliorate the catastrophic present.

Delirious Forms

Dystopia's form is delirium. In this, dystopia shares the discursive topos of madness, which according to Foucault evinces a tendency toward reason while preserving a deep skepticism of rational truths. Dystopias of the present challenge the idea that modernity is reasonable and that its rational terms are beneficial. They insist instead on the necessity of thinking modernity as irrational and for sustaining counter-rational narrative forms as part of their perceptual and aesthetic critique of modern society.

Delirium, Foucault writes in his enormous study of madness in the age of reason, is "that essential and constitutive structure which had secretly sustained madness from the first" (114). Foucault's influential study shows that in the classical period when reason came to be valued and everywhere proclaimed, and madness hidden and confined because "irrational," discourses of the mad and about madness participated fully and in extreme fashion in the language of reason (95). In short, madness and sanity were discursive wars about *how* to reason and to what extent. Foucault identifies delirium as the crux of mad reasoning precisely because delirious form subverts the claims of reason from within; delirium is reason taken too far. "Why should it be," Foucault asks about delirium, "in this discourse, whose forms we have seen to be so faithful to the rules of reason, that we find all those signs which will most manifestly declare the very absence of reason?" (101).

Extending Foucault, Kristeva credits psychoanalysis with inventing a new interpretive method, one that accounts for enigmatic forms of subjective desire so crucial to delirious expressions. To her, delirium is important because it accounts for a truth that analytic rational thought misses. If delirium strays from reality, Kristeva writes, quoting Freud, it nevertheless "owes its convincing power to the element of historical truth which it inserts in the place of the rejected reality" (82). In other words, delirious discourse marks a cleavage in subjective relations to reality such that there can no longer be a simple knowing subject who represents the world as "objectively perceptible and objectively knowable" (81).

In masking or sparing itself from a certain reality, delirium insistently reveals alternate ones. This is why the delirious form is so well suited to the ends of dystopia. Symptoms of delirium include holding on obstinately to an alternate reasoning, no matter how disjointed this version may seem to others (Kristeva 82). Formal eruptions of delirium in dystopias confer narrative with the capacity for dazzlement, a quality Foucault imputes to madness. Madness, Foucault asserts, should not be understood "as reason diseased, or as reason lost or alienated, but quite simply as reason dazzled" (108). In dystopian narratives, the delirious form intervenes to dazzle the rational forms of modernity as it is made to objectively appear. Delirium invokes forms of reason and desire that are counterfactual to modernity's rational organization of life.

In postcolonial dystopias, delirious moments tear the fabric of the real. Delirium distorts a text's objective assumptions about reality through a cascade of other subjective realities that are discontinuous with and resistant to the story's normative form. Unlike magical realism, in which strangeness routinely deranges a story's reality anchors, delirious form in dystopias is never escapist. It consorts with other realities and yet remains pointedly a part of the desperate scene that produces it. Hence, unlike magical realism, which may veer toward the absurd, comedic, or romantic, the delirious realism of dystopias remains savagely, surreally tragic in its indictment of present conditions.

Animal's People and *Narcopolis* are replete with delirious moments. The delirious strands in both novels confirm the ethos of dystopia in particular ways: by arresting narrative temporality and by collapsing a humanist or anthropocentric instrumentality that parses life into animate and inanimate, human and brute forms. A survivor of that fiery night in Khaufpur, the elderly nun Ma Franci's delirious utterances remain fixated on the effects that the spread of poison creates, relentlessly rematerializing the bleakest hour of the blast. "'Listen,'" Ma Franci says, "'injustice will triumph, thousands will die in horrible ways. Well, what else happened on that night? Nous sommes le peuple de l'Apokalis.' We are the people of the Apokalis" (63). This refrain of the apocalyptic now is a delirious mantra Ma Franci utters in her post-poisoned pidgin language, and one that recurrently stalls the forward moving, reparative impulses of others in the book as they undertake hunger strikes, boycotts, and riots to force the Kampani to compensate for a damage that is beyond material reparation. Ma Franci's intermittent rants remind us that in the poison zone time and history alter shape. For Animal, his life originates in devastation: "My first memory," he confesses, "is that fire" (15).

Likewise, Animal's uncanny ability to "[talk] to people who aren't there," including mutilated fetuses preserved in jars, ensures that the savage perversity of the blast remains always in play (56). Animal describes Khâ-in-the-Jar, as he calls his formaldehyde-submerged fetal "mate," in terms both everyday and surreal: "Glaring at me from inside the jar is a small crooked man. An ugly little monster, his hands are stretched out, he has a wicked look on his face" (57). Khâ's presence in the novel is inconstant, he appears unpredictably from time to time, disrupting the other story the novel tells of Animal's romancing of Nisha and Ellie, and his hope for a cure. When present, Khâ speaks: "Your back is twisted" he tells Animal, "but at least you are alive. Me, I'm still fucking waiting to be born" (58). The delirious tie between Animal and Khâ reignites dystopia's ethical charge. If dystopia is concerned with forms of the real fully cognizant of social brutality, delirious scenes instantiate this alternate reality. "You must free me," Khâ implores to Animal (59), an ethopoetic moment that underscores the emphatic address that damaged life makes and that delirious narratives provoke.

Narcopolis too traffics in delirium where delirious stories spiral into each other to foment a view of the present as dystopian. Again, apocalypse is the motif through which the delirious form erupts. Apocalypse myths abound in this novel, especially in the form of novels within the novel. From the novels about the eccentric Ah Chu that Mr. Lee's father authors in China and is persecuted for, to the stories Dimple compulsively reads, to the poet Newton Xavier's postmodern "rhyming quatrains" set in a "wasteland of war or famine or disease, where some unnamed catastrophe had culled much of the world's population," *Narcopolis* dismantles any notion of an abundant present with delirious invocations of damage (31). We're given, for instance, exquisite portraits of "a ruined world" that Dimple encounters in her favorite book, a collection of prophesies in Konkani written by a nun, Sister Remedios (60). The nun's tale is so expansive in its delirium that it telescopes the future into the present and the past. What is presented in such moments are fully sketched elements of delirious form.

Of course, the main delirious ruse that *Narcopolis* advances is the idea that we are reading a story told by an opium pipe. The tale is framed as one that issues out of "I and I" – that is, a story told by "the two I machines, the man and the pipe" (4). In the throes of a high, the narrator too transubstantiates into a drug: "The powder hit the back of my nose with a hard chemical burn, and ... I thought ... I'm no longer human or animal or vegetal; I am unplugged from the tick of metabolism; I am mineral" (216). These moments ensure that delirious form remains the mainstay of dystopia in this work. The melding of animate and inanimate presences, as well as the deliberate confusion over what constitutes the fiber and corporeal reality of mortal life, forces us to attend to non-instrumental possibilities for how we rationalize our social world. Thayil's novel is so perforce dystopic because even its hallucinatory moments are devastating revelations that meditate on conditions of dehumanization.

Coda: Unreasoned Damage

What are the implications of conjoining dystopia with delirium in literature of the new millennium? Kristeva offers an opening: "I would suggest," she writes, "that the wise interpreter give way to delirium so that, out of his desire, the imaginary may join interpretive closure, thus producing a perpetual interpretive creative force" (81). Similarly, Aarthi Vadde argues that "delirious reading" constitutes the genre of world literature itself (24–5). For both, deliriousness is simultaneously form and habit, albeit a straying one. Delirium represents the form of a literary work and the method of its consumption; that is, a reader must be transported into a similar delirious reading of the novel as its form impels.

Such an approach compels us to confront the ripple effect, if any, of a world cast dismally adrift. We may then take seriously the despair with which Theodor Adorno asked after the war whether in our world "horror [was not] indeed perennial," as he condemned all that is commonplace about modernity's civilizing process as hideous (*Minima* 233). Our cultural texts, he argued, offer pointless digressions on a terribly deformed and wounded world. "For the world is deeply ailing" (200), Adorno admonished in that desolate tome of aphorisms *Minima Moralia*, and our artistic representations provide but shallow cosmetic salves. If nothing else, the negative horizon of some contemporary dystopic novels forces us to consider the salience of Adorno's gloomy outlook particularly for disfigured subaltern lives, and then perhaps to ask, how can we change things?

Notes

1 Quoted as preface to Comaroff and Comaroff, "Millennial" (291). I echo it here to mark the overlap between the Comaroffs' essay and my ideas on the dystopian genre of millennial Indian fiction.
2 The flourishing of these genres is attested to by well-known Anglophone South Asian novels: Aravind Adiga's *The White Tiger* (2008), Mohsin Hamid's *How to Get Filthy Rich in Rising Asia* (2013), Vikram Seth's *A Suitable Boy* (1993), Upamanyu Chatterjee's *Weight Loss* (2006), and Shashi Tharoor's *The Great Indian Novel* (1989).
3 Renowned for their social realism are Raja Rao's *Kanthapura* (1938), Mulk Raj Anand's *Untouchable* (1935) and *Coolie* (1936), R. K. Narayan's *Waiting for the Mahatma* (1955), Bhabani Bhattacharya's *So Many Hungers* (1947), and Kamala Markandaya's *Nectar in a Sieve* (1954).
4 Quoted in Baccolini and Moylan 4.
5 See Jameson, *Archaeologies*, chapters 6 and 13 for more on "the Utopian wish."
6 See Introduction and chapter 4 of Spivak, *Critique*.
7 See also Comaroff and Comaroff, "Alien-Nation," for a fuller discussion of occult economies and the uneven expansion of transnational capital.
8 As Upamanyu Pablo Mukherjee notes, the explosion at the American-owned pesticide factory in Bhopal released a fatal dose of toxic gases, mainly methyl isocyanite, that poisoned more than 200,000 people. An estimated 5–10,000 were killed immediately, with more than 60,000 others injured ("Tomorrow" 216). See also Everest.
9 Spivak's essay, "Can the Subaltern Speak?" clarifies the ties between violence as an actual practice and its discursive and structural forms.
10 Kevin Rushby's review in the *Guardian* discusses *Narcopolis* as part of the decadent genre of intoxication novels.
11 Many reviews of the novel note how Thayil makes Bombay ground zero of his descriptions of devolution: "This is Old Bombay as seen from the slums and the gutter, the city illuminated in all its sweat and temper, stories lifting from the streets like the smoke from an opium pipe" (Evers).

CHAPTER 18

"Which Colony? Which Block?": Violence, (Post-) Colonial Urban Planning, and the Indian Novel

Upamanyu Pablo Mukherjee

"Lashings of the Ultraviolent"

Consider two explosive moments in two Indian novels from opposite ends of the first decade of the twenty-first century. In the first, frenzied denizens of one of Delhi's gated communities – or "colonies" – surround a truck driver:

> The man with the rod is now poking the driver in the throat with it. The other man is speaking. "And who was going to drive the truck? Your daughter-fucking father? ... What will my children drink tomorrow, you fucking pimp? What do we pay your owner so much for?" He lands another slap. Flecks of blood from the driver's bleeding mouth fall on his overalls. A line of red trickles down, impossibly straight, through the middle of the 'M' of the *Mehrotras Water Supply* printed across his chest. (R. Joshi 278)

At this point, the novel's central character and narrator Paresh, accompanied by some of his friends, intervenes, and all are quickly embroiled in a fracas during which the tables are turned. Now, it is the Sikh driver who is standing with the two scions of Delhi's *nouveau riche* at his feet:

> The driver has the rod now and he is a strong man. He swings the rod into Green Jacket's neck, just once, but it is enough. Then he turns to Shibu and hisses, "Hat jaao!" Shibu tries to fling himself back but he is still close enough when the rod smashes into the back of the second man's skull and the man's forehead catches him on the nose. He reels back, holding his nose, blood pouring out from under his hand. (280)

The analogous moment from the second novel comes as the narrator, a chauffeur, asks his employer, another elite Delhi businessman, to step out of the car and help him with an imaginary problem with the wheels. As the unsuspecting man bends down to inspect them, Balram engages in what *A Clockwork Orange* calls "lashings of the old ultraviolent":

> I rammed the bottle down. The glass ate his bone. I rammed it three times into the crown of his skull, smashing through to his brains. It's a good,

strong bottle, Johnnie Walker Black – well worth its resale value. The stunned body fell into the mud. A hissing sound came out of its lips, like wind escaping from a tire. (Adiga, *White* 244–5)

We can immediately register certain similarities between the two passages – stranded automobiles in deserted corners of an otherwise crowded metropolis; the speed with which social norms and hierarchies are overturned; the sheer *excessiveness* of the violence with which the servants and workers attack the objects of their *ressentiment*; the specific kinds of labor that mark the assailants (they both drive cars that serve as conspicuous status symbols for their owners). Let us also note that in a contemporary India that is one of the most heavily militarized spaces in the world, and where the army, paramilitary, police, and private security forces are combating at least three major armed insurgencies, fables of class and caste violence carry more than the usual whiff of subversion. The first extract, from Ruchir Joshi's 2001 novel *The Last Jet-Engine Laugh*, for example, provocatively foregrounds the figure of the avenging Sikh truck driver in a city whose collective memory is forever scarred by the four-day pogrom against members of this community in 1984, which saw at least 2,733 people killed and around 50,000 "internally displaced."[1] The second extract, from Aravind Adiga's 2008 novel *The White Tiger*, recalls the various instances of media-orchestrated hysteria in Delhi and other Indian metropolises regarding murderous servants and workers – such as during the Noida serial killings of 2005 and 2006, when Surindar Koli, a domestic worker, was convicted and sentenced to death for molesting and murdering a number of children, while his employer, also one of the accused, was acquitted.

Clearly, urban violence is not a recent, or even a post-colonial, phenomenon. As Raymond Williams showed long ago, the city has been the site of certain kinds of violent energies right through the 500-odd years of modernity (R. Williams). What is recent, however, is the scale and velocity of what Stephen Graham has called the "new military urbanism":

> the paradigmatic shift that renders cities' communal and private spaces, as well as their infrastructure – along with their civilian populations – a source of targets and threats. This is manifest in the widespread use of war as the dominant metaphor in describing the perpetual and boundless condition of urban societies ... the stealthy militarization of a wide range of policy debates, urban landscapes, and circuits of urban infrastructure ... [and] the creeping and insidious diffusion of militarized debates about "security" in every walk of life. (xiii–xiv)

Graham's argument focuses on the synergies between the boom in the U.S. "homeland security" services and what are being called the "9/11" wars in Afghanistan, Iraq, Pakistan, and elsewhere. But a similar situation also obtains in the so-called BRIC countries – Brazil, Russia, India, and China – that are allegedly poised to gain political and economic parity with the United States, Western Europe, and Japan. Many of the features of Graham's "military urbanism" – retina-scanning, ID cards, e-borders, CCTVs, private security firms, heavy paramilitary and military presence, police holding and detaining powers – already saturate much of Delhi, Mumbai, São Paulo, Rio de Janeiro, Shanghai, Hong Kong, and Beijing. This militarization results in the embedding of what theorists call, in a lovely Orwellian doublespeak, permanent and "low-intensity violence" within the urban fabric.

In what follows, I want to consider the literary representation of, and productive relationship between, the human subjectivities, material histories and infrastructural dimensions of one Indian city's colonial and post-colonial lives. It can be argued that Indian English-language novelists, especially those who belong to the generation famously dubbed by Salman Rushdie "midnight's children" and their successors, have always been attentive to the specific kinds of violence that have marked the country since 1947. It is difficult to miss this in depictions of communal riots, state repression, and the various dimensions of gendered acts of violence in writers as different as Manohar Malgonkar, Khushwant Singh, Attia Hosain, Nayantara Sahgal, and the writers who came after them, such as Amitav Ghosh, Rohinton Mistry, Arundhati Roy, and, of course, Rushdie himself. But my contention here is that increasingly evident in recent Indian novels in English is the relationship between the less visible spatial and infrastructural logic of India's cities and the more obvious and spectacular outbursts of violence that have scarred their citizens.[2] I support this argument by reading the two aforementioned novels by Ruchir Joshi and Aravind Adiga in relation to the policies, planning, and development of one iconic Indian city, Delhi. The novels interweave colonial and post-colonial histories to suggest that although the militarization and consequent embedding of "low-intensity" violence that Graham talks about might be new in regards to the scale and dimension of its privatization, their genesis can be traced to the past and present manifestations of modern colonialism and imperialism. Moreover, in their own globalized outlook, these novels intimate that what I call Delhi's infrastructural violence is emblematic not only of the urban condition in India but also of the global post-colonial urban condition as such. In this way, the Indian English novel has been one of the most successful forms in representing and interrogating the crisis of post-colonial urban development.

Colonial Planning, Post-Colonial City

Scholars of urban planning and development have noted the continuities between colonial and post-colonial cities. As Brenda Yeoh suggests:

> Not only are the "colonial city" and the "imperial city" umbilically connected in terms of economic linkages as well as cultural hybridization, but their "post-equivalents" cannot be disentangled one from the other and need to be analysed within a single "postcolonial" framework of intertwining histories and relations. (457)

Anthony D. King further extends Yeoh's insights to suggest that the colonial ancestors of today's postcolonial cities were "sites" where the first significant "encounter[s] ... between representatives of capitalist and pre-capitalist social formations, between what today we term 'developed' and 'developing' societies and peoples" took place (7). One could argue that the violence of this clash between contrasting spatio-temporalities is embedded in the DNA of today's global cities. The massive process of continuous "creative destruction" and the classification and replacement of the old, the disorderly, and the outmoded by the gleaming forms of modernity are immediately seen, heard, and felt in (post-)colonial cities in India and around the world.

Indeed, from the moment the British government decided to move their Indian capital away from politically turbulent Bengal to the then more passive and pacified Delhi, the city's urban development plans carried within them the manifold contradictions of colonial modernity. As Stephen Legg has observed, while these plans declared their commitment to the material progress and well-being of all the inhabitants of the city, the imperatives of colonialism meant that in practice this meant radically uneven distribution and allocation of resources along the lines of race, class, and gender. Thus, a *rhetorical* commitment to modernist ideas of equality, liberty, and justice went hand in hand with a *practical* commitment to preserving the apartheid hierarchies of the colonial order. In Delhi, this could be most clearly seen in the systematic segregation between the "old" and "new" cities, where resources were drawn away from the former to the latter and old Delhi's inhabitants were visualized as problems to be governed, and as markers of the persistence of the obsolete and the primitive. Legg finds this same apartheid ethos maintained in postcolonial Delhi:

> Beneath the discontinuous criticism of the colonial *ethos* and the technology of practice lay a continuity of *vision* and calculation.... This mode of visualizing the problem cast slum dwellers as a national rather than a human problem.... The *ethos* of directing resources away from Old Delhi was retained.... The approach consistently gravitated towards the dehumanizing language of modern planning, such as the sinister statement that "residential densities in the heart of the city have to be rationalized by eliminating disparities." (197–8)

That colonial violence should have been embedded in the infrastructure of the city should come as no surprise, since this was one of the central aims of the Town Planning Commission headed by Edwin Lutyens and Herbert Baker, which was charged with designing British India's new capital. Baker, who had delighted Cecil Rhodes with his monumental designs of colonial power in South Africa, wanted to create an imperial acropolis on the Delhi Ridge (a site suffused with memories of the siege of the city conducted by the ultimately victorious British force in 1857) (Irving 65). Lutyens designed sketches of the viceroy's residency that bristled with British Palladian palaces, piazzas, and fore-courts and that was the terminal point of a grand processional axis (Irving 53–6). Both Baker and Lutyens were concerned more with the projection of imperial power than with the reformation or redistribution of civic values or resources.

This ideology was reflected in their architectural planning as well as practices. Neither the Indian workers who built the city nor the families whose lands were confiscated were resettled in New Delhi. They were forced to find whatever shelter they could in Old Delhi, increasing the congestion there (Batra 20). Although the colonial planning commission declared that its general guiding principles were beauty, comfort, and convenience, in practice it became clear that these were values that had been reserved only for the lucky few. The new city-space carefully reproduced the logic of colonialism itself:

> Fanning out from this core along radial avenues at an increasing distance were the residences of Deputy Secretaries, Under-Secretaries ... and then the higher ranks of European and Indian clerks ... Lutyens drew a diagram for the King's Private Secretary in which the pattern of seniority housing clearly reinforced racial distinctions, and segregation was made even more emphatic by placing bungalows of junior European officials on rising ground above junior Indians (labeled "thin white" and "thin black"), with the residences of senior officers ("rich white") still higher. (Irving 77–8)

Such segregationist planning of the capital, implemented more overtly along class and caste, rather than racial, lines, has remained a feature of Delhi's urban infrastructure since independence. The first "master plan" of the Delhi Development Agency, published in 1957, bore the marks of the uneasy amalgamation of colonial urban ideology and Nehruvian socialist vision. Like the 1913 plan, it cast the "old" city as a problem but conceded that "large clearance and reconstruction was not immediately practicable" (Delhi Development Authority, *Master* ii). The planners, unlike their colonial counterparts, did pay attention to the housing and settlement of disenfranchised Indian citizens. They pledged their commitment to building the city from "the bottom upwards," since "only in a healthy environment life for the common man can become varied, rich and satisfying" (Delhi Development Authority, *Master* 7). But the segregationist ethos also persisted, and the keystone of the plan was to push the "excess population" out of the central city to six, self-contained "ring towns" (1).

If the 1957 document displayed the contradictions between the Nehruvian concern for the "common man" and the planned violence of displacing, uprooting, relocating, and creating, at least the former was acknowledged to have some palpable existence in the independent country. In the most recent "Delhi Master Plan 2021," the "common man" seems to have disappeared from sight, only to be replaced by the breathless prose of "globalization," the "global city," "business plans," and the "optimal utilization of land" (Delhi Development Authority, "Delhi"). This document quite explicitly declares that it is no longer the state's responsibility to house its citizens or to plan and deliver infrastructures, and calls for a model of development founded in "public-private partnership." Less of a master plan, it is more of an advertisement for the fire sale of state-owned land and a promise to lift most restrictions on building heights and health and safety standards in favor of rampant "development" (or "optimal utilization of land," in the document's favored formula) ("Delhi"). Alongside this disappearance of the citizen and the triumphant enshrining of "private enterprise" and "business opportunities," the original colonial target of "improving" the old city of Shahjahanabad is retained. The proposal now is to ban all vehicles in the Chandni Chowk area and convert it into a "heritage" tourism site, with a theme-parked mélange of rides, "craft bazaars," and walking routes.

To be sure, the violence guaranteed by colonial urban development is not identical to, and cannot be subsumed entirely within, the "new militarist" paradigm but it does provide a fertile stratum on which privatized or corporatized militarism can flourish. When "informal" laborers have already been pooled in slums, *favelas*, derelict inner-city zones or "new housing initiatives," often without the guarantee of such basic amenities as water or health care, monitoring or pacifying them via a mixture of state and private-sector security providers becomes both feasible and "logical."[3]

This is only exacerbated by other forms of everyday infrastructural violence, including the price of water and electricity, death by exposure, and the habitat squeeze that affects large segments of the urban poor.[4] The Yamuna River, still a major source of water for Delhi's off-grid population, has 3.8 billion liters of Delhi's sewage and industrial effluents poured into it. In 2007, the stretch near Nizamuddin Bridge, a densely populated low-income area, contained 18,000 times more coliform bacteria than the permissible level for bathing (M. Mishra 74–5). Under such conditions, terms such as "homelessness" or "nomadism" in Delhi accrue very different meanings from their normative use in academic postcolonial theories. Around 1 million people have been displaced because of "slum-clearing" drives in the city between 1998 and 2010, most of them "resettled" on the peripheries of the city or next to toxic landfill sites, with sporadic electricity and water supplies (Batra 29–30). Lalit Batra does not hesitate to declare that "Nowhere is Delhi's descent towards becoming an apartheid city more visible than in the way it is being systematically emptied out of its poor citizens.... Exclusionary city-planning processes, though far more pervasive and powerful now, have long been a part of Delhi's development as a modern city" (18). For Amita Baviskar, this permanent "low-intensity" conflict is forever trembling at the edge of a general conflagration:

> What happens when they slowly discover that the empress-city, the capital of India, has no clothes? Will there be riots? ... Or will the city become more segregated, the poor confined to apartheid enclaves.... Will the rich flee the city or wrest an uneasy armistice? Will there be a truce more favourable to the poor than is the case now? (14)

It is in this state of "low-intensity" war that we can sense the continuities between the colonial and the postcolonial to an extent that requires us to rethink the often-debated prefix of the latter term.

Infrastructural Fiction

The psychological and behavioral effects of such an organization of Delhi's space are major concerns of writers such as Adiga and Joshi. In these effects they see a key component of India's postcolonial malaise. The excessive violence that erupts in the two passages with which we began our discussion – not unique to these two novels but apparent in the works of other contemporary writers as well[5] – is directly related to planned urban development. Joshi's novel, as I have written elsewhere, is in part built on the historical crisis of South Asia's current war for natural resources – in particular, for water (U. Mukherjee, *Postcolonial* 163–87). But Joshi also pays careful attention to urban spaces, both colonial and post-colonial, and the role they play in the flow, toxicity, choking up and parceling out of India's rivers. Together, these two basic elements of human lives – water and built space – are used as focal points for Joshi's state-of-the-nation novel.

Joshi tracks his major characters – the narrator Paresh Bhatt, his daughter Para, his parents Mahadev and Suman, his friends, his former wife Ana, and his lovers – over three major historical moments. First, there is the era of the struggle for Indian independence – the late-colonial 1930s and 1940s – where we are told how Mahadev and Suman met while engaged in "direct action" against the colonial regime and of their subsequent romance. The second period, more diffuse, ranges from the 1970s to 2010 and tells of Paresh's childhood and youth in Calcutta, his nascent and then successful career as a photographer of international reputation, his meeting with the German artist Ana, and the birth and childhood of their daughter Para. This personal story is always interwoven with the many historical scars borne by India throughout this period – wars with Pakistan, astonishing degrees of state repression, militant separatist movements, millions condemned to unending poverty, and the fight for collective survival. The final segment occupies the near future – 2010 to 2030. Para is now an ace fighter pilot and a veteran of preemptive air assaults on Pakistan. Her new mission is to command India's most important space station. Paresh is living out his last days in Calcutta with a young lover. The narrative dances in a non-linear fashion across these time-segments, but certain recurring sites and topographical features – the cities of Kolkata, Ahmedabad, Delhi, and to a certain extent Paris, and the various rivers that flow through them – provide clues to decode the novel's understanding of the global (post-)colonial condition.

Just before the killing of two members of the "colony gangs" in the dispute over the delivery of water that we witnessed earlier, Joshi's narrative speeds through the streets of Delhi along with Paresh and his friends as they drive through the night. Mathura Road, Nizamuddin, Jangpura, Bhogal Market – Delhi is crisscrossed by the huge trucks of private companies contracted to deliver water to the various wealthy colonies as the rest of the city goes thirsty. The city's plight is graphically realized in the

pariah dogs, caught in their car's headlights, that give chase to the tankers
and latch on to its taps in the hope of drinking a few streaks of leaking
water (R. Joshi 257). And what is desperation in the animals turns into a
murderous, raging battle among the humans, as vigilante "colony gangs"
patrol the streets in a turf-battle over access to water trucks. On Paresh's
radar display, we can see the "big oblong" of the trucks gathered around
road blocks or hemmed in by the "smaller oblongs" of cars. As they try
and edge their way to home and safety, Paresh, Shibu, and Talukdar are
trapped between a stalled truck and a "colony patrol":

> Which colony? The question comes across her from the driver's seat. A man
> turned towards them, wearing a shiny black ski jacket with the word
> *RUTGERS* in white on the front... New Friends, says Shibu, but we have
> nothing to do –
> New Friends which block? snarls the woman." (268)

After checking out their address, the vigilantes let them go:

> The woman switches off her torch and says, You can go. The man leans
> over her and says, You are damn lucky buddy. If you were from Maharani
> Bagh your ass would be grass by now. If you are New Friends you should be
> with us on patrol. Either you are with your Colony or you should get the
> fuck out. (269)

Joshi uses deliberately exaggerated markers – the U.S. college apparel,
slang, and echoes of George Bush's "war on terror" rhetoric – to signal the
co-option of the Indian ruling classes into a U.S.-centric world *political*
system for which the term "globalization" is often employed as a blunt
shorthand. But the dystopic vision of a city divided into privatized spaces,
where water and land are secured by informal, private armies, is the extension of the logic of a neoliberal world *economic* system into urban planning regimes such as the "Delhi Master Plan 2021" that we mentioned
earlier. Joshi's work is thus a part of a global *cultural* system that reflects
on and debates the historical substrate through a series of inventive
stylistic moves.

   This contemporary post-colonial urban segregation is for Joshi both an
extension of and a step change from colonial planning. In a typical passage, the narrative breaks away from 2030 to provide a commentary on the
planning and building of the sewage system of late nineteenth- and early
twentieth-century Calcutta. While the network of underground tunnels
and drains that was built between 1864 and 1874 was on an unparalleled
scale anywhere in the world, it reflected the apartheid logic of colonialism insofar as it was meant to service the white town (R. Joshi 121–2).

However, as elsewhere, this was defeated by the reality of everyday lives. It is in the sewers and their contents that Joshi celebrates the irrefutable, earthy evidence of the everyday breachings of racialized borders:

> What was designed to carry small amounts of transformed porridge, cabbage soup, beef stew, roast chicken ... ended up carrying a far more thickly cosmopolitan mixture than that.... The system received the waste of the great kitchens of Bengal, the remains of meals from the great babu-badis of north Calcutta, intestinal translations of the ordinary daal and rice and fish of the majority of Calcutta's citizens. (123)

In this commingled sludge is wasted the logic of colonial planning. But no such transcendence is evident in the postcolonial "present" and "future" sections set in Delhi. If the Sikh driver's vengeance is achieved by a momentary alliance with the "liberal" bourgeois (Paresh and his friends who emerge from their BMW to come to his assistance), their intervention remains a fleeting occasion of *ressentiment* rather than a decisive revolutionary gesture. In Paresh's India, war is the normal state of things – his daughter grows up on military strategic video games, goes on to lead a "preemptive" air strike on Pakistan, and finally survives a U.S. attack on an Indian space station that starts a new world war. The war for water and space in Delhi is merely the local manifestation of this all-pervasive militarism.

Aravind Adiga's novel pays less attention to India's "water wars" and more to the inequities coded into the land, especially the built fabric of Indian cities. The life of the narrator, Balram Halwai, unfolds chiefly around three kinds of spaces – his childhood in a village of north Bihar, his "legal" life as the chauffeur of Mr. Ashok, a wealthy Delhi businessman, and his "illegal" life as an "entrepreneur" in the south Indian city of Bangalore, to which he has escaped after killing his employer and stealing a large amount of money. From his hiding place in Bangalore, Balram writes a series of letters to the Chinese premier, not as a confession of his guilt, but as a declaration of his pride in having imbibed the murderous logic of "globalized" India in which the only thing that counts is making it to the top by climbing over the dead bodies of its expendable citizens. Balram's internalization of this logic is intimately tied to the spatial arrangement of his habitats.

Balram's childhood in the Gaya district of Bihar is that of a modern serf working for landlords who have diversified from agricultural to other commercial interests that bind them closer to cities at regional, national, and global scales. Mr. Ashok, for example, whom Balram eventually murders, is a son of the local landlord family who has been to management school in the United States and has returned to Delhi to start a business. Among Balram's earliest memories is the recognition of an elemental, physical difference between the powerful and the powerless in India:

> A rich man's body is like a premium cotton pillow, white and soft and blank. *Ours* are different. My father's spine was a knotted rope.... Cuts and nicks and scars, like little whip marks in his flesh, ran down his chest and waist, reaching down below his hip bones into his buttocks. (Adiga, *White* 22)

This difference is concretized in the layout of Balram's village. Most of the people live around the one main street with "a bright strip of sewage" down its middle and among "shops selling more or less identically adulterated and stale items" (15). The landlord's quarter is outside this main residential area: "All four of the Animals lived in high-walled mansions just outside Laxmangarh.... They had their own temples inside the mansions, and their own wells and ponds, and did not need to come out into the village except to feed" (21). When Balram manages to escape this tightly structured apartheid of semi-feudal rural India (what he calls "Darkness") to the lights of Delhi, the initial impression is that of a baffling chaos: "See, the rich people live in big housing colonies like Defence Colony or Greater Kailash or Vasant Kunj, and inside their colonies the houses have numbers and letters, but this numbering and lettering system follows no known system of logic.... One house is called A231, and then the next is F378" (98). But this chaos, apparently a benign index of the long history of globalization, is merely cosmetic and the same iron laws of apartheid that plagued Balram's village obtain in a modernized version in the metropolis. Outside the Delhi colonies, the displaced rural poor flock on the pavement and beneath the bridges, "making fires and washing and taking lice out of their hair while the cars roar past them" (99). Inside the colonies, the buildings of the rich are strictly segregated:

> I don't know how buildings are designed in your country, but in India every apartment block, every house, every hotel is built with a servants' quarters.... When our masters wanted us, an electric bell began to ring throughout the quarters – we would rush to a board and find a red light flashing next to the number of the apartment whose servant was needed upstairs. (108–9)

The shopping malls are guarded by private security personnel who only let respectable customers in. Balram witnesses a fellow chauffeur burst out in rage as he is turned away for wearing unsuitable footwear. Even the cars, such as the one driven by Balram, act as barriers between those who are forced to breathe in Delhi's toxic air and those who can afford to stay out of it (112).

Just as in the "darkness" of northern Bihar, this informal apartheid reflects unequal access to powers and privileges. Balram drives Mr. Ashok to the President's House, on the top of Lutyens' and Baker's Raisina Hill complex, in order to offer bribes to a minister. As Balram himself puts it, "The jails of Delhi are full of drivers who are there behind bars because they are taking the blame for their good, solid middle-class masters" (145). Chauffeurs gather outside the malls and colonies, flicking through the popular crime and murder weeklies and dreaming of committing lurid acts of violence.

What becomes quickly evident in Adiga's novel, as was the case with Joshi's, is that the violence of this informal apartheid is *planned*. Not only do residential building plans, traffic layout, commercial zonal regulations, and water provisions have a systematic segregationist ethos embedded in them, but the very way in which the growth and expansion of the city are managed reflects the continuity of colonial planning ideology in Delhi's post-colonial life. Gurgaon, Jangpura, and other "satellite townships" that were envisaged as absorption points for refugees in the 1950s are now the preferred habitats of Delhi suburbanites, and the play of their excess capital is in line with the neoliberal vision of the "Delhi Master Plan 2021":

> Ten years ago, they say, there was nothing in Gurgaon.... Today it's the *modernest* suburb of Delhi. American Express, Microsoft, all the big American companies have offices there. The main road is full of shopping malls – each mall has a cinema inside! So if Pinky Madam missed America, this was the best place to bring her. (Adiga, *White* 101)

In these corporatized spaces circulate formal and informal circuits of desire and consumption – Microsoft as well as a thriving sex industry – in which Eastern European "students" and aspiring Indian "actresses" are served up to the appetites of Delhi's politicians and businessmen. It is when Mr. Ashok accepts an offer made by a politician to be entertained by a Ukrainian hostess in a nameless hotel in Jangpura that Balram makes his decision to kill him (188).

It is no accident that Balram's simmering internal conflicts take shape in a murderous rage around the consumption of the exoticized figure of the blonde prostitute. Adiga's purpose in the novel is to show that Balram's violence, when it erupts, is neither a progressive revolutionary moment nor an expression of archaic feudal notions of "honor." Rather, it is the moment when his mimicry of his employers reaches perfection. In other words, it is the moment when he becomes a full (male) citizen of "world-class" India, exercising his right to consume exotic foreign products. He wants nothing more than to, as the expression has it, eat as his master does.

Balram has already tried to mimic Mr. Ashok once by hiring a less expensive European prostitute; he had flown into a violent rage on discovering that she was a fake blonde. His contempt for Mr. Ashok grows as the latter asks to share his food; after eating it, Mr. Ashok declares it to be far superior to his own rich diet: "I ordered okra, cauliflower, radish, spinach, and *daal*. Enough to feed a whole family, or one rich man.... 'This food is fantastic. And just twenty-five rupees! You people eat so well!' ... I smiled and thought, *I like eating your kind of food too*" (203). Appropriately, then, Balram's coronation as a modern Indian entrepreneur – the moment when he slays his employer – occurs in one of those interstitial urban spaces from where the state has withdrawn its governance but that is yet to be fully penetrated by private capital:

> Now the road emptied. The rain was coming down lightly. If we kept going this way, we would come to the hotel – the grandest of all in the capital of my country.... But Delhi is a city where civilization can appear and disappear within five minutes. On either side of us right now there was just wilderness and rubbish. (241)

Between the hotel and the urban wasteland, between light and darkness, Balram acts out the fantasy that drives postcolonial Delhi – and creates wealth out of human blood.

The attention paid to the relationship between violence and caste, class, or gender configurations in the contemporary Indian novel in English is usually taken as an acknowledged fact. But what I have tried to show here with the help of two recent novels is that Indian writers have become increasingly aware of the spatial and environmental dimensions of this entrenched violence. The maimed human beings who populate their fictions are shown as products of the segregationist ideology and practices of contemporary Indian urban development. At the same time, these infrastructural practices are shown to be part of the dead weight of the country's imperial past. And with this deliberate linking of imperialism, development, and urban infrastructure, these novels achieve a critical understanding of the lived world of globalized post-colonialism.

Notes

1 For an account of the state-orchestrated riots against the Sikh community in Delhi and other Indian cities, see "The Original Sin of November 1984," http://www.thehindu.com/opinion/editorial/the-original-sin-of-november-1984/article4051648.ece, accessed September 3, 2013 – along with Van Dyke; and G. Singh.

2 There is also a growing body of critical writing that has accompanied this trend in recent Indian novels in English. I am thinking here of essays by Nixon ("Neoliberalism"; as well as the relevant chapter on Indra Sinha in his book [Nixon, *Slow*], especially 45–68); Schotland; and B. Joseph.

3 For example, see the recent report on slum clearance and resistance in Rio de Janeiro: "Rio Slum Dwellers Resist Relocation: Started in 1962," http://select.nytimes.com/gst/abstract.html?res=F10911FD355F107A93CBAB1789D95F4087 85F9, accessed September 3, 2013.

4 Such instances of everyday infrastructural violence are discussed in *Finding Delhi*, a recent collection of essays and oral testimonies by scholars, activists, workers, and "informal" laborers (Chaturvedi [ed.]).

5 See, for example, depictions of Mumbai in Rohinton Mistry's *A Fine Balance* (1995), Vikram Chandra's *Sacred Games* (2006), and Aravind Adiga's *Last Man in Tower* (2011); as well as Aman Sethi's *A Free Man* (2012) and Hirsh Sawhney (ed.), *Delhi Noir* (2009) for further depictions of infrastructural violence in Delhi.

CHAPTER 19

Post-Humanitarianism and the Indian Novel in English

Shameem Black

In the late twentieth century, Indian novels in English exploded in the world market. With the critical success of Salman Rushdie's *Midnight's Children* (1981) and the "midnight's grandchildren" who followed, Indian writing in English began to glitter with glossy paperback covers in airport bookstores all over the world. While this explosion of Indian fiction was diverse in approach, the literature that gained the most international traction in this generational shift included works that sought to grapple with major crises of modern South Asian history, such as Partition, Emergency, and the spread of religious, gendered, caste, and state violence. As these works inaugurated a late-twentieth-century boom in South Asian Anglophone writing in a globalized marketplace, they resonated internationally in part because they tapped into a powerful discourse of human rights.[1]

Novels have long shaped, and been shaped by, the emergent discourse of human rights. When the General Assembly of the United Nations adopted its Universal Declaration of Human Rights in 1948, it promulgated a language that has served as a foundation for activism and debate around the globe. As Joseph Slaughter has shown, the definition of human rights in the Universal Declaration drew heavily on visions of personhood first articulated in the novel (Slaughter 45–55). If novels gave a conceptual vocabulary to the drafters of the Declaration, suggesting what a free, rights-bearing human being could look like, the Declaration in turn generated a powerful discourse of human rights that has shaped the cultural work of twentieth-century fiction. In their ability to dramatize legacies excluded from history books, novels have often been seen to shatter official silences on histories of atrocity. In the comforting linearity of their narrative form, they have been thought to restore the moral and psychological order that trauma destroys. And in the dialogic intimacy between writer and reader, they have been seen to perform the public act of testimony and witness that underpins such human rights mechanisms

as the truth commission. Many Indian novels in English have, to varying degrees, participated in such projects. Novelists such as Shauna Singh
Baldwin and Amitav Ghosh, for instance, conducted groundbreaking oral
histories and archival research to write about histories of Partition and
the expulsion of Indians from Burma, respectively, while writers such as
Rohinton Mistry turned to the form of the realist novel to make sense of
the grotesque abuses of India's Emergency.

But even as novels share a commitment to speak out against violence,
Indian novels in English have also sought to raise crucial questions about
the exclusions and assumptions behind human rights' modern configuration. In this chapter, I will explore the ambivalences that mark Indian
novels' engagement with human rights discourse at the turn of the millennium. While these novels draw on this discourse, they also chart changing
roles for fiction in the twenty-first century.

I would like to suggest that these questions signal the rise of new modes
of humanitarian affect that circulate in the Anglophone world of these
novels' international reception. Even while deeply concerned with injustice and injury, these novels register skepticism about grand narratives
of human rights, humanitarian action, and rights-dispensing that in the
twenty-first century has become a self-critical part of the human rights
tradition. Once given to a discourse of heroism, human rights advocates
have now become more suspicious of elevated claims to right wrongs, or
to do so without in turn committing new acts of violence. Narratives of
individuals who aim to alleviate suffering reveal that a growing number of
people present their participation in the classical humanitarian project in
ironic, parodic, and even perverse terms (Black). In this post-millennial
era, groups such as Amnesty International have turned to playful and
deceptive visual traditions, such as those of optical illusions and video
games, to conscript individuals into supporting human rights. These technologies, which foreground their affinities with the consumer pleasures
of advertising and social media, stand in stark contrast to the heartrend-
ing images of ostensibly innocent victims that tended to proliferate in
the 1980s (Chouliaraki). While Indian novels in one sense offer shocking
exposés of atrocities in India for elite Indian and Western readers, they
also conform to an emergent logic in which human rights activism is
acutely aware of its own complicities with hidden forms of violence.

In this chapter, I will focus on three increasingly radical lines of questioning that reveal the Indian novel's often fractious relationship with the
discourse of human rights. I look first at the work of Arundhati Roy, whose
internationally successful novel *The God of Small Things* (1997) provided

a powerful platform for impassioned political polemics on national and international human rights abuses. In her nonfiction writing, Roy appears committed to a traditional human rights framework, where she is particularly critical of how colonialism, and its successor globalization, have served as sources of oppression in India's modern history. Yet in her fiction, even as she shows how "big" ideals of colonialism and globalization lead to staggering abuses against the "small" scale of the human individual, Roy charts deep anxieties about how colonialism and globalization might themselves become "small things" in need of protection, rather than forces always easily confined to the "big" and oppressive side of the ethical register. Her fiction thus inquires how human rights discourses, in their desire to eradicate oppression, can themselves become master narratives that confuse oppressive structures with the frail individuals who inhabit and embody those structures.

A second line of questioning in this literature interrogates the category of the human, a concern that has grown increasingly prominent in modern discourses of human rights. Drawing our attention to traditional debates between environmental and human rights perspectives, such fiction invites us to envision a way forward in which these two modes of advocacy need not always compete with one another. Wrestling with this problem lies at the core of Amitav Ghosh's *The Hungry Tide* (2004), which juxtaposes concerns for endangered animals with competing concerns for displaced humans. Indeed, novels such as Ghosh's suggest that it is only by recognizing that humans are indeed animals, part of an environment and an ecosystem, that their human rights can most fully be realized.

Finally, the third and most radical line of questioning in the Indian novel in English asks us to think about human rights through postmodern discourses of perversity. This mode of the novel takes some distance from the classical narrative contours of human rights stories, which have tended to identify clear perpetrators, victims, and channels of sympathy. As exemplified by Aravind Adiga's *The White Tiger* (2008), this newer mode reflects deep suspicions about the possibility of telling a triumphant narrative about India's progress as a national democracy. Its interest in antiheroic approaches to human rights intervention bespeaks a need to trouble the discourse of India as a land in need of saving, either by itself or by the international community.

Taken together, these three novels suggest the uneven emergence of what might be called, paradoxically, a post-humanitarian approach to human rights in the Indian novel in English. While these novels remain committed to confronting legacies of violence and atrocity, they register increasing skepticism about the progressive optimism that characterizes the mid-century codification of human rights discourse. These novels instead draw on, and help to create, new modes of humanitarian affect that serve as symptoms of India's changing status in a new globalizing century.

Small Global Things

Arundhati Roy is the Indian novelist working in English perhaps most associated with human rights discourse at home and abroad. Roy's *The God of Small Things* tells the agonizing story of Rahel and Estha, a pair of twins whose childhoods are marked by trauma. In a lyrical prose that serves to heighten the horror of its tale, the novel forces its readers to confront violence against women, deaths in police custody, caste prejudice and oppression, and child abuse. As authorities at all levels of power, large and small, take advantage of those more vulnerable than they are, the novel articulates the possibility of ethics only through "faith in fragility" (A. Roy, *God* 321). "Stick to Smallness" (321), think two of the novel's characters on the last page of the novel, as they consummate their forbidden cross-caste love in the period before one of them will be killed by the police and the other will lose her children.

While the novel charts many large ideals and institutions that oppress individuals, from religion to caste to patriarchy, among the most debilitating discourses is India's colonial legacy, perpetuated by Indians themselves long after independence. Roy's work links this colonial legacy with the forces of globalization that have worked to alter India's modern landscape. While she excoriates the national abuses in India that make a mockery of its status as a democracy, she reserves a special contempt for the international forces that perpetuate colonial structures through globalization. In her essay "The Greater Common Good," published shortly after *The God of Small Things*, Roy envisions the conflict of interest that characterizes international consultants called to evaluate big projects such as dams:

> In 1994, British consultants earned $2.5 billion on overseas contracts.... In the development racket, the rules are pretty simple. If you get invited by a government to write an [Environmental Impact Assessment] for a big dam project and you point out a problem (say, you quibble about the amount of water available in a river, or, God forbid, you suggest that the human costs are perhaps too high) then you're history. You're an OOWC. An Out-of-Work Consultant. And oops! There goes your Range Rover. There

goes your holiday in Tuscany. There goes your children's private boarding
school. There's good money in poverty. Plus perks. (A. Roy, *Cost* 31)

Pointing out the continuities between missionary colonialism and modern development work, Roy has been keen to emphasize how these forces
have enabled human rights abuses in India.

In *The God of Small Things*, this legacy of colonialism appears as one
of the many forces that marginalize the most vulnerable of India's population. Baby Kochamma, the twins' tyrannical grandaunt, forbids them
from speaking in Malayalam and "made them write lines – 'impositions'
she called them – *I will always speak in English, I will always speak in
English*" (36). Chacko, the twins' uncle, is an acknowledged Anglophile,
a casualty in, as he puts it, "'a war that has made us adore our conquerors
and despise ourselves'" (52). Such adoration takes concrete form in his
preoccupation with his British ex-wife and daughter. Chacko's daughter,
Sophie Mol, is consistently held up to the twins as the kind of idealized
and elevated subject that they can never be: she is seen as the beautiful,
light-skinned, beloved true heir of the estate who can only displace Rahel
and Estha in their already tenuous home. Yet seven-year old Sophie Mol
herself meets with tragedy. During her stay, she follows Rahel and Estha
to the powerful river that runs through the novel and drowns in its waters.
Is Sophie Mol, then, best understood as the confident and brash afterlife
of colonial superiority, or as a small thing, a victim of the metaphorical
forces that swallow her life?

The novel is divided on this question. It creates structural parallels
between Sophie and Rahel and Estha, all of whom have lost their fathers
and all of whom share a vulnerable child's perspective on their world. Yet
the novel also takes pains to distance Sophie from the twins, not dwelling
on how Sophie, as a multiracial subject in 1960s Britain, may have less of
a confident claim on the "*clean white*" (101) status of Britishness that is
often projected upon her. The novel plays with extending and withholding
compassion; unlike Rahel and Estha, who are consistently aligned with
the reader's sympathy,[2] Sophie Mol is not figured as a focalizing narrator
and is often mystified by the colonialist Anglophilia that the novel invites
us to critique. Yet, unlike the British environmental consultant imagined
in Roy's political writing, whom readers are expected to disdain without
sympathy, Sophie Mol's status as a child instantly commands shock and
horror at the idea of her death. This formal difficulty bespeaks the larger
question of how Sophie Mol's subject position confuses the clarity of the
human rights narrative to be found in so many other strands of the novel.

In her nonfiction work, Roy seems comfortable placing globalization on the "oppressive" side of moral accounting; in her novel, she allows herself the freedom to challenge the limits of this way of thinking.

Indeed, in a different novel, Sophie Mol's death – a natural accident – would not be legible as a human rights abuse. Through this river drowning, the novel takes her death out of the social discourses of religion, caste, and patriarchy that account for so many of the other abuses in its pages: "Just a quiet handing-over ceremony. A boat spilling its cargo. A river accepting the offering. One small life. A brief sunbeam. With a silver thimble clenched for luck in its little fist" (277). In this description of Sophie Mol's death, the short sentences that mirror the smallness of the child's body refuse to identify clear responsibility even as, in the language of "one small life," they link her death to the many other "small things" that are crushed and ruined in the novel. The colonial and global small is threatened by something that cannot be held accountable – the river, and the mythic powers that course through it.

What can the Indian novel do with the colonial small, when fragility and vulnerability are not simply the status of the politically marginalized but are also to be found in the history of structural oppression? Through the liminal body of Sophie Mol, *The God of Small Things* tests its commitment to the ethical value of little things. It asks if its political views – egalitarian, secular, feminist, and anti-colonial – can be reconciled with its strongest human rights imperative to have faith in fragility and to stick to smallness. The novel thus wrestles with the way in which human rights discourses deal with the politicization of bodies. As it shows us how Sophie Mol's body is produced and interpreted through oppressive discourses of colonial superiority, it then exposes how the human rights imperative to eradicate colonial traces can attack bodies that, viewed from another angle, are just as vulnerable as those they ostensibly oppress. In giving Sophie, in death, the "smallness" that it does not always allow her in life, the novel asks if human rights discourses may in some ways only recognize value when it is already too late.

Humans as Animals

Human rights discourse, by definition, privileges the human. Such has been its power to create social and political connections between diverse forms of violence and to generate ties between survivors and advocates who may have no language, history, or other social links to bind them. Yet this discourse has also sparked a counter-rhetoric that questions the privileging of "human" above other modes of life. Environmental, ecological, and animal rights perspectives have all put pressure on the ways in which human rights have claimed a self-evident status for transnational ethical concern. In response, human rights discourse – particularly in postcolonial contexts – has sometimes responded with the charge that environmentalist concerns enact problematic racial and class privileges, often placing the needs of environment and animals above those of people who are poor, displaced, and of color (Huggan). This tension has emerged in Indian novels in English, many of which both participate in and urge skepticism toward transnational discourses of human rights and environmentalism.

One key space in which we witness singularly productive modes of this struggle is Amitav Ghosh's novel *The Hungry Tide*, which interweaves narratives about animal conservation with ghostly histories of displaced human migrants. The struggle chronicled in *The Hungry Tide* is at one level a political struggle. The novel uncovers a past in which refugees compete for legitimacy on tideland islands with endangered tigers, and where the enforcement of animal conservation laws harms humans who seek respite from the political violence of other parts of the region. At the end of the novel, an Indian American marine scientist who wishes to protect Gangetic dolphins decides, in light of this history, to place her conservation efforts under the auspices of a distinctly human-centered trust. But if the novel in this sense seems to encourage readers to privilege human rights first, animals and ecology second, it does so through an insistent questioning of the divide between the two. By asking humans to think of themselves as animals, with needs for habitat and sustenance, the novel seeks to change what we mean when we say "human rights" and "environmentalism."

In doing so, the novel invites us to think about the forms of knowing that are invested in discourses of human rights and environmental advocacy. Human rights discourse has relied on translation to circulate stories of suffering in a globalized marketplace, while environmentalism has pointed to the important forms of communication (for example, within an ecosystem) that lie beyond human speech. This tension plays out in *The Hungry Tide* through its interrogation of the kinds of language through which the characters struggle to make sense of their world. The novel attempts to critique both these modes of knowing and to forge a synthesis between human-oriented translation and environment-oriented nonhuman communion.

Through the focalizing perspective of a marine scientist who distrusts human language for its capacity to mislead and betray, the novel offers a powerful critique of human speech and translatability. After meeting the Sundarban fisherman Fokir, with whom she shares no language, the Indian American scientist Piya muses, "there was the immeasurable distance that separated her from Fokir. What was he thinking about as he stared at the moonlit river? ... Speech was only a bag of tricks that fooled you into believing that you could see through the eyes of another being" (132). Speech and translatability, the cornerstones of human rights narratives, seem elusive and even illusory; even the very traditional work of the novel is called into question as "a bag of tricks." Instead, Piya favors a natural language, figured through the dolphins, that seems much more utopian:

> She imagined the animals circling drowsily, listening to echoes pinging through the water, painting pictures in three dimensions – images that only they could decode. The thought of experiencing your surroundings in that way never failed to fascinate her: the idea that to "see" was also to "speak" to others of your kind, where simply to exist was to communicate. (132)

When Piya and Fokir travel together through the tidal rivers, they develop a way of communicating that seems to replicate that form of dolphin speech. When Fokir tries to help Piya find dolphin pods, he calls out when he sees them. Since she cannot understand his words, they become a form of sonic "pinging" for her: what he sees becomes what she sees, so the divide between sight and sound, as with the dolphins, seems to melt away. This dolphin-language allows the two individuals to connect outside of their minds as their views converge on a shared object.

But the novel also critiques this vision of a perfect natural language, since its pages are also filled with tigers, which offer a much more frightening emblem of this seamless merger between seeing and communicating. The tiger appears as the devastating specter of uncontrollable violence that attacks human settlements without provocation. For many of the locals, the very word "tiger" cannot be spoken aloud, because to say its name is to summon its presence, and to see a tiger is surely to die.

The climax of the novel, when Piya and Fokir endure a lethal typhoon, suggests that this nonverbal communication reaches its fullest extent in the moment when it ends. Lashed together to a tree, Piya and Fokir are battered by the storm:

> Their bodies were so close, so finely merged, that she could feel the impact of everything hitting him, she could sense the blows raining down on his back. She could feel the bones of his cheeks as if they had been superimposed on her own; it was as if the storm had given them what life could not; it had fused them together and made them one. (321)

This perfect union is made possible only by Fokir's imminent death. While the novel begins with an idealization of communication beyond words, it leaves us with grave doubts about where such language points. When the novel reports that "he had seemed to understand her, even without words" (324), that "seemed" suggests the precariousness of this nonverbal form.

If the novel admires but critiques a nonhuman form of physical knowing, it critiques, only to rehabilitate, the hyperverbal world of translation required by human rights discourse. Through the figure of Kanai, a professional translator, the novel marks the hubristic tendencies of the hyperverbal in a scene in which Kanai faces a challenge to his authority from Fokir's wife:

> She smiled, as if to herself. "You wouldn't understand," she said.
>
> He was nettled by the certainty in her voice. "*I* wouldn't understand?" he said sharply. "I know five languages. I've traveled all over the world. Why wouldn't I understand?" (130)

Kanai's arrogance invites skepticism toward translation and its claims to mastery. But the novel also appreciates how translation is potentially capable of affording real intimacy with another point of view. Kanai realizes this through a fall into the mud – one of the novel's key images for the in-between world that is neither earth nor water. Suspended in the mud, Kanai is forced to see himself through new eyes, an experience that reminds him of the transfigurations he has experienced as a translator:

> It was as if the instrument of language had metamorphosed – instead of being a barrier, a curtain that divided, it had become a transparent film, a prism that allowed him to look through another set of eyes, to filter the world through a mind other than his own. (270)

The passage goes on to record Kanai's "vision of human beings in which a man such as Fokir counted for nothing, a man whose value was less than that of an animal" (270). As the content of Kanai's thought approaches a new awareness of the exclusions that can potentially constitute environmental advocacy, the form of this revelation signals a language that is both linked to human speech *and* anchored in the mud of the natural world.

The novel thus forwards a vision of a robust human rights that is integrated with environmental concerns: a vision that acknowledges different modes of knowing.[3] Its governing metaphor for this synthesis, a religious narrative called "The Glory of Bon Bibi," provides a vision of how this integration might take place. First introduced as a form of unintelligible chanting, the narrative weaves its way through much of the novel in different guises. It offers a syncretic melding of different faiths, languages, literary forms, and performance styles. It passes through oral lineage, but it also exists in written form. Though written in Bangla, it reads from the right as in Arabic; it strings its words out in sentences but uses the meter of Bangla prosody. The novel links it to its anchoring image of the mohona, or estuary: "*the tide country's faith is something like one of its great mohonas, a meeting not just of many rivers, but a roundabout people can use to pass in many directions*" (205–6). The novel's syncretism is performative as well as metaphorical, since readers experience the story of Bon Bibi first as a nonverbal sensation (as chanting) and then in English translation only much later in the novel. In bringing together a human-oriented world of language with an ecological appeal to alternate forms of knowing, the novel suggests that it is through the cosmopolitan form of Indian English that such philosophical reconciliation might take real shape.

Perverse Human Rights

In Salman Rushdie's *The Moor's Last Sigh* (1995), a novel deeply concerned with the rise of Hindu fundamentalism, the hero, Moor, abandons his place as the heir to Nehruvian secular pluralism and takes up a new life as the hit man of a Hindu fundamentalist gang. But while Rushdie eventually pulls his perverse antihero back into a narrative that tends to restore faith in the secular pluralism of Indian modernist art as the best guarantor of human rights, other writers have been more bracing in their attraction to postmodern perversity. This approach is emblematized in Aravind Adiga's wildly successful novel *The White Tiger*, a fictional account based on the writer's journalistic investigations that challenges neoliberal descriptions of India as a reinvigorated modern nation with a globalizing economy. Against these "rise of India" political narratives, Adiga's protagonist Balram Halwai offers a distinctly disturbing counter-rise. Adiga tells the story of a man who emerges from servitude to kill his wealthy master and take on a new life as the exceptional "White Tiger," the social entrepreneur of his day. Echoing earlier modernist antiheroes, such as Richard Wright's Bigger Thomas, Adiga's anti-Gandhian novel suggests the way in which those deprived of human rights may only come to feel like fully realized subjects through the exercise of terror. As Lena Khor argues, *The White Tiger* refuses a narrative in which some dispense rights and others receive them; instead, it foregrounds how individuals might dispense rights to themselves in a context of neoliberal globalization. Discomfiting social realist traditions through postmodern literary gestures, the novel raises crucial challenges to liberal strands of international human rights discourse.

One powerful and controversial response to the predicament of structural injustice is to embrace violence as a path to human rights. As a chauffeur, Balram exists in a liminal state of visibility and invisibility, power and dependence. Associated with mobility, masculinity, and modernity, the place of the chauffeur is a transitional place between the world of the servant and the world of the master. The nexus for this transition, in Adiga's novel, is violence. When Balram is forced to take the blame for his employer's wife Pinky Madam, who hits a child while driving the household car, he experiences a kind of secondary violence that magnifies the original violence against the child. The injury is not only to the child's body but also to the child's very status as human and as the bearer of human rights. When the child is hit, the first impulse of both servant and master is to pretend the body is inhuman:

> "A dog?" Mr. Ashok asked me. "It was a dog, wasn't it?"
>
> . . .
>
> "It wasn't a dog! It wasn't a – "
>
> Without a word between us, Mr. Ashok and I acted as a team. He grabbed her, put a hand on her mouth, and pulled her out of the driver's seat; I rushed out of the back.
>
> . . .
>
> "We hit something, Ashoky." She spoke in the softest of voices. "We have to take that thing to the hospital." (Adiga, *White* 138–9)

Whether or not the child has died, its humanity is snuffed out by Balram and Ashok; and even Pinky, who knows that she has hit a child, can only gesture at this realization through a language that scrupulously avoids any mention of human identity: "it wasn't a dog," "something," and "that thing." Moreover, the novel emphasizes the point of connection between the child and Balram through the repeated mention of dogs more generally. In the next scene, we see the Mongoose tell Balram:

> "Sit, sit, make yourself comfortable, Balram. You're part of the family."
>
> My heart filled up with pride. I crouched on the floor, happy as a dog, and waited for him to say it again. (141)

As an allegory for a middle-class gesture of recognizing the humanity of the servant classes, this offer constitutes a paradigm of human rights as something to be dispensed by the well-off to the rest of human society. But beneath that seeming generosity lurks the specter of Balram's willingness to

be "happy as a dog." Since the whole point of Balram's inclusion in the family in this scene is to persuade him to take the blame for hitting the child
with the car, Balram comes to realize that he too is considered disposable
and inhuman: "Even to think about this again makes me so angry I might
just go out and cut the throat of some rich man right now" (145). The novel
foregrounds the logical end of servitude, in which the individual serves as
the abject exclusion that renders the category of the human possible.

Balram thus takes up the provocative task of embracing this role as an
inhuman perpetrator of violence. If the masters want to script Balram for
their convenience as the perpetrator of violence against the child, they
find that this script is all too amenable to a different kind of violence –
a violence against the class of the master. Only in inhabiting this space
of violence does Balram come to feel any sense of adult freedom. When
Balram kills Ashok, even though he knows that this act will lead to the
torture and murder of his family back in his village, the violence against
his family only intensifies the sense of personhood that Balram comes to
claim in his escape. He comes to embody a logic in which all the subject of human rights can own is violence, whether against oppressors,
against family, or against the self. This terrifying mode of being, one that
cannot be easily accommodated in liberal traditions, conjures the alternative Dostoyevskian tradition of the perverse subject, in which individuals experience their humanness by choosing against their happiness, by
choosing negativity, violence, and suffering.

While this purposeful negativity of human identity would seem to
be the antithesis of the narratives of upward mobility that mark entre-
preneurship in an age of global capital, the novel suggests that entre-
preneurship – Balram's final role – is in fact the logical endpoint of this
foundational violence. Against human rights and developmentalist narratives that emphasize a right to capital, in ways that make humanity visible only through capitalist pursuits, Adiga invites a much darker reading
of entrepreneurial activity. Behind the successful entrepreneur, a symbolic sacrifice haunts the pursuit of riches. In her reading of the novel
as an allegory for neoliberalism, Betty Joseph describes its critique in
these terms: "when the White Tiger is the mouth-piece, we hear neoliberal entrepreneurial shibboleths *as* criminality" (72). Figuring global capitalism at large, Balram's predicament suggests that freedom, happiness,
wealth, and even human rights are all the creations of foundational and
ongoing trauma.

The question that has haunted readers is whether this neoliberal violence
improves upon the traditional feudal violence of patriarchy, corruption,

and caste it strives to escape. When Balram finds himself in a position where he has structurally injured another (a driver in his employ kills a young man), he visits the bereaved family, apologizes, and offers money as a material sign of his responsibility for the young man's death. In this sense, Balram sees himself as quite different from the feudal patrons of his youth, yet he also embraces his own continuity with that old order. He ends his story by saying:

> I think I am ready to have children, Mr. Premier.
> Ha!
>
> Yours forever,
> Ashok Sharma. (276)

Even as his rhetoric moves from his violent past of killing a man to a creative future in which children are possible, it undercuts and questions this narrative of progress. Is the "Ha!" triumphant, or is it ironic? And, if Balram sees himself as different from the old order he displaces, he simultaneously accepts, "forever," the name of his former employer. If violence seems to be the only way Balram can claim his own human rights, that same violence binds him ever more closely to the forces of oppression. The novel's unsettling vision of perversity thus both triumphs and despairs of the possibilities that such revolutionary human rights can yield.

Why might the novel work this way? I'd like to suggest that this turn to perversity signals the rise of new modes of humanitarian affect in mainstream human rights discourses. Whereas earlier Indian novels in English emerged in eras when the project of human rights activism seemed like an optimistic and ennobled undertaking, Adiga's novel reveals distinct suspicions about the work of human rights. But such suspicions, far from being the antithesis of human rights discourse, are now part and parcel of this discourse in its post-humanitarian phase. Even as his novel raises distinct challenges to optimistic tales of human freedom, Adiga still manages to talk about his desire to be part of a social realist tradition in which novels, by exposing social crimes, push their societies toward reform. An interview recorded in Rediff India Abroad, for instance, reports:

> "At a time when India is going through great changes and, with China, is likely to inherit the world from the West, it is important that writers like me try to highlight the brutal injustices of society," [Adiga] said, adding that the criticism by writers like Flaubert, Balzac and Dickens of [sic] in the 19th century helped England and France become better societies" ("I Highlighted").

Perverse post-humanitarianism is thus not the antagonist of human rights but instead its latest incarnation.

In their distinct engagements with human rights discourse, Indian novels in English have gestured toward both the possibilities and the problematics of human rights in a globalizing world. Rather than passively accepting an international discourse, which might replicate traditional and confining representations of India as a land in need of intervention from abroad, these novels wrestle with the foundational assumptions of human rights discourse even as they critique practices of atrocity in modern India. They actively participate in the self-critical, self-seeking turn of modern humanitarian discourse as it tries to reinvent itself in a disillusioned world that no longer accepts the idea of human rights as a bright and shining promise for the future. Inviting us to consider how such understandings of human rights can respond to the very phenomena that often trouble them – such as the legacy of colonialism, the claims of environmentalism, or the disruptive forces of antiheroic perversity – these novels work to envision post-humanitarian modes of representation in India and beyond.

Notes

1 In a recent account of human rights literature, for instance, two of the four novelists considered are Indians writing in English (Anker).
2 The novel, as Joanne Lipson Freed argues, often encourages readers to think critically about sympathy. However, as Freed also points out, this kind of critical accounting is perhaps impossible for the reader, who sees the world through the twins' eyes (233).
3 On the novel's challenge to "the dead-end logic of human struggles verses [sic] ecological struggles," see Marzec (435).

CHAPTER 20

Chetan Bhagat: Remaking the Novel in India

Priya Joshi

A curious thing happened to the Indian novel in English on the way to the twenty-first century. It stopped being a child of midnight. It even stopped being a child. Its "midnight" is now spent at the call center, and its "children" are twenty- and thirty-something readers in small towns with weak English and few literary demands, who nevertheless appear to have transformed the publishing landscape in India. In contrast to prize-winning literary novelists such as Aravind Adiga, Amitav Ghosh, and Kiran Desai, whose status is underwritten by recognition overseas rather than in India, writers of the twenty-first century Indian novel in English thrive because of a loyal base in India that keeps them on domestic bestseller lists with print runs of over a million that easily outpace the polite printings of 300 that internationally renowned literary novelists enjoy. India's robust market for English books has led some observers to predict that it will become "the biggest English language book-buying market in the world" by 2020 (Burke). The claim is hardly hyperbolic: in a dense entertainment ecosystem that includes television, print, the internet, radio, cricket, social media, and gaming, all nimbly delivering content skillfully niched to consumers, annual revenues from print in India are double the revenues from film and just behind television. A 2013 report on the Indian media and entertainment industry by the global consulting firm KPMG remarks that "India is an outlier country where print is still a growth market."[1]

For helpful comments on earlier drafts, grateful thanks to: Ulka Anjaria, Nancy Armstrong, Ian Duncan, Eric Hayot, and Peter Logan; audiences at a 2013 talk at George Washington University, especially Kavita Daiya, Nathan Hensley, and Cóilín Parsons; the Center for the Humanities at Temple University; a 2014 MLA roundtable on "New Theories of the Novel"; and the participants in a workshop on "Asia's Anglophone Novel" at the University of Pittsburgh organized by Susan Andrade. Special thanks to Amal Nanavati for insisting so long ago that I read Chetan Bhagat's novels. I'm glad I did. Research for this chapter was generously supported by a Summer Research Award from Temple University.

The novel comprises a slice of India's total print revenues, and the English[2] novel until recently an even smaller crumb. But then the twenty-first century arrived, and the publishing landscape was turned on its head by writers unheard of outside India who nevertheless seem to have reconceived the economic and social horizons of the novel, of reading, and even possibly of India. No writer better illuminates the transformations in Indian print and readership than Chetan Bhagat (b. 1974), whose novels since 2004 and their adaptation into blockbuster films since 2009 have inaugurated the phenomenon that this chapter describes. All of Bhagat's novels to date have sold over a million copies each, some reaching that milestone in three months – as *Revolution 2020* did in 2011. His latest novel, *Half Girlfriend*, published in October 2014, reportedly had an initial print run of 2 million.[3] Bhagat has been hailed as "the biggest-selling English-language novelist in India's history" (Greenlees), with some such as Gautam Padmanabhan, CEO of the publishing firm Westland, noting that Indian publishing today falls into two periods: "BC" (before Chetan) and after (as quoted in Kapoor). Author of five novels and a collection of essays, commentator in a national Hindi newspaper (*Dainik Bhaskar*), motivational speaker, and pundit on "national development" matters (the phrase is his own), Bhagat targets his writing to India's twenty- and thirty-something readers who, he argues, prefer a "Bollywood comedy sort of format" (as quoted in Greenlees). His essay collection, *What Young India Wants* (2012), communicates a canny gift for interpellating readers through catchy titles. Bhagat's novels are published at extremely low prices that appeal to his youth readership (Rs. 95, rather than Rs. 500 for literary fiction by novelists such as Ghosh and Desai) and are distributed outside the metropolitan bookstore circuit, in gas stations and traffic stops, convenience stores and footpaths. As he explains: "My readers do not go to bookstores. They don't even live in metropoles."[4] Long ignored by literary writers and respectable publishers, these readers flock to Bhagat and others like him, whose writing captures their pressure-cooker world with its consuming exam culture, family expectations, professional anxieties, and often stifling horizons.

Bhagat's pricing and outreach model have been rapidly copied and modified by others hoping to reach readers whom they insist are keen for new writing that addresses their lives in a post-liberalization India:

> I think India is changing, and people frankly don't care for the kind of books big publishers were coming out with – stories of the British Raj or the struggles of NRIs. After a century, India is rich again, and people want

to hear stories about themselves – about our call centre generation. (quoted in Reddy)

insists the novelist Amish Tripathi, who used his business school marketing skills and professionally produced YouTube videos to launch his bestseller *The Immortals of Meluha* (2010). Other novelists, such as Ravinder Singh, worked with the matrimonial website shaadi.com to help sell *I Too Had a Love Story* (2013) (Reddy).

The forms in which the English novel flourishes in India today are decidedly lowbrow and, in some cases, downright antiliterary, less because of their themes (whose key preoccupations include intimacy, community, and personal fulfillment) than because of the *treatment* of these themes in forms that closely resemble what is frequently dismissed as pulp fiction. Thus, romances, college novels, and the very Indian form of crick(et) lit have dominated purchases – with some breaking the million plus mark – while more literary writers such as Kiran Desai and Vikram Seth languish at sales of fewer than 300 copies per year. The language in Bhagat's novels is colloquial; plot and dialogue dominate over character; and SMS and chats replace narrative alongside a backdrop of combustible social and economic matters such as land grabs and religious tension. The format, combining the casual with the consequential, works. As the scholar Rashmi Sadana observes in her ethnography of Indian publishing, "There are few if any novelistic passages [in Chetan Bhagat's novels], where people, ideas, or places are described in any kind of depth. And yet whatever is described, even if brief and mostly in the form of dialogue, is compelling enough and moves the story along" (Sadana, *English* 176).

The worlds captured by new writers such as Bhagat and his readers index a phenomenon that is paradoxically old and even familiar in publishing history if one looks back far enough. Uncovering it alongside Bhagat's contemporary writings provides an opportunity to rethink the Indian novel and to place it in broader contexts than the national or the linguistic, even when both nation and language are intrinsic to the phenomenon that Bhagat's work illuminates.

This chapter proceeds in three parts. The first outlines the culture of books and reading in which the English novel circulates in India today; the second describes what might be identified as India's "writing" culture; and the conclusion offers remarks on the social purpose of the novel in the twenty-first century.

The Culture of Books

India is a literary destination, a place replete with books, and a culture that supports books in many languages, of which English is just one. When books are published, their circulation is enabled by a culture that acknowledges them (e.g., reviews) and enables their consumption. The country boasts major literary festivals (such as in Jaipur, for example), supportive publishers, multiple review outlets, book societies, prizes, and serials that together form a node that publishing historians call a *book culture*. A thriving book culture acknowledges production and inspires it as well. India is no different. The prestige of the English novel has penetrated its book culture so deeply that by some half-exasperated accounts, every student in Delhi University has a novel in his back pocket, and every other graduate of the elite Indian Institutes of Technology (IIT) uses his job bonus to publish one.[5]

This narrative of unalloyed bookishness urges nuance. India, indeed, has a sophisticated book culture – as the festivals, reviews, prizes, and sellers indicate – yet its book culture is concentrated in a few major cities (notably Delhi, which headquarters a third of India's 225 publishers) and is focused on a few forms, such as fiction, self-help, and business.[6] This concentration obscures a matter of greater interest to scholars – namely, India's widespread *reading culture*, a term that designates the many locations where readers and reading flourish (P. Joshi, "Futures" 89–90). A decade ago, it was possible to show a congruence between the country's prominent book culture (centered on production and circulation) and its thriving reading culture (centered on consumption by readers and their reading practices). Both matched, supported, and paralleled the other.

The congruence between a book culture and a reading culture is not inevitable (see P. Joshi, "Futures"). In countries such as Nigeria and Colombia that also claim prominent symbolic capital on the world literary landscape, with Nobel and Booker prizes to their credit, a noticeable gap between a book culture and a reading culture remains evident. Thus, while Gabriel García Márquez lamented the paucity of books as a youth in Bogotá, he recalled the vivid culture of reading that made much of the few books around (García Márquez 100). In other words, while Bogotá had a limited book culture, it had a thriving reading culture, and readers met regularly to discuss books and ideas in cafes and bars, even when the actual books were far beyond their means.

The sociologist Wendy Griswold observes a similar trend in contemporary Nigeria: despite a total output of approximately 500 novels published between independence in 1960 and 2000, despite few libraries and even fewer institutions to publish and circulate books, Nigeria reveals a thriving and visible reading culture (Griswold 107ff). The two examples divulge a paradox: the cultures of books and reading do not necessarily require each other to prosper, nor do they necessarily always parallel each other. That India's cultures of books and reading so closely parallel each other is an anomaly that merits closer attention, especially since the situation appears to be changing dramatically, and a cleavage between book culture and reading culture appears on the horizon.

"New" Fictions: Chetan Bhagat

Over the past decade, a vibrant, daring, and different publishing industry for the English novel has emerged in India. Forms such as crick lit, workplace novels, and the regionally specific IIT novels have taken off to hitherto unimagined heights. The previous "Hindu" print run of 500 copies has now been replaced by 30,000 to 1 million-plus first printings for writers such as Chetan Bhagat and Anuja Chauhan (author of the cricket novel *The Zoya Factor* [2008]).

The Indian Novel celebrated at the landmark Jaipur Literature Festival is quite evidently *many* Indian novels, most of them not even especially literary – as a glance at Bhagat, Chauhan, or Vikas Swarup amply documents. More to the point, these novels indicate authorial ambitions quite different from those of novelists typically featured in Jaipur, such as Salman Rushdie, Arundhati Roy, Amitav Ghosh, Vikram Chandra, and so on. Bhagat and Swarup outspokenly claim "blockbuster" status for their works, a term more typically associated with popular cinema, in which their titles have enjoyed successful adaptation. Bhagat's 2004 debut, *Five Point Someone: What NOT to do at IIT!* was adapted into *3 Idiots* (dir. Rajkumar Hirani, 2009), which became the second highest grossing Bollywood film of the new millennium at the box office.[7] Vikas Swarup's *Q&A* (2005) was adapted as the Oscar-winning *Slumdog Millionaire* in 2008 (dir. Danny Boyle). In contrast, the 2012 screen adaptation of the iconic *Midnight's Children* (dir. Deepa Mehta) had a sluggish thirteen-week run and is widely considered a flop with worldwide grosses barely crossing $1 million.[8] When Bhagat and Swarup eventually made it to Jaipur, it was as much for their novels' adaptations into successful films as for their literary ambitions. Thus, while these are novels, to be sure, they are quite clearly not literary, *nor do they intend to be.*

The journalist Sheela Reddy names new Indian writers such as Bhagat "lo-cal literati," a moniker that perceptively identifies the very local nature of their immense popularity alongside their evidently lowbrow status. Bhagat, Swarup, Chauhan, and their cohort write to and for India's youth market, which loyally keeps their titles on the bestseller lists *in India only* in marked contrast with writers such as Adiga, Ghosh, Desai, and so on, whose overseas prestige underwrites the respect they enjoy in India. When mainstream Indian publishers rejected these popular writers in the early 2000s, new houses rapidly emerged to capture them and their readers. As Jayant Bose of Srishti Publishers (one of the speediest of the publishing firms to capitalize on the "new" writers) explains, these new pulp novels "have stories set in India and about Indians, preferably from small towns," where the newest and hungriest generation of Indian readers proliferate (as quoted in Reddy). In contrast to the highbrow literary novels of Ghosh and others, those by Bhagat and Durjoy Datta easily incorporate Hindi and Gujarati into their English and adopt a laddish style that addresses the reader with endearing intimacy.

Following the success of his debut, *Five Point Someone*, Bhagat developed a device that he repeats in most of his novels: a direct address to the reader and the conceit that the narrative that follows is a story told to the real Chetan Bhagat by a living reader who engages Bhagat's previous novels, revises them, and then provides him the narrative that forms the current work. The "living reader's stories" include IIT's cut-throat culture, the humiliation of call-center work, the Godhra riots of 2002, and the unregulated coaching centers in India that try to capture lower-middle-class students desperate to enter a competitive university program in high-value fields such as business, engineering, and technology. Bhagat's intimate voice and colloquial English pervade throughout, as does his evident respect for his readers. In *One Night @ the Call Center*, Bhagat asks his readers to "Write down something that ... you fear ... [something that] makes you angry and ... [something that] you don't like about yourself." A page later, he queries, "Have you done it? If not, please do ... If yes, thanks. Sorry for doubting you.... Enjoy the story" (ix, x). The novel proceeds with a prologue: "The night train ride from Kanpur to Delhi was the most memorable journey of my life. For one, it gave me my second book" (1).

The 3 Mistakes of My Life is even more direct. Its acknowledgments border on an *ars poetica*:

> My readers, you that is, to whom I owe all my success and motivation.
> My life belongs to you now, and serving you is the most meaningful thing
> I can do with my life. I want to share something with you. I am very ambi-
> tious in my writing goals. However, I don't want to be India's most admired
> writer. I just want to be India's most loved writer. *Admiration passes, love
> endures.* (*3 Mistakes* ix; emphasis added)[9]

Bhagat's claim that "admiration passes, love endures" conveys a daring calculus for a novelist. The language of admiration and love parses placement: one sentiment is reserved for those up above (admiration), the
other for those at the same level as the subject. Dismissing the esteem
("admiration") commanded by those held on high, Bhagat instead pursues
adulation ("love") claimed from equals ("admiration comes with expectations. Love accepts some flaws," he explains in *Half Girlfriend* [vii]). The
metaphor of high and low placement further parses the *kinds of* esteem
certain literary forms command: "admiration" for the highbrow, love for
the popular. Bhagat's writing goals insist on the lowbrow, invoking the
passion that popular forms command (they are "most loved") rather than
the more sedate regard enjoyed by the highbrow. And his reasons are simple: admiration passes, love endures. In the world that Bhagat invokes,
the claim is likely accurate. However, in arbitrating prestige, book culture
tends to have its way and insist otherwise: admiration endures, love passes,
or, put another way, the literary highbrow prevails over the popular lowbrow. Eager to contest such an economy of prestige, Bhagat cannily coun-
ters with an alternative in his most recent novel: "People sometimes ask
me how I would like to be remembered.... All I tell them is this: I don't
want to be remembered, I just want to be missed" (*Half Girlfriend* vii-viii).
For Bhagat and the world that his writing indexes, the lowbrow prevails
by claiming a trifecta: it is loved; it endures in popular affection; and it is
missed when absent. In short, Bhagat's writing inhabits a zone hitherto
reserved in book culture exclusively for the highbrow.

   The ongoing contest between high and low is played out in the cultures of books and reading and is especially evident in Indian publishing today. Research on India's recent fiction helps elaborate the cleavage
between the presence of a book culture in India and the readerly culture
noted earlier. As India's book culture reaches new heights in global visibility (creating many internationally admired writers), and as new forms
of the English novel thrive in the domestic context, a new landscape is
becoming visible for the novel in India, which Bhagat helps bring to
focus. In addition to a book culture and a reading culture, a third "culture" is also becoming evident, which I name a writing culture. Again,

Bhagat illuminates this transformation especially effectively in a number of salient registers.

First, India's "new" English fiction, in contrast to its literary predecessors (by Rushdie, Seth, Ghosh, Roy, etc.) circulates widely across languages and media. Bhagat's *Five Point Someone* is perhaps better known as the film *3 Idiots* rather than as a novel (other film adaptations include Bhagat's *One Night @ the Call Center* [2005] as *Hello* [2008]; *The 3 Mistakes of My Life* [2008] as *Kai Po Che!* [2013] to rave reviews; and *2 States: The Story of My Marriage* [2009] as *2 States* [2014]). *Slumdog Millionaire* also enjoyed wider circulation in film than it did as the novel *Q&A*. Moreover, Bhagat, in marked contrast to India's monolingual literary novelists – feted in Jaipur and named earlier – writes in both the English and Hindi presses with biweekly columns in both the staid *Times of India* and the Hindi national *Dainik Bhaskar*. "*Dainik Bhaskar* has a readership in crores [tens of millions].... The Hindi audience gave me a chance to reach the majority, the real India," Bhagat explains (*What Young India* xix). In his newspaper columns, he has gone from fictionalizing India to excoriating it in writing, which gets him and his causes attention among those otherwise likely to dismiss him as a pulp novelist who writes only "stories about young people making out in confined spaces, or drinking vodka on the terrace, or falling in love" (*What Young India* vii–viii).

Bhagat targets his writing to lower-middle-class youth from the long-ignored Tier 2 and 3 cities, who reward his attention with a zeal that no "famous" literary writer can quite summon. His portrayal of their cities is affectionate if unvarnished: "[Kota] looked like any other small town in India, with too much traffic and pollution and too many telecom, underwear and coaching-class hoardings. I wondered what was so special about this place" (*Revolution* 49). Bhagat's ethnography has a light touch: "I figured out what made Kota different. Every one was clued into the entrance exams.... This complex vortex of tests, classes, selections and preparations is something every insignificant Indian student like me has to go through to have a shot at a decent life" (*Revolution* 49, 55). And the grind of competition and corruption (Bhagat's self-described "big muse" [*What Young India* xxi]) that the "billion sparks of India" undergo daily for a shot at a decent life is what Bhagat captures in his novels.[10] They are about insignificant students whose interiority and even subjectivity he inspires and conveys. By the end of each of his novels, their pallid outer life is given a Technicolor inner one by a series of events that seem farfetched (a cellphone call from God in *Call Center*) and utterly quotidian (a pogrom in *3 Mistakes*). "The obvious dilemma," writes the journalist Mini Kapoor, "is that [Bhagat's] writing does not have the complexity to be diced by the established instruments of literary analysis" (Kapoor). Bhagat's readers do not demur at all: "He's talking to my generation; we connect to him," insists an eighteen-year old (quoted in MacRae). Even Bhagat's detractors have had to admit that he captures audiences unreached by India's literary fiction in *any* language.

Bhagat's novels describe a social world in which corruption rules and meritocracy proves elusive. From a call center where his indentured characters slave, one finally explodes: "An entire generation [is] up all night, providing crutches for the white morons to run their lives. And then big companies come and convince us … [to] do jobs we hate so that we can buy stuff" (*One Night* 253). *Half Girlfriend*, with its ambition to "change … the mindset of Indian society" (vii), has its protagonist, Madhav, indulge in a "desi-invasion daydream": "If the Industrial Revolution had taken place here, there would be Indian ex-colonies around the world. White men would have had to learn Hindi to get a decent job. White teachers would tell white men how to say cow in Hindi with a perfect accent" (*Half* 129–30). No wonder the books sell in unprecedented fashion. For some such as Shagun Sharma, the Hindi-language publisher of Tulsi Paper Books: "[Chetan Bhagat] has done what television channels could not do. He has single-handedly wiped out the Hindi language reader with his easy-to-read English" (quoted in Kaur).

Bhagat's cross-platform circulation paradoxically illuminates and possibly explains the cleavage between book culture and reading culture increasingly evident in India. Precisely because the "new" fictions successfully capture an audience far beyond the precincts of a book culture, their presence is largely negligible in the metrics of a book culture. Bhagat's novels have mostly been ignored in the culture of reviews, prizes, and metropolitan bookstores and most markedly by literary critics – a neglect that explains why so many of the citations in the present study come from journalists obliged to attend to the world of publishing he has inaugurated.

In short, India's "new" fictions are texts and titles that actively short-circuit a book culture of metropolitan acknowledgement and prestige and indicate a whole world of consumption and circulation in which "reading" is simply one part. Let me provisionally name this a writing culture and define it as a node in which writing and ideas prevail, sometimes beyond the spheres of books and reading. Bhagat illuminates one way in which this may work: his writing and ideas circulate in and beyond print, in film, Facebook (where he has over 13 million Friends), Twitter (with over 4 million followers), TV, and radio, alongside more "traditional" forms of publication. Rather than one medium obliterating the other, the multiple platforms enhance Bhagat's writing and its reach and even consolidate it. Thus, the term "writing culture" conveys a place where writing appears alongside its forms of consumption. In this example, it is the anti-literary novel that elucidates a new phenomenon and future for the novel in India.

A New Purpose and Presence?

What might the gulf between book culture and reading culture say about the story of the novel broadly, or about India's literary landscape? And might this gulf indicate new futures for the novel – or book culture – in India specifically and possibly more broadly? Let me address these questions in order, with the caveat that further research is likely to urge refinement of what is an ongoing phenomenon.

While the specific forms that Bhagat currently produces might be new (i.e., not previously present, such as the IIT novel, for example), the production of such writing itself is not new, nor, more keenly, is the gulf between book culture and reading culture especially new. The rupture between popular and literary forms of the novel has been around for some time, as evidenced in the case of the novel in late nineteenth-century Britain. As Q. D. Leavis's research documents (and as Andreas Huyssen's and Lawrence Rainey's later research adumbrates), at some point British modernism manufactured the gulf between popular fiction and what it deemed elite forms in English writing. Confronting the "difficult" and "selective" modernist literary field, averred Leavis, readers stayed with the popular for pleasure and ventured, on rare occasion, toward the modernist for purpose or prestige (see Leavis 35–9).

Not only did modernism precipitate the gulf between popular and mainstream; it created the very conditions to perpetuate that gulf. The elaborate and finely grained networks of patronage, prizes, and reviews (read "book culture") that espoused Anglo-American literary modernism effectively excluded anti-modernist (read "popular") forms from serious purview. In essays and reviews, writers such as Virginia Woolf (*Mr. Bennett and Mrs. Brown* and "Modern Fiction") and T. S. Eliot ("Tradition and the Individual Talent") systematically created a book culture and defined the titles and forms that were permitted into it. The institutionalization of Anglo-American modernism and its subsequent prestige in the academy actively perpetuated this gulf and further separated the two domains of books and reading to an extent that one now has to work quite hard to recover a period (and a critical perspective) in which the popular was *also* the mainstream, as it was through the eighteenth to mid- nineteenth centuries, roughly from Defoe to Dickens, when book culture and reading culture were largely the same.

If India's "new" fictions by Bhagat and others vex the separation between a book culture and a reading culture, they do so in a marketplace that resembles in form if not degree that of a previous century and culture. Bhagat's writing and the exuberant range of his activities recall Dickens's; motivational speaker, journalist, policy wonk, national development columnist, banker, and mechanical engineer are just some of the activities alongside novelist that Bhagat claims.[11] There is no evidence in any of Bhagat's work that he is troubled by his apparent exclusion from India's book culture or that he seeks it out ("the book critics, they all hate me," he shrugs [quoted in Greenlees]). In the field of ideas that he and others following him have created, if a single culture matters, it is a *writing* culture that captures audiences before readers, often in film before the novel – as was the case with the adaptations of *Five Point Someone* and, later, *3 Mistakes*. When asked why he pursues "all this other . . . non-book work" in film and newspapers, Bhagat explained:

> I write for change. In order to change, I want to first reach as many Indians as possible through entertainment and then influence them with my non-fiction writings and views. For this, I want to be flexible with the medium, be it books, TV, films, stage or the Internet. *I do not see myself as an author alone, and my job is to reach and communicate with as many people as possible, using any available means.* (chetanbhagat.com; emphasis added)

The landscape of million-copy print runs that circulate below and outside the purview of institutional and institutionalizing book culture in India indicates a new chapter in the story of the novel in India and elsewhere. If British modernism's academizing split readers from books and kept them apart, then the Indian academy's longstanding reluctance to take Indian literature seriously or to give it curricular presence in the university is possibly a boon.[12] The logic of the market is quite different from that of the academy: in the market, success is measured by vast numbers and economic returns; in the academy, by exclusiveness and symbolic capital. In short, the *book* culture of admiration and prestige that Bhagat and his followers ignore presents no peril to their "love" or popularity in India's *reading* and *writing* cultures.

Bhagat's multilingual presence in Hindi and English, his presence in print and film, and his output in numerous discursive fields (finance, management, policy) recall a cultural moment when books *mattered* far beyond their immediate literary circuits. Again, the Victorian example is instructive. Bhagat may not be Dickens who commanded stage, newsprint, and paperboard equally, a colossus in each medium, but he might be closer to Dickens's compatriot, colleague, and later foe, G. W. M. Reynolds (1814–79), whose Chartist sympathies and reformist zeal were evident in half a century of massively populist journalism, best-selling serial fiction, and self-help books that were published in quantities and audiences to easily rival Dickens's, and that themselves inspired India's important early novels (see P. Joshi, *In Another Country* 74–87). The idea is not to restore Bhagat to some neglected pantheon. Rather, Bhagat's popularity recalls a moment and place when figures like him and the work they did – intrusively, insistently, and popularly – inserted themselves into a culture in which they *made* themselves matter. Love endures, even though readers fade.

And that, in the end, may be the next future of the English novel in India. Writers of popular fiction such as Bhagat speak to a new purpose and presence of the novel in a country that "discovered" the form relatively "late." India's "new" English novel, like India's Urdu poetry before it, has a powerful partner in popular film. Bhagat and Swarup are not the only figures whose works are adapted to widespread acclaim in Hindi cinema. Their often clumsy critiques of the "national development" story are nuanced and streamlined in blockbusters such as *3 Idiots* and *Slumdog Millionaire*, in the collaborative hands of other writers and the fingers of the world's most-skilled production teams. Absent pretensions themselves (Bhagat cheerfully accepts his moniker as an "unliterary" writer [S. Dasgupta, "Leading"]), their work unabashedly enters that most popular of zones, the Bollywood film, where it participates and shapes dialogues about nation and citizen, modernity and social purpose in realms far removed from print, literacy, and even the novel. That, finally, may be the future of the novel: inhabiting a zone in which it actively coexists with other forms and media, rather than obliterating or being obliterated by them.

Notes

1 Revenues from television dominate at Rs. 370 billion; then print a close second at Rs. 224.1 billion, followed from afar by film at Rs. 112.4 billion. See data compiled in KPMG-FICCI's 2013 report, *The Power of a Billion: Realizing the*

Indian Dream, Indian Media and Entertainment Report, 2013, p. 10. https://www.in.kpmg.com/Securedata/FICCI/Reports/FICCI-KPMG-Report-13.pdf.

2 The "English" novel in this chapter refers to the novel written in English. It does not refer to novels that come from the UK, as earlier practice might demand. In the twenty-first century, when English is an Indian language claimed by more people in India than in the UK and US combined, insisting on national origins for "English" or using terms such as "Anglophone" rehearses outdated colonial approaches. For an elaboration of some of these themes, see P. Joshi, *In Another Country* chapter 1.

3 Data on the sales of Bhagat's novel was reported in Kapoor, accessed August 2014. *Five Point Someone* took three years to sell a million copies, *One Night @ the Call Center* took four years, and *Revolution 2020* reached the million-books-sold milestone in three months.

4 "I spend half my time in Mumbai and the other half in small towns where I give motivational speeches in colleges. . . . 70 percent of my readers are from small towns," notes Chetan Bhagat in an interview with Yamini Deenadayalan (Deenadayalan).

5 The masculine pronoun is intentional here: the overwhelming number of campus novels in this publishing "boom" have been written by men. Research into gender and authorship in the last decade urgently merits further study.

6 Statistics on publishing houses in major metropolises are as follows: Delhi/New Delhi/Noida registers seventy-three publishers; Chennai sixteen publishers; Mumbai eleven; Bangalore ten; and Kolkata (once the center of Indian print and publishing) today lists only seven publishers. See publishersglobal.com, accessed April 2012.

7 The top grossing film since 2000 (adjusted for inflation) is *Gadar* (dir. Anil Sharma, 2001). See http://ibosnetwork.com/asp/topgrossersbyyear.asp?year=200, accessed July 14, 2014.

8 Box office returns from www.boxofficemojo.com/movies/?page=main&id=midnightschildren.htm, accessed July 14, 2014. The website rottentomatoes.com provides this composite review of the *Midnight's Children* film: "Though *Midnight's Children* is beautiful to look at and poignant in spots, its script is too indulgent and Deepa Mehta's direction, though ambitious, fails to bring the story together cohesively." See http://www.rottentomatoes.com/m/midnights_children/, accessed July 14, 2014.

9 Like *Call Center*, *3 Mistakes* has a prologue that frames it, where "Chetan," writing in the first person, receives an email from a suicidal fan. Spurred to action, he tries to save the man's life, and the man tells him the story that forms Bhagat's third novel. *Revolution 2020* echoes the now-familiar thanks to the reader: "once again, you, dear reader, for wanting a revolution," conclude the acknowledgments. The prologue begins with a conversation with a man whose story Bhagat putatively conveys in *Revolution* (1). The essay collection *What Young India Wants* begins, "Dear Reader, Thank you for picking up this book" (vii). And the acknowledgments of *Half Girlfriend*

(2014), his most recent novel, begin with "Thank you, dear reader and friend, for picking up *Half Girlfriend*. Whatever I have achieved today in life is thanks to you" (vii).

10 The phrase "billion sparks" comes from the motivational speech Bhagat delivered at the Symbiosis Business School, Pune, in 2008 that went viral on the Internet ("I come from the land of a billion sparks"). "Sparks" is collected in *What Young India Wants* (102–9).

11 See chetanbhagat.com for Bhagat's self-profile (accessed December 2013).

12 On the academy's reluctance to include Indian literature in its curriculum, see M. Mukherjee, "Mapping a Territory." The elite New Delhi college St. Stephen's produced critically acclaimed novelists such as Amitav Ghosh and Shashi Tharoor, among others, along with an elaborate and approving culture of academic reviewers who sometimes doubled as groupies. See the account provided by Trivedi, "St. Stephen's."

CHAPTER 21

"New India/n Woman": Agency and Identity in Post-Millennial Chick Lit

E. Dawson Varughese

This chapter examines post-millennial, Indian "Chick Lit"[1] narratives against older narratives of Indian female experience, both written by female Indian authors in English. I focus on key moments of decision-making from both eras of fiction production, with an overarching interest in demonstrating how the post-millennial Indian Chick Lit novel is a site for the articulation and contestation of modernity in India. Given that the two post-millennial works discussed here have been primarily marketed and distributed within India, resulting in restricted sales outside of India (and/or the wider region of South Asia) at the time of their initial publication, this chapter also considers how India's literary scene makes connections with today's world literature paradigms. In doing so, I hope to challenge the orthodoxy of the "postcolonial Indian novel." The fact that Chick Lit has seen exponential growth in India post millennium demonstrates that traditional hierarchies of fiction are being somewhat dismantled. Through the rise of popular or "commercial" fiction, the Indian literary scene has changed considerably in the last decade, and Chick Lit has played a fundamental role in this shift in terms of both production and consumption.

This chapter focuses on moments of women's decision-making in what I see as two distinct eras of women's writing in the Indian novel: the more literary, postcolonial phase of the 1980s into the late 1990s, and a new phase of Chick Lit in the last ten or so years. Looking at how decisions are made and followed through on, along with society's responses to those decisions, the chapter considers important changes in women's writing in the last few decades. I suggest that today's post-millennial female protagonists make life-changing decisions with a certain freedom of choice that was less readily available to their earlier counterparts. This point is important given the common perception that decision-making in Chick Lit novels is flippant and frivolous, revolving around which shoes to wear or which outfit to buy. In the Chick Lit discussed here, "serious" moments of decision-making are presented within a larger context in which female characters feel "lost" in the world. As in the earlier texts, decision-making is presented as difficult. Yet despite their difficulty, these texts' post-millennial women emerge as more settled and fulfilled characters by the end of their narratives. Interestingly, these female characters are less impacted by outside influences in their decision-making; if anything, it is their own, personal pressure that pushes them to take the decisions they do.

At the same time, female protagonists from the earlier era of fiction – from the more "literary" of the two bodies of fiction investigated here – are presented as facing difficulties caused by their identities as women, mothers, or daughters. The moments of decision-making in these earlier works are stressful and at times deeply emotional and disturbing, particularly in the case of Shashi Deshpande's narrative of marital rape in *The Dark Holds No Terrors* (1980). In contrast to post-millennial Chick Lit in which female protagonists arrive at a point of stability by the close of the novel, in earlier texts, women are left in states of irresolution: their domestic situations are not significantly improved, and thus the narratives close disconcertingly. Moreover, these female protagonists are often pressured and impacted by others in their decision-making processes. As Sen and Roy remind us: "Today's Indian English fiction ... mirrors the socio-cultural dynamics of a country changing so swiftly that it inevitably inspires new forms and content" (17). One such manifestation of this "new content" is the post-millennial Indian woman and her urban life, a new context of living and lifestyle choices and, in turn, myriad new possible identities. In contrast to the earlier female narratives, the norms of social pressure and expectation seem to have shifted, finding themselves now more intrinsically bound to pressures of globalization, economics, and the very real possibility of personal choice.

The Rise of the Literary Popular: Chick Lit

The nature of Indian writing in English has changed significantly and also relatively quickly in the last fifteen years; this is due in part to the rise of commercial Indian fiction over Indian "literary" fiction. The latter, often "regarded as coeval with 'Indian English literature' per se" (S. Gupta, "Indian" 47), dominated the postcolonial Indian English literary scene through the names of Arundhati Roy, Salman Rushdie, and others. By contrast, post-millennial Indian English publishing has witnessed significant areas of growth in commercial fiction, notably in Chick Lit, crime writing and young "urban India" narratives (see Dawson Varughese). For Suman Gupta, this new commercial fiction is

> consumed primarily within India, seen to display a kind of "Indianness" that Indians appreciate, and is not meant to be taken "seriously" or regarded as "literary." Literary fiction is the respectable public face of Indian literature in English abroad and at home, while commercial fiction is the gossipy café of Indian writing in English at home. (47)

McCrum, writing on Indian commercial fiction, describes the demographic of this readership:

> This new middle-class audience – small entrepreneurs, managers, travel agents, salespeople, secretaries, clerks – has an appetite for literary entertainment that falls between the elite idiom of the cultivated literati, who might be familiar with the novels of Amitav Ghosh or Salman Rushdie, and the Indian English of the street and the supermarket. Theirs is the Indian English of the outsourcing generation.

This new writing is a significant departure from the literary fiction of Rushdie and Roy, yet it is useful to return to Gupta to understand the common ground these two bodies of fiction share: "Despite numerous efforts to describe these terms according to content – as if texts have immanent qualities of commercialness and literariness – both are plausibly understood as market-led categories" (S. Gupta, "Indian" 46).

Indian Chick Lit is certainly a market-led genre within the wider body of commercial fiction in English for sale within India. As I have illustrated elsewhere, "'Chick lit' is mainly written by women, with a female protagonist who, in various ways, faces challenges, questions and changes in contemporary Indian society, these narratives often include a 'love' or 'romance' element" (Dawson Varughese 41). Narratives by female Indian authors, however, are not new: Shashi Deshpande, Anita Desai, Shama Futehally, Temsula Ao, Nisha da Cunha, and Kamala Markandaya are representatives of an earlier generation of authors, of whom Lau writes: "Their writings frequently include detailed descriptions of the interior spaces of home, the negotiation of roles and hierarchies, and the emotional lives played out against a background of the bedroom and the kitchen" (1098).[2]

The motif of domestic territories that Lau discusses appears in much of the earlier body of Indian writing in English by female authors but less so in paradigmatic Chick Lit narratives of the post-millennial period. However, both generations of narratives explore, as Deshpande herself puts it, "'what it is to be a woman in our society ... [and] the conflict between my idea of myself as a human being and the idea that society has of me as a woman'" (quoted in Bhalla 1). However, contemporary Chick Lit narratives reimagine and reconfigure these concerns. The moments of decision-making in both the earlier novels and the more recent ones illustrate how gendered concerns play out differently in these two time periods, especially regarding changing limitations on individuals' freedom of choice.

Desai and Deshpande: Deciding on Silence

Anita Desai's novel *Where Shall We Go This Summer?*, first published in 1975, is the story of Sita, a young woman who wrestles with her comfortable yet tedious middle-class life as she yearns for a more fulfilling existence. The novel charts this struggle and her realization that the ties that bind her to the life she is living are not easily broken. A turning point in the novel is Sita's decision, when seven months pregnant, to travel without her husband to an island called Manori, a place she knew in her younger days (Dawson Varughese 42). Her desire to leave her family home pregnant, in the raging heat of the monsoon, to go to an island with rough living arrangements, is difficult for her husband to comprehend or accept and thus illustrates the predominant androcentric positioning of the family's lived reality. As Bharucha writes:

> Female space is biologically recessed. The enclosure of the womb affords protection to the growing foetus and is therefore a positive factor. An androcentric world, however, has extended the analogy of biological female inwardness to create a feminine reductiveness. This has turned a biological virtue into a societal and cultural handicap. ("Inhabiting" 93)

Sita's desire to travel to Manori is motivated by her belief that the island can work miracles. She is tired of her everyday life in the city – and, moreover, she is terrified to bring her fifth child into the world:

> "But you were always so pleased about the babies, Sita," [her husband] said, closing his fists, unclosing them, uncertainly. "They always pleased you."
>
> "I'm *not* pleased, I'm frightened," she hissed through her teeth. "*Frightened.*"
>
> "Why? Why?" he spoke gently. "Everything will go well. I thought it grows easier and easier."
>
> "It's not easier. It's harder – harder. It's unbearable," she wept. (A. Desai, *Where* 32, emphasis in original)

Here, Sita's husband fails to understand the complexity of Sita's emotions. For her, the family home is anything but a refuge; she feels trapped in its daily routines and domestic monotony. She needs space to breathe.

In choosing to leave against her husband's wishes, Desai's protagonist contravenes all that Sita of the Ramayana enacts in her devotion to her husband Rama when she follows him into exile, suffering the indignity of his banishment. Desai's Sita is defiant in her decision to go to Manori, even if that means leaving her husband behind. By naming her protagonist "Sita," Desai speaks directly to the question of gender in 1970s India, when female identities were beginning to change in response to continued modernization.

Yet this insistence does not come without certain costs. Despite Sita's independent decision, she also faces sanction by the wider society. When she arrives at Manori, the villagers question why she is there without her husband; hers is an act of madness in both her husband's and the villagers' eyes. For Sita's husband, her emotional state with regard to their unborn baby is completely irrational. The villagers of Manori also fail to understand her; when Moses, the watchman, sees Sita playing with her son in the mud and sand, he interprets this as an act of lunacy given her age and advanced pregnancy. He also understands Sita's constant anger as a clear sign of madness, and in conversation with Jamila, the tea-shop owner's wife, Moses contrasts Sita with her late father, who was "like a god – a magic man" (156), for having rid Moses' house of scorpions, dug a well with his own hands and treated a villager for "fits and boils with powdered pearls and rubies and charged nothing" (11–12). Thus where Sita's father was idolized, Sita is deemed mentally unstable.

Moreover, Sita's decision to remain on the island is ultimately overruled by her daughter, who contacts her father, worried about missing school and their established life in the city. It is through this father-daughter collusion that Sita is forced to leave the island. Her agency – her ability to carry out a decision she made about her own life – is compromised by one of her children; the sense of betrayal, the idea that her own daughter made a decision above her, diminishes Sita's independence. Moreover, the necessity for her husband to join them on the island further feeds ideas of Sita's alleged state of madness and her inability to care for herself and her children, despite Sita having raised four children already.

In a similar vein, Shashi Deshpande's novel *The Dark Holds No Terrors* (1980) represents the difficult reality of marital rape.[3] The protagonist, Saru, returns to her parental home to look after her father following her mother's death. Her return to the family home is fraught with ensuing memories that she would care to forget – her harsh, unloving mother and the drowning of Saru's brother, an event that only embittered her mother further – but her father's house is the only place Saru can escape to in order to flee the brutality she is enduring in her own home. Her violent circumstances compel Saru to make important decisions about her own life. This begins early on in the novel, when we learn of Saru's forthrightness to pursue medical studies against her parents' wishes:

> But then it had been a king [sic] of miracle anyway, her joining medical college in spite of her mother. Standing up against her, asserting her will against her ... that had seemed impossible. But she had done it. I won that time. But I was not alone then. Baba was with me. He helped me. Without him, I would never have succeeded. (Deshpande, *Dark* 139)

Although Saru succeeds in this decision, she is simultaneously plagued by the worry that her father helped her go to medical school *only* to hurt his wife. Saru questions whether she had been used as a pawn, fuelled by her father's emotions. Furthermore, she worries that one day such betrayal will come back to her by way of her own children.

Likewise, even when Saru decides to study medicine, she is bound both financially and emotionally to her father in order to follow her decision through. Saru's mother, Kamala, feels that their money should be spent on a wedding and not on a medical education, so Saru is compelled to choose between education and marriage. Since Saru opts for education, she is ironically free to choose her own husband, given that her parents will not be involved in arranging a marriage for her. Whereas making a "suitable" choice would help mend her relationship with her parents, Saru once again defies her parents by choosing Manu, a man from a non-Brahmin family and thus considered unsuitable by her mother in particular (Manohar 98). Her decision to marry Manu is based on her feelings for him; it is clear that she has little regard for the impact this decision will have on her parents. Saru values her education and her worldliness above family, tradition, and brahminical culture, a position that further alienates her from her mother and father.

Yet despite the agency Saru claims over her own life, ultimately she fails to speak out about the marital violence she is suffering. As readers, we are left wondering what becomes of Saru, her marriage and her children and, moreover, whether she continues to suffer at the hands of her husband. As readers, we do not know whether Saru will decide to speak out about her marital rape when she meets her husband after a period of time away from him, despite (and this is key) having taken a decision to remove herself from the domestic and marital context in order to flee the violence. When Saru's husband decides to come and take Saru back home, even before his arrival, Saru rushes off to help a neighbor who is in need of medical attention. Deshpande's novel thus closes on an eerie silence that shouts of irresolution and uncertainty.

Thus Deshpande "speaks" of rape through the medium of her novel, even as her female protagonist fails to do so, and thus rejects what Rajeswari Sunder Rajan calls "a measure of liberation, a shift from serving as the object of voyeuristic discourse to the occupation of a subject-position as 'master' of narrative" (*Real* 78). What complicates any potential resolution between Saru and her husband is the fact that marital rape is represented as a desire to express violence (toward Saru), rather than as motivated by sexual desire. This echoes Sunder Rajan: "rape as a phenomenon in contemporary India is more properly understood as the expression of (male) violence – sanctioned by various modes of social power – rather than of sexual desire" (*Real* 78). In the novel, violence emerges out of Saru's husband's resentment at Saru's success as a doctor. By presenting marital rape as a form of violence, the novel makes it clear that she might decide *not* to speak of it because of what such a conversation might disclose and thus lead to (more violence?).

Choosing silence is also evidenced in *Where Shall We Go This Summer?* when Sita responds to her husband's yearly question, "Where shall we go this summer?" through silent speech: "To Manori, she instantly replied, but in silence because with this idea there also sprang to her mind the idea that she would go alone" (57). Like Saru, Sita chooses not to speak because to speak out is to articulate the unsayable: "Physically so resigned, she could not inwardly accept that this was all there is to life, that life would continue thus, inside this small, enclosed area, with these few characters churning around and then past her, leaving her always in this grey, dull-lit, empty shell" (54).

Both Desai and Deshpande craft female protagonists who are defiant in their decision-making, but it is their compulsion to silence that sees their decisions undermined by both their husbands and their own sense of acceptability within society. Both novels close in eerie uncertainty – will Saru decide to speak to her husband about the marital rape? Will Sita resolve her domestic situation? The women's lives hang in a state of irresolution: their domestic situations are not significantly improved, and, despite their self-enacted desire to bring change to their lives, and despite the fact that they both leave their husbands to be in a different environment, they return to the very position of domesticity that they attempted to flee from. Their "freedom" hangs in the balance of one final decision – to speak out or not.

Kala and Hasan: Deciding on Choice

In *Reading New India*, I explored Advaita Kala's *Almost Single* (2007) as a paradigmatic Chick Lit novel and Anjum Hasan's *Neti, Neti: Not This, Not This* (2009) as a female-centered narrative of urban New India. Here, however, I wish to consider these two post-millennial texts in relation to the fiction of Desai and Deshpande to highlight both the continuities and the transformations in the female-centered narrative over the last generation. I suggest that the newer female protagonists make decisions with a certain freedom of choice and as an antidote to feeling "lost" in the world. Dhar reminds us that the estrangement experienced by post-millennial protagonists is often,

> due to rising levels of human dissatisfaction with the acquisition of mate-
> rial possessions, individuals' self-directed questions about personal worth
> and purpose of existence, fears and feelings of inadequacy, loneliness
> and friendlessness, radical disquietudes, all aggravated by the tensions of
> a highly technologised and urban-centred existence in a contemporary
> postindustrial world scenario. (S. Dhar 165)

Dhar suggests that it is from this angst that popular Indian fiction writer Chetan Bhagat's "inspi-lit" collection of novels has grown and come to know immense success in terms of sales and appeal to "young India." Indian post-millennial Chick Lit echoes facets of this angst, compounded by the genre's own particular preoccupations (see Davis-Kahl; Ponzanesi).

Almost Single follows the lives of three close friends, Aisha, Misha, and Anushka. As I have pointed out in my previous work, the novel engages with matters of "social acceptability" in a woman-centered narrative (Dawson Varughese 46–7). Aisha constantly challenges notions of social acceptability; for instance, she flouts the regulation uniform at the Grand Orchid Hotel, where she works, insisting instead on Reebok trainers and wearing her sari over her jeans. She also engages in "unlady-like" behavior as she hitches up her sari to jump over a partition in the hotel to retrieve a piece of paper from a guest's patio area. As I detail in *Reading New India*, Aisha's "unacceptable" behavior as guest relations manager further empha-sizes her independence (47) and disregard for societal norms. Like Desai's Sita and Deshpande's Saru, Aisha also challenges society's views of women, their roles and their responsibilities. However, she does so in a different manner, and, of course, the stakes are different. Aisha's decision to jump into the guest's patio area puts her job at risk, but that is different from entrapment or forced domesticity as in Desai and Deshpande. Sunder

Rajan reminds us how "the image of the 'new Indian woman' is ... derived primarily from the urban educated middle-class career woman" (*Real* 130), an identity that runs throughout *Almost Single*. Aisha's close friend, Misha, has similar escapades. Neither woman conforms to a pre-established idea of how middle-class women should conduct their lives.

However, this is not just a rejection of Indian tradition but rather a re-articulation of it. In a bid to pacify their neighbors – as well as having a vested interest in finding a husband – the three women decide to keep the Karva Chauth fast as part of their building's social and religious calendar. This decision is taken mindfully, rather than frivolously or lightly, and to demonstrate their commitment, the three women contribute money to the association for the ceremony: "good PR for Misha, an opportunity for her to integrate with the bhadralok in her neighbourhood" (Kala 111). As the ceremony takes place, Aisha observes how much Misha is enjoying the proceedings and muses: "She is made for this stuff, and if our traditions are to withstand India's sprint towards the western way, women like Misha have to get married" (115).

This scene embodies a sense of both the articulation and contestation of modernity in India. As Sunder Rajan writes: "women in history and myth who are 'modern,' as well as contemporary women who are 'traditional' ... are made to serve as harmonious symbols of historical continuity rather than as conflictual subjects and sites of conflict" (*Real* 135). Post-millennial Indian Chick Lit appropriates such a statement – demonstrating in moments like the Karva Chauth fast that "contemporary" women can be both "traditional" and "modern" at the same time.

Ferriss and Young remind us that topics such as identity and "friends as family" are compelling motifs of Chick Lit, as are sexuality and the balancing of work and relationships. In Kala's novel, pre-marital sex is another issue around which the female protagonist actively makes her own decision. Near the end of *Almost Single*, Misha meets up with Gurinder, a childhood friend (Dawson Varughese 50–1). Misha is reluctant to meet him, but her father asks her to go, so she agrees. At the meeting, Misha is taken aback by how much Gurinder has changed; in Kala's words, he has had "more than just a growth spurt" (270). The two get on well, and the next day, as Gurinder prepares to leave for Bhatinda, Misha decides to follow him. It is from Bhatinda that Misha phones Aisha to tell her that she has decided to sleep with Gurinder, in order to determine if they are sexually compatible.

The decision-making around pre-marital sex in this novel sits uncomfortably alongside Deshpande's narrative of Saru, who suffers sexually at the hands of her husband. Aisha's suggestion that women today need to know if they are sexually compatible with their partner before they marry signifies a position of independence and choice around sexual matters in the relationship. Saru, however, is trapped in her sexual encounters with her husband, devoid of choice and independence.

The generational difference is also evident at the end of *Almost Single*, when Aisha decides to tell Karan, her love interest, how she feels about their relationship. In a scene characteristic of commercial fiction, Aisha, on a twenty-two hour journey to Nashik, jumps off the train at Bhopal and gets into a taxi to take her to the airport, where she boards the next flight for Mumbai to meet Karan. While this sudden decision echoes Sita's fervent decision to leave the city for Manori, Aisha's journey will bring her closer to her boyfriend, while Sita's journey is motivated by her desire to leave the family home and her husband behind. Saru, too, travels away from her marital home in order to flee her husband, but there it is suggested that she is fleeing for her life. Yet despite these differences, in all cases the female character is unsure of what she will do at her destination; Kala's Aisha also admits to not knowing what she will do once she arrives in Mumbai.

Just as the female protagonists of Desai and Deshpande's novels challenge accepted norms, Aisha too challenges the expected. When she meets Karan in a hotel in Mumbai, Aisha announces that she does not wish to get married immediately but would rather spend some time with him. This is something of an unexpected ending to their story so far, given that the genre of commercial fiction might presuppose a rather more "filmy" closing scene ending in marriage. The fact that such an ending does not take place accentuates the agency of the female character in shaping her future and taking charge of her relationship on her own terms.

Like *Almost Single*, Anjum Hasan's *Neti, Neti: Not This, Not This* is a female-centered narrative of urban New India. At various points in the novel, the protagonist Sophie Das is "lost in life" and wonders about her existence and her place in it all. This fact is significant when we realize that Sophie's move to Bangalore is of her own volition and that she is there to make a life for herself. Unlike Kala's Aisha, however, Sophie is a more subdued character: "And Sophie, standing there blinking, was suddenly overtaken by a powerful sense of disorientation. *Who were these people and what place was this and why was she here?* For a moment she had no clue" (Hasan 119). Sophie, like Aisha, has a group of friends, but unlike Aisha, her bond with these friends is still being formed, as these are friends who are part of the Bangalore Sophie has come to construct for herself. Despite Sophie's courage in coming to live and work in Bangalore without her family, there are times in the novel when Sophie's decision to live in the metropolis is experienced as stressful and emotionally challenging – not least because in these moments she is overtaken by a strong sense of estrangement. Sophie's existence in Bangalore lightly echoes the estrangement that Sita experiences in *Where Shall We Go This Summer?* and that Saru faces in *The Dark Holds No Terrors*. Saru, having studied and worked hard all her life to become the "lady doctor" (42), questions why, after all she has done to achieve her professional status, she should be punished by a husband who resents her accomplishments. Such karmic reflection is also found in Desai's protagonist Sita as she sits on the balcony of her apartment smoking, not reading the book that is in her lap, and gazing out at the sea (54). The title of Hasan's novel captures this sense of the ethereal and the otherworldly that estrangement in its various forms might bring about. As I have illustrated elsewhere (Dawson Varughese 32), the novel *Neti, Neti* takes its name from Hindu sources, as a chant or mantra and also as a saying found in the Vedic texts (the Upanishads). "Neti, neti" as a philosophical process looks to identify something by looking at what it is not, and this is particularly true when understanding the Divine in Hinduism. As human beings, we are unable to capture and express in words the exact nature of the Divine. We might be able to say what the Divine is *not* but not necessarily what it *is* (Dawson Varughese 32). Interestingly, Desai's Sita and Deshpande's Saru are both able to identify what they want – to get to Manori, to flee a brutish husband – but they seem unable to articulate what they *don't* want ("neti neti: not this, not this"). Sita is silent when asked where she wants to go for the summer holiday and Saru is silent when she needs to speak out about being subjected to marital rape. Sophie is also caught up in articulating and enacting what she wants and what she does not want. In deciding to move to Bangalore, Sophie is, like many other characters in the book, on a journey to find herself, and to be independent and free is part of this journey. In Bangalore, Sophie is "free" in the sense that her life and her decisions are her own. Thus, while, like Sita, Sophie too feels suffocated, Bangalore is the site of her own agency. Sophie's reality is thus both an articulation and contestation of her life in New India.

Conclusion

Although both Sita and Saru take decisions independently, they are hampered in their execution of these decisions. Such interference is usually caused by a male character – although, in Sita's case, her daughter is in collusion with her husband. Desai's and Deshpande's women also suffer from self-censorship and the pressure to remain silent. This state of being affects the women in various ways, to the detriment of their own psychological states as well as their relationships with others. Thus, although they are bold in their decision-making, it is their respective husbands and/ or society's ideas of acceptable behavior that inhibit them from enacting these decisions or being more content in their lives in general. The novels' disconcerting closures mean that their narratives are left in irresolution and in fear; Sita fears for the imminent delivery of her baby into this world, and Saru for the impending meeting with her husband.

In the cases of Aisha and Sophie, by contrast, husbands or expectations from wider society do not impinge on their decision-making to the degree that they do on Saru's and Sita's. Aisha and Sophie do not self-censor or choose silence – although they still face difficult and uneasy situations. Societal pressures above and beyond those of a traditional nature are present in the lives and narratives of these two characters, with globalization and a growing Indian economy intersecting in their lives through both work opportunities and financial responsibility. In turn, pressure is generated from within the individual's mind and experience, as she struggles with the knowledge that the decisions are her own and equally so are any consequences of such decisions. Configurations of "success" and "failure," therefore, are drawn up anew, moving beyond notions of a successful (or otherwise) marriage and family life and, by extension, one's husband's profession. It is the specter of New India that looms over these post-millennial female protagonists in their decision-making, rendering them at times confused (Hasan's Sophie) or alienated (Kala's Aisha), despite being surrounded by friends. These two characters do, however, emerge from their respective struggles as settled and fulfilled in their decisions, and, as a result, their futures appear positive and fruitful.

Not only does the emergence of the genre of commercial fiction in English in India over the past decade say much about the continued development of Indian writing in English, but the immense sales of commercial fiction say even more about writers, readers, and consumers in India today. As Sen and Roy state: "With Indian English publishing registering exponential growth, new writers emerged from all walks of life in numbers larger than ever before – journalists and academics expectedly, but also doctors, engineers, scientists, civil servants, businessmen and housewives" (16). The traditional hierarchies of fiction are being somewhat dismantled, and the genre of Chick Lit pulls apart this traditional platform on a number of levels. The authors of Chick Lit are often drawn from the pool of writers described by Sen and Roy, rather than from an established literary ilk; the language of these novels often challenges ideas of "standard" or "correct" English; the genre *is* popular, and, although sometimes criticized for its lack of literary merit, the sales and confidence in the genre cannot be easily ignored. In short, the narratives of these post-millennial female protagonists dismantle traditional hierarchies, both in literature and in life.

Notes

1 See Davis-Kahl for an overview of current definitions of "Chick Lit," including her own: "modern women struggling and succeeding with work, relationships, motherhood, infertility, finances and yes, the right shoes to wear with the right dress" (18). See also Ponzanesi for a more detailed account of the defining features of Chick Lit.
2 Also quoted in Dawson Varughese (41).
3 This is a topic Sundaram takes up in her chapter on "Marriage, Sexual Violence and Indian Masculinity," in which she discusses both *The Dark Holds No Terrors* and Anita Nair's *Mistress* (2005).

CHAPTER 22

The Politics and Art of Indian English Fantasy Fiction

Tabish Khair and Sébastien Doubinsky

Fantasy fiction seems to have little to do with the fantastic in a literary-theoretical sense – as defined by Todorov for instance – although it lives in constant tension with it. In general, there seems to be a divide between fantasy fiction and fantastic literary fiction (such as magic/al realism): while both inevitably seep into one another, they tend to be read, critiqued, and sold separately. One can argue that in the European context, this divide replicates the old eighteenth and nineteenth-century tension between "fancy" and "imagination," as well as "low" and "high" cultures. In the non-European context, the matter gets even more convoluted, partly but not only because of matters of anglocentric discursive hegemony and the colonial gaze (as examined by John Rieder in the context of science fiction). For instance, as Khair has noted with reference to magic realism, no matter what the intentions of the authors and the interpretations of theorists, twentieth-century magic realism, from Carpentier to Rushdie, echoed a prevalent European mode of looking, ranging from ancient Roman histories to medieval and colonial accounts, in which non-Europe was often portrayed as a mix of the magical and the real, the fantastic and the mundane (Khair, *Gothic*).

Hence, before we can even get to grips with fantasy fiction in English from India, we will have to put on record the fact that a dominant mode of literary fiction – often called magic realism – employs similar thematic and stylistic modes as fantasy fiction. But while the latter is usually bunched together with popular genre fiction, even pulp at times, the former enjoys the prestige of being considered "high" "literary" fiction. After all, Salman Rushdie's *Midnight's Children* features elements from Eastern epics and myths, as do the fantasy novels of writers such as Amish Tripathi. Shashi Tharoor's critically acclaimed *The Great Indian Novel* (1989) is a rewriting of the Mahabharata, but so, for instance, is the "Krishna Coriolis"[1] series by Ashok Banker, who is often also called the

Dan Brown of Indian English pulp. All such acclaimed "literary" novels share a mix of the fantastic and the "real" that is also the province of usually much less acclaimed fantasy fiction.

"Sultana's Dream" and the Origins of Political Fantasy

One way to comprehend this uneasy and often unacknowledged coexistence is to go back to the genesis of Indian English (henceforth IE) fantasy fiction. Most literary historians consider Rokeya Sakhawat Hossain's "Sultana's Dream" (1905) to be a major early example of fantasy fiction in English by an Indian. However, this work did not come out of the blue. It was heralded by a certain type of novel written by many Indian English authors in the nineteenth century. In terms of genre, Toru Dutt's *Bianca* (1878), K. K. Lahiri's *Roshinara* (1881), and K. Chakravarti's *Sarata and Hingana* (1895) were all different kinds of *romances*. Their generic affinity pulled them toward pulp and genre fiction, while their intellectual and "high" literary colonial concerns pulled them away from it. If Dutt's novel was heavily, allusively "literary," Lahiri's and Chakravarti's novels were historical romances with a "post-colonial"-type agenda. They set out to narrate a glorious past and, implicitly or explicitly, contrast it with the inglorious (colonial) present. This strong literary and socio-historical underpinning is probably a defining element of IE pulp, although one can argue that many European and American works of science or gothic fiction also have such an underpinning.[2] An element of fantasy – as a rewriting of history – is always present in such works too.

However, "Sultana's Dream" is clearly a work that can fit into the genres of fantasy as well as literary fiction; one could compare it not just to major dystopian and utopian novels from the genres of science and fantasy fiction but also to major literary and feminist works, such as Charlotte Perkins Gilman's "The Yellow Wallpaper." It contains, as does Hossain's later novel *Padmarag* (1924),[3] a strong utopian element, and the space and time in which it is enacted is clearly not historical or contemporary. It is narrated as a fable and a kind of alternative feminist fantasy. As Barnita Bagchi puts it in the introduction to the Penguin Modern Classics edition of both "Sultana's Dream" and *Padmarag*,

> In the unconventional, inverted world of *Sultana's Dream*, the men, whose advantage is brawn rather than brain, remain confined to the *mardana* [a satirical neologism by the author to parallel the *zenana*, or the women's quarters in traditionally segregated homes] and perform the daily mundane

chores, while the women, headed by a queen who is ably supported by her deputies – the female principals of the two women's universities – use their superior intellectual ability to govern the country wisely and well. (Introduction xii)

"Sultana's Dream" is a work of fantasy fiction with clear political and feminist overtones. As Suchitra Mathur puts it, "Dubbed 'a terrible revenge!' (against men) by her husband, who proudly arranged for its publication … this short utopian tale of gender role inversion forcefully articulated Hossain's views regarding the power of modern education to transform the position of women in contemporary Muslim society" (Mathur 119). Another (minor) work of fantasy, with a clear political agenda, that was written half a century before "Sultana's Dream" was Shoshee Chunder Dutt's *The Republic of Orissa: A Page from the Annals of the 20th Century*. Published in 1845, it narrates the bid, in 1916, of the people of the state of Orissa to break away from the British Empire. Is this element of political relevance then one of the factors that makes novels such as *Midnight's Children* "literary" and not an example of fantasy fiction?

Such an assumption would be misleading, although it is true that the recent upsurge in IE fantasy fiction is not distinguished – with some rare exceptions – by its political perception, and hence it is more likely to (inadvertently or not) provide fictional fodder for triumphalist narratives of Shining India. One of the ways this is done is by rewriting epics and mythical "histories" as novels. The large and glittering canvas and heavily contemporary thought processes employed for such a rewriting are immediately acceptable to readers in a country aspiring for future glory by highlighting its glorious, part-mythical past. More negatively, it can be argued that such fantasy fiction provides a mass(ive) release similar to that offered by Bollywood "masala" films.

Mythical Predecessors

Another origin for IE fantasy fiction are nineteenth-century romances, which were themselves aided by a certain slant in Orientalist studies: the narration and recuperation of ancient India as well as, to a lesser extent, medieval India. The current boom in IE fantasy fiction depends heavily on a rewriting of ancient Indian epics, Vedic narratives, popular religious myths, and folkish "histories." The bestselling Amish Tripathi was offered a one million (U.S.) dollar advance, an astronomical and very unusual sum in Indian publishing, to write his next fantasy novels following the success of his trilogy based on the Hindu deity, Shiva.[4] The fantasy fiction trend, notes Hartosh Singh Bal, began in 2003 with the publication and success of Ashok Banker's *The Prince of Ayodhya*, based on some of the myths of the Ramayana and the popular Hindu god Rama (H. Bal). One can, as we have suggested, take the trend further back to nineteenth-century romances, as well as so-called Bollywood mythologicals in the early and middle parts of the twentieth century. It is also necessary to bear in mind that the phenomenal rise of the Hindu revivalist-nationalist (and some would say, fundamentalist) Bharatiya Janata Party in the last decade of the twentieth century was also closely related to a certain emotive and political evocation of the myths of Lord Rama.

As noted earlier, much fantasy fiction can be called "pulp," rather than "genre" – if one distinguishes between the two, which we do, by considering "pulp" as merely repetitive of established generic forms and "genre" as engaging creatively with them.[5] But there is a difference – between IE fantasy fiction, even in its pulp forms, and IE pulp – that needs to be put on record. In a separate paper, one of us (Khair, "Indian") has noted that Indian pulp fiction was, until very recently, mostly written in languages other than English. As Meenakshi Mukherjee has illustrated, traces of both the (semi-)canonical European novels and Victorian pulp can be found in a "curious amalgam" in early novels in the "other" Indian languages – known as *bhashas* (M. Mukherjee, *Perishable*; and M. Mukherjee, *Realism*). And long before Shobha Dé (in the late 1980s), railway and bus station stalls in India – though probably not airport ones – stocked novels with covers full of semi-clad women, speeding cars, and haunted mansions, either translated into such languages as Hindi, Urdu, Tamil, Bangla, and Marathi or written originally in such languages. At least in the popular genre of detective novels in Indian bhashas (*jasoosi upanayas*), a degree of easy transference existed between such languages as Urdu and Hindi in the twentieth century: the same novel could be found in the Perso-Arabic and Devanagari scripts.

In fact, one could argue that in India, at least until very recently, pulp fiction was only feasible in languages other than English. The market-markers of the genre (which imply commerciality and substantial readership) make it viable only in the larger languages spoken and read by the "masses" – and Urdu, Hindi, Bangla, Tamil, and so on do have a host of pulp fiction writers, the earliest ones dating back to the end of the nineteenth century. How, then, can it be possible to have pulp fiction in English – a language that is a mother tongue to less than 4 percent of the Indian population?[6] It turns out, if we translate this tiny percentage into a number of individuals, we come up with forty million people – and, hence, a putative market larger than that of most European languages. To this should be added the facts that "India ... is the third largest English book-producing country after the United States and [UK]," that "it ranks eighth in the world" in book publishing, and that "the average number of English titles per million of population published each year is 360, which is higher than the world average" (Kachru 528).

As the rise of Dé, Banker, and others proved in the last two decades of the twentieth century, English readership of a non-elite and non-literary type has reached a kind of critical mass in urban Indian circles. This, however, does not erase the parallel fact that many bhashas offer a much bigger pulp readership. In this connection, it ought also to be noted (although this paper cannot go into the matter) that a non-anglocentric – or "anglo-phonic," as Boddhisattva Chattopadhyay puts it in a very useful paper – reading of fantasy fiction would not only bring in such important Indian writers of the genre as Satyajit Ray (better known internationally as a film-maker) but also significantly nuance our understanding of fantasy fiction in general.

However, even though such fantasy fiction can often belong to pulp, it appears that fantasy fiction *qua* fantasy fiction is particularly thriving in English in India today as *fantasized* rewritings of religious and cultural myths. This is not exactly the case in bhasha literatures, at least from what we have seen: fantasy fiction in languages such as Bangla or Marathi seems to be closer to science fiction and similar genres rather than fantasized rewritings of epics and religious myths. This might be so because the epics and popular myths that such IE fantasy fiction draws upon are already so entrenched and commonly deployed and rewritten in bhasha cultures that one needs the remove of English to turn them into both fiction *and* fantasy.

Hence, the success of Tripathi and Banker, and the others who have followed in their footsteps, is tied to the rise of a middle class that needs to access its myths and "histories" in English. A rewriting of the Ramayana in Hindi or Marathi will either translate into "literary" fiction – if the author wants to highlight its art-ificiality – or it will become just another rewriting of an epic that has been rewritten a thousand times, without becoming fantasy or fiction. For it to become *fantasy fiction*, a residue of English seems necessary. Hence, the return of such myths as IE fantasy fiction does not just suggest a resurgence of Hindutva and Hindu revivalism; it also suggests a remove (often unconscious) from a prior universe of belief and reality.

However there are novels, such as Ashwin Sanghi's *Chanakya's Chant* (2010), that share mythological, folklore-based and other thematic concerns with "literary" fiction, even as the latter employs such themes with more mediated literary overtures to contemporary times. In some ways it is difficult, for instance, to distinguish *Chanakya's Chant*, which is usually categorized as IE fantasy fiction, from, say, Tharoor's *The Great Indian Novel*, which is an acclaimed literary novel. Both take mythical and semi-historical tales and insert them into contemporary times. Such a text reminds us that generic definitions need to be more nuanced; they cannot simply depend on the source of the stories or even their usage. In general, though, Bal is right in noting that IE fantasy fiction that draws upon mythologies

> often fails to convey that the classical stories explicitly reinforced existing social hierarchies, a kind that are unpalatable today. In previous versions of the Ramayana and the Mahabharata, a sweeping war epic, conflict and decay are direct consequences of the mixing of the castes and a lack of respect for the Brahmins. Perhaps this loss at least is as it should be: The retelling of India's myths, its gloss over the past, does reflect a more modern India, shorn of some of its earlier complexities and given to a more equitable view of people. (H. Bal)

Indeed, whereas early fantasy fiction often had a clear political overtone, much of today's IE fantasy fiction lacks this. The Mahabharata or Ramayana are usually evoked not to grapple with contemporary issues and problems but, with some vague references, to provide entertainment or a sense of comfortable identity. This is a problem that other fantasy fiction traditions also confront today, although there is always a radical trend too. For instance, one can think of reams of "entertainment" fantasy novels in English that deploy, consciously or subconsciously, established Christian myths for their appeal: Dan Brown's *The Da Vinci Code* is by no means the only obvious candidate. At the same time, one also has novels such as Michael Moorcock's *Behold the Man*, in which the myth of Jesus is ironically retold as a science fiction story: Karl Glogauer, a time traveler, assumes the Messiah's identity up to the ultimate sacrifice because of his utter disappointment in the real Jesus, who is a cretin. One should also note that Michael Moorcock is also the creator of the *Elric of Menilbone* saga and the inventor of what is now called "Dark Fantasy." Moorcock's creation comes as a direct critique of Tolkien's fantasy world – which Moorcock sees as plagued with Christian subliminal messages and references[7] – and thus calls for an internal questioning and criticism of the cultural standards of fantasy.

This radical option exists in some IE fantasy fiction as well. The two significant strands in this minority stream are represented by Samit Basu's *Turbulence* (2012) and the GameWorld Trilogy (*The Simoqin Prophecies* [2004], *The Manticore's Secret* [2005], and *The Unwaba Revelations* [2007]) and by Samhita Arni's *The Missing Queen* (2014). *Turbulence* is a funny and fast-paced fantasy yarn that makes tongue-in-cheek use of almost everything in contemporary life: politics, socio-historical trends, comic books, super hero films, and so on. The story is simple: Everyone on BA flight 142 from London to Delhi exits the plane with a unique superpower, the power that they wanted most in life. For instance, Tia, an oppressed and homebound housewife who loves her children but also dreams of other lives, gets the ability to split into multiple selves; Vir, an Indian Air Force pilot, becomes a flying superman; a school girl becomes a Manga comic figure at will; an aspiring starlet gets the power of being adored by everyone; and so on. There are worse powers too. And very soon it appears that someone is killing off some of the passengers.

Basu stands the usual "super men and women" storyline of comics, graphic books, and, increasingly, films on its head by creating characters with superpowers that reflect and comment ironically on real life. Despite its Indian setting, this is a fantasy novel that sets out to subvert the dominant "global" tradition of comic book fantasies, along with their assumptions, inherited by Indians from the West. One can see something similar in Basu's earlier works, known as the GameWorld Trilogy, in which he mixes folklore, popular icons, and legends from the West and from Asia, creating a "global" parodic-fantasy setting with a tongue-in-cheek mish-mash of legends, religions, and myths from all over the world. Although the intention of his books is clearly humorous – even sarcastic at times – they nonetheless helped in opening the path to a rewriting of dominant cultural and literary paradigms, also evident in authors such as Lavie Tidhar, for example.[8]

By contrast, Arni's *The Missing Queen* targets Indian myths directly, in that it presents a rewriting of aspects of the Ramayana. In this context, it can also be read in tandem with the literary fiction of a host of other Indian English authors, ranging from Rushdie and Tharoor to Manjula Padmanabhan and Githa Hariharan, who have also mined dominant Indian myths for radical purposes. *The Missing Queen* constructs a world where, in keeping with a radical tradition in the fantasy genre internationally as well, utopia tapers into dystopia. Or rather, one person's utopia is another person's dystopia. The novel is based in a fictionalized Ayodhya a decade after Rama's return from exile and Sita's banishment.

Set in contemporary-like times, a young female journalist becomes obsessed with the question of what happened to Sita and where she went after her banishment. Her investigation soon attracts Ayodhya's secret police and its mysterious, terrifying head, the Washerman. It also exposes her to stories never told or hastily forgotten, because they belonged to the losers. In this speculative thriller, Arni creates an atmosphere redolent of dystopian fiction, from Orwell and Auster to Lavie Tidhar, with disturbing echoes of the "War on Terror" but also of more local conflicts in Kashmir, Assam, and Sri Lanka. The Ramayana has also been mined for highly topical stories – which can be variously classified as "fantasy," "science fiction," and "literary fiction" – in *Breaking the Bow* (2012), described by its editors as a collection of "speculative fiction inspired by the *Ramayana*" (Menon and Singh). These works demonstrate that the boom in IE fantasy fiction – especially in its mythological versions – does not necessarily entail the replacement of excellent literature and "genre" writing with "pulp."

The Success of Fantasy Fiction

One way to understand the more "pulpish" versions of IE fantasy fiction today would be to pay attention to the popularity of Shobha Dé, whose novels are often credited with the advent of "pulp fiction" by Indians in English. Dé's novels are not fantasy fiction; they ostensibly set out to chronicle the lives of the upper and higher middle classes in India, mostly in or around Bombay. But they share two elements with the pulpish main body of IE fantasy fiction: the use of comfortable clichés and the employment of a journalistic English. The driving forces behind the popularity of this type of writing are economic and cultural. On the economic side, as indicated by various studies, the consumption expenditure of the urban 20 percent of the population rose by a historically unprecedented 30 percent between 1997 and 2002, while that of more than 95 percent of the rural population – the majority of Indians – has actually fallen. On the cultural side, the big cities in India have witnessed the rise of a middle class that speaks English (often mixed with other Indian languages) as a matter of convenience rather than of cultural choice. Their English is not the same as the English of literary novels, even though writers such as Rushdie have borrowed from it, but it is also not the supposedly bumbling English of semi-urban character-types (who may be imagined along the exaggerated lines of

Peter Sellers' comic caricature in Blake Edwards' 1968 film *The Party*). These cultural and economic changes have created a distinctive type of middle-class Indian. Dé's characters and her readers – and, one can argue, Dé herself – belong to this type.

As in the case of Rushdie, Dé's English is a product of more than two centuries of English use by Indians and of the gradual indigenization of English in India, but it is also the result of the rise of a certain class of culturally and economically confident – even, at times, brash – Indians, who feel no need to apologize for their English or to educate themselves into literary English. To use a Bombay cinema image, Dé's English is the long-lost twin of Rushdie's English. Actually, one can even argue, if pressed, that Dé's use of the Hindustani interpolation is more convincing than Rushdie's. However, unlike Rushdie, Dé produces a largely flat reproduction of these kinds of Englishes. Rushdie's achievement is that he can take ingredients from these kinds of Englishes and shape/batter/twist them into a dozen different literary loafs. At its best, his language is capable of many registers of expression and emotion. That is something Dé, like most writers of pulp *qua* pulp, remains largely incapable of. A similar use of language can be noticed in some of the more popular versions of IE fantasy fiction, though not in the work of serious artists such as Basu or Arni.

Conclusion

Whatever its status or readability, IE fantasy fiction is an interesting marker of significant cultural and economic changes in India. It inevitably exists in fruitful tension with serious/literary Indian English fiction. For these reasons alone, it deserves a better fate than being summarily trashed. What is it that makes it "Indian"? One can argue that it is identified as "Indian" or as using "Indian English" on the basis of four factors: 1. authorship; 2. the location of the narrative; 3. the cultural affinities of its fantasy; and 4. the cultural/racial identities of the protagonist and characters. These, one can argue, are not foolproof generic markers, but they are not unimportant – as too strong an assertion of local identity could cost the writer much in terms of visibility and sales. It is obvious that the success of some genres – the Raj romance, for instance – requires an exotic, "different" location. But in other genres, especially the more popular ones, too much exoticism can either reduce readership[9] or warp access to the author.

It is this double bind that partly explains the relative invisibility of IE fantasy fiction in world markets in general – although this has been slightly dented in recent years by the best fantasy "genre" writers such as Basu. It is likely to be further dented from another angle, as the regional popularity and commercial success of fantasy fiction, such as the novels of Amish Tripathi, is bound to be noticed internationally. Whether this will translate into corresponding international success remains to be seen. One can argue that Indian audiences, no matter how Anglophone, still have enough cultural background to read fantasy fiction based on myths about Shiva or Rama without any trouble. This would not be the case with international audiences. Thus, would an international readership mean a further dilution of cultural specificities and context in the pulp branches of IE fantasy fiction? It is too early to say yet. What can be said is that IE fantasy fiction is here to stay, and it exists in both pulp and genre versions. In at least the latter versions, it has full claim to being considered equally with so-called literary fiction.

Notes

1 Banker's "Krishna Coriolis" series includes the following novels: *Slayer of Kamsa* (2010), *Dance of Govinda* (2011), *Flute of Vrindavan* (2011), *Lord of Mathura* (2012), *Rage of Jarasandha* (2012), and *Fortress of Dwarka* (2012).
2 See also Parrinder.
3 Unlike "Sultana's Dream," *Padmarag* was written in Bangla.
4 H. Bal, accessed August 22, 2013.
5 By this token, some "literary" novels can also be considered "pulp." We think this is a valid option.
6 The authoritative Central Institute of Indian Languages quotes 1991 census figures to the effect that 0.021 percent of all Indians list English as their mother tongue. This comes to about 2 million, but the actual number of Indians who have native-level fluency in English as a second language can only be guessed at. This number would, at a conservative estimate, be around 4 percent of the total population, as quoted by the British Library at http://www.bl.uk/learning/langlit/sounds/case-studies/minority-ethnic/asian/. English, despite being listed as a national language, is not one of the eighteen Indian languages included in the Eighth Schedule to the Constitution as spoken by more than five million people. See Mathews 132.
7 Moorcock's essay, "Epic Pooh," was originally published by the British Science Fiction Association in 1978.
8 Tidhar's recent novel, *Osama* (2012), is a good example of what fantasy fiction can do to comment, radically, on our times.

9 Ed Christian notes that postcolonial detective fiction "is marginalised (especially in terms of sales and income) when it is not available in English. Even if it is written and printed in English, it is not generally sold in the major markets unless published there, and it won't be published there unless editors think it will sell. It is marginalised [in the home regions] because detective fiction is often considered unworthy of a country's best writers" (5).

CHAPTER 23

The Indian Graphic Novel

Corey K. Creekmur

At first glance, the "Indian graphic novel" has only recently appeared as both a material artifact and a marketing category, and it may look like the confluence of two previously distinct narrative forms: Indian comics and the contemporary Indian novel – the latter especially in its highly visible postcolonial and globalized form, written in English.[1] As such a hybrid, the Indian graphic novel would appear to balance, on one hand, elite literary modes and, on the other, mass cultural images – a combination perhaps akin to the occasional mainstream film adaptation of a work of "serious" Indian fiction. But the Indian graphic novel may in fact be less a melding of now assimilated (if not "native") forms – Indian comics and the Indian novel – or even a "mature" development of the earlier Indian comic, than an appropriation of a format that arrived with – rather than acquired – legitimate artistic credentials.

At least since Sarnath Banerjee's *Corridor* was self-proclaimed on its cover "a graphic novel" in 2004, Indian writers, artists, publishers, critics, and readers have largely accepted the English-language term (rather than, say, the more common European designation "album") as a means to explicitly or implicitly affiliate Indian examples with their international counterparts. Recognized (although with frequent imprecision and lingering resistance) in the United States as a means to legitimate the marketing of previously dismissed "comics" or "funny books" in bookstores and to draw their ideal readers from culturally literate adults, the "graphic novel" implicitly carries an air of sophistication and, in its global reach, cosmopolitanism, if not pretension.[2] Deployed in India only within the first decade of the twenty-first century, the term tends to therefore associate Indian examples with an international network rather than affirming their (debatable) indigenous cultural roots in earlier Indian narrative forms. This is to say that the texts most often identified as Indian graphic novels seem *not* to derive from earlier Indian comics, except perhaps in an oppositional way, positioning earlier or even contemporaneous mainstream

Indian comics as counter-examples rather than precursors or peers. The graphic novel thus appears to have arrived in India fully formed, whereas its American counterpart at least partly emerged directly out of mainstream comics, even if it has also at times boldly asserted its independence from the mainstream. (In the United States, at least, mainstream publishers such as DC and Marvel, along with the publishing industry more generally, have embraced the term "graphic novel," rendering its once "alternative" stance more or less moot.)

Yet even as this international affiliation is being drawn, the most prominent Indian graphic novels, as well as more mainstream Indian comic books, are often emphatically "local" or "national" in their content and concerns, frequently taking on notably controversial or culturally specific subjects that may have little interest or familiarity for international audiences. Although almost entirely written in English, like many contemporary South Asian novels, they frequently employ words and idioms from Indian languages without translation, presuming that these will be accessible to their (mostly South Asian) readers. The persistent cultural specificity of Indian graphic novels perhaps explains why no individual work has yet enjoyed international "crossover" success, although the globalized market and (limited) international distribution, along with online publication in some cases, have allowed many recent Indian comics to reach the worldwide audience that seeks them out. The Indian graphic novel, in other words, often appears prominently and explicitly "Indian" in content and address, while its formal features frequently, simultaneously, place it in dialog with American, European, and East Asian (especially Japanese *manga*) comics traditions. Thus, while Indian comics may appear to draw upon "native," even ancient, South Asian visual and narrative traditions – such as the scrolls of *chitrakatha*, the narrative frescoes of Ajanta, or more modern media, including poster art and popular Indian cinema – the Indian graphic novel often asserts its status as a distinctly Indian contribution to what is simultaneously emphasized as a fully contemporary and increasingly international network of comics creators and consumers.

Comics in India before the Graphic Novel

As noted, the contemporary Indian graphic novel should be distinguished from the longer and earlier (and ongoing) history of Indian comics, which includes a significant history of editorial, newspaper, and magazine cartoons, such as (among many other examples) the wildly popular *Chacha Chaudhary* comics by Pran (Pran Kumar Sharma), published by Diamond

Comics, as well as the work of the legendary cartoonist and illustrator R. K. Laxman, whose "Common Man" has appeared in his "You Said It" comic strip in *The Times of India* for decades. The format of the Indian comic book – a magazine or periodical publication despite its misleading designation as a "book" – is most visible through the immensely popular series promoting India's historical and cultural heritage published under the banner *Amar Chitra Katha* ("Immortal Picture Stories"), founded by Anant Pai in 1967 and eventually selling tens of millions of copies of more than 400 titles published in twenty languages.[3] Earlier and then alongside *Amar Chitra Katha*'s rise to prominence, Indrajal Comics (1964–90) reprinted American newspaper strips such as Lee Falk's "The Phantom" and "Mandrake the Magician" before launching a successful series featuring Aabid Surti's Indian superhero Bahadur, while in 1986 Rajkumar Gupta created Raj Comics and began to publish (mostly) Hindi-language titles also featuring South Asian superheroes.[4] Other attempts to create "indigenous" Indian comics have followed, and while it has become increasingly common for these initially cheap and ephemeral publications to get collected and reprinted in more durable formats, it seems misleading to identify these volumes as "graphic novels."[5] For better or worse, the label seeks and often accords an aesthetic legitimacy that even the "wholesome," "educational," but formally conventional and industrially produced *Amar Chitra Katha* comics lack.

The Indian Graphic Novel Appears

In direct contrast to the creators of mainstream Indian comics, "the Indian graphic novelist," according to Suhaan Mehta, "has created an alternative space by accommodating voices that habitually fall outside the realm of Indian socio-politico-cultural discourses" (173).[6] This "alternative space" and these diverse "voices" are most often associated with the modern, culturally valued exercise of individual artistic expression. Although many "independent" graphic novels are created collaboratively (often by a separate writer and illustrator), these works stand in marked contrast to the typically anonymous work produced in generic "house styles" enforced by strong editorial control within the mainstream comics industry. And while many Indian graphic novels tell "dramatic" stories, they are often deeply invested in realistic representations of everyday life and the ways in which relatively ordinary people experience it, unlike the fantastic, extraordinary adventures found in superhero comics.

By most accounts, the graphic designer and illustrator Orijit Sen's *River of Stories* (1994), self-published with funding support from the environmentalist NGO Kalpavriksh, can be identified as India's first graphic novel.[7] The designation seems reasonable insofar as it was conceived as a complete, coherent, isolated work in comics form rather than as part of a larger series or a "chapter" in a serial publication; although the work derives from Sen's activism, it is explicitly the work of a single artist rather than a factory-like team. Only sixty-two pages in length and in black and white rather than the gaudy colors characteristic of most mainstream comics, *River of Stories* explicitly announces its ambition by treating a serious topic: the controversial construction of the Sardar Sarovar Dam on the Narmada river (identified by the local name Rewa in the book) in Gujarat and the displacement of *adivasis* (indigenous people) that was one of its social consequences. Rather than employing an "invisible" or generic style, *River of Stories* employs two distinct visual modes to tell two initially isolated stories featuring two narrators. The first is the traditional *gayan* (singer) Malgu, who tells the mythic tale of the creation of the river Narmada, rendered in richly textured pencil drawings. By contrast, starker, more conventional comic book panels trace the story of the journalist Vishnu, who is investigating the Narmada dam project and its impact on the local population. Eventually, the stories and styles flow together in a dramatic and formal confluence that echoes the pattern of the river itself. Sen's volume therefore resembles in general form and serious content the kinds of independent comics first identified and marketed as graphic novels in the United States, such as Will Eisner's *A Contract with God and Other Tenement Stories* (1978), which Eisner himself labeled a "graphic novel." In fact, both Sen's and Eisner's pioneering works suggest novellas or short stories rather than the typically longer novel: Eisner's text is actually a series of linked stories. (Again, the term "graphic novel" is notoriously imprecise.) In retrospect, Sen's apparently unprecedented book resembles the kind of nonfiction journalism in comics form associated with comics creators such as Joe Sacco, rather than the fictional narrative the term "novel" actually implies. (The original, limited publication of *River of Stories* went out of print almost immediately, but the work remains available via internet downloads. A reprint has been announced a number of times but has not yet appeared as of this writing.)

After a gap of almost a decade, subsequent Indian graphic novels would similarly present themselves as sophisticated, complex narratives treating difficult, often controversial subjects. They are also clearly marked as the products of individual artists and a medium of personal expression, thereby claiming a status that has not been assumed for mass-produced comics. In many cases, their contemporary narratives and realistic characters suggest that they are semi-autobiographical, aligning themselves with the now-common publication of memoirs and autobiographies in comics form in other countries: the protagonists of many Indian graphic novels are young, urban adults, much like their creators and presumably their primary audiences. Only a superficial glance at contemporary Indian graphic novels would mistake them for children's reading material or even comics in line with the culturally respectable but artistically formulaic *Amar Chitra Katha*. Their frequent reliance on black and white images – while often a necessary cost-saving measure (and hardly a defining feature, as the following examples will demonstrate) – also exhibits a marked contrast with the bright colors that characterize mainstream comic books in India and elsewhere.

Following Sen, the first Indian graphic novel as such to receive widespread attention was Sarnath Banerjee's slice-of-urban-life narrative *Corridor* (2004). This is in part because *Corridor* was published by Penguin Books India, which could provide the level of advertising and distribution impossible for Sen's in effect self-published work. Like *River of Stories*, however, *Corridor* presents itself as a work to be taken seriously by adults: its complex narrative moves among a half-dozen complex characters and between Delhi and Calcutta, and the work is also visually inventive, shifting between stark black and white and color sections, the latter often incorporating elements of collage that function as correlatives for the fragmented existence of its realistic characters (see Figure 2).

Banerjee's subsequent graphic novels – *The Barn Owl's Wondrous Capers* (published by Penguin in 2007; the odd title derives from Kaliprasanna Sinha's 1862/1864 Bengali novel *Satik Hutom Pyanchar Naksha*) and *The Harappa Files* (published by HarperCollins in 2011) – have established him as a key figure in contemporary Indian comics. Both are, again, thematically ambitious and formally complex, relying on willfully clashing rather than easily blended stylistic devices (including, as in *Corridor*, mixed-media collage and selective color). *The Barn Owl's Wondrous Capers* travels boldly through time (ranging across centuries) to reinvent the legend of the Wandering Jew, in this case tracing the search for an elusive book – a scandalous account of the British administrators of colonial Calcutta – that self-reflexively bears the same title as Banerjee's work. *The Harappa Files* is even more fragmentary as a narrative and visual artifact,

Figure 2. One of *Corridor*'s black-and-white images.
© Penguin India

summarizing the work of a mythic, secret committee charged with conducting a survey of "current ethnography and urban mythologies of a country on the brink of great hormonal changes" (*Harappa* 11). Less character-driven than Banerjee's previous works, *The Harappa Files* taps into the sometimes buried "comic" abilities of "comics," although in the form of often bitter and mordant satire.

Based upon his success, Banerjee and a partner established the short-lived Phantomville Publishing in order to produce additional graphic novels by other Indian creators: the company released *The Believers* (2006), written by Abdul Sultan PP and drawn by Partha Sengupta, followed by *Kashmir Pending* (2007), by Naseer Ahmed and illustrated by Saurabh Singh. *The Believers*, set in Kerala, depicts two brothers in a story that centers on religious extremism; *Kashmir Pending*, set in Srinagar, tackles the painful issue of militancy in Kashmir. Written by professional journalists and often relying on photographs as visual references for their images, such works confront controversial topics with a documentary style that many traditional readers might feel is improper in a form still commonly associated with children and humor. Yet at the same time that it relies on factual material, *Kashmir Pending* employs bold, stylized images with flat, primary colors that often resemble the powerful graphic style of propaganda posters. In contrast, the more realistic images in *The Believers* consistently feature delicate brown and yellow tints that visually unify a work that is otherwise a narrative exploration of the terrible impact of family and community disunity. Despite their "regional" specificity, therefore, such works clearly align the Indian graphic novel with works from around the world that have also demonstrated the ability of comics to effectively engage with complex events and vexed political issues.

In a somewhat similar vein, Vishwajyoti Ghosh's *Delhi Calm*, published by HarperCollins India in 2010, explores another difficult topic, albeit a historical one: the Emergency imposed by Prime Minister Indira Gandhi in the mid-1970s, as experienced though the distinct perspectives of three young men living in the nation's capital. Whereas works like *The Believers* and *Kashmir Pending* draw upon journalistic models, *Delhi Calm* presents itself as an explicitly historical investigation in its visual style as well as its narrative: its newly drawn images suggest earlier archival origins by being washed in a sepia tint, and Ghosh often effectively imitates the look of faded newspapers in a story that emphasizes the psychic impact of the historical event of the Emergency on the personal ties between his three main characters. At the same time, Ghosh employs a very unrealistic, "cartoonish" style in drawing his characters. This exaggeration extends to his rendering of actual historical figures, including Indira Gandhi, her sons Rajiv and Sanjay, and opposition activist Jayaprakash Narayan through thinly veiled fictional caricatures, a device that creates a curious tension between playful exaggeration and careful historical reclamation throughout the work.

Also noteworthy is Amruta Patil's *Kari*, published by HarperCollins India in 2008. Most likely India's first lesbian-themed graphic novel, *Kari* effectively balances the vivid first-person prose narrative of a young woman's survival of a break-up (with an American named Susan Lush) with panels and dialog balloons that clash as often as they mesh with the handwritten text they accompany. Patil also alternates between muted black and white and carefully selected color images in a work that increasingly illuminates the protagonist Kari's intimate relationship with Mumbai, where the story is set. Like the graphic novels previously mentioned that are implicitly affiliated with historical and political comics from America, Europe, and East Asia, Patil's *Kari* links the Indian graphic novel to the significant, ongoing exploration of gay, lesbian, or queer identities in comics within those traditions as well.

In addition to works centered on specific social concerns, identity politics, or historical events, the Indian graphic novel has allowed for more fantastic or experimental work that often verges on non-narrative. One example of this tendency is the cryptic dystopian work *Moonward: Stories from Halahala* by Appupen (George Mathen, also known for his murals) and published by the Chennai-based Blaft in 2009, as well as an anthology by the same writer of five wordless stories set in the same bizarre world: *Legends of Halahala*, published by HarperCollins India in 2013. Possibly inspired by some of the more unconventional and self-consciously grotesque strains of Japanese *manga*, the first of these is entirely in black and white with grey shades, whereas the later work incorporates muted but effective color. Populated by strange creatures that are simultaneously cute and horrific, Appupen's comics offer Indian readers a fantasy world that is often as disturbing as the society depicted in more realistic and socially engaged graphic novels.

In a relatively brief period, and through what may only be a handful of examples to date, the Indian graphic novel has nevertheless emerged and developed as a significant form for social, political, and historical inquiry, as well as a medium allowing for intimate and even experimental narratives. Like its more numerous Western counterparts, it has also relied upon a remarkably diverse range of visual styles and compositional formats, extending from rough pencil drawings to slick computer-created comics, with a notable incorporation of collage techniques.

Recent and Future Developments of the Indian Graphic Novel

By all appearances, and despite the varied fortunes of Indian comics publishers, the future looks promising for bold, innovative, and original graphic novels to continue to be created in India. On the more commercial side, the noir-inflected crime saga *Mumbai Confidential*, by writer Saurava Mohapatra and artist Vivek Shinde, may represent one version of that future, insofar as its creators are Indian-born but based in the United States: the work originally appeared in digital form, serialized on the website Comixology, and was published as a book by Los Angeles-based Archaia in 2013. Mohapatra had previously worked on the Shakti line of comics developed by filmmaker Shekhar Kapur for the short-lived, London-based Virgin Comics (2006–8) which published a number of series with Indian characters and settings, including *Devi* and *The Sadhu*. (Another line of Virgin comics was created by the Indian-American "New Age guru" Deepak Chopra.) While such examples have met with only limited success, as products of the Indian diaspora they represent what is likely to be a continuing attempt to infuse comics designed for international audiences with "exotic" Indian characters and content while adhering to mainstream generic conventions.

Another future of comics and graphic novels in India might be glimpsed in the range of comics-related activities they increasingly support. For instance, comics conventions now regularly take place in larger Indian cites, including Delhi, Hyderabad, and Bangalore, not only highlighting "local" comics activity and artists but establishing productive international connections; notably, in 2012, the legendary underground cartoonist Robert Crumb and influential independent comics publisher Gary Groth visited Comic Con India in New Delhi for a lively interview that was recorded and posted online. It seems likely that Indian comics festivals and conventions will continue to expand as events with both national and international appeal. As elsewhere, Indian comics have also established a significant presence across contemporary social media: among other ongoing projects, The Hyderabad Graphic Novel Project, founded by journalist Jai Undurti in collaboration with artist Harsho Mohan Chattoraj, seeks to support the creation of comics that capture the history and memories of the city of Hyderabad. As part of this initiative, the Project has released *The Hyderabad Graphic Novel* both online and in a print edition. Another organization, World Comics India, founded by cartoonist Sharad Sharma in the 1990s, is devoted to supporting grassroots comics creation through collaborative workshops (termed

"Comics Power!") for non-professionals that are held in rural India as well as in other countries.[8] World Comics India has also created and published black-and-white collections of comics on social issues by activists – works described on their covers as "development stories by comics journalists," including *Whose Development?* (2009) and *Parallel Lines* (2010). Also made available online, such work effectively integrates grassroots activism, collaborative artistic production, and communication via new media.

Educational graphic novels have also been produced by Delhi's Sarai Media Lab, including Bhagwati Prasad and Amitabh Kumar's *Tinker. Soldier. Tap* (2009), illustrating the lived experience of media transformations (such as the arrival of the VCR in India in the 1980s) and Bhagwati Prasad's more impressionistic *The Water Cookbook* (2011), on peri-urban sustainability and daily life in Ghaziabad. Earlier, the Sarai Media Lab also published *Raj Comics for the Hard Headed* (2008), Amitabh Kumar's witty graphic novel examining the history and significance – especially for urban Indians – of a mainstream comics publisher, as well as a collaborative work on open source software, *FLOSS is Not Just Good for Teeth* (2006). Such work extends the artistic claims of the graphic novel into the realms of social engagement and pedagogy, further justifying the reliance of a new generation of Indian creators as well as activists on comics, a heretofore popular but frequently undervalued form of visual and verbal communication. As elsewhere, but in a remarkably brief period, the graphic novel in India has demonstrated its ability to compete with more established literary as well as popular narrative forms while establishing and exploring its often unique aesthetic capabilities.

Notes

1 On the "politics" of English in Indian writing, see (in addition to this volume) Sadana, "Writing."
2 Among the many discussions of the term "graphic novel" within the emerging field of "comics studies," see Hatfield.
3 Although I am setting them aside to focus on graphic novels, I do not wish to dismiss or disparage *Amar Chitra Katha*, which has recently been the focus of significant scholarly attention (see N. Chandra; McLain; and Sreenivas). Earlier critical discussions of *Amar Chitra Katha* include Hawley; and Pritchett.
4 For a useful survey of these mainstream Indian comics companies, see A. Rao.
5 This would include the international attention-grabbing *Spider-Man: India*, by Sharad Devarajan, Suresh Seetharaman, and Jeevan J. Kang, which relocated the famous Marvel Comics character to Mumbai and identified him as Pavitr Prabhakar (rather than the original Peter Parker). Published in India in 2004 by Gotham Entertainment Group, the series was released the

following year in the United States by Marvel as a limited series and later a trade paperback.

6 This chapter is indebted to Mehta's pioneering essay on the Indian graphic novel, which it seeks to extend and update.

7 I am following Mehta's lead in locating Sen's work at the start of the recent tradition of Indian graphic novels.

8 See www.worldcomicsindia.com.

CHAPTER 24

"Coming to a Multiplex Near You": Indian Fiction in English and New Bollywood Cinema

Sangita Gopal

The story of the adaptation of Chetan Bhagat's best-selling 2004 debut, *Five Point Someone*, into the blockbuster Bollywood film *3 Idiots* (dir. Rajkumar Hirani, 2009) is an interesting one. While most discussions around an adaptation stress how different the film is from the book, Bhagat and his fans stress how similar the two properties¹ are, insisting that perhaps the author should have received greater prominence in the film's credits and promotion than he did. Bollywood has a long history of borrowing (to be generous) plots and ideas from other (especially Hollywood) films, but the case of *3 Idiots* is not one of intellectual property, as both parties agree that no legal injury has been done to the author. The film's producer, Vidhu Vinod Chopra, director, Rajkumar Hirani, and star, Aamir Khan, have averred that although Bhagat had been given his due, he was generating controversy in order to cash in on the film's success. Bhagat and his supporters agree in a sense by suggesting that his claims are moral rather than legal. Given how closely the film resembles the novel – down to such details as the red Maruti 800 car featured in several scenes – Bhagat's supporters stress that the author of the bestselling novel on which *3 Idiots* is based should have received a little more airtime in the media blitz that preceded and followed the release of the film. They repeatedly contrast Bhagat's shoddy treatment at the hands of a Bollywood producer to that of Vikas Swarup, on whose novel *Q&A* (2005) the international hit *Slumdog Millionaire* (dir. Danny Boyle, 2008) was based. While Swarup was front and center at all events celebrating the film's phenomenal success, including at the Oscars, Bhagat's name appeared just once in the credits for *3 Idiots* and that too at a very low billing!

For an English-language novelist such as Bhagat to desire a closer association with a blockbuster Hindi film such as *3 Idiots* is indeed noteworthy if we consider the cultural dynamics that have historically kept the Indian novel in English at a great remove from the Hindi popular cinema. Until Salman Rushdie's nostalgic (some might allege orientalist) and entirely postmodern evocation of the excesses of Bollywood and its "masala" movies in his many novels, which in itself activated a minor trend of such works in Indo-Anglian fiction, English novels and Hindi films had belonged to two entirely different social realms in postcolonial India; one might even say that a rejection of the demotic pleasures of Hindi popular cinema was a measure of one's (Anglicized) modernity in the Nehruvian era. The Mumbai film – in turn – lampooned Western and Westernized sensibilities as elite and inauthentic and had little truck with the rarefied world of the Indian novel in English. In short, there was little intersection between the social and imaginary milieux of the English novel and its (ideal) readership on one hand and the so-called masses to whom the Hindi film was supposedly addressed on the other.

How then do we account for the recent flurry of Indian novels in English that are being adapted to Bollywood screens? Four of Chetan Bhagat's five novels have already been made into mainstream Hindi films, while the remaining one – *Revolution 2020* – is in production.[2] With one exception (*Hello*), they have all proved blockbusters at the box office, including most recently *2 States*, which garnered over 100 crore rupees, a significant achievement for a romantic comedy starring two relative newcomers and set in the world of the Indian Institute of Management, Ahmedabad. Several other writers belonging to the "Lo-Cal Literati"[3] – writers who attempt to reach the masses without attempting to win the Booker prize or secure fancy advances – have films in the works. They include genre writers such as Mukul Deva and Amish Tripathi as well as bestselling chick-lit author Anuja Chauhan, whose novels *The Zoya Factor* (2008) and *Those Pricey Thakur Girls* (2013) have been acquired by prestigious production houses, Red Chillies Entertainment and Anil Kapoor Communications, respectively. Even a niche writer like Anirban Bose has licensed film rights for his novel *Bombay Rains, Bombay Girls* (2008) to Pooja Bedi of Owl Village Films, while Princeton-based historian Gyan Prakash's *Mumbai Fables* (2011) – a novelistic account of the city's rise from colonial times to the present with a special focus on the 1950s – is being turned by Anurag Kashyap into a neo-noir set in the 1950s entitled *Bombay Velvet*.

While this rush to acquire properties is no doubt fueled in part by the box office success of Bhagat-based films such as *3 Idiots* and *Kai Po Che!*, I will argue that we need to view this unprecedented exchange between the worlds of English fiction and Hindi cinema as a transmedia – or multiplatform – phenomenon, in which a narrative is constructed and dispersed differentially across multiple platforms, in this case print and celluloid. Here, the commercial fiction in English and what I have called New Bollywood cinema are engaged in the making of one (fictional) world inhabited by the denizens of Young India.[4] Whether appearing in a newsstand or a multiplex near you, these novels and the movies to which they give rise need to be thought of as constructing a world that is part-real and part-virtual, insofar as its potential will be realized in the future. These stories simultaneously represent and are addressed to "Young India" and have a decidedly "domestic" – one might even say "nationalist" – orientation. Moreover, they imagine "Young India" as undoing the distinctions of class, caste, and region that have been entangled with linguistic hierarchies in India.[5] In the process, English is claimed not only as an Indian language but as one that is potentially accessible to the masses. A free and fluid interchange between English and other Indian languages (preeminently Hindi) emerges as characteristic of "Young India." This diglossic mode – once the province of elites – is now identified by both English fiction and New Bollywood cinema as constitutive of Indian identity.[6] New writers are very aware of the significance of this change. Thus, Chetan Bhagat says, "Most publishers here are very fake. The only writers they admire are those who are popular in the UK. It's like saying only Hindi films that succeed in UK are good. But books that work in UK are tailor-made for them, not for us" (quoted in Reddy). Similarly, Amish Tripathi sums up the Indian Anglophone novel in these blunt terms: "Before us, there were mostly stories of the British Raj or NRIs. Frankly, who cares? When I read about an NRI's struggle, I want to go: Dude, it's a foreign country. Get used to it, or come back" (quoted in Reddy). This desire to reach an "Indian" reader is precisely what aligns the "world" of this new Indian fiction with New Bollywood cinema that is also (notwithstanding Bollywood's global presence) focused on growing the domestic multiplex market. While the Indian popular cinema has always distinguished itself as a mass medium, it is the new Indian fiction's discovery of the masses as potential readers that creates this hitherto unprecedented synergy between the novel and cinema.

In what follows, I will suggest that the relative absence of adaptations from literature to Hindi popular cinema might be attributed to an absence of a shared world – both sociologically and aesthetically speaking. I will then locate this current wave of adaptations in the context of the transmedia creation of such a world – again, sociologically but perhaps even more significantly as an imagined space that might be shorthanded "Young India."[7] I will then focus on three novels by Chetan Bhagat and their film versions to assess the degree to which each might be viewed as building on this world.

Worlds Apart

The Mumbai-based Hindi popular film has very occasionally turned to literary sources for inspiration – although, in those instances, almost always to sources written in the vernacular. Works by Bengali, Hindi, and Urdu writers such as Saratchandra Chatterjee, Munshi Premchand, Rajendra Yadav, Manohar Shyam Joshi, Mohan Rakesh, Amrita Pritam, and Ismat Chughtai have been made into films, but the "literary film" in Hindi remains the exception rather than the rule.[8] When filmmakers have turned to literature, they have done so because a cinematic adaptation of the literary work already exists (as in the case of the serial adaptations of Saratchandra Chatterjee's *Devdas*) or in order to self-consciously break the mold of the formulaic Hindi film by drawing on the novelty and cultural capital offered by a literary work. Good examples would be Mohan Rakesh, on whose eponymous short story *Uski Roti* Mani Kaul's 1971 landmark Indian "new wave" film was based; and Ismat Chughtai, whose unpublished short story was turned into M. S. Sathyu's iconic film on the partition of India and Pakistan, *Garam Hawa* (1973).

While accounting for this lack of exchange between literature and the commercial Hindi cinema is beyond the scope of this chapter, looking at two instances of how literary properties have fared onscreen might help illuminate the cultural politics of this relation. The history of the *Filmfare* awards for Best Story (given to the author of the story on which a film has been based in any given year) shows that Gulshan Nanda has been nominated for more awards than any other author. We can credit him with the story and screenplay behind many of the major hits of the 1960s and early 1970s, including *Kaajal* (1965), *Kati Patang* (1970), *Sharmeelee* (1971), and *Daag* (1973) – to name just a few. Nanda was part of a group of bestselling writers of Hindi pulp fiction that emerged during the 1960s and 1970s – first in the pages of magazines such as *Manohar Kahaniya*, *Maya*, *Apradh Katha*, and *Satyakatha* and then in the publishing industry that mushroomed in Meerut and around the Daryaganj area of New Delhi. While Allahabad was the epicenter of serious Hindi literature, these pulp paperbacks that ranged in genre from crime to romance to family dramas were targeted to the burgeoning middle classes moving from villages into the smaller towns in northern India in the post-independence period.[9] Priced between Rs. 20 and Rs. 40, they easily sold upward of 500,000 copies, and the most popular titles went into the millions. Among the best-known authors of Hindi pulp were Ved Prakash Sharma, Pyarelal Aawara, Rajhans, Akram Allahabadi, Sarla Ranu, Surendra Mohan Pathak, and, of course, Gulshan Nanda. Nanda's success as a screenwriter for Hindi film was clearly allied to his ability to write mass fiction; even so, he frequently adapted his own (and others') stories for the movies, including *I Married a Dead Man* (turned into *Kati Patang*) and Thomas Hardy's *The Mayor of Casterbridge* (which was the basis for *Daag*). Nanda's modus operandi was quite unusual: in the course of adapting a novel such as Hardy's to a Hindi film, he first turned it into a story to appear serialized in a magazine, and its success in this format would lead subsequently to a scenario (Pande). Nanda's successful dual career as novelist and scenarist in some sense anticipates that of Chetan Bhagat and other contemporary novelists of commercial English fiction whose work is being converted into Bollywood movies now. In each case, mass-market paperbacks rather than "good" literature serve as the basis for desirable film properties.

In the rare instances that a producer in the film industry acquired more highbrow literary titles, these had to be thoroughly worked over to fit the generic idiom and narrative formulas of popular film. Consider for instance the curious case of Keshab Kumar Mishra's novel *Kohbar ki Shart*, first published in 1965 (Chaudhury). It is hard to imagine that this delicately-crafted, subtly-realized novel about the negotiations of desire and responsibility within the framework of an extended family in rural Uttar Pradesh became the basis for Bollywood's first glittering global hit, *Hum Aapke Hain Koun!* (*HAHK*, dir. Sooraj Barjatya, 1994). Rajshri Productions first acquired this novel in the 1970s and turned it into a film called *Nadiya Ke Paar* in 1982. This film retained the novel's rural milieu but changed the ending to a happy one in which the hero, Chandan's older brother Omkar, on learning about Chandan's prior relationship with his fiancé, Gunja, steps aside so the couple can be united. When *Nadiya Ke Paar* was remade in 1994 as *Hum Aapke Hain Koun!*, Mishra's novel became almost unrecognizable as its source; even the realistic setting of *Nadiya Ke Paar* was replaced with the majestic palaces and beautiful landscapes of *HAHK*, against which the hero and heroine enact numerous lavish song-dance routines. When a conflict arises, it is resolved with such ease that it hard to see any link between the film's facile take on social relations and Mishra's original text, with its trenchant critique of feudal family mores. Further, as the author of a recent article on Mishra points out, Bollywood played fast and loose not only with Mishra's narrative but even in commercial terms, as the publisher Rajkamal failed to cash in on the property.

While Mishra was consigned to anonymity by the film industry, Nanda succeeded by fully accepting and assimilating its aesthetic norms. He used novels as raw material from which he generated screenplays that would accord with the prevailing formulas of the film industries. Thus, his screenplays are not adaptations proper, since they do not really involve a transfer from one medium to another, but are complete do-overs, in which characters and plot points from novels are reconstituted for the cinema. Here, Nanda's successful command of a mass-market literary idiom probably helped him write for the screen. The decline of the market for mass paperbacks and the rise of the scriptwriter in the form of the duo Salim-Javed in the 1970s[10] further weakened the transactions between literature and cinema in the next three decades.

If film adaptations from Hindi and vernacular literatures were sporadic and disorganized at best, film versions of English novels, especially those written by Indian writers, were almost unheard of. The works of Indo-Anglian writer Ruskin Bond have been adapted from time to time – Shyam Benegal's *Junoon* (1978) was based on Bond's *A Flight of Pigeons*, while more recently Vishal Bharadwaj's *Saat Khoon Maaf* (2011) was inspired by *Susanna's Seven Husbands* – but other than a few random experiments here and there, the most memorable adaptation remains the bilingual version of R. K. Narayan's novel *The Guide* (1958).[11] It is now almost a cliché that there was such a mismatch between Narayan and Navketan Films over this adaptation that Narayan went on to write an essay about his experiences, entitled "Misguided Guide," as well as an article in *Life* magazine detailing his unhappiness with the productions (especially the English one, which was scripted by Pearl S. Buck and directed by Ted Danielski). Early in the process, Narayan realized that neither the Hindi nor the English version of the movie was going to pay much attention to the book or its author. If Narayan's fictional world – the thickly-described provincial town that is the scene of the unfolding of Raju and Rosie's entanglements – is one of the principal accomplishments of the novel, neither Danielski nor Vijay Anand, the Hindi version's director, felt any attachment whatsoever to this setting when making their film adaptations. Thus, the American told Narayan, "We are out to expand the notion of Malgudi. Malgudi will be where we place it, in Kashmir, Rajasthan, Bombay, Delhi, even Ceylon" (Narayan, *Writer's* 211) – while Dev Anand recounted, "We, of course, did not shoot the movie in the villages near Mysore since R. K. Narayan had told me that the villages depicted by him were fictitious" (D. Anand 206). This tussle over Malgudi concretely illustrates not only the different worlds that the realist novel and the commercial cinema inhabit but also how the concept of the world itself is differently evaluated by each medium. While Narayan may have bitterly said of the film *Guide*, "It is a bastard offspring from my book, has much less to do with me and far more to do with Dev,"[12] the fact remains that *Guide* is a canonical Hindi film, beloved and remembered for its magical soundtrack and dazzling performances.

Thus while even in its early years, Hollywood has always turned to literary properties as a significant source of its narrative material, this has never been a widespread industrial practice in Bollywood cinema. While there are some celebrated films based on literary sources, the absence of a large-scale public that both reads literature and goes to the movies for leisure has meant that the exchange between these two worlds has been quite limited. Neither the sociology nor the imaginary of these two publics (literature and mass cinema) have intersected in any significant sense. Rather, films have sought inspiration in other sources, including epics, myths, current events, and other cinemas, including Hollywood. Further, if we look from the vantage of production culture, until recently, the mainstream Bollywood film has had a pretty stable multigeneric identity – first called the "social" and then, from the 1970s onward, "masala" – whereby a story is merely one component of a wide array of attractions that include stars, thrills, songs, dances, dialogues, and so on. The assembled nature of the Bollywood film with its own logic of what counts as new and entertaining has meant that narrative novelty is not usually or solely anchored in the story, and most films, at the level of plot, do reprise a few popular formulas. Thus, almost all calls for reform of this product usually start by demanding new stories. However, this call has typically been issued to scriptwriters and not novelists, since the novel, notwithstanding Hindi pulp fiction, has remained an elite and literate form.

World-Building

A reviewer of Chetan Bhagat's first novel called *Five Point Someone* "a book version of *Dil Chahta Hai*" – referring to Farhan Akhtar's landmark film from 2001 about the joys and sorrows, friendships and loves of three young men negotiating adulthood in a rapidly-globalizing India. It was indeed an astute comment, as Akhtar's film and Bhagat's novel are both foundational cultural texts of "Young India."[13] They feature characters who are somewhat real and somewhat idealized, operating in milieux that exist but remain aspirational for most readers/viewers. As such, both works reflect what has been called an "enterprise culture," in which the young are exhorted to pursue their desires for a better future no matter what their status in the present (Gooptu 14).[14] Thus, Akhtar's film carries a self-explanatory title that translates as "What the heart desires," while Bhagat's book shows that even "Five Pointers" (i.e., students with very low GPAs) can become "someone" in the new India where human worth inheres in enterprise and initiative and not mere academic accomplishment. Both Bhagat and Akhtar are actively engaged in building a *world* peopled by the young (and the young at heart) whose spatio-temporal coordinates can accommodate this free play of enterprise and aspiration. Chetan Bhagat puts it in these terms: "From Amravati ... to Gorakhpur to Kochi and Guwahati to Jaipur[,] I learnt more about India and its youth. I realized that even though the regional cultures were different, all Indians wanted the same thing – a better life in a good society" (*What* xviii). The world that Bhagat's novels and their successful New Bollywood adaptations build is structured by this underlying logic – to imagine a *different* future where personal betterment and social progress are inextricably linked. Thus, in an interview Bhagat sums up what "Young India" wants in these succinct terms: "*Meri Naukri, Meri Chokri* [my job, my girl] ... [and] the social causes must be linked to this ambition."[15] If the "old India" demanded that personal desires be sacrificed to the needs of family, community, and nation, the new generation resets this equation such that personal fulfillment and social good are now aligned. Both *Dil Chahta Hai* and *Five Point Someone* are "coming of age stories" that also crucially recalibrate the self-society antinomy and tradition-modernity dialectic that have thus far structured the worlds of Hindi popular cinema and Indian English fiction. If the former, inevitably and perhaps conventionally, settled in favor of a resolution of these contradictions, the latter refused such reconciliation to reveal how individuality is (tragically) foreclosed by a society that is postcolonial but not yet fully modern. However, in New Bollywood cinema as well as in the English commercial fiction of the past two decades, a new calculus begins to emerge between the individual and the family/community/nation that identifies – as we see in the Bhagat quote – happiness for *all* as inhering in upward mobility and self-actualization. This linking of economic liberalization (markets) to personal liberty (subject) and national progress is the "lesson" that Bhagat's novels and their film versions teach over and over again. The protagonists end up with the good life only after they learn to stand up for themselves in the face of filial encumbrances and social injustices. Though each work takes up a particular social problem in contemporary India – alienated labor in the service economy, religious intolerance, orthodoxy and higher education, parochialism, rogue capitalism – the solution seems to lie in the individual taking charge of his or her life by recognizing and then gradually reforming the structures that hinder and oppress his or her economic and romantic futures. The novels and films are youth-focused in two senses: they are concerned with problems that particularly affect youth, and they provide solutions that are conducive to a better future for the youth. We might call it world-building through problem-solving.

Further, this new fiction in English represented (and in some senses founded) by Bhagat's novels not only shares a worldview with its film adaptations but also imagines a very similar audience – the mass of young Indians who are going to comprise and create the nation's future. While Hindi popular cinema has historically imagined its audience to be the "masses," the last two decades – as several recent studies have shown – have witnessed quite a radical shift in this conception of the audience. The rise and spread of the multiplex, from major metropolitan centers to provincial cities and then small towns, has entailed a recalibration of the audience of mainstream Hindi cinema as largely young, middle-class and urban. Though this represents a decline in numbers in real terms, higher ticket prices and ancillary revenue streams have put in place a fiscal model that can produce robust returns without actually growing the movie-going population.[16] While the audience imagined by New Bollywood cinema is actually quite attenuated when compared to the "masses" addressed by popular Hindi cinema in the past, from the vantage of Indian fiction in English this population represents a vast expansion of the market.

When books are priced like movie tickets (between \$2 and \$4), it makes sense to imagine viewers/readers as one unified market. Thus Chetan Bhagat notes: "Many writers upgrade, get agents in London. I want to reach masses. The day I reach Indian farmers I'll consider myself a true Indian writer."[17] Rashmi Bansal, author of the aptly-titled *Stay Hungry Stay Foolish*, similarly states, "I'm on top of the bestseller list, same as Amitav Ghosh. But nobody is going to interview me as they do him. It doesn't bother me as long as I'm reaching real people" (Reddy). Almost without exception, the authors of the commercial fiction in English embrace this populist rhetoric (in real terms, a print run between 100,000 and 200,000 is considered a bestseller) and tie their thematic and aesthetic choices to the desires of the authentic urban (if non-metropolitan) Indian reader. Publisher Jayanta Bose of Srishti Books – an imprint that has churned out several bestsellers – thus describes Bhagat's winning formula: "Love sells, ... especially in small towns. And when you combine love with the anxiety that goes with growing up in the New India – coping with board exams, parental aspirations, girlfriend troubles, job stress – it sells lakhs of copies" (quoted in Reddy). Clearly, Bhagat's assertion that this generation is all about "Meri naukri, meri chokhri" is borne out.

Indeed Saugata Mukherjee, head of HarperCollins India, says: "In the last year or so, if I have seen cinematic possibility in a book I have sent copies to filmmakers and followed it up aggressively.... That's because film rights are gradually becoming all about some serious money" (N. Joshi). Anuja Chauhan, author of *The Zoya Factor*, concurs that "You can't live on royalties but you can live off a good film deal" (quoted in N. Joshi). But the commercial imperative alone cannot fully account for why many professionals in the publishing world now approach commercial fiction as "screenplays in novel form." The novel form is seen as the first stage in the evolution and dissemination of the world that the writer conjures. Thus, Ashvini Vardi of Grazing Goat Pictures sees books as a "readymade platform" for subsequent celluloid conversion while Ashwin Sanghi, author of *Chanakya's Chant* (2010), sees novels as story banks for Bollywood in light of the decline of the star system. If a novel is but a precursor to its cinematic iteration, what is a film in relation to the novel whose content it channels in visual form? For Bhagat, "the film is a chance to improve on the story as now the book is out and we have feedback. For *Kai Po Che*, we changed whatever didn't work so well in the book."[18] For producer Manish Goswamy, a film is a simplification of content that has been worked out in greater detail in written form (Dasgupta and Sengupta). Others view books as "a great starting point for filmmaking" not because of the story they tell but for their sales figures and reader data, which can be used to "graph engagement level" and assess "what kind of audience will watch your film and shape marketing strategy as well."[19] At Disney India, the creative team searches for materials at the manuscript stage and actively collaborates with authors to create scriptworthy novels – leading to their 100 percent success rate in adapting print properties to screen (namely *Kai Po Che!* and *2 States*). Mukul Deva, whose military thriller *Lashkar* (2008) is currently in production by Planman Pictures, was careful to hand over the rights to the most appropriate director, not because he feared that his book might get devalued in its adaptation to screen but because he wanted to make sure that this page-turner that was always-already visualized as a film found someone who understood how inherently cinematic this property was.[20] Authors and filmmakers alike see the migration of content from print to screen and the inevitable transformations this process entails as a broadening of the audience base – a way to reach a greater number of people. It is as though the book's readers are a focus group whose response can then be used to shape a wider release of the material via film.

It is useful to think about fiction and film alike as engaged in world-building, whereby "Young India" is a space analogous to that of Dickens's London, Hardy's Wessex, or, for that matter, R. K. Narayan's Malgudi. For example, the opening of *One Night @ the Call Center* precisely calls for this kind of demographic extension in order for Bhagat to be thought of as a truly pan-Indian writer. In the framing device that structures the novel, Bhagat the writer meets one of the denizens of "Young India," who chides him for restricting himself in his first novel, *Five Point Someone*, to the elite world of the IITs. He thus reckons that his authorial task henceforth is to elaborate on "Young India" as a totality. Thus, the job of these novels is to connect the different chronotopes that are inhabited by young India – IITs, call centers, private universities – in a manner that follows a certain logic so that the insertion of new stories makes sense within this world and its underlying rationalities. If we regard the novels and their film versions together, what we witness is the creation of an ecology that is evolving but is underwritten nonetheless by certain imperatives: self-actualization, fiscal well-being, romantic love, friendship, nuclear families, social reform. While such acts of world-building are much more easily comprehended with regard to fantastical works such as Amish Tripathi's Vayuputra novels or even Mukul Deva's military thrillers, I would suggest that Chetan Bhagat is a trailblazer in this regard. He creates a fictional world and realizes its commercial potential for seriality and transmedia storytelling.

For narrative theorist Marie Laure Ryan, a transmedia text in any media is apprehended as a window on something that exists outside of language and signs and extends in time and space well beyond the window frame. While her insight works most obviously when we refer to genres such as fantasy or science fiction, in which indeed a "world" needs to be created and mapped in order for the story to work and in which, once such a world is in place, it can be requisitioned serially for subsequent works across different media wherein each iteration is merely another exploration of a part of this world. However, such a perspective is also applicable to neo-realist cinema, for example, where each film is a window onto a reality that the celluloid frame refers us to. But if in the latter case, the reality of the world we live in supports and authorizes its putative onscreen capture, in the scenario described by Ryan, textuality melts away, opening into a world that now seems to exist for real (Ryan). However, in the case of a writer such as Bhagat, we seem to be engaged in building a world that is not fantastical but rather as yet virtual. It is concerned with the quotidian goals of getting an education, finding a job, discovering true love, realizing one's potential, and creating a social infrastructure that enables us to be who we want to be. These goals, supposedly shared by all of "Young India," entail confronting and dealing with all the obstacles – filial, social, structural – that come in their way. Both novel and film are ordered by these simple rules.

Notes

1 The term property here is being used in the sense of a copyrighted object. This term is becoming increasingly common in both the publishing and entertainment sectors to differentiate between "legal" and "illegal" goods and services.

2 In addition to *3 Idiots*, *One Night @ the Call Center* (2005) was turned into a film called *Hello* (dir. Atul Agnihotri, 2008); *The 3 Mistakes of My Life* (2008) was adapted as *Kai Po Che!* (dir. Abhishek Kapoor, 2013), while *2 States: The Story of My Marriage* (2009) was shortened to *2 States* (dir. Abhishek Varman, 2014). *Revolution 2020* (2013) is being produced by UTV and directed by Rajkumar Gupta.

3 For more on this phrase as one of self-description by a new breed of best-selling English language novelists in India, see Reddy.

4 The phrase "Young India" is from Chetan Bhagat's book *What Young India Wants*. This is a collection of his columns for the *Times of India*, motivational speeches, and sundry writings. Two recent research titles that examine the complex lived worlds as well as the political economy of Young India include Lukose, *Liberalization's Children* and J. Kapur, *The Politics of Time and Youth in Brand India*.

5 The structural bilingualism claimed for "Young India" by Bhagat et al. reprises an earlier phase in Indian nationalism. According to Sudipta Kaviraj, elites gained political influence and formed a national coalition by embracing bilingualism, meaning English plus a regional language. However, in postcolonial India, such bilingualism was replaced by a unilingual and English-using elite on the one hand and an equally unilingual user of regional languages on the other. See Kaviraj, *Imaginary*.

6 For a fascinating ethnographic analysis of the shifting place of English within the hierarchy of languages among publishers, authors, and literary academies in contemporary India, see Sadana, *English*.

7 India is characterized by what a recent editorial in the *New York Times* called a "youth bulge." The statistics are well known – about half of India's 1.2 billion people are under twenty-five. This suggests that in years to come this demographic will emerge as the world's biggest labor force and largest consumer market. In the same editorial, it is noted that while most of this population remains poor and ill-educated, India's youth nonetheless came of age in the

1990s and 2000s and had access growing up to televisions and cell phones that allowed them to see how the rest of the world as well as the elite in India live. Channeling these aspirations toward productive ends is "India's Youth Challenge," the editorial concludes. I discuss this editorial at some length for it reprises the two key features that characterize all discussions of "Young India" – that it is at once "real" (in demographic terms) and "potential" (in terms of its aspirations for a better world). See "India's Youth Challenge."

8 Other Indian language cinemas have turned more frequently to literary sources. These would include cinemas in Marathi and Kannada. However, the film industry that is most strongly allied to a literary tradition is Bengali cinema. Novels by Bengali writers have been routinely adapted to the screen, ranging from Satyajit Ray's celebrated adaptations of the novels of Rabindranath Tagore and Bibhutibhushan Bandopadhyay to the routine adaptations of works by novelists such as Premendra Mitra, Pratibha Ray, and Sunil Gangopadhyay. "Literariness" is thus a defining feature of Bengali film. The term "literary film" refers not only to adaptations but also to a certain aesthetic and narrative predisposition of the Bengali cinema that has been called novelistic.

9 For scholarly and historical accounts of these fictions, see Orsini (*Hindi*); and Stark. Also, for a general account of the rise of the popular press, see Anindita Ghosh, *Power*.

10 For an account of the importance of Salim-Javed to the rise of the "script-writer" in Bollywood, see Chopra, and also Gruben (40).

11 A detailed and lively account of this is available in the following blog: http://maddy06.blogspot.in/2013/02/the-writer-showman-and-guide.html.

12 I thank Maddy for this quote (http://maddy06.blogspot.com/2013/02/the-writer-showman-and-guide.html).

13 For an excellent reading of *Dil Chahta Hai* in particular and of the "youth film" more broadly as a genre that captures certain key social shifts, see Anjaria and Anjaria, "Text."

14 For an excellent recent analysis of various aspects of this enterprise culture, see Gooptu.

15 "Young India wants jobs, girls and social status," NDTV Interview, August 7, 2012, http://www.ndtv.com/article/india/young-india-wants-jobs-girls-soci al-status-chetan-bhagat-252152.

16 There are a number of recent works that address the issue of audience in recent Indian cinema, especially in the wake of the transformation of the exhibition and production sectors. See Athique and Hill; Ganti; S. Gopal; Rai; and Vasudevan, among others.

17 "Chetan Bhagat Penning Script for Salman Khan's Kick." *Hindustan Times*, October 26, 2012, http://www.hindustantimes.com/entertainment /bollywood/chetan-bhagat-penning-script-for-salman-khan-s-kick /article1-950423.aspx. It is important to note that in this era of corporate farming and industrial agriculture, the "Indian farmer" is no longer synon-ymous with "real India"; yet Bhagat clearly uses this phrase to refer to his

books as mass-market publications. Bhagat is actually more interested in the urban – if non-metropolitan – youth, who have also been the subject of much recent Hindi cinema. A seminal film in this regard is *Bunty Aur Babli* (dir. Shaad Ali, 2005), but there are numerous other examples spanning the gamut from action blockbuster to broad comedy to lush romance.

18 Rashmi Daryanani, "Interview with Chetan Bhagat," April 3, 2013. http://www.missmalini.com/2013/03/04/interview-chetan-bhagat-reveals -which-bollywood-movie-hed-love-to-write-a-book-on/.

19 Ajit Andhare, COO, Viacom 18 Pictures, quoted in S. Dasgupta and Sengupta.

20 Anuj Kumar, "The Action Shifts: Interview with Mukul Deva," *The Hindu*, July 14, 2011. http://www.thehindu.com/todays-paper/tp-features /tp-metroplus/the-action-shifts/article2225139.ece.

CHAPTER 25

Caste, Complicity, and the Contemporary

Toral Jatin Gajarawala

This chapter insists on two dueling frameworks: "caste" and "contemporaneity." Presumed to be mutually exclusive, one is marked, the other clear and transparent; one archaic, the other heralding the new; one evoking dirty realisms and realpolitik, the other, the freedoms of abstraction. This chapter will insist on the intertwining of caste and the contemporary in order to argue that the contemporary is a category constructed by and around caste, rather than a radical break from it, or a true Novum in the Blochian sense; the time/space of the contemporary is, in fact, in complicity with caste.

It is now a truism to say that caste does not disappear with what we refer to as modernity but takes new and subtle forms. Caste "prejudice," caste conflict, casteist violence, and caste humiliation have all accommodated themselves to institutions and bureaucracies, colleges and community gyms. And caste identitarianism, of which Dalit literary movements are no small part, has become increasingly important for both structural and affective reasons. How does caste insert itself into the discourse of the casteless contemporary? We will examine here the modalities via which caste politics makes itself visible in Dalit autobiography, the Anglophone novel, the contemporary Hindi novel, and new Dalit fiction.

Contemporaneity, as a concept, poses a kind of problem. Unlike modernity, large and long enough to include vernacular, subaltern, and other downtrodden if politically suspect versions of itself, contemporaneity is presumed to be secular, post-identitarian, and fleeting; most importantly, its globality is implicit.[1] There are many different contemporaries, but contemporaneity is not the province of one region, sector or "world"; it is not, in other words, a gift granted to the colony by the metropole. The contemporary is theorized and represented by both honor killings and occupation, footloose construction and air travel. This is why in one of Hindi Dalit writer Ajay Navariya's stories, the chaiwallah in his ramshackle stand is glued to both "an international channel ... now

373

showing pictures of Saddam Hussein" ("New" 74) and the vulture-like investigation of a passerby's caste identity. Contemporaneity need not be progressive, in either sense of the word, but rather collagist. And in this inheres the tragedy of the contemporary, which, though ringing with newness and emergence in the work of many postmodern theorists, is a problematic continuity of time past. In this chapter, I will capture some elements of the casteist contemporary as it emerges in the realm of fiction and autobiography of the last decade, namely the Hindi short stories of Ajay Navariya (written between 2004 and 2012), the Anglophone novel *Serious Men* (2010) by Manu Joseph, the Dalit autobiography of Narendra Jadhav (2003), written in Marathi, then English, and the eminent Hindi novelist Uday Prakash's *Peeli chatri wali ladki* (*The Girl with the Golden Parasol*, 2001). In doing so, I suggest a transition from an older, social and socialized model of literary resistance toward one in which revolt hinges on the question of the personal.

Modernity and Contemporaneity

Beyond our most basic historical markers, what flags a Dalit writer such as Ajay Navariya as "modern," "modernist," or "contemporary"? It is winter in some of these stories, and that sea change seems to indicate metaphorically a swerve from the paradigmatic overheated India of colonial memoir as well as realist fiction. But more importantly, Ajay Navariya's work marks its distinction both from any abstract notion of the casteless Indian novel, as well as from the twentieth-century traditions of Dalit literature. If the first generation of Dalit writers in Hindi, like those who came before them in Marathi, were concerned primarily with the articulation of modes of subjection in order to forge a collective Dalit consciousness, Navariya's work stands apart. Beyond the question of the landlord and the peasant, uppercaste atrocity and village exodus, in Navariya's writings, there is the office space, the birthday party, urban anomie and existential reverie. Navariya's rise as an intellectual owes less to labor, land, or traditional Dalit movements than to the literary public sphere, where he has been a fiction writer, a guest editor at *Hans*, and a professor of ethics at Jamia Millia.[2] In the collection *Unclaimed Terrain* (2013), the translator has compiled short stories from two collections of Navariya's work, *Patkatha aur anya kahaniyam* (2006) and *Yes Sir* (2012). This allows for the juxtaposition of stories that consider animal skinning and Ambedkarite Buddhism alongside those that feature young college graduates in the city. Caste is no longer the thing that cannot be spoken, but rather can be

named, and named, and named, as the central locus of contention; as one
character puts it to his father in the story "Sacrifice [Bali]," in a classic
moment of intergenerational warfare, "You've eaten us alive! Caste, caste,
caste.... What are we – dogs and cats? Who I married, who I shouldn't
have ... this is my business" (21). Here, caste is considered to be exces-
sively communitarian ("What are we –") as well as backward and primitive ("dogs and cats?"). And it poses an ethical problem for the freedom of
the individual. In this story, sacrifice refers to both the animal under the
knife as well as the relinquishment of tradition: the traditions of endogamy, of caste-based occupation, and of Dalit Hinduism. In a complex formulation, the brutality of father-son relations in the story circles around a
conflict between Khatiks and Chamars and the irruption of Ambedkarite
Buddhism into the household; caste conflict is no longer figured as a dialectical struggle between the landowner and the landless or the Brahmin
and the Dalit. But the battle between the father and son, in this case, and
in others, veers toward the question of freedom; it is the individual who
wins, both the argument, and in the story.

As these stories suggest, the zeitgeist has shifted from early Dalit writing (1970s–90s) – which in Marathi, its first iteration, as well as in other
regional languages, was a literary movement committed to a socially
responsible art form that both articulated grievance and raised political consciousness. It drew attention to the crisis of caste in every incarnation: bonded labor, rape, debt, marriage, the classroom. It advocated
a modern subjectivity but by and large worked within a framework of
realism.[3] The literature of contemporaneity has thrown off this banner for a proliferation of politics and forms. This is not to say that this
recent fiction has entirely abandoned the paradigms of early Dalit writing: anti-Brahminism, the foregrounding of caste-based violence and
atrocity, the privileging of the Dalit subject, or the strident identitarianism of a casteist worldview: "People said that her damned in-laws were
absolute monsters. They shaved her head. They starved her. These upper
caste people are really cruel. Among us, if a woman becomes a widow, she
can remarry. No one would think of shaving her head" ("Sacrifice" 36).
Like much Dalit literature, Navariya's stories too insist on a casteist ontological divide and espouse a position of Dalit-bahujan superiority. And
yet, the clarity of Dalit positionality that marked the first generation of
Dalit sahitya is no longer available. In "Bali," the Dalit contemporary is
a tangled web of affiliations. For the rigid identitarianism of the father's
Khatikness is not only a product of the history of caste endogamy and
other socio-cultural structures but the dialectical response to his thwarted

love for a Brahmin girl. As one character says, in another story, "This is a man's world, where women are treated like objects and men are deluded into believing themselves to be the consumers. In this game, it is hard to know who the product is and who the customer; everyone is stirred around in the same pot" ("New" 68). As we shall see in Uday Prakash's writings, as well, capitalist modernity has produced a confusion in the various forms of subjectivity, one that no longer allows for the neat delineation between the outcasted and the privileged.

These works raise the question: Does a novel have to be about caste in order to "be about caste"? In other words, does it need to cite caste as character and present a critique of untouchability? If the strident identitarianism of the last few decades of Dalit literature has taught us anything, it is this: that to name names is a radical act, as it casteizes what for too long had passed as a secular space. But what Uday Prakash's recent novel *Peeli chatri wali ladki (The Girl with the Golden Parasol)* demonstrates is the smooth way in which caste does not *infiltrate* but rather has gradually accommodated itself to discourses of meritocracy, globalization, and capitalism.

The central figure in Hindi literature today, Uday Prakash, former journalist and contemporary poet, is best known for his short fiction, which has been published, circulated, and translated widely since the early 1980s. Prakash's stories are experimental, meditative, and historical and play with a range of modes of narration and style. *Peeli chatri wali ladki*, which he refers to as a "long short story," was published in 2001. The novella, alongside its narrative of inter-caste love, offers a compelling portrait of the new "angry young man" – theorized by Aravind Adiga in his novel *The White Tiger* (2008) and subject to much speculation by the media. Who is this new subject who has abandoned movements and collectivities and craves luxury and pleasure for the individual? In Prakash's formulation, these are men of small family income, "farmers, small businessmen and low-grade civil servants" (*Girl* 125). They are marginally educated and medium fed, and without jobs to be had, they hang around at tea stalls, railway stations, and abandoned lots. This is how they speak:

> "If only I could get a lakh from somewhere, I'll show them ... behnchod."
> "I haven't gone home in three days. The old man's started counting the rotis I eat. Got any money? Can you fix us up with some chai...?" ...
> "Five thousand, that's all I'm asking for, and I swear I'd kill anyone."
> "That Deepa, you know, the crochety baker's daughter? Ever since she opened that beauty parlour, her parents' luck totally turned around ..."

"What beauty parlour? That's just a cover for another hobby of hers. Junior engineer Sharma and builder Satvinder are both in on it, and in on her ..."

"Don't let her brother hear that, he'll sort you out." – ...

"Hey Kishore, didn't you do an MSc in physics?"

"Yeah, but I've fucking forgotten everything. Now I think I'll get into politics. Listen, I've got a plan. I'll get some fake papers to make it look like I have a job, show them to some lucky parents, get married with a big dowry, go on the honeymoon, fuck her for a week, and then sell her and take off for Dubai. God knows, I'm tired of this kind of life." (126)

The context of the novel is a college in a provincial town, which, despite its desire to introvert itself, must consistently fight against the problem of the social that surrounds it. By the end of the novel, we see very clearly that the problem of social inequity outside the university is very much in complicity with the one inside its halls. In the previous citation, Prakash constructs the vile social atmosphere of contemporary India through male chatter, in which familial relations are strained by stringent economizing and female endeavor. This dialogue – extemporaneous, non-identified, taken to be expressive of a general social malaise – is the atmosphere in which the major figures of the text are suspended. A naked ressentiment is accompanied by a palpably violent misogyny, which expresses itself with lascivious candor. Women are making money, and the assumption that they have traded on their honor is the necessary balm for this gendered anxiety. Entrepreneurialism is crushed by lack of capital. There is an affective continuity here between the young men figured by Navariya and those by Prakash, and that continuity may be the emotive mark of the contemporary.

The Politics of Humiliation

In Ajay Navariya's story of a Brahmin peon who works for a Scheduled Caste manager, "Yes Sir," the Brahmin is casteized by the text. Rather than the casteless contemporary figured by many Anglophone texts, here the Brahmin character is not the figure of the secular imaginary: post-caste, post-identitarian. It is he who mediates on caste politics, it is he who snarls over reservations, and it is he who wrestles with the institutions and structures that preceded him. The dominant affect in this story is a kind of caste humiliation, directed at his superior: " 'Bastard, asshole, dog, lowborn, scum.... The father's not killed so much as a frog, and the son's a marksman!' " (Navariya, "Yes" 57). The peon's manager is younger, has passed only in the third division, never uses the honorific, and is a Dalit.

Figure 3. Cartoon by K. Shankar Pillai.
© Children's Book Trust.

Humiliation has emerged as a critical category of importance in Dalit
studies and has reverberated into the larger literary sphere. The recent
debate around the inclusion of a "demeaning" cartoon of B. R. Ambedkar,
the father of the modern Dalit movement, in the NCERT standard textbooks, gestures to this (see Figure 3). In the cartoon, Ambedkar is seated
on a snail he is riding before a crowd; as he is about to whip the slow snail,
he is also about to be whipped by Jawaharlal Nehru, in classic cap and
vest. Meant to criticize Ambedkar for the putative delays in the drafting of

the constitution, the father of the Dalit movement is clearly imagined as the figurative beast of burden.

As I have discussed elsewhere, critiques of the cartoon have taken several forms, some of which attempt to historicize the original political context, others of which remind us of the fraught site of modern education, in which texts and images of denigration have a long and complicated genealogy (Gajarawala 204). However, most of the discussion surrounding this debate, as well as other, more recent ones, hinges on the relationships between art, broadly speaking, and insult, and between insult and action. In other words, a lineage of (particularly masculine) caste humiliation is a legible form of historical causality. Dalit philosopher Gopal Guru criticizes this strain of logic, which relies, he claims, on the "thick emotionalism" of the Dalit, who must react rather than think: the Dalit who is not capable of rational deliberation. In his work on humiliation, Guru writes that "the realization of desire for recognition is not without social cost" (210). One legitimate question that arises from the variegated sphere of caste contemporaneity is: What is the nature of literary and cultural recognition, and what are its social costs?

In his reading of the Gandhi-Ambedkar contestation over the question of separate electorates and of Gandhi's "fast unto death," critic D. R. Nagaraj excavates the story of the "untouchable youth" who was to bring an orange to break Gandhi's fast but claimed he was denied entry to Gandhi's camp. He later confessed that he had lied. Nagaraj writes:

> By deliberately missing the appointment with Gandhi on that historical day, the unnamed youth had metaphorically begun the Dalit movement. The Gandhian project had no real role for untouchables.... The boy's lie was a truthful act to protect his self-respect, and thus began the strain-filled, necessary, imaginative search for the politics of Dalit identity. (102)

Nagaraj's reading is unusual in many respects: it resurrects the buried actor, it rereads his intentionality, and it makes of him a symptom of something as yet unnamed that can only be read anachronistically.

Self-respect thus strains the upper-caste imagination and, as Guru says, establishes its own moral parameters: "The more one delays the response the more one creates the possibility of retaining one's self-respect. Dragging foot is the subaltern method of restoring self-respect" (Guru 215). The snail that appears as the mark of disdain, the orange that is too late, then become the signs of Ambedkarite patient deliberation. In other words, the cultural framework that reads the tragedy and humiliation of the whipped snail needs to be reread without "thick emotionalism" but with the will of the orange-bearing youth.

The Politics of Ressentiment

The problem that we see in the contemporary literary sphere, however, is that of the affective reliance on humiliation to produce a politics of ressentiment. Contemporary fiction demonstrates a kind of consonance between the abject Brahmin peon in Navariya's story, the murderous chauffeur Balram Halwai of Aravind Adiga's *The White Tiger*, the aimless, provincial, lower middle-class men of *Peeli chatri wali ladki*, and the Dalit subject imagined by a novel such as Manu Joseph's *Serious Men*. That consonance, I would argue, is the narrative framework of humiliation and ressentiment. In Navariya's story "New Custom," the protagonist who is returning to his home in the village is humiliated by the chaiwallah, who is himself fixated on the television displaying Saddam Hussein's open mouth, humiliated by the Americans. Upon being revealed as a Dalit and cast out for defiling the tea stall, he smashes a glass into pieces.

Ressentiment circulates in these texts as a causal agent. Theorized first by Friedrich Nietzsche in *On the Genealogy of Morals*, ressentiment is characteristic of what he defines as the "slave morality." The slave morality is the province of the weak – a secondary, belated condition; it is the philosophical other of the morality of the noble. In Nietzsche's formulation, ressentiment is the defining feature of the slave, and its tragedy is its reactive and negative quality. Ressentiment, in other words, responds to the conditions laid by others:

> The man of ressentiment is neither upright nor naïve nor honest and straightforward with himself. His soul squints; his spirit loves hiding places, secret paths and back doors; ... he understands how to keep silent, how not to forget, how to wait, how to be provisionally self-deprecating and humble. A race of such men of ressentiment is bound to become eventually cleverer than any noble race; it will also honor cleverness to a far greater degree. (Nietzsche 38)

And yet, within ressentiment lies the potential creativity and passion of he who has been subjected. If hegemonic cultural and moral structures are to be challenged at all, the location of that challenge is ressentiment: "One would undoubtedly have to regard all those instincts of reaction and ressentiment through whose aid the noble races and their ideals were finally confounded and overthrown as the actual instruments of culture" (Nietzsche 42). Beyond any petty caricature of resentment, the ideal of ressentiment is not simply the transformation of the subject but its constitutive structure.

How does Joseph's novel *Serious Men*[4] imagine the new Dalit subject? Or, more to the point, what kind of literary Dalit is available to the contemporary cultural imaginary? Here is one indication:

> Sometimes he saw bitterness in the eyes of his old friends who thought he had gone too far in life, leaving them all behind. That bitterness reassured him. The secret rage in their downcast eyes also reminded him of a truth which was dearer to him than anything else. That men, in reality, did not have friends in other men. That the fellowship of men, despite its joyous banter, old memories of exaggerated mischief and the altruism of sharing pornography, was actually a farcical fellowship. Because what a man really wanted was to be bigger than his friends. (M. Joseph, *Serious* 7)

The question of the ideological imaginary available to contemporary fiction is a crucial one in general, but it is particularly so for the Anglophone novel, which has largely ignored the problem of caste, while also solidifying an upper-caste literary space.[5] In that sense, the contribution of *Serious Men* is that it participates in a discourse of caste in the public sphere that was inaugurated by Dalit literature. It is thus able to raise questions of Dalit Buddhism and reservations, urban anonymity, and institutional caste prejudice that were unavailable a decade ago. But here our protagonist, Ayyan Mani, is an embittered personal assistant to a brilliant astronomer at the Institute of Theory and Research, and distantiated from coworker and comrade. He seeks to endow his son with a kind of preternatural gift and does so by feeding him bits of knowledge and test answers in order to rig his success on competitive mathematics and physics exams for geniuses. Humiliated by a series of minor failures and the meager privileges of lower middle-class life, Mani's is a cynical project that circumvents the possibility of genuine effort or social recognition and requires a series of collusions. It is in this novelistic "reality" that the Dalit subject has learned the cynical truths of "fellowship," "banter," and "altruism," which reveal their true philosophical character when put to the historical test. These bonds of horizontality and sharing have been given lie by the dominant atmosphere of "bitterness," "rage," and "farce." Fellowship, solidarity even, is a performance, "exaggerated," and man is defined in the singular as agonist to the plural of friends. What historical and social context rereads fellowship as farce? The moment of *Serious Men* is the same as that of *The White Tiger*, *The Girl with the Golden Parasol*, Ajay Navariya's *Unclaimed Terrain* – marked by either resentment and misery if not a utopian hope that borders on fantasy – as well as the last section of Narendra

Jadhav's *Outcaste* (2003), with its move toward flight, emigration, diaspora, and the emancipation these provide. Twenty-first-century contemporaneity may be no more than a continuation of the various forms of injustice of the past, but it is also the political moment of a re-privileging of competition, meritocracy, jostling and climbing, and new forms of verticality, in which fellowship shows its true face to be farce. Humiliations carry forward from the past, and ressentiment creates futures.

Of this variegated cultural production, Prakash's novel is one that does suggest moments of student solidarity as young people band together to fight crime and assault, the general lack of personal security, and perennial administrative corruption and complacency. But what a tragedy this political affiliation becomes! Students are forced to develop their own paramilitary force in the name of security – to become the state, in other words – in a situation in which the governing body is absent. And their activism is local and temporary; though cross-caste and cross-region, they do not coalesce around any party, ideology, or political structure beyond public safety (the murder of a friend prompted by his assault by "locals") and private property (the continual theft of tuition sent by parents).

Is it any accident, then, that Ayyan Mani dreams of the subjugation of women, whose "haughty face [it] would be a pleasure to tame. With love, poetry or a leather belt, perhaps" (M. Joseph, *Serious* 4)? For *Serious Men*, love is farcical as well. In the late century heyday of V. S. Naipaul, whose oeuvre stands as one of the most powerful testaments to literary misogyny – and perhaps not coincidentally, a body of work occasionally transfixed by caste – Jimmy Ahmed's rape of Jane in *Guerrillas* or Salim's assault and battery of Yvette in *A Bend in the River* were contextual but primarily characterological: in the colonies, the native subject goes awry and veers toward pathology. The more recent texts, however, have raised this affect to an ethnographic dominant that the contemporary throws in relief. In *Serious Men*, patriarchy is renewed and revivified as the prosperity of the poor: "These days," muses Mani, the neo-Buddhist, "men live like men only in the homes of the poor" (79). For men to "live like men," they must be friendless, disenfranchised, and gender equity averse. The intertwining of Dalit depravity and a deep misogyny in the space of the text confirms a longstanding link between gendered and casteist relations of power that structure the contours of the contemporary novel.[6]

The central question raised by the collation of caste and the contemporary is that of the political future. Now that both the Dalit subject and caste as deep structure seem visible, how does culture move beyond the problem of social and cultural recognition? What the casteist contemporary suggests is that it is no more immune to the various crises of late modernity than other geographic spaces. Humiliation plus ressentiment functions as genealogy, but as a unit it is unable to construct new forms of being. In that sense, what these new texts offer, beyond the very fleeting moment of utopian or romantic pleasure, is a critique of the possibility of "resistance" in any straightforward way. The framework of resistance literature has been the dominant one in which to interpret Dalit literature, in which atrocity and exclusion are named and then challenged or overturned.[7] As both a literary and political movement, Dalit literature sought this burden of distinction, in contradistinction to a history of cultural passivity, subjection, and degradation. Navariya, in particular, is clearly participating in a conversation with this body of work, as his rewriting of Premchand shows ("Hello Premchand"). But the "Chikh" ["Scream"], as one of his stories is titled, is the trope of anomie par excellence, and the manipulative love affairs of its protagonist only heighten his isolation. In "Bali," the presence of Ambedkarite Buddhism, the classic indication of modernity, modernization, and a post-Premchandian discourse of pity for the Dalit subject, is made anodyne; it is given expression only by the final acceptance of the wife's tea by her casteist father-in-law. Commensality has historically been a radical kind of solution: Gandhian, Ambedkarite, populist, and Dalit. But for the contemporary moment, the taking of tea and the smashing of glass indicate a tragic spectrum of possibility. Individualist, contained, and domestic, resistance to casteist structures can only be figured through the personal. This is why love and sex – powerful tropes that theorize the functioning of caste (arranged marriage, for example, and of course rape and sexual domination) – have now become markers of freedom. Most telling is that the final act of "Chikh," the murder of a man – the narrator? The landlord's son? The jealous husband? The possessive mistress? – is left radically in doubt, its perpetrator unknown. The inability to properly name "the other" is what justifies this epistemological uncertainty and clearly marks a kind of turn in casteist fiction. Contemporary writing on caste might be said to theorize precisely the inability of culture to do the work of protest – aesthetically, generically, and narratively – that it for so long has been able to do.

Conclusion

Complicity is one way to frame the dominant ethos of new literature on caste that advocates, by and large, for some degree of participation in a social structure rather than outright challenge to it. Different from collusion – which is conscientious, deliberate, secretive – complicity is structural, rather than individual; it can also be low-level and occasional, rather than constant and thematic. In the Adornian sense, complicity is an inherent problem of the modern subject, who participates in his own alienation. But complicity is also a problem for contemporary culture, which, in the period of new materialism, cannot properly distinguish itself from the commodity. As a result, culture participates, as do its actors, in the structures of the present, even while it may also seek to extricate itself from them.[8] Complicity thus accepts all the minor advantages gifted by the status quo: sexual opportunity, information culled by accident, cash dropped on the floor. On occasion, this might be transformed into outright sabotage.

The contemporaneity of caste is itself an intellectual conundrum: neither extinct nor extinguishable, the politics of caste remain. This is the irony of any teleology of Dalit progress. As the Dalit economist Narendra Jadhav writes so poignantly in his parting question, produced by a meditative reverie on an airplane – "no better place or time to be philosophical" (*Outcaste* 206): "Why should the caste into which I was born count *now*?" (207). Implicit in the "now" is that the now is a radical break from that which came before it; not only is it *after*, chronologically, the past, but it is constituted differently.

Typically, Dalit autobiography spends its time in the past: reverie is a formal element that links narrative meandering and past injustice with the contemporary moment. In other words, Dalit autobiography requires a contemporaneous subject who speaks to the reader in present time, through a process of differentiation from the suffering subject, the elaboration of which takes up the vast majority of the text. The majority of Dalit autobiographies, and there are so many now – those of Omprakash Valmiki and Mohandas Naimishraya in Hindi; of Baby Kamble and Daya Pawar in Marathi, and of course Narendra Jadhav's *Outcaste: A Memoir* – focus primarily on the reconstruction of the past. Jadhav is an economist who worked for decades with the Reserve Bank of India and then the International Monetary Fund, but he became known in the literary sphere with the 1993 publication of *Amcha baap aan amhi*, his life narrative in Marathi. *Outcaste*, and the eventual *Untouchables: My Family's Triumphant Journey out of the Caste System in Modern India* (2005), are English retellings and expansions of the earlier Marathi version.

In Dalit autobiography, the present subject, assumed to be the slow accretion of the various phases of atrocity, education, and exodus that often structure the text, is putatively self-evident; he is the one, after all, who constructs the long backward glance. His narrative elaboration, then, is not typically a priority in the text, and I have suggested elsewhere why that might be (Gajarawala chapter 5). The subject of the text in the present, then, the figure of the "now," does not spend much time with the reader, which is what makes Jadhav's memoir interesting and unusual. Concluding with a section entitled "Making of the Second Generation," the date of 1997 clearly marked (despite the subtitle "Chotu: Looking Back"), Jadhav spends some pages reflecting on the contemporary moment. In the crowded Mumbai international airport where his family has gathered to send him off, Jadhav muses on the irony of his condition: economist, soon to take up residence in Washington DC, appointed by the International Monetary Fund, and yet condemned by caste.

Serious Men makes a similar point in the radical juxtaposition of a phone conversation, straining against the Brownian hum of the receiver's immediate hubbub: subsidized kerosene and brideburning alongside space-time geometry and its relation to string theory. And in *The Girl with the Golden Parasol*, the non-Brahmin student at the provincial college falls in love with the daughter of a minister. In his zeal to pursue her he drops anthropology and takes up an M.A. in Hindi. It is the Hindi department that is the site of one of the newly banal contradictions of the contemporary, the smooth intertwining of Brahminism and globalization. The department prepares for the arrival of an eminent guest scholar of Hindi mannerist poetry from the prestigious Benares Hindu University. A banner is hung (with misspellings). Professors arrive in new cars: the trappings of debt-ridden life. And the performance of prostration begins, in ritual order: Vice Chancellor, Head of Department, Padma Sri honoree. From a corner, the only three non-Brahmin students observe "at a distance from this sacred ritual ... prohibited from the ceremonial site by the precepts of the Dog Shastra" (144). One student, ecstatic with joy, begins chanting, "Hurray for our Derrida! Hurray for our Derrida!" (143). Beyond the routine admixture of clichés of tradition and modernity, the performance is parodic, both of cultural rites, and the spirit of intellectualism. A post-colonial cultural nationalism ("our Derrida!") has done nothing to challenge the strategic exclusion of the outcaste, which is reaffirmed by the academy, entirely contiguous with the world outside. One by one, each student and professor (numbered by the narrator) is complicit in that structure of exclusion, even as the very desire for inclusion is ironized!

This is the formal correlative, to use Roberto Schwarz's terminology (*Two Girls*), of the wealth and knowledge differential but also of that contradiction that inheres in the contemporary, no longer wholly subject to the ongoing trammeling of modernity. "The very thing that made him want to die back in the village was considered 'work' here. And one got paid for it. Here, labor had value" (Navariya, "Chikh" 171). It is under a new value regime that various forms of labor – sexual, sanitation, and so on – can be resignified. But this is not utopian enclave, this is capitalism in the city, where anonymity, but also anomie, can produce its own humiliations.

Notes

1 See, for example, Agamben; Nancy.
2 Ajay Navariya is one of the most important figures in contemporary Dalit literature in Hindi. He has published two collections of short stories and a novel, *Udhar ke log* (2008). He has also guest edited an important issue of the literary magazine *Hans* on new writing in Hindi literature. Navariya received his Ph.D. from Jawaharlal Nehru University and now teaches Hinduism in the Hindi department at Jamia Millia Islamia University. Often described as "modernist," Navariya's writing has at times sat uneasily with a more conventional and programmatic Dalit literary establishment. As he himself told *The Sunday Guardian*, "They simply refuse to believe that I'm a part of 'Dalit writing'" (http://www.sunday-guardian.com/artbeat/on-the-great-truth-of-indian-society-and-its-arbiters, accessed September 8, 2014).
3 In Hindi in particular, see the work of Omprakash Valmiki, Mohandas Naimishraya, Kusum Meghwal, and Rajat Rani Meenu.
4 Manu Joseph is a career journalist who was until recently an editor for *Open Magazine* and has contributed to the international *New York Times* and *The Independent*. *Serious Men*, his first novel, was shortlisted for the Man Asian literary prize and awarded The Hindu Literary Prize. His most recent book, *The Illicit Happiness of Other People*, came out in 2013.
5 Important exceptions would be Mulk Raj Anand's *Untouchable* (1935), Raja Rao's *Kanthapura* (1938), Rohinton Mistry's *A Fine Balance* (1995), Arundhati Roy's *The God of Small Things* (1997), and Aravind Adiga's *The White Tiger* (2008).
6 See S. Anand's dark reading of *Serious Men*, which argues that "the garb of satire – where almost every character cuts a sorry figure – gives the author the license to offer one of the most bleak and pessimistic portrayals of urban Dalits."
7 See, for example, Brueck.
8 See Adorno, *Culture*. While Adorno's theorization is conditioned by the postwar landscape and the problem of mass, rather than high modernist, culture, the question of complicity seems relevant in the moment I describe

as a casteized contemporaneity. Theories of postmodernity, to which contemporaneity is generally held, strike me as inappropriate to categorize the cultural field I describe here, not least because of the problem of relying on Fredric Jameson's analysis of late capitalism to characterize contemporary India. In general, theories of postmodernity do not seem able to take into account new formations of caste and class and the unfinished business of "resistance."

Works Cited

PRIMARY SOURCES

2 States. Dir. Abhishek Varman. 2014. DVD. Dharma Productions.

3 Idiots. Dir. Rajkumar Hirani. 2009. DVD. Vinod Chopra Productions.

Aag. Dir. Raj Kapoor. 1948. DVD. R. K. Films Ltd.

Adiga, Aravind. *Between the Assassinations*. New York: Free Press, 2009.

Last Man in Tower. London: Atlantic, 2012.

The White Tiger. New York: Free Press, 2008.

Agyeya. *Tar-saptak*. New Delhi: Bharatiya Jnanpith, 2000.

Ahmed, Naseer, writer. *Kashmir Pending*. Art by Saurabh Singh. New Delhi: Phantomville, 2007.

Ali, Ahmed. Afterword. *The Prison House: Short Stories*. Karachi: Akrash Publishers, 1985. 162–9.

The Prison-House: Short Stories. Karachi: Akrash Publishers, 1986.

"Progressive View of Art." *Marxist Cultural Movement in India*, vol. 1. Ed. Sudhi Pradhan. Calcutta: National Book Agency Pvt. Ltd., 1979. 67–83.

"The Progressive Writers' Movement and Creative Writers in Urdu." *Marxist Influences and South Asian Literature*. Ed. Carlo Coppola. Delhi: Chanakya Publications, 1988. 42–53.

Twilight in Delhi. New York: New Directions, 1994.

Anand, Mulk Raj. *Across the Black Waters*. London: Jonathan Cape, 1940.

Apology for Heroism: A Brief Autobiography of Ideas. Bombay: Kutub-Popular, 1957.

The Bubble. New Delhi: Gulab Vazirani for A. Heinemann (India), 1984.

Conversations in Bloomsbury. New Delhi: Vision Books, 2001.

Coolie. London: Penguin, 1936.

"The Making of an Indian-English Novel: Untouchable." *The Eye of the Beholder: Indian Writing in English*. Ed. Maggie Butcher. London: Commonwealth Institute, 1983. 34–43.

"On the Genesis of *Untouchable*: A Note by Mulk Raj Anand." *South Asian Review* 32.1 (2011): 133–6.

"On the Progressive Writers' Movement." *Marxist Cultural Movement in India*, vol. 1. Ed. Sudhi Pradhan. Calcutta: National Book Agency Pvt. Ltd., 1979. 1–22.

Private Life of an Indian Prince. London: Bodley Head, 1970.

"Reason and Romanticism: A Talk with T. S. Eliot in Schmidt's Restaurant in Charlotte Street." *Mulk Raj Anand: A Reader.* Ed. Atma Ram. New Delhi: Sahitya Akademi, 2005. 611–18.

"The Sources of Protest in My Novels." *South Asian Review* 32.1 (2011): 121–31.

The Sword and the Sickle. London: Jonathan Cape, 1942.

Untouchable. New Delhi: Penguin, 1940.

The Village. London: Jonathan Cape, 1939.

Anantha Murthy, U. R. *Samskara.* Trans. A. K. Ramanujan. Delhi: Oxford University Press, 1978.

Appupen. *Legends of Halahala.* Noida: HarperCollins, 2013.

Moonward: Stories from Halahala. Chennai: Blaft Publications, 2009.

Arni, Samhita. *The Missing Queen.* New Delhi: Zubaan, 2014.

Aslam, Nadeem. *The Wasted Vigil.* New York: Alfred A. Knopf, 2008.

Baldwin, Shauna Singh. *What the Body Remembers.* New York: N.A. Talese, 1999.

Bandyopadhyay, Bhabanicharan. *Naba Babu Bilas* [*A Pleasant Tale of the New Babu*, 1825]. Kolkata: Subarnarekha, 1979.

Banerjee, Sarnath. *The Barn Owl's Wondrous Capers.* New Delhi: Penguin, 2007.

Corridor: A Graphic Novel. New Delhi: Penguin, 2004.

The Harappa Files. New Delhi: HarperCollins India, 2011.

Banker, Ashok K. *Dance of Govinda.* Noida: HarperCollins, 2011.

Flute of Vrindavan. Noida: HarperCollins, 2011.

Fortress of Dwarka. Noida: HarperCollins, 2012.

Lord of Matura. Noida: HarperCollins, 2012.

Rage of Jarasandha. Noida: HarperCollins, 2012.

Slayer of Kamsa. Noida: HarperCollins, 2010.

Bansal, Rashmi. *Stay Hungry Stay Foolish.* Chennai: Westland, 2012.

Basu, Samit. *The Manticore's Secret.* New Delhi, Penguin, 2005.

The Simoqin Prophecies. New Delhi: Penguin, 2004.

Turbulence. London: Titan, 2012.

The Unwaba Revelations. New Delhi: Penguin, 2007.

Bhagat, *2 States: The Story of My Marriage.* New Delhi: Rupa, 2009.

The 3 Mistakes of My Life. New Delhi: Rupa, 2008.

Five Point Someone: What Not To Do At IIT. New Delhi: Rupa, 2004.

Half Girlfriend. New Delhi: Rupa, 2014.

One Night @ the Call Center. New Delhi: Rupa, 2005.

Revolution 2020: Love, Corruption, Ambition. New Delhi: Rupa, 2011.

What Young India Wants: Selected Essays and Columns. New Delhi: Rupa, 2012.

Bhattacharya, Bhabani. *So Many Hungers!* London: V. Gollancz, 1947.

Bond, Ruskin. *A Flight of Pigeons.* Bombay: IBH, 1980.

Susanna's Seven Husbands. New Delhi: Penguin, 2011.

Bose, Anirban. *Bombay Rains, Bombay Girls.* New Delhi: HarperCollins India, 2008.

Bunty Aur Babli. Dir. Shaad Ali. 2005. DVD. Yash Raj Films.

Chakraborty, Novoneel. *That Kiss in the Rain: Love Is the Weather of Life*. New Delhi: Srishti Publishers, 2010.

Chakravarti, K. *Sarata and Hingana*. Calcutta: Basu and Mitra, 1895.

Chandra, Vikram. "The Cult of Authenticity." *Boston Review*. February 1, 2000. http://bostonreview.net/vikram-chandra-the-cult-of-authenticity, accessed October 17, 2014.

Love and Longing in Bombay. New Delhi: Penguin, 1997.

Red Earth and Pouring Rain. Boston: Little, Brown, and Co., 1995.

Sacred Games. London: Faber and Faber, 2006.

Chandu Menon, Oyyarattu. *Indulekha*. Trans. Anitha Devasia. Delhi: Oxford University Press, 2005.

Chatterjee, Saratchandra. *Devdas*. Trans. Sreejata Guha. New Delhi: Penguin, 2002.

Chatterjee, Upamanyu. *English August: An Indian Story*. New York: New York Review Books, 1988.

Weight Loss. London: Penguin, 2007.

Chattopadhyay, Bankimchandra. *Anandamath*. Trans. Julius Lipner. New York: Oxford University Press, 2005.

"Bangadarshaner Patra-Suchana [Foreword to *Bangadarshan*]." *Bankim Rachanabali*, vol. 2. Ed. Jogesh Chandra Bagal. Kolkata: Sahitya Samsad, 2004. 244–7.

"Bangala Sahityer Adar [The Prestige of Bengali Literature]." *Bankim Rachanabali*, vol. 2. Ed. Jogesh Chandra Bagal. Kolkata: Sahitya Samsad, 2004. 41–3.

"Bangalar Itihash Sambandhe Kayekti Katha [A Few Words Concerning the History of Bengal]." *Bankim Rachanabali*, vol. 2. Ed. Jogesh Chandra Bagal. Kolkata: Sahitya Samsad, 2004. 290–3.

Bankim Rachanabali [Collected Works]. Ed. Jogesh Chandra Bagal. Kolkata: Sahitya Samsad, 3 vols. Vol. 1 (2003), vol. 2 (2004), vol. 3 (1998).

"Bengali Literature." *Bankim Rachanabali*, vol. 3. Ed. Jogesh Chandra Bagal. Kolkata: Sahitya Samsad, 1998. 103–24.

Bishabriksha. *Bankim Rachanabali* [Collected Works], vol. 1. Ed. Jogesh Chandra Bagal. Kolkata: Sahitya Samsad, 2003. 205–84.

"The Confession of a Young Bengal." *Bankim Rachanabali* [Collected Works], vol. 2. Ed. Jogesh Chandra Bagal. Kolkata: Sahitya Samsad, 2004. 137–41.

Debi Chaudhurani. *Bankim Rachanabali* [Collected Works], vol. 1. Ed. Jogesh Chandra Bagal. Kolkata: Sahitya Samsad, 2003. 727–808.

Debi Chaudhurani, or The Wife Who Came Home. Trans. Julius J. Lipner. Oxford: Oxford University Press, 2009.

Durgeshnandini. *Bankim Rachanabali* [Collected Works], vol. 1. Ed. Jogesh Chandra Bagal. Kolkata: Sahitya Samsad, 2003. 1–83.

Kapalkundala. *Bankim Rachanabali* [Collected Works], vol. 1. Ed. Jogesh Chandra Bagal. Kolkata: Sahitya Samsad, 2003. 85–134.

Kopal-Kundala: A Tale of Bengali Life. Trans. H. A. D. Phillips. London: Trübner, 1885.

Krishnakanter Will. Bankim Rachanabali [Collected Works], vol. 1. Ed. Jogesh Chandra Bagal. Kolkata: Sahitya Samsad, 2003. 481–548.

Mrinalini. Bankim Rachanabali [Collected Works], vol. 1. Ed. Jogesh Chandra Bagal. Kolkata: Sahitya Samsad, 2003. 205–84.

Rajmohan's Wife. Ed. Meenakshi Mukherjee. New Delhi: Ravi Dayal/Penguin India, 2009.

"Samya [Equality]." *Bankim Rachanabali* [Collected Works], vol. 2. Ed. Jogesh Chandra Bagal. Kolkata: Sahitya Samsad, 2004. 328–51.

Chaturvedi, Bharati, ed. *Finding Delhi: Loss and Renewal in the Megacity.* New Delhi: Penguin, 2010.

Chauhan, Anuja. *Those Pricey Thakur Girls.* Noida: HarperCollins India, 2013.

The Zoya Factor. New Delhi: HarperCollins India, 2008.

Daag. Dir. Yash Chopra. 1973. DVD. Yash Raj Films.

Datta, Durjoy and Maanvi Ahuja. *Now That You're Rich… Let's Fall in Love!* New Delhi: Srishti Publishers, 2011.

Of Course I Love You..! Till I Find Someone Better. New Delhi: Srishti Publishers, 2008.

Day, Lal Behari. *Bengal Peasant Life, Folk Tales of Bengal, and Recollections of My School Days.* Ed. Mahadevprasad Saha. Calcutta: Editions Indian, 1969.

Deb, Siddhartha. *The Point of Return.* Delhi: HarperCollins, 2004.

Desai, Anita. *Clear Light of Day.* New York: Harper and Row, 1980.

Where Shall We Go This Summer? New Delhi: Orient Paperbacks, 2001.

Desai, Kiran. *The Inheritance of Loss.* New York: Atlantic Monthly Press, 2006.

Desani, G. V. *All About H. Hatterr.* New York: Farrar, Straus and Giroux, 1970.

Deshpande, Shashi. *The Binding Vine.* London: Virago Press, 1993.

The Dark Holds No Terrors. New Delhi: Penguin Books, 1990.

Roots and Shadows. Hyderabad: Sangam Books, 1983.

That Long Silence. London: Virago Press, 1988.

Devarajan, Sharad, Suresh Seetharaman, and Jeevan J. Kang. *Spider-Man: India.* New York: Marvel Age, 2005.

Devi, Mahasweta. "Douloti." *Imaginary Maps: Three Stories.* Trans. Gayatri Chakravorty Spivak. New York: Routledge, 1995. 19–94.

"The Hunt." *Imaginary Maps: Three Stories.* Trans. Gayatri Chakravorty Spivak. New York: Routledge, 1995. 1–18.

Dil Chahta Hai. Dir. Farhan Akhtar. 2001. DVD. Excel Entertainment.

Dutt, Govin Chunder, et al., ed. *The Dutt Family Album.* London: Longman, Greens and Co., 1870.

Dutt, Kylas Chunder. "A Journal of 48 Hours of the Year 1945." *Calcutta Literary Gazette* 3. 75 (June 6, 1835). Reprinted in *Wasafiri*, 21:3(2006): 15–20.

Dutt, Michael Madhusudan. *Madhusudan Rachanabali* [Collected Works]. Ed. Kshetra Gupta. Kolkata: Sahitya Samsad, 1990.

Dutt, Shoshee Chunder. "The Republic of Orissa: A Page from the Annals of the Twentieth Century." *The Saturday Evening Harakuru,* May 25, 1845. Reprinted in *Bengaliana: A Dish of Rice and Curry, and Other Indigestible Ingredients.* Calcutta: Thacker, Spink and Co., 1885. 347–56.

Dutt, Toru. *Ancient Ballads and Legends of Hindustan*. London: Kegan Paul, 1882.
Bianca, or, The Young Spanish Maiden: The First Novel by an Indian Woman. New Delhi: Prachi Prakashan, 2001.
Collected Prose and Poetry. Ed. Chandani Lokugé. Delhi: Oxford University Press, 2006.
Le Journal de Mademoiselle D'Arvers. Paris: Didier, 1879.
A Sheaf Gleaned in French Fields. London: Kegan Paul, 1880.
Dutt, Toru and Aru Dutt. *A Sheaf Gleaned in French Fields*. Bhowanipore: Saptahik Sambad Press, 1876.
Faiz, Faiz Ahmed. *Naqsh-e-faryadi*. Delhi: Urdu Ghar, 1941.
Futehally, Zeenuth. *Zohra*. Bombay: Hind Kitabs, 1951.
Gadar. Dir. Anil Sharma. 2001. DVD. Zee Telefilms.
Gandhi, Mohandas Karamchand. *Hind Swaraj [Indian Home Rule]*. *The Selected Works of Mahatma Gandhi*, vol. 4. Ed. Shriman Narayan. Ahmedabad: Navajivan, 1968.
Garam Hawa. Dir. M. S. Sathyu. 1974. DVD. Film Finance Corporation.
Gargi, Balwant. *The Naked Triangle: An Autobiographical Novel*. Ghaziabad: Vikas, 1979.
Ghosal, Swarnakumari Devi. *The Fatal Garland*. London: T. Werner Laurie, 1915.
An Unfinished Song: A Tale. London: T. Werner Laurie, 1913.
Ghosh, Amitav. *The Calcutta Chromosome*. New York: Avon Books, 1995.
The Circle of Reason. New York: Viking, 1986.
The Hungry Tide. Boston: Houghton Mifflin, 2005.
"The Imam and the Indian." *Granta* 20 (1986): 135–46.
In an Antique Land. Harmondsworth: Penguin, 1992.
River of Smoke. New Delhi: Penguin India, 2011.
Sea of Poppies. New Delhi: Penguin India, 2008.
The Shadow Lines. London: Bloomsbury, 1988.
"The Slave of MS. H. 6." *Subaltern Studies VII: Writings on South Asian History and Society*. Eds. Partha Chatterjee and Gyanendra Pandey. Delhi: Oxford University Press, 1992. 159–220.
Ghosh, Sarath Kumar. *The Prince of Destiny*. London: Rebman, 1909.
Ghosh, Vishwajyoti. *Delhi Calm*. New York: HarperCollins, 2010.
ed. *This Side That Side: Restorying Partition*. Delhi: Yoda Press, 2013.
Gill, Raj. *Torch-Bearer: A Novel*. Ghaziabad: Vikas Publishing House, 1983.
Guide. Dir. Vijay Anand. 1965. DVD. Navketan International Films.
Gupta, Sunetra. *The Glassblower's Breath*. New York: Grove Press, 1993.
Memories of Rain. London: Phoenix House, 1992.
Moonlight into Marzipan. London: Phoenix House, 1995.
A Sin of Colour. London: Phoenix House, 1999.
Hamid, Mohsin. *How To Get Filthy Rich in Rising Asia*. New York: Riverhead Books, 2013.
Hariharan, Githa. *In Times of Siege*. New York: Vintage, 2004.
Hasan, Anjum. *Neti, Neti: Not This, Not This*. New Delhi: IndiaInk, 2009.

Hello. Dir. Atul Agnihotri. 2008. DVD. Funky Buddha Productions.

Hosain, Attia. *Sunlight on a Broken Column.* New Delhi: Penguin Books, 1992.

Hossain, Rokeya Sakhawat. "Padmarag." *Sultana's Dream and Padmarag: Two Feminist Utopias.* Trans. Barnita Bagchi. New Delhi: Penguin Books, 2005. 15–193.

"Sultana's Dream." *Sultana's Dream and Padmarag: Two Feminist Utopias.* Trans. Barnita Bagchi. New Delhi: Penguin Books, 2005. 1–14.

Hum Aapke Hain Koun! Dir. Sooraj Barjatya. 1994. DVD. Rajshri Productions.

Hussain, Iqbalunnisa. *Changing India: A Muslim Woman Speaks.* Bangalore: Hosali Press, 1940.

Purdah and Polygamy: Life in an Indian Muslim Household. Bangalore: Hosali Press, 1944.

Hyder, Qurratulain. *River of Fire (Aag ka darya).* New Delhi: Kali for Women, 1998.

Jadhav, Narendra. *Amcha baap aan amhi.* Mumbai: Granthali, 1993.

Outcaste: A Memoir. New Delhi: Viking, 2003.

Untouchables: My Family's Triumphant Journey Out of the Caste System in Modern India. New York: Scribner, 2005.

Joseph, Manu. *The Illicit Happiness of Other People.* New York: W. W. Norton, 2013.

Serious Men. New York: Norton, 2010.

Joshi, Arun. *The City and the River.* New Delhi: Vision Books, 1990.

Joshi, Ruchir. *The Last Jet-Engine Laugh.* London: Flamingo, 2002.

Junoon. Dir. Shyam Benegal. 1978. DVD. Film-Valas.

Kaajal. Dir. Ram Maheshwari. 1965. DVD. Kalpanalok.

Kabir, Humayun. *Men and Rivers.* London: The New India Publishing Company, 1947.

Kai Po Che! Dir. Abhishek Kapoor. 2013. DVD. UTV Motion Pictures.

Kala, Advaita. *Almost Single.* New Delhi: HarperCollins, 2007.

Kapur, Manju. *Difficult Daughters.* London: Faber and Faber, 1998.

Kati Patang. Dir. Shakti Samanta. 1970. DVD. Shakti Films.

Kesavan, Mukul. *Looking Through Glass.* London: Vintage, 1996.

"To Be Ever More Itself – From an Indian Point of View, South Asia is a Well-Meant Fiction." *Telegraph* [Calcutta]. March 27, 2005. http://www.telegraphindia.com/1050327/asp/opinion/story_4517236.asp, accessed September 4, 2014.

Khan, Panchkouree. *The Revelations of an Orderly.* Benares: E.J. Lazarus & Co., 1866.

Kumar, Amitabh. *Raj Comics for the Hard Headed.* New Delhi: Sarai Media Lab, 2008.

Kunzru, Hari. *Transmission.* New York: Dutton, 2004.

Lahiri, Jhumpa. *The Interpreter of Maladies.* New York: Mariner Books, 1999.

The Lowland. New York: Alfred A. Knopf, 2013.

Lahiri, Kali Krishna. *Roshinara: A Historical Romance.* Chittagong: R.R. Sen, 1912.

Lal, Ranjit. *The Crow Chronicles.* New Delhi: Penguin Books, 1996.

Madgulkar, Vyankatesh. *Bangarwadi [The Village Had No Walls]*. Trans. Ram Deshmukh. New York: Asia Publishing House, 1958.

Malgonkar, Manohar. *The Garland Keepers*. New Delhi: Vision Books, 1980.

Manto, Saadat Hasan. "Toba Tek Singh." *Mottled Dawn: Fifty Sketches and Stories of Partition*. Trans. Khalid Hasan. New Delhi: Penguin, 1997. 1–10.

Markandaya, Kamala. *Nectar in a Sieve*. New York: J. Day Co., 1954.

Menon, Anil and Vandana Singh, eds. *Breaking the Bow: Speculative Fiction Inspired by the Ramayana*. New Delhi: Zubaan, 2012.

Mera Naam Joker. Dir. Raj Kapoor. 1970. DVD. R.K. Films Ltd.

Midnight's Children. Dir. Deepa Mehta. 2012. DVD. David Hamilton Productions.

Mishra, Keshab Prasad. *Kohbar ki Shart*. New Delhi: Rajkamal Peparabaiksa, 1993.

Mishra, Manoj. "Dreaming of a Blue Yamuna." *Finding Delhi: Loss and Renewal in the Megacity*. Ed. Bharati Chaturvedi. New Delhi: Penguin, 2010. 71–86.

Mistry, Rohinton. *Family Matters*. London: Faber and Faber, 2003.

A Fine Balance. New York: Vintage, 1995.

Such a Long Journey. London: Faber and Faber, 1992.

Swimming Lessons: and Other Stories from Firozsha Baag. Boston: Houghton Mifflin Company, 1989.

Tales from Firozsha Baag. London: Faber and Faber, 1992.

Mitra, Peary Chand. *Alaler Gharer Dulal. Pyarichand Rachanabali* [Collected Works]. Ed. Asit Kumar Bandyopadhyay. Calcutta: Mandal Book House, 1971. 1–135.

The Spoilt Child: A Tale of Hindu Domestic Life. Calcutta: Thacker, Spink, 1893.

Mohapatra, Saurava, writer. *Mumbai Confidential*. Art by Vivek Shinde. Los Angeles: Archaia Entertainment, 2013.

Mughal-e-Azam. Dir. K. Asif. 1960. DVD. Sterling Investment Corp.

Mukhopadhyay, Trailokyanath. *Bhut o Manush [Ghosts and Men]. Trailokya Rachanabali* [Collected Works], vol. 2. Kolkata: Granthamela, 1974. 1–73.

Mullens, Hannah Catherine. *Phulmani o Karunar Bibaran*. Kolkata: General Printers and Publishers, 1958.

Nadiya ke Paar. Dir. Govind Moonis. 1982. DVD. Rajshir Productions.

Nagarajan, K. *Athavar House*. Madras: Higginbothams, 1937.

Chronicles of Kedaram. Bombay: Asia, 1961.

Nagarkar, Kiran. *Seven Sixes Are Forty-Three [Saat Sakkam Trechalis]*. Trans. Shubha Slee. Oxford: Heinemann, 1995.

Naipaul, V. S. *A Bend in the River*. New York: Knopf, 1979.

Guerrilas. New York: Knopf, 1975.

A House for Mr Biswas. New York: Knopf, 1961.

India: A Wounded Civilization. London: André Deutsch, 1977.

Nair, Rukmini Bhaya. *Mad Girl's Love Song: A Novel*. Noida: HarperCollins, 2013.

Narayan, R. K. *The Bachelor of Arts* [1937]. Chicago: University of Chicago Press, 1980.

The English Teacher [1946]. Chennai: Indian Thought Publications, 1955.

The Financial Expert. East Lansing: Michigan State College Press, 1953.

The Guide. London: Heinemann, 1958.

The Man-Eater of Malgudi. London: Heinemann, 1961.

Mr. Sampath. London: Eyre, 1949.

The Painter of Signs. New York: Viking Press, 1976.

Swami and Friends. London: Hamish Hamilton, 1935.

The Vendor of Sweets. London: Heinemann, 1967.

Waiting for the Mahatma. Chennai: Indian Thought Publications, 1967.

A Writer's Nightmare: Selected Essays, 1958–88. New Delhi: Penguin Books, 1983.

Navariya, Ajay. "Chikh [Scream]." *Unclaimed Terrain*. Trans. Laura Brueck. New Delhi: Navayana, 2013. 155–91.

"Hello Premchand [Uttar Katha]." *Unclaimed Terrain*. Trans. Laura Brueck. New Delhi: Navayana, 2013. 123–54.

"New Custom [Naya Kaayda]." *Unclaimed Terrain*. Trans. Laura Brueck. New Delhi: Navayana, 2013. 65–79.

Patkatha aur anya kahaniyam. New Delhi: Vani Prakashan, 2006.

"Sacrifice [Bali]." *Unclaimed Terrain*. Trans. Laura Brueck. New Delhi: Navayana, 2013. 9–43.

Udhar ke log. New Delhi: Rajkamal Prakashan, 2008.

Unclaimed Terrain. Trans. Laura Brueck. New Delhi: Navayana, 2013.

Yes Sir. New Delhi: Samayik Prakashan, 2012.

"Yes Sir." *Unclaimed Terrain*. Trans. Laura Brueck. New Delhi: Navayana, 2013. 45–64.

Ondaatje, Michael. *Anil's Ghost*. New York: Alfred A. Knopf, 2000.

P. P., Abdul Sultan, writer. *The Believers*. Art by Partha Sengupta. New Delhi: Phantomville, 2006.

Padmanji, Baba. *Yamuna Paryatan*. Bombay: T. Graham, 1857.

Pather Panchali. Dir. Satyajit Ray. 1955. DVD. Sony Pictures, 2003.

Patil, Amruta. *Kari*. New Delhi: HarperCollins, 2008.

Prakash, Uday. *The Girl with the Golden Parasol*. Trans. Jason Grunebaum. New Delhi: Penguin, 2008.

Peeli chatri wali ladki. New Delhi: Vani Prakashan, 2001.

Prasad, Bhagwati. *Tinker. Soldier. Tap: A Graphic Novel*. Delhi: Centre for the Study of Developing Societies, 2009.

The Water Cookbook. Delhi: Centre for the Study of Developing Societies, 2011.

Premchand. "Upanyasa – 1." *Premchand rachanavali*, vol. 7. Ed. Ram Anand. Delhi: Janvani Prakashan, 1996. 291–6.

Qaidi. Dir. Najam Naqvi. 1962. Evernew Pictures.

Ramabai, Pandita. *High-Caste Hindu Woman*. New York: Fleming H. Revell, 1901.

United Stateschi Lokasthiti ani Pravasavritta. Mumbai: Nirnayasagar Press, 1889.

Ramanujan, A. K. Afterword to *Samskara* by U. R. Anantha Murthy. Delhi: Oxford University Press, 1978. 139–47.

"Annayya's Anthropology." *From Cauvery to Godavari: Modern Kannada Short Stories*. Ed. Ramachandra Sharma. Trans. Narayan Hegde. New Delhi: Penguin, 1992. 44–53.

The Oxford India Ramanujan. Ed. Molly Daniels-Ramanujan. New Delhi: Oxford University Press, 2004.

"Three Hundred Ramayanas: Five Examples and Three Thoughts on Translation." *Many Ramayanas: The Diversity of a Narrative Tradition in South Asia.* Ed. Paula Richman. Berkeley: University of California Press, 1991. 22–49.

"Translator's Note." *Samskara* by U. R. Anantha Murthy. Delhi: Oxford University Press, 1978. viii.

Rao, Raja. "Entering the Literary World." *World Literature Today* 62.4 (Autumn, 1988): 536–8.

Kanthapura. New Delhi: Oxford University Press, 1989.

Renu, Phaniswarnath. *Maila Anchal [The Soiled Border].* Trans. Indira Junghare. Delhi: Chanakya Publications, 1991.

Roy, Arundhati. *The Cost of Living.* New York: Modern Library, 1999.

The God of Small Things. New York: Random House, 1997.

Rushdie, Salman. *Fury.* New York: Random House, 2001.

Grimus. Woodstock, NY: Overlook Press, 1975.

The Ground Beneath Her Feet. New York: Henry Holt, 1999.

Introduction. *Mirrorwork: 50 Years of Indian Writing, 1947–1997.* Eds. Salman Rushdie and Elizabeth West. New York: Henry Holt an Co., 1997. vii–xx.

Joseph Anton. New York: Random House, 2012.

Midnight's Children. New York: Random House, 2006.

The Moor's Last Sigh. New York: Vintage, 1995.

The Satanic Verses. New York: Random House, 2008.

Shalimar the Clown. London: Jonathan Cape, 2005.

Shame. New York: Knopf, 1983.

Rushdie, Salman and Elizabeth West, eds. *Mirrorwork: 50 Years of Indian Writing 1947–1997.* New York: Henry Holt, 1997.

Saat Khoon Maaf. Dir. Vishal Bhardwaj. 2011. DVD. UTV Spotboy.

Sahgal, Nayantara. *The Day in Shadow.* New Delhi: Penguin Books, 1991.

Indira Gandhi: Her Road to Power. New York: F. Ungar, 1982.

Indira Gandhi: Tryst with Power. Delhi: Penguin Books, 2012.

Indira Gandhi's Emergence and Style. New Delhi: Vikas Publishing House, 1978.

Prison and Chocolate Cake. New York: Knopf, 1966.

Rich Like Us. London: Heinemann, 1985.

A Situation in New Delhi. London: London Magazine Editions, 1977.

A Voice for Freedom. Delhi: Hind Pocket Books, 1977.

Sanghi, Ashwin. *Chanakya's Chant.* Chennai: Westland, 2010.

Satthianadhan, Krupabai. *Kamala: A Story of Hindu Life.* Madras: Srinivasa, Varadachari and Co, 1894.

Miscellaneous Writings of Krupabai Satthianadhan. Madras: Srinivasa, Varadachari & Co., 1896.

Saguna: A Story of Native Christian Life. Madras: Lawrence Asylum, 1891.

Sawhney, Hirsh, ed. *Delhi Noir.* New Delhi: HarperCollins India, 2009.

Sealy, I. Allan. *The Trotter-nama: A Chronicle.* New York: Knopf, 1988.

Sen, Orijit. *River of Stories.* New Delhi: Kalpavriksh, 1997.

Senapati, Fakir Mohan. *Six Acres and a Third [Chha Mana Atha Guntha]*. Berkeley: University of California Press, 2005.

Seth, Vikram. *The Golden Gate: A Novel in Verse*. New York: Random House, 1986.

  A Suitable Boy. New York: HarperCollins, 1993.

  Two Lives. New York: HarperCollins, 2005.

Sethi, Aman. *A Free Man*. London: Jonathan Cape, 2012.

Shamsie, Kamila. *Burnt Shadows*. New York: Picador, 2009.

Sharma, Sharad. *Parallel Lines*. Delhi: World Comics India Publications, 2010.

  Whose Development? Delhi: World Comics India Publications, 2009.

Sharmeelee. Dir. Samir Ganguly. 1971. DVD. Subodh Mukherjee Productions.

Shree 420. Dir. Raj Kapoor. 1955. DVD. R. K. Films Ltd.

Shukla, Srilal. *Raag Darbari*. New Delhi: Rajkamal Prakashan, 1968.

Sidhwa, Bapsi. *Cracking India*. Minneapolis: Milkweed, 1992.

Singh, Khushwant. *Train to Pakistan*. London: Chatto and Windus, 1956.

Singh, Ravinder. *I Too Had a Love Story*. New Delhi: Penguin Metro Reads, 2012.

Sinha, Indra. *Animal's People*. New York: Simon and Schuster, 2007.

Sinha, Kali Kumar. *Sanjogita: or the Princess of Aryavarta*. Dinapore: Watling Printing Works, 1903.

[Sinha, Kaliprasanna]. *Satik Hutom Pyanchar Naksha*. Ed. Arun Nag. Kolkata: Ananda Publishers, 2008.

Sinha, Kaliprasanna. *Sketches by Hootum the Owl: A Satirist's View of Colonial Calcutta*. Trans. Chitralekha Basu. Kolkata: Samya, 2012.

Slumdog Millionaire. Dir. Danny Boyle. 2008. DVD. Warner Bros.

Swarup, Vikas. *Q&A*. New York: Scribner, 2005.

Tagore, Rabindranath. *Gora*. Trans. Sujit Mukherjee. Delhi: Sahitya Akademi, 1997.

  The Home and the World [Ghare Baire]. Trans. Surendranath Tagore. London: Penguin, 1985.

  Jivansmrti [Reminiscences, 1912]. *Rabindra Rachanabali* [Collected Works], vol. 17. Kolkata: Vishva Bharati, 1954. 261–432.

  Quartet. Oxford: Heinemann, 1993.

Tharoor, Shashi. *The Great Indian Novel*. New York: Arcade, 1989.

Tharu, Susie and K. Lalitha, eds. *Women Writing in India, Volume I: 600 B.C. to the Early Twentieth Century*. New York: Feminist Press, 1991.

Thayil, Jeet. *Narcopolis*. New York: Penguin, 2012.

Tripathi, Amish. *The Immortals of Meluha*. New Delhi: BahriSons, 2011.

Uski Roti. Dir. Mani Kaul. 1970. DVD. NDFC.

Valmiki, Omprakash. *Joothan: A Dalit's Life*. Trans. Arun Prabha Mukherjee. Kolkata: Samya, 2007.

Vassanji, M. G. *The Assassin's Song*. Edinburgh: Canongate, 2009.

Vijayan, O. V. *After the Hanging and Other Stories*. New Delhi: Penguin, 1989.

  The Saga of Dharmapuri. New Delhi: Penguin, 1988.

Yashpal. *Jutha Sach*. Lucknow: Viplava, 1963.

Zaheer, Sajjad. *The Light: A History of the Movement for Progressive Literature in the Indo-Pak Subcontinent*. Trans. Amina Azfar. Karachi: Oxford University Press, 2006.

Zaheer, Sajjad, Ahmed Ali, Rashid Jahan, and Mahmud uz-Zafar. *Angaaray: The Firebrands*. Trans. Snehal Shingavi. New Delhi: Penguin, 2014.

SECONDARY SOURCES

Achebe, Chinua. "The African Writer and the English Language." *Chinua Achebe's Things Fall Apart: A Casebook*. Ed. Isidore Okpewho. Oxford: Oxford University Press, 2003. 55–65.

Adorno, Theodor. *The Culture Industry*. London: Routledge, 1991.

  Minima Moralia: Reflections on a Damaged Life. New York: Verso, 2006.

Afzal-Khan, Fawzia. "Post-Modernist Strategies of Liberation in the Works of Salman Rushdie." *Journal of South Asian Literature* 23.1 (1988): 137–45.

Agamben, Giorgio. "What is the Contemporary?" *Nudites*. Trans. David Kishik and Stefan Pedatella. Stanford, CA: Stanford University Press, 2011.

Agarwalla, Shyam S. "Jameson's Third Worldist National Allegory and Salman Rushdie's *Midnight's Children*." *Salman Rushdie: Critical Essays*, vol. 1. Eds. Mohit Kumar Ray and Rama Kundu. New Delhi: Atlantic Publishers, 2006. 12–32.

Ahmad, Aijaz. "Jameson's Rhetoric of Otherness and the 'National Allegory.'" *In Theory: Classes, Nations, Literatures*. Bombay: Oxford University Press, 1993. 95–122.

  "Reading Arundhati Roy Politically." *Frontline*, August 8, 1997: 103–8.

Ahmed, Talat. *Literature and Politics in the Age of Nationalism: The Progressive Episode in South Asia, 1932–56*. London: Routledge, 2009.

Alam, Asiya. "Polygyny, Family and Sharafat: Discourses amongst North Indian Muslims, circa 1870–1918." *Modern Asian Studies* 45 3 (2011): 631–68.

Ali, Kamran Asdar. "Progressives and 'Perverts': Partition Stories and Pakistan's Future." *Social Text* 29.3 (2011): 1–29.

Almond, Ian. "On Re-Orientalizing the Indian Novel: A Case Study of Rohinton Mistry's *A Fine Balance*." *Orbis Litterarum: International Review of Literary Studies* 59.3 (2004): 204–17.

Alter, Tom. "The Flawed Paradise." *India Today*, January 28, 2012. http://indiatoday .intoday.in/story/narcopolis-by-jeet-thayil/1/170869.html.

Amur, G. S. "Raja Rao: The Kannada Phase." *Journal of the Karnatak University* 10 (1966): 40–52.

Anand, Dev. *Romancing with Life*. New York: Penguin, 2007.

Anand, S. "Lighting Out for the Territory." *The Caravan*. February 1, 2011.

Anderson, Benedict. *Imagined Communities*. London: Verso, 1991.

Anderson, David D. "Ahmed Ali and *Twilight in Delhi*: The Genesis of a Pakistani Novel." *Mahfil* 7.1–2 (Spring–Summer 1971): 81–6.

Anjaria, Ulka. *Realism in the Twentieth-Century Indian Novel: Colonial Difference and Literary Form*. Cambridge: Cambridge University Press, 2012.

Anjaria, Ulka and Jonathan Shapiro Anjaria. "Text, Genre, Society: Hindi Youth Films and Postcolonial Desire." *Journal of South Asian Popular Culture* 6.2 (2008): 125–40.

Anker, Elizabeth S. *Fictions of Dignity: Embodying Human Rights in World Literature.* Ithaca, NY: Cornell University Press, 2012.

Appadurai, Arjun. *Fear of Small Numbers: An Essay on the Geography of Anger.* Durham, NC: Duke University Press, 2006.

Appiah, Kwame Anthony. "Is the Post- in Postmodern the Post- in Postcolonial?" *Contemporary Postcolonial Theory: A Reader.* Ed. Padmini Mongia. London: Arnold, 2003. 55–71.

Arendt, Hannah. *The Origins of Totalitarianism.* New York: Harcourt, Brace and World, 1966.

Athique, Adrian and Douglas Hill. *The Multiplex in India: A Cultural Economy of Urban Leisure.* New York: Routledge, 2010.

Attridge, Derek. *J.M. Coetzee and the Ethics of Reading: Literature in the Event.* Chicago: University of Chicago Press, 2004.

Auden, W. H. "September 1, 1939." *Another Time.* New York: Random House, 1940. 98–101.

Austen, Jane. *Northanger Abbey.* Oxford: Oxford University Press, 1990.

Baccolini, Raffaella and Tom Moylan. "Introduction: Dystopia and Histories." *Dark Horizons: Science Fiction and the Dystopian Imagination.* Eds. Raffaella Baccolini and Tom Moylan. New York: Routledge, 2003. 1–12.

Baden-Powell, B. H. *The Indian Village Community.* London: Longmans, Green, and Co., 1896.

Bader, Clarisse. *La Femme dans l'Inde Antique: Etudes, Morales, et Litteraires.* Paris: Didier, 1867.

Bagchi, Barnita. "Hannah Arendt, Education, and Liberation: A Comparative South Asian Feminist Perspective." *Heidelberg Papers in South Asian and Comparative Politics* 35 (2007): 1–20.

Introduction. *Sultana's Dream and Padmarag* by Rokeya Sakhawat Hossain. New Delhi: Penguin Books, 2005. vii–xxvi.

Bahri, Deepika. *Native Intelligence: Aesthetics, Politics, and Postcolonial Literature.* Minneapolis: University of Minnesota Press, 2003.

Bal, Hartosh Singh. "The Return of the Ramayana." *The New York Times* blog, April 9, 2013. http://latitude.blogs.nytimes.com/2013/04/09/the-return-of-the-ramayana/?_r=0.

Bal, Mieke. "Meanwhile: Literature in an Expanded Field." *Journal of the Australasian Universities Language and Literature Association* 99.1 (2003): 1–22.

Balzac, Honoré. *La Comédie Humaine.* Paris: Gallimard, 1976.

Lost Illusions. New York: Modern Library, 1951.

Banerji, Brajendra Nath. Preface [1935]. In Bankimchandra Chattopadhyay, *Rajmohan's Wife.* Ed. Meenakshi Mukherjee. New Delhi: Ravi Dayal/ Penguin Books, 2009. xii–xiii.

Batra, Lalit, "Out of Sight, Out of Mind: Slum Dwellers in 'World-Class' Delhi." *Finding Delhi: Loss and Renewal in the Megacity.* Ed. Bharati Chaturvedi. New Delhi: Penguin, 2010. 16–36.

Baviskar, Amita. "Urban Exclusions: Public Spaces and the Poor in Delhi." *Finding Delhi: Loss and Renewal in the Megacity*. Ed. Bharati Chaturvedi. New Delhi: Penguin, 2010. 3–15.

Benjamin, Walter. *Illuminations*. Ed. Hannah Arendt. Trans. Harry Zohn. London: HarperCollins/Fontana, 1992.

Berlant, Lauren. "Intimacy: A Special Issue." *Intimacy*. Ed. Lauren Berlant. Chicago: University of Chicago Press, 2000. 1–8.

Berlant, Lauren and Michael Warner. "Sex in Public." *Intimacy*. Ed. Lauren Berlant. Chicago: University of Chicago Press, 2000. 311–30.

Berman, Jessica. *Modernist Commitments: Ethics, Politics, and Transnational Modernism*. New York: Columbia University Press, 2011.

Bhabha, Homi. "How Newness Enters the World: Postmodern Space, Postcolonial Times and the Trials of Cultural Translation." *The Location of Culture*. London: Routledge, 1994. 212–25.

The Location of Culture. London: Routledge, 1994.

"Representation and the Colonial Text: A Critical Exploration of Some Forms of Mimeticism." *The Theory of Reading*. Ed. Frank Gloversmith. Brighton: Harvester, 1984. 93–122.

Bhalla, Amrita. *Shashi Deshpande*. Devon, UK: Northcote House Publishers, 2006.

Bharucha, Nilufer E. "Inhabiting Enclosures and Creating Spaces: The Worlds of Women in Indian Literature in English." *ARIEL: A Review of International English Literature* 29:1 (January 1998): 93–107.

Rohinton Mistry: Ethnic Enclosures and Transcultural Spaces. Jaipur: Rawat Publications, 2003.

Bhasin, Kamla and Ritu Menon. *Borders and Boundaries: Women's Voices from the Partition of India*. New Delhi: Kali for Women, 1998.

Bhattacharya, Amitrasudan. *Bankimchandra Jibani* [*Life of Bankimchandra*]. Kolkata: Ananda Publishers, 1991.

Black, Shameem. "Fictions of Humanitarian Responsibility: Narrating Microfinance." *Journal of Human Rights* 12.1 (2013): 103–20.

Bloch, Ernst. *The Principle of Hope*. Cambridge, MA: MIT Press, 1995.

Boehmer, Elleke. *Colonial and Postcolonial Literature*. Oxford: Oxford University Press, 1995.

Bose, Brinda. "In Desire and Death: Eroticism as Politics in Arundhati Roy's *The God of Small Things*." *ARIEL: A Review of International English Literature* 29:2 (April 1998): 59–72.

Bose, Rupleena. "Writing 'Realism' in Bombay Cinema: Tracing the Figure of the 'Urdu Writer' Through *Khoya Khoya Chand*." *Economic and Political Weekly* 44.47 (November 21–7, 2009): 61–6.

Boyd, Richard. "Metaphor and Theory Change: What Is 'Metaphor' a Metaphor For?" *Metaphor and Thought*. 2nd ed. Ed. Andrew Ortony. New York: Cambridge University Press, 1993. 481–532.

Boym, Svetlana. "On Diasporic Intimacy: Ilya Kabakov's Installations and Immigrant Homes." *Intimacy*. Ed. Lauren Berlant. Chicago: University of Chicago Press, 2000. 226–52.

Braudel, Fernand. *The Mediterranean and the Mediterranean World in the Age of Philip II*. Vol 1. Trans. Siân Reynolds. New York: Harper & Row, 1972.

Brennan, Timothy. "The National Longing for Form." *Nation and Narration*. Ed. Homi Bhabha. London: Routledge, 1990. 44–70.

    Salman Rushdie and the Third World: Myths of the Nation. New York: St Martin Press, 1989.

Brueck, Laura. *Writing Resistance: The Rhetorical Imagination of Hindi Dalit Literature*. New York: Columbia University Press, 2013.

Buckland, C. E. *Bengal under the Lieutenant-Governors*, vol. 2. Calcutta: S.K. Lahiri & Co., 1901.

Buelens, Gert, Samuel Durrant, and Robert Eaglestone, eds. *The Future of Trauma Theory: Contemporary Literary and Cultural Criticism*. London and New York: Routledge, 2013.

Buford, Bill. "Declarations of Independence: Why Are There Suddenly So Many Indian Novelists?" *New Yorker*, June 23, 1997. 6–8.

Burke, Jason. "Mills and Boon Answer Call of India's New Middle Class for English Novels." *The Guardian* (London). March 4, 2010.

Butalia, Urvashi. *The Other Side of Silence: Voices from the Partition of India*. New Delhi: Penguin India, 1998.

Calinescu, Matei. *Five Faces of Modernity: Modernism, Avant-garde, Decadence, Kitsch, Postmodernism*. Durham, NC: Duke University Press, 1987.

Carter, David. "Tasteless Subjects: Postcolonial Literary Criticism, Realism and the Subject of Taste." *Southern Review* 25 (1992): 292–303.

Castle, Gregory. Introduction. *Postcolonial Discourses: An Anthology*. Ed. Gregory Castle. Oxford: Blackwell, 2001. xi–xxiii.

Chakrabarty, Dipesh. *Provincializing Europe: Postcolonial Thought and Historical Difference*. Princeton, NJ: Princeton University Press, 2000.

    "The Time of History and the Times of the Gods." *The Politics of Culture in the Shadow of Capital*. Eds. Lisa Lowe and David Lloyd. Durham, NC: Duke University Press, 1997. 35–60.

Chakravorty, Mrinalini. "The Dead That Haunt Anil's Ghost: Subaltern Difference and Postcolonial Melancholia." *PMLA* 128.3 (2013): 542–58.

Chandra, Nandini. *The Classic Popular: Amar Chitra Katha, 1967–2007*. New Delhi: Yoda Press, 2008.

Chari, Hema. "Imperial Dependency, Addiction, and the Decadent Body." *Perennial Decay: On the Aesthetics and Politics of Decadence*. Eds. Liz Constable, Dennis Denisoff, and Matthew Potolsky. Philadelphia: University of Pennsylvania Press, 1999. 215–34.

Chatterjee, Indrani. Introduction. *Unfamiliar Relations: Family and History in South Asia*. Ed. Indrani Chatterjee. New Delhi: Permanent Black, 2004. 1-59.

Chatterjee, Partha. *The Nation and its Fragments: Colonial and Postcolonial Histories*. Princeton, NJ: Princeton University Press, 1993.

    Nationalist Thought and the Colonial World: A Derivative Discourse? London: Zed, 1986.

    Our Modernity. Rotterdam: SEPHIS, 1997.

Chattopadhyay, Boddhisattva. "Recentring Science Fiction and the Fantastic: What would a non-Anglocentric understanding of science fiction and fantasy look like?" *Strange Horizons*, September 23, 2013. http://www .strangehorizons.com/2013/20130923/1chattopadhyay-a.shtml.

Chattopadhyay, Shachishchandra. *Bankim-Jibani* [*Life of Bankim*], 4th edition. Eds. Alok Ray and Ashok Upadhyay. Kolkata: Pustak Bipani, 1988.

Chaudhuri, Amit. *Clearing a Space: Reflections on India, Literature and Culture*. Ranikhet: Black Kite, 2008.

"The Construction of the Indian Novel in English." *The Picador Book of Modern Indian Literature*. Ed. Amit Chaudhuri. London: Picador, 2001. xxiii-xxxi.

"Modernity and the Vernacular." *The Picador Book of Modern Indian Literature*. Ed. Amit Chaudhuri. London: Picador, 2001. xvii–xxii.

"Salman Rushdie." *The Picador Book of Modern Indian Literature*. Ed. Amit Chaudhuri. London: Picador, 2001. 484-6.

Chaudhuri, Rosinka. "Cutlets or Fish Curry?: Debating Indian Authenticity in Late Nineteenth-Century Bengal." *Modern Asian Studies* 40.2 (2006): 257–72.

Gentlemen Poets in Colonial Bengal: Emergent Nationalism and the Orientalist Project. Calcutta: Seagull, 2002.

"The Politics of Naming: Derozio in Two Formative Moments of Literary and Political Discourse, Calcutta, 1835-31." *Modern Asian Studies* 44.4 (2010): 857–85.

Chaudhuri, Supriya. "The Bengali Novel." *The Cambridge Companion to Modern Indian Culture*. Eds. Vasudha Dalmia and Rashmi Sadana. Cambridge: Cambridge University Press, 2012. 101–23.

"Phantasmagorias of the Interior: Furniture, Modernity, and Early Bengali Fiction." *Journal of Victorian Culture* 15:2 (2010): 173–93.

Chaudhury, Abhishek. "Terms of Engagement." *Caravan*, December 1, 2013. http://caravanmagazine.in/lede/terms-engagement, accessed October 7, 2014.

Chopra, Anupama. *Sholay: The Making of a Classic*. New Delhi: Penguin, 2000.

Chouliaraki, Lilie. "Post-Humanitarianism: Humanitarian Communication Beyond a Politics of Pity." *International Journal of Cultural Studies* 13 (March 2010): 107–26.

Christian, Ed. "Introducing the Post-Colonial Detective: Putting Marginality to Work." *The Post-Colonial Detective*. Ed. Ed Christian. Basingstoke and New York: Palgrave, 2001. 1–16.

Chuh, Kandice. *Imagine Otherwise: On Asian Americanist Critique*. Durham, NC: Duke University Press, 2003.

Churchman, C. West. "Guest Editorial: Wicked Problems." *Management Science* 14. 4 (December 1967): B141–2.

Comaroff, Jean and John L. Comaroff. "Alien-Nation: Zombies, Immigrants, and Millennial Capitalism." *South Atlantic Quarterly* 101.4 (Fall 2002): 779–805.

"Millennial Capitalism: First Thoughts on a Second Coming." *Public Culture* 12.2 (Spring 2000): 291–343.

Coppola, Carlo. "Ahmed Ali (1910–1994): Bridges & Links East & West." *Journal of South Asian Literature* 33/34.1/2 (1998/1999): 112–16.

"Ahmed Ali in Conversation: An Excerpt from an Interview." *Annual of Urdu Studies* 9 (1994): 11–26.

"The All-India Progressive Writers' Association: The Early Phases." *Marxist Influences and South Asian Literature.* Ed. Carlo Coppola. Delhi: Chanakya Publications, 1988. 1–41.

"Premchand's Address to the First Meeting of the All-India Progressive Writers Association: Some Speculations." *Journal of South Asian Literature* 21.2 (1986): 21–39.

Coronil, Fernando. Contribution to "Editor's Column: The End of Postcolonial Theory?" *PMLA* 122.3 (2007): 636–7.

Cowasjee, Saros. *So Many Freedoms: A Study of the Major Fiction of Mulk Raj Anand.* Delhi: Oxford University Press, 1977.

Cronin, Richard. *Imagining India.* Oxford: Basil Blackwell, 1990.

Cundy, Catherine. *Salman Rushdie.* Manchester: Manchester University Press, 1996.

Daiya, Kavita. " 'No Home But in Memory': Migrant Bodies and Belongings, Globalization and Nationalism in Amitav Ghosh's Novels." *Amitav Ghosh: Critical Perspectives.* Ed. Brinda Bose. New Delhi: Pencraft International, 2003. 36–55.

"Refugees, Gender, and Secularism in South Asian Literature and Cinema." *Representations of War, Migration, and Refugeehood: Interdisciplinary Perspectives.* Eds. Daniel H. Rellstab and Christiane Schlote. London: Routledge, 2014. 263–79.

Violent Belongings: Partition, Gender and National Culture in Postcolonial India. Philadelphia: Temple University Press, 2008.

Dalmia, Vasudha. *Poetics, Plays, and Performances: The Politics of Modern Indian Theatre.* Delhi: Oxford University Press, 2006.

Das, Harihar. *Life and Letters of Toru Dutt.* Oxford: Oxford University Press, 1921.

Das, Sisir Kumar. *A History of Indian Literature, 1800–1910.* New Delhi: Sahitya Akademi, 1991.

Dasgupta, Rana. *Capital: A Portrait of Twenty-First Century Delhi.* London: Canongate, 2014.

Dasgupta, Sagarika and Somita Sengupta. "Novel Strategy." *Box Office India.* May 10, 2014.

Dasgupta, Shougat. "Leading the Idiocracy." August 18, 2012. http://www.tehelka.com/leading-the-idiocracy, accessed March 2013.

Davis-Kahl, Stephanie. "The Case for Chick Lit in Academic Libraries." *Collection Building* 27.1 (2008): 18–21.

Dawson Varughese, E. *Reading New India: Post-Millennial Indian Fiction in English.* London: Bloomsbury, 2013.

de Souza, Eunice, ed. *The Satthianadhan Family Album.* New Delhi: Sahitya Akademi, 2005.

Deenadayalan, Yamini. "The Snobs Hate Him, but Chetan Bhagat has 13,332,315 Fans on Facebook." http://www.highbeam.com/doc/1P3-2442125781.html, accessed September 1, 2011.

Delhi Development Authority. "Delhi Master Plan 2021." http://delhi-masterplan .com.

Master Plan for Delhi. New Delhi, 1957.

Dhar, Subir. "Inspiring India: The Fiction of Chetan Bhagat and the Discourse of Motivation." *Writing India Anew: Indian English Fiction 2000–2010*. Eds. Krishna Sen and Rituparna Roy. Amsterdam: Amsterdam University Press, 2013. 161–9.

Dhar, Tej Nath. *History-Fiction Interface in Indian English Novel: Mulk Raj Anand, Nayantara Sahgal, Salman Rushdie, Shashi Tharoor, O.V. Vijayan*. New Delhi: Prestige, 1999.

Dharwadker, Vinay. "Constructions of World Literature in Colonial and Postcolonial India." *The Routledge Companion to World Literature*. Eds. Theo D'haen, David Damrosch, and Djelal Kadir. New York: Routledge, 2012. 476–86.

"The Historical Formation of Indian-English Literature." *Literary Cultures in History: Reconstructions from South Asia*. Ed. Sheldon Pollock. Berkeley: University of California Press, 2003. 199–267.

"The Internationalization of Literatures." *New National and Post-Colonial Literatures: An Introduction*. Ed. Bruce King. Oxford: Clarendon Press, 1996. 59–77.

Dharwadker, Vinay and A. K. Ramanujan, eds. *The Oxford Anthology of Modern Indian Poetry*. New Delhi: Oxford University Press, 1994.

Dixon, Robert. "Travelling in the West: The Writings of Amitav Ghosh." *Amitav Ghosh: A Critical Companion*. Ed. Tabish Khair. New Delhi: Permanent Black, 2003. 9–35.

Doyle, Laura and Laura Winkiel, eds. *Geomodernisms: Race, Modernism, Modernity*. Bloomington: Indiana University Press, 2005.

During, Simon. "Postmodernism or Post-Colonialism Today." *Textual Practice* 1.1 (1987): 32–47.

Dutheil, Martin Hennard. *Origin and Originality in Rushdie's Fiction*. Bern: Peter Lang, 1999.

Dwivedi, A. N. *Indian Writing in English: Genres Other than Poetry*, vol. 2. Delhi: Amar Prakashan, 1991.

Eisner, Will. *A Contract with God and Other Tenement Stories*. New York: DC Comics, 1996.

Elias, Amy J. "Faithful Historicism and Philosophical Semi-Retirement." *The Limits of Literary Historicism*. Eds. Allen Dunn and Thomas Haddox. Knoxville: University of Tennessee Press, 2012. 29–53.

Eliot, George. *Adam Bede*. New York: Harpers and Brothers, 1859.

Eliot, T. S. "Tradition and the Individual Talent." *The Sacred Wood: Essays on Poetry and Criticism*. London: Barnes & Noble, 1960. 42–53.

Ermarth, Elizabeth Deeds. *Realism and Consensus in the English Novel*. Princeton, NJ: Princeton University Press, 1983.

Everest, Larry. *Behind the Poison Cloud: Union Carbide's Bhopal Massacre*. Chicago: Banner, 1986.

Evers, Stuart. "Narcopolis by Jeet Thayil: Review of Man Booker prize 2012 shortlist." *Telegraph* (U.K.), February 8, 2012. http://www.telegraph .co.uk/culture/books/9057255/Narcopolis-by-Jeet-Thayil-review-of -Man-Booker-prize-2012-shortlist.html.

Ewing, Katherine Pratt. *Arguing Sainthood: Modernity, Psychoanalysis, and Islam*. Durham, NC: Duke University Press, 1997.

Fairweather, Elizabeth. "Andrey Tarkovsky: The Refrain of the Sonic Fingerprint." *Music, Sound and Filmmakers: Sonic Style in Cinema*. Ed. James Wierzbicki. New York: Routledge, 2012. 32–44.

Faris, Wendy B. *Ordinary Enchantments: Magical Realism and the Remystification of Narrative*. Nashville, TN: Vanderbilt University Press, 2004.

Ferriss, Suzanne and Mallory Young. "A Generational Divide Over Chick Lit." *Chronicle of Higher Education* 52.38 (2006): B13–14.

Fisher, Marlene. "Mulk Raj Anand: The Novelist as Novelist." *Marxist Influences and South Asian Literature*. Ed. Carlo Coppola. Delhi: Chanakya Publications, 1988. 67–82.

Forster, E. M. Preface. *Untouchable* by Mulk Raj Anand. London: Penguin, 1940. v–viii.

Foucault, Michel. *Madness and Civilization: A History of Insanity in the Age of Reason*. Richard Howard, trans. New York: Vintage, 1988.

Fox, Richard G. *Gandhian Utopia: Experiments with Culture*. Boston: Beacon, 1989.

Freed, Joanne Lipson. "The Ethics of Identification: The Global Circulation of Traumatic Narrative in Silko's *Ceremony* and Roy's *The God of Small Things*." *Comparative Literature Studies* 48.2 (2011): 219–40.

Frye, Northrop. *Anatomy of Criticism: Four Essays*. Princeton, NJ: Princeton University Press, 1971.

Fukuyama, Francis. *The End of History and the Last Man*. New York: Free Press, 1992.

Gabriel, Sharmani Patricia. "Diasporic Hybridities and the 'Patchwork Quilt': Contesting Nationalist History and Other Fictions in Rohinton Mistry's *A Fine Balance*." *Commonwealth Essays and Studies* 25:2 (2003): 83–94.

Gajarawala, Toral Jatin. *Untouchable Fictions: Literary Realism and the Crisis of Caste*. New York: Fordham University Press, 2013.

Gallop, Jane. "The Historicization of Literary Studies and the Fate of Close Reading." *Profession* (2007): 181–6.

Gandhi, Leela. "Novelists of the 1930s and 1940s." *A Concise History of Indian Literature in English*. Ed. Arvind Krishna Mehrotra. New York: Palgrave Macmillan, 2009. 169–92.

Ganguly, Debjani. "Dalit Life Stories." *The Cambridge Companion to Modern Indian Culture*. Eds. Vasudha Dalmia and Rashmi Sadana. Cambridge: Cambridge University Press, 2012. 142–62.

Ganti, Tejaswini. *Producing Bollywood: Inside the Contemporary Hindi Film Industry*. Durham, NC: Duke University Press, 2012.

García Márquez, Gabriel. "The Challenge." *The New Yorker*, October 6, 2003: 100–5.

Geertz, Clifford. "Found in Translation: Social History of Moral Imagination." *Local Knowledge: Further Essays in Interpretive Anthropology*. New York: Basic Books, 1983. 36–54.

George, Rosemary Marangoly. *Indian English and the Fiction of National Literature*. Cambridge: Cambridge University Press, 2013.

Ghosh, Anindita. *Power in Print: Popular Publishing and the Politics of Language and Culture in Colonial Society*. New Delhi: Oxford University Press, 2006.

Gooptu, Nandini. Introduction. *Enterprise Culture in Neoliberal India: Studies in Youth, Class, Work and Media*. Ed Nandini Gooptu. London: Routledge, 2013. 1–24.

Gopal, Priyamvada. *The Indian English Novel: Nation, History, and Narration*. Oxford: Oxford University Press, 2009.

Literary Radicalism in India: Gender, Nation and the Transition to Independence. New York: Routledge, 2005.

Gopal, Sangita. *Conjugations: Marriage and Film Form in New Bollywood Cinema*. Chicago: University of Chicago Press, 2012.

Gordin, Michael D., Helen Tilley, and Gyan Prakash. *Utopia/Dystopia: Conditions of Historical Possibility*. Princeton, NJ: Princeton University Press, 2010.

Graham, Stephen. *Cities under Siege: The New Military Urbanism*. London and New York: Verso, 2010.

Greenlees, Donald. "An Indian Banker Finds Fame off the Books." *New York Times*, March 26, 2008.

Griswold, Wendy. *Bearing Witness: Readers, Writers, and the Novel in Nigeria*. Princeton, NJ: Princeton University Press, 2000.

Gruben, Patricia. "Who Wants to Be a Screenwriter? Script Development in Globalizing India." *CineAction* 78 (2009): 40–5.

Guha, Ramachandra. *Environmentalism: A Global History*. New York: Longman, 2000.

India after Gandhi. New York: HarperCollins, 2007.

Gunning, Dave. "Ethnicity, Authenticity, and Empathy in the Realist Novel and Its Alternatives." *Contemporary Literature* 53:3 (2012): 779–813.

Gupta, Prasenjit. "Refusing the Gaze: Identity and Translation in Nirmal Verma's Fiction." *World Literature Today* 74.1 (2000): 53–9.

Gupta, Suman. "Indian 'Commercial' Fiction in English, the Publishing Industry, and Youth Culture." *Economic and Political Weekly* 46.5 (2012): 46–53.

Guru, Gopal. *Humiliation: Claims and Context*. New Delhi: Oxford University Press, 2009.

Hai, Ambreen. "Adultery Behind Purdah and the Politics of Indian Muslim Nationalism in Zeenuth Futehally's *Zohra.*" *Modern Fiction Studies*, 59.2 (2013): 317–45.

Hatfield, Charles. *Alternative Comics: An Emerging Literature.* Jackson: University Press of Mississippi, 2005.

Hawley, John Stratton. "The Saints Subdued: Domestic Virtue and National Integration in *Amar Chitra Katha.*" *Media and the Transformation of Religion in South Asia.* Eds. Lawrence A. Babb and Susan S. Wadley. Philadelphia: University of Pennsylvania Press, 1995: 107–34.

Heffernan, Teresa. "Apocalyptic Narratives: The Nation in Salman Rushdie's *Midnight's Children.*" *Twentieth Century Literature* 46.4 (Winter 2000): 470–91.

Heimsath, Charles H. *Indian Nationalism and Hindu Social Reform.* Princeton, NJ: Princeton University Press, 1964.

Herbert, Caroline. "'Dishonourably Postnational?' The Politics of Migrancy and Cosmopolitanism in Rohinton Mistry's *A Fine Balance.*" *Journal of Commonwealth Literature* 43:2 (2008): 11–28.

Huggan, Graham. "'Greening Postcolonialism': Ecocritical Perspectives." *Modern Fiction Studies* 50.3 (Fall 2004): 701–33.

Hunter, William Wilson, ed. *Imperial Gazetteer of India*, vol. xvi, new edition. Oxford: Clarendon Press, 1908.

Hussein, Aamer. "That Little Bird: Remembering Qurratulain Hyder." Introduction. *Fireflies in the Mist* by Qurratulain Hyder. New Delhi: Women Unlimited, 2008. vii–xxiv.

Husserl, Edmund. *Ideas.* New York: Routledge Classics, 2012.

Hutcheon, Linda. *A Poetics of Postmodernism: History, Theory, Fiction.* New York: Routledge, 1988.

Huxley, Aldous. *Brave New World.* New York: Harper Perennial Modern Classics, 2010.

Huyssen, Andreas. *After the Great Divide: Modernism, Mass Culture, Postmodernism.* Bloomington: Indiana University Press, 1986.

"I Highlighted India's Brutal Injustices: Adiga." *Rediff India Abroad*, October 16, 2008. http://www.rediff.com/news/2008/oct/16adiga.htm. Accessed November 18, 2013.

"India's Youth Challenge." *New York Times*, April 14, 2014. http://www.nytimes.com/2014/04/18/opinion/indias-youth-challenge.html, accessed October 7, 2014.

Irving, Robert Grant. *Indian Summer: Lutyens, Baker, and Imperial Delhi.* New Haven, CT, and London: Yale University Press, 1981.

Iyengar, K. R. Srinivas. *Indian Writing in English.* Jalandhar: Sterling Publishers Pvt. Ltd., 1984.

Jain, Jasbir. *Nayantara Sahgal.* Jaipur: Printwell, 1994.

Jain, Jyotindra. *Kalighat Painting: Images from a Changing World.* London: Mapin Publishing, 1999.

Jalal, Ayesha. *The Pity of Partition: Manto's Life, Times, and Work across the India-Pakistan Divide.* Princeton, NJ: Princeton University Press, 2013.

Self and Sovereignty: Individual and Community in South Asian Islam Since 1850. London: Routledge, 2000.

Jameson, Fredric. *Archaeologies of the Future: The Desire Called Utopia and Other Science Fictions.* New York: Verso, 2005.

"Third-World Literature in the Era of Multinational Capitalism." *Social Text* 15 (1986): 65–88.

Jamkhandi, Sudhakar Ratnakar. "Raja Rao: A Selected Checklist of Primary and Secondary Material." *Journal of Commonwealth Literature* 16.1 (1981): 132–41.

Jani, Pranav. *Decentering Rushdie: Cosmopolitanism and the Indian Novel in English.* Columbus: Ohio State University Press, 2010.

Joseph, Betty. "Neoliberalism and Allegory." *Cultural Critique* 82 (Fall 2012): 68–94.

Joshee, Reva. "Citizenship Education in India: From Colonial Subjugation to Radical Possibilities." *SAGE Handbook of Education for Citizenship and Democracy.* Eds. James Arthur, Ian Davies, and Carole Hahn. New Delhi: Sage, 2008. 175–89.

Joshi, Namrata. "Booking a Story." *Outlook,* December 21, 2009. http://www.outlookindia.com/printarticle.aspx?263236, accessed October 7, 2014.

Joshi, Priya. "Futures Past: Books, Reading, Culture in the Age of Liberalization." *Books Without Borders: Perspectives from South Asia,* vol. 2. Eds. Robert Fraser and Mary Hammond. Basingstoke: Palgrave Macmillan, 2008. 85–99.

In Another Country: Colonialism, Culture, and the English Novel in India. New York: Columbia University Press, 2002.

Jussawalla, Adil, ed. *New Writing in India.* Harmondsworth: Penguin Books, 1974.

Kabir, Ananya Jahanara. "Affect, Body, Place: Trauma Theory in the World." In Gert Buelens, Samuel Durrant, and Robert Eaglestone, eds. *The Future of Trauma Theory: Contemporary Literary and Cultural Criticism.* London and New York: Routledge, 2013. 63–75.

Partition's Post-Amnesias: 1947, 1971 and Modern South Asia. Delhi: Women Unlimited, 2013.

"Postcolonial Writing in India." *Cambridge History of Postcolonial Literature.* Ed. Ato Quayson. Cambridge: Cambridge University Press, 2011. 412–45.

"Secret Histories of Indian Modernism: M.F. Husain as an Indian Muslim Artist." *M.F. Husain.* Ed. Sumathi Ramaswamy. London and New York, Routledge, 2010. 100–15.

"Subjectivities, Memories, Loss of Pigskin Bags, Silver Spittoons and the Partition of India." *Interventions* 4.2 (2002): 245–64.

Kachru, Braj B. "English in South Asia." *The Cambridge History of the English Language: English in Britain and Overseas,* vol. 5. Ed. Robert Burchfield. Cambridge: Cambridge University Press, 1994. 497–551.

Kafer, Alison. *Feminist, Queer, Crip.* Bloomington: Indiana University Press, 2013.

Kamala, N. "Toru Dutt: Écrivaine francophile et francophone." *Synergies Inde* 4 (2009): 101–13.

Kant, Immanuel. "An Answer to the Question: 'What Is Enlightenment?'" *Political Writings*, 2nd ed. Ed. Hans Reiss. Trans. H. B. Nisbet. Cambridge: Cambridge University Press, 1991. 54–60.

Kapoor, Mini. "What Makes Chetan Bhagat the One-Man Industry and Change Agent that He Is." *India Today*, August 28, 2017. http://indiatoday.intoday .in/story/chetan-bhagat-novel-half-girlfriend-two-million-copies-set-to- roll-off-press/1/379631.html.

Kapur, Geeta. *When Was Modernism: Essays in Contemporary Cultural Practice in India*. New Delhi: Tulika, 2000.

Kapur, Jyotsna. *The Politics of Time and Youth in Brand India*. London: Anthem Press, 2013.

Kaur, Pawanpreet. "The Sad Demise of Hindi Pulp Fiction." May 16, 2012. http:// www.sunday-guardian.com/artbeat/the-sad-demise-of-hindi-pulp-fiction, accessed May 2012.

Kaviraj, Sudipta. *The Imaginary Institution of India: Politics and Ideas*. New York: Columbia University Press, 2013.

"Languages of Secularity." *Economic and Political Weekly* 48.50 (December 14, 2013). http://www.epw.in/revisiting-secularisation/languages-secularity .html, accessed August 18, 2014.

"The Two Histories of Literary Culture in Bengal." *Literary Cultures in History: Reconstructions from South Asia*. Ed. Sheldon Pollock. Berkeley: University of California Press, 2003. 503–66.

The Unhappy Consciousness: Bankimchandra Chattopadhyay and the Formation of Nationalist Discourse in India. New Delhi: Oxford University Press, 1995.

Khair, Tabish. *The Gothic, Postcolonialism and Otherness: Ghosts from Elsewhere*. London: Palgrave Macmillan, 2009.

"Indian Pulp Fiction in English: A Preliminary Overview from Dutt to Dé." *Journal of Commonwealth Literature* 43.59 (2008): 59–74.

Khilnani, Sunil. *The Idea of India*. London: Hamish Hamilton, 1997.

Khor, Lena. "Can the Subaltern Right Wrongs? Human Rights and Development in Aravind Adiga's *The White Tiger*." *South Central Review* 29.1–2 (2012): 41–67.

Kickasola, Joseph G. "Kieślowski's *Musique concrète*." *Music, Sound and Filmmakers: Sonic Style in Cinema*. Ed. James Wierzbicki. New York: Routledge, 2012. 61–75.

King, Anthony D. *Urbanism, Colonialism, and the World-Economy: Cultural and Spatial Foundations of the World Urban System*. London and New York: Routledge, 1990.

Kingston, Maxine Hong. "The Novel's Next Step." *Mother Jones* 14 (December 1989): 37–41.

Kipnis, Laura. "Adultery." *Intimacy*. Ed. Lauren Berlant. Chicago: University of Chicago Press, 2000. 9–47.

Against Love: A Polemic. New York: Vintage, 2003.

Komalesha, H. S. *Issues of Identity in Indian English Fiction*. London: Peter Lang, 2008.

Kopf, David. *The Brahmo Samaj and the Shaping of the Indian Modern Mind*. Princeton, NJ: Princeton University Press, 1979.

British Orientalism and the Bengal Renaissance. Calcutta: Firma K. L. Mukhopadhyay, 1969.

Kosambi, Meera. *Women Writing Gender: Marathi Fiction before Independence*. New Delhi: Permanent Black, 2012.

ed. *Feminist Vision or "Treason Against Men"?: Kashibai Kanitkar and the Engendering of Marathi Literature*. Trans. Meera Kosambi. Ranikhet: Permanent Black, 2008.

Kothari, Rita. *Translating India: The Cultural Politics of English*, Delhi: Foundation Books, 2003.

Kripal, Viney and Mukta Atrey. *Shashi Deshpande: A Feminist Study of Her Fiction*. New Delhi: BR Publishing Corporation, 1998.

Kristeva, Julia. "Psychoanalysis and the Polis." Trans. Margaret Waller. *Critical Inquiry* 9.1 (September 1982): 77–92.

Kulezic-Wilson, Danijela. "Gus Van Sant's Soundwalks and Audio-visual *Musique concrète*." *Music, Sound and Filmmakers: Sonic Style in Cinema*. Ed. James Wierzbicki. New York: Routledge, 2012. 76–88.

Kumar, Girja. *The Book on Trial: Fundamentalism and Censorship in India*. New Delhi: Har-Anand Publications, 1997.

Lau, Lisa. "Emotional and Domestic Territories: The Positionality of Women as Reflected in the Landscape of the Home in Contemporary South Asian Women's Writings." *Modern Asian Studies* 40.4 (2006): 1097–1116.

Lazarus, Neil. "The Politics of Postcolonial Modernism." *Postcolonial Studies and Beyond*. Ed. Ania Loomba et al. Durham, NC: Duke University Press, 2005. 423–38.

The Postcolonial Unconscious. Cambridge: Cambridge University Press, 2011.

Leavis, Q. D. *Fiction and the Reading Public*. London: Chatto & Windus, 1974.

Legg, Stephen. "Post-Colonial Developmentalities: From Delhi Improvement Trust to the Delhi Development Authority." *Colonial and Post-Colonial Geographies of India*. Eds. Saraswati Raju, M. Satish Kumar, and Stuart Corbridge. New Delhi: Sage, 2006. 182–205.

Lipner, Julius J. Introduction. *Debi Chaudhurani, or The Wife Who Came Home by Bankimchandra Chattopadhyay*. Oxford: Oxford University Press, 2009. 1–35.

Lukács, Georg. "Realism in the Balance." *Aesthetics and Politics: The Key Texts of the Classic Debate within German Marxism*. Trans. Rodney Livingstone. New York: Verso, 1980. 28–59.

The Theory of the Novel. Trans. Anna Bostock. London: Merlin, 2003.

Lukmani, Yasmeen. Introduction. *The Shifting Worlds of Kiran Nagarkar's Fiction*. Ed. Yasmeen Lukmani. New Delhi: Indialog, 2004. vii–xxi.

Lukose, Ritty. *Liberalization's Children: Gender, Youth and Consumer Citizenship in India*. Durham, NC: Duke University Press, 2009.

Macaulay, Thomas Babington. "Minute on Indian Education." *Archives of Empire, Volume I: From the East India Company to the Suez Canal.* Eds. Mia Carter and Barbara Harlow. Durham, NC: Duke University Press, 2003. 227–38.

MacCabe, Colin. "Salman Rushdie Talks to the London Consortium about *The Satanic Verses*." *Critical Quarterly* 38.2 (1996): 51–70.

Mach, Ernst. "On Thought Experiments." *Knowledge and Error: Sketches on the Psychology of Enquiry.* Trans. Thomas J. McCormack and Paul Foulkes. Dordrecht Holland: Reidel, 1976. 134–47.

Macpherson, G. *Life of Lal Behari Day, Convert, Pastor, Professor and Author.* Edinburgh: T&T Clark, 1900.

MacRae, Penny. "He's Talking to my Generation." *Ottawa Citizen.* March 29, 2009. B1.

Maharaj, Neelam. "Amitav Ghosh and the Forgotten Army." *Postcolonial Text* 2.2 (2006).

Mahmud, Shabana. "Angare and the Founding of the Progressive Writers' Association." *Modern Asian Studies* 30.2 (1996): 447–67.

Maine, Henry Sumner. *Village-Communities in the East and West.* London: John Murray, 1907.

Majeed, Javed. Introduction. *The Reconstruction of Religious Thought in Islam* by Muhammad Iqbal. Stanford, CA: Stanford University Press, 2013. xi–xxx.

Majumdar, Nivedita. "When the East is a Career: The Question of Exoticism in Indian Anglophone Literature." *Postcolonial Text* 4.3 (2008): 1–18.

Majumdar, Ramesh Chandra, ed. *British Paramountcy and Indian Renaissance.* Bombay: Bharatiya Vidya Bhavan, 1965.

Malik, Hafeez. "The Marxist Literary Movement in India and Pakistan." *Journal of Asian Studies* 26.4 (1967): 649–66.

Manohar, D. Murali. *Indian English Women's Fiction: A Study of Marriage, Career and Divorce.* New Delhi: Atlantic Publishers and Distributors, 2007.

Mantel, Hilary. "States of Emergency." *The New York Review of Books* 43:8 (1996): 4–6.

Marzec, Robert P. "Speaking Before the Environment: Modern Fiction and the Ecological." *Modern Fiction Studies* 55.3 (Fall 2009): 419–42.

Mathews, Mohan M. *India: Facts and Figures.* Delhi: Sterling, 2001.

Mathur, Suchitra. "Caught Between the Goddess and the Cyborg: Third-World Women and the Politics of Science in Three Works of Indian Science Fiction." *Journal of Commonwealth Literature* 39.3 (2004): 119–38.

Mazzarella, William. *Shoveling Smoke: Advertising and Globalization in Contemporary India.* Durham, NC: Duke University Press, 2003.

McCrum Robert. "Chetan Bhagat: The Paperback King of India." *The Observer.* January 24, 2010.

McLain, Karline. *India's Immortal Comic Books: Gods, Kings, and Other Heroes.* Bloomington: Indiana University Press, 2009.

McLeod, James. *Postcolonial London: Rewriting the Metropolis.* London: Routledge, 2004.

McQuiston, Kate. "The Stanley Kubrick Experience: Music, Firecrackers, Disorientation, and You." *Music, Sound and Filmmakers: Sonic Style in Cinema*. Ed. James Wierzbicki. New York: Routledge, 2012. 138–50.

McRuer, Robert. *Crip Theory: Cultural Signs of Queerness and Disability*. New York: New York University Press, 2006.

Mehrotra, Arvind Krishna. Introduction. *An Illustrated History of Indian Literature in English*. Ed. Arvind Krishna Mehrotra. Delhi: Permanent Black, 2003. 1–26.

     ed. *A History of Indian Literature in English*. New York: Columbia University Press, 2003.

Mehta, Suhaan. "Wondrous Capers: The Graphic Novel in India." *Multicultural Comics: From Zap to Blue Beetle*. Ed. Frederick Luis Aldama. Austin: University of Texas Press, 2010. 173–88.

Mendes, Ana Cristina, ed. *Salman Rushdie and Visual Culture: Celebrating Impurity, Disrupting Borders*. London: Routledge, 2012.

Metcalf, Thomas R. *An Imperial Vision: Indian Architecture and Britain's Raj*. Berkeley: University of California Press, 1989.

Michael, R. Blake. *The Origins of Virasaiva Sects*. Delhi: Motilal Banarsidass, 1992.

Mignolo, Walter D. and Madina Tlostanova. "The Logic of Coloniality and the Limits of Postcoloniality." *The Postcolonial and the Global*. Eds. Revathi Krishnaswamy and John C. Hawley. Minneapolis: University of Minnesota Press, 2007. 109–23.

Mikics, David. "Derek Walcott and Alejo Carpentier: Nature, History and the Caribbean Writer." *Magical Realism: Theory, History, Community*. Ed. Lois Parkinson Zamora and Wendy B. Faris. Durham, NC: Duke University Press, 1995. 371–404.

Mishra, Pankaj. "R. K. Narayan." *An Illustrated History of Indian Literature in English*. Ed. A. K. Mehrotra. Delhi: Permanent Black, 2003. 193–208.

Mishra, Vijay. "Rushdie and Bollywood Cinema." *The Cambridge Companion to Salman Rushdie*. Ed. Abdulrazak Gurnah. Cambridge: Cambridge University Press, 2007. 11–28.

     "Salman Rushdie, Aesthetics and Bollywood Popular Culture." *Thesis* 11.113 (December 2012): 112–28.

     "Tuneless Soloists in Salman Rushdie: Cinema, Sound and Sense." *Delhi University Journal of the Humanities and the Social Sciences* 1 (2014): 15–23.

Mitchell, David T. and Sharon L. Snyder. *Narrative Prosthesis: Disability and the Dependencies of Discourse*. Ann Arbor: University of Michigan Press, 2001.

Mitchell, Timothy. *Colonising Egypt*. Cambridge: Cambridge University Press, 1998.

Mitchell, W. J. T. *Picture Theory: Essays in Verbal and Visual Representation*. Chicago: University of Chicago Press, 1994.

Mitter, Partha. *The Triumph of Modernism: India's Artists and the Avant-garde, 1922–1947*. New Delhi: Oxford University Press, 2007.

Mohanty, Satya P. "Can Our Values Be Objective? On Ethics, Aesthetics, and Progressive Politics." *New Literary History* 32.4 (Autumn 2001): 803–33.

"The Dynamics of Literary Reference." *Thematology: Literary Studies in India*. Ed. Sibaji Bandyopadhyayay. Calcutta: Jadavpur University Press, 2004. 23–48.

Introduction. *Six Acres and a Third* by Fakir Mohan Senapati. Berkeley: University of California Press, 2005. 1–31.

Literary Theory and the Claims of History: Postmodernism, Objectivity, Multicultural Politics. Ithaca, NY: Cornell University Press, 1997.

ed. *Colonialism, Modernity and Literature: A View from India*. New York: Palgrave Macmillan, 2011.

Mohapatra, H. S. and J. K. Nayak. "Writing Peasant Life in Colonial India." *Toronto Review of Contemporary Writing Abroad* (Spring 1996): 29–40.

Moorcock, Michael. "Epic Pooh." http://www.revolutionsf.com/article.php?id=953.

Morey, Peter. *Fictions of India: Narrative and Power*. Edinburgh: Edinburgh University Press, 2000.

Rohinton Mistry. Manchester: Manchester University Press, 2004.

Morgan, Daniel. "Max Ophüls and the Limits of Virtuosity: On the Aesthetics and Ethics of Camera Movement." *Critical Inquiry* 38.1 (Autumn 2011): 127–63.

Morton, Stephen. "Beyond the Visible: Secularism and Postcolonial Modernity in Salman Rushdie's *The Moor's Last Sigh*, Jamelie Hassan's *Trilogy*, and Anish Kapoor's *Blood Relations*." *Salman Rushdie and Visual Culture: Celebrating Impurity, Disrupting Borders*. Ed. Ana Cristina Mendes. London: Routledge, 2012. 32–49.

Salman Rushdie: Fictions of Postcolonial Modernity. New York: Palgrave Macmillan, 2008.

Moss, Laura. "Can Rohinton Mistry's Realism Rescue the Novel?" *Postcolonizing the Commonwealth: Studies in Literature and Culture*. Ed. Rowland Smith. Waterloo, Ontario: Wilfrid Laurier University Press, 2000. 157–65.

"An Infinity of Alternate Realities: Reconfiguring Realism in Postcolonial Theory and Fiction." Unpublished doctoral dissertation, 1998.

"'The Plague of Normality': Reconfiguring Realism in Postcolonial Theory." *Jouvert* 5:1 (2000). http://english.chass.ncsu.edu/jouvert/v5i1/moss.htm, accessed January 2014.

Mossman, Mark. "Salman Rushdie's *Midnight's Children*: National Narrative as a Liminal Voice." *Midwest Quarterly* 41:1 (Autumn 1999): 66–78.

Moylan, Tom. *Scraps of the Untainted Sky: Science Fiction, Utopia, Dystopia*. Boulder, CO: Westview Press, 2000.

Mufti, Aamir. *Enlightenment in the Colony: The Jewish Question and the Crisis of Postcolonial Culture*. Princeton, NJ: Princeton University Press, 2007.

"A Greater Short-Story Writer Than God." *Subaltern Studies XI: Community, Gender and Violence*. Eds. Partha Chatterjee and Pradeep Jeganathan. New York: Columbia University Press, 2000. 1–36.

"Towards a Lyric History of India." *boundary 2* 31.2 (2004): 245–74.

Mukherjee, Aditya, Mridula Mukherjee, and Sucheta Mahajan. *RSS, School Texts and the Murder of Mahatma Gandhi: The Hindu Communal Project*. New Delhi: Sage, 2008.

Mukherjee, Arun. "The Exclusions of Postcolonial Theory and Mulk Raj Anand's *Untouchable*: A Case Study." *Ariel* 22.3 (July 1991): 27–48.

Mukherjee, Arun, Alok Mukherjee and Barbara Godard. "Translating Minoritized Cultures: Issues of Caste, Class and Gender." *Postcolonial Text* 2.3 (2006): 1–23.

Mukherjee, Meenakshi. Afterword to *Rajmohan's Wife* by Bankimchandra Chattopadhyay. New Delhi: Ravi Dayal/Penguin India, 2009. 128–45.

"The Anxiety of Indianness: Our Novels in English." *Economic and Political Weekly* 28.48 (November 27, 1993): 2607–11.

"Epic and Novel in India." *The Novel*, vol. 1. Ed. Franco Moretti. Princeton, NJ: Princeton University Press, 2007. 596–631.

Introduction. *Gora* by Rabindranath Tagore. Trans. Sujit Mukherjee. Delhi: Sahitya Akademi, 1997. ix–xxiv.

"The Local and the Global: Literary Implications in India." *English Studies* 43.2 (2000): 47–56.

"Mapping an Elusive Terrain: Literature." *India International Centre Quarterly* 33.1 (2006): 79–92.

"Mapping a Territory: Notes on Framing a Course." *The Lie of the Land: English Literary Studies in India*. Ed. Rajeswari Sunder Rajan. New Delhi: Oxford Univeristy Press, 1992. 229–45.

"Narrating a Nation." *Indian Literature* 35.4 (1992): 138–49.

The Perishable Empire: Essays on Indian Writing in English. New Delhi: Oxford University Press, 2000.

Realism and Reality: The Novel and Society in India. New Delhi: Oxford University Press, 1995.

"The Theme of Displacement in Anita Desai and Kamala Markandaya." *World Literature Written in English* 17.1 (1978): 225–33.

The Twice Born Fiction: Themes and Techniques of the Indian Novel in English. New Delhi: Arnold-Heinemann, 1971.

Mukherjee, Sujit. *Translation as Recovery*. Delhi: Pencraft International, 2009.

Mukherjee, Upamanyu Pablo. *Postcolonial Environments: Nature, Culture and the Contemporary Indian Novel in English*. Basingstoke: Palgrave Macmillan, 2010.

"Tomorrow There Will Be More of Us: Toxic Postcoloniality in *Animal's People*." *Postcolonial Ecologies: Literatures of the Environment*. Eds. Elizabeth DeLoughrey and George B. Handley. Oxford: Oxford University Press, 2011. 216–35.

Nagaraj, D. R. *The Flaming Feet: A Study of the Dalit Movement in India*. Bangalore: South Forum Press, 1993.

Naik, M. K. *A History of Indian English Literature*. New Delhi: Sahitya Akademi, 1982.

Raja Rao. New York: Twayne, 1972.

Nair, Rukmini Bhaya. "Acts of Agency and Acts of God: The Discourse of Disaster." *Economic and Political Weekly* 32:11 (March 1997): 535–42.

"Bringing English into the 21st Century: A Perspective from India." *International Journal of Language, Translation and Intercultural Communication* 1.1 (2012): 103–22.

"Gandhi's Assassination." *Speaking of Gandhi's Death*. Eds. Tridib Suhrud and Peter Ronald deSouza. Hyderabad: Orient Blackswan, 2010. 17–30.

"Language, Youth Culture and the Evolution of English." *Language in South Asia*. Eds. Braj B. Kachru, Yamuna Kachru, and S. N. Sridhar. Cambridge: Cambridge University Press, 2008. 466–94.

"The Life and Death of Salman Rushdie." *American Review of Books* (July–August 1998): 10–12.

"The Linguistic Qualities of the Satanic Verses." *Salman Rushdie: From Midnight's Children to the Satanic Verses*. Ed. David Smale. London: Palgrave Macmlllan, 2003. 80–7.

Lying on the Postcolonial Couch: The Idea of Indifference. Minneapolis: University of Minnesota Press, 2002.

Narrative Gravity: Conversation, Cognition, Culture. New Delhi: Oxford University Press, 2002.

"The Nature of Narrative: Schemes, Genes, Memes, Dreams and Screams!" *Religious Narrative, Cognition and Culture: Image and Word in the Mind of Narrative*. Eds. Armin W. Geertz and Jeppe Sinding Jensen. London: Acumen. 2011. 117–46.

"The Pedigree of the White Stallion: Postcoloniality and Literary History." *The Uses of Literary History*. Ed. Marshall Brown. Durham, NC: Duke University Press, 1995. 159–86.

"Philological Angst: Or How the Narrative of Census, Caste and Race in India Still Informs the Discourse of the 21st Century." *Wort Macht Stamm: Rassismus und Determinismus in der Philologie*. Eds. Markus Messling and Ottmar Ette. Munich: Wilhelm Fink Verlag, 2012. 55–87.

Poetry in a Time of Terror: Essays in the Postcolonial Preternatural. Delhi: Oxford University Press, 2009.

"The Road from Mandalay: Reflections on Amitav Ghosh's *The Glass Palace*." *Amitav Ghosh: A Critical Companion*. Ed. Tabish Khair. Hyderabad: Permanent Black, 2003. 162–74.

"Sappho's Daughters: Postcoloniality and the Polysemous Semantics of Gender." *Journal of Literary Semantics* 32.2 (2003): 113–35.

"Singing a Nation into Being." *Seminar* 497 (January 1, 2001): 95–100.

"Text and Pre-Text: History as Gossip in Rushdie's Novels." *Economic and Political Weekly* 24:18 (May 1989): 994–1000.

"Thinking out the Story Box: Creative Writing and Narrative Culture in South Asia." *TEXT* 10 (2011): 1–22.

"Twins and Lovers: Arundhati Roy's *The God of Small Things*." *Desert in Bloom: Contemporary Indian Women's Fiction in English*. Ed. Meenakshi Bharat. New Delhi: Pencraft International, 2003. 176–98.

"The Voyeur's View in *Midnight's Children* and *Shame*." *Bulletin of the Association of Commonwealth Language and Literature Studies* 7.1 (1985): 57–75.

"Writing the Future and the Future of Writing." *Biblio* 13.9–10 (September–October 2008). http://biblio-india.org/showart.asp?inv=1&mp=SOo8, accessed October 17, 2014.

"Yudhishthira's Lie: The Fiction of India." *Poetiques Comparatistes/Comparative Poetics* (2010): 227–42.

Nair, Rukmini Bhaya, ed. *Translation, Text and Theory: The Paradigm of India.* New Delhi: Sage, 2002.

Nair, Rukmini Bhaya and Rimli Bhattacharya. "Salman Rushdie: The Migrant in the Metropolis." *Third Text* (Summer 1990): 16–30.

Nancy, Jean Luc. "Art Today." *Journal of Visual Culture* 9.1 (April 2010): 91–9.

Nandy, Ashis. *The Intimate Enemy: Loss and Recovery of Self under Colonialism.* Delhi: Oxford University Press, 1983.

Narasimhaiah, C. D. *The Writer's Gandhi.* Patiala: Punjabi University, 1967.

Nietzsche, Friedrich. *On the Genealogy of Morals.* New York: Vintage, 1989.

Nixon, Rob. "Neoliberalism, Slow Violence, and the Environmental Picaresque." *Modern Fiction Studies* 55.3 (2009): 443–67.

Slow Violence and the Environmentalism of the Poor. Cambridge, MA: Harvard University Press, 2011.

Nubile, Clara. *The Danger of Gender: Caste, Class and Gender in Contemporary Indian Women's Writing.* Delhi: Sarup and Sons, 2003.

Orsini, Francesca. *The Hindi Public Sphere 1920–1940: Language and Literature in the Age of Nationalism.* New York: Oxford University Press, 2002.

"India in the Mirror of World Fiction." *New Left Review* 13 (2002): 75–88.

Orwell, George. *1984.* New York: Signet Classics, 1949.

Pande, Mrinal. "The Life and Death of Indian Pulp Fiction." *Livemint*, October 20, 2008. http://www.livemint.com/Politics/Lc2BrUPpwJLWgOXVo6WTtK/The-life-and-death-of-Hindi-pulp-fiction.html, accessed October 7, 2014.

Panikkar, K. N. "History as a Site of Struggle." *The Hindu*, August 15, 2007.

"Secular and Democratic Education." *Social Scientist* 27.9–10 (1999): 70–5.

Paranjape, Makarand. "The Allegory of *Rajmohan's Wife* (1864): National Culture and Colonialism in Asia's First English Novel." *Early Novels in India.* Ed. Meenakshi Mukherjee. New Delhi: Sahitya Akademi, 2002. 141–60.

Parashkevova, Vassilena. "Living Art: Artistic and Intertextual Re-envisionings of the Urban Trope in *The Moor's Last Sigh*." *Salman Rushdie and Visual Culture: Celebrating Impurity, Disrupting Borders.* Ed. Ana Cristina Mendes. London: Routledge, 2012. 50–79.

Parrinder, Patrick. *Science Fiction: Its Criticism and Teaching.* London and New York: Methuen, 1980.

Phillips, H. A. D. Introduction. *Kopal-Kundala: A Tale of Bengali Life.* Trans. H. A. D. Phillips. London: Trübner, 1885. ix–xxix.

Piciucco, Pier Paolo, ed. *A Companion to Indian Fiction in English.* New Delhi: Atlantic Publishers, 2004.

Ponzanesi, Sandra. "Postcolonial Chick Lit: Postfeminism or Consumerism?" *The Postcolonial Cultural Industry: Icons, Markets, Mythologies.* Basingstoke: Palgrave Macmillian, 2014. 156–227.

Povinelli, Elizabeth A. "The State of Shame: Australian Multiculturalism and the Crisis of Indigenous Citizenship." *Intimacy.* Ed. Lauren Berlant. Chicago: University of Chicago Press, 2000. 253–88.

Prabha, M. *The Waffle of the Toffs: A Sociocultural Critique of Indian Writing in English.* New Delhi: Oxford & IBH Publishing Co. Pvt. Ltd., 2000.

Pradhan, Sudhi ed. *Marxist Cultural Movement in India*, vol. 1. Calcutta: National Book Agency Pvt. Ltd., 1979.

Prakash, Gyan. *Mumbai Fables.* Princeton, NJ: Princeton University Press, 2010.

Prashad, Vijay. "India's Left Will Be Back." *The Guardian.* May 23, 2014. http://www.theguardian.com/commentisfree/2014/may/23/india-communists-bjp-neoliberalism-left, accessed October 28, 2014.

Pratt, Mary Louise. "Scratches on the Face of the Country; or, What Mr. Barrow Saw in the Land of the Bushmen." *"Race," Writing, and Difference.* Ed. Henry Louis Gates Jr., Chicago: University of Chicago Press, 1986. 138–62.

Pritchett, Frances W. "The World of *Amar Chitra Katha*." *Media and the Transformation of Religion in South Asia.* Eds. Lawrence A Babb and Susan S. Wadley. Philadelphia: University of Pennsylvania Press, 1995. 76–106.

Puar, Jasbir. *Terrorist Assemblages: Homonationalism in Queer Times.* London and Durham, NC: Duke University Press, 2007.

Pushkin, Alexander. *Eugene Onegin: A Novel in Verse.* Trans. James E. Falen. Oxford: Oxford University Press, 1990.

Rai, Amit. *Untimely Bollywood: India's New Media Assemblage.* Durham, NC: Duke University Press, 2009.

Rainey, Lawrence. *The Institutions of Modernism: Literary Elites and Public Culture.* New Haven, CT: Yale University Press, 1998.

Rajan, Gita and Shailja Sharma. "Theorizing Recognizion: South Asian Authors in a Global Milieu." *New Cosmopolitanisms: South Asians in the US.* Eds. Gita Rajan and Shailja Sharma. Stanford, CA: Stanford University Press, 2006. 150–69.

Ramamurti, K. S. "Kanthapura, Kedaram, Malgudi and Trinidad as Indias in Miniature – A Comparative Study." *Alien Voice: Perspectives on Commonwealth Literature.* Ed. Avadesh K. Sinha. Lucknow: Print House, 1981. 61–74.

Ramone, Jenni. "Paint, Patronage, Power, and the Translator's Visibility." *Salman Rushdie and Visual Culture: Celebrating Impurity, Disrupting Borders.* Ed. Ana Cristina Mendes. London: Routledge, 2012. 87–105.

Rancière, Jacques. "The Aesthetic Dimension: Aesthetics, Politics, Knowledge." *Critical Inquiry* 31.1 (Autumn 2009): 1–19.

Rao, Aruna. "From Self-Knowledge to Super Heroes: The Story of Indian Comics." *Illustrating Asia: Comics, Humour Magazines, and Picture Books.* Ed. John A. Lent. Richmond, Surrey: Curzon Press, 2001. 37–63.

Ray, Bharati. "A Voice of Protest: The Writings of Rokeya Sakhawat Hossain (1880–1932)." *Women of India: Colonial and Post-Colonial Periods*. Ed. Bharati Ray. New Delhi: Sage, 2005. 427–53.

Ray, Sangeeta. *En-Gendering India: Woman and Nation in Colonial and Postcolonial Narratives*. Durham, NC: Duke University Press, 2000.

Reddy, Sheela. "The Lo-Cal Literati." *Outlook*, July 18, 2011. http://www.outlookindia.com/article/The-LoCal-Literati/277582, accessed October 7, 2014.

Reder, Michael R. *Conversations with Salman Rushdie*. Jackson: University of Mississippi Press, 2000.

Rieder, John. *Colonialism and the Emergence of Science Fiction*. Middletown, CT: Wesleyan University Press, 2008.

Rittel, Horst W. J. and Melvin M. Webber. "Dilemmas in a General Theory of Planning." *Policy Sciences* 4 (1973): 155–69.

Rooney, Ellen. "Form and Contentment." *Modern Language Quarterly* 61.1 (2000): 17–40.

Ross, Robert. "Seeking and Maintaining Balance: Rohinton Mistry's Fiction." *World Literature Today* 73:2 (1999): 239–44.

Rothberg, Michael. *Multidirectional Memory: Remembering the Holocaust in an Age of Decolonisation*. Palo Alto, CA: Stanford University Press, 2009.

Roy, Anjali Gera. "What's Punjabi Doing in an English Film? Bollywood's New Transnational Tribes." *The Global-Local Interface and Hybridity: Exploring Language and Identity*. Eds. Rani Rubdy and Lubna Alsagoff. 153–69.

Roy, Anuradha. *Patterns of Feminist Consciousness in Indian Women Writers*. New Delhi: Prestige Books, 1999.

Roy, Nilanjana. "Silencing Ramanujan." 2011. http://akhondofswat.blogspot.co.uk/search/label/Ramanujan, accessed April 2, 2014.

Rushby, Kevin. "*Narcopolis* by Jeet Thayil – review." *Guardian*, February 17, 2012. http://www.theguardian.com/books/2012/feb/17/narcopolis-jeet-thayil-review.

Ryan, Marie-Laure. "Transmedia Storytelling and Transfictionality." http://users.frii.com/mlryan/transmedia.html, accessed October 7, 2014.

Saberwal, Satish. "Societal Designs in History: The West and India." *Situating Indian History*. Eds. Sabyasachi Bhattacharya and Romila Thapar. Delhi: Oxford University Press, 1986. 434–60.

Sadana, Rashmi. *English Heart, Hindi Heartland: The Political Life of Literature in India*. Berkeley: University of California Press, 2012.

"Writing in English." *The Cambridge Companion to Modern Indian Culture*. Eds. Vasudha Dalmia and Rashmi Sadana. Cambridge: Cambridge University Press, 2012. 124–41.

Saha, Mahadevprasad. Introduction. *Bengal Peasant Life* by Lal Behari Day. Calcutta: Editions Indian, 1969. iii–xi.

Said, Edward W. *Culture and Imperialism*. London: Chatto and Windus, 1993.

Orientalism. New York: Vintage Books, 1979.

The World, the Text, and the Critic. Cambridge, MA: Harvard University Press, 1983.

Sanga, Jaina C. Introduction. *South Asian Novelists in English: An A-to-Z Guide.* Ed. Jaina C. Sanga. Westport, CT: Greenwood Press, 2003. xi–xvi.

Salman Rushdie's Postcolonial Metaphors: Migration, Translation, Hybridity, Blasphemy and Globalization. Westport, CT: Greenwood Press, 2001.

Sangari, Kumkum. "Viraha: A Trajectory in the Nehruvian Era." *Poetics and Politics of Sufism and Bhakti in South Asia: Love, Loss and Liberation.* Ed. Kavita Panjabi. New Delhi: Orient Blackswan, 2011. 256–87.

Sangari, Kumkum and Sudesh Vaid, eds. *Recasting Women: Essays in Indian Colonial History.* New Brunswick, NJ: Rutgers University Press, 1999.

Sargent, Lyman Tower. "The Three Faces of Utopianism Revisted." *Utopian Studies* 5.1 (1994): 1–37.

Sarkar, Susobhan. *Bengal Renaissance and Other Essays.* New Delhi: People's Publishing House, 1970.

Sarkar, Tanika. *Hindu Wife, Hindu Nation.* New Delhi: Permanent Black, 2001.

Sarma, Gobinda Prasad. *Nationalism in Indo-Anglian Fiction.* New Delhi: Sterling Publishers Private Limited, 1990.

Saunders, Kate. "*Narcopolis* by Jeet Thayil. *Sunday Times* (London), February 18, 2012. http://www.thetimes.co.uk/tto/arts/books/fiction/article3318967.ece.

Schneller, Beverly. " 'Visible and Visitable': The Role of History in Gita Mehta's Raj and Rohinton Mistry's *A Fine Balance*." *Journal of Narrative Theory* 31:2 (2001): 233–54.

Schotland, Sara. "Breaking out of the Rooster Coop: Violent Crime in Aravind Adiga's *White Tiger* and Richard Wright's *Native Son*." *Comparative Literature Studies* 48.1 (2011): 1–19.

Schouten, Jan Peter. *Revolution of the Mystics.* Kampen: Kok Pharos, 1991.

Schwarz, Roberto. *Two Girls and Other Essays.* New York: Verso, 2013.

Sen, Amartya. *The Argumentative Indian: Writings on Indian History, Culture and Identity.* London: Macmillan, 2005.

Sen, Krishna and Rituparna Roy. Introduction. *Writing India Anew: Indian English Fiction 2000–2010.* Eds. Krishna Sen and Rituparna Roy. Amsterdam: Amsterdam University Press, 2013. 9–25.

Sengupta, Padmini. *Pandita Ramabai Saraswati: Her Life and Work.* London: Asia Publishing House, 1970.

The Portrait of an Indian Woman. Calcutta: YWCA, 1956.

Sarojini Naidu: A Biography. London: Asia Publishing House, 1966.

Toru Dutt. New Delhi: Sahitya Akademi, 1968.

Sharma, Alpana. "Decolonizing the Modernist Mind." *South Asian Review* 33.1 (2012): 13–29.

Shingavi, Snehal. *The Mahatma Misundersood: The Politics and Forms of Literary Nationalism in India.* London: Anthem, 2013.

Singh, Gurharpal. "The Punjab Crisis Since 1984: A Reassessment." *Ethnic and Racial Studies* 18.3 (1995): 476–93.

Singh, Rashna B. "Traversing Diacritical Space: Negotiating and Narrating Parsi Nationness." *Journal of Commonwealth Literature* 43 (June 2008): 29–47.

Singh, Sushila, ed. *Feminism and Recent Fiction in English*. New Delhi: Prestige Books, 1991.

Sinha, Mrinalini. *Colonial Masculinity: The "Manly Englishman" and the "Effeminate Bengali" in the Late Nineteenth Century*. Manchester: Manchester University Press, 1995.

Slaughter, Joseph R. *Human Rights, Inc.: The World Novel, Narrative Form, and International Law*. New York: Fordham University Press, 2007.

Sleeman, William Henry. *Rambles and Recollections of an Indian Official* [1844]. Ed. Vincent A. Smith. London: Oxford University Press, 1915.

Sorensen, Eli Park. "Novelistic Interpretation: The Travelling Theory of Georg Lukács's *Theory of the Novel*." *JNT: Journal of Narrative Theory* 39:1 (2009): 57–86.

Postcolonial Studies and the Literary: Theory, Interpretation and the Novel. London: Palgrave Macmillan, 2010.

Spivak, Gayatri Chakravorty. "Can the Subaltern Speak?" *Marxism and the Interpretation of Culture*. Ed. Cary Nelson and Lawrence Grossberg. Urbana: University of Illinois Press, 1988. 271–313.

A Critique of Postcolonial Reason: Toward a History of the Vanishing Present. Cambridge, MA: Harvard University Press, 1999.

In Other Worlds: Essays in Cultural Politics. New York: Methuen, 1987.

"Three Women's Texts and a Critique of Imperialism." *Critical Inquiry* 12.1 (1985): 243–61.

Sreenivas, Deepa. *Sculpting the Middle Class: History, Masculinity and the Amar Chitra Katha*. New Delhi: Routledge India, 2010.

Srivastava, Neelam. *Secularism in the Postcolonial Indian Novel: National and Cosmopolitan Narratives in English*. London: Routledge, 2007.

Stadtler, Florian. *Fiction, Film and Indian Popular Cinema: Salman Rushdie's Novels and the Cinematic Imagination*. New York: Routledge, 2014.

Standten, Cecile. "Intermedial Fictions of the 'New' Metropolis: Calcutta, Delhi and Cairo in the Graphic Novels of Sarnath Banerjee and G. Willow Wilson." *Journal of Postcolonial Writing* 47.5 (2011): 510–22.

Stark, Ulrike. *An Empire of Books: The Naval Kishore Press and the Diffusion of the Printed Word in Colonial India*. Ranikhet: Permanent Black, 2009.

Sterne, Laurence. *Tristam Shandy*. London: J.M. Dent & Sons, 1950.

Subramanian, Samanth. "India After English?" *New York Review of Books* blog. http://www.nybooks.com/blogs/nyrblog/2014/jun/09/india-newspapers-after-english/, accessed October 20, 2015.

Suleri, Sara. *The Rhetoric of English India*. Chicago: University of Chicago Press, 1992.

Sundaram, Aparna. "Marriage, Sexual Violence and Indian Masculinity: A Study of Shashi Deshpande's *The Dark Holds No Terrors* and Anita Nair's *Mistress*." *Postcolonial Indian Fiction in English and Masculinity*. Eds. Rajeshwar Mittapalli and Letizia Alterno. New Delhi: Atlantic Publishers and Distributors, 2009. 18–31.

Sunder Rajan, Rajeswari. "After *Midnight's Children*: Some Notes on the New Indian Novel in English." *Social Research* 78.1 (Spring 2011): 203–30.

Real and Imagined Women: Gender, Culture and Postcolonialism. London: Routledge, 1993.

Tarlo, Emma. *Unsettling Memories: Narratives of the Emergency in Delhi*. Berkeley: University of California Press, 2003.

Taylor, Philip Meadowes. *Confessions of a Thug*. London: Richard Bentley, 1839.

Teverson, Andrew. "Merely Connect: Salman Rushdie and Tom Phillips." *Salman Rushdie and Visual Culture: Celebrating Impurity, Disrupting Borders*. Ed. Ana Cristina Mendes. London: Routledge, 2012. 12–31.

Tickell, Alex. "Terrorism and the Informative Romance: Two Early South-Asian Novels in English." *Kunapipi* 25.1 (2003): 73–82.

Terrorism, Insurgency and Indian-English Literature, 1830–1947. London: Routledge, 2012.

Tidhar, Lavie. *Osama*. Oxford: Solaris, 2012.

Tiffin, Helen. "Post-Colonialism, Post-Modernism and the Rehabilitation of Post-Colonial History." *Journal of Commonwealth Literature* 23.1 (March 1988): 169–81.

Tod, James. *Annals and Antiquities of Rajasthan*. London: H. Milford, 1920.

Todorov, Tzvetan. *The Fantastic: A Structural Approach to Literary Genre*. Trans. Richard Howard. Ithaca, NY: Cornell University Press, 1985.

Tokaryk, Tyler. "Keynes, Storytelling, and Realism: Literary and Economic Discourse in Rohinton Mistry's *A Fine Balance*." *Studies in Canadian Literature/Etudes en Littérature Canadienne* 30.2 (2005): 1–31.

Toor, Saadia. *The State of Islam: Culture and Cold War Politics in Pakistan*. London: Pluto, 2011.

Trilling, Lionel. *Beyond Culture*. Harmondsworth, Middlesex: Penguin Books, 1967.

Trivedi, Harish. "Ahmed Ali, Twilight in Delhi." *Major Indian Novels: An Evaluation*. Ed. N. S. Pradhan. Atlantic Highlands, NJ: Humanities Press, 1986. 41–73.

"Gandhian Nationalism: Kanthapura." *Literature and Nation: Britain and India 1900–1990*. Eds. Richard Allen and Harish Trivedi. London: Routledge, 2000. 107–20.

"The Progress of Hindi, Part 2: Hindi and the Nation." *Literary Cultures in History: Reconstructions from South Asia*. Ed. Sheldon Pollock. Berkeley: University of California Press, 2003. 958–1018.

"The St. Stephen's Factor." *Indian Literature* 145 (September–October 1991): 183–7.

Uraizee, Joya Farooq. *This is No Place for a Woman: Nadine Gordimer, Buchi Emecheta, Nayantara Sahgal, and the Politics of Gender*. Trenton, NJ: Africa World Press, 2000.

Vadde, Aarthi. "Reading Deliriously." *Novel: A Forum on Fiction* 45:1 (Spring 2012): 23–6.

Van Dyke, Virginia. "The Anti-Sikh Riots of 1984 in Delhi: Politicians, Criminals, and the Discourse of Communalism." *Riots and Pogroms*. London: Macmillan, 1996. 201–20.

van Elferen, Isabella. "Dream Timbre: Notes on Lynchian Sound Design." *Music, Sound and Filmmakers: Sonic Style in Cinema*. Ed. James Wierzbicki. New York: Routledge, 2012. 175–88.

Vasudevan, Ravi. *The Melodramatic Public: Film Form and Spectatorship in Indian Cinema*. New York: Palgrave, 2011.

Verma, K. D. "Mulk Raj Anand and Realism." *South Asian Review* 32.1 (2011): 137–51.

Viswanathan, Gauri. *Outside the Fold: Conversion, Modernity, and Belief*. Princeton, NJ: Princeton University Press, 1998.

Walkowitz, Rebecca L. *Cosmopolitan Style: Modernism Beyond the Nation*. New York: Columbia University Press, 2006.

Wierzbicki, James. "Sonic Style in Cinema." *Music, Sound and Filmmakers: Sonic Style in Cinema*. Ed. James Wierzbicki. New York: Routledge, 2012. 1–14.

Williams, H. M. *Indo-Anglian Literature, 1800–1970: A Survey*. Madras: Orient Longman, 1976.

Williams, Raymond. *The Country and the City*. London: Chatto and Windus, 1973.

Wolmark, Jenny. *Aliens and Others: Science Fiction, Feminism, and Postmodernism*. Iowa City: University of Iowa Press, 1994.

Woolf, Virginia. "A Letter to a Young Poet." *The Death of a Moth and Other Essays*. New York: Harcourt Brace Jovanovich, 1942. 208–26.

"Modern Fiction." *The Common Reader*. Ed. Andrew McNeillie. New York: Harcourt, 1925.

Mr. Bennett and Mrs. Brown. London: Hogarth Press, 1924.

Yaseen, Mohammad. "Aesthetic of Indo-English Political Novel." *Indian Writing in English: A Critical Response*. Ed. Syed Mashkoor Ali. New Delhi: Creative Books, 2001. 11–16.

Yeoh, Brenda. "Postcolonial Cities." *Progress in Human Geography* 25.3 (2001): 456–68.

Zamindar, Vazira Fazila-Yacoobali. *The Long Partition and the Making of Modern South Asia: Refugees, Boundaries, Histories*. New York: Columbia University Press, 2007.

Zamyatin, Yevgeny. *We*. New York: Modern Library, 2006.

Zvelebil, K. V., trans. *The Lord of the Meeting Rivers: Devotional Poems of Basavanna*. Delhi: Motilal Banarsidass, 1984.

Index